T0191612

Communications in Computer and Information Science 1226

Commenced Publication in 2007
Founding and Former Series Editors:
Simone Diniz Junqueira Barbosa, Phoebe Chen, Alfredo Cuzzocrea,
Xiaoyong Du, Orhun Kara, Ting Liu, Krishna M. Sivalingam,
Dominik Ślęzak, Takashi Washio, Xiaokang Yang, and Junsong Yuan

More information about this series at http://www.springer.com/series/7899

Constantine Stephanidis ·
Margherita Antona (Eds.)

HCI International 2020 - Posters

22nd International Conference, HCII 2020
Copenhagen, Denmark, July 19–24, 2020
Proceedings, Part III

 Springer

Editors
Constantine Stephanidis
University of Crete
and Foundation for Research
and Technology – Hellas (FORTH)
Heraklion, Crete, Greece

Margherita Antona
Foundation for Research
and Technology – Hellas (FORTH)
Heraklion, Crete, Greece

ISSN 1865-0929   ISSN 1865-0937 (electronic)
Communications in Computer and Information Science
ISBN 978-3-030-50731-2   ISBN 978-3-030-50732-9 (eBook)
https://doi.org/10.1007/978-3-030-50732-9

This Springer imprint is published by the registered company Springer Nature Switzerland AG
The registered company address is: Gewerbestrasse 11, 6330 Cham, Switzerland

Foreword

The 22nd International Conference on Human-Computer Interaction, HCI International 2020 (HCII 2020), was planned to be held at the AC Bella Sky Hotel and Bella Center, Copenhagen, Denmark, during July 19–24, 2020. Due to the COVID-19 coronavirus pandemic and the resolution of the Danish government not to allow events larger than 500 people to be hosted until September 1, 2020, HCII 2020 had to be held virtually. It incorporated the 21 thematic areas and affiliated conferences listed on the following page.

A total of 6,326 individuals from academia, research institutes, industry, and governmental agencies from 97 countries submitted contributions, and 1,439 papers and 238 posters were included in the conference proceedings. These contributions address the latest research and development efforts and highlight the human aspects of design and use of computing systems. The contributions thoroughly cover the entire field of human-computer interaction, addressing major advances in knowledge and effective use of computers in a variety of application areas. The volumes constituting the full set of the conference proceedings are listed in the following pages.

The HCI International (HCII) conference also offers the option of "late-breaking work" which applies both for papers and posters and the corresponding volume(s) of the proceedings will be published just after the conference. Full papers will be included in the "HCII 2020 - Late Breaking Papers" volume of the proceedings to be published in the Springer LNCS series, while poster extended abstracts will be included as short papers in the "HCII 2020 - Late Breaking Posters" volume to be published in the Springer CCIS series.

I would like to thank the program board chairs and the members of the program boards of all thematic areas and affiliated conferences for their contribution to the highest scientific quality and the overall success of the HCI International 2020 conference.

This conference would not have been possible without the continuous and unwavering support and advice of the founder, Conference General Chair Emeritus and Conference Scientific Advisor Prof. Gavriel Salvendy. For his outstanding efforts, I would like to express my appreciation to the communications chair and editor of HCI International News, Dr. Abbas Moallem.

July 2020   Constantine Stephanidis

HCI International 2020 Thematic Areas and Affiliated Conferences

Thematic areas:

- HCI 2020: Human-Computer Interaction
- HIMI 2020: Human Interface and the Management of Information

Affiliated conferences:

- EPCE: 17th International Conference on Engineering Psychology and Cognitive Ergonomics
- UAHCI: 14th International Conference on Universal Access in Human-Computer Interaction
- VAMR: 12th International Conference on Virtual, Augmented and Mixed Reality
- CCD: 12th International Conference on Cross-Cultural Design
- SCSM: 12th International Conference on Social Computing and Social Media
- AC: 14th International Conference on Augmented Cognition
- DHM: 11th International Conference on Digital Human Modeling and Applications in Health, Safety, Ergonomics and Risk Management
- DUXU: 9th International Conference on Design, User Experience and Usability
- DAPI: 8th International Conference on Distributed, Ambient and Pervasive Interactions
- HCIBGO: 7th International Conference on HCI in Business, Government and Organizations
- LCT: 7th International Conference on Learning and Collaboration Technologies
- ITAP: 6th International Conference on Human Aspects of IT for the Aged Population
- HCI-CPT: Second International Conference on HCI for Cybersecurity, Privacy and Trust
- HCI-Games: Second International Conference on HCI in Games
- MobiTAS: Second International Conference on HCI in Mobility, Transport and Automotive Systems
- AIS: Second International Conference on Adaptive Instructional Systems
- C&C: 8th International Conference on Culture and Computing
- MOBILE: First International Conference on Design, Operation and Evaluation of Mobile Communications
- AI-HCI: First International Conference on Artificial Intelligence in HCI

Conference Proceedings Volumes Full List

http://2020.hci.international/proceedings

HCI International 2020 (HCII 2020)

The full list with the Program Board Chairs and the members of the Program Boards of all thematic areas and affiliated conferences is available online at:

http://www.hci.international/board-members-2020.php

HCI International 2021

The 23rd International Conference on Human-Computer Interaction, HCI International 2021 (HCII 2021), will be held jointly with the affiliated conferences in Washington DC, USA, at the Washington Hilton Hotel, July 24–29, 2021. It will cover a broad spectrum of themes related to Human-Computer Interaction (HCI), including theoretical issues, methods, tools, processes, and case studies in HCI design, as well as novel interaction techniques, interfaces, and applications. The proceedings will be published by Springer. More information will be available on the conference website: http://2021.hci.international/.

General Chair
Prof. Constantine Stephanidis
University of Crete and ICS-FORTH
Heraklion, Crete, Greece
Email: general_chair@hcii2021.org

http://2021.hci.international/

Contents – Part III

Smartphones, Social Media and Human Behaviour

Interacting with Cultural Heritage

Human-Vehicle Interaction

Transport, Safety and Crisis Management

Security, Privacy and Trust

Product and Service Design

Universal Access, Accessibility and Design for the Elderly

Brain-Computer Interaction and Silent Speech Recognition on Decentralized Messaging Applications

Luís Arteiro[✉], Fábio Lourenço, Paula Escudeiro, and Carlos Ferreira

Polytechnic of Porto - School of Engineering (ISEP), 4200-072 Porto, Portugal
{1150625,1150434,pmo,cgf}@isep.ipp.com

Abstract. Peer-to-peer communication has increasingly gained prevalence in people's daily lives, with its widespread adoption being catalysed by technological advances. Although there have been strides for the inclusion of disabled individuals to ease communication between peers, people who suffer hand/arm impairments have scarce support in regular mainstream applications to efficiently communicate privately with other individuals. Additionally, as centralized systems have come into scrutiny regarding privacy and security, development of alternative, decentralized solutions has increased, a movement pioneered by Bitcoin that culminated on the blockchain technology and its variants.

Within the inclusivity paradigm, this paper aims to showcase an alternative on human-computer interaction with support for the aforementioned individuals, through the use of an electroencephalography headset and electromyography surface electrodes, for application navigation and text input purposes respectively. Users of the application are inserted in a decentralized system that is designed for secure communication and exchange of data between peers that are both resilient to tampering attacks and central points of failure, with no long-term restrictions regarding scalability prospects. Therefore, being composed of a silent speech and brain-computer interface, users can communicate with other peers, regardless of disability status, with no physical contact with the device. Users utilize a specific user interface design that supports such interaction, doing so securely on a decentralized network that is based on a distributed hash table for better lookup, insert and deletion of data performance. This project is still in early stages of development, having successfully been developed a functional prototype on a closed, testing environment.

Keywords: Brain-computer interface · Silent speech recognition · Peer-to-peer communication · Decentralization · Distributed hash table

1 Introduction

With the advent of messaging applications, there is an apparent lack of support for disabled individuals to communicate on these platforms and use such

© Springer Nature Switzerland AG 2020
C. Stephanidis and M. Antona (Eds.): HCII 2020, CCIS 1226, pp. 3–11, 2020.
https://doi.org/10.1007/978-3-030-50732-9_1

applications to interact efficiently with other people. There has been significant progress addressing such issues mainly through electroencephalography (EEG) sensors capable of recording brain activity that, powered by machine learning, can translate it into actions [6]. Similarly, electromyography (EMG) electrodes can measure activity from muscle responsible for speech, enabling silent speech recognition (SSR) [11], that can be used for private and silent text input into the application.

Additionally, privacy and security of data within centralized systems have been under the spotlight, especially on mobile applications [2], contributing to the rise of the development of alternative, decentralized solutions have increased, a movement first created by Bitcoin [8] that effectively stapled blockchain as a growing technology. The latter has shown tremendous potential and applicability on a wide range of scenarios, boosted by the introduction of smart contracts by Ethereum [13], going beyond currency exchange. These assets allow trustless, secure, peer-to-peer value transfer that can easily be applied to the messaging paradigm, thus allowing immutable, secure messaging between nodes. The surge of this technology paved the way for variants that maintain blockchain's main advantages but change their scope. These have set a precedent and strides for decentralization across many fields [10].

2 Related Work

Regarding brain-computer interfaces (BCI) using non-invasive EEG, research projects have emerged allowing users to control virtual keyboards and mouses, empowering individuals with motor disabilities in their interaction with computers. Regarding app's navigation using this approach, there are experiments on cursor movement that allow a user to move it by a BCI. Tests with different approaches within movements for one or two dimensions showed an accuracy of approximately 70% [5]. A similar project utilizes a hybrid near-infrared spectroscopy-electroencephalography technique trying to extract four different types of brain signals, decoding them into direction symbols, namely, "forward", "backward", "left", and "right". The classification accuracy for "left" and "right" commands was 94.7%, for "forward" was 80.2% and 83.6% for "backward" [6]. Later in this document, it will be shown that our system uses a similar approach for the set of commands used for navigation in the platform.

Since this project concerns a messaging platform, text input is a key feature that must offer support for the target audience - disabled subjects. Experiments have been made using EEG to input text using virtual keyboards, allowing a user to make binary decisions and iteratively splitting a keyboard in half until one letter remains, having a spelling rate of about 0.5 char/min [1]. Another approach, which instead of doing binary choices, allows the selection of one between six hexagons, enabling the input of about 7 chars/min [12]. Although input speed is not the central focus of these projects, it must be user-friendly for instant messaging to be conceivable. Yet another studied approach to allow text input was through a silent speech interface (SSI), which also enables input by people with speech impairments (e.g. laryngectomy). Researches on this field still have a high word error rate (WER), as some have achieved around 50% WER for their SSR attempt, using a vocabulary of 108 words through the EMG-UKA corpus [11]. Another group proposed another solution, using the same corpus, attaining around 30% char accuracy [9]. Studies for this approach do not yield satisfactory results for a wide-range vocabulary, although appearing to be more promising when compared to EEG-based interfaces.

Regarding messaging platforms and their dedicated backend, there have been attempts to develop decentralized messaging applications that aim to address many issues present in centralized applications that are usually perceived as secure (e.g. Telegram) and allow decentralized authoritative messaging [7]. Applications that follow the classic blockchain approach towards the messaging panorama include Adamant, which showcases an example of a fully anonymous, private and secure messaging between peers. Relying on its own token that is used for each transaction, such application relies on having no personal or sensitive data being extracted from the user [4]. A decentralized solution which follows a distributed hash table (DHT) approach is Jami, where the DHT is used to locate peer addresses and establish peer-to-peer connection without any personal sensitive data associated, with undelivered messages being stored locally.

3 Our Solution

The proposed solution encompasses a new approach to the interaction of an application that partakes in a decentralized ecosystem that is user-centric, with high throughput and maintaining a bottom-line of privacy of data and message exchange. It envisions a way for people with arm/hand to be able to communicate with anyone. It is, therefore, divided into two distinctive counterparts: human-machine interaction, through BCI and SSI, and decentralized communication between peers. This is further outlined in Fig. 1.

3.1 Human-Machine Interaction

Aiming towards a hands-free controlled application with text input through silent speech, this project proposes a synthetic telepathy-based solution to messaging. It allows individuals with arm motor disabilities to interact with the platform and also creates a multitude of use cases for people without these limitations (e.g. privacy and mitigation of background noises when using speech-to-text features in public; multitasking while navigating with mental commands).

Brain-Computer Interface. For the BCI component in this project, Emotiv EPOC+ is being used for EEG recordings and the Emotiv BCI software for training and classification of the data gathered from the user. This device and related software are of great advantage since it accelerates the overall project development considering it already has predefined mental commands for a subject to

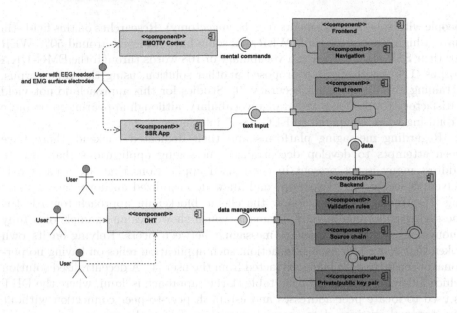

Fig. 1. Overall conceptual view of the platform, outlining the interaction between the user and interface, as well as showcasing the decentralized system where the user is inserted into (DLT - Distributed Ledger Technology), outlining the different components that make up the backend.

train, which can be applied for the user interface (UI) navigation. Considering the UI must be accessible and intuitive for both users with or without impairments, a new design idea had to emerge to accomplish these goals. Thus, besides from regular click/tap to interact, the user can also navigate through different chat rooms using four different commands, "pull", "push", "left", and "right". Simulating a three-dimensional space, the "pull" and "push" commands pull closer to and push away from the user view, respectively (see Fig. 2), and the remaining "left" and "right" commands are used to slide through a carousel-type view with each chat room, always fixing a chat room in the middle, until the user pulls the one selected (see Fig. 3). Furthermore, more commands may be added for others minor tasks, or these already implemented commands can correspond to multiple actions depending on the state of the application or feature that is being used.

Silent Speech Interface. Regarding SSI, it is being used the aforementioned EMG-UKA corpus for implementation and testing of the system in its early stages. Approaches for this system are still being studied, and the first experiments are being conducted on a session-dependent model attempting to classify phones (speech sounds) from EMG data. Further developments will allow users to input full words into the system. In order to reach a broader audience and using the exiting corpus, the system is tailored for the English language.

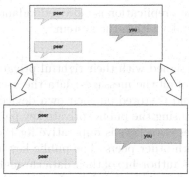

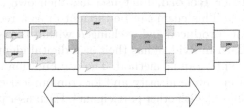

Fig. 2. "Pull" and "push" commands effect the UI, allowing the user to enter and leave chatrooms.

Fig. 3. The user can slide right or left and navigate through his/her chatrooms through "right" and "left" mental commands.

3.2 Decentralized Backend

As it was aforementioned, individuals who make use of the platform, whether these suffer from any impairment or not, will partake in a decentralized ecosystem that is intended to provide secure peer-to-peer communication with data integrity. The system is agent-centric, meaning each user runs a copy of the backend, have their own identity and their private and public shared data. Being on the same encrypted peer-to-peer network entails each user can communicate with each other directly to maintain its integrity. Having each peer hold the same application bundle with the respective logic, it is possible to verify other peer's transactions and data created. Each data has proof of authorship (i.e. a signature). Since every data is recorded and validated by the peers within the system, it is tamper-resistant - this showcases data integrity.

Data resilience is also important in any messaging platform. That is, data must not get lost when users go offline. To address this issue, each piece of public data is witnessed, validated according to the system's logic that is present in every user and stored by a random selection of peers. This makes it that the community and cooperating parties detect invalid data, gossip such evidence of harmful agents and take action to deal with malice data/users. This is a synonym to peer data replication and data validation.

The system shares similarities with Jami in a way that it is based on a distributed hash table (DHT). This table, contrary to blockchain-based applications, is not replicated in each node. To attain a higher transactions per second (TPS), throughput and lookup, each peer stores a segment of the table. This DHT is where the data resides and, in cases where users go offline, is stored to later be retrieved by the recipient. The implementation of this table is based on top of the Holochain framework, allowing for easier data replication and validation between peers. As more users join in the network, more computational power is contributed to the environment and data replication is more redundant, allowing the system to scale as more users partake within the system.

User Record. Each user has their own chain signed with their rightful private key. This chain can be thought of as a record of all the messages/data the user has produced and exchanged within the app and is stored on their own device. Each individual has their own digital identifier using the public/private key pair cryptographic method. The combination of these two keys is imperative for the user online identity and for communication with other peers. The public key is shared with other participants. Each user proves authorship of their data through digital signatures stemming from their private key. Any tampering is promptly detected by simply using the correspondent public key to verify the signature. If such validation fails, the data is considered invalid and this finding is gossiped and broadcasted to the rest of the network. The distributed hash table is where all public data resides in. The word "public" is used very loosely. Every entry is hashed so as to make it untraceable so it is not necessarily public as in it is available for everyone to see. Each and every entry that resides within the DHT are essentially user chain entries that are merely marked as public.

Validation and Direct Peer-To-Peer Communication. The security, state and integrity of the whole system is maintained by logic that is hard-coded and bundled in every node. Data integrity is ruled by these rules which, in turn, uphold the security of the system. All data, whether it is in the user private chain or in the public DHT, is validated according to these rules. Normal messaging occurs when two users are online and is made through direct peer-to-peer connection in an end-to-end encrypted channel by resolving each agent's IP address. This method only works when both peers are online. To circumvent this, private messages are encrypted using the recipient's public key and published to the DHT, to later be retrieved by the recipient when they are back online.

Most of these networking protocols and distributed computing scenarios are handled by the Holochain framework, from which the architecture is based from. Not only it resolves many concerns regarding encryption but also allows for inter-operatibility with other systems that take part within the Holochain network.

4   Preliminary Evaluation

As this is a work-in-progress and with no tangible results yet yielded, it is possible to define an assessment strategy for it. BCI evaluation process will consist of usability tests performed by hand/arm impaired individuals to gather feedback on how the platform improves the user's communication and overall navigation compared with similar apps. Prior to testing, the subjects ought to train the BCI headset and tailor it to their mental activity for the model to recognize the commands from a specific user. Afterwards, subjects will be asked to perform a planned set of actions that entails navigating in the platform and interact with it. Lastly, a survey will be conducted following the System Usability Scale [3], with 10 items answered in a degree of agreement or disagreement with each statement on typical five-level Likert scale. For SSI, the datasets used for each model created will be divided into smaller training and testing sets, allowing to evaluate their accuracy, aiming to obtain the lowest WER possible.

The Holochain framework provides support for both unit and functional tests. These are useful to provide a measurement of code coverage and respective reliability. End-to-end tests will ultimately leverage a way to measure performance as the solution scales. The throughput is tracked as the number of users grows and its consistency is assessed. Early results have showcased successful data creation on the public DHT on a small number of users (five) with a step duration of 1000 ms, where the period is halved at every stage. In this, the stress test is conducted indefinitely and increases pace at every stage. Additionally, a small increase of throughput was noticed when more users joined the network, from two peers to five. These experiments have not shown any sensible traces of data corruption nor delay, although more tests on a higher scale are be needed to form more conclusive results.

5 Conclusion

This project mitigates communication barriers between subjects with or without hand/arm impairments and allows the inclusion of everyone into a single messaging system, using a new strategy to this type of platform, applying a synthetic telepathy approach for the interaction with it. Additionally, if the project produces positive results, the range of applicability for both BCI and SSI approaches can extend beyond the messaging paradigm.

The system that was outlined showcases a new proposal on the decentralized messaging platform, either from human-machine interaction standpoint or the distributed ecosystem counterpart. Following an user-centric approach towards the problem, utilizing a DHT with ad hoc peer consensus instead of data replication in its entirety with global consensus is more adequate to the messaging panorama. These design choices have a direct effect on performance and throughput of the system: more TPS can occur whilst the exchange of data is still secure, private and resilient against tampering attacks. This essentially means that scalability does not pose as a problem on a long-term perspective, unlike many solutions that are based on the classic blockchain concept.

6 Future Work

With the drafted architecture and design choices, there is still room for improvement for future project prospects so as to be providable to a broader audience and maintain a performance bottom line. On the human-machine interface counterpart, for the BCI component, other commands can be mapped and used by the platform, giving the user more options for navigation and control over the application, for a wider set of features, but keeping the interaction as intuitive as possible. SSI-wise, aiming for a more natural and reliable text input system for any user, efforts will be made for a session and user-independent system, enabling the its usage by multiple users and sessions without much accuracy fluctuations.

One of the objectives regarding the decentralized backend would be to go beyond message exchange and also extend to file sharing. Approaches could be developed similar to InterPlanetary File System (IPFS). However, this topic is sensitive since file storage takes up more space than common messages. Replication of data between peers would need to be addressed differently, perhaps through parallel channel or DHT altogether. Furthermore, voice calling could be another feature present within the application that could co-exist and be made through node-to-node channels.

References

1. Birbaumer, N., et al.: A spelling device for the paralysed. Nature **398**, 297–298 (1999). https://doi.org/10.1038/18581
2. Bouhnik, D., Deshen, M., Gan, R.: Whatsapp goes to school: mobile instant messaging between teachers and students. J. Inf. Technol. Educ. Res. **13**(1), 217–231 (2014)
3. Brooke, J., et al.: SUS-a quick and dirty usability scale. In: Usability Evaluation in Industry, vol. 189, no. 194, pp. 4–7 (1996)
4. Evgenov, P., et al.: White paper: Adamant messaging application. Technical report (2017). https://adamant.im/whitepaper/adamant-whitepaper-en.pdf
5. Fabiani, G.E., McFarland, D.J., Wolpaw, J.R., Pfurtscheller, G.: Conversion of EEG activity into cursor movement by a brain-computer interface (BCI). IEEE Trans. Neural Syst. Rehabil. Eng. **12**(3), 331–338 (2004). https://doi.org/10.1109/TNSRE.2004.834627
6. Khan, M.J., Hong, M.J., Hong, K.S.: Decoding of four movement directions using hybrid NIRS-EEG brain-computer interface. Front. Hum. Neurosci. **8**, 244 (2014). https://doi.org/10.3389/fnhum.2014.00244. https://www.frontiersin.org/article/10.3389/fnhum.2014.00244
7. Leavy, T.M., Ryan, G.: Decentralized authoritative messaging, 27 November 2018. US Patent 10,142,300
8. Nakamoto, S., et al.: Bitcoin: a peer-to-peer electronic cash system (2008). https://bitcoin.org/bitcoin.pdf
9. Rosello, P., Toman, P., Agarwala, N.: End-to-end neural networks for subvocal speech recognition. Stanford University (2017). http://www.pamelatoman.net/wp/wp-content/uploads/2018/06/subvocalspeechrecognitionpaper.pdf
10. Wan, Z., Guan, Z., Zhuo, F., Xian, H.: BKI: towards accountable and decentralized public-key infrastructure with blockchain. In: Lin, X., Ghorbani, A., Ren, K., Zhu, S., Zhang, A. (eds.) SecureComm 2017. LNICST, vol. 238, pp. 644–658. Springer, Cham (2018). https://doi.org/10.1007/978-3-319-78813-5_33
11. Wand, M., Janke, M., Schultz, T.: The EMG-UKA corpus for electromyography speech processing. In: INTERSPEECH-2014, pp. 1593–1597 (2014)

12. Williamson, J., Murray-Smith, R., Blankertz, B., Krauledat, M., Müller, K.R.: Designing for uncertain, asymmetric control: interaction design for brain-computer interfaces. Int. J. Hum. Comput. Stud. **67**, 827–841 (2009). https://doi.org/10.1016/j.ijhcs.2009.05.009
13. Wood, G., et al.: Ethereum: a secure decentralised generalised transaction ledger. Ethereum Project Yellow Paper **151**(2014), 1–32 (2014)

TACTILE – A Novel Mixed Reality System for Training and Social Interaction

Elisabeth Broneder[1]([⊠]), Christoph Weiß[1], Monika Puck[3],
Stephanie Puck[3], Emanuel Sandner[2], Adam Papp[1],
Gustavo Fernández Domínguez[1], and Miroslav Sili[2]

[1] Center for Digital Safety & Security, AIT Austrian Institute of Technology
GmbH, Vienna, Austria
elisabeth.broneder@ait.ac.at
[2] Center for Health & Bioresources, AIT Austrian Institute of Technology
GmbH, Vienna, Austria
[3] GTA GedächtnistrainingsAkademie, Salzburg, Austria
office@gedaechtnistraining.at

Abstract. Elderly people are frequently affected by a decline of mental and physical abilities, which results in anxiety, frailty and reclusiveness. Often, they live alone, spatially separated from their families or friends, unable to meet them on a regular basis. The TACTILE project addresses these challenges and fosters an active lifestyle and well-being of older adults via an enjoyable, innovative, and user-friendly Mixed Reality (MR) solution. The system enables training both the cognitive and physical state using MR technology and maintaining social contacts by connecting seniors with family and friends. Cognitive trainings are provided by conventional and physically available board games - such as Ludo - that are completed with virtual game pieces of a remote partner. Since the system uses real physical game pieces, the user experiences a tactile feedback that enables a more familiar feeling and thus novel way of digital interaction. Physical trainings are provided by a virtual avatar that explains and shows dedicated exercises, adaptable to the individual needs and physical restrictions of the user. Thus, the avatar accompanies the user during the physical training in a more natural way.

Keywords: Mixed Reality · Cognitive & physical training · Social inclusion · Tangible interaction · User experience · UX

1 Introduction

27% of older adults are completely inactive [1]. If elderly citizens are motivated to do more cognitive and physical exercises, it may have the potential to slow down mental and physical decline [2, 3]. Even 75 min a week of light physical activity could reduce the risk to develop a cardiovascular disease by as much as 14% [4]. Furthermore, the risk of developing dementia can also be reduced by playing challenging games, interacting with other people and doing physical exercises [5, 6]. Augmented Reality (AR), Virtual Reality (VR) and Mixed Reality (MR) technologies offer novel opportunities for an interactive learning style and new ways of interaction. There are some

© Springer Nature Switzerland AG 2020
C. Stephanidis and M. Antona (Eds.): HCII 2020, CCIS 1226, pp. 12–20, 2020.
https://doi.org/10.1007/978-3-030-50732-9_2

existing solutions for the elderly regarding physical or cognitive training using VR or AR but not MR like in TACTILE. Regarding VR, various solutions and projects can be found like the project Rehabilitation Gaming System (RGM) that reports a system for the rehabilitation of elderly people at home after suffering a brain lesion due to stroke [7]. Quintero et al. [8] survey the use of AR for education including minorities and students with impairments, noting that only 2% of the reviewed studies aim elderly people to improve their physical and mental health. Further research regarding VR and AR applications for the elderly target group can be found in [9–14]. However, existing solutions mainly aim to entertain, some have a focus on rehabilitation, but there is no communication or possibility to play together with a real person especially combined with a training aspect.

The goal of the EU project TACTILE is to foster an active lifestyle and well-being of older adults, through a solution that enables training both, the cognitive and physical state, and maintaining social contacts by connecting seniors with their family and friends. TACTILE provides an easy to use MR software for elderly people to play board games and do physical training exercises on MR glasses (Fig. 1).

Fig. 1. The idea of the TACTILE system. Left: User plays Ludo in Mixed Reality. Right: User is doing physical exercises together with a virtual avatar. © AIT/www.einstellungssache.at

2 The TACTILE System

The TACTILE system consists of the MR app that provides board games and physical trainings; and the portal that holds user accounts that can be managed by the secondary end-users like caregivers. The app runs on the MR glasses "Magic Leap One" (ML1)[1], which was chosen because of user requirements and market availability at project start. As development environment we are using the game engine Unity3D[2]. The final system will offer two board games – Ludo and Halma – as well as eight training

---

[1] https://www.magicleap.com/en-us/magic-leap-1.

[2] https://unity.com/.

exercises. At the current stage of the project, we implemented the first version of the board game – Ludo - along with four exercises. This setup is currently tested at the end-user partners GedächtnistrainingsAkademie (GTA) in Austria and TanteLouise (TAL) in the Netherlands.

2.1   Board Games

The MR app provides familiar board games that are played in a MR setting with a remote partner, which can be a family member, a friend or another secondary end-user like a caregiver. The user plays with physical game pieces on a real game board that he is looking at. The game board and pieces are detected and tracked via computer vision (CV) algorithms. To detect the game board, AprilTag [15] visual markers are used, which are mounted on the game board, as depicted in Fig. 2. Based on the detected pose of the markers, the location and rotation of the game board in real-world coordinates can be determined. Game pieces are detected using the geometry information of the detected game board and the derived well-known locations of the game fields, as well as CV algorithms based on image segmentation. The detected game pieces are displayed in the right position on the opponent's game board as virtual game figures. To avoid problems regarding occlusions and different light conditions, repainted pink Checkers figures are used for the first prototype to improve their detection. Figure 2 shows the board game in the MR glasses from the user's perspective.

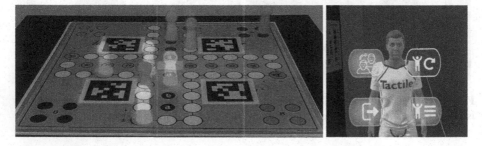

Fig. 2. Left: Virtual game figures are projected on the real game board. The red figures are belonging to the real Checker figures of the local player; the green ones are the projected figures of the remote player. Right: Training menu is overlaid on the avatar.

2.2   Physical Exercises

The TACTILE system provides physical trainings that are done together with a virtual avatar. The avatar explains the exercises and guides the user through the training. Since the virtual avatar is standing next to the user in the real environment in MR, the user is expected to be able to follow the instructions and demonstrations more easily. To adapt the physical trainings to the individual user needs, the trainings can be adjusted via a user portal in the browser. The secondary end-user can choose different exercises and combine them to a training. Difficulty levels can be defined and adapted according to the individual user needs. This makes sure that users with physical limitations are not excluded by the developed system.

3 Design and Development Methodology

TACTILE follows a user-centered design process. In a first step, end-user requirements were collected both in Austria and in the Netherlands by the end-user partners GedächtnistrainingsAkademie (GTA) and TanteLouise (TAL). In Austria, a requirements analysis with 11 workshops took place. 75 primary users (elderlies at an age >65 years) and 35 secondary users (relatives and caregivers) were asked by two psychologists about basic requirements. The requirements workshop for the primary users included questions about favorite and well-known board games, physical and visual disorders and conditions at home like the amount of space they have for the physical training. The secondary users were asked about requirements regarding the online portal (e.g. statistics, options to adjust the settings for the primary users). The exercises for the physical training were selected by literature research and expert interviews with occupational therapists and physiotherapists.

During development, end-users are constantly providing feedback via end-user workshops that are taking place at the end-user organizations in Austria and the Netherlands. The first user workshop took place in October 2019, where focus was on the user interface and interaction design as well as on the avatar design. Further, the first two training exercises were evaluated. The results of the first end-user workshop are described in Sect. 4. In the second workshop, which takes place in March 2020, four new exercises as well as the first board game – Ludo are tested by the end-users. In the final workshop, which will take place in August 2020, the end-users will evaluate the 3rd prototype, which will include all planned exercises as well as both board games. The feedback will support the further improvement of the prototype for the field trials that will start in February 2021 in Austria and the Netherlands.

3.1 UI Design and Interaction

Since older adults often have troubles handling technical devices, it is from uttermost importance to pay special attention to the user interaction during the development process of the MR solution. MR offers new opportunities to interact in a natural way that is familiar to this generation. In TACTILE, the MR application is designed in a way that only a minimal number of UI elements - such as buttons – are implemented, because it is important to keep the natural interaction that is familiar to the target group. Since the UI exists in the same 3D space as the other virtual elements, it is challenging to position it as to not disturb the user interaction when playing board games and doing physical exercises (see Fig. 2). For the first user workshop, we developed a UI prototype, where the user had to choose buttons of different size (see Fig. 3) with three different modes of interaction. One interaction mode is controller-based, the others are based on hand movement. The controller-based approach used the controller as laser pointer, selecting buttons with the laser beam and pressing a controller button. For both hand-based modes, a button is highlighted by holding the open hand over it. In the first mode, selection is achieved by keeping the hand over it for a few seconds and in the other one by closing the hand. Apart from the interaction modes, we investigated how the UI design must look in MR to easily select UI elements. Therefore, the interaction modes were tried out on UI screens with different number of buttons. Further, different font sizes and the color scheme were reviewed. The results are described in Sect. 4.

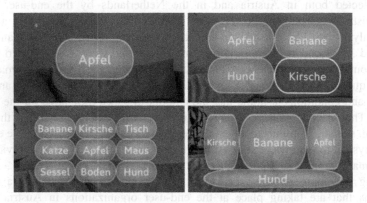

Fig. 3. Different button sizes with different interaction methods were tested in the first user workshop to find out how buttons have to be designed for the elderlies.

3.2 Avatar Design & Training Exercises

According to the collected end-user requirements, the first training exercises were implemented. Two avatars – one male and one female – were designed with respect to the older target group. In the first end-user workshop the avatar design as well as the first exercises were evaluated (see Fig. 4). Further, the sequence of the exercises and overall understanding of the avatar's explanation were assessed. The results are described in Sect. 4.

3.3 Board Games

Based on the outcome of the collected user requirements and the technical feasibility, the board games Ludo and Halma are chosen. Since elderlies often have problems with their fine motor skills, game pieces and dice larger than found in common board games are used. This also comes handy for the developed algorithms to detect the game board and the game pieces. As described in Sect. 2.1, we decided to choose game figures of the game "Checkers". In the second end-user workshop we want to find out if these figures are accepted by the elderlies or if they prefer the original game figures. Further, the end-users test the first board game - Ludo. The end-user feedback will define our future developments towards the third prototype.

4 Results

In October 2019 the first end-user workshop took place in Austria and the Netherlands. In the following the results of the first workshop in Austria are described. N = 20 primary users (PUs) (13 female, 7 male) and N = 19 secondary users (SUs) (13 female, 6 male) participated. The workshop lasted for one and a half hours and included interviews, several exercises wearing the ML1, and questions about usability and accessibility. The sociodemographic data shows that the PUs in Austria were on average 76.7 years old ($\pm$5.57 standard deviation N = 20) and the SUs were 42.2 years old ($\pm$14.2 standard deviation N = 19). Three of the PUs had no laptop, PC or mobile phone. 75% of PUs and 90% of SUs agreed to the sentence "technologies enrich my daily life" and 80% of the PUs and 95% of the SUs agreed to the sentence "I am critical about new technology". None of the PUs had any previous experience with AR or VR systems. 25% of the SUs had tried VR glasses for gaming before.

Fig. 4. Left: A virtual avatar (male or female) is guiding the user through the training exercises. Middle: User is following the movements of the avatar. Right: User is choosing a button

4.1 Test Sequence During the Workshop

The first user workshop was split in four different tasks. In the first task the participants had to put on the MR glasses, adjust them, turn them on and start the application. The exercise has been completed by all participants and only 15% of the PUs needed help by one of the workshop leaders. In the second task the participants had to select virtual buttons in the user interaction prototype as described in Sect. 3.1 the different number and sizes of the buttons made no difference for the participants. Great differences appeared when the participants rated the different interaction methods for choosing the buttons as shown in Table 1. The PUs and SUs rated the three possibilities from 1 "very good" to 5 "very bad". In the third task two players tried to connect to each other and choose a board game. All participants described the procedure as easy to understand and straightforward.

Table 1. Percentage of participants that rated the interaction methods as "very good" or "good".

	Controller	Hand over button	Fist making
Primary user (AT)	95%	55%	55%
Secondary user (AT)	100%	50%	15.79%

The last task was about the physical training. The participants had to choose between the male and female avatar, place it into the room, start the physical training and provide feedback about the training exercises. None of the SUs and 5 PUs needed help to complete this task. The main problems were the positioning of the avatar and the differentiation between the exercise explanation and the avatar's instruction to actually start the training exercise.

4.2 Usability/Accessibility

After completing the tasks, participants were asked to answer questions regarding the usability and accessibility. A 5-point Likert scale ranging from "I absolutely agree" to "I absolutely disagree" was used. 18 PUs and 18 SUs completed the questionnaire. 50% of the PUs and 88.89% of the SUs claimed that they want to use the system more often. Another 25% of the PUs answered neutral and claimed that they have to see more of the system in the next workshop to evaluate it properly. 83.3% of SUs and 63.3% of PUs rated the system as not unnecessarily complex. 100% of SUs and 83.3% of PUs claimed that the system was easy to use. 27.76% of PUs and 5.56% of the SUs claimed that they would need help of a technically more experienced person, but 94.45% of SUs and 66.67% of PUs think that they would easily learn to use the system. Only one SU and 3 PUs said that the system was strange to use. 94.44% of the SUs and 77.78% of the PUs agreed to the sentence "I felt very comfortable while using the system". In terms of accessibility 100% of SUs and 83.3% of the PUs agreed that the meaning of the buttons was clear, but only 50% in each group agreed that the information in the system was highlighted properly. 2 PUs and 1 SU rated the contrast between foreground and background in the user interface as not clear enough. None of the asked participants disagreed to the sentence "the navigation to go ahead in the system was clear" and 100% of the asked participants agreed that the feedback of the system was sufficient to know if the steps were done right.

5 Summary and Outlook

This work highlights the aim, the technical prototype, and the first user involvement results of the EU co-funded project TACTILE. The paper underlines that MR-based solutions have various supporting potentials but are not widely used, especially not in the target group of older adults. As outlined in Sect. 4, the TACTILE prototype highly motivates seniors to use, learn from, and enjoy the solution even if it is still in an early development stage. The feedback of the first user workshop was incorporated into the second prototype that is currently tested in Austria and the Netherlands. In our future activities we will evaluate and incorporate the feedback of the current end-user workshops and implement the second board game "Halma" and the remaining training exercises that will be tested in the 3rd end-user workshop. These results will further support the final development phase before the final TACTILE prototype will be tested and evaluated by the primary- and secondary target group in a long-lasting field trial phase in Austria and the Netherlands.

Acknowledgment. The project TACTILE is co-funded by the AAL Joint Programme (AAL-2018-5-143-CP) and the following National Authorities and R&D programs in Austria, Switzerland, and the Netherlands: FFG, Schweizer Eidgenossenschaft, ZonMw.

References

1. Townsend, N., Wickramasinghe, K., Williams, J., Bhatnagar, P., Rayner, M.: Physical activity statistics. British Heart Foundation, pp. 1–128 (2015)
2. Cohen, G., Perlstein, S., Chapline, J., Kelly, J., Firth, K., Simmens, S.: The impact of professionally conducted cultural programs on the physical health, mental health, and social functioning of older adults. Gerontologist **46**(6), 726–734 (2006). https://doi.org/10.1093/geront/46.6.726
3. Seeman, T., Lusignolo, T., Albert, M., Berkman, L.: Social relationships, social support, and patterns of cognitive aging in healthy, high-functioning older adults: MacArthur studies of successful aging. Health Psychol. **20**(4), 243–255 (2001). https://doi.org/10.1037/0278-6133.20.4.243
4. Barnes, A.: Obesity and sedentary lifestyles: risk for cardiovascular disease in women. Tex. Heart Inst. J. **39**(2), 224–227 (2002). http://www.ncbi.nlm.nih.gov/pubmed/22740737
5. Verghese, J., Lipton, R., Katz, M., Hall, C.: Leisure activities and the risk of dementia in the elderly. N. Engl. J. Med. **348**(25), 2508–2516 (2003)
6. Hikichi, H., Kondo, K., Takeda, T., Kawachi, I.: Social interaction and cognitive decline: results of a 7-year community intervention. Havard T.H, Chan School of Public Health (2017)
7. http://www.aal-europe.eu/projects/rgs. Accessed 10 Mar 2020
8. Quintero, J., Baldiris, S., Rubira, R., Cerón, J., Velez, G.: Augmented reality in educational inclusion. a systematic review on the last decade. Front. Psychol. **10** (2019). Article 1835
9. https://rendever.com/. Accessed 10 Mar 2020
10. http://www.agedcarevirtualreality.com. Accessed 10 Mar 2020
11. Optale, G., Urgesi, C., Busato, V., Marin, S., Piron, L., Priftis, K., Gamberini, L., Capodieci, S., Bordin A.: Controlling memory impairment in elderly adults using virtual reality memory training: a randomized controlled pilot study. Neurorehabil. Neural Repair **24**, 348–357 (2010)
12. Freeman, D., Reeve, S., Robinson, A., Ehlers, A., Clark, D., Spanlang, B., Slater M.: Virtual reality in the assessment, understanding, and treatment of mental health disorders. Psychol. Med. **47**(14), 2393–2400 (2017)

13. Dey, A., Billinghurst, M., Lindeman, R.W., Swan, J.: A systematic review of 10 years of augmented reality usability studies: 2005 to 2014. Front. Rob. AI **5**, 37 (2018)

14. Cao, S.: Virtual reality applications in rehabilitation. In: 2016, Part I Proceedings of the 18th International Conference on Human-Computer Interaction. Theory, Design, Development and Practice, vol. 9731, pp. 3–10 (2016). https://doi.org/10.1007/978-3-319-39510-4_1

15. Olson, E.: A robust and flexible visual fiducial system. In: Proceedings of the IEEE International Conference on Robotics and Automation, pp. 2400–2407, May 2011

Affordance Requirements in Product Interface Design for Elderly User

Hui-Qing Cai[✉] and Li-Hao Chen

Fu Jen Catholic University, No. 510, Zhongzheng Road, Xinzhuang District,
New Taipei City 24205, Taiwan
chuiqing8@gmail.com, ahao55@gmail.com

Abstract. The elderly find they have difficulty interacting with products as their physiological functions deteriorate. In interaction design, affordance, a design concept, provides a direction that guides the intuitive behaviors of users. Affordance is considered differently among design applications, and also plays different roles in designing user interfaces. This research aims to discuss the applications of affordance in designing product interfaces for the elderly through focus group interviews. With rice cooker interfaces as the research tool, we have invited 10 elderly people to express and exchange their subjective opinions on the operation and use of product interfaces. The research results show that: the product interfaces for the elderly should be designed to simplify functional affordance (FA), thus reducing the cognitive load of the elderly; conventional affordance (CA) should be designed based on the previous experience and knowledge of the elderly; and physical affordance (PA) should be presented in a streamlined and consistent manner. The research results can provide a reference for the intuitive design of product interfaces for the elderly, and promote effective interaction between elderly users and product interfaces, thereby improving the living quality of the elderly.

Keywords: Affordance · Product interface · Elder users

1 Introduction

With the advent of an aging society, the elderly are receiving much attention. The elderly are facing the threat of physiological deterioration, including impaired perception, motor skills, and cognitive abilities. Physiological deterioration makes it difficult for the elderly to operate or use products. For example, reduced visual acuity prevents the elderly from seeing tiny things [1], and memory loss also makes the elderly often forget their previous experiences. In recent years, affordance has been valued in interaction design. Affordance is proposed by Gibson [2] to represent the interaction between living organisms and the environment. Hartson [3] believes that users should achieve their goals by perceiving, understanding and utilizing affordance when operating products. The affordance of a certain product allows users to know how to operate the product through observation [4]. This research discusses the roles and requirements of various types of affordance in the interaction between elderly users and

© Springer Nature Switzerland AG 2020
C. Stephanidis and M. Antona (Eds.): HCII 2020, CCIS 1226, pp. 21–28, 2020.
https://doi.org/10.1007/978-3-030-50732-9_3

product interfaces. Future product interfaces for the elderly could be designed on the basis of the research results.

Due to the different perspectives on affordance in interaction design, this research will use the types of affordance proposed by Chen [5] to divide affordance into functional affordance, conventional affordance, and physical affordance.

1.1 Functional Affordance

Functional affordance refers to the design function [3] that can help users complete their work, which is used to indicate the usage of products [5]. Gibson [2] holds that affordance contains all the possibilities of any person taking a certain action in the environment, such as eating an apple either by biting or swallowing. Any product to be used also provides users with all possible usages, while the users' current intention determines what possible usage they may select. Chen [6] points out that users should perceive the affordance of product during their interaction with the product. During the interaction, users will decide the usage of product according to their behavior intention and product features at that time. If their intention and goals can be satisfied by the usage of product, it proves that the functional affordance of product can be perceived by its users [5].

1.2 Conventional Affordance

Conventional affordance allows users to understand the features of product. For example, a button logo can help users understand what will happen when they click the button [3]. Conventional affordance is indicated in the form of icons, symbols or texts [7]. Blacker [8] believes that designing products based on the previous knowledge of target users can improve the ease of use of products. The previous knowledge and experience of users are highly related to conventional affordance, because they often perceive conventional affordance through culture and convention [5]. In other words, the conventional affordance of product interfaces should be designed taking into account the previous experience and knowledge of users.

1.3 Physical Affordance

Physical affordance can help users to actually operate on product interfaces. For example, a button large enough is convenient for users to press it [3]. Physical affordance is generally expressed by the size, shape, and material of product [9]. Blackler et al. [10, 11] propose that the appearance characteristics of products have the greatest influence on operation time and intuitive use. In interaction design, users perceive the affordance of products on their own, and the appearance characteristics of products are clues to help users operate products correctly [4]. In addition, Chen [5] also believes that physical affordance should correspond to the behaviors, abilities, and body size of users. Therefore, the product interfaces for elderly users should be designed considering the correspondence between the conditions of users and product features.

1.4   Relevance of Affordance to Product Usage

As shown in Fig. 1, users will determine whether the functional affordance supports the intended use according to their own goals. If so, users will start operating their products. During the use of products, users will utilize physical affordance and conventional affordance to achieve their goals by operating these products. For the rice cooker interfaces, we get to know the influence of their affordance on elderly users through focus group interviews.

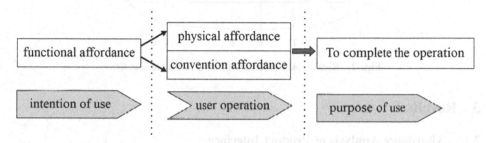

Fig. 1. Relevance of affordance to user operation (Chen 2007).

2   Method

2.1   Design Process

First, we divide affordance into functional affordance (FA), conventional affordance (CA), and physical affordance (PA). Second, we analyze the affordance of each functional component in a rice cooker interface, and carry out focus group interviews (fully recorded by video and audio means) according to the two basic operation procedures of rice cooker interface. Finally, we analyze the interface operation problems, causes, and subjective opinions proposed by the participants of interviews, and summarize the operation behaviors of elderly users and the requirements of all types of affordance in the interface.

2.2   Participants and Product Interfaces

In this research, 10 elderly users aged over 65 are invited to participate in 2 focus group interviews, 5 of which are included in Group A (mean age: 76.0; SD: 6.6) and another 5 of which are included in Group B (mean age: 79.0; SD: 4.7). These two interviews are conducted in two nursing homes in Taiwan. A rice cooker interface, as shown in Fig. 2, is selected as the research tool: "Function Select" button (A), "Cooking" button (B), "Close" button (C), "Timer" button (D), "Hour" button (E), "Minute" button (F), Display Panel (G).

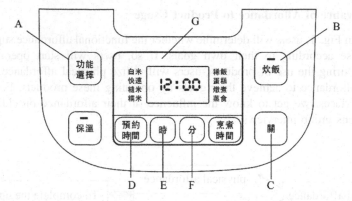

Fig. 2. Rice cooker interface (drawn in this research).

3 Results

3.1 Affordance Analysis of Product Interface

The rice cooker interface herein consists of 7 components (see Fig. 2), of which 6 components are operational, including: "Function Select" button (A), "Cooking" button (B), "Close" button (C), "Timer" button (D), "Hour" button (E), and "Minute" button (F). The Display Panel (G) is for viewing only and is not operable. This paper evaluates and analyzes the components of rice cooker interface with three types of affordance, as shown in Table 1. The functional affordance of components is their main functions; the conventional affordance is the operation information expressed by texts, symbols and images on the components; and the physical affordance is the operation mode of components. For example, for the "Function Select" component, its FA is to select cooking mode; its CA is expressed by text; and its PA is expressed by "press with fingers".

Table 1. Requirements analysis of functional, conventional and physical affordance (prepared by this research).

Components	Main functions	Description of CA	Description of PA
A	To select cooking mode	Text: Function Select	Press with fingers
B	To start cooking	Text: Cooking	Press with fingers
C	To power off	Text: Close	Press with fingers
D	To set the starting time	Text: Timer	Press with fingers
E	To set cooking time (hour)	Text: Hour	Press with fingers
F	To set cooking time (minute)	Text: Minute	Press with fingers
G	To display function status and information	Display Panel	Display information

3.2   Affordance Analysis of Operating Task

This paper analyzes two operating tasks of rice cooker, i.e. Cooking and Timer, and their subtasks, along with user operations, as shown in Table 2. For example, for the "Cooking" task, its sub-tasks include "click the 'Function Select' button", "click the 'Cooking' button", and "click the 'Close' button". Involved components include "Function Select" button (A), "Cooking" button (B), and "Close" button (C).

Table 2. List of test operating tasks (prepared by this research).

Operating	Subtask and operation	Involved component
1. Cooking	1.1 Click the "Function Select" button	A: Function Select
	1.2 Click the "Cooking" button	B: Cooking
	1.3 Click the "Close" button	C: Close
2. Timer	2.1 Click the "Function Select" button	A: Function Select
	2.2 Click the "Timer" button	D: Timer
	2.3 Click the "Hour"/"Minute" button	E: Hour F: Minute
	2.4 Click the "Close" button	C: Close

3.3   Analysis of Interview Results

This paper collects the opinions from elderly users in focus group interviews and finds out relevant affordance types for analysis, as shown in Table 3.

Table 3. Affordance analysis for operating tasks (prepared by this research).

Operating task	Problems and findings	Relevant affordance
1. Cooking	1. Operation steps are complicated and difficult to remember	CA
	2. Tasks are inconsistent with the previous experience of participants	CA
	3. All participants can see the text on interface	PA
2. Timer	1. Participants do not know the function of "Timer" button	CA
	2. Participants may forget to click the "Cooking" button in the "Timer" mode	CA
	3. Participants fail to select the right button because there are too many buttons on the interface	PA
	4. Participants do not know the correct operation steps	CA
	5. Participants believe that only a few of the buttons in the interface are necessary	FA

CA: conventional affordance PA: physical affordance FA: functional affordance

The results show that most of the problems encountered by participants in Operating Task 1 are arising from CA. For example, participants think that operation steps are complicated and difficult to remember. It is because that this task is inconsistent with the previous experience of participants. Many participants mention that previous products allow them to start cooking by clicking only one button, while the operation steps of new rice cookers are too complicated for them. In Operation Task 2, participants propose that they do not know the function of Timer button, which indicates that the CA of "Timer" button (D) could not be perceived by participants; participants also point out that there are many unnecessary functions on the interface, which indicates that the FA of current rice cooker interface has placed a burden on elderly users and prevented them from direct and quick interaction with products. In both interviews, all participants are able to see the text on the interface and know that they can operate components by pressing relevant buttons. However, participants also think that there are too many components on the interface, indicating that the PA of interface has caused operational obstacles against the participants.

4 Discussion

The interview results show that: In terms of FA, elderly users think that operating tasks are too complicated and many functions are unnecessary. Due to the decline of cognitive abilities, the memory and judgment of elderly users are not as good as average people. The complicated operation steps and excessive functions of current rice cookers increase the cognitive load of elderly users. Norman [4] takes the ease of steps required by users to operate any product as the assessment criteria for product usability. FA is a design function that can help users complete their goals. Excessive functions of current rice cooker interface are unaffordable to the cognition of elderly users. Therefore, the product interfaces for elderly users should be designed to remove unnecessary functions or simplify complicated functions, so that FA can be presented in a simple and clear manner.

In terms of CA, participants find it hard to understand the text on components. In any product interface, CA is indicated in the form of texts, symbols or icons, while the texts, icons, and symbols perceived by users come from their previous knowledge and experience. When the CA of current rice cooker interface is inconsistent with the previous experience of participants, they will not be able to operate the rice cooker effectively. Hartson [3] states that among usability problems, 75% of which relate to CA, and CA is the main mechanism for the learning and memory of all users. His statement is also confirmed in this research. Most of the interface problems of elderly participants of focus group interviews are arising from CA because they fail to learn and remember the CA of interface. Therefore, in the design of product interfaces, the previous experience and knowledge of elderly users can be used to strengthen the CA of components, so that elderly users can use their experience to interact with product interfaces.

In terms of PA, all participants can see the text on interface and know that they can operate components by pressing relevant buttons. However, participants point out that excessive components of interface have prevented them from completing their operation goals. This paper proposes to reduce the number of components, and improve the consistency by the functions, appearance, location and other forms of interfaces as suggested by Blacker [12]. Therefore, the interface components should be designed in a streamlined, regular, and consistent manner, so that PA can be presented in the most effective way.

5 Conclusion

Product design is paying more attention to elderly users due to the aging of population. The understanding and operation abilities of elderly users on product interfaces have gradually declined along with the continuous deterioration of physiological functions, especially cognitive abilities. This research discusses different types of affordance among product interfaces for elderly users, and aims to promote the intuitive interaction between elderly users and product interfaces. The research results show that: (1) Excessive functions on product interfaces place a burden on elderly users. These product interfaces should be designed to reduce the memory load of elderly users by simplifying the FA of interface; (2) the major problem in the interaction between elderly users and product interfaces is that the CA of interface is inconsistent with the cognition of elderly users. The CA of interface should be designed based on the previous experience and knowledge of elderly users; (3) the interface components should be designed in a streamlined, regular, and consistent manner, so that PA can be presented in an effective way to reduce the operating time of elderly users. As a pre-test, this research aims to discuss the affordance requirements of elderly users for product interfaces and provide a basis for the subsequent design of interface affordance. This research only uses rice cooker interfaces as its research tool, and explores the design of product interfaces for elderly users with qualitative methods. In the subsequent researches, different product interfaces and operating tasks will be included and further analysis will be performed by quantitative methods. The affordance of product interfaces for elderly users can be designed based on the conclusions.

Acknowledgement. This research was supported by the grant from the Ministry of Science and Technology, Taiwan, Grant 107-2410-H-030-059-MY2.

References

1. Welford, A.T.: Changes of performance with age. In: Charness, N. (ed.) Aging and Human Performance. Wiley, New York (1985)
2. Gibson, J.J.: The Ecological Approach to Visual Perception. Houghton Mifflin Company, Boston (1979)
3. Hartson, H.R.: Cognitive, physical, and perceptual affordances in interaction design. Behav. Inf. Technol. 22(5), 315–338 (2003)
4. Norman, D.A.: The Design of Everyday Things. Basic Books Inc., New York (1990)
5. Chen, L.H., Lee, C.F., Ho, M.C.: Application of affordance concept on product design. J. Sci. Technol. Sci. Technol. 16(2), 143–151 (2007)
6. Chen, L.H.: Affordance requirements for intuitive user-product interaction. Bull. Jpn. Soc. Sci. Des. 60(1), 61–68 (2013)

7. Chen, L.H., Cheng, P.J.: Affordances of virtual touch button in user-computer interaction. In: Proceedings of 5th International Congress of International Association of Societies of Design Research, Tokyo, Japan, pp. 3610–3616 (2013)
8. Blackler, A., Hurtienne, J.: Towards a unified view of intuitive interaction: definitions, models and tools across the world. MMI-Interaktiv 13(2007), 36–54 (2007). ISSN 1439-7854
9. Chen, L.H., Liu, Y.C.: Affordance design requirements to promote intuitive user-product interaction for elderly users with dementia (I). J. Sci. Des. 2(2), 53–62 (2018)
10. Blackler, A., Popovic, V., Mahar, D.: Intuitive interaction with complex artefacts. In: Proceedings of Futureground Design Research Society International Conference, Melbourne (2004)
11. Blackler, A., Popovic, V., Mahar, D.: Intuitive interaction applied to interface design. In: Proceedings of International Design Congress, Douliou, Taiwan (2005)
12. Blackler, A., Popovic, V., Mahar, D.: Towards a design methodology for applying intuitive interaction. In: Proceedings of Wonderground, Design Research Society International Conference, Lisbon, Portugal (2006)

A Resort or A Remote Village? - Using Jobs-To-Be-Done Theory to Understand Elderly's Thinking Toward Senior Residences in Taiwan

Miao-Hsien Chuang[1]([⊠]), Ming-Shien Wen[2], and You-Shan Lin[2]

[1] Department of Visual Communication Design,
Ming Chi University of Technology, New Taipei City, Taiwan
joyceblog@gmail.com
[2] Cardiology, Chang Gung Medical Foundation, New Taipei City, Taiwan
wenms123@cgmh.org.tw, sherrylin0824@gmail.com

Abstract. Contrary to westerners' recognition towards senior residences, Asians have a deep-rooted concept of "Bring up children for the purpose of being looked after in old age". In Asian society, it is considered a blessing for elderly to live with their family among many generations. Thus, living in a senior residence is considered an indignity, in which the elderly are perceived to have been abandoned by their children. Society in Taiwan does not have a positive attitude toward senior residences. In fact, an effective health and wellness organization that senior residences can provide will help improve the "twilight years" of the elderly, and at the same time, reduce the proportion of the "disability population" of the entire society.

This research uses the Progress Making Forces Diagram in Jobs-to-be-Done theory to understand the attitudes of residents in a seniors health and care village and the attitudes of "hesitants" (i.e., those who have doubts about living in senior residences). This research adopts the research method of focus interviews in order to explore the residents' ideas of the two forces of "push" of the situation and "magnetism" of the new solution as well as those of the hesitants regarding their "habit" of the present and "anxiety" of the new solution.

In our research, a total of six focus group interviews were conducted. Three groups of interviewees, which included 22 people in total, were already occupants of a senior home village. The other three groups of interviewees, which also included 22 people in total, focused on hesitants who were living at home with their families. Based on the analysis of grounded theory, we found that safety, health, and learning were most attractive for the residents, who viewed an seniors health and care village as "a free resort". In contrast, the hesitants were satisfied with living their families and their living environment and did not want to be isolated in "a remote village". These findings provide preliminary concepts for quasi-elderly on the attitudes of their peers with regard to senior residences. Furthermore, these findings also provide a reference for senior residences that will aid in marketing and promotion.

Keywords: Jobs-to-be-done · Senior residences · Progress Making Forces diagram

© Springer Nature Switzerland AG 2020
C. Stephanidis and M. Antona (Eds.): HCII 2020, CCIS 1226, pp. 29–34, 2020.
https://doi.org/10.1007/978-3-030-50732-9_4

1 Introduction

Aging society is a prominent global problem caused by the large population of baby boomers (those born between 1946 and 1964). Public and private agencies in Europe, the United States, and Asia have been forced to proactively face this phenomenon. In the United States, approximately 76 million people who were born during the baby boom period are now entering their senior years. Currently, approximately 3 million older adults in Taiwan are 65 years or older. The aging speed of Taiwanese society is on par with countries such as Hong Kong, South Korea, and Singapore. In 2018, Taiwan became an aged society (i.e., older adults constitute more than 14% of the population) and is expected to become a super-aged society (i.e., older adults constitute more than 20% of the population) by 2026. By 2061, every 1.2 young adults in Taiwan would need to support an older adult. According to the 2017 Report of the Senior Citizen Condition Survey published by the Taiwan Ministry of Health and Welfare, 55% of adults who are 55 years or older prefer to "live with their children"; only 10%–20% intend to enter a care institution. However, 30%–40% of adults intended to enter a care institution if they lost the ability to perform self-care. Younger people are more open to the idea of living in a care institution. However, adults older than 55 years currently residing in a care institution only constitute 1.22% of the total population. In both Western and Eastern countries, the baby boomer generation, which possesses both high financial capability and high academic qualifications, will eventually enter their senior years. Thus, retirement care and living arrangements for this population group pose a problem for governmental agencies, space providers, and space users.

2 Literature Review

2.1 Living Preferences of Older Adults

Older adults in Western countries have three types of living arrangements: long distance migration, aging in place, and age segregation. The details of each stage are explained as follows: (1) Long distance migration involves older adults migrating to live in an area with a milder climate (e.g., Florida, USA) and is further divided into three stages. Stage 1 typically occurs after retirement (65–74 years old). In this stage, older adults typically possess good health, intact marriages, and sufficient financial resources at this stage. Therefore, long distance migration at this stage is known as "amenity migration". Stage 2 typically occurs during the mid- or late 70s of older adults. During this stage, older adults begin facing physical or cognition problems, and most have a deceased spouse and reduced financial resources. At this stage, older adults move from the areas they migrated to in Stage 1 to their original residences to receive care from their family members or adult children. In Stage 3, the long distance migration is derived from dependency; it typically involves severely disabled older adults in need of high-level care and whose needs cannot be fulfilled by informal care from family members. (2) Aging in place refers to the condition in which older adults continue living in their original residences. However, they may require assistance for transport, shopping, house repair and cleaning, and meal preparation. (3) Age segregation refers to when older adults move to live in houses specially designed for older adults. This accommodation option typically involves the provision of services such as meals, social events, short tour trips, transportation, and medical healthcare (Huang and Yang 2010). Compared to older adults in Western countries, the proportion of those in Eastern countries who experience long distance migration is relatively smaller. Currently, accommodation service organizations for Stage 3 (age segregation) are rapidly growing.

Based on her experience of volunteering at senior care institutions in the United States and Japan, Chen (2010) asserted that older adults in the United States are more magnanimous in their expectations toward their children. Older adults in the United States believe that it is their duty or responsibility to bring up their children and that they are responsible for taking care of themselves when they enter their senior years. Therefore, American older adults who stay in senior care institutions are happy with the occasional visit of their children. By contrast, older adults in Japan who live in senior care institutions believe that it is obligatory for their children to regularly visit them. Because of these expectations, they experience a sense of loss when their children do not make the visit. Chu (2011) asserts that core families in the United States disintegrate after the children have grown up and moved out for work. Older adults then enter the empty nest period during this time. Therefore, situations in which older adults are surrounded by their children and grandchildren and can frequently play with their grandchildren only appear in Eastern societies.

2.2 Senior Health and Care Villages

Currently, the institutional care system in Taiwan is classified based on the extent of older adults' degree of (1) ability to perform self-care and (2) requiring living assistance from others. (1) Care institutions for older adults who can perform self-care are divided into senior apartments and senior care institutions; the former of which gives leasing priority to older adults from low and middle income households and those who do not possess self-use residences, the latter of which are open for self-financing older adults. The "senior health and care villages" mentioned in this study belong to this category. (2) Care institutions for older adults who require living assistance from others include long-term care institutions, nursing institutions, welfare service institutions for the disabled, and veterans' homes.

In this study, the researchers defined "health and care villages" as follows (1) a health preservation and promotion organization that provides accommodation services for senior citizens. (2) Their customer base is the retired population in good health and who possess self-care ability and mobility. Accommodation space in the organizations is leased. (3) Service provision methods include institutions providing professional medical services, high quality retirement living environments (including a gym, sports area, cultural classes, cultural classroom, library, restaurant facilities, and fine dining) and various learning courses and recreational activities.

2.3   Job-To-Be-Done Theory

In the past, the Product Development and Management Association of the United States regarded customers' needs as a "fuzzy front end" in which customers' needs are unpredictable and can only be roughly inferred through inaccurate market surveys. Therefore, successful innovation is completely dependent on luck. Christensen et al. (2017) noted that 84% of senior executives around the world believe that innovation is crucial for business growth. However, 94% of senior executives are unsatisfied with the innovation performance of their organizations. Christensen et al. (2017) reported that innovation should be independent of luck, and aspiring innovators should instead try to use the "right questions" to understand situations in which customers want to "hire" or "fire" their products or services. By using the "right questions," innovation performance can be highly predictable.

Christensen et al. (2017) stated that customers do not actually buy products or services, but rather incorporate products and services to progress in their lives. In job-to-be-done theory, progress is referred to as a "job". Therefore, customers hire certain products or services to accomplish certain tasks in their lives. However, customers' decision-making process begins before they step into a store. The decision-making process is complex and dominated by two opposing forces that constantly contest each other to dominate a customer's decisions.

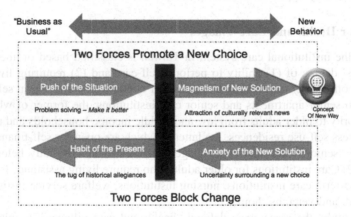

Fig. 1. Progress Making Forces diagram (Source: Moesta and Spiek 2013)

The coauthors of job-to-be-done theory, Moesta and Spiek (2013), used the idea of tugging forces and developed the Progress Making Forces diagram. According to this diagram (Fig. 1), consumers may choose new behavior because of a push or pull force (also known as magnetism) or may maintain their old behavior because of anxiety and inertia. In the Progress Making Forces diagram, (1) push refers to force exerted by a situation (i.e., the "push" of the situation). This represents instances or situations in which customers truly feel that an old solution or habit does not work and various dissatisfactions gradually accumulate. (2) Pull represents the attractiveness of a new solution (i.e., its "magnetism") and elements that catch the attention of customers when they see a new method or new solution. (3) Inertia refers to the "habit" of the present. This element concerns how customers lament an old method and attachments to old solutions and habits. (4) Anxiety is the "anxiety" of a new solution, which is the type of worries and concerns customers have upon seeing a new solution.

3 Research Methods

This research used the Progress Making Forces diagram from jobs-to-be-done theory to understand the attitude of residents toward senior health and care villages and the attitude of "hesitants" (i.e., those with doubts about living in senior residences). Six focus group interview sessions were conducted; three of which featured 22 current occupants of senior health and care villages, the other three which focused on 22 hesitants.

A focus group interview is a group interview research method that involves using a moderator as the leader of the interview session. Features of focus group interviews include the follows: (1) Participants generate thoughts, opinions, and attitudes after interacting with others and brainstorming. (2) Researchers have the opportunity to directly interact with participants. (3) Researchers can acquire answers that participants construct using their own "language" (4) The method can obtain diverse answers to a question more rapidly than with one-on-one in-depth interviews. The researchers of this study aimed to understand the decision-making mentality of two groups on living in a senior health and care village through the following procedures. First, the interviewees were invited to freely express their opinions regarding a certain problem. The interview sessions were audibly taped, and the audio recordings were used to produce verbatim transcripts that are useful for concept extraction analysis.

4 Results and Discussions

The study results indicated that the push factors that caused current occupants to enter a seniors health and care village were its safety; that fact that it is a lodging place for themselves; their unwillingness to trouble their children, family, or friends; the availability of around-the-clock help from others (i.e., management personnel and other village occupants), their urgency to check themselves into the village while they were healthy to prevent losing their eligibility to enter after falling ill, and to help care for parents who also live in the village. However, intense attractive features (magnetism) include the exquisite environment, availability of space in the village, quiet environment, the chance to engage in diverse learning, and the chance to lead a new, simple, and comfortable life. Many village occupants feel that they live in a resort and that they feel young again by having fun with other village occupants of similar age.

Some hesitants choose to remain in the inertia of stable old habits because they believe that they and their partners are in good health and can take care of each other, they current have a comfortable living space, and they are familiar with the local environment. Factors causing their hesitation include obligations to elderly parents, yearning for their children and grandchildren, negative opinions that family and friends have toward care institutions (i.e., living in a care institution means being abandoned by one's children), and adaptation problems. Some hesitants believe that the traffic inaccessibility of health and care villages may cause them to feel "imprisoned". This results in their decision-making anxiety.

5   Conclusions and Suggestions

This research used the Progress Making Forces diagram of jobs-to-be-done theory to understand the thoughts of current occupants of senior health and care villages and the attitude of hesitants regarding living in such villages. The focus group interview results indicated that under two pushing and tugging forces, both groups exhibited meticulous considerations regarding themselves. Many studies have indicated that having a positive and happy village life helps maintain the curiosity of older adults. This then promotes physical and mental health and ultimately enhances their "healthy years". However, given the close-knit emotional bonds between Eastern older adults and their children and adaptation problems associated to moving in senior health and care villages, the considerations of hesitants may serve as reference for senior health and care village operators.

References

Chen, H.H.: Happy Silver Go (2010). https://reurl.cc/4RyWRR
Christensen, C.M., Hall, T., Dillion, K., Duncan, D.: Competing Against Luck- The Story of Innovation and Customer Choice (H. F. Hong, Trans.). Common Wealth, Taipei (2017). (Original Work Published 2016)
Chu, N.H.: Elderly people in the United States and elderly issues. In: Lou, S. (ed.) Age of Creation: Silver Storm Strikes. LiHsu, Taipei (2011)
Huang, F.S., Yang, K.D.: Gerontology. WuNan, Taipei (2010)
Moesta, B., Spiek, C.: Jobs to be Done: Switch Workshop (2013). https://www.slideshare.net/marklittlewood/jobs-to-be-doneswitch-workshop
Taiwan Ministry of Health and Welfare: Report of the Senior Citizen Condition Survey (2017). https://dep.mohw.gov.tw/DOS/lp-1767-113.html

Design Method of Online Health Education with Service Interaction System for the Elderly

Binliang Chen, Yongyan Guo[✉], Yinjun Xia, Yiyang Mao, and Guanhua Wang

School of Art Design and Media, East China University of Science and Technology, Meilong Road 130, Shanghai, China
1009694856@qq.com, g_gale@163.com

Abstract. The demand for elderly health education and health counseling is increasing and the quality of health services for the elderly needs to be improved. Therefore, the purpose of this study is to explore the factors that affect the elderly adults' access to health education, and to establish the design method of related service system to improve the user experience. Research method: In this research a user journey map and an elderly user's emotional experience map for the current health education service were drawn to find the pain points and the improvement suggestions. The focus group and the co-design workshop were held to get the design elements and suggestions of the aging health education service system.

Keywords: Service design method · Aging · Health education · User experience

1 Introduction

With the deepening of aging population degree, medical and nursing problems are increasingly prominent, and the demand for elderly health services is increasing. The mainstream health education services mainly include community offline lectures, offline free consultation, TV health programs, etc. In recent years, some health service software has also been available on mobile clients, WeChat mini programs, and WeChat public accounts. However, there are some problems such as poor systematic knowledge, lack of pertinence and inconvenient note taking, which make the elderly adults unable to remember health information even if they listen to lectures repeatedly. With the rapid development of computer technology and information technology, it is possible to replace human services with new technologies of online health education. Health education service system need to be developed to suit the aging trend combining with the current background.

© Springer Nature Switzerland AG 2020
C. Stephanidis and M. Antona (Eds.): HCII 2020, CCIS 1226, pp. 35–41, 2020.
https://doi.org/10.1007/978-3-030-50732-9_5

2   Related Work

2.1   The Problems of Health Education Information

Due to the low threshold of Internet access and the weak supervision ability of network information, the reliability of health education information is difficult to guarantee [1]. In terms of user experience, the existing health education platform has two problems. First, the growth of health knowledge is inconsistent with the change of health behavior. It may because that the change of eating behavior and lifestyle is not achieved in a short period of time, it needs a process, so long-term health education for the elderly should be valued. The second is the lack of consideration for the unique needs of elderly users. Because the elderly population has differences in the desire for health knowledge, economic conditions, and the expanse they can afford, which leads to different needs for health education. To meet the special physical health needs of the elderly adults, so that the elderly can always maintain a good mentality [2]. The main contents of health education for the elderly should be to improve health level, cultivate health awareness and build up self-confidence of the elderly. Xue Zhi'an believes that there should be diversity in the methods of health education for the elderly, and it will be explained in a variety of forms by collecting various vivid examples of feedback from the masses, which is easy to understand [3].

2.2   Design Principles of Health Education System

According to the analysis of existing products, the design principles of the health education system in the mobile phone platforms are summarized as follows: (1) Systematic and standardized curriculum settings. Health education information should be authoritatively certified to avoid misleading elderly users with incorrect information. (2) Personalized customization should be provided. Digital health education products need to be designed according to the assessment of the user's physical condition and health knowledge. (3) The interaction mode and visual interface should be optimized for the elderly users. (4) Persuasion mechanism should be used in system design. As the learning ability of the elderly group declines, the group's initiative to learn systematic knowledge has also decreased to a certain extent. Elderly health education products should lastingly and efficiently stimulate elderly people to learn health knowledge, and at the same time help elderly users form positive feedback in the learning process.

3   Research Methods

3.1   Research Steps

1. Learned the service design trend, research models, related technology and interaction mode of health education for the elderly at home and abroad by doing literature research. Then the research method of health education for the elderly in line with China's national conditions was proposed.

2. Focus group was held in the elderly health service center in nearby community. The existing health service design was analyzed, so as to get a deep understanding of the health education system design.
3. Used the service design thinking to analyze the existing services of health education and got the idea of improving design. Studied the behavioral habits and mental models of the elderly adults through questionnaires and focus group method [4], so as to make sure the system design conforms with the elderly's behavioral habits.
4. Drew user journey map [5] and valued the user experiences of the existing health education service system. Then the pain points of the existing service were found. By holding a co-design [6] workshop, stakeholders were invited together to discuss each touch point of the service and find out how to improve it.
5. Completed the research content arrangement of health education service for the elderly adults. The information architecture of the health education applications was proposed.

4   Case Study

4.1   Focus Group Method

Discussion Guides. Based on the results of the initial survey, this section applies the focus group method to study the motivation, touch points and pain points of elderly users when using the health education service systems. Focus group method was used to get in-depth understanding of users' behaviors and psychological activities, ensuring efficient and thorough information collection.

First, the content and purpose of the focus group discussion was introduced to users through a simple dialogue and the user's basic information and experience in participating in health education activities were collected.

The basic discuss questions were as follows:

① Environmental background
   1. Please briefly introduce your age, cultural background, and family income.
   2. What is your current physical condition? Do you usually pay attention to health information?
   3. What is your motivation for focusing on health education information?
   4. Do you have a health education app on your mobile phone?

② Touch points of service
   1. Please briefly recall the entire process of participating in health education activities in the community.
   2. What are the inconveniences when receiving the "Health Lecture" notice from the neighborhood committee?
   3. What are the good experiences and bad experiences during the community health lecture?
   4. What are your gains and difficulties after the community health lecture?

③ Function definition
1. What kind of health knowledge do you usually pay attention to on your mobile phone?
2. In what way do you think health knowledge is presented that can be accepted more easily on your mobile phone?
3. What persuasion methods do you think can help you learn more effectively?
4. What problems do you usually worry about when using the software?

4.2   Selection of Participants

The research object of this paper is 60–70-year-old people, because their physiological conditions are gradually declined and this group is prone to various chronic diseases. Compared with other groups, they are more concerned about health information, and have basic smart phone operation capabilities. This article adopted a semi-open interview. According to the above requirements, 10 qualified target users were selected. The discussion lasted about 100 min. The place of discussion was the elderly health service center in Lingyun community in Shanghai.

4.3   User Journey Map of Health Education Design

According to the focus group result, the user journey map of health education service in this community was drawn with the whole process of participating in the community health education activities (Fig. 1). The existing user journey map was mainly divided into four stages: receiving the notice, entering the classroom, listening to the lecture and leaving the place.

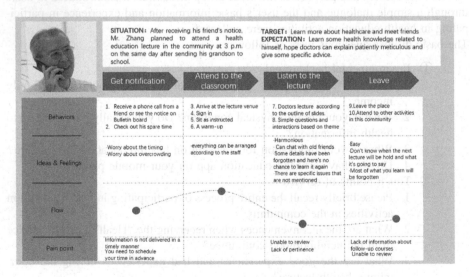

Fig. 1. User journey map of health education service

Through the user's emotional experience, we find that the main touch points of the elderly user's emotional decline in participating in health education services are:

(1) The dissemination of offline health education information is limited and less influential. (2) The lecture time is fixed and cannot be played back if it conflicts with the user's time. (3) Some important details in lectures are easy to be ignored. (4) Content cannot be customized according to personal situation. (5) Lack of long-term schedule and feedback tracking for health lectures. (6) Health knowledge is hard to remember after leaving the lecture room. From the analysis of the service journey map, the design gap in the current health education service was found, and new requirements and research contents for the design of online health education system were put forward.

4.4 Co-design Workshop

According to the collected user interview information and user demand feedback, we invited stakeholders to participate in the co-design workshop, and rethink the structure of the whole service process by card sorting method. First, the host of the workshop invited participants to classify the cards according to the closed card classification method, that is, according to the information structure logic determined by the designer. The cards were classified into different categories, and the categories of the cards were compiled according to the content of the user interviews in the previous stage. Secondly, the interview content cards of 10 users were classified in the Table 1 for further research.

Table 1. First card classification

First level information	Use background	Service touch point	Demand factors
Second level information	Age	Flexible time	Provide relevant-information
	Cultural background	Notice of -	
	Family situation	lecture/activity	Interesting text
	Consumption situation	Inner pleasure	Less intensive-typesetting
	Income situation	Social contact	
	Learning purpose	Pertinence	Text simplification
	Learning time	Review	Information-collection
	Learning knowledge	long-term memory	Mark key points
	Prevention of disease	Forget	Video guidance
	Conditions of body and mind	Course arrangement	Real person explanation
		Outline presentation	Reduce the bomb box
	Chat topics	Share	Trust software
	Learning time		
	Surrounding hospitals		

Finally, for the second card classification, it was required to supplement the second level information in the first card classification according to the experience and creativity of participants. Then participants were asked to re-classify and summarize the second level information. The classification logic was not limited (Table 2).

Table 2. Part of the second card classification

Interaction process	Online learning	Main education modules	Short question and answer
			MOOC
			Daily behavior record
		Auxiliary learning module	Remind
			Collection
			Mark
			Accumulated points exchange
			Share
			Learn together
			Learning progress
	Online-offline interaction	Doctor-patient interaction	Live broadcast online
			Online consultation
		Doctor-patient interaction	Exchange health services
			Gift exchange

Through two card-classifications, the experience elements of the elderly health education service and the system information architecture were obtained by stakeholders' co-design. Online health education service system was mainly divided into three parts: personal information, content design and interaction process.

5   Conclusion

The purpose of this paper is to study the design method of health education service system which meets the needs of the elderly users. Firstly, by studying many health education products, we found the problems in existing systems and summarized the design principles. Secondly, through focus group user research and service experience analysis, the pain points were found out in the aging health education system. Thirdly, a new service design information architecture was proposed through users' co-design workshop. This design method may contribute to the relevant work for improving the elderly adults' experience of the service system. In the future works, we will design the interaction prototype and test users' feedback to the system with different persuasive strategies.

Acknowledgements. This study is supported by the Youth Fund for Humanities and Social Sciences Research of the Ministry of Education, No. 17YJCZH055. This study is supported by the College Students' innovation project of East China University of science and technology, No. X19233.

References

1. Zhao, D.: The Trick of Internet Thinking, pp. 14–15. Mechanical Industry Press, Beijing (2014)
2. Jia, L.: On health education for the elderly. In: Vocational Education Research and Practice, pp. 42–46 (2008)
3. Xue, Z.: Principles of health education for the elderly. Chin. J. Health Educ. **14**(4), 132–137 (1998)
4. Wang, Y., Hu, W., Tang, J., Liang, Q.: Travel postcard service design based on user experience trip. Packag. Eng. **37**(22), 158–159 (2016)
5. Cooper, A.: Software Concept Revolution: The Essence of Interaction Design, pp. 56–57. Publishing House of Electronics Industry, Beijing (2012)
6. Laitinen, I., Kinder, T., Stenvall, J.: Co-design and action learning in local public services. J. Adult Contin. Educ. **24**(1), 58–80 (2018)

Shaping Social Relationships Digitally: WhatsApp's Influence on Social Relationships of Older Adults

Veronika Hämmerle[✉], Rhea Braundwalder, Cora Pauli,
and Sabina Misoch

Institute for Ageing Research, University of Applied Sciences St.Gallen,
Rosenbergstrasse 59, 9001 St. Gallen, Switzerland
`veronika.haemmerle@fhsg.ch`

Abstract. Ageing societies and digitalisation are prominent topics in industrialised nations. Although research suggests that technology use could positively influence the social contexts of older adults, there is not enough empirical evidence on this topic.

In order to bridge this research gap, we conducted a qualitative study on the WhatsApp use of older adults in Switzerland. A qualitative study with 30 older adults (65+) in Switzerland should shed light on motivational aspects of usage and the effects of the instant messaging App on their subjectively perceived quality of social relationships. Data collection was based on two methodological elements: the creation of ego-centered network maps and the implementation of qualitative, semi-structured face-to-face interviews. Data was analysed by qualitative content analysis. Our research shows that adults are willing to participate in digitalisation and accept new technologies if they benefit from them. Upholding and intensifying social relationships, increasing a sense of belonging to groups and the practical aspect of WhatsApp were essential categories we derived from our data. We conclude that older adults' use of WhatsApp is in line with prominent life-span theories and models (socioemotional selectivity theory, SOC) and that WhatsApp has a positive effect on the social relations of older users. WhatsApp is used consciously to achieve positive ends, allowing older users to select and invest time in meaningful relationships.

Keywords: Older adults · Technology · Instant messaging · WhatsApp · Socioemotional selectivity theory · SOC · Social relations

1 Introduction

The Swiss Federal Council sees digitalisation as an opportunity and has set itself the goal to ensure the participation of the whole Swiss society in information and communication technology (Bundesamt für Statistik 2017). In parallel demographic changes are leading to an increased proportion of older adults and studies show that there still is a difference in adoption and use of the internet depending on age, older adults using digital services less than their younger counterparts (Friemel 2016; Seifert and Doh 2016). Now that the number of older adults using the internet is on the rise

C. Stephanidis and M. Antona (Eds.): HCII 2020, CCIS 1226, pp. 42–49, 2020.
https://doi.org/10.1007/978-3-030-50732-9_6

(Seifert and Doh 2016) the question of how digitalisation affects older people should be further examined.

In this paper, based on a qualitative study conducted in 2019, we ask whether theories such as the socioemotional selectivity theory and models of aging remain valid in the face of rapidly developing digital communication services by examining the effects of the instant messaging service WhatsApp on the subjective perception of social relationships of older people aged 65+ in Switzerland. We focus on WhatsApp, as according to data on Switzerland, WhatsApp was the most popular App installed on smartphones in Switzerland in 2017 (Y&R Group Switzerland 2017).

1.1 Theoretical Framework

Theories on aging such as the socioemotional selectivity theory (SST) (Carstensen et al. 2003) or the selection, optimization and compensation (SOC) model (Baltes 1997) describe age related changes in motivations, goals and priorities in the course of an individual's life span. The SST states that older adults carefully select and invest time in meaningful social relationships in the light of the shorter lifetime left to live (Carstensen et al. 2003). Since time is perceived as more limited with increasing age, older adults mainly invest their cognitive and social resources in emotionally rewarding (inter)actions (Carstensen and Mikels 2005; Barber et al. 2016). This strategy allows them to achieve as much emotional gratification as possible in their remaining lifetime. Older adults focus on the quality of a fewer number of close relationships and are better at regulating emotions in everyday life (Carstensen et al. 2003).

Whereas the SST concentrates on emotion regulation and social relationships the SOC model, developed by Baltes (1997), more broadly describes three strategies (selection, optimization and compensation) used to lead a successful life while aging. Selection indicates a field in which an individual decides to invest resources in. Optimization relates to strategies learnt to better achieve the selection and compensation refers to actions undertaken to counteract losses, in the case of old age often related to loneliness, physical constraints or illnesses.

In the light of these theories and models, considering age in research on instant messaging is essential, as emphasised by Rosales and Fernández-Ardèvol in their study on smartphone usage of older adults in Spain (2016). As needs and values change in the course of the lifetime and social norms influence ageing, the dimension of age should be considered in studies on technology use (Rosales and Fernández-Ardèvol 2016).

However, not only personal life development must be considered. Kamin et al. (2016), in their study on social contexts of technology use in old age, develop a model of technology use and social contexts in later life which shows how technology use and social contexts are interrelated. Wahl et al. (2012) similarly propose a framework including personal aspects such as agency and belonging as well as contextual resources and state that there is not much empiric research on the relationship of theories of aging such as SOC and SST and technological solutions offered for older adults. They suggest that usage decisions are also influenced by environmental resources and demands and that further studies should address how specific technologies influence the regulation of social relationships in old age.

We found evidence in our data that for the context we examined, which consists of well educated, socially connected and physically fit older adults, the use of WhatsApp acts beneficially and in accordance with strategies and goals indicated in theories of aging such as the SOC model and SST.

2 Study

In our explorative and qualitative study on the subjective effects of WhatsApp on social relationships of older adults aged 65+ in Switzerland our sample consisted of 15 men and 15 women aged between 66 and 84 (average age: 72.5), all WhatsApp users. One-third had followed schooling up to secondary education, two-thirds had completed tertiary education. We included people with (22) and without children (8) and grandchildren (19 with grandchildren, 11 without grandchildren) and living alone (9) or with their spouses/partners (21). Participants were required to be over 65 years of age, German-speaking and to have used WhatsApp within the last three months. Data collection was based on two methodological elements: the creation of ego-centered network maps, situating all social contacts of the informant within three concentric circles from close to distant (Kahn and Antonucci 1980), and qualitative, semi-structured face-to-face interviews. The interviews focused on the content, frequency and form of messages exchanged over WhatsApp, the history of use, advantages and disadvantages concerning WhatsApp and the subjective experienced effects of WhatsApp on social relations. We also asked for misunderstandings and topics our informants would not discuss via WhatsApp. All interviews were audio-recorded and fully transcribed. The data is currently being analysed by qualitative content analysis (Mayring 2015). After project completion, the anonymized transcriptions of the interviews will be made accessible through a data repository of our choice. Descriptive analysis was conducted with SPSS.

3 Preliminary Findings

3.1 Social Networks and Usage Habits

The social network of our participants consisted of 23.3 persons on average (Max = 45; Min = 23). Our informants communicated with an average of 18.1 people via WhatsApp (Max = 36; Min = 6). The communication via WhatsApp ran through all network circles. On average, 6.1 people in circle 1 communicated via WhatsApp, 6.6 in circle 2 and 5.3 in circle 3. Most of the participants used WhatsApp daily (23), some used it weekly (2), one participant used it several times per month (missing = 3). Persons that the participants used WhatsApp most frequently with were family and friends located in the circles 1 or 2. However, WhatsApp was also used for club activities (often WhatsApp groups) and voluntary work in different social areas.

3.2   Usage History

Most of the interviewees were introduced to WhatsApp and motivated to use it by family and friends. For many interviewees, their own children provided the initial motivation to use the app and were also there to help in case of technical problems or questions. The respondents largely reported an uncomplicated and self-sufficient adaption process. The preferred way to learn the use of WhatsApp was through friends or family. However, some informants reported they learned how to use WhatsApp through trial and error. Over time, our informants often expanded their usage to new features (e.g. telephony or voice messages) they either learned from others or tried out themselves. Many of the interviewees reported that they had installed the app without great expectations. The recommendation of their surroundings and the possibility to connect with other people was the main motivation to use WhatsApp. Our interviewees found WhatsApp to be a very useful tool for many situations and most of them stated that their frequency of use regarding WhatsApp was clearly increasing over the years.

3.3   Content

In general, WhatsApp was associated with light, interesting and pleasurable contents. Informants stated that they would never discuss sensitive matters over WhatsApp. They were unanimously of the opinion, that conflicts and serious discussions should be done face-to-face or at least on the telephone, where they would be able to hear their counterpart's voice. Some reported forwarding jokes, funny pictures or videos to others, after careful consideration, whether the recipient would be interested in a specific content or not. If irrelevant or inappropriate content was received it was either ignored or immediately deleted. In general, our informants stressed the positivity and the pleasure of messages received and sent.

Next to sending text messages, exchanging pictures was one of the most used functions of WhatsApp. Besides pictures of grandchildren, a very popular motif was travel impressions but also pictures of outstanding or special moments in everyday life. Many of the interviewees emphasized that they liked to receive pictures of their loved ones' travels or to follow the status of others. Informants pointed out they send and share contents carefully and selective (e.g. a picture of a flower is sent only to somebody who is interested in plants and gardening). At the same time, some of the informants pointed out that they send or share fewer pictures they took themselves. This was explained either by reluctance to stage themselves (on the WhatsApp status) or by the fact that they themselves did not feel as they have as much exciting content to share.

3.4   Purpose and Effects on Social Relations

The analysis of the interviews showed that Whatsapp was used for different purposes and had several impacts on the social relations of older adults.

Maintaining relationships was one purpose of our interviewee's WhatsApp use. Although some of the interviewees reported that they added new contacts if the occasion arose, the informants focused their communication strongly on people they knew and who were important to them. One informant even reported that she would rather contact a new acquaintance via sms, as WhatsApp seemed more intimate to her. Many interviewees stated that they sent greetings to friends and family, checking up on them when they were on their minds, asking them how they and their families were. Some were inspired to contact people they had not contacted in a while by scrolling through their WhatsApp chats.

However, the use of WhatsApp to simplify the maintenance of relationships was especially salient in case of close family members or friends, especially when they were physically separated by large distances. Informants described how they appreciated receiving information from their children about their whereabouts and safe arrival at home or holiday destinations. Sharing holiday impressions or impressions from everyday life in the form of pictures, videos or texts made the geographic distance bridgeable and allowed for the continuation of relationships to people abroad. Further aspects addressed were costs and the time difference, which both could be ignored while sending WhatsApp messages to family and friends living abroad.

Creating opportunities for social exchange summarizes another important purpose of WhatsApp according to our findings. Some of the participants mentioned the advantage of WhatsApp in interaction with friends or family that have less time, due to family and work. The app made it easier to keep in touch with them, as their loved ones could answer their messages when they had time and with less effort than writing an e-mail, card or letter. The nonintrusive way of communication via WhatsApp was stressed by many participants. Many of them used WhatsApp before a phone call to make sure their friend/relative was willing to talk. Users said that they could write a message or extend an invitation without worrying about bothering their counterparts at an inappropriate time. Sending a WhatsApp message was assumed to be less disturbing than calling.

Many reported that WhatsApp was used to arrange meetings or discuss organizational matters. Whether this meant arranging to go to the cinema with a friend, inviting their children to dinner, going on a day trip with a group of friends, managing a shared holiday home, coordinating telephone calls, the care of grandchildren or confirming attendance to club events, WhatsApp was widely used to arrange appointments of all sorts. Group chats were especially mentioned as practical to organise and coordinate reoccurring or one-time events. Another use and motivation of family chats was the coordination of the care for a sick or older family member.

Intensifying relationships was one of the outcomes of our informants' WhatsApp use on their relations. In addition to the broad scale of possibilities in expressing themselves, our interviewees stated that the frequency of exchanges with social ties had increased by using WhatsApp. This increased the feeling of intensity of relationships, as the contacts were more present and closer to our interviewees day to day lives. Through exchanging small and everyday events as well as emotional milestones, like a grandchild's first steps, our informants gained insights into the day to day lives of their family and friends and which made them feel closer to them. Especially thanks to the various functions of WhatsApp used by our interviewees in different intensity (text messages, pictures, videos, voice messages and emojis) a multi-dimensional exchange was created, which could be shaped according to personal preference.

Grandparents described how WhatsApp complemented the face-to-face meetings with their grandchildren. Via videos and photos, they were able to witness important milestones even in the early stages of life of their grandchildren. The interviewed grandparents reported that they enjoyed receiving new videos or photos showing their grandchildren and being able to react via chat on the received content. With the shared photos and videos, the app use made the interviewed grandparents feel more involved in the life and progress of their grandchildren.

Strengthening of the sense of belonging was another effect of the WhatsApp use on our interviewee's social contexts. Some of the interviewees stated that WhatsApp was especially important to them because they lived alone. One woman described WhatsApp as a present and very important to her life. The uncomplicated way of hearing from others on a regular basis seemed to be especially important here.

Not only regarding individuals, but also groups, WhatsApp seemed to have a positive effect on the perception of closeness and sense of belonging of our informants. WhatsApp group chats amongst families, siblings, friends and hobby or club groups were widely used, mostly for planning and coordinative purposes. While exchanges in group chats were sometimes perceived as uninteresting or irrelevant, especially in groups located in the outermost circles of our informant's network maps, the exchanges with groups involving close friends and family made our informants feel more included. Most used were family WhatsApp groups, which included the informant, their spouse, their children and in case old enough, grandchildren. Here, information, extraordinary and every-day occurrences, greetings, pictures, thoughts, jokes and memories were exchanged. Regarding WhatsApp groups with social contacts our informants listed in the inner two circles on the network map (usually family and close friends), our informants felt more included and a stronger sense of belonging and community.

4 Conclusion

How our informants used WhatsApp shows that WhatsApp could be described as an instrument of socio-emotional selection for older adults. WhatsApp allowed our informants to select their contacts and contents carefully and enhance the positive outcome on quality of relations and perceived closeness. It made it easier for our informants to keep in touch and even intensify contacts. Older adults' communication via WhatsApp is motivated by the encouragement of emotionally meaningful persons (family and friends; circle 1–2) and focused strongly on socio-emotionally meaningful interactions. The app was used most frequently with members of the core family (mostly the children) or close friends (located in the two inner circles of the network map) that were not living in the same household.

WhatsApp was further used to support the investment of behavioral resources to achieve the regulation of social context. It enabled communication that requires less time and effort, than other media (e.g. phone, letter, e-mail) and gave the user more freedom and flexibility. This might be especially relevant in the social interaction with family and friends that do not have time resources, due to work and other duties. Our interviewees pointed out that WhatsApp helped them to stay in touch regardless of their friends or family member's daily schedule or lifestyle. Moreover, the technology with its various functions and interaction possibilities allowed social interactions and participation in the lives of others (e.g. grandchildren) that would not have happened without using the app. Using WhatsApp led to an enhanced relationship quality and intensified the feeling of closeness to others, since it enables continuous communication and thus a state of connected presence (Licoppe and Smoreda 2005).

Older adults further used WhatsApp to maximize their positive experience in social contexts (Kamin et al. 2016). For seniors, WhatsApp communication means an easy, light and joyful communication without the worries of bothering their counterparts in inappropriate moments.

Or findings also indicate that WhatsApp helps seniors to compensate loss in their social contexts. We use the term "loss" for geographical distance and lost synchronous life rhythms. Older adults used WhatsApp to bridge geographical distances to family and friends abroad. Furthermore, WhatsApp helped people that live alone feel more connected and to achieve a greater sense of belonging. As children start their own family and are less available in terms of time and space the family chat was used to keep in touch in the small moments of time available. These findings support the assumption, that technology use can help combat loneliness (Kamin et al. 2016) and goes in line with previous studies on cellphone/internet use and social isolation, loneliness and depression (Minagawa and Saito 2014; Cotten et al. 2014).

Taken together, our findings for this context of well connected, well-educated and physically fit older adults, show evidence that aging processes are not fundamentally changed by digitalisation, and instead that older adults actively integrate technology into their lives to reach their social goals and motivations.

References

Baltes, P.B.: On the incomplete architecture of human ontogeny: selection, optimization, and compensation as foundation of developmental theory. Am. Psychol. **52**(4), 366 (1997)

Barber, S.J., Opitz, P.C., Martins, B., Sakaki, M., Mather, M.: Thinking about a limited future enhances the positivity of younger and older adults' recall: support for socioemotional selectivity theory. Mem. Cogn. **44**(6), 869–882 (2016). https://doi.org/10.3758/s13421-016-0612-0

Bundesamt für Statistik: BFS Medienmitteilung, Internetnutzung in den Haushalten 2017, Neuchâtel (2017)

Carstensen, L.L., Fung, H.H., Charles, S.T.: Socioemotional selectivity theory and the regulation of emotion in the second half of life. Motiv. Emot. **27**(2), 103–123 (2003). https://doi.org/10.1023/A:1024569803230

Carstensen, L.L., Mikels, J.A.: At the intersection of emotion and cognition: aging and the positivity effect. Curr. Dir. Psychol. Sci. **14**(3), 117–121 (2005)

Cotten, S.R., Ford, G., Ford, S., Hale, T.M.: Internet use and depression among retired older adults in the United States: a longitudinal analysis. J. Gerontol. B Psychol. Sci. Soc. Sci. **69**(5), 763–771 (2014)

Friemel, T.N.: The digital divide has grown old: determinants of a digital divide among seniors. New Media Soc. **18**, 313–331 (2016)

Kahn, R.L., Antonucci, T.C.: Convoys over the life course: a life course approach. In: Life Span Development and Behavior, pp. 253–286 (1980)

Kamin, S.T., Lang, F.R., Kamber, T.: Social contexts of technology use in old age. In: Gerontechnology. Research, Practice, and Principles in the Field of Technology and Aging. Springer (2016)

Licoppe, C., Smoreda, Z.: Are social networks technologically embedded? Soc. Netw. **27**(4), 317–335 (2005)

Mayring, P.: Qualitative content analysis: theoretical background and procedures. In: Bikner-Ahsbahs, A., Knipping, C., Presmeg, N. (eds.) Approaches to Qualitative Research in Mathematics Education. AME, pp. 365–380. Springer, Dordrecht (2015). https://doi.org/10.1007/978-94-017-9181-6_13

Minagawa, Y., Saito, Y.: An analysis of the impact of cell phone use on depressive symptoms among Japanese elders. Gerontology **60**(6), 539–547 (2014)

Rosales, A., Fernández-Ardèvol, M.: Beyond WhatsApp: older people and smartphones. Rom. J. Commun. Public Relat. **18**, 27–47 (2016)

Seifert, A., Doh, M.: Internetnutzung im Alter – Diffusion, Alltagsrelevanz und Kompetenzvermittlung. Report Psychologie **41**, 394–402 (2016)

Wahl, H.W., Iwarsson, S., Oswald, F.: Aging well and the environment: toward an integrative model and research agenda for the future. Gerontologist **52**(3), 306–316 (2012)

Y&R Group Switzerland: Media Use Index 2017, Zürich (2017)

Process Automation in the Translation of Standard Language Texts into Easy-to-Read Texts – A Software Requirements Analysis

Claudia Hösel[✉], Christian Roschke, Rico Thomanek, Tony Rolletschke, Benny Platte, and Marc Ritter

University of Applied Sciences Mittweida, 09648 Mittweida, Germany
{hoesel,roschke,rthomane,rolletsc,platte,ritter}@hs-mittweida.de

Abstract. Many people are denied access to information and communication because they cannot read and understand standard texts. The translation of standard texts into easy-to-read texts can reduce these obstacles and enable barrier-free communication. Due to the lack of computer-supported tools, this is a primarily intellectual process, which is why very little information is available as easy-to-read text. Existing approaches dealing with the automation of the intralingual translation process focus in particular on the sub-process of text simplification. In our study, we look at the entire translation process with the aim of identifying the characteristics of a software system that are required to digitize the entire process as needed. We analyse the intralingual translation process and create a model. In addition, we conduct a software requirements analysis, which we use to systematically analyse and document the demands put to the software architecture. The results of our study form the foundation of the development of a software system that can make the intralingual translation process more efficient and effective.

Keywords: Easy-to-read · Text simplification · Process automation · Requirements engineering · Requirements analysis

1 Introduction

We are on the way to an information technology society where there is a tendency to digitize information of all kinds in order to make it accessible to users. However, we are still a long way from the ideal of a uniformly digitized society in which everyone can use information without barriers. Access to information and communication is still closely linked to language skills [2]. Many groups of people, e.g. people with learning difficulties, the ones affected by prelingual deafness, but also people with aphasia, are denied comprehensive participation in the socio-economic activities of society because they cannot read and understand standard language texts. In order to provide these people with unhindered access

© Springer Nature Switzerland AG 2020
C. Stephanidis and M. Antona (Eds.): HCII 2020, CCIS 1226, pp. 50–57, 2020.
https://doi.org/10.1007/978-3-030-50732-9_7

to information resources, barrier-free communication is required. The easy-to-read approach, which has experienced an upswing in recent years as a result of inclusion movements, is regarded as a central building block for creating this barrier-free environment [10]. The easy-to-read approach aims at simplification at all levels of the source language with the aim of providing easily readable and comprehensible information. The transformation of standard language texts into easy-to-read texts can be regarded as an intralingual translation process, since no language boundary is crossed, but rather a variety boundary within a single language [13]. While numerous computer-supported tools are available for interlingual translation processes, the translation of standard source texts into easy-to-read ones is primarily intellectual, which is why so far only a few high-quality easy-to-read texts are available. In order to be able to provide more information resources as easy-to-read with constant quality, the intralingual translation process needs to be optimized by means of adequate computer-supported tools.

Approaches that deal with the optimization of the intralingual translation process look in particular at the sub-process of text simplification. Initial approaches to text simplification, such as Chandrasekar et al. [6], Caroll et al. [5], Siddharthan [18], investigate the grammatical complexity of a text with the aim of transforming it into a simpler structure and thus aim at syntactical simplification. Later work focuses on simplification at the lexical level by adding information from dictionaries or other sources [8,14] or by substituting difficult words [4,19]. Recent works, such as Van den Bercken et al. [3], Nisioi et al. [16], Paetzold and Specia [17], focus on automated lexical text simplification using machine learning methods. To optimize the entire intralingual translation process, however, automation and digitization of further process steps are required. Nevertheless, approaches that deal with process automation and process digitization focus in particular on workflows in the industrial sector [15,20] and can only be used to a limited extent for the specific workflow of the intralingual translation process. The present study takes up this problem and examines which technical, qualitative and quantitative characteristics a software system must have in order to digitize the entire intralingual translation process according to demand and thus make it more effective, efficient and user-oriented.

2   Methodical Approach

Requirements form the basis of any software architecture. Systematic management and a structured approach to requirements analysis are fundamental to the development of efficient and error-free systems, as they ensure that the software system developed meets the needs of users [1,12]. For the determination, analysis, specification and validation of the properties and framework conditions of the required software system, we used the following systematic procedure, which is divided into three processes:

Process 1 – Define Scope of Requirements: The first process aimed to clearly define the scope of requirements. To this end, we analysed the intralingual translation process through extensive literature research in online databases (e.g. ACM, IEEE, Elsevier/Science Direct), conducted interviews with translators and practiced the intralingual translation process under the guidance of experts. In addition, we examined the process environment by looking at the intralingual translation process as a black box and identifying relevant areas of influence through systematic analysis.

Process 2 – Identification of Stakeholders and Primary Actors: Based on the analysis of the environment carried out in the first process, we then detected the stakeholders with the aim of identifying their requirements for the systems to be created. Since not all stakeholders were equally relevant, we prioritized the detected stakeholders according to their influence on and interaction potential with the system.

Process 3 – Requirements Assessment: This process focused on the assessment and specification of requirements. For systematic determination, a distinction was made between functional, non-functional, qualitative and technical requirements. The requirements were collected using two sub-processes (SP) described below.

SP 1 – Survey of Functional Requirements: To determine the functional requirements, we adapted the systematic approach of use-case analysis [7,11]. From the stakeholder survey, we generated use cases, which we converted into use-case diagrams.

SP 2 – Determination of Qualitative and Technical Requirements: In determining the qualitative requirements, we were guided by the international standard ISO/IEC 25000 "Software engineering - Software product Quality Requirements and Evaluation (SQuaRE)" [9].

3   Results

The complex processes of the intellectual translation process from standard source texts into easy-to-read text were made transparent by a process and environment analysis and presented in a model-based activity diagram. Figure 1 shows the results of the process and environment analysis. The activity diagram consists of four sections, which are described as activities below: 1) Analysis of the standard source text, 2) Development of the translation strategy, 3) Preparation of the translation and 4) Verification of the translation. The individual activities are discussed below.

The first section is the analysis of the standard source text of the intralingual translation process. The analysis focuses, among other things, on the text length, the type of text as well as the function and information structure of the source text. If contradictions are found or information is missing, the translator establishes contact with the client. Based on the results of the first section and any further specifications, the translator develops a translation strategy for the source text in section 2. This strategy is tested for effectiveness by translating a small extract of the standard source text into an easy-to-read text. A direct

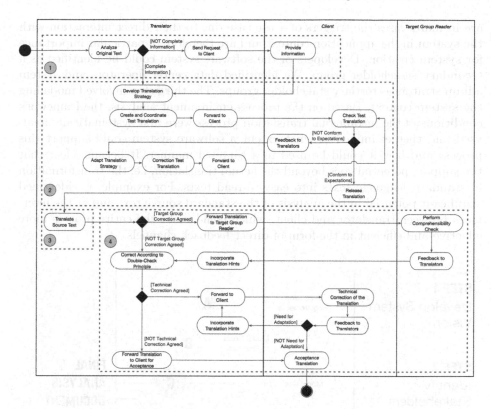

Fig. 1. Process activity diagram

feedback channel to the client can ensure that the intralingual translation is carried out in line with expectations. Section 3 then translates the entire standard source text into an easy-to-read text. The basis for this is the translation strategy, which determines how to proceed with the source text at word, sentence, text and character level. In Section 4, the easy-to-read text is then checked on the basis of a catalogue of criteria previously agreed with the client. If a target group correction is applied, the translation is forwarded to target group readers who check the easy-to-read text for comprehensibility and provide the translator with appropriate feedback. If the client wishes to have the text checked by a specialist, appropriate actions are taken before the text is forwarded to the client for final approval.

The results of the requirements analysis are described below based on the process shown in Fig. 2. In the first step, a system vision was developed based on the activity diagram and the essential system goals of the software to be developed were described. By means of the environment analysis we identified the primary, secondary and tertiary stakeholder groups. The primary stakeholder groups of the system to be created were translators, clients and easy-to-read readers. In addition, the group of translators was identified as the primary actor, as these are in many cases the triggers of a use case due to their direct interaction with the system in the application context and are therefore of particular importance for system creation. Developers of the software system could be identified as a secondary stakeholder group. We identified data center operators and system administrators as tertiary stakeholder groups. The third step involved modelling the system context. Based on the process environment analysis, the framework conditions of the intralingual translation process were first systematically analysed and then examined to what extent a software system could support this process and how it could be used in a targeted manner. It became clear that the support potential goes beyond the actual translation, i.e. the transformation of standard language texts into easy-to-read texts. For example, we identified significant potential in the analysis of the standard source text and at the interfaces between translator and client, which could make the entire process more effective and efficient in the form of direct feedback channels.

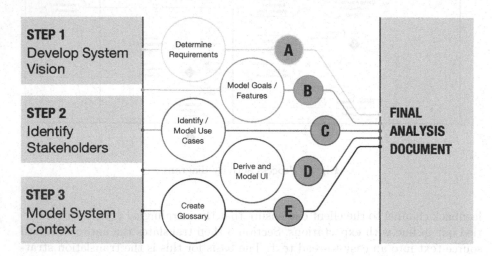

Fig. 2. Process of requirements analysis

The implementation of steps one to three enabled the parallel execution of analysis steps A-E, the results of which are presented below: (A) From the activity diagram created and the survey of all stakeholders, in particular the primary actors, requirements for the software system were determined and specified by an iterative procedure. The functional requirements could first be formulated in natural language using a requirements template and then recorded in tabular form in requirement lists. In the interview procedure, goals and characteristics were worked out and precisely described (B). It became clear that all stakeholders were looking for a cross-platform solution, with a general increase in interest in digitization. This was mostly due to expected increased efficiency. The creation of use case diagrams (C) made it possible to visualize the findings recorded in the interview. These were used to check existing requirements for correctness iteratively with the stakeholders and to determine further requirements, in particular technical and qualitative ones. In this context, it became apparent that the stakeholders consider the scalability and maintainability of the software system to be particularly important. In a status quo analysis, we were able to determine the technical framework conditions of the stakeholders. It became clear that the majority of the stakeholders surveyed use desktop PCs with older Windows versions (Windows XP, Windows 7) and have little technical affinity. (C) Based on the findings, interface prototypes were developed using interactive mock-ups, tested together with stakeholders and the resulting feedback directly implemented. From this, it was also possible to identify missing requirements. It turned out that the users need a complex role concept and that the meta information for texts to be uploaded should also be adaptable and extendable for technically less experienced users. (D) A common glossary was created to ensure that all participants could use the same terminology. This was necessary because of the interdisciplinary nature of the work and the fact that certain terms may have different meanings in different fields. On the basis of all collected findings, it was possible to create a comprehensive final analysis document, which was optimized in several iteration phases together with the stakeholders and forms the basis for the development of a first prototype.

4   Conclusion

In our study, we conducted a systematic requirements analysis with the aim of identifying the qualitative and quantitative characteristics of a software system that are required to digitize the intralingual translation process according to the needs. To this end, we analysed the complex processes involved in the intellectual translation of standard source texts into easy-to-read texts and set out the process sequence in an activity diagram based on a model. By means of the activity diagram and the survey of stakeholders and primary actors, we conducted a systematic requirements analysis. We generated comprehensive requirement documents for the functional, non-functional, technical and qualitative requirements. In our future work, we will use the requirement documents created for the prototype development and implementation of a software system that can adequately support the previously intellectually executed translation process from standard source texts into easy-to-read texts. In this context, it is also necessary to check the identified requirements on the basis of test cases and, if necessary, to specify them further. This enables iterative optimization of the complex process.

References

1. Banerjee, S., Sarkar, A.: A requirements analysis framework for development of service oriented systems. ACM SIGSOFT Softw. Eng. Not. **42**(3), 1–12 (2017). https://doi.org/10.1145/3127360.3127366

2. Bautista, S., Hervás, R., Gervás, P., Bagó, A., García-Ortiz, J.: Taking text simplification to the user. In: Proceedings of the 8th International Conference on Software Development and Technologies for Enhancing Accessibility and Fighting Info-exclusion - DSAI 2018, pp. 88–96. ACM Press, New York (2018). https://doi.org/10.1145/3218585.3218591

3. van den Bercken, L., Sips, R.J., Lofi, C.: Evaluating neural text simplification in the medical domain. In: The World Wide Web Conference on - WWW 2019, vol. 2, pp. 3286–3292. ACM Press, New York (2019). https://doi.org/10.1145/3308558.3313630

4. Biran, O., Brody, S., Elhadad, N.: Putting it simply: a context-aware approach to lexical simplification. In: Proceedings of the 49th Annual Meeting of the Association for Computational Linguistics: Human Language Technologies: Short Papers - Volume 2, HLT 2011, pp. 496–501. Association for Computational Linguistics, Stroudsburg (2011)

5. Carroll, J., Minnen, G., Canning, Y., Devlin, S., Tait, J.: Practical simplification of English newspaper text to assist aphasic readers. In: Proceedings of AAAI-98 Workshop on Integrating Artificial Intelligence and Assistive Technology, vol. 1324, pp. 7–10 (1998)

6. Chandrasekar, R., Doran, C., Srinivas, B.: Motivations and methods for text simplification. In: COLING 1996 Proceedings of the 16th Conference on Computational Linguistics, vol. 2, no. 9, pp. 1041–1044 (1996)

7. Cockburn, A.: Writing Effective Use Cases. Addison-Wesley, Boston (2000)

8. Elhadad, N.: Comprehending technical texts: predicting and defining unfamiliar terms. In: Annual Symposium Proceedings, AMIA Symposium, pp. 239–243. Association for Computational Linguistics (2006)

9. IEC International Electrotechnical Commission: Software engineering. Software product quality requirements and evaluation (SQuaRE) (2005). https://www.iso.org/obp/ui/#iso:std:iso-iec:25000:ed-1:v1:en. Accessed 10 Jan 2020

10. Inclusion Europe: Inclusion Europe (2016). https://easy-to-read.eu/de/. Accessed 10 Jan 2020

11. Jacobson, I.: Object-Oriented Software Engineering: A Use Case Driven Approach. Addison Wesley Longman Publishing Co., Inc., Redwood City (2004)

12. Jain, P., Verma, K., Kass, A.: Automated review of natural language requirements documents: generating useful warnings with user-extensible glossaries driving a simple state machine. In: Proceedings of the 2nd India Software Engineering Conference, pp. 37–45 (2009)

13. Jakobson, R.: On linguistic aspects of translation. In: Brower, R.A. (ed.) On Translation, pp. 232–239. Harvard University Press, Cambridge (1959)

14. Kaji, N., Kawahara, D., Kurohash, S., Sato, S.: Verb paraphrase based on case frame alignment. In: Proceedings of the 40th Annual Meeting of the Association for Computational Linguistics (ACL 2002), pp. 12–15 (2002)

15. Kattepur, A.: Towards structured performance analysis of Industry 4.0 workflow automation resources. In: Proceedings of the 2019 ACM/SPEC International Conference on Performance Engineering - ICPE 2019, pp. 189–196 (2019). https://doi.org/10.1145/3297663.3309671

16. Nisioi, S., Štajner, S., Ponzetto, S.P., Dinu, L.P.: Exploring neural text simplification models. In: Proceedings of the 55th Annual Meeting of the Association for Computational Linguistics, pp. 85–91 (2017). https://doi.org/10.18653/v1/P17-2014

17. Paetzold, G., Specia, L.: Reliable lexical simplification for non-native speakers. In: Proceedings of the 2015 Conference of the North American Chapter of the Association for Computational Linguistics: Student Research Workshop, pp. 3761–3767. Association for Computational Linguistics, Stroudsburg (2016). https://doi.org/10.3115/v1/N15-2002
18. Siddharthan, A.: Preserving discourse structure when simplifying text. In: Proceedings of the European Natural Language Generation Workshop (ENLG), 11th Conference of the European Chapter of the Association for Computational Linguistics (EACL 2003), pp. 103–110 (2003)
19. Walker, A., Starkey, A.: Investigation into human preference between common and unambiguous lexical substitutions. In: Proceedings of the 13th European Workshop on Natural Language Generation (ENLG), pp. 176–180 (2011)
20. Wang, Z., Liffman, D.Y., Karunamoorthy, D., Abebe, E.: Distributed ledger technology for document and workflow management in trade and logistics. In: Proceedings of the 27th ACM International Conference on Information and Knowledge Management - CIKM 2018, pp. 1895–1898. ACM Press, New York (2018). https://doi.org/10.1145/3269206.3269222

Development of Behavior-Based Game for Early Screening of Mild Cognitive Impairment: With the Plan for a Feasibility Study

Hyungsook Kim[1], David O'Sullivan[2], and Yonghyun Park[1(✉)]

[1] HY Global Development Center, Hanyang Convergence Research Center,
Hanyang University, Seoul, Republic of Korea
yhpark81@gmail.com
[2] Division of Sports Science, Pusan National University,
Busan, Republic of Korea

Abstract. The purpose of this study is to develop serious game content that can test cognitive ability by using digital media such as smartphones and a beam projection. The main idea of the serious game is that the physical movements of the elderly control the game. The different scenarios of the game promote the physical activity of the elderly while at the same time measuring the cognitive characteristics of the elderly through their behavioural reaction to the contents. The contents are aimed at the use of the general healthy adult population to prevent and screen for dementia and cognitive decline in memory loss and temporal-spatial awareness. The content will be designed based on the mini-mental state examination for cognitive domains and on sit to walk gait analysis for a screening of both physical and mental issues. To improve the user's experience, we plan to measure the user's behaviors and interaction with the reaction-stimulating serious game content. Though the analysis of the user's movements, such as reaction times and movement speeds, we plan to measure the state of the cognitive function. The reliability and validity of the content will be checked through a series of clinical pilot tests. The contents will be developed to deal with all the different severity in the stages of dementia from the asymptomatic stage to severe dementia. Through the continuous practice of these whole-body interactive contents, we expect that it will help to slow down the progression and prevention of cognitive and physical decline.

Keywords: Dementia · Digital therapeutics · Gait analysis · Behavior · Cognition · Physical activity

1 Introduction

With the worldwide increase in an ageing population [1], many related cognitive impairment issues, such as dementia, and Parkinson's Disease, are critical societal challenges that need to be solved [2]. Therefore, there has been a rapid increase in investment in the research and development of related digital technologies (mental

C. Stephanidis and M. Antona (Eds.): HCII 2020, CCIS 1226, pp. 58–63, 2020.
https://doi.org/10.1007/978-3-030-50732-9_8

health applications and digital therapeutics) that can help tackle the concerning cognition and mental health issues [3].

The purpose of this study is to develop serious game content that can test cognitive ability by using digital media such as smartphones, beam projection, and a robot. The main idea of the serious game is that the physical movements of the elderly control the developed game. The different scenarios of the game promote the physical activity of the elderly while at the same time measuring the cognitive characteristics of the elderly through their behavioural reaction to the contents. Additionally, weekly and daily practice of these interactive contents is to monitor the elderly user's neurocognitive function in terms of memory loss, spatial-temporal awareness. The contents are aimed at the use of the general healthy adult population to prevent and screen for dementia and cognitive decline. In contrast, the content is to help delay the onset of symptoms for the mild cognitive impairment group, whereas, for the more severe it will be used to help manage and slow the progression of the cognitive impairments in memory loss and temporal-spatial awareness domains.

2   Content Development Method

There are a vast number of studies highlighting the secure link between the various physical activity intensities and types and the neurotransmitters in the brain [4–6]. Additionally, there are strong links between the cognitive training contents and improvement in cognition by the varying ages of the participants from university students to the elderly [7–9]. We, therefore, propose a mixture of these two methods to aid in the stimulation of cognitive-based physical activity. From this point of view, the game will allow the elderly users to perform the tasks in reaction to the content with their whole-body movement (Fig. 1).

Fig. 1. The three scenarios to be tested and trained using the proposed contents for dementia detection, screening, prevention, and management.

The contents were developed to be able to manage with users of different severities in the stages of dementia. We targeted the users from the asymptomatic stage to mild cognitive impairment, early dementia, mild dementia, moderate dementia, and severe dementia. The game will present a high level of difficulty for the lower severities of the mental/cognitive decline, whereas, for the more severe patients with dementia, the level of content will be easier. Through the continuous practice of this whole-body interactive content, we expect that the contents will be applicable for slowing down progression and the prevention of cognitive and physical decline. The content was designed based on the mini-mental state examination for cognitive domains and on sit to walk gait analysis for a screening of both physical and mental issues. Gait analysis is a common method that can be used to screen for cognitive decline and predict frailty in the elderly population [10–12].

The interactive program opens with the choice of the user to select between 3 choices, gait analysis (top), memory evaluation (middle), and temporal-spatial awareness (bottom) (Fig. 2).

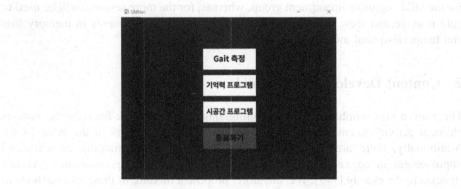

Fig. 2. Opening screen with the three options to choose form.

For the gait analysis task, the user is instructed to walk around the projection of the path on the floor while their time is measured. Here are two screenshots showing the path and the user's walking time. The gait test is to replicate the sit to walk test, which has been validated in research to be able to predict cognitive decline in the elderly [13] (Fig. 3).

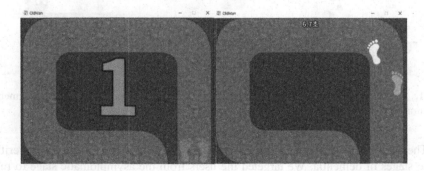

Fig. 3. The user starts on the bottom left of the screen projected on the floor then must walk around the edge as shown.

For the memory loss task, the user a choice of 3 levels. Each time the level increases the time that the position of the animals on the 3 × 3 grid becomes shorter. The level 1 test shows the full grid of the three different animals, the rabbit, turtle, and tiger for 10 s then will disappear. Then two of the same animals are shown and the user must go and stand on the position of the same third animal. The user must go to the designated square and stand there until the next option is given. The second level is the same, but the time to show the position of the animals becomes shorter, and for the third level, the time showing the positions of the animals is even shorter again (Fig. 4).

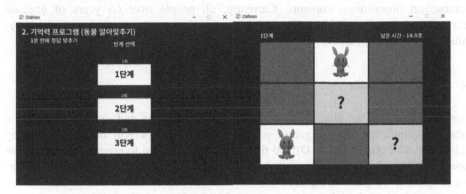

Fig. 4. (Left) Screenshot with the 3 levels to choose from, (right) the user must stand on the position where the third rabbit was shown in the previous screen

For the spatial-temporal awareness task, the user has the choice to do all three levels or choose one of the levels. The difficulty of the levels increases by showing a path projected on the ground, either in a straight line, curving line or a combination of both. The difficulty is increased by showing the path for a shorter time and making a more complex path with more turns (Fig. 5).

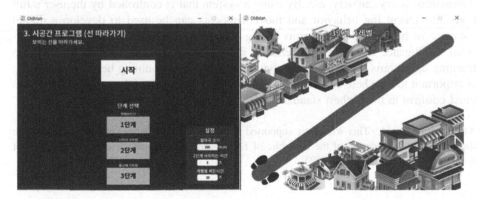

Fig. 5. (Left) Screenshot with the 3 levels to choose from, (right) the user must follow the path projected onto the ground correctly

3 Validity of Content

The reliability and the face validity of the content will be checked through a series of clinical pilot tests. As the contents is based on the cognitive tests used by neurologists to screen and diagnose any cognitive decline, the contents will be checked by neurologists by comparing the results of the behavior recorded in the clinical trials with the results of the existing data that they have from the participants regular hospital checkup. In other words, the existing clinical data and the results of the user's reactions and performance of the proposed contents will be used to validate the effectiveness of the interaction intervention contents. Currently, all people over 65 years of age are expected to attend a clinic to fill out a mini mental state examination and other cognitive related questionnaires every year [12, 14].

4 User Analysis

For user analysis, we plan to measure the user's behaviors and interaction with the reaction-stimulating media (game) content. Their behavior will be recorded using Kinect depth cameras (RGB-D) and their movement is used to control the interactive contents. Though the analysis of their movements, such as reaction times and movement speeds, we plan to measure the state of the cognitive function in the various domains (short- and medium-term memory loss, and temporal-spatial awareness).

5 Future Work

The intervention contents developed in this study for the screening, prevention, management of cognitive decline for the elderly needs to be continually improved and additional contents for other cognitive domains needs to be further developed. Furthermore, content based on the innovative methods in this study should be examined for other target groups of people and other mental/cognitive related declines, such as depression, worry, anxiety, etc. By using a system that is controlled by the user's full body movement the behavior and movement data can be used to develop a digital database of human behavior norms during various set scenarios. As explanatory artificial intelligence develops this behavior database will possibly be used to develop learning algorithms that may detect abnormal or possibly troubling behavior queues. It is important to note here that the privacy of the user during all of these future endeavors must confirm to the highest standards to protect any user or participant.

Acknowledgement. This work was supported by Global Research Network program through the Ministry of Education of the Republic of Korea and the National Research Foundation of Korea (NRF-2016S1A2A2912583).

References

1. Mealy, A., Sorensen, J.: Effects of an aging population on hospital costs related to elective hip replacements. Public Health **180**, 10–16 (2020)
2. Bray, J., Atkinson, T., Latham, I., Brooker, D.: Practice of Namaste Care for people living with dementia in the UK. Nurs. Older People **32**(1) (2020)
3. Khirasaria, R., Singh, V., Batta, A.: Exploring digital therapeutics: the next paradigm of modern health-care industry
4. Ejima, K., et al.: Exceptional reported effects and data anomalies merit explanation from "A randomized controlled trial of coordination exercise on cognitive function in obese adolescents" by Liu et al. Psychol. Sport Exerc. **46**, 101604 (2018)
5. Redwine, L.S., Pung, M.A., Wilson, K., Bangen, K.J., Delano-Wood, L., Hurwitz, B.: An exploratory randomized sub-study of light-to-moderate intensity exercise on cognitive function, depression symptoms and inflammation in older adults with heart failure. J. Psychosom. Res. **128**, 109883 (2020)
6. Ichinose, Y., Morishita, S., Suzuki, R., Endo, G., Tsubaki, A.: Comparison of the effects of continuous and intermittent exercise on cerebral oxygenation and cognitive function. In: Ryu, P.-D., LaManna, J.C., Harrison, D.K., Lee, S.-S. (eds.) Oxygen Transport to Tissue XLI. AEMB, vol. 1232, pp. 209–214. Springer, Cham (2020). https://doi.org/10.1007/978-3-030-34461-0_26
7. Lee, P., Cai, S., Lu, E.Y., Ng, B.F., Jensen, M.P., Tsang, H.W.: Qigong reduces depressive symptoms of Taiwanese elderly with chronic physical illness: a randomized controlled trial. J. Altern. Complement. Med. **26**(1), 76–78 (2020)
8. Li, K.Z.H., Bherer, L.: Cognitive training and mobility: implications for falls prevention. In: Montero-Odasso, M., Camicioli, R. (eds.) Falls and Cognition in Older Persons, pp. 289–308. Springer, Cham (2020). https://doi.org/10.1007/978-3-030-24233-6_17
9. Hohenfeld, C., et al.: Changes in brain activation related to visuo-spatial memory after real-time fMRI neurofeedback training in healthy elderly and Alzheimer's disease. Behav. Brain Res. **381**, 112435 (2020)
10. Pieruccini-Faria, F., Montero-Odasso, M., Hausdorff, J.M.: Gait variability and fall risk in older adults: the role of cognitive function. In: Montero-Odasso, M., Camicioli, R. (eds.) Falls and Cognition in Older Persons, pp. 107–138. Springer, Cham (2020). https://doi.org/10.1007/978-3-030-24233-6_7
11. Seo, M., Won, C.W., Kim, S., Yoo, J.H., Kim, Y.H., Kim, B.S.: The association of gait speed and frontal lobe among various cognitive domains: the Korean frailty and aging cohort study (KFACS). J. Nutr. Health Aging **24**(1), 91–97 (2019). https://doi.org/10.1007/s12603-019-1276-9
12. Shim, H., Kim, M., Won, C.W.: Motoric cognitive risk syndrome is associated with processing speed and executive function, but not delayed free recall memory: the Korean frailty and aging cohort study (KFACS). Arch. Gerontol. Geriat. **87**, 103990 (2020)
13. Montero-Odasso, M., Camicioli, R.: Falls as a manifestation of brain failure: gait, cognition, and the neurobiology of falls. In: Montero-Odasso, M., Camicioli, R. (eds.) Falls and Cognition in Older Persons, pp. 3–20. Springer, Cham (2020). https://doi.org/10.1007/978-3-030-24233-6_1
14. Doi, T., et al.: Spatio-temporal gait variables predicted incident disability. J. NeuroEng. Rehabil. **17**(1), 1–7 (2020)

Robot Use for Older Adults – Attitudes, Wishes and Concerns. First Results from Switzerland

Stephanie Lehmann[✉️][ID], Esther Ruf, and Sabina Misoch

Institute for Ageing Research, FHS St.Gallen, University of Applied Sciences,
Rosenbergstrasse 59, 9001 St. Gallen, Switzerland
stephanie.lehmann@ost.ch

Abstract. Due to demographic change, the increasing shortage of skilled professionals in the care sector, and the desire of older adults to stay independent as long as possible, it is predicted that robots will be used more often in the future to support older adults. To achieve accepted solutions, the opinions and concerns of the population need to be considered. Studies so far have shown different results, focus on a specific type of robot, and there is little knowledge about the attitudes and concerns of the population regarding the general use of robots for older adults. Based on established models of technology and robot acceptance, a questionnaire was compiled. To gain nationwide representative data, the survey includes questions on different factors of robot acceptance, preferred appearance, preferred functions and field of application, as well as ethical considerations. Here, data for Switzerland is published for the first time and evaluated descriptively. So far, 189 participants answered the survey, 57.6% of them women. Most participants had a positive attitude towards robots and would personally use a robot. But some functions are judged to be more conceivable than others. The main ethical concerns were a lack of interpersonal contact or problems with data security. The data collection will continue to achieve representativeness and to provide an overview of the attitudes and concerns about the implementation of robots for older adults in Switzerland and will be the basis for later in-depth analyses.

Keywords: Robot use · Older adults · Attitudes

1 Background

Due to demographic change, the proportion of people over 65 is rising [1] and most older adults wish to live at home as long as possible [2–4] which is beneficial for their quality of life [5]. This will lead to an increase in the number of people in need of support in the future, which may exacerbate the existing shortage of nursing staff in the out- and inpatient sector and increase health care costs [6–10]. To address the problems in the out- and inpatient sector, more and more technical innovations are being developed and used to support older adults at home and caregivers in institutions. It is to be expected that the use of robots in older adults' homes or institutions will also play an increasingly important role, in maintaining the independence and well-being of older adults [11–13] and to relieve caregivers [14].

© Springer Nature Switzerland AG 2020
C. Stephanidis and M. Antona (Eds.): HCII 2020, CCIS 1226, pp. 64–70, 2020.
https://doi.org/10.1007/978-3-030-50732-9_9

To achieve accepted robotic solutions, the opinions and concerns of the population need to be considered. Despite the actuality (popularity) of the topic, ambivalent results exist indicating low acceptance [15] as well as positive attitudes toward robots [16] and there is currently little detailed knowledge about the attitudes and concerns of the Swiss population regarding the use of robots for older adults. Previous surveys focus on specific robots such as special humanoid robots [e.g. 17] or industrial robots [18] but do not address robots for older adults.

In the present study, attitudes, wishes and concerns of the Swiss population towards robot use for older adults are surveyed in order to support further research and development of successful and accepted robots for older adults. Different findings, cultural sensitivity [17], rapid technical development, and a universal approach were considered in developing an innovative questionnaire that addresses robot use for older adults specifically, the situation in Switzerland, and robots in general. The study is ongoing, with the aim of collecting national representative data for later in-depth analyses of the acceptance of robots.

2   Method

As part of a project funded by the University of Applied Sciences St.Gallen in 2018, a questionnaire for the survey study was developed. Based on a literature search, various models of technology/robot acceptance and attitude research were compiled and evaluated for their suitability for the objective of the questionnaire to be prepared. Factors that were present in theories, models and scales concerning robot acceptance often cited in literature were selected by two researchers of the study group and included the following: Multi-dimensional robot attitude scale [19], Almere Model [20, 21], Usability, social acceptance, user experience and societal impact (USUS) [22], Acceptance model for industrial context [18], Technology acceptance model 3 (TAM 3) [23], Model of domestic social robot acceptance [24], Theory of Reasoned Action (TRA) [25], Technology Acceptance Model (TAM) [26], and the Unified Theory of Acceptance and Use of Technology Model (UTAUT) [27]. The selected factors were discussed in an internal scientific colloquium.

Based on this, 13 factors were identified as variables that can influence robot acceptance. Factors related to the person/individual are general attitude toward robots, negative emotions, positive emotions, self-efficacy and trust. Factors related to the robot and its functions are usefulness, perceived barriers (later renamed to effort), joy/fun, safety, control and usability. Factors related to the context are the attitude of the social network and social support. The factors were each collected with one to two items. Further aspects considered relevant for acceptance in literature are included: ethical concerns (seven items), effects on society (one item), preferred appearance of the robot (one item), conceivable functions of the robot (eight items) and possible application areas of robots (two items) [28–33]. A Likert scale with seven categories was chosen as answer format for the variables. Sociodemographic variables were recorded according to the recommendations of Flandorfer [34]. Experience with robots [35], technical experience, interest in technology, and the area of professional activity (self-developed) were included, one question each. This resulted in a three-page questionnaire with 48 items that can be completed in 10–15 min.

The questionnaire was pretested by 61 participants. After the pretest, linguistic adjustments were made, and the response scale was reduced to six categories (from 1 "totally disagree" to 6 "totally agree"). Internal consistency resulted in a Cronbach's Alpha of >.9. The online version of the final questionnaire can be viewed on the website of the Institute (http://www.fhsg.ch/alter). The questionnaire was then distributed via online-link and paper-pencil version at events for relatives and older adults in nursing homes, at municipal events, by e-mail to persons of the institute's database, and to persons of the institute's broad network organized in various associations and societies, and by posting the link to the questionnaire on the institute's homepage. All statistics were calculated using the IBM SPSS 24 software package. The survey started in January 2019 and data are collected continuously. Descriptive statistics are shown for variables described above, based on the data available on March 2020. Answer categories 1, 2, and 3 are taken together to calculate disagreement, and answer categories 4, 5, and 6 to calculate agreement.

3   Results

3.1   Participants

So far, 189 people filled out the questionnaire. The respondents were on average 65.4 years old (SD 16.6 years, range 17 to 96 years). 57.6% were women and 64.5% lived with a partner. 9.2% completed mandatory school education and 65.8% have a tertiary level qualification. The majority (96.8%) lived in a private household and 50.3% rated their residential area as rather rural. 29.4% considered themselves to be very interested in technology, 52.4% as interested, 14.4% as less interested and 3.7% as not at all interested in technology. 59.7% valued themselves as experienced with technology. 54.6% had no previous experience with a robot.

3.2   General Attitudes Towards Robots

The majority of respondents said they were interested in robots, stated having a positive view of robots and would themselves use a robot: 72.3% agreed with the statement that they were interested in robot use and robotic solutions for older adults, 67.5% said they had a generally positive view of robots, and 69.7% said they would personally use a robot. Most of the respondents stated that they could imagine the support of older adults by a robot mainly in the private home (78.6%) or also in a retirement or nursing home (74.3%). 59.9% could imagine the support in a hospital. 68.4% said they could imagine using a robot for themselves, 20.9% for their parents or grandparents, and 61.5% for other people.

3.3   Assessment of Ability to Handle Robots

Most respondents rated themselves as competent in handling robots: 86.0% agreed that they would be able to use a robot after instruction, and 83.1% agreed with the statement that they had all the skills to handle a robot.

3.4   Desired Functions and Application Areas of Robots

Of the eight functions asked, five were conceivable for most respondents. 85.0% could imagine the robot calling for help if something happened (e.g. a fall), 84.0% a reminder function (e.g. taking medication), 72.7% support in everyday activities (such as picking up things), 69.0% monitoring and reporting vital signs (e.g. pulse or blood pressure), and 68.4% the joint performance of movement exercises. For most of the respondents talking and conversing with a robot was not imaginable (72.2%), for 69.0% nursing activities (e.g. washing) by a robot were not imaginable, and the robot as a communication aid to communicate with friends and relatives were not imaginable for 58.3%.

3.5   Preferred Appearance of Robots

In terms of appearance, a robot was preferred that looks more like a machine (25.3%), like a human being (22.5%), 21.9% would not care about appearance, 14.6% preferred a look like an object of utility, 11.2% preferred a look like a fantasy creature, and 4.5% preferred an animal-like appearance. The evaluation separated by gender showed that male participants preferred a machine-like appearance (28.8%) or they would not care about appearance (26.0%), and female participants preferred the human appearance (27.2%) or the machine-like appearance (22.3%).

3.6   Ethical Concerns Regarding the Use of Robots for Older Adults

Participants indicated their agreement to various ethical concerns, which must be considered when using robots with older adults. Concerns mainly related to the lack of interpersonal contact and problems with handling sensitive data. 76.5% and 60.4% respectively agreed with these statements. 49.3% expressed concern that workers will lose their jobs and 45.6% expressed the fear that privacy is not guaranteed. Concerns that the older adults could be deceived (42.4%), that the self-determination of older adults could be restricted (40.0%), and that the dignity of older adults is being violated (38.1%) were expressed.

4   Discussion

To collect attitudes, wishes and concerns about robot use for older adults, a survey study was conducted in Switzerland. The participants up to now were highly educated and highly interested in technology. Therefore, the actual sample is not yet representative of Switzerland. However, it is known from other studies, that well integrated, educated and technology-oriented people are more likely to take part in studies [36–

39]. Due to the recruitment procedure, it was not possible to collect any information about return rates.

Most respondents were generally interested in robots and had positive thoughts about robots in general. That means that not all user-groups and functions of robots seem accepted. Most respondents would use robots for themselves or others but not for their (grand)parents, although many respondents indicated that the use in a retirement or nursing home would be quite conceivable. Possible explanations that should be further investigated are whether the respondents consider their (grand)parents not to be able to handle a robot, or whether respondents feel guilty considering a robot caring for their (grand)parents. The most problematic ethical concerns stated were a lack of interpersonal contact and data security. Developers must address these findings when creating or adapting a robot.

To be able to consider as many factors as possible for a comprehensive opinion, each aspect of robot acceptance was realized with 1-2 items. In the original scales, the respective factors often contained several items. Direct comparability with specific individual scales is therefore not always possible.

The participants were not shown a specific picture of a robot, which could have influenced the answers: Some relied on experience, others only on an internal picture [see 33]. This must be considered for interpretation but is handled like this in other studies too [16, 35].

So far, the data was published for the first time and evaluated descriptively. The aim is to continue the data collection, to achieve representativeness and to provide knowledge for research and development, and to adapt robots to the wishes and needs of the population. There is a need for further research on attitudes and concerns about robots and in-depth, multivariate analyses. Whether the desired or imaginable functions of robots are influenced by other moderating aspects should be assessed. It could make a difference whether the use of a robot is compared to a subjectively less attractive alternative (e.g. entering a nursing home), or whether the robot is used alone or together with a caregiver. Currently, the different age-groups are too small for in-depth analysis. Sub-group analyses (age, gender, educational level) will be carried out with a larger sample. In addition, a theoretical model of robot acceptance will be tested.

References

1. Vaupel, J.: Setting the stage: a generation of centenarians? Wash. Q. **23**(3), 197–200 (2000)
2. Hedtke-Becker, A., Hoevels, R., Otto, U., Stumpp, G., Beck, S.: Zu Hause wohnen wollen bis zuletzt. In: Pohlmann, S. (ed.) Altern mit Zukunft, pp. 141–176. Springer, Wiesbaden (2012). https://doi.org/10.1007/978-3-531-19418-9_6
3. Marek, K.D., Rantz, M.J.: Ageing in place: a new model for long-term care. Nurs. Adm. Q. **24**(3), 1–11 (2000)
4. Oswald, F., Kaspar, R., Frenzel-Erkert, U., Konopik, N.: "Hier will ich wohnen bleiben!" Ergebnisse eines Frankfurter Forschungsprojekts zur Bedeutung des Wohnens in der Nachbarschaft für gesundes Altern. Goethe Universität, Frankfurt am Main (2013)
5. Sixsmith, A., Gutman, G.: Technologies for Active Aging. International Perspectives on Aging. Springer, New York (2013). https://doi.org/10.1007/978-1-4419-8348-0

6. Afentakis, A., Maier, T.: Projektionen des Personalbedarfs und -angebots in Pflegeberufen bis 2025 (S. 990–1002). Statistisches Bundesamt, Wiesbaden (2010)
7. Mercay, C., Burla, L., Widmer, M.: Gesundheitspersonal in der Schweiz. Bestandesaufnahme und Prognosen bis 2030 (Obsan Bericht 71). Schweizerisches Gesundheitsobservatorium, Neuchâtel (2016)
8. Mercay, C., Grünig, A.: Gesundheitspersonal in der Schweiz – Zukünftiger Bedarf bis 2030 und die Folgen für den Nachwuchsbedarf (Obsan Bulletin 12/2016). Schweizerisches Gesundheitsobservatorium, Neuchâtel (2016)
9. Petek, C., et al.: Kompetenzmodell für Pflegeberufe in Österreich. Österreichichscher Gesundheits- und Krankenpflegeverband, Wien (2011)
10. World Health Organization: World report on ageing and health. World Health Organization, Geneva (2015)
11. Graf, B., Heyer, T., Klein, B., Wallhoff, F.: Servicerobotik für den demographischen Wandel. Mögliche Einsatzfelder und aktueller Entwicklungsstand. Bundesgesundheitsblatt-Gesundheitsforschung-Gesundheitsschutz **56**(8), 1145–1152 (2013)
12. Ray, C., Mondada, F., Siegwart, R.: What do people expect from robots? In: Proceedings of the IEEE/RSJ International Conference on Intelligent Robots and Systems, Nice, pp. 3816–3821. IEEE (2008)
13. Wu, Y.-H., Wrobel, J., Cornuet, M., Kerhervé, H., Damnée, S., Rigaud, A.-S.: Acceptance of an assistive robot in older adults: a mixed-method study of human-robot interaction over a 1-month period in the Living Lab setting. Clin. Interv. Aging **9**, 801–811 (2014)
14. Becker, H., et al.: Robotik in Betreuung und Gesundheitsversorgung. Vdf Hochschulverlag AG, Zürich (2013)
15. Payr, S., Werner, F., Werner, K.: Potential of robotics for ambient assisted living. FFG benefit, Vienna (2015)
16. European Commission: Einstellungen der Öffentlichkeit zu Robotern. Zusammenfassung. Spezial Eurobaometer 382 (2012)
17. Mavridis, N., et al.: Opinions and attitudes toward humanoid robots in the Middle East. AI Soc. **27**, 517–534 (2012). https://doi.org/10.1007/s00146-011-0370-2
18. Bröhl, C., Nelles, J., Brandl, C., Mertens, A., Schlick, C.M.: Entwicklung und Analyse eines Akzeptanzmodells für die Mensch-Roboter-Kooperation in der Industrie. In: Gesellschaft für Arbeitswissenschaft e.V., Dortmund (eds.) Frühjahrskongress 2017, Brugg und Zürich: Soziotechnische Gestaltung des digitalen Wandels – kreativ, innovative, sinnhaft, pp. 1–6 (2017)
19. Ninomiya, T., Fujita, A., Suzuki, D., Umemuro, H.: Development of the multi-dimensional robot attitude scale: constructs of people's attitudes towards domestic robots. In: Tapus, A., André, E., Martin, J.C., Ferland, F., Ammi, M. (eds.) ICSR 2015. LNCS (LNAI), vol. 9388, pp. 482–491. Springer, Cham (2015). https://doi.org/10.1007/978-3-319-25554-5_48
20. Heerink, M., Kröse, B., Evers, V., Wielinga, B.: Measuring acceptance of an assistive social robot: a suggested toolkit. In: 18th IEEE International Symposium on Robot and Human Interactive Communication, Toyama, pp. 528–533. IEEE (2009)
21. Heerink, M., Kröse, B., Evers, V., Wielinga, B.: Assessing acceptance of assistive social agent technology by older adults: the almere model. Int. J. Social Robot. **2**(4), 361–375 (2010). https://doi.org/10.1007/s12369-010-0068-5
22. Ludewig, Y.: Untersuchung des Einflusses sozio-emotionaler Faktoren auf die soziale Akzeptanz und Nutzungsintention bei Lotsenrobotern. Disserttaion, Weimar (2016)
23. Venkatesh, V., Bala, H.: Technology acceptance model 3 and a research agenda on interventions. Decis. Sci. **39**(2), 273–315 (2008)
24. De Graaf, M.M.A., Allouch, S.B., van Dijk, J.A.G.M.: Why would I use this in my home? A model of domestic social robot acceptance. Hum. Comput. Interact. **34**(2), 115–173 (2019)

25. Fishbein, M., Ajzen, I.: Belief, Attitude, Intention, and Behavior: An Introduction to Theory and Research. Addison-Wesley, Reading (1975)
26. Davis, F.D., Bagozzi, R.P., Warshaw, P.R.: User acceptance of computer technology: a comparison of two theoretical models. Manage. Sci. **35**(8), 982–1003 (1989)
27. Venkatesh, V., Morris, M.G., Davis, G.B., Davis, F.D.: User acceptance of information technology: toward a unified view. Manag. Inf. Syst. Q. **27**(3), 425–478 (2003)
28. Beer, J.M., Prakash, A., Mitzner, T.L., Rogers, W.A.: Understanding Robot Acceptance. Georgia Institute of Technology, Atlanta, GA (2011)
29. Coco, K., Kangasniemi, M., Rantanen, T.: Care personnel's attitudes and fears toward care robots in elderly care: a comparison of data from the care personnel in Finland and Japan. J. Nurs. Scholarsh. **50**(6), 634–644 (2018)
30. Pino, M., Boulay, M., Jouen, F., Rigaud, A.-S.: «Are we ready for robots that care for us?» Attitudes and opinions of older adults toward socially assistive robots. Front. Aging Neurosci. **7** (2015). Article 141
31. Rantanen, T., Lehto, P., Vuorinen, P., Coco, K.: The adoption of care robots in home care – a survey on the attitudes of Finish home care personnel. J. Clin. Nurs. **27**, 1846–1859 (2018)
32. Richter, K.: Gesundheits-Roboter für Senior/innen. Neue Informations- und Kommunikationstechnologien in der alternden Gesellschaft. Dissertation. Universitätsverlag, Ilmenau (2017)
33. Savela, N., Turja, T., Oksanen, A.: Social acceptance of robots in different occupational fields: a systematic literature review. Int. J. Social Robot. **10**(4), 493–502 (2017). https://doi.org/10.1007/s12369-017-0452-5
34. Flandorfer, P.: Population ageing and socially assistive robots for elderly persons: the importance of sociodemographic factors for user acceptance. Int. J. Popul. Res. **2012**, 13 p. (2012). Article no. 829835. https://doi.org/10.1155/2012/829835
35. Nitto, H., Taniyama, D., Inagaki, H.: Social acceptance and impact of robots and artificial intelligence –findings of survey in Japan, the U.S. and Germany–. NRI Papers No. 211. Nomura Research Institute (2017)
36. Classen, K., Oswald, F., Doh, M., Kleinemas, U., Wahl, H.-W.: Umwelten des Alterns: Wohnen, Mobilität, Technik und Medien. Kohlhammer, Stuttgart (2014)
37. Kubiak, M.: Ist Beteiligung immer gut und sinnvoll? Partizipation und/oder politische Gleichheit. Impu!se **88**, 4–5 (2015)
38. Mies, C.: Akzeptanz von Smart Home Technologien: Einfluss von subjektivem Pflegebedarf und Technikerfahrung bei älteren Menschen. Untersuchung im Rahmen des Projekts «Accepting Smart Homes». Diplomarbeit, Wien (2011)
39. Stadelhofer, C.: Möglichkeiten und Chancen der Internetnutzung durch Ältere. Zeitschrift für Gerontologie und Geriatrie **33**, 186–194 (2000)

Evaluation of Musical Playing Ability of Children with Intellectual Disabilities by Using Keyboard-Playing-Software with the Figurenotes System

Kazuyuki Mito[1(✉)], Chiharu Watanabe[1], Rui Sotome[1], Aya Shirai[1], Tota Mizuno[1], Naoaki Itakura[1], and Manami Matsuda[2]

[1] The University of Electro-Communications,
1-5-1 Chofugaoka, Chofu, Tokyo 182-8585, Japan
k.mito@uec.ac.jp
[2] General Incorporated Association the Spread of Figurenotes HappyMuse,
4-34-7 Nishinogawa, Komae, Tokyo 201-0001, Japan

Abstract. Figurenotes is an intuitive music notation system developed for people who have difficulty reading musical score such as people with intellectual disabilities and it is a simple system to uses color and shape to convey all the information of traditional music notation. The aim of this study is to clarify the effectiveness of application software to learn musical performance using the Figurenotes system and to identify the causes of stumbling in musical instrument performance in people with intellectual disabilities. In this research, we created a keyboard-playing application software of the tablet terminal with a learning support function using the Figurenotes system. 9 subjects aged 7 to 16 with intellectual disabilities used the application software for one month. Then, the number of correctly played sounds and the number of taps of the keyboard were obtained from the usage history. As a result of the analysis, the mistake factors of the musical performance of children with intellectual disabilities were 1) tapping according to the rhythm, 2) matching of the symbol for a musical score and 3) quickness of the eye and hand cooperative operation. Furthermore, from the questionnaire of the music behavior, the children who could tap and match the symbol according to the rhythm had a high degree of development of the musical aspect. Thus, it was found that two factors, playing in accordance with the rhythm and symbol matching, particularly affected the development of musical learning.

Keywords: Piano · iOS application · Matching of a musical score · Intellectual disability

1 Introduction

Playing musical instruments is known to be effective in developing sensory organs and cognitive functions in children with intellectual disabilities [1]. In addition, it can be expected to be able to express oneself by means of music and expand exchanges with others. Generally, children with intellectual disabilities are poor at understanding

C. Stephanidis and M. Antona (Eds.): HCII 2020, CCIS 1226, pp. 71–75, 2020.
https://doi.org/10.1007/978-3-030-50732-9_10

traditional music notation. There are also a few reading support tools for them. Figurenotes is an intuitive music notation system developed for people who have difficulty reading musical scores such as people with intellectual disabilities, and it is a simple system to uses color and shape to convey all the information of traditional music notation [2]. The Figurenotes are used in 13 countries, mainly in Europe, and have proven effective in learning children with intellectual disabilities. Yamada has reported that the Figurenotes system makes learning music easier and makes the delight and the sense of accomplishment by the progress of performances cause the confidence, the intention and the concentration for people with intellectual disabilities [3]. Watanabe et al. [4] had developed tablet-based application software that plays the musical score of the Figurenotes by a keyboard, and has verified its usefulness for children with intellectual disabilities. Their interest grew and they concentrated on using the application. However, there were individual differences in playing the correct keyboard in rhythm. And it became clear that it was important to provide learning support according to the ability. The purpose of our study is to development of an application to learn piano playing using the Figurenotes system and to clarify its effectiveness. And more identify the causes of stumbling in musical instrument performance in children with intellectual disabilities.

2 Design of Application Software

The application software was created with consideration for the number of choice menus and the size of the buttons, based on the advice of the teacher of special education school and music therapist. An example of the screen layout of the application software is shown in Fig. 1. The music score of the figurenote system, the keyboard, and the symbol of the figurenote system are displayed on the keyboard. When the start button is tapped, the accompaniment plays and the user plays with the keyboard. The musical notes to be played are indicated by red arrows. The musical performance song is "ABC song". The number of musical notes to be played in one musical bar increases in three stages, one-note (Stage 1), two-notes (Stage 2) and four-notes (Stage 3) per bar. At each stage, there are three modes: a) rhythm learning, b) guided musical performance learning, and c) non-guided musical performance learning, and steps up in the order a, b and c. In a) rhythm learning, the background color of the applause picture turns yellow according to the rhythm of the song, and the user taps the screen accordingly. In b) guided musical performance learning, the color of the keyboard changes to yellow according to the notes of the musical score and the user taps the keyboard. In c) non-guided musical performance learning, the color of the keyboard does not change according to the notes of the score. The total learning steps are nine with three stages of musical notes and three types of learning modes. Also, when the user taps the button of the example, the user can watch the explainer video at each step. When the user could play correctly, the mark ◎ appears below the score. After the performance, an illustration of the character indicating the degree of the correct answer rate is displayed on the screen. When the correct rate is above 75%, the user can learn the next step. This application software works on iOS devices and installed on iPad Pro 9.7 in.

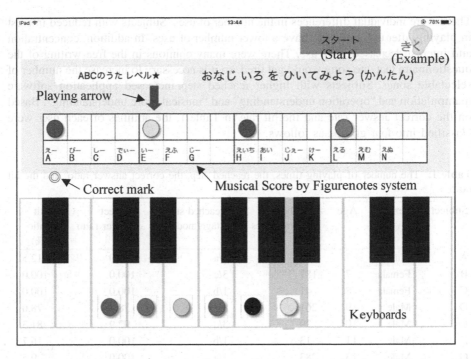

Fig. 1. Example of the screen layout of the application software (mode of guided musical performance learning)

3   User Test

The purpose of the user test is to verify that people with intellectual disabilities can use the proposed application software and to identify the causes of stumbling in musical instrument performance. This experiment was performed with the approval of the Ethics Review Committee of the University of Electro-Communications (control number: No. 18046). The subjects were 9 persons (6 males and 3 females) aged 7 to 16 with intellectual disabilities. Since all the subjects were minors, the contents of the experiment were explained to their parents in writing and informed consent was obtained. The subjects used the application for one month. For each subject, the date and time of use, the learning step, and the timing of tapping were recorded. Subject's parents responded to musical behavior questionnaires before and after user testing. The questionnaire items are "Concentration", "Interest", "Score understanding", "Operation understanding". Parents evaluated each item on a six-point scale (1: yes, 6: no).

4   Results and Discussion

Table 1 shows the number of playing times, the reached step, the correct answer ratio, and the hit ratio. The hit ratio is the ratio between the number of correct answers and the number of taps. Table 2 shows the results of the questionnaire on musical behavior.

There were individual differences in the number of uses. Subjects with reduced interest in playing after use tended to have a lower number of uses. In addition, concentration and interest decreased after use. There were many opinions in the free writing of the questionnaire that one song would get tired, so it is necessary to increase the number of selectable songs. Subjects with higher reached step increased application software manipulation and "operation understanding" and "musical score understanding". Based on the correct answer rate and the hit rate in Table 1, the abilities of each user were classified into four groups as follows.

Table 1. The number of playing times, the reached step, the correct answer ratio, and the hit ratio.

Subject	Sex	Age	Number of playing times	Reached step (stage/mode)	Correct answer ratio (%)	Hit ratio (%)
A	Male	7	180	1/a	100.0	12.5
B	Female	7	187	3/c	100.0	100.0
C	Female	8	41	1/b	100.0	100.0
D	Male	9	261	3/c	78.6	78.6
E	Male	10	29	3/c	92.9	81.3
F	Male	11	13	1/b	100.0	16.7
G	Male	13	283	1/a	100.0	9.5
H	Male	14	139	1/a	100.0	100.0
I	Female	16	122	3/a	92.9	65.0

Table 2. Questionnaire of musical behavior (6: Yes, 1: No)

Subject	Concentration		Interest		Operation understanding		Musical score understanding	
	Before	After	Before	After	Before	After	Before	After
A	4	5	1	2	3	3	2	2
B	5	5	5	6	5	6	5	6
C	4	4	2	2	2	2	2	4
D	5	5	6	6	6	6	5	5
E	3	4	5	3	4	4	4	6
F	4	2	4	1	1	6	2	2
G	2	2	2	2	2	2	2	2
H	6	4	2	2	3	3	2	2
I	4	5	5	5	5	5	4	5
Mean	4.1	4.0	3.6	3.2	3.4	4.1	3.1	3.8
SD	1.1	1.2	1.7	1.8	1.6	1.6	1.3	1.7

- Group 1 (subject A, F, and G): the subjects tap the keyboard many times without being in rhythm.
- Group 2 (C, H): the subjects can play along with the rhythm if there is a guide due to a change in the color of the keyboard, but cannot play without the guide. This is, it is not possible to match symbols between the score and the keyboard.
- Group 3 (I): the subject can match the symbols between the keys of the score according to the rhythm. However, when the number of notes increases, the fingers cannot be moved quickly to perform.
- Group 4 (B, D, and H) the subjects can play with the eyes and hands coordinating quickly to the rhythm.

From the characteristics of Groups 1 and 2, rhythm learning and symbol matching learning in the Figurenotes system is considered important.

5 Conclusion

In this study, we developed a piano playing application software using the Figurenotes system and investigated the learning characteristics of children with intellectual disabilities. Analysis of the playing history revealed that the cause of the stumbling was the tapping according to the rhythm, the matching between the score and the keyboard symbol, and the quickness of eye-hand coordination. In addition, the subjects whose learning steps increased had a higher understanding of the application operation and the Figurenotes system. Thus, it was found that two factors, tapping in accordance with the rhythm and symbol matching, particularly affected the development of musical performance learning.

References

1. Takahashi, T.: An outline of music therapy. Jpn. J. Complement. Altern. Med. 1(1), 77–84 (2004)
2. Drake Music Scotland. https://drakemusicscotland.org/. Accessed 3 Oct 2020
3. Yamada, M.: Finnish Figurenotes music therapy method: a tool of improving the quality of life of the mentally disabled people. Bull. Lifelong Learn. Res. Inst. Hokkaido Asai Gakuen Univ. 8, 215–224 (2005)
4. Watanabe, C., Mizuno, T., Itakura, N., Mito, K.: The effectiveness of keyboard playing application using Figurenotes in music education for people with intellectual disabilities. In: Proceeding of the 59th Conference of Japan Ergonomics Society, 2C4-2 (2018)

Constructing a Highly Accurate Japanese Sign Language Motion Database Including Dialogue

Yuji Nagashima[1]([✉]) [iD], Keiko Watanabe[1], Daisuke Hara[2], Yasuo Horiuchi[3], Shinji Sako[4], and Akira Ichikawa[1]

[1] Kogakuin University, 2665-1 Nakano, Hachioji, Tokyo 192-0015, Japan
nagasima@cc.kogakuin.ac.jp, ed13001@ns.kogakuin.ac.jp
[2] Toyota Technological Institute,
2-12-1 Hisakata, Tempaku-ku, Nagoya 468-8511, Japan
[3] Chiba University, 1-33, Yayoicho, Inage-ku, Chiba-shi, Chiba 263-8522, Japan
[4] Nagoya Institute of Technology,
Gokiso-cho, Showa-ku, Nagoya, Aichi 466-8555, Japan

Abstract. Sign language is a visual language. Research into Sign language, including in related areas such as linguistics and engineering is lagging behind spoken language. One reason for this is the absence of a common database available to researchers from different areas.

This paper defines how to words are selected for inclusion in the sign language database, how to select informants, what format the data are included in and how to record the data. Also, the database includes three-dimensional behavioral data based on dialogue. The following explains the results.

Keywords: Japanese sign language · Database · Optical motion capture · Dialogue

1 Introduction

Sign language is used by deaf people, and is a natural interactive language different from and independent of oral language. Although it is a language, research on sign language remains underdeveloped in linguistics, engineering, and other related fields when compared to spoken languages. One reason for this is the lack of a multi-purpose database for shared use by linguists, engineers, and researchers in other fields.

However, differences are expected between the data formats desired by linguists, engineers, and those working in cognitive science. To standardize sign language research in many areas, it is desirable to record the same sign language movements in a data format compatible with researchers' needs. Analyzing the same sign language movements from different perspectives and in different ways may multiply opportunities to obtain new insight.

© Springer Nature Switzerland AG 2020
C. Stephanidis and M. Antona (Eds.): HCII 2020, CCIS 1226, pp. 76–81, 2020.
https://doi.org/10.1007/978-3-030-50732-9_11

This paper defines how to words are selected for inclusion in the sign language database, how to select informants, what format the data are included in and how to record the data. Also, the database includes three-dimensional behavioral data based on dialogue. The following explains the results.

2 Selecting the Words to Be Included in the Database and the Informants

The selection of JSL expressions to be included in the database was based on data about the frequency of use of Japanese words. The informants, are native signers, were chosen based on a criterion to use a type of Japanese sign language which is ease to read.

2.1 Selecting JSL Words

For JSL data, referring to the corpora of spoken Japanese such as the "Lexical Properties of Japanese [1]" made by NTT and the "Corpus of Spontaneous Japanese [2]", as well as sign language corpora such as the "NHK sign language news [3]" and the "Japanese-JSL Dictionary [4]" published by Japanese Federation of the Deaf, we have chosen signs to be recorded.

From the list of candidates, Japanese sign language expressions to be included in the database were selected based on the expressions in the Japanese-JSL Dictionary. The Japanese-JSL Dictionary includes more expressions than any other sign language dictionary published in print form. It contains nearly 6,000 expressions.

Furthermore, the following words have been added. They are not included in the dictionary we consulted.

- Words relating to the latest IT
- Words relating the imperial family and Reiwa, the new era name in Japan
- Words relating to sports, as the Tokyo Olympics is right around the corner
- Words relating to disaster
- Words relating to disability and information security

The sign language expressions have been verified in cooperation with persons who use sign language as their primary language.

2.2 Selection of Informants

As well as selecting signs to be recorded, we have discussed requirements about the informants who we will work with. We have decided that the informants must:

- be native signers of JSL born in a Deaf family
- use a type of JSL which is ease to read
- consent to making the JSL data public

Taking these requirements into consideration, we have decided on M (male, 41 yrs.) and K (female, 42 yrs.).

3   How Data Is Recorded and in What Format

We have discussed the best source format, spatio-temporal resolution, format of data files, and storing method for academic fields such as linguistics and engineering. Detailed analyses of the distinctive features, phonemes or morphemes of sign language involve detailed analyses of manual signals and non-manual markers. Not like Audio data which are one-dimensional on a time axis, sign language data are three-dimensional with a spatial spread on a time axis. If we do numerical analyses about sign language motion data, as we do with audio data, it is highly expected to obtain new information useful for sign language research. However, compared with audio data, sign language motion data will have much higher complexity because they involve more dimensions than audio data. Accurately analyzing sign language motion and generating high-quality computer-generated models for sign language will require highly accurate three-dimensional measurements of motions. If highly accurate three-dimensional sign language motion data and two-dimensional video data of sign language can synchronize, then it will be possible to analyze how the three-dimensional motions break down into two dimensions and progress on a time axis in terms of the recognition of sign language including non-manual markers and the analysis of its motions. This will make it possible to obtain a new methodology for understanding and recognizing sign language.

In the database that we built, the following data in three different frame rates are recorded by synchronizing them.

Figure 1 shows the configuration of the recording equipment and synchronization conceptual diagram used in 2018.

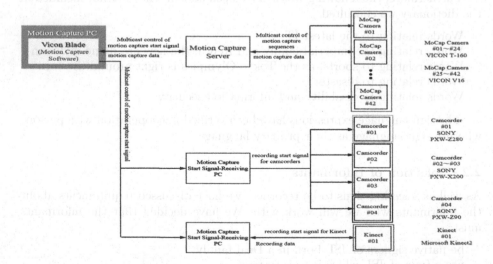

Fig. 1. The configuration of the recording equipment and synchronization conceptual diagram used in 2018

3.1 Three-Dimensional Behavior Measurement

Optical motion capture (hereinafter "MoCap") was used to measure three-dimensional data with high precision in terms of space and time. Measuring each word involved the use of forty-two T-160 cameras from VICON, each with 16 megapixels to achieve a spatial resolution of 0.5 mm and a temporal resolution of 119.88 fps. A total of 66 cameras, 33 per person, were used to shoot dialogues. MoCap data was recorded in three formats, C3D, BVH and FBX.

The frame rate of each data format is shown below.

- C3D data at 119.88 fps
- BVH data at 119.88 fps
- FBX data at 119.88 fps

3.2 Camera for Shooting

Three SONY camcorders were used to shoot videos of sign language; one located in front of an informant, one to the left and the other one to the right. For 2019, all three camcorders were 4 K. The capture frame rate is 59.94 fps.

3.3 Depth Sensor

Less expensive sensors capable of measuring distances with relatively high precision are widely available. We used the Kinect 2 ToF (Time of Flight) format. The maximum frame rate of data is 29.98 fps.

4 Recording Words in the Database

Videos for 4873 words were shot in the same shooting method and data format as described in Sect. 3 above. Table 1 shows, by year, the number of words shot in the videos. Each of the words with different movements and the same meaning (hereinafter "synonyms") are counted as a single Japanese label in the number of Japanese labels shown in the table. Therefore, each label with a synonym has different movements recorded. For numerical figures, units, the Japanese syllabary and alphabet, about 400 words were recorded in the 2019 version.

Table 1. Number of words shot in videos, by year

Year	2017	2018	2019	Total
Number of Japanese labels	400	600	3,873	4,873

The 2019 version also includes data from dialogues between two informants discussing different topics. For one of the topics (about 7 min long), post-processing (creation of BVH data, C3D data and FBX data) was performed to make the data three dimensional. Figure 2 shows how the dialogues were shot. Figure 3 shows 3D computer graphics from the FBX data of the dialogue data which underwent post processing .

Fig. 2. Dialogue shot in a video

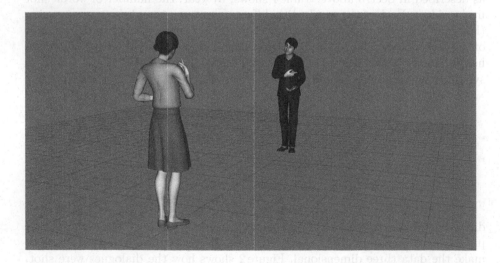

Fig. 3. 3D computer graphic of the dialogue data (drawn by FBX Reviewer)

5   Summary and Future Actions

This paper is about how the JSL database was built, how the data was recorded, and the actual recordings of words and dialogues. To date, 4873 words and dialogue data including the Japanese syllabary and alphabet have been recorded. A single set of dialogue data is transformed into three-dimensional behavioral data and can be synchronized with 4 K videos and Kinect data for analysis. Three-dimensional behavioral data are important in the analysis of sign language. Currently, we are building an annotation support system which will be capable of synchronization and analyzing the data recorded in the database. Details about the annotation support system will be reported at another time. Incidentally, we have already completed the development of the viewer [5] that will be needed for the annotation support system.

From here onward, we will concentrate on efforts to make the database publicly available. After being opened to the public, the database will become available in linguistics, engineering and other interdisciplinary domains. In that regard, the usefulness of DB will be immeasurable. This will make it possible for different researchers with different perspectives to analyze the same sign language expressions and will hopefully help to obtain new insights. Moreover, we will complete the annotation support system and open it to the public.

Acknowledgments. This work was supported by JSPS KAKENHI Grant Number 17H06114.

References

1. Amano, S., Kasahara, K., Kondo, K. : NTT database series [Lexical Properties of Japanese] volume 9: word familiarity database (addition ed.). Sanseido Co., Inc, Tokyo (2008)
2. Corpus of Spontaneous Japanese. http://pj.ninjal.ac.jp/corpus_center/csj/. Accessed 29 Nov 2018
3. Katou, N.: NHK Japanese sign language corpus on NHK news. In: 2010 NLP (the Association for Natural Language Processing) Annual Meeting, pp. 494–497 (2010)
4. Japan Institute for Sign Language Studies (ed.).: Japanese/ Japanese Sign Language Dictionary. Japanese Federation of the Deaf, Tokyo (1997)
5. Nagashima, Y. : Constructing a Japanese sign language database and developing its viewer. In: Proceedings of the 12th ACM PETRA 2019, pp. 321–322 (2019). https://doi.org/10.1145/3316782.3322738

A User-Centered Approach to Digital Household Risk Management

Cristina Paupini⑩, G. Anthony Giannoumis(✉)⑩,
and Terje Gjøsæter⑩

Oslo Metropolitan University, 0130 Oslo, Norway
{cristina.paupini,gagian}@oslomet.no

Abstract. Internet of Things (IoT) is expected to become as common as electricity (OECD 2016) and there is a high probability for connected homes to become central parts of critical societal. IoT technologies might access, manage and record sensitive data about citizens and, as they become more and more pervasive, unintended data breaches reports increase every week. However, most of the tools designed to protect users' privacy and personal data on IoT devices fail to contemplate the experience of persons with disabilities, elderly and other vulnerable categories of people. As a consequence, they are forced to rely on the help of family members or other related persons with technical skills, as frequent technical problems turn out to be the rule rather than the exception. With humans traditionally considered to be the "weak link" in technological networks there is the need of a vast educational project to raise awareness on the subject. This ongoing research paper aims to fill the existing gap in research by asking how humans deal with the risk factors linked to connected homes and how to develop a universally designed set of tools for everyday risk management in connected homes.

Keywords: Universal design · Internet of Things · Connected homes

1 Introduction

Home has always been a focal point of society's activities and decision - making, providing shelter and security to its inhabitants [1]. Recent technological innovations continue to change society through widespread and broadly accessible internet, artificial intelligence and machine learning [2]. Internet of Things (IoT), here referred to as the interconnection via the Internet of computing devices embedded in everyday objects, allowing their management, data mining and the access to the data generated [3], is expected to become as common as electricity (OECD 2016). There is therefore a high probability for connected homes to become central parts of critical societal infrastructures [1]. As a consequence, it is necessary to address the digital risks and vulnerabilities that come with the development of IoT consumer products and services. Privacy and security have emerged as two critical areas of risk when it comes to accessing and using technology [4]. This is especially relevant for IoT technologies as they access, manage and record sensitive data about people. As they become more and more pervasive, unintended data breaches reports increase every week [5].

© Springer Nature Switzerland AG 2020
C. Stephanidis and M. Antona (Eds.): HCII 2020, CCIS 1226, pp. 82–88, 2020.
https://doi.org/10.1007/978-3-030-50732-9_12

However, most of the tools designed to protect users' privacy and personal data on IoT devices are not accessible for persons with disabilities, older persons and other groups of socially disadvantaged people [6]. As a consequence, they are forced to rely on the help of family members or other related figures with technical skills [7]. With humans traditionally considered to be the "weak link" in technological networks [8], there is the need for more evidence and awareness on the relationship between privacy and accessibility concerning IoT technologies. This paper presents the ongoing research that aims to fill this gap asking the following research question: how do the perceived risks linked to connected households and homes differ from the actual risks IoT comes with and how do humans deal with those risk factors?

2 State of the Art

2.1 Internet and Communication Technology and Internet of Things

The fourth industrial revolution is bringing a drastic change of paradigm in our society by introducing widespread and broadly accessible internet, smaller, cheaper and more powerful sensors, artificial intelligence and machine learning [2]. Technology is being more and more intertwined with the very fabric of our society [9], and the more people become connected, the more they tend to inhabit connected homes. The environment itself is becoming widely connected through smart cities and vehicles, affecting industries and the public sector as well as individuals [10]. Traditional physical and societal infrastructures connecting homes to key services are currently being digitalized. According to IEC (2015), 200 million Internet connected wireless smart home security and safety products will have been installed worldwide by 2020. Scholars' interest has been drawn to explore IoT's characteristics in an numerous research works, from the pure definitions of Internet of Things and the early stages of its application [4, 11, 12] to the effects of its implementation and whether or not Europe is (was) ready for it [2]. Furthermore, several studies explore IoT possible adaptation in smart cities and environments, households and services [11, 12].

2.2 The Risks Connected to Internet of Things

While information technology benefits society in numerous ways, it also has potential to create new vulnerabilities, even while attempting to solve other problems [13]. With this in mind, our reliance on digital infrastructures implies that digital risks and vulnerabilities must be addressed, managed and reduced. Internet of Things, in particular, is the setting stone of the futuristic imaginary of a day-to-day reality where objects come alive and actively upgrade our routine [14]. It is therefore crucial to note that IoT devices, especially home-based ones, often come with a deficiency in proper security systems and upgrade opportunities [15]. In his dissertation, Angrishi argues that these smart devices should be considered as computers that "do specialized jobs", rather than as specialized devices with built-in intelligence. What really differentiates IoT devices from computers is that their design often does not include security at all [14]. Hewlett-Packard (HP) in 2014 released a study about the most popular devices in some of the most common IoT niches at the time, reporting an average of 25 vulnerabilities per device. According to the study, "80% of devices failed to require passwords of sufficient complexity and length, 70% did not encrypt local and remote traffic communications, and 60% contained vulnerable user interfaces and/or vulnerable firmware" [16]. Some of the reasons for this exposure may be found in their lack of well-defined perimeters, their highly dynamic and mobile nature and heterogeneity in respect to communication medium and protocols [17]. To sum up, most studies indicate privacy and security are the two main areas of risk individuated for digital households, but few have investigated those risks for vulnerable categories such as people with disabilities and older persons.

2.3   Human Relation with Privacy and Data Security

In addition to Internet of Things devices' default criticalities regarding privacy and security, numerous scholars focused on people's approach to data protection and privacy. Users are in fact traditionally considered to be the weak spot in technological networks [8], a belief that is frequently linked to the so called "privacy paradox" [18], also known as humans' tendency towards privacy-compromising behavior online eventually resulting in a dichotomy between privacy attitudes and actual behavior [19]. This conduct seems to characterize even privacy conscious individuals that, especially online, do not live up to their declared privacy preferences [20]. However, as observed by Acquisti and Grossklags in 2005, "individuals make privacy-sensitive decisions based on multiple factors, including (but not limited to) what they know, how much they care, and how costly and effective they believe their actions can be.", meaning that the dichotomy between stated and implemented preferences does not inevitably imply the existence of the paradox [21]. Furthermore, even when the purpose to reduce data disclosure is present, due to the unfamiliarity of the average person the actual disclosure considerably exceeds intention [18, 22]. The majority of research into the privacy paradox and users' attitude towards privacy and data security focuses on e-commerce and social networking [18] and there is a noticeable general tendency to not consider vulnerable categories of people, such as the ageing population and persons with disabilities, as particularly exposed to risks in digital environments.

2.4   Universal Design

According to the United Nations Convention on the rights of Persons with Disabilities (CRPD), "Universal design means the design of products, environments, programs and services to be usable by all people, to the greatest extent possible, without the need for adaptation or specialized design. (art.2). As shown in the previous sections, there are many studies of privacy and security in relation to IoT devices, but most of them fail to consider the experience of people with disabilities [6]. It is striking to notice how most of the tools implemented for security and privacy protection, for instance, rely on subtle visual cues or other potentially inaccessible indicators. Constant interaction with such reality might cause extreme frustration or total inability to users with perceptual limitations [6]. Due to the limitations in the design of IoT devices, including products for connected households, persons with disabilities are often dependent on the help of family members. Frequent technical problems appear to be the rule rather than the exception [7]. Acknowledging these situations means acknowledging the need for a change in the way we approach security and privacy risk factors in IoT environments and devices towards a more inclusive perspective.

3   Methods

In order to answer the research question above, a transdisciplinary and interdisciplinary approach was adopted. The projects on which this paper is based is a collaboration between the Sociology and Computer Science departments and the researchers involved come from a variety of different fields. From Universal Design to ICT and Social Media to Education and Sociology, elements from the different disciplines were brought in to contribute to the outline and realization of the research.

The project involves a group of twenty households selected with varying social and demographic characteristics. The participants are directly involved in various steps of the research. Multiple research methods from different fields were adopted during the research, including in-depth interviews, participant observation, multimedia documentary data, and a survey. First, a set of semi-structured interviews were carried out in the participants' homes. This method allowed informants the freedom to express their views in their own terms while providing reliable, comparable qualitative data [23]. The participants also drew a floor map of their house and indicated where each IoT device was typically placed. Pictures of the devices were collected as additional documentation. Second, a house visit and follow-up interviews were conducted and the participants were asked to reenact their typical home routines in order to illustrate their use of IoT devices.

Following each house visit, a risk assessment of the IoT devices in the home was performed using a Risk Assessment Model, which was developed as part of the research project. The assessment consists of 15 questions that examine different characteristics of the IoT device. The assessment is divided into five sections that evaluate 1) the device's connectivity and protocols used to connect to public and private networks, 2) data transmission and encryption, 3) user authentication, 4) the Operating System's update procedures, and 5) data storage, data protection guarantees and end user license, guide and procedures. The questionnaire ends with a subjective open question that aims to assess on a scale from 1 to 5 the negative impact that a malfunction or a data breach in the analyzed device would have over the house and its owner. A thematic analysis of documentation from the home visits and interview transcripts is to be conducted in order to disclose the perceived risks among the users and their families. These themes are meant to be compared to the results of the risk assessment in order to highlight any difference.

4 Preliminary Results and Discussion

Due to the rampant global coronavirus pandemic, the research was forced to a suspension. However, a first pilot study has been conducted and the preliminary data is being analyzed. The pilot allowed the methods to be tested and their efficacy to be confirmed by the quantity and quality of data gained in various forms. However, it is possible that the present conditions, if prolonged in time, will require a change in the approach to the methods and the whole research.

5 Conclusions and Future Work

With Internet of Things (IoT) expected to be as common as electricity (OECD 2016) there is a high probability for connected homes to become central parts of critical societal. It is therefore crucial to note that IoT devices, especially home-based ones, often come with a deficiency in proper security systems and upgrade opportunities [15]. This issue is particularly evident when addressing the experience of persons with disabilities, elderly and other vulnerable categories of people, which most tools for privacy protection fail to contemplate. With humans traditionally considered to be the "weak link" in technological networks there is the need of a vast educational project to raise awareness on the subject.

The next steps in the research include the creation of a set of tools for households IoT risk management, which will be developed in collaboration with stakeholders and designers. The intention is to emphasize the active involvement of research participants throughout the research, as co-researchers [24]. The framework adopted comes from the Participatory Action Research, as "the way groups of people can organize the conditions under which they can learn from their own experiences and make this experience available to others" [25]. In this project, action research is to be integrated by a combination of techniques from Co-design and Participatory Design. Co-design here is intended as collective creativity applied across the whole span of a design process [26], whether Participatory Design is considered as a process of investigating and supporting mutual learning between multiple participants [27].

Acknowledgements. The research this paper is based on is part of the *RELINK - Relinking the "weak link". Building resilient digital households through interdisciplinary and multilevel exploration and intervention* project. The research project is funded by the Research Council of Norway, IKTPluss, grant no. 288663, and is headed by Consumption Research Norway (SIFO) and Oslo Metropolitan University (OsloMet).

References

1. Helle-Valle, J., Slettemeås, D.: ICTs, domestication and language-games: a Wittgensteinian approach to media uses. New Media Soc. **10**(1), 45–66 (2008)
2. Kuruczleki, E., et al.: The Readiness of the european union to embrace the fourth industrial revolution. Management (18544223), **11**(4) (2016)

3. Dorsemaine, B., et al.: Internet of things: a definition & taxonomy. In: 2015 9th International Conference on Next Generation Mobile Applications, Services and Technologies. IEEE (2015)
4. Atzori, L., Iera, A., Morabito, G.: The internet of things: a survey. Comput. Netw. **54**(15), 2787–2805 (2010)
5. Ferrara, P., Spoto, F.: Static analysis for GDPR compliance. In: ITASEC (2018)
6. Sauer, G., et al.: Accessible privacy and security: a universally usable human-interaction proof tool. Univ. Access Inf. Soc. **9**(3), 239–248 (2010)
7. Fuglerud, K.S.: The barriers to and benefits of use of ict for people with visual impairment. In: Stephanidis, C. (ed.) UAHCI 2011. LNCS, vol. 6765, pp. 452–462. Springer, Heidelberg (2011). https://doi.org/10.1007/978-3-642-21672-5_49
8. Sasse, M.A., Brostoff, S., Weirich, D.: Transforming the 'weakest link'—a human/computer interaction approach to usable and effective security. BT Technol. J. **19**(3), 122–131 (2001)
9. Schwab, K.: The Fourth Industrial Revolution. Currency (2017)
10. Vulkanovski, A.: Home, Tweet Home": Implications of the Connected Home, Human and Habitat on Australian Consumers. Australian Communications Consumer Action Network, Sydney (2016)
11. Bertino, E. Data Security and Privacy in the IoT. in EDBT. 2016
12. Zanella, A., et al.: Internet of things for smart cities. IEEE Internet Things J. **1**(1), 22–32 (2014)
13. Ransbotham, S., et al.: Special section introduction—ubiquitous IT and digital vulnerabilities. Inf. Syst. Res. **27**(4), 834–847 (2016)
14. Angrishi, K.: Turning internet of things (iot) into internet of vulnerabilities (iov): Iot botnets (2017). arXiv preprint arXiv:1702.03681
15. Xi, W., Ling, L.: Research on IoT privacy security risks. In: 2016 International Conference on Industrial Informatics-Computing Technology, Intelligent Technology, Industrial Information Integration (ICIICII). IEEE (2016)
16. Rawlinson, K.: Hp study reveals 70 percent of internet of things devices vulnerable to attack. HP, **29**, July 2014
17. Bertino, E.: Data privacy for IoT systems: concepts, approaches, and research directions. In: 2016 IEEE International Conference on Big Data (Big Data). IEEE (2016)
18. Barth, S., De Jong, M.D.: The privacy paradox–Investigating discrepancies between expressed privacy concerns and actual online behavior–a systematic literature review. Telematics Inf. **34**(7), 1038–1058 (2017)
19. Acquisti, A., Grossklags, J.: Privacy and rationality in individual decision making. IEEE Secur. Priv. **3**(1), 26–33 (2005)
20. Spiekermann, S., Grossklags, J., Berendt, B.: E-privacy in 2nd generation E-commerce: privacy preferences versus actual behavior. In: Proceedings of the 3rd ACM Conference on Electronic Commerce. ACM (2001)
21. Morando, F., R. Iemma, and E. Raiteri, Privacy evaluation: what empirical research on users' valuation of personal data tells us. Internet Policy Rev. **3**(2) (2014)
22. Norberg, P.A., Horne, D.R., Horne, D.A.: The privacy paradox: personal information disclosure intentions versus behaviors. J. Consum. Aff. **41**(1), 100–126 (2007)
23. Cohen, D., Crabtree, B.: Qualitative research guidelines project (2006)
24. Bilandzic, M., Venable, J.: Towards participatory action design research: adapting action research and design science research methods for urban informatics. J. Commun. Inf. **7**(3) (2011)

25. McTaggart, R.: Principles for participatory action research. Adult Educ. Q. **41**(3), 168–187 (1991)
26. Sanders, E.B.-N., Stappers, P.J.: Co-creation and the new landscapes of design. Co-design **4**(1), 5–18 (2008)
27. Schön, D.A.: The Reflective Practitioner, vol. 1083, New York (1983)

Making the Home Accessible - Experiments with an Infrared Handheld Gesture-Based Remote Control

Heinrich Ruser[1]([⊠]), Susan Vorwerg[2], and Cornelia Eicher[2]

[1] Institute for Applied Physics and Measurement Technology,
Universität der Bundeswehr München, 85577 Neubiberg, Germany
heinrich.ruser@unibw.de
[2] Geriatrics Research Group, Charité – Universitätsmedizin Berlin,
13347 Berlin, Germany
{susan.vorwerg, cornelia.eicher}@charite.de

Abstract. A universal remote control for many different technical devices in the living environment - which should be very easy, almost intuitively to use - would be most desirable, especially for elderly and mobility-impaired persons. For this purpose, a flashlight-like handheld infrared gesture-controlled remote we call SmartPointer is being developed and evaluated. Carrying out a mid-air gesture with the SmartPointer moves the irradiated beam of structured IR light across a receiver box near the device, which detects the light pattern's trajectory and converts the identified gesture into device-specific commands. In our laboratory study, the user experience of the SmartPointer system and its gesture recognition capabilities were examined with a group of 29 elderly volunteers who were asked to repeatedly carry out quasi-intuitive gestures with the SmartPointer to operate four typical home appliances: light switch (on/off), heating device (warmer/colder), blinds (up/down) and door (lock/unlock). Applying adaptive rule-based signal processing and pattern recognition, an overall recognition rate of 94.3% could be achieved so far.

Keywords: Gestural interaction · Human-centered design · Pointing device

1 Introduction

1.1 Making the Home More Accessible

The deep-rooted desire to control and manipulate a large variety of electrical devices in the living environment remotely in a customary and simple manner stems both from user convenience and urgent necessity, especially for elderly people often plagued with (temporal or permanent) mobility impairments which affect their mobility at home and their ability to maintain an independent life altogether. However, still only very few homes are equipped with interconnected devices and a convenient or central control unit. Moreover, accessible, almost intuitive everyday-interaction procedures are generally missed.

© Springer Nature Switzerland AG 2020
C. Stephanidis and M. Antona (Eds.): HCII 2020, CCIS 1226, pp. 89–97, 2020.
https://doi.org/10.1007/978-3-030-50732-9_13

Instead of "analog" physical buttons on conventional remote controls, "digital" buttons on smartphones and tablets are often proposed to control light, blinds or temperature, with commands wirelessly sent to the devices. However, touch-based interaction can be arduous, straining and exhausting. The same is true for exact finger motion above a smartphone or tablet surface.

Moreover, the use of smartphones or tablets is still not prevalent among the elderly. The devices are not very robust – and the prevailing fear of dropping and damaging them further reduces their use. For many elderly, modern smartphones are generally perceived as being cumbersome, costly, bulky and heavy-weight. As an everyday communication device they require care, above all frequent recharging.

Among other modalities, mid-air gesture design and gestural interactions were widely investigated in the context of smart homes (see [1, 2] for reviews). A user-centered approach to deal with gesture design are elicitation studies to extract appropriate gestures that meet important criteria such as accessibility, memorability or reliability and hence ease-of-use. However, the effective use of gestures can be challenging and frustrating. In the sequel, experiments with a group of 29 elderly volunteers with a newly developed infrared handheld gesture-based remote control are reported.

1.2 Motivation for Device-Based Mid-Air Gestures

The use of mid-air gestures as means of a natural human-computer interaction has been popularized by entertainment applications e.g. in interactive sports games at distances up to several meters from the sensor or television screen. Popular commercial solutions include Nintendo's Wii™ game platform with the hand-held controller WiiMote™ (introduced 2006), Microsoft's Kinect™ which tracks the player's body movement (introduced 2010 and updated 2013, but discontinued since 2017) or LeapMotion™, which supports real-time motion tracking of palms and fingers and can be integrated with VR (Virtual Reality) Head Mounted Displays to enable controller-free, mid-air interactions in VR [3]. Also, Orbbec's Astra™ and Intel's Realsense™ can be named here.

Often, mid-air gesture-based interaction is focused on free-hand gestures, which of course have the benefit that they can be used straight away, without a dedicated device. Elicitation studies of free-hand mid-air gestures for the home appliances typically investigate user-defined gestures for interactions with particular devices, especially the TV (e.g. [4, 5]) which has evolved to a standard interactive multimedia device.

Besides the computational challenges behind the analysis of freehand gestures from video footage obtained from a set of cameras – which poses challenging demands for the technical system itself but also great concerns regarding personality rights protection – a comparison of the results of the studies (e.g. in [2]) reveals that it is difficult to define a comprehensive universal gesture vocabulary. In many interviews and elicitation studies, device-free mid-air gestures receive negative assessments. Participants explicitly state that they would not choose free-hand gestures because those are too complicated to execute, too easy to forget, and altogether not intuitive enough, because free-hand gestures - other than voice or touch control - are only rarely used as interface to everyday devices. Instead, handheld control devices facilitate the execution of gestures, compared to hands-free control [6, 7]. Therefore, a flashlight-like universal gesture-based control we call "SmartPointer" is currently being developed and optimized.

1.3 User-Centered Design

Acceptance of new technologies is generally influenced by multiple factors, the most important being (1) expected personal benefits (like perceived usefulness or increased safety) to meet experienced needs and desires, (2) available alternatives and (3) persuasions and social influence (family, friends or professional caregivers) [8].

In a preliminary study carried out in the Usability Lab of the Geriatrics Research Group at Charité – Universitätsmedizin Berlin, a group of 20 elderly volunteers (aged 74.7 ± 4.9 years) was examined, how they would respond to a gesture-based interaction with home appliances [9]. The purpose of that study was to create a 2-D hand gesture set for specific tasks, with the final selection based on user ratings and consideration of system capabilities. For this purpose, a mixed-method design was applied, involving assessments, a guideline-based interview, a task-based application and a questionnaire using a gesture catalog. Finally, the test persons were given a number of imaginative tasks to control several household devices by mid-air gestures and were asked to perform those gestures of their choice with a commercial laser pointer (as the SmartPointer system was only to be developed) that they thought would be best to execute the task.

All test persons were very interested in, and open-minded towards, the tasks given to them. In the process, qualitative requirements were collected regarding the design and haptics of the hand-held device, desired feedback and safety concerns. Above all, a simple, almost intuitive use was of utmost importance for the test persons. "Intuitive" in this context is a synonym of "familiar": A user interface is "intuitive" insofar as it resembles something the user has already learned or is exploiting existing skills [10].

The subsequent process of designing the system followed the guidelines of participatory design and was closely based on the 1) expectations and preferences of the potential users, 2) considerations regarding haptics and age-related limitations like fatigue and cognitive load and 3) experiences of the design experts among the project partners. As a result, the buttonless, lightweight ($\sim$70 g), small-sized ($\sim$10 cm) *haptic* interface, i.e. the handheld *SmartPointer*, was built in two different shapes we call 'cross' and 'pipe', see Fig. 1. (Weight and size are about half of that of usual remotes).

2   Technical Implementation

The novel gesture-based infrared remote control consists of (1) the handheld *SmartPointer* which emits a) a visible light spot to select a particular device and "switch it on" and b) an invisible, spatially structured infrared (IR) light pattern to operate the device; (2) a small receiver box near the device which detects the trajectory of motion of the projected pattern, identifies the intended gesture and converts it into the device-specific command, Fig. 2. The emitted IR light is spatially modulated by a

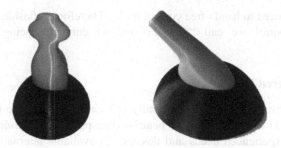

Fig. 1. Two alternative shapes of the battery-powered, handheld *SmartPointer* – 'cross' (left) and 'pipe' (right) along with the corresponding charging cradles – resulting from a participatory design process for the haptic interaction device. Assembly and functionality are identical.

diffractive optical element (DOE) [11] which has a specially designed micro-structured surface to generate a binary pseudo-random array of light beams. This concept allows to come up with a handheld device which contains only a few inexpensive mass-market components (since the IR-optical signal is both the information and transmission channel) and is very easy to use. The technical system and design guidelines to optimize its overall performance are described in more detail in [12].

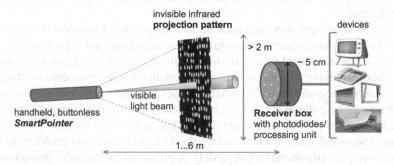

Fig. 2. The optical remote control comprises a hand-held device (left) that emits a visible beam and a large infrared pattern and is automatically activated by an acceleration sensor, a receiver box (right) with an array of photodiodes in, on or near the device to be remotely controlled and a processing unit for gesture recognition and the generation of device-specific commands.

The *SmartPointer* is used similarly to a laser pointer. Targeting the visible light beam for a short time ($\sim 1...2$ s) towards a device selects it and switches it on. (The precision required for targeting is greatly reduced compared to using a laser pointer, due to the large size of the projected visible beam pattern.) A gesture is carried out with the handheld remote describing "a trajectory in the air". This moves the invisible wide-angle beam pattern (with a large diameter > 2 m at working distances of several meters) across the receiver box, changing the light intensities at its IR-sensitive receivers (photodiodes) in a specific way. Based on the stepwise cross-correlation of these intensity changes at all pairs of photodiodes, the trajectory of the pattern is gradually reconstructed. Only the relevant, intended part is evaluated for recognition; the delivery and final movements are discarded. By assigning the trajectory features to one of the predefined gesture classes, the gesture is automatically recognized.

In short, the techniques required to reconstruct the user's hand trajectory from the recorded electrical signals and to recognize the intended gesture can be categorized into the following stages: data acquisition, pre-processing, segmentation, feature extraction and multi-class classification.

3 Gesture Vocabulary

During preliminary investigations with uninstructed persons in the Usability Lab at Charité – Universitätsmedizin Berlin, it turned out that the majority of participants used the same gestures for the same functionalities for different devices. For example, for volume control of TV and radio or for dimming light, the gesture would often be the same [9]. This helps to unify and simplify the operation of a large variety of different household devices and hence can eliminate a great concern (especially among senior users) of forgetting the control gestures. During those tests, horizontal, vertical, circular and targeting gestures were most frequently used.

All gestures used in the recent experiments (2 targeting gestures, 4 one-directional strokes and 2 circle movements) are displayed and described in Table 1. This choice was guided by those preliminary investigations and practical experience (e.g. respecting "symmetry", which refers to reverse gestures for reversed action [13]). The selected gestures are quite distinctive, but large spatio-temporal variabilities in shape and duration have to be considered for successful pattern recognition.

Table 1. Gesture lexicon used in the experiments; associated functions.

Gesture:			Associated with:	
No.	Action	Trajectory	Device	Function
1	Point at it	–	Lamp	Switch on
2	Point at it	–		Switch off
3	Move hand or arm Straight bottom-up	Line bottom-up	Blind	Lift/open
4	Move hand or arm Straight top-down	Line top-down		Lower/close
5	Move hand or arm Straight left-to-right	Line left-to-right	Door	Open
6	Move hand or arm Straight right-to-left	Line right-to-left		Close
7	Turn/rotate hand or arm to the right	Circle or ellipse clockwise	Heater	Warmer
8	Turn/rotate hand or arm to the left	Circle or ellipse counterclockwise		Colder

4 Study Procedure

In our laboratory study volunteered 29 healthy elderly persons (14 female/15 male) aged 74.9 ± 4.7 years, 23 being right-handed, 4 left-handed, and two ambidextrous. After completing the cognitive test, each test person picked one of the two differently shaped *SmartPointers* ('cross' or 'pipe', see Fig. 1) of her/his choice, sat on a chair in a distance of about 3 m opposite to the test devices (see Fig. 3) and was asked to subsequently operate the four devices by the specific associated gestures (cf. Table 1): (1) lamp: switch on/off; (2) blind: move up/down; (3) heater: draw a circle clockwise/counterclockwise; (4) door: move left/right. None of the participants had any familiarity with gesture-based devices or game consoles before. All, however, did immediately grasp how to "draw" a stroke or circle "in the air" with the flashlight-like *SmartPointer* without being primed. The test persons were only told that they had time to "draw" the gesture of up to 6 s after the starting signal.

Fig. 3. (Left) Test devices (light, blind, heater, door – from left to right) as seen from the user's perspective when carrying out the control gestures. (Right) Detector box with the array of IR-sensitive photodiodes behind the optical filter (black square) to block ambient light.

While a test person was carrying out a gesture, the electrical signals from of all photodiodes of the receiver unit were synchronously recorded. After the preset time the recording was stopped, the trajectories instantly reconstructed and displayed and the gestures recognition result given. Then the test person was asked to repeat the same gesture up to two more times and after that to proceed to the next command.

Overall, 642 gestures from 29 participants were recorded and analyzed. Participants made an average of 2.70 gestures per gesture class (referent) (SD = 0.51).

5 Results

In Fig. 4, three exemplary recorded electrical signals – each 4 s long – from one photodiode (the signals from the other photodiodes being very similar, time-shifted copies) are displayed together with the reconstructed trajectories calculated from the signal fragments within frames representing the start and end of the intended "stroke". The frames are rule-based set from amplitude gradients, velocities and accelerations. From these reconstructed trajectories, the gestures are recognized based on the match with linear or elliptical least square (LS) fits as a quality factor.

In Fig. 5, the recognition rates for all gestures from all 29 test persons are given in two bars for each test person. The left bar (in grey) represents the recognition rate with all strokes considered. The right bar (in black) represents the true positive rate (TPR), when only those strokes are taken into account where fragments of intended "strokes" could be recognized by the algorithm as well as by human observers.

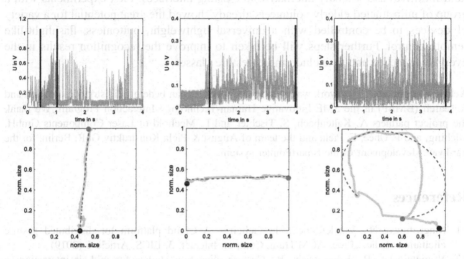

Fig. 4. (Above) Examples of recorded signals from one photodiode with rule-base found start and end of the meaningful part. (Below) Results of corresponding trajectories reconstructed from the signals within frames: line top-down, line right-to-left, circle counterclockwise (from left to right). The trajectories' beginning and end are marked by green and black dots, resp. (Color figure online)

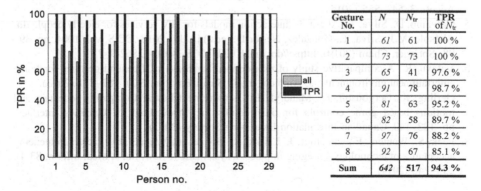

Gesture No.	N	N_{tr}	TPR of N_{tr}
1	61	61	100 %
2	73	73	100 %
3	65	41	97.6 %
4	91	78	98.7 %
5	81	63	95.2 %
6	82	58	89.7 %
7	97	76	88.2 %
8	92	67	85.1 %
Sum	642	517	94.3 %

Fig. 5. Results of gesture recognition. (Left) Results for every test person, for all attempts ('all') and meaningful signals ('TPR'). (Right) Results for each of the 8 gesture classes, with TPR for all meaningful signals (N_{tr} counts of all N attempts for one class).

As can be seen from the results, almost every test person carried out some gestures awkwardly or not during the time of recording, such that the intention could not be found from the recordings. These failed attempts were often among the first gestures carried out by a test person and are obviously caused by lacking practice. In order to evaluate the pattern recognition algorithm, only meaningful gestures were taken into consideration (see right column of the Table in Fig. 5). Note, however, that the pointing gestures 1 and 2 (switch on/off) were always correctly executed and recognized.

The presented device-based gestural remote control portrays a novel, but familiar (and intuitive) user-friendly alternative to existing interfaces. First experiments with a group of uninstructed elderly volunteers already showed the great potential for a variety of devices to be controlled with a universal lightweight, buttonless, flashlight-like remote control. Further steps will be taken to improve the recognition results in the everyday practice and to include more gesture classes.

Acknowledgments. This work was supported by the German Federal Ministry of Education and Research (BMBF) in the SME-Innovative Human-Technology Interaction Program. We thank the project partners A. Kaltenbach, S. Tischler and L. Mechold of Laser Components GmbH, Olching, and F. Obée, F. Piela and the team of August & Piela Konstruktiv GbR, Berlin, for the hardware development of the SmartPointer system.

References

1. Magrofuoco, N., Vanderdonckt, J.: Gelicit – A Cloud platform for distributed gesture elicitation studies. Proc. ACM Hum.-Comput. Interact. **3**, EICS, Article 6 (2019)
2. Vogiatzidakis, P., Koutsabasis, P.: Gesture elicitation studies for mid-air interaction: a review. J. Multimodal Technol. Interact. **2**(4), 65 (2018)
3. Hoffmann, F., Tyroller, M., Wende, F., Henze, N.: User-defined interaction for smart homes: voice, touch, or mid-air gestures? In: Proceedings of the 18th International Conference on Mobile and Ubiquitous Multimedia (2019)
4. Dong, H., Danesh, A., Figueroa, N., Saddik, A.: An elicitation study on gesture preferences and memorability toward a practical hand-gesture vocabulary for smart televisions. IEEE Access **3**, 543–555 (2015)
5. Carvalho, D., Silva, T., Abreu, J.: Interaction models for iTV services for elderly people. In: Abásolo, M.J., Silva, T., González, Nestor D. (eds.) jAUTI 2018. CCIS, vol. 1004, pp. 89–98. Springer, Cham (2019). https://doi.org/10.1007/978-3-030-23862-9_7
6. Vatavu, R.: A comparative study of user-defined handheld vs. freehand gestures for home entertainment environments, J. Ambient Intell. Smart Environ. **5**(2), 187–211 (2013)
7. Gerling, K., Dergousoff, K., Mandryk, R.: Is movement better? Comparing sedentary and motion- based game controls for older adults. In: Proceedings of Graphics Interface, pp. 133–140. Canadian Information Processing Society (2013)
8. Peek, S., Wouters, E., van Hoof, J., Luijkx, K., Boeije, H., Vrijhoef, H.: Factors influencing acceptance of technology for aging in place: a systematic review. Int. J. Med. Inform. **83**(4), 235–248 (2014)

9. Vorwerg, S., et al.: requirements for gesture-controlled remote operation to facilitate human-technology interaction in the living environment of elderly people. In: Zhou, J., Salvendy, G. (eds.) HCII 2019. LNCS, vol. 11592, pp. 551–569. Springer, Cham (2019). https://doi.org/10.1007/978-3-030-22012-9_39
10. Raskin, J.: Intuitive equals familiar. Commun. ACM. **37**(9), 17–18 (1994)
11. Katz, S., Kaplan, N., Grossinger, I.: Using Diffractive Optical Elements - DOEs for beam shaping – fundamentals and applications. Optik Photonik **13**(4), 83–86 (2018)
12. Ruser, H., Kaltenbach, A., Mechold, L.: "SmartPointer" – buttonless remote control based on structured light and intuitive gestures. In: Proceedings 6th International Workshop on Sensor-based Activity Recognition (iWOAR2019), ACM, New York (2019)
13. Pereira, A., Wachs, J., Park, K., Rempel, D.: A user-developed 3-D hand gesture set for human-computer interaction. Hum. Factors **57**(4), 607–621 (2015)

A Proposal of Rehabilitation Application System Using Sliding Block Puzzles for Prevention of Mild Cognitive Impairment (MCI)

Shun Sasaki[✉], Hiroki Takagi, Saburo Yokokura, and Meeko Kuwahara

Meisei University, 2-1-1 Hodokubo, Hino-Shi, Tokyo, Japan
17j5048@stu.meisei-u.ac.jp,
meeko.kuwahara@meisei-u.ac.jp

Abstract. Rehabilitation for the most common symptoms such as dementia is brain training, and it is thought that this type of training is highly compatible to digitalization and applications.

In this paper, we propose an application using sliding block puzzles for prevention of MCI. This will include an editing function that acquires image data, divides it into 3 * 3 or 4 * 4 and creates questions. The function determines whether the image is portrait or landscape and resizes the image accordingly. It also changes the color and brightness of the image in consideration of the user's vision.

Therefore, this proposed application is operated with intuitive movement using touch and slide operation on a tablet terminal. Intuitive operations such as touch and slide are easily understood by anyone without instruction.

As with the conventional sliding block puzzle, the user will slide the panel using the space of one frame to arrange the panel in the desired order. It is thought that the cerebral blood flow is activated by the user performing such an activity. Since the sliding block puzzle requires the memory of a goal, the arrangement of figures and special awareness, we believe that it will suppress the progress of dementia.

1 Introduction

According to the 2017 Senior Citizens White Paper (Japan), under future statistics for the number of dementia patients and prevalence for those 65 and over, senior citizens with dementia were over 4.62 million (approximately 1 in 7 senior citizens over 65), but in 2025 it is estimated that this will increase to 1 out of 5.

A lifestyle that can activate the brain through physical exercise is effective to prevent dementia. Rehabilitation for the most common symptoms of dementia is brain training, and it is thought that this type of training is highly compatible to digitalization and applications.

In Japan, smartphones outnumbered PCs within households at 75.1% vs 72.5% respectively in 2017. Therefore, we believed it was necessary to create an application

C. Stephanidis and M. Antona (Eds.): HCII 2020, CCIS 1226, pp. 98–106, 2020.
https://doi.org/10.1007/978-3-030-50732-9_14

that used a tablet terminal that was similar to a smartphone and easy for users to operate. A tablet terminal is considered best suited for the medical and nursing care fields such as rehabilitation, because it has a larger screen and is easier to operate than a smartphone.

Mild cognitive impairment (MCI) refers to a condition in which cognitive function is impaired, but the individual is living independently.

MCI is said to develop into dementia in a few years, but early detection and appropriate measures and treatment may delay the onset of dementia. Currently, no complete prevention or radical cure for dementia has been found.

We propose a rehabilitation application system using sliding block puzzles for prevention of MCI. This will include an editing function that acquires image data, divides it into 3 * 3 or 4 * 4 and creates questions. The function determines whether the image is portrait or landscape and resizes the image accordingly. It also changes the color and brightness of the image in consideration of the user's vision.

The proposed application is operated with intuitive movement using touch and slide operation on a tablet terminal. Intuitive operations such as touch and slide are easily understood by anyone without instruction.

As with the conventional sliding block puzzle, the user will slide the panel using the space of one frame to arrange the panel in the desired order. It is thought that the cerebral blood flow is activated by the user performing such an activity. Since the sliding block puzzle requires the memory of a goal, the arrangement of figures and special awareness, we believe that it will suppress the progress of dementia.

2 Dementia

Characteristics of dementia

The characteristics of dementia are roughly divided into the following three

- Obstacles are less apparent

In Alzheimer's disease, a typical form of dementia, the accumulation of amyloid β protein in the brain destroys cranial nerves, and impairs intellectual functions such as language, thinking, memory, action, learning, and attention. The symptoms are self-contained and often inconspicuous in appearance.

- The person himself cannot fully recognize the disability

As explained earlier, dementia often does not allow the person himself to recognize the disability because the symptoms are often inconspicuous in appearance. In addition, it is difficult to confront one's inability to do what one has always been able to do before because symptoms may suddenly occur, and it is often the case that they are not easily motivated for rehabilitation and consultation.

- Symptoms are more likely to appear in daily life and social activities at home than in consultation and hospitalization

Many of the typical symptoms are manifested in intellectual functions, and are likely to occur in daily life and social activities (workplace, shopping, use of transportation, procedures at government offices and banks, etc.). Therefore, unless family and doctors around them encounter the scene, they often cannot fully recognize the disability.

Mild cognitive impairment (MCI)

MCI is considered to be a pre-dementia stage and has received attention in recent years. Although it is associated with a decline in cognitive function, it is not currently considered dementia nor does it cause heavy difficulty in everyday life.

Currently, there is no complete prevention or radical cure for dementia.

MCI is a situation with a high rate of developing into dementia if it is not addressed, and is often said to be the pre-dementia stage or the middle point between a healthy state and dementia.

However, there are also those with MCI who do not develop dementia but recover to a healthy state. In addition, early stage recognition and proper measures and treatment can slow progression of dementia.

3 Proposal

In this paper, we propose a brain training application using sliding block puzzles to prevent MCI for rehabilitation of dementia. Most popular smartphones have a screen size of 6 in. or less. Smartphone screens are small for elderly people, and characters may be difficult to see, so we propose an application recommended for use on a tablet-type terminal with a size of about 10 in. These are as easy to carry as smartphones and can also be used anywhere.

Using the same operation as the conventional sliding block puzzle, the user would slide the panel using the space for one frame to arrange the panel in the desired arrangement. The cerebral blood flow is activated when the user performs a finger motion such as a slide.

It stimulates the frontal lobe, which controls memory, as the user predicts in which direction the moving panels can be moved to attain the desired arrangement. The user must shift the position of the panels in the sliding block puzzle while remembering the original shape.

The spatial recognition function of the frontal lobe is stimulated as the user comes up with the procedure to attain the correct answer by grasping the position of the panels. To complete the puzzle, the target memory, the arrangement of figures, and the ability to grasp the space is needed, so it is thought that it will prevent the progression of dementia and prevent MCI.

A terminal equipped with a camera and capable of touch panel operation can be used to create new puzzles from captured images.

The image used as a puzzle does not need to be prepared in advance, and it is possible to resize an image from the tablet terminal or the size of the image file owned by the user.

We believe that it would be effective for rehabilitation and prevention because not only can the number of puzzles could be increased, but also images taken of places familiar to the person can be easily used.

4 Implementation

We propose a brain training application using sliding block puzzles. Introduce an editing function that acquires image data in the application, divides it into 3 × 3 or 4 × 4 and creates questions.

When adjusting image data, determine whether the image is portrait or landscape and resize the image to fit the screen. Creates questions's function can Change the color and brightness of the image base on user's vision. Tapping the desired mode on the screen shown in Fig. 1 to change to be figure. Instead of starting the puzzle immediately the application will show the figure for the user first to memorize the completed figure.

In Fig. 2, a problem as an example is prepared instead of a photographed image.

If you want to change the question, tap on the "Question change" at the bottom right of Fig. 2 to change to another question. Question will changes randomly.

To avoid facing difficult problems, the user can tap 'question change' botton to finish by himself even the questions is not yet finished. You can adjust the brightness of the image with the "brightness function" for older people to see easies.

When you tap "Start", the image will be split a part then some of it will becomes a black or empty. When you start, the timers will it is display in the elapsed time in Fig. 2 the number of puzzle movements will be displayed in Fig. 2 (Figs. 3, 4, 5, 6).

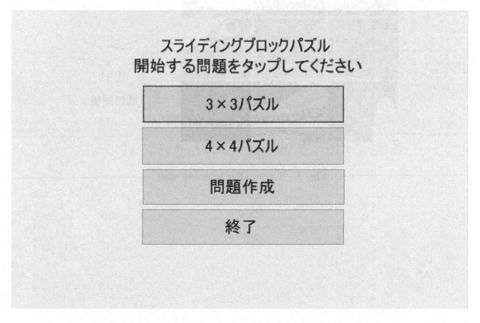

Fig. 1. Question selection screen displayed immediately after startup

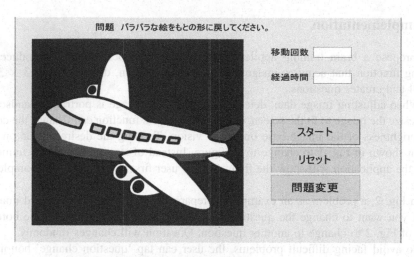

Fig. 2. Screen after selecting 3 × 3

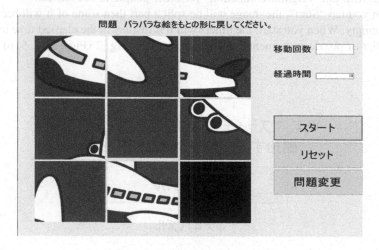

Fig. 3. Screen after selecting start

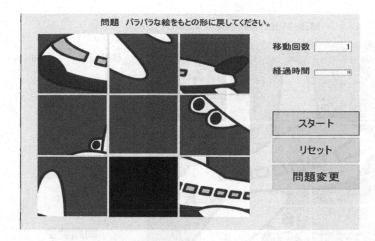

Fig. 4. Screen where you select start and slide once

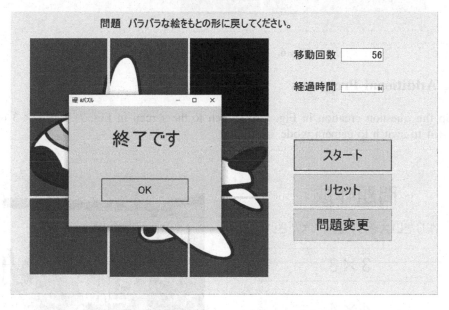

Fig. 5. Screen when puzzle is completed

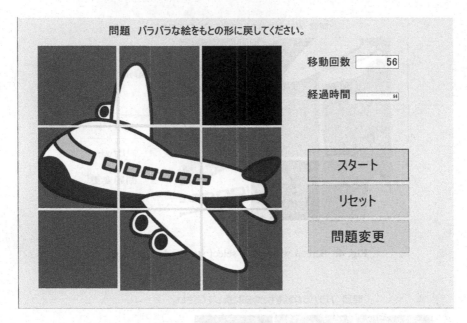

Fig. 6. Screen after selecting OK

5   Additional Programs

Tap the question creation in Fig. 1 to switch to the screen in Fig. 7. Tap 3 × 3 or 4 × 4 to switch to camera mode.

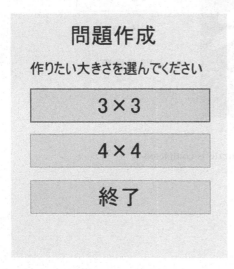

Fig. 7. Screen after selecting to create a question

Fig. 8. Photo taken

Only terminals that can operate touch panels with cameras are supported.

If the image is horizontal, adjust the puzzle frame horizontally, and if the image is vertical, adjust the puzzle frame vertically. The added image is added to the question file (Figs. 8, 9).

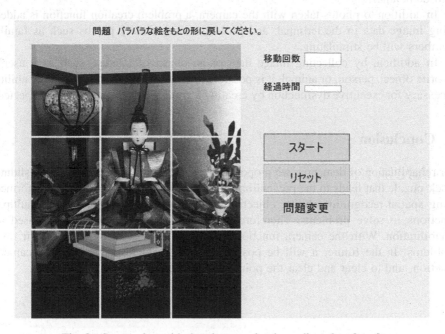

Fig. 9. Screen shot with the photograph taken adjusted to 3 × 3

6 Result

There are comments from the user that this application is user friendly, especially for older people. For some users with bad eyesight, it is difficult for them to see the press. In case where the application using physical press or key, such as keyboard, it is difficult to understand which press or key to press. The operation of the touch panel is considered appropriate for rehabilitation of elderly people.

For some users, their eyes were so bad that the letters were hard to see, and they didn't know where to press. Therefore, measures such as enlarging the button and enlarging the character have been required.

There are comments from the user that the sample illustration was easy to understand. Some users do not know how to play the sliding block puzzle, so it is necessary to prepare a way how to play for the elderly. It is difficult for people with severe dementia to communication. Even if they are interested in the application, it is difficult for them to play.

7 Discussion

For rehabilitation of dementia, we proposed an application that could prevent MCI. We think that a tablet terminal with a camera can be operated intuitively, even by people with dementia.

In addition to photos taken with the camera, a problem creation function is added using image data in the terminal, and problems using family photos such as family members will be stimulating.

In addition, by collecting image data of an object of interest, such as a user's favorite object, person, or animal, it is possible to further strengthen the thinking ability necessary for executive dysfunction by creating a problem on its own. Can be expected.

8 Conclusion

For rehabilitation of dementia, we proposed a brain training application using a sliding block puzzle that leads to the prevention of MCI. Sliding block puzzles are performed using spatial recognition ability, objective memory, figure arrangement and multiple functions to solve problems. Therefore, it can be expected that it can be used as rehabilitation. With the camera function, users can play more by adding their own problems. In the future, it will be possible to add problems other than the camera function, and to clear and clear the points and earn achievements.

Effectiveness of Color and Shape Matching Learning in Figurenotes System Using Musical Instrument Software

Rui Sotome[1](✉), Chiharu Watanabe[1], Aya Shirai[1], Manami Matsuda[2], Tota Mizuno[1], Naoaki Itakura[1], and Kazuyuki Mito[1]

[1] The University of Electro-Communications, 1-5-1 Chofugaoka, Chofu, Tokyo 182-8585, Japan
s2030061@edu.cc.uec.ac.jp
[2] General Incorporated Association the Spread of Figurenotes HappyMuse, 4-34-7 Nishinogawa, Komae, Tokyo 201-0001, Japan

Abstract. Figurenotes is an intuitive music notation system developed mainly for people with intellectual disabilities. In figurenotes system, notes are represented by a mark with a color and a shape.

However, there is a problem that when playing the piano using figurenotes system, it is difficult for people with intellectual disabilities to match a note and a mark on keyboard because of the large number of notes on a music score.

The purpose of this study is a development of the musical instrument playing application using figurenotes system with five steps starting from a simple matching of color and shape on the musical note for playing "alphabet song" and the evaluation of learning effect using the application.

The verification was conducted to three students with intellectual disabilities who have learned figurenotes system and cannot match a note and a mark on keyboard. We asked them to use the developed application freely for about a week. After that, we examined the step they could reach finally from its usage history.

As a result, two subjects could complete matching and rhythm steps, and reach final step. From this, when learning musical instrument performance, it is assumed that a matching a note and a key is important.

In conclusion, in this study, the musical instrument playing application using figurenotes system with five steps starting from a simple matching learning was developed and the evaluation of it was conducted. It is assumed that matching a note and a key on musical instrument performance is important.

Keywords: Piano · iOS application · Matching of color and shape · Intellectual disability

1 Introduction

1.1 Background

Music therapy is the therapy which uses music intentionally for the recovery of mental and physical disorders, the improvement of functions and the quality of life, and the

C. Stephanidis and M. Antona (Eds.): HCII 2020, CCIS 1226, pp. 107–113, 2020.
https://doi.org/10.1007/978-3-030-50732-9_15

modification of behavior. In Japan, about 50% subjects of the therapy are people with intellectual disabilities. Playing a musical instrument is one of the forms of music therapy for them [1]. When playing a musical instrument, we need to read musical scores. However, there are few support tools for people who can't read musical scores, relying on the ingenuity of individual instructors.

1.2   About Figurenotes

Figurenotes is an intuitive music notation system developed for people who have difficulty reading musical score such as people with intellectual disabilities. In figurenotes system, pitch names are represented by colors, and octaves are represented by shapes. In other words, in this system, musical notes are represented by a mark with a color and a shape (see Fig. 1) [2].

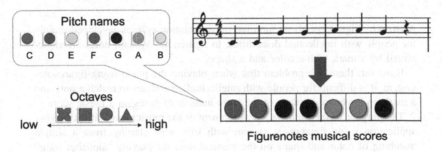

Fig. 1. Figurenotes system [2]

Several studies have reported that figurenotes system makes learning of music easier, makes cognitive ability and skill to grasp the whole developed, and the delight and the sense of accomplishment by the progress of performances cause the confidence, the intention, and the concentration for people with intellectual disabilities [3].

Watanabe developed the application which you play the piano using figurenotes system after learning the rhythm, and verified it for people with intellectual disabilities [4]. As a result, she has demonstrated that it is difficult for people with intellectual disabilities to match a musical note and a mark on keyboard because of the large number of musical notes on a music score.

1.3   Purpose

The purpose of this study is a development of the musical instrument playing application using figurenotes system with five steps starting with a simple matching learning, and evaluation of learning effect using the application.

2   The Developed Application

In this study, the musical instrument playing application using figurenotes system with five steps starting from a simple matching learning was developed. This application is for iPad. As you can see Fig. 2, the first two steps are learning to match of color and shape on the musical note. Next two steps are steps learning rhythm. Final step is a step playing the actual song. If you clear a step, you can learn in the next step. Whenever you start using this application, the step is reset to first step for the establishment of the understanding of figurenotes system.

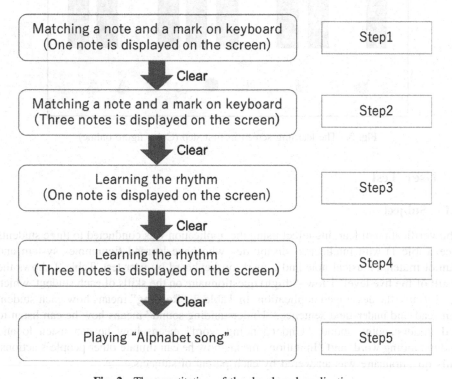

Fig. 2. The constitution of the developed application

For example, Fig. 3 shows the learning screen in first step. In the learning screen, a musical note, a keyboard, a sentence instructing an operation, and the button which playbacks the video explaining how to use this application are displayed. A sentence instructing an operation and the button which plays the video explaining how to use this application is mainly for people who don't know how to use this application and can't understand a sentence. Also, when you touched a wrong key, in other words, you failed to match a musical note and a mark on keyboard, the correct key becomes yellow for leading to touch the correct key.

Also, this application can record the use history such as used time, reached step, usage count, and total number of plays of the explainer video.

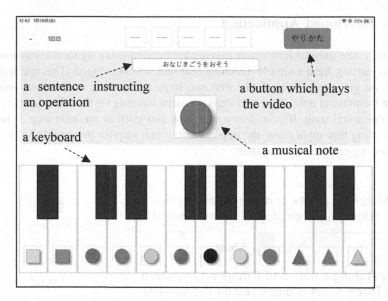

a sentence instructing an operation

a button which plays the video

a keyboard

a musical note

Fig. 3. The learning screen in first step (Color figure online)

3 User Test

3.1 Subject

The verification of learning effect using the application was conducted to three students (see Table 1) with intellectual disabilities who have learned figurenotes system and cannot match a musical note and a mark on keyboard by user test. Table 2 shows the result of the five-level (1:low–5:high) questionnaire on the skills of each student, which need to use the developed application. In Table 2, "Reading" means how each student can read and understand sentence, "Understanding sound" means how he can listen to and understanding sound, "Understanding word" means how he can listen to and understanding word, and "Imitation" means how he can imitate other people's actions. This questionnaire was answered by each parent of subjects.

Table 1. Information of each subjects

Subject	Sex	Age
A	Male	11
B	Male	15
C	Male	14

Table 2. The skills of each subject (1:low–5:high)

Subject	Reading	Understanding sound	Understanding word	Imitation
A	3	3	3	3
B	1	3	3	3
C	2	2	3	2

3.2   The Method of the User Test and Evaluation

After getting their consent and giving them iPad installed the application, we asked subjects to use the developed application freely for about a week. After that, we assessed the application by examining the step they could reach finally, usage count, and total number of plays of the explainer video from its usage history. Also, we asked each parent of subjects to answer a questionnaire on the condition of a subject before and after the experiment for the reference of the assessment. The questionnaire consists of four five-levels (1:bad–5:good) questions and free writing (see Table 3).

Table 3. A questionnaire on the condition of a subject

Question	Content
1	Did he concentrate on the application?
2	Was he interested in the application?
3	Could he operate the application?
4	Could he understand figurenotes system?
5	Free writing

4   Results

Table 4 is the summary of the result of the usage count, the total number of plays of the explainer video and the final reached step in the use test period. Also, the result of the questionnaire is shown in Table 5 and Table 6. In Table 4, subject B and subject C used the application and watched the explainer video many times compared with subject A. From this, they seem to be interested in the developed application. Also, Subject A and Subject C could reach step5, playing "Alphabet song" step. From this, they could match a musical note and a mark on keyboard and learn rhythm by the figurenotes system.

Table 4. The summary of the result of the verification

	Subject A	Subject B	Subject C
Usage count	3	29	65
Usage of the video count	2	33	105
Reached step	Step5	Step1	Step5

Table 5. The result of the questionnaire on the condition of a subject before and after the experiment (1:bad–5:good), question number refers to Table 3

Question	Subject A		Subject B		Subject C	
	Before	After	Before	After	Before	After
1	3	3	4	3	4	5
2	4	5	2	2	5	5
3	4	3	3	3	3	3
4	3	3	3	3	2	3

Table 6. The result of the questionnaire of the free comments by a parent

Subject B	He repeated watching the explainer video
	Words of animation manual were difficult to understand for him
	He was learning figurenotes system more intensively than before
Subject C	He could be learning figurenotes system more intensively than before

5   Discussion

From the results of subject A and subject C, which could reach step5, in learning matching a musical note and a key and rhythm, it is assumed that the step-by-step learning starting from learning with only one musical note is effective. Also, from this, it is assumed that the developed application is effective for people with intellectual disabilities to learn the figurenotes system. However, because there were few subjects, we need to investigate for more people.

The paper by Maeda et al. has reported that learning matching is important for people with intellectual disabilities [5]. In this study, it is assumed that the matching a musical note and a key enabled them to reach the playing "Alphabet song" step.

In Table 5 and Table 6, some subjects improved interest and concentration before and after the experiment. Sahara has demonstrated that a teaching material that repeats around 30 s is appropriate for people with intellectual disabilities [6]. In the developed application, it is assumed that introducing the explainer video about 40 s made their interest and concentration improved.

In 4 and Table 6, subjects B watched the explainer video repeatedly, but he couldn't reach after step2. Also, from Table 6, this reason is assumed that the words used in the video were difficult for him. Therefore, improving of understanding figurenotes system is expected by using easier words in the video.

6 Conclusion

In this study, the musical instrument playing application using figurenotes system with five steps starting from a simple matching learning was developed and the evaluation of learning effect using the application of it was conducted. As a result of the verification, it is assumed that a matching a musical note and a key on musical instrument performance is important. However, because there were few subjects in this study, we will need to investigate for more people after improving the developed application.

References

1. Takahashi, T.: An outline of music therapy. Jpn. J. Complement. Altern. Med. 1(1), 77–84 (2004)
2. Happy Muse - Association the Spread of Figurenotes. https://happymuse.net/how-to-use/ Accessed 10 Mar 2020
3. Yamada, M.: Finnish figurenotes music therapy method: a tool of improving the quality of life of the mentally disabled people. Bull. Lifelong Learn. Res. Inst. Hokkaido Asai Gakuen Univ. 8, 215–224 (2005)
4. Watanabe, C., Mizuno, T., Itakura, N., Mito, K., Matsuda, M.: The effectiveness of learning support function in keyboard-playing-application using figurenotes in music education for people with intellectual disabilities. In: Proceeding of 2019 Annual Conference of Electronics, Information and Systems Society, pp. 468–471, IEE of Japan (2019)
5. Maeda, N., Otomo, K.: Development of matching in young children: comparisons between typically developing children and asd children. Bull. Tokyo Gakugei Univ. 68(2), 433–440 (2017)
6. Sahara, K.: Effect and subject of tablet PC use in education with severe mental retarded children. Jpn. Soc. Educ. Inf. 29(2), 29–38 (2014)

Simultaneous Speech Subtitling Systems for Multiple Speakers

Takuya Suzuki[(✉)]

Tsukuba University of Technology, Tsukuba, Ibaraki, Japan
suzukit@a.tsukuba-tech.ac.jp

Abstract. This research is about the User Interface of subtitle displaying for the situation such as meetings or workshops, that plural speakers talk at the same time. A visual approach such as note-taking, sign language, is commonly used to support hearing-impaired person. Meanwhile, even with that kind of visual assistance, a hearing-impaired person still might not be able to get enough information in the situation plural speakers talk at the same time. To improve that problem, some assistance such as sending materials beforehand, the facilitator controlling the number of speakers, are offered occasionally. However, not all cases have that assistance as it requires human resources. A tool that makes a hearing-impaired person be able to have an equal opportunity to get information visually as a hearing person gets it aurally, is necessary. During this research, a system was developed to assist the hearing-impaired people in the situations plural speakers talk in parallel such as conferences or group workings when hearing-impaired people and hearing people participate together. This system dictates voices talked in that situation and displays dictated texts. The developed system was validated with the corporation of hearing-impaired people and hearing people.

Keywords: Deaf or hard of hearing student · Speech subtitling · Multiple speakers

1 Introduction

Support for hearing-impaired people has been centred on hearing aid systems and visual methods, such as note-taking and sign language interpretation. In recent years, methods that utilize information and communication technologies, such as voice recognition technology, have been producing better results. However, there are still problems that prove to be difficult to solve. For instance, some of the challenges that hearing-impaired people face at school and work include group work and meetings. In situations where multiple speakers are talking simultaneously, hearing-impaired people cannot obtain enough information through sign language or subtitles alone. Some solutions for this are providing materials in advance, ensuring that multiple speakers do not talk at the same time, or having a moderator to manage the speakers.

However, these solutions are not available at all times. This can result in the decrease in the amount of information exchanged and, sometimes, in the loss of participation from hearing-impaired people. To solve this problem, we need solutions that

© Springer Nature Switzerland AG 2020
C. Stephanidis and M. Antona (Eds.): HCII 2020, CCIS 1226, pp. 114–120, 2020.
https://doi.org/10.1007/978-3-030-50732-9_16

are founded on principles other than the existing types of support and accommodations. If hearing-impaired people had the opportunity to visually obtain the same amount of information that other people receive through hearing, it would help solve these problems.

I am a teaching staff of a special university for students who have a hearing impairment. My teaching experience made me realize the difficulties for hearing-impaired people when they are in the group which hearing people are the majority. If few hearing-impaired people are in the group of hearing people at a learning session or a conference, it should be one of the most difficult situation for hearing-impaired people.

2 Planning the System

In Japan, it is a tendency to have a support method that hearing people is requested to limit the amount of their statement, such as the rule that speakers need to raise a hand to take their tune so that multiple speakers do not talk at the same time.

However, such rules might be thought of as scaling back the quality and quantity of communication. Sometimes these support methods became a psychological burden for a hearing-impaired person, which made them hesitate to participate in those opportunities. To solve those issues, the methods subtitle speeches in their entirety on the situation several people speak at the same time were developed.

At first, Note-taking was considered. Showing the subtitle by Note-taking is a common method of deaf support system. It is used often in the situation such as lecture which has importance more on the accuracy of the information than simultaneity of subtitle display. Meanwhile, the simultaneity of subtitle display is more important than the accuracy of the information in the group talking.

I examined previous studies about speech and its subtitling. According to the study by Maruyama and others [1], tolerance limit of voice and subtitle is about 1 s. The study by Shimogori and others [2] indicates the timing of subtitle displaying has a bigger influence on an understanding level than the accuracy of subtitle information. These previous studies indicate the duration between speech and subtitle appearance should be within 1 s.

In the next step, I considered the method subtitling within 1 s from speech. Note-taking is known it takes some time duration from speech to subtitle displaying. The study by Ariumi reports [3] that time durations from speech to display of subtitles are 4 s by fast note-taker then 5 to 10 s by slow note-taker. It is assumed to take more time for the subtitling of several speakers' speeches as the situation requires more work to recognize who is the speaker. Accordingly, I considered it is impossible to subtitling in 1 s by a manual note-taking method.

Next, subtitling by voice recognition system was considered. The method and system developed by this study will be offered free of charge in the end. Therefore, I considered it is important to the voice-recognition system that it is free of charge. First, I tried voice recognition of Google Document and found it subtitle in 1 s from the speech. However, this recognition system on Google Documents could not subtitle several speakers' voices separately. And its submitted text is not divided by each talk, it is not suitable for the user interface to display several speakers' talk. Therefore, another method uses the voice recognition system on Google Document was examined. UDTalk [4] is a subtitling software of the Japanese language. It uses a voice recognition system. It is free for personal use. It subtitles within 1to 2 s from a voice, still, there is a delay from the result of Google Document about 2 times of duration as feeling. UD Talk doesn't have the UI adapt several speakers' talks as Google Document doesn't. To solve that issue, speakers need to pass UD Talk device to each other. That handling takes time in addition to the voice recognition process. Thus, free subtitle system displays subtitle of talk in Japanese language and have UI shows several speakers' talks was not existed. They are the methods to subtitle the talks which are hearing persons offer the information to a hearing-impaired person.

Another issue is in the situation hearing-impaired person offers the information to hearing person, which is that it is difficult for a hearing-impaired person to put in the talk at natural timing. Hearing-impaired person who can speak is able to put in the talk by uttering. Nevertheless, if uttering is not the option, the person intends to speak needs to interrupt the talk visually, raising hands, for example.

It is a psychological barrier for a hearing-impaired person. Another issue prevents support is the installation cost of the system. If the installation cost is expensive, it will not be exploited fully even the system dismisses the stress during the offering and accepting the information for a hearing-impaired person. If the installation cost is expensive, it will not be exploited fully even the system dismisses the stress during the offering and accepting the information for a hearing-impaired person.

As stated in the beginning, this study is aiming to remove difficulties in hearing-impaired person's communication in the group of hearing person. Therefore, it is essential that the system is easy to install and requires none of the special devices.

In the recognition process of the Japanese language, lots of revision will be required for mistakes on Kana to Kanji conversion process. The UI makes the revision of the text easy should be necessary.

Those were the conditions the developed software must satisfy. The points put importance on developing the system as follows;

1. The duration from utterance to display of subtitles should be within approximately 1 s.
2. The user interface, make voices of several speakers easy to recognize, is necessary.
3. The UI of this system needs to make a speech-handicapped and hearing-impaired person easy to participate in the discussion.
4. The system should be installed free of charge on any device.
5. The UI should have a function to revise the recognized text from the voice. That function needs to be easy to edit the text.

3   Developing the System

First, the voice recognition engine was considered. There are several systems that recognize and transcript the voice spoken in Japanese. In February 2019, when the development started, IBM Watson Speech to text, Microsoft Azure Speech to Text,

Google Cloud Speech-to-Text existed. Google Cloud Speech-to-Text was free of charge within 60 min in a month. However, it is obvious that the usage of data excess the 60 min limitation soon. It could not keep being free of charge. Another engine is necessary.

Next, the voice recognition system included in the Google Chrome browser was examined. It is free of charge if you use the voice recognition system via the Chrome browser, irrespective of the minutes of use. Though it works only on Google Chrome, this recognition engine is able to decrease the installation cost of the system mentioned in the previous paragraph. Therefore, this system was developed as a Web application. A brief prototype voice recognizes and the subtitle was developed and examined. The duration from utterance from subtitle was found to same as Google Document. It means it is possible to make the duration from utterance from subtitle within 1 s. This system satisfies no. 1 and 4 of the conditions described at the end of Sect. 1.

The UI was considered next. This system should have the UI easy to distinguish several speakers' voices. As a result of the research, a method was found, which separate several speakers' voices by independent Component Analysis use software. Still, it should be more definite if several speakers' voices are separated by hardware. So, the system was made to be connected via each speakers' device such as laptop computer, or smart mobile. This feature satisfies the condition no. 2 stated before.

In the next step, the function makes hearing-impaired person easy to participate in the discussion was considered. Although many hearing-impaired people speak on oral, it is difficult to speak to be processed on the voice recognition system for most of them. Therefore, text writing function was added to the UI. This text writing function will have the transcript voice and that text is able to revise on the UI. This feature satisfies the condition no. 3 and 5 stated before. Thus, those specifications satisfied every condition.

Figure 1 shows the display right after the log-in, one of the appearance image of the developed prototype. Figure 2 shows the screen after entering the room. The Japanese text in the image was translated and noted on the image in English.

Fig. 1. Appearance of Prototype (Initial Screen).

Here is how to use this system. The user logs in on Google account, then set the room. Figure 1 shows the status of only one room was set. Several rooms could be set as well. The user issues the invitation code to invite other users to the room. Image 3 shows the situation three users participate in the room and having chat. The Guest user is only able to join the room but set the room.

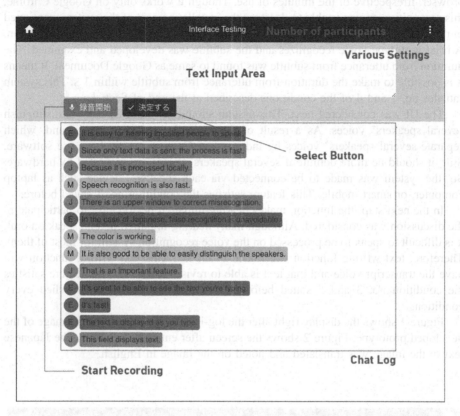

Fig. 2. Appearance of Prototype (Each Room).

The following is the explanation of image 3. "Text Input Area" is used for input text like an ordinary text editor. In the prototype phase, the Enter key was not worked. "Determine" button was used to fix the input text. "Start Recording" button is toggle style. Pushing it starts recording of sound, then the button inverted to gray. The result of voice recognition is inputted in "Text Input Area" and stay there during the time the user set. When the text appears in the window, the result text could be revised. Pushing the "Determine" button or running out the set staying time, the input was determined and appears in "Main Window" below. In the same time, inverted to the grey "Start Recording" button turn into default status. It means users need to push the "Start Recording" button at each speaking. And voice recognized result was not accessible to

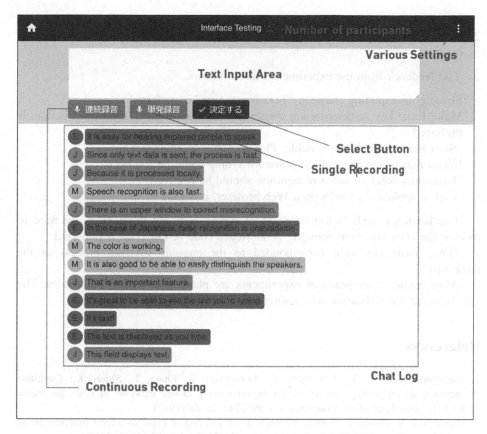

Fig. 3. Appearance of Prototype after the Adjusted (Each Room).

other users when it is in "Text Input Area". Only after the text determined, other users see the results.

4 Experiment and Feedback

After development, the prototype was examined in a practical experiment. The experiment was held at a Japanese company in the situation one hearing person speaks to nine hearing-impaired people.

However, the experiment was stopped soon because the operation was too burdensome as users need to push the "Start Recording" button at each talk. That was only feedback as experimented time was too short. The UI was adjusted to continue recognizing voice so that the user should not need to take action at each speaking. Figure 3 shows an adjusted prototype appearance.

After the adjustment of the prototype, the practical experiment was conducted. Two Japanese companies participated. The prototype used in the situation as follows;

1. The situation two hearing people and one hearing-impaired person talk
2. The situation four hearing people and two hearing-impaired people talk like a group meeting

The feedback from the experiment was as follows.

- Sharing the inputting status in "Text Input Area" is preferred.
- Make Enter key to determining the text in addition to the "Determine" button, is preferred.
- "Start Recording" is not suitable. Please change to another word.
- If you understand the context, some mistyping could be followed.
- Occasional delay of voice recognition should be resolved.
- As it is application works on a Web browser, it is easy to start using.

The invitation code is too long. As of typing, it is not impractical, we need to receive the code via some network. A shortened code or QR code is preferred.

These feedbacks have corresponded to the ongoing revising process of the prototype.

After revise, other practical experiments are planned at several companies. The development and validation will continue and further progress is expected.

References

1. Maruyama, I., Abe, Y., Sawamura, E., Mitsuhashi, T., Ehara, T., Shirai, K.: Cognitive experiments on timing differences for superimposing closed captions in news programs. I EICE Tech. Rep. Hum. Commun. Sci. **99**(123), 21–28 (1999)
2. Shimogori, N., Ikeda, T., Sekiya, Y.: How display timing of captions affects comprehension of EFL speakers. IPSJ SIG Technical reports, GN75, E1-E6, 18 March 2010
3. Ariumi, Y.: Characteristics of textual information in speech-to-text translation service with computers for university students with hearing impairment; Focusing on the factors of class situations, translators and users. University of Tsukuba, Ph. D. thesis, March 2013
4. UDTalk. https://udtalk.jp/. Accessed 20 Mar 2020

Voice and Speech Training System for the Hearing-Impaired Children Using Tablet Terminal

Hiroki Takagi[1]([✉]), Shun Sasaki[1], Megumi Kaneko[1,2,3],
Takayuki Itoh[3], Kazuo Sasaki[2], Kazuya Ueki[1],
and Meeko Kuwahara[1]

[1] Meisei University, 2-1-1 Hodokubo, Hino-shi, Tokyo, Japan
17j5060@stu.meisei-u.ac.jp,
meeko.kuwahara@meisei-u.ac.jp
[2] Tokyo University of Technology, 14041-1, Hachioji-shi, Tokyo, Japan
[3] Ochanomizu University, Otuka, Bunkyo-ku, Tokyo, Japan

Abstract. Speech is an important human capability, especially as a learning base for expression and communication. However, it is very difficult for children with hearing disorders to obtain this basic ability while they are young.

The authors have found the potential of using voice recognition in application systems for portable devices and tablet terminal for use in the speech training of children with hearing disorders since early childhood (pre-school). In this paper, we propose the creation of this application through evaluation and discussion of practicality.

The application focuses on the enjoyment of a game and a sense of accomplishment so that children can keep learning with motivation while operating. A tablet is used for this system for easy operation by children. The environment includes OS: Windows 10, Game Engine: Unity, and Voice analysis: Julius. The application has voice recognition, so it can be operated through speech. This voice recognition covers from simple sounds to utterance accuracy: it recognizes whether the child is using their voice and if the utterance is correct. In this way, the application can help children with hearing disorders to acquire speech and reduce disability in the future.

Keywords: Speech training of children with hearing disorders · Voice and speech training system · Tablet terminal application

1 Introduction

In Japan, the widespread use of newborn hearing screening tests has led to early detection of hearing impairment and increased opportunities for early treatment. However, it has been well-known in Japan that a hearing-impaired child acquires less vocabulary than a normal-hearing child, and development is delayed relative to age from infancy. The inability of hearing-impaired children to learn speech affects the display of affection with families and others around them, and hinders appropriate communication with others, thus affecting social development.

© Springer Nature Switzerland AG 2020
C. Stephanidis and M. Antona (Eds.): HCII 2020, CCIS 1226, pp. 121–127, 2020.
https://doi.org/10.1007/978-3-030-50732-9_17

Speech guidance necessary for communication using words and speech is carried out at the kindergarten of the school for the deaf. However, it is problematic that skilled persons are required for speech guidance. Another problem in the education of the hearing-impaired is the difficulty in learning words. It has also been well-known that the delay in vocabulary acquisition begins in childhood, and misuse is also noticeable. In addition, the hearing disability influences not only the delay in language acquisition but also on the development of other physical functions, the building of human relationships, and the development of emotions. With the development of technology in recent years, effective results have been obtained from research on hearing-impaired persons utilizing information technology, speech recognition, and speech synthesis technology [1, 2].

The goal of this research is to support the first steps of language acquisition and communication for hearing-impaired children using he advantages of portable terminals for young children so that the restrictions on social activities due to disabilities can be reduced as much as possible.

This paper describes the details of the proposed application as well as evaluations and discussions on practicality. This application focuses on the enjoyment of the game and a sense of accomplishment so that children can keep learning with motivation and enjoy the game and be able to operate this application. This game application is developed in the following two main types, whether the children are making a voice, and if the utterance is correct.

Ex1) A rocket flies in reaction to the voice of the user. The flight distance and direction of the rocket differ according to the voice volume and the utterance of the user.

Ex2) A character and the face of the user appear on the display. The application asks user to pronounce a certain vowel correctly. The character on the screen guides the user by indicating them how to move their mouth and what shape the mouth would be while pronouncing the vowel. When the user pronounces the vowel correctly, the sound is shown on the screen as a voice pattern.

Ex3) The user becomes the character for a role playing game and based on the sound they pronounce, they go on an adventure of catching escaped animals.

The proposed system uses a tablet terminal so that young children can practice alone, and can easily and continuously support basic pronunciation practice. This application can help children with hearing disorders to acquire speech.

2   Traditional Japanese Speech Training Methods

In the education of hearing-impaired children in Japan, it is important to teach spoken language, letters and sign language at the same time, and, not only increase vocabulary, but also promote the use of full sentences.

Language training using words and speech is carried out at the kindergarten of the school for the deaf. Speech training is conducted through practice of shaping the mouth for pronunciation of Japanese vowel sounds and by putting one's fingers in the mouth and learning the number of fingers it takes to make the sound. Many studies on hearing-impaired children have already used information technology. These studies found that the use of information terminals (tablet terminals) is effective for language and knowledge acquisition for hearing-impaired children [3].

3   Proposed System

Delaying vocabulary acquisition until entering school has a major impact on primary school education as well as communication development.

For this reason, we propose a system for vocalization training for younger hearing-impaired children using a camera-equipped tablet terminal and voice, image recognition, and voice recognition. The target of the proposed system is to check whether the hearing-impaired child can produce the sound accurately. The shape of the mouth is one of the important factors in producing accurate sound; therefore, we propose a system that can guide the child to create the correct mouth shape. By using a tablet device with a camera, the system displays the face of the trainee so that trainee can understand whether "the correct sound has been emitted" and "the correct mouth shape has been made for the pronunciation". In addition, we developed the system so that preschoolers can use to attain correct pronunciation without much explanation through the use of voice recognition because they do not understand many words. The system also shows scores through such things as cartoon animation and without the use of too many words so that the preschoolers can easily understand.

4   Prototype Application

4.1   Navigation System for Opening the Mouth Shape

Implementation

The proposed application uses a face detection method supported by image recognition libraries to navigate the shape of the mouth for checking correct vowel pronunciations. It uses OpenCV and Dlib to detect the shape of the mouth. The application shows the face using the camera, and displays the correct shape of the mouth over the shape of his/her mouth. The development environment included OS: Windows10, IDE: Visual studio2017, programing language: C ++, Library: OpenCV and Dlib, voice analysis: Julius.

The coordinates of the landmark points are stored in an array during the face detection by Dlib. Also, the number of coordinates of the feature points, the order of the coordinates, and the face part indicated by the coordinates are determined in advance. Therefore, the application also determines the position of the array in which the coordinates of the mouth necessary for the proposed system are stored in advance. The shape of the mouth is determined by comparing the coordinates of the feature point corresponding to the mouth in the array with the coordinates stored before, since it is difficult to determine the shape of the mouth using only the stored coordinates.

As a result, the shape of the mouth could be distinguished not by the coordinates but by the amount of change in the coordinates. In addition, the system uses the coordinates at which the authors were producing the desired vowel as the correct mouth shape.

The application draws the shape of the user's mouth as a line in green and the correct mouth shape as a line in red. Users can attain the correct mouth shape by changing the shape of the mouth so that the green line overlaps the red line.

Figure 1 shows a screen capture of the running application. Figure 1 (left) shows the state in which the shape of the mouth for the sound "A(a)" is being indicated while the mouth of the user is closed. Figure 1 (center) shows a state in which the mouth shape of "A(a)" is being indicated and the mouse of the user shapes for the sound "I(i)". Figure 1 (right) shows the state in which the mouth shape of "A(a)" is being indicated and the mouth of the user shapes for "A(a)". The red and green lines do not overlap in Fig. 1 (left) and (center). On the other hand, the lines greatly overlap in Fig. 1 (right).

Result
We could navigate the shape of the mouth detected by Dlib. Also, the shape of the mouth can be corrected to the desired shape of the mouth by changing the shape of the mouth to be closer to the navigation line

Fig. 1. Navigation system for opening the mouth shape (Color figure online)

4.2   Flying Rocket

Implementation
The proposed system uses a speech recognition method to convey whether or not the pronounced sound is correct, using as few words as possible. The proposed system uses Julius to determine the correctness of pronunciation. The movement of the cartoon animation changes depending on the correctness of the pronunciation. The development environment includes OS: Windows10, game engine: Unity, programing language: C++, voice analysis: Julius.

Julius can edit the words to be recognized and treat the result of speech recognition as "confidence." Therefore, the application determines the distance of the flight of the rocket based on the reliability (confidence) of the target words. We prepared four levels to the flying distance of the rocket. The higher the confidence factor, the closer the rocket would fly to the moon. In this way, the correctness of pronunciation is indicated without using words.

Figure 2 shows the start window. Voice input at this screen is recognized by Julius. The animation of a flying rocket appears as shown in Fig. 3 (left) when the target word is recognized. The higher the Julius word confidence, the more the rocket will fly. The rocket will land on the moon when the word confidence is the highest. Figure 3 (center) shows the result when the degree of certainty is 90 to 94%. Figure 3 (right) shows a result when the degree of certainty is 95 to 100%.

Result
We could practice and evaluate objective pronunciation by using Julius. In addition, we could show the evaluation of pronunciation using the minimum amount of words by using the animation of a flying rocket and by applying the word confidence of Julius.

Fig. 2. start window (Flying rocket)

Fig. 3. Play window (Flying rocket)

4.3 The Game of Capture Animals

Implementation
We propose a game where users can clear a stage once they have produced the correct pronunciation. We aimed that young children can play repeatedly to target better results by enhancing entertainment factors into the application. The User must capture animals of the Japanese zodiac while playing with this game. The development environment includes OS: Windows10, game engine: Unity, programing language: C++, voice analysis: Julius.

As with the rocket application, the confidence of the target word determines whether the animal can be captured or not. We expect that this can be played repeatedly due to the effective entertainment factor.

Figure 4 shows the start window. The voice input at this screen is recognized by Julius. Figure 4 (far left) shows the failure screen for when the confidence of the word is 0 to 84%. Figure 4 (center-left) shows the success screen for when the confidence is 85 to 89%. Figure 4 (center-right) shows the success screen for when the confidence is 90 to 94%. Figure 4 (far right) shows a success screen when the confidence is 95 to 100%.

Result

We believe that the word confidence of Julius allowed the creation of a game that can be played repeatedly thanks to the effective entertainment factor of catching animals. It is possible, however, that some children will not understand the game. More guidance is necessary for such a case.

Fig. 4. The game of capture animals

5 Discussion

We have proposed a system for voice and speech training for hearing-impaired children using a camera-equipped tablet terminal and voice, visual, and sound recognition. We created prototype applications that could be used for practice. As a result, the intended operations were performed successfully. Although we could not have young children with hearing impairment experience the applications, we received positive feedback from trainers of such children.

Feedback from teachers at a school for the deaf (who were also deaf) was that the game gave a strong sense of accomplishment to the user because they were able to control the game with their own voice and repeat the activity if they failed. It increased the possibility of enjoyment while learning speech and words. It also fills the need for a way to fix speech mistakes. Although it is possible to speak without the correct mouth shape, there is a need for a way to teach it.

From this feedback, we believe that children can learn through this game, and that it would fill the need for a correction method when the speech is incorrect.

The Speech-Language-Hearing Therapist advised that it was important to judge and fix speech to attain correct speech. But, if the purpose of correct speech is ease of communication, the addition of information other than speech such as sign language, characters, mouth shapes, and facial expressions will increase the ease of communication. It is good to have the experience of being able to communicate with others by using spoken language or other means of communication, even if it is determined to be incorrect by this application. There should be a way to indicate a way to correct pronunciation if it is incorrect but it is important to teach spoken language, character and sign language at the same time. If the application plays a part in that, it would be worthwhile.

Therefore, we believe it can be useful for pronunciation practice of younger children.

6 Conclusion

The proposed prototype applications can be used by hearing-impaired children to practice pronunciation through image recognition and voice recognition technology. The prototype applications have succeeded in operating as intended.

As a future issue, it is necessary to have a younger hearing-impaired child experience the applications that were actually created, and verify whether it will trigger the vocabulary acquisition. In addition, it is necessary to develop a system by which young children can be trained not only in speech but sign language and written language at the same time as another future work.

References

1. Ogawa, N., Hiraga, R.: A voice game to improve speech by deaf and hard of hearing persons. IPSJ SIG Technical reports 2019-AAC-9(15), pp. 1–4 (2019)
2. Higashinoi, Y., et al.: Evaluation of the hearing environment for hearing-impaired people using an automatic voice recognition software program and the CI-2004 test battery. Audiol. Jpn **61**(3), 222–231 (2018)
3. Shibata, K., Ayuha, D., Hattori, A.: Tablet-media for children with hearing-hard -language speaking and knowledge acquisition-. IPSJ SIG Technical reports 2013-DPS-156(13), pp. 1–6 (2013)

Research on Interface Design for the Elderly

Ruo-Qiao Zhao[✉] and Li-Hao Chen

Fu Jen Catholic University, No. 510, Zhongzheng Road, Xinzhuang District,
New Taipei City 24205, Taiwan
Zhaoruoqiao163@gmail.com, ahao@gmail.com

Abstract. The study aims to examine the intuitive use of different types of product interfaces by the elderly. A total of 31 elderly users were invited to participate in the test to use TV remote control interfaces. A test program was designed to present the interfaces on a tablet computer in three ways, which differ in the functional block position, and the size and shape of number buttons. The participants performed specific operations on the interfaces. The test program recorded the response time of each participant in the first operation. According to the research findings, in terms of the position of functional blocks, the participants' response in intuitive use is the fastest when the channel tuning buttons, volume buttons and number buttons are located in the lower part of the remote control. The key size had little impact on the participants. The intuitive use of the participants is better when the keys have a rectangular or round shape. The research findings also reveal that the elderly users' intuitive use of product interfaces is related to their use experience.

Keywords: The elderly · Interface design · Affordance

1 Introduction

The elderly is one of user groups that attract keen attention of product designers. When designing operation interfaces of a product, designers should take into account its intuitive use in addition to its aesthetics (Cheng et al. 2016). Modern products come with more and more functions, but the older people have difficulties in operating these products because they are physically and psychologically restricted due to physical degradation (Hawthorn 2000). Affordance proposed by Gibson (1979) has become a well-known design concept, which emphasizes that creatures perceive external forms and structures of environmental objects through visual perception, acquire characteristics of things, and learn how to interact with them. Norman (1990), a famous psychologist, believes that the perception of affordance of a product is related to past experience and knowledge. A well-designed product allows a user to easily understand how to operate it even at the first use. McGrenere and Ho (2000) proposes that viewers will interpret the perceived messages in the environment based on past experience and respond accordingly to interact with them. Blackler and Hurtienne (2007) points out that the users' familiarity with technologies depends on how often they use certain products and what functions they use. If the designers have known the intuitive use of

© Springer Nature Switzerland AG 2020
C. Stephanidis and M. Antona (Eds.): HCII 2020, CCIS 1226, pp. 128–135, 2020.
https://doi.org/10.1007/978-3-030-50732-9_18

the product by users in the first place, they could have designed an operation interface in an intuitive way.

Watching TV is an important form of entertainment for the older people, and they often use a remote control for TVs (Angeletou et al. 2009). As the older people have degraded muscles, low sensitivity of fingers and reduced cognitive ability, they are unable to operate these products smoothly by pressing small buttons. As for the size of buttons, Chen et al. (2013) proposed in related researches on the use of interfaces by the elderly that the size of buttons is related to users' posture. If the button size is smaller than 20 mm, it takes longer to complete the task when the user is standing up than that when the user is seated; if the button is larger, there is little different in operation time whether the user is standing up or is seated. Xiong et al. (2014) proposed that with the same size of buttons, the older people take about twice as long as young people to complete a task. As the size of buttons decreases, the operation time and the error rate of the elderly increase. As for the arrangement of product interfaces, Chen (2007) pointed out that the elderly are affected by the form of interface display. If the interface display can be adapted to the functions and needs of the product, it will make operation easier for the elderly. Freeman and Lessiter (2007) found in their study of TV remote controls that ordinary people can intuitively ignore buttons that are not needed, while the elderly can hardly do that. Proper arrangement of functional buttons allows operators to press the required buttons more directly and ignore buttons that are not needed. As for the shape of buttons, Breinholt and Krueger (1997) pointed out that the shapes of interface buttons have little impact on the operation speed. This is similar to the viewpoint of Chen et al. (2018), that is, the button shape has little impact on the first tap time and the completion time for the intuitive operation of the elderly. However, Tao et al. (2018) had a different viewpoint, who believes that the contact area of the finger during operation varies with the button shape; when the button is small, a square-shaped button will be easier to press than buttons of other shapes.

This study aims to explore the intuitive use of different forms of operation interfaces by the elderly with regard to the first tap on a button, and to propose a product interface design form suitable for the elderly. Focusing on TV remote controls, the study explores the effect of three design elements, that is, arrangement of button blocks, size of buttons and shape of buttons, on the operation of the elderly, and the research findings provide a reference for designers of operation interfaces of products for the older people. A Subsection Sample

2 Experimental Details

2.1 Participants and Test Interface

A total of 31 participants with a mean age of 69.22 (SD: 2.67) took part in the experiment. Participants had no speech impediment or visual impairment, and all had experience in using remote controls of TVs or other products. The test environment was a quiet classroom in a university. A total of 14 common types of user interfaces were collected for testing operations on common TV remote controls. To prevent the interference of factors such as color and material, the test interface was drawn using drawing software. The operation interfaces under test are represented by black wire frames on a white background (see Fig. 1).

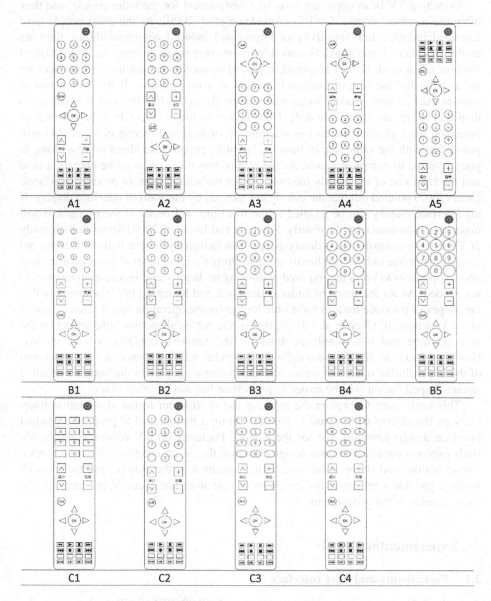

Fig. 1. Test operation interface

With the MIL-HDBK759 button size as a reference, the diameter of the button with the minimum fingertip area is 10/13 mm, the diameter of the button with the maximum fingertip area is 19 mm, and the interval between single-finger continuous operations is

6 mm. Interfaces A1–A5 are TV remote control interface block arrangement models, B1–B5 are number button size models, and C1–C4 are number button shape models. Operation time of participants is calculated in seconds, and data is quoted up to the second digit after the decimal point. The interface display device used in the experiment is a 10-inch iPad touch screen, and its layout is presented as a 1:1 simulated TV remote control interface. The first tap time of each participant is recorded.

A1 to A5 are the five most common block arrangements based on the collected samples. B1 to B5 depict round number buttons of common TV remote controls, with the maximum button diameter of about 13 mm and the minimum button diameter of about 7 mm. The dimensions of the test interfaces from B1 to B5 are 7 mm, 9 mm, 11 mm, 13 mm, and 15 mm respectively. Due to the size limitation of remote controls, button spacing is not considered here. The four types of number button are respectively of rectangle (C1), circle (C2), capsule (C3), and oval (C4) in shape. Because the button shapes are different, the horizontal spacing of the number buttons is not considered. The vertical spacing is 6 mm. The buttons of C1, C3, and C4 are equal in length and height.

2.2 Operation

Operation tasks are set based on different interfaces. For interfaces A1–A5, there are three types of operation tasks: (1) Change channel with number buttons; (2) change channel with channel tuning buttons; and (3) adjust volume with volume buttons. For interfaces B1–B5 and C1–C4, the operation task is to change channel with the number buttons. There is no time limit on the experiment. During the operation, the task interface appeared randomly. The program automatically recorded the first tap time of each participant (the time between tapping the Power button and then tapping any button on the interface). The operation process is as follows: Tap the red Power button to turn on the TV, use the number buttons to change the channel to 28 (two-digit operation task appears randomly on the screen), and tap the OK button to confirm.

3 Research Results

According to the results of the variation number, from the perspective of the block arrangement, the positions of number buttons in the five interfaces had no significant impact on the first tap time of participants (Table 1). The positions of channel tuning buttons on the five interfaces had significant impact on the results of the first tap time ($P = 0.018 < 0.05$); in this operation task, the average response time of all 31 participants was the shortest when they performed the operation on interface A5, and was relevantly long when they performed the operation on interface A1 (Table 2). The positions of the volume buttons on the five interfaces showed no significant impact on the intuitive use of participants (Table 3).

According to Table 4, the average first tap time of the participants on interface B5 is the shortest, and in comparison, the average response time for interface B2 is longer. Interfaces B2 and B5 ($P = 0.024 < 0.05$) are significantly different from each other. The other interface variations show no significant difference.

Table 1. Tasks of arranging number buttons in blocks

Sample	Mean	SD	Number	Significance				
				A1	A2	A3	A4	A5
A1	3.57	2.65	31		–	–	–	–
A2	3.21	1.95	31			–	–	–
A3	4.65	6.05	31				–	–
A4	2.83	1.81	31					–
A5	2.66	1.8	31					

(*: p < 0.05, **: p < 0.01, ***: p < 0.001, -: non-significant)

Table 2. Tasks of arranging channel tuning buttons in blocks

Sample	Mean	SD	Number	Significance				
				A1	A2	A3	A4	A5
A1	2.55	1.79	31		–	–	–	*
A2	2.14	1.25	31			–	–	–
A3	2.23	1.68	31				–	–
A4	2.16	1.17	31					–
A5	1.7	1.02	31					

(*: p < 0.05, **: p < 0.01, ***: p < 0.001, -: non-significant)

Table 3. Tasks of arranging volume buttons in blocks

Sample	Mean	SD	Number	Significance				
				A1	A2	A3	A4	A5
A1	2.11	1.24	31		–	–	–	–
A2	1.88	0.94	31			–	–	–
A3	1.82	1.33	31				–	–
A4	1.74	1.30	31					–
A5	1.61	1.07	31					

(*: p < 0.05, **: p < 0.01, ***: p < 0.001, -: non-significant)

Table 4. Size of number buttons

Sample	Mean	SD	Number	Significance				
				B1	B2	B3	B4	B5
B1	2.96	3.3	31		–	–	–	–
B2	3.42	3.21	31			–	–	*
B3	2.72	1.6	31				–	–
B4	3.15	2.85	31					–
B5	2.18	1.16	31					

(*: p < 0.05, **: p < 0.01, ***: p < 0.001, -: non-significant)

According to Table 5, interfaces C1 and C3 (P = 0.014 < 0.05) are significantly different, interfaces C2 and C3 (P = 0.03 < 0.05) are also significantly different, but interface C4 has no significant difference with the other three interfaces. The average first tap time of the participants on interface C3 is longer than that on the other three interfaces. Interfaces C1 and C2 show higher availability than other interfaces in this operation, and the average first tap time on these two interfaces is basically the same.

Table 5. Shape of number buttons

Sample	Mean	SD	Number	Significance			
				C1	C2	C3	C4
C1	2.57	1.41	31	–		*	–
C2	2.6	1.78	31			*	–
C3	3.98	2.74	31				–
C4	3.36	2.77	31				

(*: p < 0.05, **: p < 0.01, ***: p < 0.001, -: non-significant)

4 Discussion

The research results show that:

The difference in the arrangement of functional blocks on the interface results in some differences in the intuitive use of the elderly users. This conclusion coincides with the findings of Chen and Liu (2017) and Chen et al. (2018). When changing channel with channel tuning buttons, there is a significant difference between interface A1 and interface A5. The difference may be mainly caused by the fact that the "▲▼, ok, ◀▶" buttons in the digital TV block above the channel tuning buttons of interface A1 are similar to the channel tuning buttons, which caused interference to most participants (tapping the wrong button, or pausing to think about whether the buttons might serve the same purpose). The arrangement of the volume buttons has no interference on the participants when they use the buttons adjust volume; this is because there is a clear distinction between the volume button symbols "+" and "−" and the "◀" and "▶" buttons in the navigation area. The number buttons on interface A1 are separated from the channel tuning and volume buttons. In general, the intuitive use of this interface is low for the participants. At present, the most frequently used buttons on a TV remote control by the elderly are number buttons and channel tuning & volume buttons. When these two blocks are arranged side by side, the elderly may ignore other less used button blocks. In all these operation tasks, interface A5 shows the optimal intuitive use for the elderly due to two possible reasons: First, these elderly people used to grasp the lower part of a TV remote control, so this is a focal area of eyesight (this assumption needs to be further verified). Second, these 31 participants have similar life experience; some remote controls for digital TVs currently available in Taiwan are similar to this interface, and the elderly have certain use experience of this interface.

The size of number buttons has no impact on the intuitive use of the elderly. There is a significant difference between interfaces B2 and B5. However, it should be noted that, according to the average first tap time, neither interface B2 with the smallest number button size nor interface B4 with larger buttons helped the intuitive use of the participants. Related studies before mostly focus on the completion time of operation tasks. The first tap time in this experiment does not suffice to prove the impact of the button size on the operation performance. In subsequent researches, the experiment will be improved and the completion time of operation tasks will be recorded for further discussion.

In tasks related to the shape of number buttons, interface C1 (with rectangular buttons) and interface C2 (with round buttons) show better usability. The difference between the average times of the first tap of the two interfaces is very small. Jung and Im (2015) proposed that the touchable areas and areas touched by fingertips are related to the matching degree between them. The participants perceive the difference in shapes through vision and interact with buttons based on past experience. Number buttons of TV remote controls on the market are mostly of rectangular or round shape, and the participants are familiar with the two interfaces. The result confirms the theory of Blackler and Hurtienne (2007) in the aforementioned literature.

5   Conclusion

This study found that the intuitive use of the elderly mainly depends on their use experience. The arrangement of button blocks on the interface is related to the functions of the products used by the elderly. A reasonable arrangement of function button blocks can lead to better intuitive use experience for the elderly. The size of number buttons has little impact on the intuition of the elderly in terms of the first tap time. The impact of the shape of buttons on the use of interfaces by the elderly mainly depends on the users' experience.

Acknowledgement. This research was supported by the grant from the Ministry of Science and Technology, Taiwan, Grant 107-2410-H-030-059-MY2.

References

Angeletou, A., Goulati, A., Bartkowska, A., Politis, I.: TV remote control for elderly. In: CHI 2009, Boston, Massachusetts, USA, 4–9 April 2009 (2009)

Blacker, A., Hurtienne, J.: Towards a unified view of intuitive interaction: definitions, models and tools across the world. MMI-Interaktiv **13**, 36–54 (2007)

Breinholt, G., Krueger, H.: Evaluation of key shapes on a touchscreen simulation of a specialised keypad. Appl. Ergon. **27**(6), 375–379 (1997)

Chen, K.B., Savage, A.B., Chourasia, A.O., Wiegmann, D.A., Sesto, M.E.: Touch screen performance by individuals with and without motor control disabilities. Appl. Ergon. **44**(2), 297e302 (2013)

Chen, L.H., Liu, Y.C.: Affordance and intuitive interface design for elder users with dementia. Procedia CIRP **60**, 470–475 (2017)

Chen, L.H., Liu, Y.C., Cheng, P.J.: Perceived affordances in older people with dementia: designing intuitive product interfaces. In: MATEC Web of Conferences, vol. 221, p. 02001. EDP Sciences (2018)

Cheng, Y.W., Chen, L.H., Liu, Y.C.: Intuitive interface design for elderly-demented users (2016)

Freeman, J., Lessiter, J.: Research report: easy to use digital television receivers: remote control buttons and functions used by different types of consumer (2007)

Gibson, J.J.: The Ecological approach to Visual Perception. Houghton Mifflin Company, Boston (1979)

Hawthorn, D.: Possible implications of aging for interface designers. Interact. Comput. **12**, 507–528 (2000)

Jung, E.S., Im, Y.: Touchable area: an empirical study on design approach considering perception size and touch input behavior. Int. J. Ind. Ergon. **49**, 21e30 (2015)

McGrenere, J., Ho, W.: Affordance: clarifying and evolving a concept. In: Proceedings of Graphics Interface, pp. 179–186 (2000)

Norman, D.A.: The Design of everyday Things. Basic Books Inc. statista, London (1990)

Tao, D., Yuan, J., Liu, S., Qu, X.: Effects of button design characteristics on performance and perceptions of touchscreen use. Int. J. Ind. Ergon. **64**, 59–68 (2018)

Xiong, J., Muraki, S., Fukumoto, K.: The effects of touch button size on touchscreen operability. J. Mech. Eng. Autom. **4**(8), 667–672 (2014)

Smartphones, Social Media and Human Behaviour

Effect of Online Weight Loss Advertising in Young Women with Body Dissatisfaction: An Experimental Protocol Using Eye-Tracking and Facial Electromyography

Carlos A. Almenara[1](✉) ⓘ, Annie Aimé[2] ⓘ,
and Christophe Maïano[2] ⓘ

[1] Universidad Peruana de Ciencias Aplicadas, Av. Alameda San Marcos, S/N,
Lima 15067, Peru
carlos.almenara@upc.pe
[2] Université du Québec en Outaouais, 5, Rue Saint-Joseph, Saint-Jérôme,
Québec J7Z 0B7, Canada

Abstract. The weight loss industry is projected to reach USD$ 278.95 billion worldwide by 2023. Weight loss companies devote a large part of their budget for advertising their products. Unfortunately, as revealed by the Federal Trade Commission (FTC), there are many deceptive ads. The effect of weight loss advertising on consumer's diet and eating behavior is so large that it has been proposed a causal relationship between advertising and diet. Adolescents, women with appearance concerns, and obese people, are the most vulnerable consumers for this kind of advertising. Within the Internet, most weight loss products are advertised under algorithmic rules. This algorithmic regulation refers to the online advertising being established by a series of rules (i.e., algorithms). These algorithms collect information about our online identity and behavior (e.g., sociodemographic characteristics, online searches we do, online content we download, "liked" content, etc.), to personalize the content displayed while we browse the Internet. Because of it, this algorithmic regulation has been described as a "filter bubble", because most content we see on the Internet is reflecting our idiosyncratic interests, desires, and needs. Following this paradigm, this study presents a research protocol to experimentally examine the effect of online weight loss advertising in the attention (using eye-tracking) and physiological response (using facial electromyography) of women with different levels of body dissatisfaction. The protocol describes the methodology for: participants' recruitment; collecting weight loss ads; and the experimental study, which includes the stimuli (ads) and the responses (eye fixations and facial muscles activity).

Keywords: Weight loss · Online advertising · Eye-tracking · Body dissatisfaction · Algorithmic regulation · Facial electromyography · Internet

© Springer Nature Switzerland AG 2020
C. Stephanidis and M. Antona (Eds.): HCII 2020, CCIS 1226, pp. 139–148, 2020.
https://doi.org/10.1007/978-3-030-50732-9_19

1 Introduction

According with Orbis Research, the global market of the weight loss industry was USD$ 168.95 billion in 2016 and it is projected a growth to USD$ 278.95 in 2023 [1]. These companies have a large budget for advertising their weight loss products, although, as has been identified by the Federal Trade Commission (FTC), there are many deceptive ads within them [2–4].

Many consumers are aware and can identify deceptive weight loss ads. However, even the skeptic consumers are prone to buy weight loss products in Internet with the hope to lose weight [2]. For instance, adolescents, women with appearance concerns, and obese people, are the most vulnerable consumers for this kind of advertising [2, 5, 6]. Specifically, the most representative segment of consumers for these products are young adult women (below 30 years), representing up to 40% of all consumers [7]. In most of these cases, the consumers are buying these weight loss products because of their concerns with their body weight and shape.

These concerns with body weight and shape are studied under the term of body dissatisfaction, i.e., individual's cognitive and affective negative evaluations of his/her own body and its characteristics [8]. Unfortunately, body dissatisfaction is considered an important predictor in the development of eating disorders as well as risky eating behaviors and patterns, such as extreme diets for weight loss [9].

As evidenced by previous studies, the effect of advertising on consumer's diet and eating behavior is so large that it has been proposed a causal relationship between advertising and diet [10]. Particularly in the case of women with high levels of body dissatisfaction, it is important to highlight that the continuous exposure to this kind of advertising in Internet and other media, can promote unhealthy eating patterns and even the relapse in women recovering of the treatment for an eating disorder [10–13]. For that reason, it is necessary to scientifically examine the effect of the online advertising of diet and weight loss products in the most vulnerable individuals, such as young women with body dissatisfaction.

Several studies have explored the effect of online advertising on body image attitudes and eating behaviors to lose weight, in both cross-sectional and experimental studies [14]. However, to the best of our knowledge, there is not such study as the one we present here, which includes a biomarker, a behavioral marker, and experimental stimuli established by computer algorithms.

In this study, the biomarker is obtained by measuring facial muscles activity (physiological response), using facial electromyography (fEMG), whereas the behavioral marker is obtained by measuring eye movements (eye fixations), using eye tracking. fEMG has been used in media and advertising research, being considered a useful measure of emotional valence and arousal [15, 16]. Similarly, eye tracking has been used in studies of digital online advertising, and it is considered an objective measure of gaze patterns [17, 18]. Regarding computer algorithms, most online advertising is established by a series of rules (i.e., algorithms) that personalize the content for each Internet user. These algorithms collect information about our online identity and behavior (e.g., sociodemographic characteristics, online searches we do, online content we download, "liked" content, etc.), to personalize the content displayed while we browse the Internet [19]. Because of it, this algorithmic regulation has been described as a "filter bubble", because most content we see on the Internet is actually reflecting our idiosyncratic interests, desires, and needs [20].

Following the algorithmic regulation paradigm, this study presents a research protocol to experimentally examine the effect of online weight loss advertising in the attention (eye fixation) and physiological response (electrodermal activity) of women with different levels of body dissatisfaction. The current protocol describes the methodology for: participants' recruitment; collecting weight loss ads; and the experimental study, which includes the stimuli (ads) and the responses (eye fixations and fEMG).

2 Methodology

Regarding the research design, we propose an experimental design with a matched control group. In this scenario, participants are randomly assigned to either the control or experimental condition and the control group will match with the experimental group in their sociodemographic characteristics [21].

2.1 Participants

Sampling is non-random and participants (young women between 18 and 30 years old) are invited to participate in the experiment. The invitation is sent by email to university students and it is also posted on Facebook groups of students.

2.2 Instruments

Sociodemographic Questionnaire. Participants are asked to report their age, highest educational attainment, current occupation, weight, and height. The latter two are used to calculate the body mass index (BMI).

Body Dissatisfaction. In this study we will use three measures of body dissatisfaction. The first measure is the Photographic Figure Rating Scale (PFRS), which consists of pictorial stimuli composed by gray scale photographic figures of women [22]. Participants are asked to choose an image that represents their ideal body, and an image that represents their actual body. Thus, this instrument measures the discrepancy between the ideal body and the perceived body (i.e., body dissatisfaction), using culturally neutral stimuli. The second instrument includes a single-item measure of global body dissatisfaction (*"How satisfied are you with the physical appearance of your body?"*) that uses a 5-point Likert scale (from "Not satisfied at all" = 1 to "Absolutely satisfied" = 5). Moreover, this instrument asks the same to participants but regarding different body parts (e.g., stomach, buttocks, etc.). The third instrument is the Body Dissatisfaction subscale of the Eating Disorders Inventory - 3, which is a renowned instrument used in hundreds of studies [23].

Eye-Tracking. To measure eye movements, we propose the use of Pupil Labs binocular glasses (https://pupil-labs.com), which have good accuracy and precision [24]. Moreover, this eye tracker has a sampling frequency of 200 Hz, which is an acceptable sampling rate for available algorithms to detect eye fixations [25]. Although most studies apply mathematical and statistical procedures to handle eye tracking data [26], for this protocol we propose using also visualization techniques that allow, for example, to identify areas of interest [27]. The protocol of data acquisition follows recommended guidelines for eye tracking research [28].

Facial Electromyography (fEMG). fEMG data is obtained by locating gold cup electrodes in specific facial muscles (*zygomaticus major*, *corrugator supercilia*, and *levator labii*), and a ground electrode on the left mastoid, according to recommended guidelines [16, 29, 30].

2.3   Procedure

First, the research follows ethical guidelines for the study of human subjects [31], which implies the approval of this protocol by the Institutional Review Board (IRB) of our university. This also includes asking participants to sign an informed consent, in which we explain them about the experiment and all possible consequences of it. Moreover, all information gathered from participants is anonymized, to take care of the privacy of participants.

Collection of Experimental Stimuli. The procedure to collect weight loss advertising images from the Internet is presented in Fig. 1. First, seed terms are identified from previous studies [32–35], and are used for the acquisition of other terms [36] in Google trends, YouTube, Instagram, Twitter, Pinterest, and Facebook, through an iterative process. For example, the terms "diet" and "weight loss" are seed terms found in previous literature, whereas "intermittent fasting" is a term that can be found in Google trends while searching for "diet" in the geographical location of our interest. The iterative process finishes by considering keyword grouping relevant to the original seed keywords, a technique used in sponsored search advertising [37, 38].

Next, to perform the Internet searches, four virtual machines are configured, and four digital personae are created. A digital persona refers here to the digital data consolidation regarding the characteristics and attributes of a particular consumer [39]. In our case, we propose assigning the following sociodemographic characteristics to our digital personae: young women between 18 and 30 years, born and living in Lima, Peru. We propose four digital personae (one for each virtual machine), considering that word grouping in topic modeling is parsimonious between two and five (more could be considered overclustering) [40]. Moreover, four groups of keywords are also an appropriate number in online advertising. In other words, one group of keywords is assigned to each of the four digital personae.

A virtual machine is an operating system (virtually) installed within a host (native) operating system [41]. Considering the popularity of Microsoft Windows and Ubuntu Linux distribution, we propose configuring several virtual machines with Microsoft Windows (one for each digital persona), installed within a host Ubuntu operating system. Each virtual machine is configured and used in a way that has a unique Internet

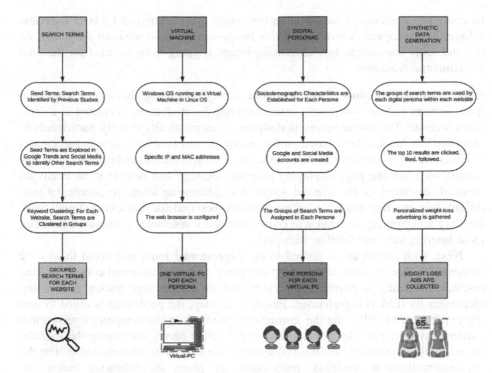

Fig. 1. Visualization of the methodology to obtain weight loss advertising images.

protocol (IP) address, and a unique media access control (MAC) address. Moreover, each virtual machine has a web browser configured by default. Google Chrome and Mozilla Firefox are the chosen web browsers given their popularity in desktop computers running Microsoft Windows.

Then, within each virtual machine (one at a time), we launch the web browser to create email and social media accounts (Google Gmail, Facebook, Instagram, Pinterest, Twitter), using the sociodemographic information that better describes our participants (young women from Lima, Peru). Next, being logged in in all these websites, we start searching the Internet using the groups of search terms we previously found. Similarly, we start to "like" the web pages devoted to weight loss and dieting that we previously identified as the most popular in social media websites. Finally, we start to collect diet and weight loss advertising images that we encounter during our web surfing in the previous step. Considering that consumers tend to prefer skyscrapers [42], only this type of advertising is selected. This process finishes after clicking on all of the first five non-sponsored links, because 90% of all clicks usually occur there [43], or until we have an appropriate number of ads to fit into a 1920 × 1080 pixels screen.

To evaluate the saliency of these pictorial stimuli, we will do a quasi-experimental pilot study with 20 university students (young women between 18 to 30 years). The participants will be in front of a projector screen displaying all collected ads which shuffle randomly every 10 s to avoid the confounding effect of their position (see preview available online: https://cybermind.ai/eye-tracking-stimuli-one). Saliency will be evaluated evaluating visual fixation time (with eye tracking) and a brief interview asking the participant *"which advertising image was the most pleasant for you?"*. At the end, only one weight loss advertising image is going to be selected for the final experimental procedure.

Experimental Procedure. First, an online survey containing the sociodemographic questionnaire and the instruments assessing body dissatisfaction, is created in a dedicated website. The online survey is designed to automatically classify participants in "satisfied" or "no satisfied" based on the responses, and randomly assigns participants to either the experimental or control condition. The experimental and control conditions consist on a website page displaying an email message and next to it: an empty ad (control condition), or the selected weight loss advertising image (experimental condition) (see preview available online: https://cybermind.ai/eye-tracking-stimuli-two). Reading and replying an email was chosen because it resembles a natural context that most Internet users are familiar with [44].

Next, each participant is invited to the experimental room and asked to sit on a comfortable chair in front of a desktop computer. Once the informed consent and the research debriefing is provided, the calibration of devices (eye tracker glasses and electrodes for fEMG) is performed. Finished this step, the participant is asked to start the experiment by following the instructions provided on the computer screen. First, participants must provide the responses to the online survey containing the sociodemographic questionnaire and the instruments assessing body dissatisfaction. For the experimental/control condition, participants are given the following instruction: "Please, read the email message and reply to the sender writing at least three lines of text".

Previous studies have identified weight-related attentional bias in people with body dissatisfaction [45]. Therefore, it is hypothesized that participants classified as dissatisfied with their bodies will display a longer total fixation time on the weight loss ad compared with their matched counterparts in the control group.

On the other hand, previous studies in young women have found that images of overweight bodies elicit facial muscle activation indicating disgust (*corrugator supercilii* and *levator labii*), whereas images of thin bodies do not [46]. Therefore, we hypothesize that participants exposed to the weight loss advertising image will display facial muscle activation indicating pleasantness.

Once collected the data, it will be analyzed with R Statistical Software 3.6.3 and Python 3.8.2.

3 Discussion

The current study was aimed to present an experimental protocol for the study of body-related attentional bias within the algorithmic regulation paradigm of online advertising. The weight loss industry devotes a large amount of money in online advertising. However, deceptive marketing strategies and weight loss products can have hazardous effects on vulnerable people such as young women with body dissatisfaction. The current study taps into this problem by providing a detailed procedure to gather weight loss ads, and an experimental protocol to examine the effect of weight loss advertising in young women with different levels of body dissatisfaction.

Although this study has strengths, is not exempt of limitations. The largest limitation is that this protocol has not been proved yet, and therefore we expect in the near future to provide further improvements along with the final results of the experiment. Meanwhile, future studies can improve this methodology by adding other neurophysiological measures and self-reports. For example, a multimodal experimental study can use galvanic skin response (electrodermal activity), facial recognition software, and self-reports of attention and bias.

Acknowledgements. This study was funded by Dirección de Investigación de la Universidad Peruana de Ciencias Aplicadas (C-04-2019).

References

1. Orbis Research Global Weight Loss and Weight Management Market 2018 Analysis, Size, Share, Facts and Figures with Products Overview, Services and Forecast 2023 (2018). http://orbisresearch.com/reports/index/weight-loss-and-weight-management-global-market-outlook-2017-2023
2. Lellis, J.C.: Waving the red flag: FTC regulation of deceptive weight-loss advertising 1951–2009. Health Commun. **31**, 47–59 (2016). https://doi.org/10.1080/10410236.2014.936334
3. Muris, T.J., Thompson, M.W., Swindle, O., et al.: Deception in weight-loss advertising workshop: Seizing opportunities and building partnerships to stop weight-loss fraud. Federal Trade Commission, Washington, DC (2003)
4. Federal Trade Commission Dietary supplements: an advertising guide for industry. Crit. Rev. Food Sci Nutr **41**, 71–85 (2001). https://doi.org/10.1080/20014091091742
5. Hobbs, R., Broder, S., Pope, H., Rowe, J.: How adolescent girls interpret weight-loss advertising. Health Educ. Res. **21**, 719–730 (2006). https://doi.org/10.1093/her/cyl077
6. Lewis, S., Thomas, S.L., Blood, R.W., et al.: 'I'm searching for solutions': why are obese individuals turning to the Internet for help and support with 'being fat'? Health Expect **14**, 339–350 (2011). https://doi.org/10.1111/j.1369-7625.2010.00644.x
7. Euromonitor International: Young Women's Health: Global Attitudes Towards Health, Fitness and Wellbeing Among the Under 30 s and Market Impact. Euromonitor International Ltd., London (2015)
8. Smahel, D., Machackova, H., Smahelova, M., et al.: Digital Technology, Eating Behaviors, and Eating Disorders. Springer, New York (2018). https://doi.org/10.1007/978-3-319-93221-7
9. Berge, J.M., Loth, K.A., Hanson, C., et al.: Family life cycle transitions and the onset of eating disorders: a retrospective grounded theory approach. J. Clin. Nurs. **21**, 1355–1363 (2012). https://doi.org/10.1111/j.1365-2702.2011.03762.x
10. Norman, J., Kelly, B.J., Boyland, E.J., McMahon, A.-T.: The impact of marketing and advertising on food behaviours: evaluating the evidence for a causal relationship. Curr. Nutr. Rep. **5**, 139–149 (2016). https://doi.org/10.1007/s13668-016-0166-6

11. Holland, G., Tiggemann, M.: A systematic review of the impact of the use of social networking sites on body image and disordered eating outcomes. Body Image **17**, 100–110 (2016). https://doi.org/10.1016/j.bodyim.2016.02.008

12. Turner, J.S.: Negotiating a media effects model: addendums and adjustments to Perloff's framework for social media's impact on body image concerns. Sex Roles **71**, 393–406 (2014). https://doi.org/10.1007/s11199-014-0431-3

13. Harrison, K.: Media, body image, and eating disorders. In: Lemish, D. (ed.) The Routledge International Handbook of Children, Adolescents, and Media, pp. 224–231. Routledge, Abingdon (2013)

14. Knobloch-Westerwick, S., Sarge, M.A.: Impacts of exemplification and efficacy as characteristics of an online weight-loss message on selective exposure and subsequent weight-loss behavior. Commun. Res. **42**, 547–568 (2015). https://doi.org/10.1177/0093650213478440

15. Bolls, P.D., Weber, R., Lang, A., Potter, R.F.: Media psychophysiology and neuroscience: bringing brain science into media processes and effects research. In: Oliver, M.B., Raney, A. A., Bryant, J. (eds.) Media effects: Advances in Theory and Research, 4th edn, pp. 195–210. Routledge, New York (2020)

16. Lajante, M.M.P., Droulers, O., Amarantini, D.: How reliable are "state-of-the-art" facial EMG processing methods? J. Advert. Res. **57**, 28–37 (2017). https://doi.org/10.2501/JAR-2017-011

17. Pfiffelmann, J., Dens, N., Soulez, S.: Personalized advertisements with integration of names and photographs: an eye-tracking experiment. J. Bus. Res. **111**, 196–207 (2020). https://doi.org/10.1016/j.jbusres.2019.08.017

18. McDuff, D.: New methods for measuring advertising efficacy. In: Rodgers, S., Thorson, E. (eds.) Digital Advertising: Theory and Research, 3rd edn, pp. 327–342. Routledge, New York (2017)

19. O'Reilly, T.: Open data and algorithmic regulation. In: Goldstein, B., Dyson, L. (eds.) Beyond Transparency: Open Data and the Future of Civic Innovation, pp. 289–300. Code for America Press, San Francisco (2013)

20. Pariser, E.: The Filter Bubble: What the Internet is Hiding from You. Penguin Press, New York (2011)

21. Shadish, W.R., Cook, T.D., Campbell, D.T.: Experimental and Quasi-Experimental Designs for Generalized Causal Inference. Houghton Mifflin Company, Boston (2002)

22. Swami, V., Salem, N., Furnham, A., Tovée, M.J.: Initial examination of the validity and reliability of the female photographic figure rating scale for body image assessment. Pers. Individ. Difffer. **44**, 1752–1761 (2008). https://doi.org/10.1016/j.paid.2008.02.002

23. Forbush, K.T., Berg, K.C.: Self-report assessments of eating pathology. In: Walsh, B.T., Attia, E., Glasofer, D.R., Sysko, R. (eds.) Handbook of Assessment and Treatment of Eating Disorders, pp. 157–174. American Psychiatric Publishing, Arlington (2016)

24. MacInnes, J.J., Iqbal, S., Pearson, J., Johnson, E.N.: Wearable eye-tracking for research: automated dynamic gaze mapping and accuracy/precision comparisons across devices. bioRxiv 299925 (2018). https://doi.org/10.1101/299925

25. Zemblys, R., Niehorster, D.C., Komogortsev, O., Holmqvist, K.: Using machine learning to detect events in eye-tracking data. Behav. Res. Methods **50**, 160–181 (2018). https://doi.org/10.3758/s13428-017-0860-3

26. Andersson, R., Larsson, L., Holmqvist, K., et al.: One algorithm to rule them all? an evaluation and discussion of ten eye movement event-detection algorithms. Behav. Res. Methods **49**, 616–637 (2017). https://doi.org/10.3758/s13428-016-0738-9

27. Blascheck, T., Kurzhals, K., Raschke, M., et al.: Visualization of eye tracking data: a taxonomy and survey. Comput, Graph. Forum **36**, 260–284 (2017). https://doi.org/10.1111/cgf.13079
28. Duchowski, A.T.: Eye Tracking Methodology: Theory and Practice, 3rd edn. Springer, New York (2017). https://doi.org/10.1007/978-3-319-57883-5
29. Fridlund, A.J., Cacioppo, J.T.: Guidelines for human electromyographic research. Psychophysiology **23**, 567–589 (1986). https://doi.org/10.1111/j.1469-8986.1986.tb00676.x
30. Tassinary, L.G., Cacioppo, J.T., Geen, T.R.: A psychometric study of surface electrode placements for facial electromyographic recording: I. the brow and cheek muscle regions. Psychophysiology **26**, 1–16 (1989). https://doi.org/10.1111/j.1469-8986.1989.tb03125.x
31. Eynon, R., Fry, J., Schroeder, R.: The ethics of Internet research. In: Fielding, N.G., Lee, R. M., Blank, G. (eds.) The Sage Handbook of Online Research Methods, 2nd edn, pp. 19–37. Sage, Thousand Oaks (2017)
32. Modrego-Pardo, I., Solá-Izquierdo, E., Morillas-Ariño, C.: Tendencia de la población española de búsqueda en Internet sobre información relacionada con diferentes dietas. Endocrinol. Diab. y Nutr. (2020). https://doi.org/10.1016/j.endinu.2019.11.003
33. Colditz, J.B., Woods, M.S., Primack, B.A.: Adolescents seeking online health information: topics, approaches, and challenges. In: Moreno, M.A., Radovic, A. (eds.) Technology and Adolescent Mental Health, pp. 21–35. Springer, Cham (2018). https://doi.org/10.1007/978-3-319-69638-6_2
34. Markey, P.M., Markey, C.N.: Annual variation in Internet keyword searches: linking dieting interest to obesity and negative health outcomes. J. Health Psychol. **18**, 875–886 (2013). https://doi.org/10.1177/1359105312445080
35. Senkowski, V., Branscum, P.: How college students search the Internet for weight control and weight management information: an observational study. Am. J. Health Educ. **46**, 231–240 (2015). https://doi.org/10.1080/19325037.2015.1044139
36. Jacquemin, C.: Spotting and Discovering Terms Through Natural Language Processing. The MIT Press, Cambridge (2001)
37. Li, H., Yang, Y.: Optimal keywords grouping in sponsored search advertising under uncertain environments. Int. J. Electron. Commer. **24**, 107–129 (2020). https://doi.org/10.1080/10864415.2019.1683704
38. Nie, H., Yang, Y., Zeng, D.: Keyword generation for sponsored search advertising: balancing coverage and relevance. IEEE Intell. Syst. **34**, 14–24 (2019). https://doi.org/10.1109/MIS.2019.2938881
39. Clarke, R.: Risks inherent in the digital surveillance economy: a research agenda. J. Inf. Technol. **34**, 59–80 (2019). https://doi.org/10.1177/0268396218815559
40. Greene, D., O'Callaghan, D., Cunningham, P.: How many topics? stability analysis for topic models. In: Calders, T., Esposito, F., Hüllermeier, E., Meo, R. (eds.) Machine Learning and Knowledge Discovery in Databases, pp. 498–513. Springer, Heidelberg (2014). https://doi.org/10.1007/978-3-662-44848-9_32
41. Rothwell, W., Kinsey, D.: Linux Essentials for Cybersecurity. Pearson, Indianapolis (2018)
42. Burns, K.S., Lutz, R.J.: The function of format: consumer responses to six on-line advertising formats. J. Advert **35**, 53–63 (2006). https://doi.org/10.2753/JOA0091-3367350104
43. Cardel, M.I., Chavez, S., Bian, J., et al.: Accuracy of weight loss information in Spanish search engine results on the internet. Obesity (2016). https://doi.org/10.1002/oby.21646
44. Reeves, B., Ram, N., Robinson, T.N., et al.: Screenomics: A framework to capture and analyze personal life experiences and the ways that technology shapes them. Hum.–Comput. Interact, 1–52 (2019). https://doi.org/10.1080/07370024.2019.1578652

45. Porras-Garcia, B., Ferrer-Garcia, M., Yilmaz, L., et al.: Body-related attentional bias as mediator of the relationship between body mass index and body dissatisfaction. Eur. Eat. Disord. Rev. (2020). https://doi.org/10.1002/erv.2730
46. Dodd, D.R., Velkoff, E.A., Forrest, L.N., et al.: Beauty in the eye of the beholder: Using facial electromyography to examine the association between eating disorder symptoms and perceptions of emaciation among undergraduate women. Body Image **21**, 47–56 (2017). https://doi.org/10.1016/j.bodyim.2017.02.002

Examining Independent Podcasts in Portuguese iTunes

Maria João Antunes[1](✉) [ID] and Ramón Salaverría[2] [ID]

[1] Department of Communication and Art, University of Aveiro,
Campus Universitário de Santiago, 3810-193 Aveiro, Portugal
`mariajoao@ua.pt`
[2] University of Navarra, School of Communication,
31080 Pamplona, Navarra, Spain
`rsalaver@unav.es`

Abstract. The purpose of this paper is to compare and analyse a sample of podcasts, using the most popular podcasts of iTunes (Top 200 podcasts - Portugal). The data was collected in two different dates (October 1st 2018 and October 15th 2019), using a Portuguese Apple ID. Results show that in October 2018 few Portuguese independent podcasts were presented among the top 200 podcasts in iTunes (22 podcasts). The authors/producers were mostly male persons. The podcasts were mainly dedicated to entertainment (comedy), and the contents were characterized by a freedom of expression impossible to include into any commercial or public media. In October 2019 the top 200 podcasts in iTunes (Portugal) presents a higher number of Portuguese independent podcasts (35 podcasts). The podcasts were included in a greater diversity of categories (e.g. entertainment, society, health & well-being, and politics). There is an increasing integration of podcasting with other services and social networks, including website/blogs, Instagram, YouTube, and Facebook. Among the most popular contents it was noticed a greater parity between authors/producers (men *versus* women).

Keywords: Independent podcasts · iTunes · Portugal

1 Introduction

Podcasts have become an important audio content over the last years, particularly in the United States of America [1]. In association with other new media, podcasts are an alternative platform to delivery contents and engage with niche audiences [2].

From an authors' perspective, podcasts offer, with a low investment, the opportunity to express themselves, to get some public attention, to create a community, and receive feedback that help them to improve their skills [3, 4]. At the same time, in the process involved in podcast production podcasters also have fun [4]. From listeners perspective, this medium offers, also at an affordable price, a means to acquire new knowledge and entertainment [5]. Podcasting is fostering a new relationship, more informal, between authors and listeners, and creating a more informal genre of audio narrative [6].

© Springer Nature Switzerland AG 2020
C. Stephanidis and M. Antona (Eds.): HCII 2020, CCIS 1226, pp. 149–153, 2020.
https://doi.org/10.1007/978-3-030-50732-9_20

In Portugal the attention to podcasting is recent. In 2019, 34,0% of Portuguese population listened to a podcast in the last month [7]. The listeners are mainly male (56,0%), and young, between 18 and 24 years old (52,4%). Smartphones and tablets are the most used devices for podcast listening [8]. However, the patterns of Portuguese podcast production were not yet examined, so this paper adds some interesting findings to understand and to map the Portuguese production of independent podcasts.

After a brief introduction to some theoretical ideas underpinning this study, this paper describes the research methodology followed for data collection. Once the methodology is introduced, the paper presents its main results. The paper ends presenting the final remarks and the limitations of the study.

2 Methodology

The paper studied a sample of audio podcasts created by Portuguese users. The sample was extracted based on the list of the 200 most popular audio podcasts on iTunes (Top Audio Podcasts), in two different dates (October 1st 2018 and October 15th 2019), using a Portuguese ID account.

The 200 podcasts were categorized in five different groups ("non Portuguese podcasts"; podcasts generated by Portuguese "radio/newspapers/tv"; Portuguese "commercial podcasts"; Portuguese "UCC podcasts" and "others"). Table 1 gives a summary of this distribution.

Table 1. Top 200 podcasts (Portugal)

Categories	October 1st 2018 (N = 200)	October 15th 2019 (N = 200)
Non Portuguese	93	88
Radio/newspaper/tv	82	72
Commercial	1	1
UCC	22	35
Others	2	4

The concept of User Created Content (UCC) can be interpreted in two senses, according to the definition of OECD [9]. Firstly, as content made publicly available over the internet, and creative effort put into its elaboration. Secondly, as content created with or without a financial reward basis.

The podcasts, integrated in the Portuguese UCC category, were analysed according to six topics:

- Authorship (female, male);
- Category (Art & Culture; Children & Youth; Entertainment; Fiction; Health & Well-being; Information; Politics; Science & Technology; Society; Sport and Other). These categories do not match the categories defined in iTunes.
- Frequency of episodes' publication;
- Longevity (number of months/years since podcast creation);

- Funding model (advertisement, crowdfunding, branded content, sponsorship, none);
- Related services/media (website and social media).

3 Findings

The presentation of results (Table 2) is organized according to the topics introduced in the previous section.

Table 2. Topics analysed in Portuguese UCC podcasts

Topics analysed	October 1st 2018 (n = 22)	October 15th 2019 (n = 35)
Authorship*		
Female	4	18
Male	33	33
Category		
Art & Culture	4	3
Children & Youth	–	–
Entertainment	13	16
Fiction	–	1
Health & Well-being	1	3
Information	–	1
Politics	1	2
Science & Technology	1	–
Society	2	6
Sport	–	1
Other	–	2
Frequency of episodes' publication		
Weekly	13	20
Fortnightly	3	–
Monthly	–	2
Variable	6	13
Longevity		
2013	1	1
2014	–	–
2015	3	2
2016	4	1
2017	9	7
2018	5	8
2019	———	16
Funding model		
Advertisement	1	3
Branded content	7	9
Crowdfunding	4	6
Sponsorship	2	2
None	8	15

(*continued*)

Table 2. (*continued*)

Topics analysed	October 1st 2018 (n = 22)	October 15th 2019 (n = 35)
Related services/Media**		
Website/blog	2	12
Facebook	16	21
Instagram	9	21
Twitter	5	10
YouTube	6	14
Pinterest	–	1
None	3	2

* Some podcasts have more than 1 author.
** Some podcasts have 2 or more related services/media.

The findings of this study indicate that the podcast production in Portugal, either as individual authorship or as co-authorship, is mainly led by men. However, in the comparison between 2018 and 2019, there was a significant increase in women's participation. Among the UCC podcasts analysed, there is a predominance of products included in the entertainment category, with emphasis on comedy. In this type of podcasts, informality and slang language are usual. In 2019, the second place in the top belongs to fictional podcast series, where the author interprets all the characters. "Society" category has, in 2019, some prominence. It includes podcasts about nowadays interests, like environment and sustainability, parenting, and personal development.

Some popular categories in traditional media (television, radio or newspapers), such as information, sports and politics, have little presence in terms of the top 200 podcasts in Portugal. There is no podcast integrating the "Children & Youth" category, and technology (gadgets) was only present at the top in 2018. Most podcasts have a weekly episode's publishing pace, which demonstrates the great involvement with their production and the desire to engage the audiences. In 2019, 13 podcasts have a variable publication periodicity, sometimes weekly, sometimes fortnightly or even monthly, which also reveals the non-professional nature of their authors.

The less recent podcasts integrate the categories of culture (2), technology (1) and some are cult products in the entertainment area (2). A high number of podcasts does not have any funding model. When authors considered to monetize their contents, they do it mainly by using branded content and crowdfunding (Patreon).

Between 2018 and 2019, there is a notable increase on the presence of podcasts programs on web service/platforms. The presence of podcasts programs on Instagram is, in 2019, equal to the presence of programs on Facebook (21 podcasts in 2019). Only one website (about parenting) also choose to have a presence on Pinterest.

4 Final Remarks and Research Limitations

The study presented in this paper was based on a sample of popular independent UCC podcasts, collected in two different dates of October 2018 and October 2019 in Portugal. Through this study, it was possible to conclude that between 2018 and 2019 there was an increase in the number of Portuguese UCC podcasts, presented in the top of 200 podcasts in iTunes (Portugal). It was noticed an empowerment of women in the authorship/presentation of podcasts, and an increase in the diversity of contents listened by audiences, with entertainment keeping its leadership. To engage with audiences, podcasts authors are using different social networks and creating related websites or blogs. In Portugal the set of independent podcasts studied seems to have the potential to offer some deviations from the mainstream sound platforms (e.g. radio), where information, music, talk-shows and magazines are common contents. Independent podcasts are offering a more specific content, aiming to target an increasingly fragmented audience.

The study has limitations inherent to the chosen methodology and the analysis performed. The analysed podcasts start from a sample of a top podcast on a single platform (iTunes). We acknowledge that drawing upon commercial rankings, such as the iTunes list of most popular podcasts, is not the most consistent way to select a sample of study, as these lists may be manipulated by platform owners or by the users themselves. Nevertheless, this is an exploratory study, so the results are at the moment indicative and not conclusive.

References

1. Reuters Institute Digital News Report 2018. http://media.digitalnewsreport.org/wp-content/uploads/2018/06/digital-news-report-2018.pdf. Accessed 17 Mar 2020
2. Symons, A.: Podcast comedy and 'authentic outsiders': how new media is challenging the owners of industry. Celebrity Stud. 8(1), 104–118 (2017)
3. Sienkiewicz, M., Jaramillo, D.: Podcasting, the intimate self, and the public sphere. Popular Commun. 17(4), 268–272 (2019)
4. Markman, K., Sawyer, C.: Why pod? further explorations of the motivations for independent podcasting. J. Radio Audio Media 21(1), 20–35 (2014)
5. Samuel-Azran, T., Laor, T., Tal, D.: Who listens to podcasts, and why?: the Israeli case. Online Inf. Rev. 43(4), 482–495 (2019)
6. McHugh, S.: Radio J. Int. Stud. Broadcast Audio Media 14(1), 65–82 (2016)
7. Reuters Institute Digital News Report 2019. https://reutersinstitute.politics.ox.ac.uk/sites/default/files/inline-files/DNR_2019_FINAL.pdf. Accessed 19 Mar 2020
8. Digital News Report 2019 – Portugal. https://obercom.pt/wp-content/uploads/2019/12/RDNRP-WEB-SETEMBRO.pdf. Accessed 19 Mar 2020
9. OECD, Participative Web: User-Created Content. http://www.oecd.org/internet/ieconomy/38393115.pdf. Accessed 17 Mar 2020

An Analysis of Trends and Connections in Google, Twitter, and Wikipedia

Gianluca Conti, Giuseppe Sansonetti[(✉)], and Alessandro Micarelli

Department of Engineering, Roma Tre University,
Via della Vasca Navale 79, 00146 Rome, Italy
{gsansone,ailab}@dia.uniroma3.it

Abstract. In this paper, we propose a system for extracting, storing, and analyzing the data provided by three well-known and widespread services available online. More specifically, the system can automatically collect a real-world dataset for a selected language and/or geographical region and match similar trends expressed through different keywords. Unlike previous studies in the same area, we avoided to focus on a specific aspect and explored which resonance different topics may have between one source and another, and how quickly each source generally reacts to external events.

Keywords: Trend analysis · Aggregated data · Social network analysis · Sentiment analysis

1 Introduction and Background

Within a few years, the Internet has become the crossroads of the active information and opinion of a huge and ever-growing number of users. Google, Twitter, and Wikipedia represent three of the main references worldwide, each of them with different perspectives and usages. All three services provide up-to-date data related to search trends: *Google Trends*[1], *Twitter Trending Topics*[2], *Wikipedia Trending Articles*[3]. Google updates its data every hour, Twitter every five minutes, and Wikipedia on a daily basis. If taken individually, this data provides useful information to comprehend the current users' interests and opinions [14,25]. However, it is possible to obtain even richer information by crossing and comparing this data with each other [17,18]. In this paper, we propose a system based on two main components: *(i)* a modular extraction architecture to collect, normalize, and enrich the trends of Google, Twitter, and Wikipedia and automatically build a dataset for a selected language; *(ii)* a set of analysis tools to extract general results, but also to examine individual case studies. The system aims to determine possible connections and general behaviors that link trends

---

[1] https://trends.google.com/trends/.
[2] https://twitter.com/.
[3] https://en.wikipedia.org/.

© Springer Nature Switzerland AG 2020
C. Stephanidis and M. Antona (Eds.): HCII 2020, CCIS 1226, pp. 154–160, 2020.
https://doi.org/10.1007/978-3-030-50732-9_21

from various sources together. The architecture allows us to collect datasets just by selecting the language and the sampling interval, thus choosing the time granularity and the geographical area. Unlike other contributions [1,16], we also evaluated the matching among keywords in every subset of the three sources. To this aim, we implemented and tested a set of matching algorithms to find the best approach in the specific domain. Furthermore, the system can also collect information about sentiment in the Google-Twitter subset. The analysis of aggregated data such as trends and time-series - apart from a few notable exceptions (e.g., see [13,24]) - is a relatively new research field, which heavily relies on the available data and their level of detail. While certain results have a relative value strongly conditioned by the time window and the events, other findings can be confirmed and generalized using multiple datasets and intervals. The main contributions of this paper are thus the following:

1. an architecture to collect and analyze data extracted from the aforementioned services;
2. algorithms for matching analysis between different keywords;
3. preliminary results on real-world datasets that demonstrate the potential offered by the system.

The paper is structured as follows. In Sect. 2, we sketch the overall system architecture and describe in detail each of the four modules that compose it. The preliminary results of the experimental evaluation performed on the collected datasets are reported and discussed in Sect. 3. In Sect. 4, we draw our conclusions and outline some possible future developments of the system as well as its feasible applications.

2   The Proposed Approach

The overall architecture of the proposed system is shown in Fig. 1. It consists of four main modules. First of all, we can find an extraction component, which provides a set of functions to get the trends through the available APIs. Then, the processing module builds a list of matching keywords for each subset of the three sources using a hybrid algorithm based on syntactic and heuristic criteria. Besides, this module also takes a sample of tweets for each topic belonging to the Google-Twitter subset and performs a sentiment analysis [9] on each topic, saving the detailed results of each tweet for further processing. The remaining modules are used to store data in a non-relational database[4] and to perform a continuous execution through an Amazon EC2[5] remote server, thus constructing the dataset. The execution interval is defined according to the desired results, and our datasets were built at hourly intervals. More specifically, the trend matching problem was addressed using a test set built out of a 1000 h dataset, generated in the United States in 40 days. The set includes all the hardest false negatives

---

[4] https://www.mongodb.com/.
[5] https://aws.amazon.com/ec2/.

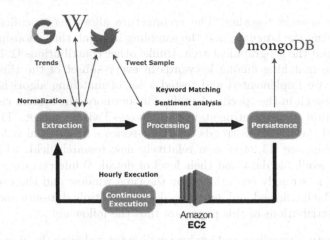

Fig. 1. The overall system architecture consisting of four main modules.

and false positives available, and a list of queries of minor difficulty. The first approach was semantic [5], using various knowledge bases such as DBpedia[6]. While this approach is reasonable for Wikipedia, the domain of trends in Google and Twitter could be considered unlimited and unpredictable, thus causing too many false negatives. The second approach was syntactic and involved the use of algorithms like sequence matching, fuzzy matching, and more. The resulting algorithm exploits a combination of fuzzy matching and a set of empirically defined domain rules, such as differentiated management of acronyms. Fuzzy matching makes use of the Levenshtein distance to estimate the basic similarity. The final algorithm can correctly recognize every couple in the test set without false positives for a certain threshold value, with encouraging values of Precision and Recall (see Fig. 2). The sentiment analysis is performed using the SentiStrength[7] tool on a set of more than 500 tweets per topic, considering scalar and trinary scores.

3 Experimental Evaluation

The experimental results were extracted from a 1000 h dataset containing the U.S. trends, and a 300 h dataset containing the Italy trends to validate the result, when possible. Another strategy to validate and generalize the results was to consider and compare different time windows on the same dataset. More specifically, the analysis functions made the most of the dataset structure, with three main types of analysis:

---

[6] https://wiki.dbpedia.org/.
[7] http://sentistrength.wlv.ac.uk/.

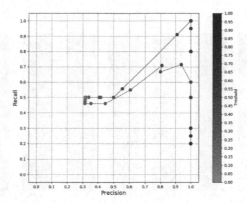

Fig. 2. Results of a comparative analysis in terms of performance between the sequence matching algorithm (red line) and the final algorithm (grey line). (Color figure online)

- **Sentiment and polarization:** we estimated how much trends were polarized or strongly polarized using the trinary score of each tweet, for each topic. Furthermore, we also evaluated the sentiment distribution for every collected topic;
- **Supervised classification:** we classified trends of each group (i.e., the three sources and each subset) in a set of predefined classes;
- **Life cycle and first-time occurrence:** we determined the life cycle of each trend, also taking into account its multiple occurrences and the possible transition interval among them. This analysis identified the first-time occurrence of trends as well, considering only those that appeared in at least two sources.

The above functions could also be combined. Looking at the reactivity value (see Fig. 3), the results for each dataset show that Twitter is the fastest service to react to new trends. Only Wikipedia has a significant delay, since it updates its data every 24 h, while Google and Twitter are updated hourly or even less. The

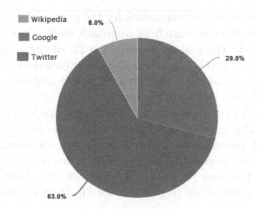

Fig. 3. The mean reactivity value of each source for each dataset.

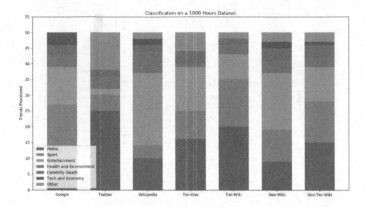

Fig. 4. Results of a topic-based classification on the U.S. dataset.

classification process is performed using a set of classes. Unlike other approaches, the number of classes for each set is minimized to avoid overlaps and difficult interpretations. The classification results are shown in Fig. 4. They were obtained through a topic-based classification, which required domain knowledge and a supervised approach. In particular, only the top 50 trends for each group are reported.

4   Conclusions

In this paper, we have presented a flexible and automatic architecture to collect data provided by Google, Twitter, and Wikipedia. The system can also analyze rich datasets of trends for a selected language and/or geographical region, using a given time granularity. We experimented with two real-world datasets to determine and explore some general behaviors and connections between different sources. We addressed the trend matching problem as well, testing a set of semantic and syntactic algorithms to connect two different queries referring to the same entity.

There are many possible developments for the proposed system. For instance, we plan to develop a different matching approach making use of a semantic [11] component and to test the real-time operation [2] of the system using stream trends data. The mentioned analysis can also be extended to obtain other results and explore other social and web platforms. The applications of the system can be manifold as well. For example, its results can be integrated with data of a different nature, such as temporal dynamics [22], attitudes [8], and web browsing activities [12]. The inferred information could also be exploited to improve the performance of personalized systems, such as recommender systems [20]. The application scenarios could be varied, from those related to points of interest [21] such as restaurants [4] to social networks [10], from news [7] to cultural heritage [23], from music [19] to movies [3], from research papers [15] to e-commerce [6].

References

1. Althoff, T., Borth, D., Hees, J., Dengel, A.: Analysis and forecasting of trending topics in online media streams. In: Proceedings of the 21st ACM International Conference on Multimedia, MM 2013, p. 907916. ACM, New York (2013)
2. Arru, G., Feltoni Gurini, D., Gasparetti, F., Micarelli, A., Sansonetti, G.: Signal-based user recommendation on Twitter. In: Proceedings of the 22nd International Conference on World Wide Web, WWW 2013 Companion, pp. 941–944. ACM, New York (2013)
3. Biancalana, C., Gasparetti, F., Micarelli, A., Miola, A., Sansonetti, G.: Context-aware movie recommendation based on signal processing and machine learning. In: Proceedings of the 2nd Challenge on Context-Aware Movie Recommendation, CAMRa 2011, pp. 5–10. ACM, New York (2011)
4. Biancalana, C., Gasparetti, F., Micarelli, A., Sansonetti, G.: An approach to social recommendation for context-aware mobile services. ACM Trans. Intell. Syst. Technol. 4(1), 10:1–10:31 (2013)
5. Biancalana, C., Gasparetti, F., Micarelli, A., Sansonetti, G.: Social semantic query expansion. ACM Trans. Intell. Syst. Technol. 4(4), 60:1–60:43 (2013)
6. Bologna, C., De Rosa, A.C., De Vivo, A., Gaeta, M., Sansonetti, G., Viserta, V.: Personality-based recommendation in e-commerce. In: CEUR Workshop Proceedings, vol. 997. CEUR-WS.org, Aachen (2013)
7. Caldarelli, S., Feltoni Gurini, D., Micarelli, A., Sansonetti, G.: A signal-based approach to news recommendation. In: CEUR Workshop Proceedings, vol. 1618. CEUR-WS.org, Aachen (2016)
8. Feltoni Gurini, D., Gasparetti, F., Micarelli, A., Sansonetti, G.: iSCUR: interest and sentiment-based community detection for user recommendation on Twitter. In: Dimitrova, V., Kuflik, T., Chin, D., Ricci, F., Dolog, P., Houben, G.-J. (eds.) UMAP 2014. LNCS, vol. 8538, pp. 314–319. Springer, Cham (2014). https://doi.org/10.1007/978-3-319-08786-3_27
9. Feltoni Gurini, D., Gasparetti, F., Micarelli, A., Sansonetti, G.: Enhancing social recommendation with sentiment communities. In: Wang, J., et al. (eds.) WISE 2015. LNCS, vol. 9419, pp. 308–315. Springer, Cham (2015). https://doi.org/10.1007/978-3-319-26187-4_28
10. Feltoni Gurini, D., Gasparetti, F., Micarelli, A., Sansonetti, G.: Temporal people-to-people recommendation on social networks with sentiment-based matrix factorization. Future Gener. Comput. Syst. 78, 430–439 (2018)
11. Fogli, A., Sansonetti, G.: Exploiting semantics for context-aware itinerary recommendation. Pers. Ubiquit. Comput. 23(2), 215–231 (2019). https://doi.org/10.1007/s00779-018-01189-7
12. Gasparetti, F., Micarelli, A., Sansonetti, G.: Exploiting web browsing activities for user needs identification. In: 2014 International Conference on Computational Science and Computational Intelligence, vol. 2, pp. 86–89, March 2014
13. Giummolè, F., Orlando, S., Tolomei, G.: Trending topics on Twitter improve the prediction of Google hot queries. Università Ca' Foscari Venezia, Dipartimento di Scienze Ambientali, Informatica e Statistica (2013)
14. Hal, V., Hyunyoung, C.: Predicting the present with google trends. Economic Record (2009)
15. Hassan, H.A.M., Sansonetti, G., Gasparetti, F., Micarelli, A., Beel, J.: BERT, ELMo, USE and InferSent sentence encoders: the Panacea for research-paper recommendation? In: Tkalcic, M., Pera, S. (eds.) Proceedings of ACM RecSys 2019 Late-Breaking Results, vol. 2431, pp. 6–10. CEUR-WS.org (2019)

16. Higgins, B., Lai, J.: Predicting mass movements with public data. Stanford University (2016)
17. Mahroum, N., et al.: Leveraging Google Trends, Twitter, and Wikipedia to Investigate the Impact of a Celebrity's Death from Rheumatoid Arthritis. Wolters Kluwer Health, Inc., Waltham (2018)
18. Marcin, I., Shiu, S.: Extracting topic trends and connections: semantic analysis and topic linking in Twitter and Wikipedia datasets. Stanford University (2012)
19. Onori, M., Micarelli, A., Sansonetti, G.: A comparative analysis of personality-based music recommender systems. In: CEUR Workshop Proceedings, vol. 1680, pp. 55–59. CEUR-WS.org, Aachen (2016)
20. Ricci, F., Rokach, L., Shapira, B.: Recommender Systems Handbook, 2nd edn. Springer, Heidelberg (2015). https://doi.org/10.1007/978-1-4899-7637-6
21. Sansonetti, G.: Point of interest recommendation based on social and linked open data. Pers. Ubiquit. Comput. **23**(2), 199–214 (2019). https://doi.org/10.1007/s00779-019-01218-z
22. Sansonetti, G., Feltoni Gurini, D., Gasparetti, F., Micarelli, A.: Dynamic social recommendation. In: Proceedings of the 2017 IEEE/ACM International Conference on Advances in Social Networks Analysis and Mining 2017, ASONAM 2017, pp. 943–947. ACM, New York (2017)
23. Sansonetti, G., Gasparetti, F., Micarelli, A., Cena, F., Gena, C.: Enhancing cultural recommendations through social and linked open data. User Model. User-Adap. Inter. **29**(1), 121–159 (2019). https://doi.org/10.1007/s11257-019-09225-8
24. Schaer, O., Kourentzes, N., Fildes, R.: Demand forecasting with user-generated online information. Int. J. Forecast. **35**, 197–212 (2018)
25. Zubiaga, A., Spina, D., Fresno, V., Martínez, R.: Classifying trending topics: a typology of conversation triggers on Twitter. In: Proceedings of the 20th ACM International Conference on Information and Knowledge Management, pp. 2461–2464. ACM (2011)

University Online Counseling: Recommended Model Using iOS and Android

Krenar Huseini, Neshat Ajruli, and Agon Memeti(✉)

Faculty of Natural Sciences and Mathematics, University of Tetova,
Tetova, North Macedonia
agon.memeti@unite.edu.mk

Abstract. The growing impact over smart phone increases the development of mobile application for educational counseling. The main idea of this paper is to recommend a mobile application model that is used for Guidance and Counselling services. The application is designed specifically for the university and university students, and as a case study it uses University of Tetova. The proposed model is an effort of helping learners develop educational and academic results, personal life, social life, learning activities, as well as planning their career development. It also helps overcome the obstacles and problems faced by learners.

The educational guidance for the students helps them gain good results, the drawbacks that they suffer with the university get recognized and the student needs within the educational system are satisfied and fulfilled. It also helps them discover and develop self-confidence, independency, responsibleness, have self-concept, accept and appreciate the unique characteristics and abilities. We have tried to focus on two main components while proposing the model and developing the app: To give the students the easiest and most convenient user experience & to make it easy for the institution to keep the students informed about school activities.

Keywords: Smart phones · Mobile application · iOS · Android · Recommended model

1 Introduction

The proposed model is designed specifically for the university and university students, and as a case study it uses the University of Tetova; it is an effort of helping learners develop educational and academic results, personal life, social life, learning activities, as well as planning their career development. It also helps overcome the obstacles and problems faced by learners.

It uses the Firebase Realtime Database to store information about students and every university event. The database has detailed information about the office of education, international relations office and their contact details. We fetch every ounce of data from our website and google sheets using REST API.

The administrator has been given permission to access the database information and make changes to this information. The students and staff are given their own university

© Springer Nature Switzerland AG 2020
C. Stephanidis and M. Antona (Eds.): HCII 2020, CCIS 1226, pp. 161–168, 2020.
https://doi.org/10.1007/978-3-030-50732-9_22

generated emails that allow them to register in our application. They log in to the application in their smart phone with the email and password provided by the university and view necessary information such as the schedule, exams, events and news. The interaction between student and staff, staff and administrator, and student and administrator is made easy.

Based on our own experience we noticed that there is a necessity for a platform where students can interact with each other and that is how we came up with the idea of building a forum inside of our proposed model. The forum will allow interaction between students that belong to the same study program because this will reduce confusion and increase the workflow and so they will use it to solve problems that are not divulged in lectures.

After logging in, the students will get the schedule and event details based on their study program and everything is only one click away.

The university library will also be included in the app so students can see which books are in stock and available. In order to improve the teaching and scientific activity, strengthen the academic freedom, institutional transparency, articulate all the different needs, demands and concerns, we have also integrated our online student platform "Kujdesi per ty/We Care".

Also included in the app will be every academic calendar so the user doesn't have to do a deep search for them on the website.

The proposed implemented model will provide a new and better experience for students. With digital spectrum evolving every single day, the paper will help in solving the gap of reducing the time a student takes to access a certain information in our user-friendly environment.

This paper is composed into three parts. The first part is review of similar work done by other people in this area. The second one represents the proposed model of the app, containing information about how the app is designed in the background whereas the last part describes the implementation and the design of the proposed model.

2   Related Work

Based on [1] authors propose a platform that offers operations to support distance learning. Northern Illinois University also is a similar application with the proposed application in this study, which helps the Northern Illinois University students have all the information in their pockets.

Harvard University's mobile application has a people directory, a map of the campus, a shuttle tracker, dining options, news and events, as well as the course administration and admission operations, and it also provides social networking, and library options. The App allows the users to customize the icons on the homepage so that they can only see the options they would like to [2].

The University of Michigan's mobile application offers course information, including grades, course resources and announcements. Users can send documents to print stations. The application also provides real-time bus routes, dining menus, news, a phone directory, a campus map, an events calendar, career Centre information, travel registry tips and emergency contacts. The students can locate open seats at campus computer labs, search in the university library catalog and use mobile library resources. The application also offers a feature to make donations from the mobile device [3].

According [4] the application supports user management and the functionality of the application changes based on user's group. Different authors also mention several benefits of using it, according [5] mobile app allows us to be aware of what is going on in our locality.

Our University shares information through the University's website and from Google Spreadsheets, the problem was that the students had to search too much for the information that they wanted to get.

The implemented model fetch this data using Restful Services. Restful Services are a set of principles, lighter than SOAP-based Web Services, due to its simplicity, heterogeneity and web-based format. Entities/Resources are identified by unique URLs, including how resource states are addressed and transferred over HTTP by a wide range of clients written in different languages. All Google Spreadsheet JSON URLs are stored in a Firebase Realtime Database and used later.

The students' information is gathered after they verify their account, we only collect simple data so that we can provide them only with the information they need and this helps us make the students user experience much better.

3   Proposed Recommended Model

Today with the rapid development in computer technology it's difficult to choose the right tools for software development.

Smartphone came onto the consumer market in the late 90s, but only gained mainstream popularity with the introduction of Apple's iPhone in 2007. The iPhone revolutionized the industry by offering customer friendly features such as a touch screen interface and a virtual keyboard. The first smartphone running on Android was introduced to the consumer market in late 2008. The smartphone industry has been steadily developing and growing since then, both in market size, as well as in models and suppliers. By 2021, over a third of the world's population is projected to own a smartphone, an estimated total of almost 3.6 billion smartphone users in the world. According to [6], Android additionally offers flexible coding and rapid development that allows a short time span of implementing of different ideas into something concrete.

There were two options, to use a native language or a cross-platform one, because of the tight deadline we went with Xamarin which is a cross-platform language developed by Microsoft. Unlike traditional hybrid solutions, based on web technologies, a cross-platform app built with Xamarin, can still be classified as native.

Component-based development is also used that re-establishes the idea of reuse. With this approach the application was built by assembling some components that already had been developed and prepared for integration. Software components are artefacts identified such as classes or frameworks, Fig. 1.

The proposed platform in this paper aims to provide a solution that will collect data from existing services that are used by the University of Tetova and represent them in a single platform, Fig. 2.

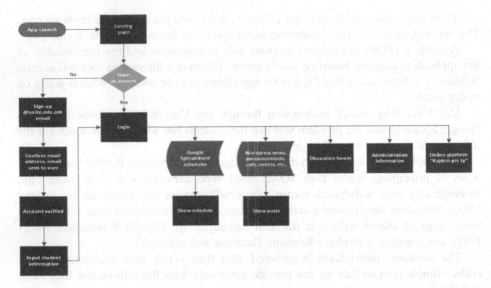

Fig. 1. Proposed recommended model scheme

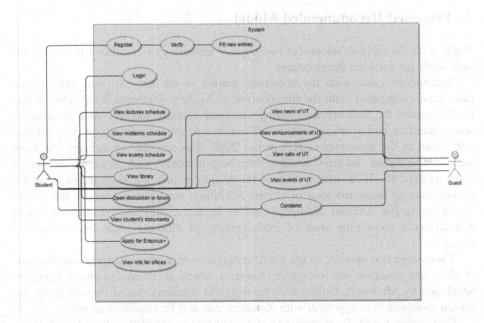

Fig. 2. Proposed platform UseCase diagram

As seen in Fig. 1, there are two types of users interacting with the platform, on one side is the registered user or the student and on the other is the guest.

The student has more privileges than the guest because this platform is meant for them and they have to get registered in order for us to have the necessary information on what they are studying. Also to be able to use the built in forum to communicate with other students of the same program.

On the other side the guest has access to only information available to the public and they don't need to register to view them.

4 Proposed Model Implementation

The mobile platform proposed in this paper, entitled UnitEd - University of Tetova consists of two main activities, collecting data from existing services using Rest API and using a cloud-hosted database to enable seamless real-time communication between students of the same study program.

The *MainActivity* as a main class of the platform is to integrate existing in-house services through Service Architecture Approach (by exporting data as basic services) based on reuse approach, and then deploying them in the cloud. Then we share these information's with the users based on the program they are studying and this way they are just one click away from the information they are searching for. Also by using Restful Services we collect data that is published directly from the university's administration, they don't need to publish data in our application and we don't need to publish it ourselves.

Following is the method of *MainActivity* that handles the JSON data, deserializes them and displays them, Fig. 3.

The first time when the user opens the schedule the JSON data gets downloaded on the users phone, this enables the user to view the data offline and allows him to update the data when he has access to the internet.

The *SecondActivity* is another activity that allows students to communicate seemlessly with each other using the build-in forum. Data is stored as JSON and synchronized in realtime to every connected user. Data is persisted locally, and even while offline, realtime events continue to fire, giving the end user a responsive experience. This is all made possible by using Firebase Realtime Database. The forum is designed to be user-friendly and responsive. In order to reduce confusion and increase productivity we decided to make the communication possible only between students of the same study program. The Firebase Realtime Database lets you build rich, collaborative applications by allowing secure access to the database directly from client-side code. It can be accessed directly from a mobile device or web browser; there's no need for an application server [7].

The forum contains two simple methods *CreatePost* and *CreateComment*. This activity can be accessed from the *Options Menu* of the application. Following are the methods *CreatePost* and *CreateComment* and how they are displayed on the app (Fig. 4):

```
public async Task<List<Models.ScheduleJSON.Entry>> DeserializeJsonAsync(string loadType, string url = "")
{
    string result = "";
    // Try to get data from phone if it exists
    if (loadType == "local")
    {
        result = helper.GetLocalData("LecturesData");
    }
    // Try to get data from internet
    else if (loadType == "internet")
    {
        result = await helper.GetLatestJsonAsync(url);
        await helper.SaveLocallyAsync(result, "LecturesData");
    }

    Models.ScheduleJSON.RootObject root = JsonConvert.DeserializeObject<Models.ScheduleJSON.RootObject>(result);
    // Remove 5 rows of unnecessary content
    root.feed.entry.RemoveRange(0, 5);
    return root.feed.entry;
}
```

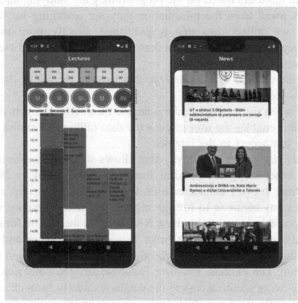

Fig. 3. Displaying the JSON data

```
public async Task CreatePost(string postid, string postauthorname, string postauthorlastname, string posttitle,
    string postcontent , DateTime posttime, string postprogram, string imageurl)
    {
        await firebase
            .Child("ForumPosts")
            .PostAsync(new ForumPosts() { PostID = postid, PostAuthorName = postauthorname,
                        PostAuthorLastName = postauthorlastname, PostTitle = posttitle,
                            PostContent = postcontent, PostTime = posttime, PostProgram = postprogram , PostImage = imageurl});
    }
public async Task CreateComment(string commentid, string postid, string commentauthorname, string commentauthorlastname,
                    string commentcontent, DateTime commentime, string commentimage)
    {
        await firebase
            .Child("ForumComments")
            .PostAsync(new ForumComments() { CommentID = commentid, PostID = postid, CommentAuthorName = commentauthorname,
                        CommentAuthorLastName = commentauthorlastname,
                            CommentContent = commentcontent, CommentTime = commentime,CommentImage = commentimage });
    }
```

Fig. 4. Displaying the build-in forum

5 Conclusion

Mobile applications are inevitable in today's modern information society and nowadays it is the era of mobile services.

Component Reusability, Restful services and a real time database are a challenging task and obviously the future trend of building web-based and mobile applications.

In this paper we have presented an architecture of a mobile application, named UnitEd - University of Tetova, which will enable students to easily check the necessary information like schedule, exams, events, news and communicate seamlessly with other students of the same study program.

In the near future we will implement more features to the application, such as push notifications, reminders, class attendance, and professor roles.

References

1. Ahmed, T.H., et al.: A design of mobile application for university management systems using android. Int. J. Inf. Technol. **3**, 6–11 (2017)
2. Harvard Mobile by Harvard University. https://itunes.apple.com/us/app/harvard-mobile/id389199460?mt=8. Accessed 20 Aug 2014
3. University of Michigan Mobile Apps Center. http://mobileapps.its.umich.edu/michigan-app. Accessed 20 Aug 2014
4. Yilmazel, O., et al.: Mobile applications at a Mega university: Anadolu university campus app. AAOU J. **10**, 13–21 (2015)
5. Abu Naser, S.S., et al.: Design and development of mobile university student guide. J. Multidiscip. Eng. Sci. Stud. **2**, 193–197 (2016)
6. Android Development. https://qz.com/826672/android-goog-just-hit-a-record-88-market-share-of-all-smartphones/. Accessed 11 Mar 2020
7. Firebase. https://firebase.google.com/docs. Accessed 13 Mar 2020

Does Social Media Close the Political Efficacy Gap to Participate in Politics?

Hyesun Hwang[✉]

Department of Consumer Science, Sungkyunkwan University, Seoul, Korea
h.hwang@skku.edu

Abstract. This study examined the effects of social media use on the intention to participate in politics. This study used Korean Youth and Children Integrated Survey published by the National Youth Policy Institute in South Korea. The effects of social media dependency and interest in socio-political issues on the intention to participate in politics were verified using a general linear model. Social media dependency, socio-political interest, and political efficacy all had significant main effects on the intent to participate in politics; the interaction effect of 'social media dependency × political efficacy' was significant. The result showed that young people who have greater political efficacy have much more intention to participate in politics when they more depend on social media for the purpose of acquiring social and political issues. Social media dependency has a moderating effect that closes the political efficacy gap.

Keywords: Social media · Political participation · Political efficacy · Social and political interests

1 Introduction

Over the past few decades, the Internet has had some prosocial effects by expanding socio-political information more than ever before, which lends consumers greater opportunities to participate in the process of establishing consumer policy. In recent years, social media has come to the fore due to its potential to change political variables strengthening the network and generating environments for discussion and participation with highly contextualized conversations based on broadly shared knowledge [1, 2]. Through the networked media based on the Internet that contributes to the collection, delivery, and exchange of the various opinions of those who would be regarded as passive audience members, democratic participation of consumers can be facilitated [3].

As social media have become tools to connect, communicate, and interact with other users of the media, people who have various opinions and values have become generative and proactive contributors of media content [4, 5]. Such consuming and generating user content on digital online media is regarded as a form of civic engagement and participation of ordinary people [6]. Consumers may benefit from the open and participatory nature of social media that enables them to be empowered and involved in the society, which indicates more sustainable community [7].

© Springer Nature Switzerland AG 2020
C. Stephanidis and M. Antona (Eds.): HCII 2020, CCIS 1226, pp. 169–176, 2020.
https://doi.org/10.1007/978-3-030-50732-9_23

This study focuses on young consumers' intention to participate in politics. In particular, the present study analyze the effects of social media use on the intention to participate in politics of Korean young consumers. Social media have had big impact on politics in Korea and the most obvious evidence is a radical change witnessed in the April 11 General Election of 2012 [8]. In this election, the voter turnout was increased for the first time since 1987, when the first direct presidential election was held in Korea. Also, the turnout among voters who were in their 20's was increased radically at 64% compared to 24.2% in the 2008 General Election, which is regarded as an outcome stimulated by social media [8].

Consumers' participation in politics is one of the important consumer behaviors to promote consumer rights. As consumers' participation in politics is the direct voice to the progress of policy toward advocacy for consumer rights, consumer participation can be considered as an important agenda of consumer education in a democratic society. The result of the present study can give implications to understand how social media affect young consumers' interests in social and political issues and stimulate them to participate in politics by raising their voice toward a society.

2 Background

2.1 Media Dependency

Media play a role in informing the public about social issues and facilitating communication in a society (Happer and Phiol 2013). Ball-Rokeach and DeFleur (1976) explained the interdependent relationship among media, audiences, and society using the media system dependency model. According to this model, an individual's dependency on media as resources of information changes both personal and social processes. According to this model, an individual's dependency on media as resources of information changes both personal and social processes.

Media dependency may be related to media use, but the influence of the message delivered through the media is more contingent on media dependency than on media use (Ball-Rokeach 1985); DeFleur and Ball-Rokeach (1989) emphasized that dependency alters the audience's cognition, feelings, and behaviors. In this sense, the present study employed the concept of social media dependency to investigate the relationship between social media use and political participation, focusing on the intrinsic meaning of media use.

Knowing that digital media have horizontal and decentralized dispositions, social media can be regarded as creating a civic space where individuals from diverse backgrounds are allowed to take part in political movements by reading, posting, and sharing various opinions, even though digitally networked activism is criticized for mobilizing less committed actions that have weak ties (Gil de Zúñiga, Jung, and Valenzuela 2012; Gladwell 2010; Juris 2012). In this sense, a research question (RQ1) and hypotheses (H1 and H2) were established:

RQ1. What are the relationship between young consumers' social media dependency and the interests in social and political issues?

H1. People who depend more on social media (High SMD) have more general and specific interests in social and political issues.

H2. High SMD's peer groups have more interests in social and political issues.

2.2 Social Media and Political Participation

According to a study on the relationship between media and political efficacy, the advent of the Internet carries a connotation for political effects [9], which is closely connected to the characteristics of the Internet, especially its openness. In this regard, the role of social media has been addressed as tools for coordinating social and political movements [10]. As social media can deliver messages about globalized social movements based on its decentralized and horizontal structure, individuals who have limited opportunity to express opinions and to participate in politics are empowered. In addition, it is asserted that larger and diversified networks deliver more mobilizing information and have a positive effect on participation [1].

Political information on social media provides a mix of content including the information itself, the publisher's previous posts, the publisher's friends, and the reactions of others [1, 11]. It means that the composition of one's network may influence on what information will be shared and how political issues will be discussed. By accessing political information through social media, individuals may feel united and that they are building a community, and they may perceive the possibility of expressing their opinions and influencing others. Thus, social media can inspire individual consumers to perceive the political world as if they can connect strong lines of force to the officialdom, which is defined as political efficacy that means a belief of a communicative relationship between oneself and the institutions that govern society [12].

To sum up, social media may function as resources for political information; in the process of information delivery, consumers acquire political information by sharing and discussing it with other social media users, which generates additional information that leads to better understanding. In line with this, RQ2 was established:

RQ2. How does social media use affect the intention to participate in politics?

3 Methods

3.1 Data

The data analyzed for this study is from the Korean Youth and Children Integrated Survey, published by the National Youth Policy Institute (2012) in South Korea. This survey provides not only general information on the social media usage of youths but also their political efficacy and intention to participate in politics. From 16 provinces in South Korea, 2,574 high school students and 2,302 young people in college responded to this survey; they were sampled using the stratified multi-stage sampling method. The respondents were face-to-face interviewed with a questionnaire. For the purpose of this study, young people who are using social media (Facebook or Twitter), who are 19 years and older, and who are entitled to vote were analyzed. There were 1,866 study subjects, 81.1% of the total sample of young people.

3.2 Measures

To measure social media dependency (SMD), a 4-point Likert question was asked: 'To what extent do you depend on social media for the purpose of acquiring social and political information?' (1 = *never depend on* to 4 = *heavily depend on*). To measure the interests in social and political issues, two 4-point Likert questions were asked. In particular, general interest (GI) and specific interest (SI) were measured using a 4-point Likert scale: 'To what extent are you interested in political and social issues in comparison to your friends?' and 'To what extent are you interested in the general election in 2012 in comparison to your friends?' (1 = *not at all* to 4 = *very much*). The peer group's interest in social and political issues (PI) was measured using a 4-point Likert scale: and 'To what extent are your friends on social media interested in social and political issues?' (1 = *not at all* to 4 = *very much*). The political efficacy (PE) is generally measured in two subparts: internal and external efficacy. This study focuses on internal political efficacy, which refers to one's confidence in his or her own political capacities. To measure internal efficacy, three items were made based on the prior studies [13–15]. The items referred to the subject's perceived capabilities to make a rational decision about national policy, about election candidates, and the extent to which he/she believes his/herself to be qualified to participate in politics. The intention to participate in politics (IPP) was measured by a question that asks about the extent of willingness to contribute to politics through active participation using a 4-point Likert scale (1 = *not at all* to 4 = *very much*).

3.3 Analysis

The mean differences of the interests in social and political issues including individual's general interests (GI), individual's specific interests (SI) and peer group's interests (PI) were verified using a t-test according to the level of social media dependency (SMD). The effects of interest in social issues and social media dependency on the intention to participate in politics in the future were verified with the interaction effects using a general linear model (GLM). Statistical analyses were conducted using the IBM SPSS 21.0 program.

4   Results

4.1   Description of Respondents

In this study, Facebook and/or Twitter users were analyzed. As shown in Table 1, 49% and 51% of respondents were men and women, respectively. The usage rates of other social media were 52% for Blog and 69% for Youtube. Of the respondents, 63% use social media almost every day.

Table 1. Description of the respondents (n = 1,866)

		Frequency (%)	
Gender	Male	912	(48.9)
	Female	954	(51.1)
Social media use	Facebook	1815	(97.3)
	Twitter	648	(34.7)
	Blog	972	(52.1)
	YouTube	1284	(68.8)

4.2 Media Dependency and Interest in Social and Political Issues

To analyze the difference of social and political interests according to one's SMD, the respondents were firstly classified into two groups: High SMD and Low SMD (High SMD = *'depend on'* and *'heavily depend on'*, Low SMD = *'never depend on' and 'not depend on'*). Of the respondents, 58.8% were classified into the high SMD group. As shown in Table 2, individuals had higher GI and SI in the group with higher SMD. Thus, H1 was supported. The mean differences between the groups were 0.154 ($t = 4.656$, $p < .001$) and 0.155 ($t = 4.230$, $p < .001$), respectively. In addition, the mean difference of PI between the groups was statistically significant ($t = 6.990$, $p < .001$) and H2 was supported. The results indicate that people who depend on social media tend to have more general and specific interest in social and political issues; their peer group is likely to be involved in social and political issues to a greater degree.

Table 2. Interest in social and political issues

	High SMD (n_1 = 1097)	Low SMD (n_2 = 769)	t
	Mean (SD)	Mean (SD)	
Individual general interests (GI)	2.39 (0.680)	2.24 (0.733)	4.656[***]
Individual specific interests (SI)	2.43 (0.764)	2.28 (0.802)	4.230[***]
Peer group interests (PI)	2.38 (0.691)	2.15 (0.738)	6.990[***]

***$p < .001$

4.3 Intention to Participate in Politics in the Future

As shown in Table 3, the effect of SMD on the IPP and the interaction effects were verified using a general linear model (RQ2). In this model, SMD, PE, and PI had significant main effects on the IPP. As shown in Table 3, the main effect of SMD, PI and PE had positive effects on IPP. The interaction effect of 'SMD × PE' was verified at a 5% significance level. As shown in Fig. 1, for the group possessing higher PE, the mean score of the IPP for those who depended more on social media was 2.17 and the mean difference was 0.22 ($t = 3.321$, $p < .001$). For the group of lower PE, the mean difference was only 0.08. This result shows that people who depend on social media more for political information have greater intention to participate in politics despite perceiving themselves as having less political efficacy.

Table 3. Result of general linear model of intentions to participate in politics

	Sum of squares	df	Mean square	F-value
SMD (high = 1)	5.197	1	5.197	10.064**
PI (high = 1)	21.583	1	21.583	41.796***
PE (high = 1)	99.352	1	99.352	192.402***
SMD × PE	1.983	1	1.983	3.841*
SMD × PI	.586	1	.586	1.135
PI × PE	.009	1	.009	.018

*$p < .05$. **$p < .01$. ***$p < .001$

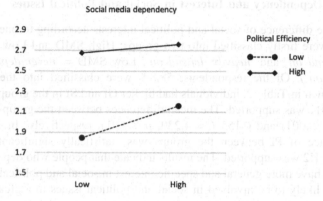

Fig. 1. Interaction effect of social media dependency × political efficacy

5   Conclusion

The advent of new media is closely associated with social processes by transforming methods of communication and expanding the parties involved in communication in society. This study focused on social media's effect on young consumers' political participation as a sphere of changing social processes. The results of this study imply that the conditions for political participation are changing with new media development, which may differentiate participation opportunities.

According to the level of social media dependency, the interest of individuals and that of their peer groups in social issues was higher for those with greater dependency on social media. The interest of individuals and their peer groups in social issues were higher for the group with high dependency, which shows that members of a social media network may have an interrelated influence on each other. As suggested in the previous study [1], the interaction among members of social media has a synergy because social media members build trusting relationships by exchanging information, which increases the media's potential. Thus, it can be assumed that young people who depend on social media and join a network would be exposed to more social and political information than those who do not. As social media becomes influential regarding social and political issues, a question is raised about the lack of opportunity to acquire political information and to participate in the social process for those who do not use, or who depend less on, social media. By understanding the phenomenon that young people are more likely to depend on social media for access to political information, progress can be made to close the gap caused by different media usage.

Lastly, social media dependency, political efficacy and peer group interest all had significant main effects on the intent to participate in politics and the interaction effect of 'social media dependency × political efficacy' was significant. In particular, the association between political efficacy and intention to participate in politics was moderated by social media dependency. The intention was much higher for the group with greater political efficacy; the mean difference between the low and high social media dependency groups was greater for the low political efficacy group. As the conditions for political participation are changing, discussion of how to take advantage of the changing conditions for a democratic society has taken place and been tracked for decades; with the changing media environment, a way to enhance political participation may also be found. According to the result, social media dependency has a moderating effect that closes the political efficacy gap.

A major contribution of this study lies in its demonstrating the association between young consumers' social media use and their political participation. In the perspective of the role of social media as an intermediary of social processes, the effect of social media on political participation was verified. From the viewpoint that democracy is comprised of the people who are engaged in, it is important to find a way to enable people to engage proactively by providing opportunities to do so. This study shows that social media can be conducive to increased opportunity and lowered barriers to young consumers' participation in politics.

Future research should collect longitudinal data to address the causal relationship between social media use and actual political participation. In the case of tracing media consumption longitudinally, strategies that are more practical would be suggested for enhancing political participation in accordance with changing media use. This study is limited to young people who are in college. Therefore, the general young population should be included in order to investigate the effect of social media on the general young consumers in the future research.

References

1. de Zúñiga, H.G., Jung, N., Valenzuela, S.: Social media use for news and individuals' social capital, civic engagement and political participation. J. Comput.-Mediat. Commun. **17**, 319–336 (2012)
2. Malouf, R., Mullen, T.: Taking sides: user classification for informal online political discourse. Internet Res. **18**, 177–190 (2008)
3. Bimber, B., Cunill, M.C., Copeland, L., Gibson, R.: Digital media and political participation: the moderating role of political interest across acts and over time. Soc. Sci. Comput. Rev. **33**, 21–42 (2015)
4. Hansen, D., Shneiderman, B., Smith, M.: Analyzing Social Media Networks with NodeXL: Insights from a Connected World. Morgan Kaufmann, Burlington (2010)

5. Veil, S.R., Buehner, T., Michael, J.P.: A work-in-process literature review: incorporating social media in risk and crisis communication. J. Conting. Crisis Manag. **19**(2), 110–122 (2011)
6. Bennett, W.L.: Changing citizenship in the digital age. In: Bennett, W.L. (ed.) Civic Life Online: Learning How Digital Media Can Engage Youth, pp. 1–24. The MIT Press, London (2008)
7. Civille, R.: A national strategy for civic networking: a vision of change. Internet Res. **3**, 2–21 (1993)
8. Chang, D., Bae, Y.: The Birth of Social Election in South Korea. Fesmedia Asia, Germany (2012)
9. Moffett, K.W., Rice, L.L.: College students and online political expression during the 2016 election. Soc. Sci. Comput. Rev. **36**(4), 422–439 (2017)
10. Shirky, C.: Political power of social media: technology, the public sphere and political change. Foreign Aff. **90**, 28–41 (2011)
11. Mitchell, A., Gottfried, J., Kiley, J., Matsa, K.E.: Section 2: social media, political news and ideology. In: The Pew Research Center (2014)
12. Coleman, S., Morrison, D.E., Svennevig, M.: New media and political efficacy. Int. J. Commun. **2**, 771–791 (2008)
13. Craig, S., Niemi, R.G., Silver, G.E.: Political efficacy and trust: a report on the NES pilot study items. Polit. Behav. **12**, 289–314 (1990)
14. Morrell, M.E.: Survey and experimental evidence for a reliable and valid measure of internal political efficacy. Public Opin. Q. **67**(4), 589–602 (2003)
15. Niemi, R.G., Craig, S.C., Mattei, F.: Measuring internal political efficacy in the 1988 national election study. Am. Polit. Sci. Rev. **85**(4), 1407–1413 (1991)

An Analysis on Digital Note-Taking Using Social Media in Japan

Toshikazu Iitaka$^{(\boxtimes)}$

Kumamoto Gakuen University, Oe 2-5-1, Kumamoto, Japan
iitaka2@yahoo.co.jp

Abstract. The present study is related to the use of social media among young people in Japan. The main focus herein is digital note-taking, i.e., taking notes by using social media. A previous study reported that many young Japanese people tend to use social media, particularly Twitter, for note-taking. Hence, this study reconfirms the note-taking tendency and analyzes its background.

Keywords: Note-taking · Social-media · Big-data

1 Objective

The focus of this study is the use of social media for digital note-taking that can be observed among students in Japan. Recently, many people use social media, often utilizing it for learning. Social media is used for building communities of learning.

The tendency to use social media was predicted by literature [1]. In 2010, the researcher did not mention that social media is directly used for learning, but he reported in 2018 that these media are utilized for note-taking nowadays.

The objective of this study is to confirm the reproducibility of the analysis of literature [3]. Hence, we perform a similar survey herein and obtain the same result, as well as further data regarding the background on the social media use for learning.

2 Significance

The current study has two significant factors; namely, digital note-taking research and analysis on social media use for learning.

We believe that taking notes is one of the most important parts of learning. Hence, researchers' investigation on digital note-takings in the network age is very common. According to a discussion of Literature [5], people not only take notes digitally, but also share these notes through online networks. This process is considered to be a significant advantage of digital note-taking.

T. Seo who is a journalist reported that users of the note-taking application Clear often communicate through social media [6]. Literature [3] mentioned that people might notice that the interface of the Clear application is similar to that of Twitter. Thus, the researcher assumed that Twitter itself can also be used and is possibly already used for digital note-taking. Based on this assumption, Internet users are surveyed

© Springer Nature Switzerland AG 2020
C. Stephanidis and M. Antona (Eds.): HCII 2020, CCIS 1226, pp. 177–184, 2020.
https://doi.org/10.1007/978-3-030-50732-9_24

online. The result revealed that students in Japan tend to use Twitter for digital note-taking.

According to Seo, the main criterion of younger people for selecting social media for learning is whether their privacy is protected [6]. Seo insisted that Twitter is mostly utilized because its privacy protection is higher than Facebook. However, such tendency was not observed.

Furthermore, a presentation based on literature [3] has pointed out that trust on major Internet companies (We name the variable "trust of companies and government") probably has a positive effect on the frequency of digital note-taking by using social media. However, online research was not designed to verify the influence of such trust. The influence of trust on major Internet companies must be analyzed more precisely. The samples of online research were selected randomly. Thus, the number of samples is not sufficient for a precise examination because the number of young samples who are often learning is not much.

3   Methods

3.1   Research Questions and Hypotheses

The research questions are the following:

RQ1 Do younger Japanese students use social media for digital note-taking?
RQ2 How does the "trust on companies" affect the digital note-taking by using social media?

The hypothesis based on RQ1 is as follows:

H1 Approximately 40% of younger Japanese people (students) use social media, especially Twitter, for digital note-taking.

Verifying H1 involves confirming the reproducibility of the analysis of literature [3]. However, the analysis in the current study is described more precisely than that of literature [3].

The hypothesis based on RQ2 is as follows:

H2 Positive relationship between "trust on companies and government" and frequency of digital note-taking must be confirmed.

RQ2 is not accurately examined by literature [3], because "trust of companies and government" is not defined well in this research. Hence, we must obtain important factors of "trust on companies and government" that affect digital note-taking and online learning. The current study will also perform an exploratory analysis regarding RQ2.

3.2   Research Description

The survey design is similar to that of literature [3]. The surveys used a research company with about 870,000 samples. The feature of the samples is shown in web site

[7]. The company selected 560 samples randomly. However, the target of the survey is controlled differently this time. The samples of literature [3] are controlled only by age and gender. But more students are present in the current survey because we assume that students learn and take notes more frequently (Table 1).

Table 1. Feature of the research.

Type of survey	Online research
Period	2018.3.14–3.19
Number of samples	560

Gender	%	Number of samples
Male	50.0%	280
Female	50.0%	280

Age	%	Number of samples
10-19	25.2%	141
20-29	31.8%	178
30-39	10.4%	58
40-49	10.2%	57
50-59	10.0%	56
60-	12.5%	70

The current survey implemented is online research. The samples are controlled this time, i.e., 50% of the samples are students. In the present study, many samples that use social media for digital note-taking are gathered.

Then, we describe the independent variable for RQ2. The variable is 'Trust on companies and government'. The variable contains answers of the questions which examine if the respondents agree or disagree following statements (Table 2).

The answer to Q11 "No problem with information availability" is considered to be "trust on companies and government" in the study of literature [3]. These questions are all five-scale questions and are related to privacy. Several of them can measure the tendency of allowing trustworthy companies to access users' private information. Regarding the factor analysis (Extraction Method: Principal Axis Factoring, Rotation Method: Varimax with Kaiser Normalization), four significant factors are obtained. The first factor is composed of "Camera set," "Information use," "Trust on companies," "Distinguishing information availability and watching," and "Information access relieves us." We call this factor "No privacy" and its reliability is sufficient ($\alpha = 0.765$). The second factor consists of "Hate to gather information," "Distinguishing information availability and watching," "Information availability is privacy invasion," "Free speech invasion," "Viewable communication," and "Inactivity identification." We call this factor "Protection privacy" and its reliability is sufficient ($\alpha = 0.565$). The third factor is composed of "Use without awareness," "Convenience of information gathering," and "No problem with information availability." We call this factor

Table 2. Questions for the independent variables.

	Text	Abbreviation
Q1	Surveillance cameras set in your town for security reasons are helpful	Camera set
Q2	The information collected by surveillance cameras should be carefully controlled to prevent abuse	Controlled information
Q3	The information collected by surveillance cameras may be used for survey if private information is not leaked	Information use
Q4	We should entrust the management of our private information to trustworthy companies to avoid leak and destruction of information	Trust on companies
Q5	Companies and government can make use of information of network service positively to realize better service	Authority use
Q6	There is no problem when private information and access logs are gathered by networks without our awareness	Use without awareness
Q7	We hate when access logs are gathered even if it is for survey purposes and private information are not accessed	Hate to gather information
Q8	It is convenient that we can obtain recommendation through accurate information gathering and management	Convenience of information gathering
Q9	Availability of private information on servers of companies does not mean that they are watching our private information	Distinguishing information availability and watching
Q10	Availability of private information on servers of companies is a background of invasion of privacy	Information availability is privacy invasion
Q11	It is no problem that there are private information on servers of trustworthy companies	No problem with information availability
Q12	It relieves us that police can access our private information on data servers in the case of emergency	Information access relieves us
Q13	Free speech must be invaded if we allow third persons to access private information on data servers	Free speech invasion
Q14	The contents of our online communication must not be viewable when we do not want to show it to anyone	Viewable communication
Q15	We cannot discuss actively online when we are easily identified	Easy identification

"Convenience and trust" and its reliability is sufficient ($\alpha = 0.659$). The fourth factor consists of "Trust on companies" and "Authority use." We refer this factor as "Authority trust" and its reliability is sufficient ($\alpha = 0.533$). The reliability of these four factors is sufficient. We establish four variables that are the sum of the components of the four factors.

Table 3. Crosstab analysis.

	Never	Seldom	Sometimes	Often
I take notes as text data on Facebook				
Not student	233	26	18	3
	83.2%	9.3%	6.4%	1.1%
Student	164	55	44	17
	58.6%	19.6%	15.7%	6.1%
Total	397	81	62	20
	70.9%	14.5%	11.1%	3.6%
I take notes as text data on Twitter				
Not student	229	24	21	6
	81.8%	8.6%	7.5%	2.1%
Student	149	61	48	22
	53.2%	21.8%	17.1%	7.9%
Total	378	85	69	28
	67.5%	15.2%	12.3%	5.0%

3.3   Statistical Analysis

We examine the first research question here. We can examine it by comparing students and others.

More than 40% of Japanese students are using social media to record their learning and for digital note-taking. This result is in agreement with our expectations. Thus, H1 is confirmed to be accurate. T-test is performed and statistically significant difference between student and not student is confirmed $(t(481.08) = 6.5$, $p < 0.01$; $t(502.3) = 6.851$, $p < 0.01)$.

Moreover, we examine the second research question (Table 4).

Table 4. Correlation between trust and digital note-taking.

	I record what I have learned on that day on Facebook	I record what I have learned on that day on Twitter
No problem with information availability	0.16 ***	0.191***

The number is Pearson correlation coefficient, *** $p < 0.001$.

As shown in Table 3, correlation coefficient between "trust on companies" (No problem with information availability) and digital note-taking is positive and statistically significant. We can say H2 is confirmed.

As discussed in the last section, "No problem with information availability" is component of "Convenience and trust." The variable is created on the basis of questions related to privacy.

As listed in Table 5, "Protection privacy" is not related to digital note-taking at all, and only "Convenience and trust" has a clear relation to digital note-taking. Thus, H2 is confirmed to be accurate.

Table 5. Relationship among factors regarding privacy and digital note-taking.

	I record what we have learned on Facebook	I record what we have learned on Twitter	I take notes as text data on Facebook	I take notes as text data on Twitter
No privacy	−.156**	−.157**	−.154**	−.124**
Protection privacy	.013	.016	.018	.054
Convenience and trust	.286**	.266**	.299**	.290**
Authority trust	.165**	.179**	.139**	.138**

The number is Pearson correlation coefficient, **$p < 0.001$.

Further, we perform the multiple regression analysis to accurately examine what items of "Convenience and trust" have influence on digital note-taking.

As shown in Fig. 1 and 2, both models are statistically significant, and only the "Use without awareness" has influence in both models. A similar tendency is observed when we examine other uses of social media for digital note-taking. Moreover, we can assume that "Use without awareness" is a condition of frequent network use. When we are very concerned about privacy invasion, we should not use social media networks frequently. Generally, this feature has also a positive effect on frequencies of digital note-taking by using social media. However, we will need to examine the background of "Use without awareness" in the future work.

4   Discussion of Result

This study analyzed the use of social media for digital note-taking. We initially explained more precisely the discussion of literature [3]. We attempted to examine the reproducibility of the analysis of literature [3]. In addition, we sought a solution for the question of literature [3], i.e. influence of "Trust on companies" on digital note-taking by using social media.

Generally, teaching and learning methods that are accurate for each student are necessary. Thus, the recommendation engine that can realize such methods was investigated by literature [2, 4]. Such an engine will probably create recommendation data based on big data. In addition, social media must be one of important sources of these big data. Therefore, social media networks that are directly used by young Japanese people must be very important. Moreover, further investigation for the background and influence of digital note-taking by using social media must be useful.

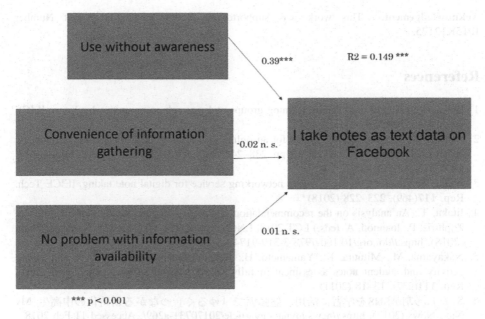

Fig. 1. Multiple regression analysis on "Convenience and trust" and digital note-taking by using Facebook.

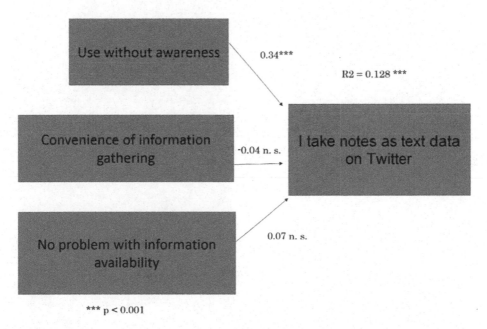

Fig. 2. Multiple regression analysis on "Convenience and trust" and digital note-taking by using Twitter.

Acknowledgement.   This work was supported by JSPS KAKENHI Grant Number JP15K12175.

References

1. Iitaka, T.: Integration of online learning groups and research communities by Xoop. IEICE Tech. Rep. **109**(387), 1–6 (2010)
2. Iitaka, T.: Recommendation engine for an online drill system. In: Zaphiris, P., Ioannou, A. (eds.) LCT 2015. LNCS, vol. 9192, pp. 238–248. Springer, Cham (2015). https://doi.org/10.1007/978-3-319-20609-7_23
3. Iitaka, T.: A survey on use of social networking service for digital note taking. IEICE Tech. Rep. **117**(469), 223–228 (2018)
4. Iitaka, T.: An analysis on the recommendation engine of a course introduction module. In: Zaphiris, P., Ioannou, A. (eds.) LCT 2018. LNCS, vol. 10924, pp. 243–255. Springer, Cham (2018). https://doi.org/10.1007/978-3-319-91743-6_19
5. Nakayama, M., Mituura, K., Yamamoto, H.: Relationship between factors of note-taking activity and student notes assessment in fully online learning environment. IEICE Tech. Rep. **111**(237), 13–18 (2011)
6. Seo, T.: 9割がSNSを学習に活用、勉強垢で「ゆるく」つながる新時代の中高生, My Navi News (2017). https://news.mynavi.jp/article/20170731-a269/. Accessed 11 Feb 2018
7. Mellinks Ltd.: リサーチモニター登録、属性, Mellinks Ltd. https://www.mellinks.co.jp/speedmel_monitor.html. Accessed 3 Mar 2020

A Study to Understand Behavioral Influencers Related to Carpooling in India

Abhishek Jain[1](✉) and Sundar Krishnamurthy[2]

[1] KPIT Technologies Ltd., Pune, India
abhishek.jain3@kpit.com
[2] KPIT Technologies Ltd., Bangalore, India
sundar.krishnamurthy@kpit.com

Abstract. Shared mobility is increasingly being considered by travelers in last few years due to increase in traffic, economic advantages, reduced travel time, concern for the environment and more. Carpooling which is one of the more popular variants of shared mobility is projected to exponentially grow at a CAGR of 19.87% from 2018 to 2025, to reach a market size of USD 218.0 billion by 2025 from USD 61.3 billion in 2018. While carpooling is increasingly becoming popular its adoption is varied across the geographies and dependent on a multitude of expectations and considerations of the traveler. Furthermore, divergences in infrastructure and policies implemented by the government as well as the social strata and ethnographic constraints play an important part in the adoption of carpooling. For instance, working professionals make up over significant chunk of the carpooling market in India leading to major ride sharing companies to offer carpooling services while newer enterprises aim to capitalize on carpooling as a venture. In this study, we have attempted to understand the current state of carpooling in India and identified key factors impacting the adoption of carpooling. For this study we conducted an online survey with 850+ working professional participants. Post the survey, personal interviews and inferential analysis has been done to draw meaningful insights. The study identifies key influencers such as safety, convenience, flexibility, reliability, economics, personal space and time consumption etc. The study provides a view of travelers' behavioral considerations in choosing carpooling and aims to present key findings that influence carpooling.

Keywords: Carpool · Shared mobility · Human computer interaction · Travel · User experience

1 Introduction

The last decade of mobility has made possible vehicle ownership primarily driven by lower costs of vehicles while also better ability for the consumer to afford one. In the last decade alone the motor vehicle sales increased from 1.9 million units in 2008 to 4.4 million units in 2018 [2]. However, the advent of the mobility boom was followed by traffic woes which has steadily increased, proportionally, driving congestion on the streets while also contributing to environmental damage due to pollution and increasing CO2 emissions. Another impact has been longer commuting times especially work

© Springer Nature Switzerland AG 2020
C. Stephanidis and M. Antona (Eds.): HCII 2020, CCIS 1226, pp. 185–193, 2020.
https://doi.org/10.1007/978-3-030-50732-9_25

driven commute where its common to see miles long traffic during peak hours. Compounding the above-mentioned issues were infrastructure challenges including lack of good public transport. To mitigate some of these challenges, carpooling was envisioned as a possible solution. In the last few years carpooling has emerged as a favored commute option particularly among the working populace. The presence of tech-parks or workplace clusters means that more of the office workers drive similar routes and to similar destinations. This makes carpooling a cogent candidate for office commute, signifying a paradigm shift from single ownership vehicles to shared mobility.

There are different types of carpooling options. Personal carpooling which is between a vehicle owner and acquaintances while workplace carpooling is primarily for carpooling between office workers. The latters' burgeoning market for carpooling has inspired many services which aim to simplify the planning and riding part. While major ride sharing companies like Uber [3] and Ola [4] offer pooling services these are more structured with a driver who picks up passengers along a predetermined source and destination. Carpooling market is scheduled to grow by CAGR of 19.87% to reach a total valuation of USD 218.0 billion by 2025 [1]. Number of carpooling vehicles worldwide has increase from 7.67 millions in 2015 to 23.16 millions unit in 2020 and is expected to reach 44.98 millions unit by 2025 [2–7]. This has prompted newer entrants into this market like sRide [5] and QuickRide [6] which offer services aimed at the corporate employee. Many of these services provide the service by allowing a vehicle owner to become a 'ride giver' and anyone who wants to carpool in the vehicle to become a 'ride seeker'. The service connects the ride giver to one or more potential ride seekers who can request to ride along with the ride seeker for a predefined sum which is calculated based on the distance and fuel economy. One of the major plus factors in favor of carpooling is the frugality of cost.

While the carpooling market seems to be poised to grow even further with more services entering the marketplace with lucrative offerings for the consumer, there are many factors which affect the behaviors of the ride giver and the ride seeker. It's imperative that these are considered to ensure that there are no detrimental experiences for the consumer of the service while also to ensure that the usability of the service would lend itself to the mind model of expectations and motivations based on which the users of the services sign up. The study involved research of behavioral dynamics of the carpooling userbase; both ride giver and ride seeker from a perspective of understanding the key goals, motivations and challenges as also various other behavioral traits. For instance, Malodia and Singla's study of carpooling in Indian cities discuss extra travel time, walking time to reach the meeting point, waiting time and cost savings as the influencing factors [8]. This study, however, was primarily conducted metro cities in India with the corporate workers for whom majority of the services are targeted. The study included both a quantitative component to understand the statistical segmentation and a qualitative component to understand the behavioral markers.

2 Method

A total of 852 subjects participated in this study (Male = 599, Female = 253). The criterion used for selecting subject were a) subjects should be corporate sectors professionals (IT professionals etc.) in Pune & Bangalore city, b) Regular intra city travelers for office-home commute. While in the analysis phase the samples have been distributed in additional groups with respect to gender, age range and type of carpool offerings.

There were two research methods employed in this study starting from unmoderated online survey. After the survey, factor and inferential analysis has been done to draw meaningful insights and another set of participants from same sample group were identified with respect to additional parameters for in-person semi structured qualitative interviews.

Primary goal of online survey was to identify the participants who are the current consumers of carpool services and those who wish to use carpool in near future. As result of this, around 26% survey participants were found as the consumers of carpool services and around 41% participants showed their interest towards carpool in future (Fig. 1).

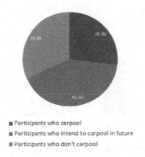

■ Participants who carpool
■ Participants who intend to carpool in future
■ Participants who don't carpool

Fig. 1. Total participants distribution against carpooling (%)

3 Results

3.1 Gender Wise Age Distribution Analysis of Survey Participants

From the survey 230 participants (150 Male, 80 Female) were identified as current consumers and users of carpool service. Age range wise distribution of participants who carpool is depicted in Fig. 2. In the sample of male participants ≈23% were under 'below 25 years', ≈65% in between 25 to 40 years and ≈11.33 & above 40 years who carpool. Similarly, in sample of female participants, 40% were under 25 years, ≈58% in between 25 to 40 years and ≈1.25% above 40 years who carpool.

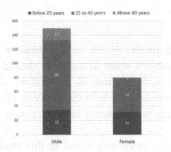

Fig. 2. Gender wise age range distribution of carpool participants

3.2 Gender Wise Utilization of Carpool Services

Participants who carpool and utilize carpool services were also analysed with respect to gender as behavioral indicator. In total sample of male participants ≈28% participants 'offer rides' in carpooling, ≈41.66% seek rides and 30% utilize both (offering & taking rides) at different times. Whereas in female participants sample, 5% offer rides, ≈82.5% seek rides and ≈12.5% utilize both (Fig. 3).

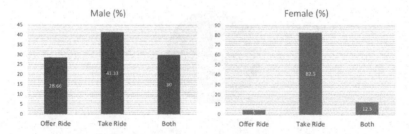

Fig. 3. Gender wise utilization of carpool services

3.3 Frequency of Carpool

Majority of participants (aggregated male & female) who carpool on regular basis, ≈52% participants use carpool almost every workday, ≈28% use 2–3 times a work week and ≈19.5% use carpool once a week (Fig. 4).

3.4 Analysis of Top Reasons for Not Using Carpool

There were plenty of factors which affect the carpooling behavior and decision making while choosing carpool as option for commute. Some reasons have been identified and analyzed as the outcome of survey research such as 'preference of other mode', 'time consumption', 'reliability', 'flexibility', 'safety', 'privacy', 'convenience' etc. In Fig. 5 percent wise distribution of reasons is depicted for not using carpool.

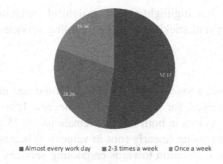

■ Almost every work day   ■ 2-3 times a week   ■ Once a week

Fig. 4. Frequency of carpool (%)

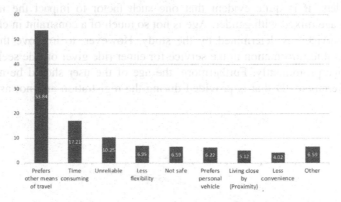

Fig. 5. Analysis of top reasons for not using carpool (%)

4 Observations and Analysis

With respect to the carpool service like ride sharing and ride seeking, there are 2 different primary actors involved ride giver and ride seeker. Ride seeker's key objectives are identified as to get a ride to their destination which will take lesser time, economically and safely, whereas for ride giver key objectives are to share their vacant seat with a passenger who is traveling in a similar direction, which will help save some money and also the environment. Majority of participants (ride giver and seeker) uses more than one channel for getting carpooling rides. Omni-channel dedicated and non-dedicated, online and offline platforms are used to avail carpool services. Many participants reported that initially they use multiple apps to find the riders and familiarity ensured same group taking rides together. In Fig. 5 key issues are by carpoolers and non-carpoolers alike which affects carpooling behavior and user experience. One of biggest factor affecting overall experience of ride giver and seeker is wrong ETA (estimated time of arrival) provided by dedicated carpooling services. Apart from this, other participants have described error in live location tracking, inconsistent response from riders and privacy issues as reasons for their wariness with carpooling. With the help of data, the study has highlighted few insightful behavioral indicators which affects the riders' affinity and stickiness with carpooling services.

4.1 Age

The preference for carpool services were similar for some age ranges while a sudden difference has been observed for later ages in male and female riders. Inclination towards the carpooling services in both male & female under 25 years and between 26 to 40 years were seen increasing linearly (not in values). Whereas for age range above 40 years, a sudden fall in inclination towards carpooling services has been observed in female riders. This was not a case with male participants (Fig. 6). Reduction in the preference with male riders above 40 years has also been observed but not to the extent of female riders. It is quite evident that one such factor to impact the interest for carpooling is age mixed with gender. Age is not so much of a constraint in choosing of the carpool services as determined by the study. However, to improve the veracity service, the profile information in the service for either ride giver or ride seeker should display the age prominently. Furthermore, the age of the user should be ascertained from the government ID that is provided during the registration and not as a manual input.

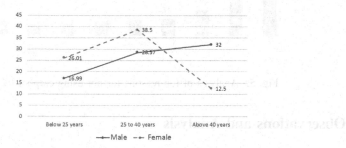

Fig. 6. Preference on carpool service with respect to age range (%)

4.2 Gender

This study has unearthed key behavioral insights related to gender of the rider. Male participants have been observed as leading in offering rides as compared to female riders. Whereas female participants primarily preferred seeking rides (Fig. 7). Given the importance of gender as a parameter which influences the choice of carpooling participants, the service should have an option for ride seekers to select the gender of co-riders as well as allowing ride givers to predefine the gender of the ride seekers and vice versa. This will allow the users to see other ride givers/seekers based on their gender preference and would improve the usability of the service.

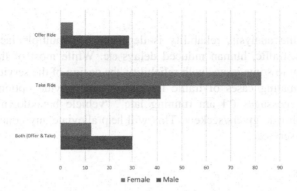

Fig. 7. Comparison of carpool service usage with respect to gender (%)

4.3 Privacy

Most of the respondents in the study indicated privacy as one of the most important aspects which influenced their preference for carpooling. Since a typical carpooling service involved ride seekers and ride givers who are typically strangers, the service should ensure to obfuscate private details like the actual address of the residence (in case of pickup) and provide a nearby point for the ride seeker to wait for the pickup. Furthermore, other details than name, age and gender should be obfuscated; like phone number. Instead the service can provide call anonymization service which will ensure neither party can see the other's phone numbers. This will improve the usability vastly.

4.4 Safety

In case of carpooling aspects of safety are applicable both during the ride and before/after as well. The design of the service should surface elements of safety for the users to be able to access without any effort in case of need. During ride planning, provide feature like being able to set an emergency contact and, as indicated by many of the female respondents of the survey, allow sharing of the ride details so that a family member or loved one can track the ride.

During the ride, safety features in form of one touch access to emergency service (panic button) is essential (as again indicated largely by female respondents). Furthermore, there are aspects of contextual safety that can be enabled especially for a country like India. This includes providing doorstep drop off for female users (with consent) during late hours, ability to inform emergency contacts that the ride seeker has reached destination successfully etc. The design should also account for a command center (remote monitoring by service provider) to be able to receive and display any emergency notifications like speeding, harsh driving, route deviation and panic SOS. As indicated in our study, safety and privacy are the topmost areas that the service providers must focus on in order to influence a positive carpool experience.

4.5   Reliability

As noted from the analysis, reliability is dependent on multiple factors including location services, traffic, human induced delays etc. While most of the respondents were able to adapt to some issues with reliability, the design of the service can be more proactive in intimating cases of traffic led delays and provide options for rides to exchange quick messages ("I am running late", "vehicle breakdown", "waiting at pickup" etc.) with ride givers/seekers. This will help alleviate any concerns about the reliability of the service.

4.6   Economics

One of the reasons why respondents of the study preferred carpooling over cabs or private commute was the cost which can be extremely attractive. As evinced from the study, the ride giver sets the cost of the ride which is also influenced by the distance, space available in the vehicle and the fuel price. One area where user experience can help is provide some guide to the ride given on how much each ride seeker would have to pay as that would help the ride giver set costs to be more optimal. Alternatively, the ride seeker should be able to see a proper breakup of the costs so that they can upfront consent for the same. The study also identified areas where group of ride givers and seekers, after developing familiarity from riding together over time, decided to eschew the service (and consequently the service charge levied) for a more personal arrangement of cash transaction. However, this was not always a successful system due to noncompliance among the riders in the group.

5   Conclusion

Carpooling as a market is poised to grow in the next decade particularly in the face of growing traffic and infrastructure inadequacies. While the study was targeted at the working populace- the ones that are most likely to use carpooling services to commute to work, the implications of the study is clear that there is a significant interest in the urban working community to embrace carpooling as a mainstream commute option. However, from a behavioral standpoint, the key indicators point to a majority male ride giver segment. Further, the study also indicates that the ride seeker segment has expectations around privacy and safety, particularly the female ride seekers. Understanding and assimilating these behavioral expectations would be quintessential to ensure maximum users embrace carpooling.

References

1. Market, R.: Ride sharing market size, share, trends & industry forecast by 2025 (2020). https://www.marketsandmarkets.com/Market-Reports/mobility-on-demand-market-198699113.html
2. Wagner, I.: Vehicle sales: India 2018, 15 August 2019. https://www.statista.com/statistics/265958/vehicle-sales-in-india/

3. Uber: uberpool vs. uberx - how does uberpool work? (2020). https://www.uber.com/in/en/ride/uberpool/
4. Olacabs.com: Book share cabs—buy share pass—hire taxi nearby online at olacabs.com (2020). https://www.olacabs.com/share
5. sRide - Carpool, bikepool, office ride, rideshare (2020). https://sride.co/
6. Quick Ride - Carpooling app & bike pooling app in India. https://quickride.in/
7. Statista: Carpooling worldwide - number of vehicles 2025—Statista (2020). https://www.statista.com/statistics/867668/carpooling-vehicles-worldwide/
8. Malodia, S., Singla, H.: A study of carpooling behavior using a stated preference web survey in selected cities of India. Transp. Plan Technol. **39**(5), 538–550 (2016). https://doi.org/10.1080/03081060.2016.1174368

A Study on Self-awareness Development by Logging and Gamification of Daily Emotions

Jungyun Kim, Toshiki Takeuchi[✉], Tomohiro Tanikawa[✉], Takuji Narumi[✉], Hideaki Kuzuoka[✉], and Michitaka Hirose[✉]

The University of Tokyo, Hongo 7-3-1, Bunkyo-ku, Tokyo, Japan
{jungyun,take,tani,narumi,kuzuoka,
hirose}@cyber.t.u-tokyo.ac.jp

Abstract. Lifelogging records personal data generated from one's own physical and emotional activities in daily life. It is widely used to discover sleep, exercise, or socializing patterns. In recent years, wearable devices and mobile applications have been used to automatically log daily activities, expanding the capabilities of lifelogging applications for a variety of purposes. One such application is the development of self-awareness, comprehensive knowledge about the self with which one may discover their inclinations and set clear goals to enhance future performance. This study proposes an approach for improving self-awareness that allows users to precisely review personal standards and levels of happiness and stress using a smartwatch and mobile application. Related work is investigated to understand the various types of methods and purposes involved, and a survey is conducted to gain insights on daily activities that induce specific emotional states. The findings support dividing one's daily activities into seven categories, which are socialization, leisure, eating, sleeping, working, studying, and other, and an effective mobile application is thus designed. The potential for behavioral changes and the positive effects of the gamification of data visualization to be deployed in the mobile application are also discussed.

Keywords: Self-awareness · Lifelog · Gamification · Emotions

1 Introduction

Self-awareness is the understanding of different aspects of the self, such as emotions, personality, and behavior [1]. Such understanding will enable a person to more effectively discern their own level of subjective wellbeing as well as the values and perspectives of others. Furthermore, one can find methods to improve one's own quality of life through self-awareness [2]. Happiness and stress are critical elements of self-awareness, as these states are profoundly present in daily life [3]. However, the interpretation of happiness can vary between individuals, as it is based on one's daily routines, interests, and behavior [4]. Additionally, both happiness and stress levels may change frequently, and thus, instantaneous data may not accurately describe a person's current emotional state.

© Springer Nature Switzerland AG 2020
C. Stephanidis and M. Antona (Eds.): HCII 2020, CCIS 1226, pp. 194–201, 2020.
https://doi.org/10.1007/978-3-030-50732-9_26

The development of self-awareness is an important issue in any society [5], because it is relevant to individuals' subjective well-being [6]. A lack of self-awareness, which is caused by various factors such as busy routines, often results in a reduced quality of life. For example, it is common for individuals to feel stressed without knowing the reason behind it; this may be due to mental health issues, including depressive disorders. To prevent such issues and deepen self-awareness, it is important to under-stand happiness and stress beforehand. Prior studies have attempted to measure happiness and stress levels using a questionnaire, accelerometer, and smartphone, following which advice is provided based on the result. The present study will further investigate the causes of such states and provide an opportunity to develop self-awareness through reflecting and providing insights on personal standards of happiness and stress in detail.

The primary objective of this study is to justify how self-awareness can be developed by measuring and analyzing personal happiness and stress levels through lifelogging. The lifelog data will be collected from a smartwatch and analyzed in a mobile application. Gamification of the data visualization is proposed to encourage behavioral changes from self-reflection, the cultivation of a positive lifestyle, and to contribute to the improvement of subjective well-being. Consequently, this study also supports finding the best method to enable such improvements.

2 Related Work

2.1 The Oxford Happiness Questionnaire

The Oxford Happiness Questionnaire was created and developed by psychologists Michael Argyle and Peter Hills in 2002 [7] to allow users to periodically check their happiness levels. The questionnaire focuses on user satisfaction and attitude towards life, relationships, and themselves. In the study, 172 participating undergraduate students were asked to respond to the questionnaire on a six-point Likert scale, where 1 indicates 'strongly disagree,' and 6 indicates 'strongly agree.' This questionnaire is used in order to collect granular feedback rather than simple yes/no responses.

The mean of the reverse-scoring of the responses represents the overall happiness level of the students. Happiness level values between 1 and 2 suggest that the respondent may be in an unhappy or stressful situation, and the respondent may be advised to undertake a depression test in some cases; 3 to 4 is considered to be a neutral range, while 5 indicates an ideal happiness level. Moreover, 6 is interpreted as 'too high' according to interpretations of the questionnaire, and such conditions may decrease work, study, and health performance because it may cause mental emptiness and loss of motivation towards an improved quality of life.

2.2 Datawear

Developed by Ahmad Beltagui from the University of Wolverhampton and Tom Rodden and others from the Horizon Digital Economy Research Institute of the University of Nottingham in 2015, Datawear applies an experience sampling method using a mobile application and wearable camera [8]. It is designed to enable users to perform self-reflection on daily life, particularly on work routines, by reviewing images captured by the camera and providing quantitative and qualitative feedback. Users can add comments, name events, and rate their emotions, which include drowsy, relaxed, sad, tense, alert, and happy. Images containing personal data can be deleted from the mobile application before sending them to the research team.

In the study, participants were asked to wear a wearable camera for at least three hours per day for a duration of five days and to install the Datawear mobile application on their smartphone. The application sends out notifications during the day, asking users to perform self-reflection. A post-study interview was conducted to review image details and discuss participants' overall experience of the study.

2.3   Hitachi Happiness Planet

In 2015, Hitachi introduced a new wearable sensor that embedded an accelerometer to collect and analyze data on distinctive physical movements patterns from the behavior of users [9, 10], which is then used to measure happiness levels. Hitachi was strongly influenced by the recent research conducted at the University of Warwick stating that there is a strong correlation between happiness and productivity [11], and they aimed to enhance work efficiency and productivity of employees by monitoring employees' happiness level using the sensor.

Hitachi continued to further research this and developed an artificial intelligence (AI) tool to provide users with advice through smartphones. The user may wish to improve their happiness levels but may not know what actions to take to achieve this; the AI tool will present them with relevant steps. As the sensor is targeted to company employees, the advice is based on employees' work style, such as communication with colleagues and higher-ups or time management techniques, and the users gain the opportunity to apply the advice [12]. For privacy reasons, as the data and advice are personalized, users can only view their own data.

3   Survey of Daily Emotional States

In the present study, a survey was conducted to understand the daily activities that cause happiness or stress. It aims to discover the happiness and stress levels and any daily activities that influence such levels via self-reflection based on the past month. The daily activities in this context only include events or situations that require active participation. Moreover, to help participants to gain awareness of their emotional changes, the survey requires them to describe an experience of feeling happy or stressed without knowing the reason.

The survey was conducted with 70 participants aged between 18 to 44 years. The scale used in The Oxford Happiness Questionnaire was followed; on a scale of 1 to 6, where 1 is the lowest and 6 is the highest, the participants showed average happiness and stress levels of 3.4 and 3.9 during weekdays and 3.9 and 3.4 during weekends, respectively. Furthermore, 24 and 29 people stated that they feel unwarranted happiness on weekdays and weekends, while 25 and 27 people stated that they feel unwarranted stress on weekdays and weekends, respectively. Based on the answers collected from the survey, the daily activities were organized into seven categories: socialization, leisure, eating, sleeping, working, studying, and other. The details of the survey are shown in Table 1 and Table 2. Within these categories, leisure has sub-categories, including sports, shopping, Internet surfing, TV/movies, art/music, and rest. These subcategories will be enforced during usability testing when classifying the types of activities conducted by mobile application users in the form of a pie graph, as shown in Fig. 1.

Table 1. An excerpt from the survey.

What daily activities made you happy over the past month?
Going to karaoke with friends
Having dinner with my family
Going for a drink at the izakaya with friends
Going on a date with my partner
Going for a walk
Watching movies
Working out at the gym to stay fit
Shopping at the mall
Staying in bed all day doing nothing
Listening to music and drinking tea
Internet surfing

Table 2. Activity categories organized for mobile application.

Main category	Subcategory
Socialization	None
Leisure	Sports
	Shopping
	Internet
	TV/Movie
	Art/Music
	Rest
	Other
Eating	None
Sleeping	None
Studying	None
Working	None
Other	None

4   Mobile Application for Self-awareness Development

The mobile application is designed to demonstrate the user's personal standard and level of happiness and stress in detail. The user will gain insight into the types of activities that make them happy or stressed, and thus understand minor emotional changes which they may not recognise in daily life; this will support the development of self-awareness and help them to find methods to improve their mental well-being. The mobile application will have minimalistic design for better usability and be divided into two sections, of which one displays the results of data analysis as a pie graph and the other displays the user's happiness level in the form of a house. The application will use data from a smartwatch, which will be collected through brief interactions.

4.1   Data Collection

A smartwatch will be used to collect lifelogs, as it can be connected to mobile phones and has wearability, which can prevent interference with daily activities during usability testing. Moreover, it is suitable for the collection of precise user data because it can continuously track user's activities both physically and emotionally.

If there are any significant changes in the user's physical activity or heart rate, the mobile application sends out a pop-up message asking to rate the user's current happiness and stress level from 1 to 6, where 1 is the lowest and 6 is the highest. This rating action will identify the user's emotional disposition in different situations. Having direct input of the current happiness and stress level from users can reveal patterns in their emotional states while conducting specific activities. The mobile application will be developed to retain activity information and data inputs from users and utilize the collected data in a similar situation. The pop-up may show frequently during the initial stage of data collection; however, it is expected to gradually decrease with the accumulation of data.

4.2   Usability Testing

Usability testing will be conducted on the mobile application to analyze and evaluate the user's happiness and stress levels. The usability testing will involve around five to ten users, a range suggested by the Nielsen Norman Group [13, 14]. The users participating in usability testing are limited to those who have different types of activities involved during the day, such as work, exercise, or leisure. The target user for this study is an individual between the ages of 18 to 34, an age group that is familiar with the Internet and smartphones [15] and are currently studying at an educational institution or have an occupation. These criteria have been set to avoid data collection from users with an exceptionally small variation of daily activities, which may interfere with data analysis.

4.3   Data Analysis and Gamification

The analyzed data will display on a mobile application. As shown in Fig. 1, it displays what caused users to feel happy or stressed in their daily activities as a pie graph, and it is divided into days, weeks, months, and years. Figure 2 shows a 'house of happiness.' The color, shape, and size of the house are based on the pie graph from Fig. 1. Each of them represents different aspects of the user's happiness status. The color of the house allows users to discover the types of daily activities that made them feel happy. The variation of colors may change depending on the portion of each activity in a day; for example, if socialization makes up the largest portion of the pie graph and uses an orange color to represent its data, orange makes up the most significant part of the house. This would indicate that the user feels the most happiness when they are socializing with others. The shape and size of the house represent the overall level of happiness, and a higher level of happiness makes the house decorative. The use of gamification and logging to develop the houses allows users to reflect and review their standards of happiness and stress levels and encourages them to change their behavior to build a house with an ideal design [16]. Achieving the ideal house indicates that the user has gradually understood how to handle their happiness and stress levels, thus developing self-awareness.

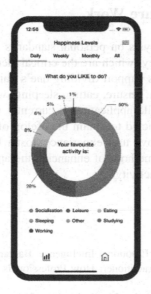

Fig. 1. Mobile application used for data analysis.

Fig. 2. House of happiness.

5   Conclusion and Future Work

This study performed an analysis on personal standards and levels of happiness and stress collected from the survey, which are the critical elements in the development of self-awareness. These findings support dividing one's daily activities into seven categories, which are socialization, leisure, eating, sleeping, working, studying, and other. The development of the mobile application is currently in progress. On completion, usability testing will be conducted to obtain the lifelog of its users. Gamification will also be implemented to improve user experience, foster behavioral change for better self-awareness, and discover methods of enhancing the application quality to improve the detailed tracking of user activity.

References

1. Goldman, D.: Working with Emotional Intelligence. Bantam, New York (1998)
2. Schön, D.: The Reflective Practitioner: How Professionals Think in Action. Basic Books, New York (1983)
3. Seligman, M.E., Csikszentmihalyi, M.: Positive psychology: an introduction. Am. Psychol. Assoc. **55**(1), 5–14 (2000)
4. Calvo, R.A., Peters, D.: Positive Computing: Technology for Wellbeing and Human Potential. The MIT Press, Cambridge (2017)
5. Harvard Business Review. https://hbr.org/2018/01/what-self-awareness-really-is-and-how-to-cultivate-it. Accessed 2 Mar 2020

6. Diener, E., Tay, L.: A scientific review of the remarkable benefits of happiness for successful and healthy living. In: Happiness: Transforming the Development Landscape, pp. 90–117. Centre for Bhutan Studies and GNH, Thimphu (2017)
7. Hills, P., Argyle, M.: The Oxford happiness questionnaire: a compact scale for the measurement of psychological well-being. Personal. Individ. Differ. **33**(7), 1073–1082 (2002)
8. Skatova, A., Shipp, V.E., Spacagna, L., Bedwell, B., Beltagui, A., Rodden, T.: Datawear: self-reflection on the go or how to ethically use wearable cameras for research. In: Proceedings of the 33rd Annual ACM Conference Extended Abstracts on Human Factors in Computing Systems, pp. 323–326 (2015)
9. Yano, K., et al.: Measuring happiness using wearable technology —technology for boosting productivity in knowledge work and service businesses—. Hitachi Rev. **64**(8), 517–524 (2015)
10. Hitachi. http://www.hitachi.com/New/cnews/month/2015/02/150209.html. Accessed 14 Mar 2020
11. Oswald, A.J., Proto, E., Sgroi, D.: Happiness and productivity. J. Labor Econ. **33**(4), 789–822 (2015)
12. Hitachi. http://www.hitachi.com/New/cnews/month/2016/06/160627.html. Accessed 14 Mar 2020
13. Nielsen, J., Landauer, T.K.: A mathematical model of the finding of usability problems. In: Proceedings of the INTERACT 1993 and CHI 1993 Conference on Human Factors in Computing Systems, pp. 206–213. ACM, New York (1993)
14. Schmettow, M.: Sample size in usability studies. Commun. ACM **55**(4), 64–70 (2012)
15. Poushter, J.: Smartphone ownership and internet usage continues to climb in emerging economies. Pew Res. Center **22**, 1–44 (2016)
16. Francisco-Aparicio, A., Gutiérrez-Vela, F.L., Isla-Montes, J.L., Sanchez, J.L.G.: Gamification: analysis and application. In: Penichet, V., Peñalver, A., Gallud, J. (eds.) New Trends in Interaction, Virtual Reality and Modeling. HCIS, pp. 113–126. Springer, London (2013). https://doi.org/10.1007/978-1-4471-5445-7_9

How Much Should I Pay? An Empirical Analysis on Monetary Prize in TopCoder

Mostaan Lotfalian Saremi, Razieh Saremi[✉],
and Denisse Martinez-Mejorado

Stevens Institute of Technology, Hoboken, NJ 070390, USA
{mlotfali,rsaremi,dmartin2}@stevens.edu

Abstract. It is reported that task monetary prize is one of the most important motivating factors to attract crowd workers. While using expert-based methods to price Crowdsourcing tasks is a common practice, the challenge of validating the associated prices across different tasks is a constant issue. To address this issue, three different classifications of multiple linear regression, logistic regression, and K-nearest neighbor were compared to find the most accurate predicted price, using a dataset from TopCoder website. The result of comparing chosen algorithms showed that the logistics regression model will provide the highest accuracy of 90% to predict the associated price to tasks and KNN ranked the second with an accuracy of 64% for K = 7. Also, applying PCA wouldn't lead to any better prediction accuracy as data components are not correlated.

Keywords: Monetary prize · Crowdsourced software development · Crowd software worker · TopCoder

1 Introduction

Available literatures on motivation patterns of crowdsourcing workers have reported that the monetary prize associated with tasks is one of the top motivating factors to attract and involve potential workers in task competition [1]. The monetary prize usually represents the degree of task complexity as well as required competition levels [2, 3]. In practice, task requesters frequently employ expert-based methods to price tasks, which may involve a high degree of subjectivity, while the challenge of validating the associated prices across different tasks is a constant issue.

As of today, multiple pricing models are introduced with a focus on pricing strategy [4], the Context-Centric Pricing approach [5], the impact of price on workers' behavior [6] and using machine learning methods [7] to help task requesters with predicting reasonable price range. However, none of these papers applied PCA to evaluate the accuracy of the presented. In this work, we aim to investigate that gap.

To address this issue, three different classifications of multiple linear regression, logistic regression, and K-nearest neighbor were compared to find the most accurate predicted price, using data extracted from TopCoder website [8]. The result of comparing chosen algorithms showed that the logistics regression model will provide the highest accuracy of predicting the associated price to tasks. Also, applying PCA wouldn't lead to any better prediction accuracy as data components are not correlated.

© Springer Nature Switzerland AG 2020
C. Stephanidis and M. Antona (Eds.): HCII 2020, CCIS 1226, pp. 202–208, 2020.
https://doi.org/10.1007/978-3-030-50732-9_27

The rest of the paper is organized as follows: Sect. 2 introduces the research design; Sect. 3 presents the result and discussion of the research conducted; Sect. 4 gives a conclusion and outlook to future work.

2 Research Design

2.1 Dataset and Metrics

The dataset used contains 514 component development tasks from Sep 2003 to Sep 2012, extracted from the TopCoder website. All tasks are completed, meaning receiving acceptable submissions with a score higher than 75. The total monetary prize is divided into the top-2 winners with a 2:1 ratio.

The initial analysis on the dataset implies that a typical task on TopCoder is priced as $750 [6] (i.e. $500 and $250 for the top-2 winners respectively), the average size of 2290 lines of code, and the median numbers of registrations and submissions are 16 and 4 respectively. And the median score of the winning submission is 94.16 out of 100. A current common impression is that crowdsourcing is more feasible for easy and simple tasks, the data shows that it is also feasible for complex component development at the scale of 21925 lines of code. The maximum number of registrants of 72 is surprising since the nature of the task is competitive considering that only top-2 winner gets paid.

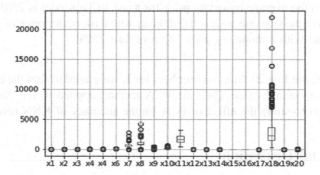

Fig. 1. Overall distribiution of the dataset

2.2 Dataset Preparation

The outlier for each variable was identified and removed. To do so we applied 1.5 of interquartile to add and subtract to the third and first quartiles respectively. Figure 1 illustrates the distribution of data.

Also deeper analysis in the database, it became clear that 8 variables have the least relation with the monetary prize, therefor we ignored them in our analysis. Table 1 summarized the remaining data statistics in the clean database.

Table 1. Summary of metric data in the whole dataset

Metric	Min	Max	Median	Average	STDEV
Monetary prize	112.5	3000	750	754	372.4
Size	310	21925	2290	2978	2267.9
#Reg	1	72	16	18	11
#Sub	1	44	4	5	4
Score	75	100	94.1	92.5	6.2

2.3 Empirical Studies and Design

In order to predict the monetary prize associated with each task this research studied three predictive modeling methods: linear regression, logistic regression, and KNN.

Multilinear Regression

The analysis on the training data suggested that monetary prize (MP_i) follows a multiple linear regression, Eq. 1:

$$MP_i = \alpha + \sum i^{20} \beta_i . X_i \qquad (1)$$

In which α is the constant term and β_i is the coefficient for the variable (X_i).

Logistic Regression

As it is reported the average monetary prize for a task in TopCoder is 750\$. Therefor to apply logistics regression, we assigned 0 to tasks with a monetary prize of less than 750 \$ and 1 to tasks with a monetary prize of more than 750\$.

KNN

To apply KNN, the first 20 different numbers for K were used to find the best neighbor numbers on the clean dataset. Then the PCA method applied to the dataset and the KNN was rerun to study the effect of PCA on the accuracy of KNN results.

3 Result and Discussion

3.1 Multilinear Regression

Monetary prize is a continuous number, ranging from 75 to 2000. This suggests that the multi linear regression model would be a good match for predicting the monetary prize. Because of this, we first used a multiple regression model to analyze the data. The initial result provides the R2 value of 0.5448 and degree of freedom on 376, which indicates a decent fitting line passing through the dataset. However, a significant number of task variables provide no significant impact on the prediction. Therefore, the insignificant variables were removed and the model re-run. The second model provides the R2 value of 0.5108 and the degree of freedom on 389, which is a worse fit to use for Monetary prize prediction.

The multilinear regression model is created based on 70% training and 30% testing data. The accuracy of the model is shown in Fig. 2. As it is clear, the prediction model tended to underestimate the monetary prize, however, the median of both actual and predicted monetary prize remained similar.

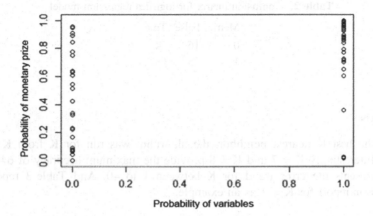

Fig. 2. Predicted monetary prize by multi linear regression

3.2   Logistic Regression

To apply logistic regression to our dataset, the first step is to convert monetary prize to discrete data. Therefore we assigned 0 to price less than 750$ and 1 to price more than 750$. This allowed applying logistics regression to the dataset. Similar to multiple linear regression, the initial model showed that a significant number of task variables were not influential in the equation. Therefore, to make a more efficient model, we only used the significant variables to create the prediction model. Figure 3 presents the classification of Task variables v.s probabilistic prediction of the monetary prize by the logistics regression model. A natural S-Curve shape that the model tends to take is clear.

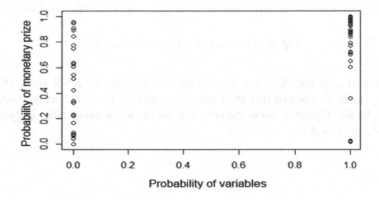

Fig. 3. Classification of variables v.s. probebilistics on monetary prize

Moreover, the confusion matrix of the model with the threshold for prediction at 50% provides a promising result, Table 2. The presented model successfully predicts the assigned monetary prize with an accuracy of 90%.

Table 2. Confusion metrix for logistics regression model

Metric	False	True
0	16	4
1	5	68

3.3   KNN

To find the best K nearest neighbor, the algorithm was run for K from K = 1, to K = 40. Interestingly K = 7 and K = 8 provide the maximum accuracy of 64%. Figure 4 represents the error trend for K between 1 to 40. And Table 3 reports the classification report for K = 7 as an example.

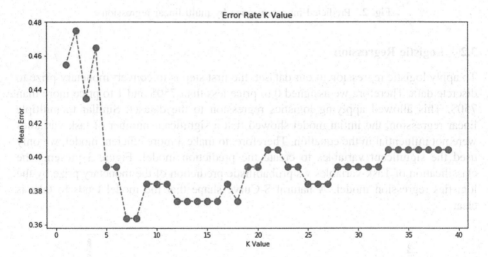

Fig. 4. Error trend for K between 1 to 40

In the next step, the PCA was applied and the accuracy of KNN under PCA was analyzed. The result showed that PCA not only could not improve accuracy but also it decreased by 4%. Figure 5 shows the error rate for the KNN model after applying PCA for K between 1 to 40.

Table 3. Classification report of K = 7, KNN model

	Precision	Recall	F1-score	Support
75	0	0	0	0
96	0.67	1	0.8	2
100	0.67	0.67	0.67	3
144	0	0	0	1
150	0	0	0	3
250	0	0	0	3
300	0.33	0.5	0.4	2
400	0	0	0	7
500	0	0	0	1
600	0	0	0	4
700	0	0	0	4
750	0.67	0.98	0.8	59
800	0	0	0	2
900	0	0	0	1
1000	0	0	0	4
1250	0	0	0	1
1500	0	0	0	1
1800	0	0	0	1
Micro avg	0.64	0.64	0.64	99
Macro avg	0.13	0.17	0.15	99
Weighted avg	0.44	0.64	0.52	99

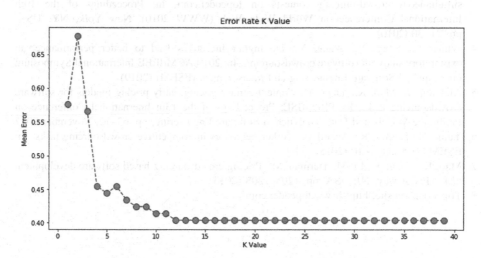

Fig. 5. Error trend for K between 1 to 40 after applying PCA

4 Conclusions

The monetary prize usually represents the degree of task complexity as well as required competition levels. In practice, task requesters frequently employ expert-based methods to price tasks, which may involve a high degree of subjectivity, while the challenge of validating the associated prices across different tasks is a constant issue.

To address this issue, three different classifications of multiple linear regression, logistic regression, and K-nearest neighbor were compared to find the most accurate predicted price, using a dataset from the TopCoder website. The result of comparing chosen algorithms showed that the logistics regression model will provide the highest accuracy of 90% to predict the associated price to tasks and KNN ranked the second with an accuracy of 64% for K = 7. Also, applying PCA wouldn't lead to any better prediction accuracy as data components are not correlated.

In the future, we would like to focus on the similar crowd worker behavior and performance based on task similarity level and try to analyze a task- worker performance to report more decision elements according to the monetary prize, task size task utilization, and crowd workers' performance.

References

1. Stol, K.-J., Fitzgerald, B.: Two's company, three's a crowd: a case study of crowdsourcing software development. In: The 36th International Conference on Software Engineering (2014)
2. Faradani, S., Hartmann, B., Ipeirotis, P.G.: What's the right price? Pricing tasks for finishing on time. In: Proceedings of the Human Computation (2011)
3. Archak, N.: Money, glory and cheap talk: analyzing strategic behavior of contestants in simultaneous crowdsourcing contests on topcoder.com. In: Proceedings of the 19th International Conference on World Wide Web (WWW 2010), New York, NY, USA, pp. 21–30 (2010)
4. Wang, L., Yang, Y., Wang, Y.: Do higher incentives lead to better performance?-an exploratory study on software crowdsourcing. In: 2019 ACM/IEEE International Symposium on Empirical Software Engineering and Measurement (ESEM) (2019)
5. Alelyani, T., Mao, K., Yang, Y.: Context-centric pricing: early pricing models for software crowdsourcing tasks. In: PROMISE: Proceedings of the 13th International Conference on Predictive Models and Data Analytics in Software Engineering, pp. 63–72, November 2017
6. Yang, Y., Saremi, R.: Award vs. worker behaviors in competitive crowdsourcing tasks. In: ESEM 2015, pp. 1–10 (2015)
7. Mao, K., Yang, Y., Li, M., Harman, M.: Pricing crowdsourcing-based software development tasks, Piscataway, NJ, USA, pp. 1205–1208 (2013)
8. Topcoder website. http://www.topcoder.com

Time to Log Off

An Analysis of Factors Influencing the Willingness to Participate in a Long-Term 'Digital Detox' with the Smartphone

Catharina Muench[✉], Lena Feulner, Ricardo Muench, and Astrid Carolus

Julius-Maximilians University Wuerzburg,
Oswald-Kuelpe-Weg 82, 97074 Würzburg, Germany
catharina.muench@uni-wuerzburg.de

Abstract. Studies showed that habitualization of smartphone use may result in a compulsive usage. Resolutions to reduce overuse also known as a 'digital detox' are an emerging trend. Previous studies analyzing the effects of a short voluntary smartphone separation focused on anxiety and 'Fear of Missing Out' (FoMO) and revealed positive correlations between the separation of the smartphone and these factors. First studies have started to widen the perspective and analyze three weeks of separation. A considerably long-term 'smartphone detox' has not been studied, yet. To close the gap, our study aimed to analyze a list of factors, which were shown to be associated with problematic smartphone usage (frequency of usage, age, FoMO, Nomophobia), regarding their impact on participants' ($N = 120$) willingness to limit one's smartphone usage for the six-week-period of the Christian Lent. Results showed a significant relation between frequency of smartphone usage, FoMO, Nomophobia and the willingness to abstain from one's smartphone for six weeks. Overall, this study serves as an initial research on the underlying psychological effects of smartphone usage and a long-term 'digital detox'.

Keywords: Smartphone usage · Digital detox · FoMO · Nomophobia

1 Introduction

Since the launch of the first smartphone, interpersonal communication as well as the reception and the creation of media content evolved substantially. Instant messaging replaced the classic SMS, media content is read, watched, listened to and created on the go. Nowadays, smartphones are ubiquitous and accompany their user throughout the day - from switching off the alarm clock when waking up to checking the messages for the last time when going to bed [6]. Despite the increasing smartphone usage, attempts arise to turn off the smartphone more often and use it less. A study by Deloitte [13] showed that 48% of smartphone users report to use their smartphone too often. Approximately 80% of these self-proclaimed over-users would like to spend less time

© Springer Nature Switzerland AG 2020
C. Stephanidis and M. Antona (Eds.): HCII 2020, CCIS 1226, pp. 209–216, 2020.
https://doi.org/10.1007/978-3-030-50732-9_28

with their smartphones [13]. Accordingly, one out of four smartphone users had tried a 'digital detox' already but did not persevere [3].

In sum, people seem to be aware of their potential overuse. However, the various functions the smartphone offers seem to be too important to easily refrain from one's phone and to log off. Taking these findings as a starting point, our study focuses on the elaboration of factors, which have been shown to be associated with problematic smartphone usage to gain insights into their influence on the willingness to limit one's smartphone usage.

2 Background and Hypotheses

Smartphones are used intensively with a usage time of 159 min per day [12]. Research has shown that problematic smartphone usage is related to the frequency of usage [21] as well as to the amount of time spent on the phone [22]. In this rather unsurprising context, problematic smartphone usage is defined by the fact that people spend so much time with their phone that this may have a negative impact on user's health [19], on their body posture and respiratory functions [20], on academic and cognitive performances [2, 27] and on users' psychological wellbeing leading to symptoms of depression [11].

Users' constant interaction with the phone has been shown to result in some kind of relationship between owner and device which was referred to as a 'digital companionship' [6]. They even compared this relationship with characteristics of a human-human relationship leading to the idea that the smartphone is more than just a technical device but rather a digital companion. From that perspective, smartphone separation seems to be more than only the waiving of a technological device, leading to changes in users' emotions [24]. Accordingly, Anrijs et al. [2], for example, showed that a 'smartphone detox' is associated with short-term changes in the experience of stress. The authors recorded the behavior of a control group (normal smartphone use) and of an experimental group ('smartphone detox') on seven days. Results showed significantly lower stress levels of the detox group compared to the group using their smartphones regularly [2]. Adelhardt, Markus and Eberle [1] examined the effects of smartphone separation on teenagers and revealed through in-depth interviews and short essays about teenagers' experiences that adolescents with lower smartphone usage and lower technological dependency were not significantly affected by the three weeks of smartphone separation. In contrast, teenagers with higher usage either reported difficulties at the beginning of the separation to which they could adapt or a rather easy beginning but increasing difficulties over time. However, the underlying willingness to take part in a detox program has not been studied so far.

To summarize the existing body of literature, a more intensive smartphone usage has been shown to be associated with a compulsive usage behavior, which resembles addictive behaviors [21, 24]. Similar to the symptoms of dependence already classified by the WHO [28], smartphone users seem to have a strong desire to use the device, report an impaired capacity to control the usage and seem to fear withdrawal. Referring to first studies analyzing the effects of separation as well as to the literature on behavioral addictions, we postulate a correlation between usage intensity and the willingness to refrain from the phone and assume that higher smartphone usage is related to less willingness to limit their smartphone usage for a longer period of time. Thus, the first hypothesis (H1) postulates: *There is a significant negative relationship between daily smartphone usage frequency and the willingness to limit one's smartphone usage.*

According to statistics by Bitkom [5], more than 73% of all smartphone users cannot imagine a life without their smartphone, 45% of children and adolescents between 16 and 29 years prefer to be permanently online [4]. Due to the early contact of digital natives with the device, the smartphone has a particularly high priority for this generation [18]. In addition, previous research has shown that even a short-term disconnection from the phone can lead to more negative outcomes such as anxiety [7, 9] and stress, especially for young adults [14, 29]. Referring to the studies presented, which emphasize the importance of the device especially for younger users, H2 says: *There is a significant, positive relationship between age and the willingness to limit one's smartphone usage.*

Problematic smartphone use has already been linked to nomophobia. For example, Yildiz [30] showed a positive relation between nomophobia and problematic smartphone use of high school students. Gezgin [17] showed that nomophobia was significantly higher for students who use their smartphone more often. Referring to users who are afraid of being without their smartphone and users who even report to experience panic attacks when their phone is unlocatable [25]. Consequently, H3 postulates: *There is a significant, negative relationship between nomophobia and the willingness to limit one's smartphone usage.*

Furthermore, a relation between problematic smartphone use and FoMO has already been investigated. Elhai et al. [15] showed that people who score high on FoMO tend to use their smartphones problematically aiming to satisfy their need for constant connection. An excessive use of digital technologies is positively related to developing burnout, depression or anxiety [15]. Wolniewicz et al. [27] revealed a positive relation between FoMO and problematic smartphone use and on social smartphone use in particular: using the smartphone to maintain relationships for example seems to be a kind of compensation for the fear of missing out on something. Thus, H4 assumes: *There is a significant, negative relationship between FoMO and the willingness to limit one's smartphone usage.*

Finally, we focus on the combined predictive value of the variables, which have been focused on separately, so far, with the research question asking: *Do relationships exist between the factors and the criterion in a combined analysis?*

3   Methods

3.1   Participants

Participants were recruited through online forums and social networks. A total of $N = 120$ participants answered the survey: 92 (76,7%) women and 28 (23,3%) men between 17 to 62 years ($M = 26.85$, $SD = 8.40$). 45.0% ($n = 54$) had a university degree, 34.2% ($n = 41$) a high school diploma, 20.0% ($n = 24$) a secondary school diploma and 0.8% ($n = 1$) a secondary modern school qualification. Participants reported to use their smartphone 147 min ($SD = 87.53$) a day.

3.2   Data Collection

The basic idea of our study was to ask for participants' willingness to abstain from their smartphone during Christian Lent. For 40 days - from Ash Wednesday to Easter vigil - Christians traditionally fast and refrain from food or limit their eating behavior. As a sign of penance and reflection, they refrain from pleasant activities that are unhealthy and have negative physical effects. More recently, the period was used to refrain from sweets or alcohol, for example. Furthermore, a limited usage of technological devices and services has become popular.

To assess participants' willingness to limit their smartphone usage, an online survey was conducted involving questions about the frequency of smartphone usage, FoMO, nomophobia, as well as demographics including gender and age.

Willingness to limit one's smartphone usage during the Christian Lent was measured with a single item ("To what extent could you imagine limiting your smartphone usage during the 40 days of Christian Lent?"). This item was answered on a 7-point Likert scale, ranging from 1 = "I could not imagine at all" to 7 = "I could well imagine" ($M = 3.08$, $SD = 1.78$). *Frequency of smartphone usage* ("How often do you use your smartphone?") was answered on a 9-point Likert scale (1 = "never" to 9 = "several times an hour" ($M = 8.09$, $SD = 1.03$). *Nomophobia* was measured using the Nomophobia Questionnaire (NMP-Q) [29] on a 7-point Likert scale, ranging from 1 = "strongly disagree" to 7 = "strongly agree" ($M = 3.03$, $SD = 1.10$, $\alpha = .94$). To examine *FoMO* we used the Fear of Missing Out Scale (FoMOs) [23] on a 5-point Likert scale, ranging from 1 = "strongly disagree" to 7 = "strongly agree" ($M = 2.63$, $SD = 0.70$, $\alpha = .87$). Additional demographic information such as age and gender were collected. Data collection started two days before Christian Lent.

4   Results

One-sided Pearson correlations were calculated to test the four hypotheses. Results show that the frequency of daily smartphone usage correlated significantly negatively with the willingness to limit the smartphone usage during Christian Lent, $r (118) = -.256$, $p = .002$. Thus, H1 can be confirmed. Regarding H2, there was a weak, insignificant correlation between age and willingness to limit smartphone usage, $r (118) = .138$, $p = .067$. H2 must be rejected, therefore. Analyzing H3, a significant negative correlation was found between nomophobia and the willingness to limit one's smartphone usage, $r (118) = -.191$, $p = .018$. H3 can be accepted. Finally, FoMO and the willingness to limit one's smartphone usage correlated weakly but significantly, $r (118) = -.158$, $p = .043$, which resulted in the acceptance of H4. Table 1 gives an overview of the correlations.

Finally, the variables analyzed separately before (smartphone usage, age, nomophobia, FoMO), were then combined in a multiple linear regression to predict participants' willingness to limit their smartphone usage. The model fulfilled the statistical

Table 1. One-sided Pearson correlations of frequency of smartphone usage, age, FoMO, Nomophobia and the willingness to limit the smartphone usage during Christian Lent (N = 120).

	M	SD	1	2	3	4	5
Willingness to limit SP-usage	3.08	1.78	1				
SP-usage	8.09	1.03	−.256**	1			
Age	26.9	8.40	.138	−.323**	1		
Nomophobia	3.03	1.10	−.191*	.338**	−.349**	1	
FoMO	2.63	.70	−.158*	.357**	−.428**	.560**	1

Note: SP = smartphone, p < .05. **p < .01.

requirements with the Durbin-Watson Test statistic ($d = 1.64$) indicating a positive autocorrelation which is 'relatively normal' [16]. A significant regression equation was found ($F(4, 115) = 2.46$, $p = .05$), with an R^2 of .08 (adjusted $R^2 = .05$), which indicated a weak goodness-of-fit according to Cohen [10]. Participants' predicted willingness to limit their smartphone usage is equal to 6.41 + .01 (age) − .04 (FoMO) − .17 (nomophobia) − .36 (smartphone usage). Only smartphone usage was a significant predictor of participants' willingness to limit smartphone usage ($p = .04$). All the other variables did not contribute statistically significant to the prediction.

5   Discussion and Limitations

This study aimed for an analysis of factors associated with the willingness to limit smartphone usage for a longer period of time. Results partially support our hypotheses. Hypotheses 1, 3, and 4, which predicted a significant, negative relation between the willingness to limit the smartphone usage and frequency of average smartphone usage, nomophobia and FoMO, were confirmed supporting previous research [21, 27, 29]. Consequently, the more often people interact with their smartphone and the more they are afraid of not being accessible or of missing social interactions, the less they can imagine to refrain from their phone. From a psychological perspective, these users seem to associate certain relevant gratifications with their phone usage such as staying in touch with others (need to belong) and being informed or keeping up with the (social) news. Perhaps, they intensively use their phone to communicate with important others, with family members or friends. Losing their phone would mean to lose the connection to them. What is important to learn, here: Although the participants' age does not significantly correlate with their willingness to limit their phone usage, both variables do correlate positively revealing that younger participants are less motivated to give away their phones. However, the explanatory power is limited due to the rather young age of our participants (mean age: 27 years) resulting in a reduced variance and in, probably, smaller effects. Future research needs to widen the perspective involving a more heterogeneous sample regarding age. Finally, we asked for the combined predictive value of all predictors analyzed. Results show a significant but weak regression equation with only one significant predictor of the willingness to limit phone usage. When analyzed in combination, FoMO and nomophobia did not significantly contribute to the prediction, anymore, and the frequency of smartphone usage remained to be the only relevant predictor. Following this result, FoMO and nomophobia seem to be constructs, which do not create added value indicating that the mere duration of usage is a sufficient predictor of smartphone abstinence.

However, the regression equation indicated very limited explanation of variance. Therefore, we argue for a future re-analysis of the factors of the willingness to reduce smartphone usage, which needs to (1) incorporate a more heterogeneous sample and (2) variables allowing a more profound analysis of psychologically relevant factors. First, the sample presented was not only limited regarding its young age but also regarding a gender bias: about 80% of the participants were female. To analyze potential gender differences, future studies need to work with a more balanced sample [8]. Second, the use of the translated items of the NMP-Q [29] and the FoMO questionnaire [23], which were not empirically tested, need to be criticized. Additionally, data were self-reported and therefore not robust against social desirability. Future research could consider alternative measures such as peripheral psychological measurements, implicit association tests or app-based measurements of the actual usage. Furthermore, the survey approach should be transferred to an experimental approach implementing long-term separation in real life. Finally, to gain more detailed insights into the psychological nature of smartphone abstinence, we need to incorporate variables like personality and self-esteem into the analysis. These have been shown to be important predictors of phone usage in general or of specific applications such as social media apps [21].

6 Conclusion

The concept of 'digital detox' refers to problematic usage of technological devices resulting in overuse or even 'digital overload'. Especially our smartphones are discussed to be associated with addictive behavior patterns and resulting in negative effects. Its overwhelming success and its penetration of the market result in an ubiquity of the smartphone which has changed our lives substantially. Furthermore, the use of the phone seems to happen rather unconsciously or automatically: many users seem to not notice or to deny the amount of time spent with the device. Research has shown that smartphone abstinence or a 'digital detox' was regarded to be desirable but hard to realize. In this context, the study offers first steps towards an understanding of the underlying processes of smartphone separation - and of smartphone usage, in return. Smartphone usage, FoMO and Nomophobia were found to be negatively correlated to the willingness to limit the time spent with the smartphone. However, when analyzed in combination, only smartphone usage remained as a significant predictor. Future research needs to build up on these first results to refine and extend the analysis regarding further potentially influencing factors. To conclude, it can be seen that the research area of 'digital detox' provides various research opportunities, which promise multifaceted insights into the use of technological devices, which future research needs to establish.

References

1. Adelhardt, Z., Markus, S., Eberle, T.: Teenagers' reaction on the long-lasting separation from smartphones, anxiety and fear of missing out. In: Proceedings of the 9th International Conference on Social Media and Society, pp. 212–216 (2018)
2. Anrijs, S., et al.: MobileDNA: relating physiological stress measurements to smartphone usage to assess the effect of a digital detox. In: Stephanidis, C. (ed.) HCI 2018. CCIS, vol. 851, pp. 356–363. Springer, Cham (2018). https://doi.org/10.1007/978-3-319-92279-9_48
3. Bitkom Homepage. https://www.bitkom.org/Presse/Presseinformation/Digital-Detox-Smartphone. Accessed 29 Mar 2020
4. Bitkom Homepage. https://www.bitkom.org/sites/default/files/2019-05/bitkom_pk-charts_kinder_und_jugendliche_2019.pdf. Accessed 29 Mar 2020
5. Bitkom Homepage. https://www.bitkom.org/Presse/Presseinformation/Smartphone-Markt-waechst-um-3-Prozent-auf-34-Milliarden-Euro. Accessed 29 Mar 2020
6. Carolus, A., Binder, J.F., Muench, R., Schmidt, C., Schneider, F., Buglass, S.L.: Smartphones as digital companions: characterizing the relationship between users and their phones. New Media Soc. 21(4), 914–938 (2019)
7. Cheever, N.A., Rosen, L.D., Carrier, L.M., Chavez, A.: Out of sight is not out of mind: the impact of restricting wireless mobile device use on anxiety levels among low, moderate and high users. Comput. Hum. Behav. 37, 290–297 (2014)
8. Chen, B., Liu, F., Ding, S., Ying, X., Wang, L., Wen, Y.: Gender differences in factors associated with smartphone addiction: a cross-sectional study among medical college students. BMC Psychiatry 17(1), 341 (2017)
9. Clayton, R.B., Leshner, G., Almond, A.: The extended iSelf: the impact of iPhone separation on cognition, emotion, and physiology. J. Comput.-Mediat. Commun. 20(2), 119–135 (2015)
10. Cohen, J.: Statistical Power Analysis for the Behavioral Sciences. Erlbaum, Hillsdale (1988)
11. Demirci, K., Akgönül, M., Akpinar, A.: Relationship of smartphone use severity with sleep quality, depression, and anxiety in university students. J. Behav. Addict. 4(2), 85–92 (2015)
12. Deng, T., et al.: Measuring smartphone usage and task switching with log tracking and self-reports. Mob. Media Commun. 7(1), 3–23 (2019)
13. Deloitte Homepage. https://www2.deloitte.com/ch/de/pages/technology-media-and-telecom munications/articles/smartphones-sind-nuetzlich-bereiten-aber-auch-sorgen.html. Accessed 29 Mar 2020
14. Dongre, A.S., Inamdar, I.F., Gattani, P.L.: Nomophobia: a study to evaluate mobile phone dependence and impact of cell phone on health. Natl. J. Commun. Med. 8(11), 688–693 (2017)
15. Elhai, J.D., Levine, J.C., Dvorak, R.D., Hall, B.J.: Fear of missing out, need for touch, anxiety and depression are related to problematic smartphone use. Comput. Hum. Behav. 63, 509–516 (2016)
16. Field, A.P.: Discovering Statistics Using SPSS, 3rd edn. Sage, London (2009)
17. Gezgin, D.M.: Exploring the influence of the patterns of mobile internet use on university students' nomophobia levels. Eur. J. Educ. Stud. (2017)
18. Güzeller, C.O., Coşguner, T.: Development of a problematic mobile phone use scale for Turkish adolescents. Cyberpsychol. Behav. Soc. Netw. 15(4), 205–211 (2012)
19. İnal, E.E., Demİrcİ, K., Çetİntürk, A., Akgönül, M., Savaş, S.: Effects of smartphone overuse on hand function, pinch strength, and the median nerve. Muscle Nerve 52(2), 183–188 (2015)

20. Kang, K.W., Jung, S.I., Lee, D.Y., Kim, K., Lee, N.K.: Effect of sitting posture on respiratory function while using a smartphone. J. Phys. Therapy Sci. **28**(5), 1496–1498 (2016)
21. Kwon, M., et al.: Development and validation of a smartphone addiction scale (SAS). PLoS ONE **8**(2), e56936 (2013)
22. Lin, Y.-H., et al.: Time distortion associated with smartphone addiction: identifying smartphone addiction via a mobile application (App). J. Psychiatr. Res. **65**, 139–145 (2015)
23. Przybylski, A.K., Murayama, K., DeHaan, C.R., Gladwell, V.: Motivational, emotional, and behavioral correlates of fear of missing out. Comput. Hum. Behav. **29**(4), 1841–1848 (2013)
24. Schmidt, C., Muench, R., Schneider, F., Breitenbach, S., Carolus, A.: Generation "always on" turned off. Effects of smartphone separation on anxiety mediated by the fear of missing out. In: Stephanidis, C. (ed.) HCI 2018. CCIS, vol. 851, pp. 436–443. Springer, Cham (2018). https://doi.org/10.1007/978-3-319-92279-9_58
25. Sharma, N., Sharma, P., Sharma, N., Wavare, R.: Rising concern of nomophobia amongst Indian medical students. Int. J. Res. Med. Sci. **3**(3), 705 (2015)
26. Wilmer, H.H., Sherman, L.E., Chein, J.M.: Smartphones and cognition: a review of research exploring the links between mobile technology habits and cognitive functioning. Front. Psychol. **8**, 605 (2017)
27. Wolniewicz, C.A., Tiamiyu, M.F., Weeks, J.W., Elhai, J.D.: Problematic smartphone use and relations with negative affect, fear of missing out, and fear of negative and positive evaluation. Psychiatry Res. **262**, 618–623 (2018)
28. World Health Organization Homepage. https://www.who.int/substance_abuse/terminology/definition1/en/. Accessed 29 Mar 2020
29. Yildirim, C., Correia, A.-P.: Exploring the dimensions of nomophobia: development and validation of a self-reported questionnaire. Comput. Hum. Behav. **49**, 130–137 (2015)
30. Yildiz Durak, H.: Investigation of nomophobia and smartphone addiction predictors among adolescents in Turkey: demographic variables and academic performance. Soc. Sci. J. **56**(4), 492–517 (2019)

Me Without My Smartphone? Never!
Predictors of Willingness for Smartphone
Separation and Nomophobia

Ricardo Muench[(⊠)] and Catharina Muench

Julius-Maximilians University of Wuerzburg,
Oswald-Kuelpe-Weg 82, 97074 Würzburg, Germany
ricardo.muench@uni-wuerzburg.de

Abstract. The smartphone as a ubiquitous mobile computer can be regarded as
a 'digital companion', being with us 24/7 and supporting us in every aspect of
modern life. This companionship might lead to a psychological attachment to
the device comparable to the attachment to social (human) partners, and ultimately even compulsive usage. Here, a relevant construct is the fear of missing
out (short: FoMO) leading to a constant checking of one's phone. Furthermore,
users can develop a fear called 'nomophobia' (no-mobile-phone phobia).
Despite this fear, resolutions to reduce overuse also known as a 'digital detox' is
an emerging trend. Our research aims at revealing predictors of nomophobia and
the willingness to limit one's smartphone usage, and which sub-factors of
nomophobia are dominating. N = 220 participants filled out an online survey
including factors like compulsive usage, FoMO, nomophobia, frequency of
smartphone usage and willingness to separate from one's smartphone. Multiple
regression analyses revealed potential predictors for nomophobia and willingness for smartphone separation.

Keywords: Smartphone separation · Nomophobia · Digital companion

1 Introduction

There are numerous occasions in everyday life, in which people are seen using their
smartphone non-stop. It is used in every situation thinkable - on public transport or at
home, as a primary activity or as a second screen when watching television. While its
basic function is a means to communicate, it can also be used for work-related tasks, to
access information or to entertain oneself. The constitution of the smartphone as an
ubiquitous and multi-functional mobile computer is also reflected in daily usage time,
which was an average of 3 h and 35 min in the US in 2018 [16]. There are even fashion
trends like the smartphone neck-strap, which always enable the (in this case predominantly female) users to have their device close-by. It allows direct smartphone access
even without pulling it out of pants pockets or bags. It seems that the time spent with
this technology needs to be maximized at all cost.

There is a lot of research regarding mobile phone usage and the effects on the user.
Studies address questions concerning a typical psychological predisposition of an

© Springer Nature Switzerland AG 2020
C. Stephanidis and M. Antona (Eds.): HCII 2020, CCIS 1226, pp. 217–223, 2020.
https://doi.org/10.1007/978-3-030-50732-9_29

'over-user' [3] or decreases in productivity due to constant distractions by the smartphone [9]. Consequently, there is also a field of research interested in the benefits of consciously limiting one's smartphone usage by conducting a digital detox [1, 2, 14]. But are people willing to separate from their own smartphone? And if so, what factors influence and predict the willingness to engage in such self-limitation?

2   Theoretical Framework

Due to the multi-functionality of smartphones, they can be described as the perfect devices to gratify users' needs. As described above, users stay connected with their phone throughout the day and interact with it frequently. The smartphone can be conceptualized as a "digital companion", which is more than mere technical equipment [5]. The interaction of users with their device can even evolve in human-like relationships and psychological attachment comparable to other social (human) partners [4].

The tendency to form social and emotional attachments is deeply rooted in humans, and even extends to the attachment with non-living objects, e.g. technology. Especially younger age-groups seem prone to form such relationships with the smartphone: they are constantly trying to stay connected with the device and feel distressed when separated from it [11]. This attachment even goes so far that the smartphone is used while driving a car. Using a representative sample of young drivers (17–28 years) it was determined that high mobile attachment predicts distracted driving behavior, e.g. by checking social media app notifications [17]. People highly attached to their smartphone are prone to an overuse of the device, also labeled a problematic smartphone use. This problematic overuse is often linked to negative feelings like stress and decreased life satisfaction [12].

Research has also been looking at the usage motives to explain why we are using the smartphone as frequently as we do. One motive is the constant connectedness with friends, family and all types of acquaintances by communicating directly or using social media applications. A possible underlying factor is the so called 'fear of missing out' (short: FoMO) [13]. It is defined as a omnipresent fear, that others might have exciting experiences, which we do not know about or cannot attend to. In a study about problematic smartphone overuse, FoMo was shown to be related to high social media usage [10]. FoMO is argued to lead to increased smartphone usage, as it gives users the opportunity to gather information about related people and ongoing events in one's peer group. This is further underlined by the findings of Wolniewicz and colleagues: high FoMO was shown to be related to increased social uses of the smartphone compared to functional uses [18]. Therefore, FoMO seems to be predicting not only increased smartphone usage time overall, but also social application usage especially.

In this context, users can develop a fear called 'nomophobia', an acronym for 'no mobile phone phobia'. It describes the fear of not being in touch with the smartphone and the various functions it enables. Thus, this concept contains four factors: (1) not being able to communicate, (2) losing the connectedness with the online (social) world, (3) discomfort of losing pervasive access to information and (4) giving up the convenience a smartphone gives [19]. A study with students from India showed, that approximately 75% of participants suffered from nomophobia [15].

Despite these fears and other psychological factors like mobile attachment, or maybe because of them, resolutions to limit smartphone use also known as 'digital detoxing' is an emerging trend. Digital detox is mostly conducted in a private social environment, in order to improve the quality time spent with family and friends. However, studies analyzing the effects of a short-term separation from one's own smartphone showed that this may lead to higher levels of anxiety [6], mediated by FoMO [14] and an increase of blood pressure and a decrease of task performance [7]. Research analyzing long-term separation effects of smartphone separation, like a digital detox, show contrary results as participants report significantly lower stress levels compared to the control group using their smartphones regularly [2].

Based on previous research, there are several factors that seem to be relevant regarding the willingness to separate from one's smartphone. Nevertheless, the most intuitive predictor is nomophobia, as the fear to be without one's smartphone should influence the willingness to engage in a limitation of said device. To further analyze which users experience nomophobia in the first place we ask for underlying factors of this fear:

RQ1: Which of the factors FoMO, mobile attachment, compulsive smartphone usage, frequency of smartphone usage and well-being significantly predict nomophobia?

Furthermore, we were interested in examining the relevant factors in willingness for smartphone separation besides nomophobia:

RQ2: Which of the previous factors plus nomophobia significantly predict the willingness for smartphone separation?

3   Method

3.1   Participants

The sample consisted of 220 (139 female, 80 male, 1 unspecified gender) people, recruited by posting in social networking sites. Participation was voluntary. The age ranged from 12 to 77 years with a mean age of 27.89 years ($SD = 11.58$). Approximately 80% of participants were of ages 30 and younger. Most participants were enrolled in education (student, apprentice, etc.), only 34.7% were employed.

3.2   Measures

To assess the underlying factors of nomophobia and willingness to separate from one's smartphone, participants filled out an online questionnaire, which was created with an online tool called "SosciSurvey". The questionnaire included various scales, as well as several demographic questions.

Frequency of smartphone usage was gathered by asking how long in minutes the smartphone was used on average daily ($M = 287.74$ min, $SD = 180.09$ min).

Willingness for smartphone separation was measured with a single item stating 'I would be willing to give up my smartphone for one week'. The item could be answered on a 5-point Likert scale from 1 = 'strongly disagree' to 5 = strongly agree' ($M = 3.14$, $SD = 1.49$).

Well-Being was assessed with the 'Flourishing Scale' by Diener and colleagues [8]. The scale consists of eight items, all answerable on a 7-point Likert scale from 1 = 'strongly disagree' to 7 = 'strongly agree' ($M = 5.67$, $SD = .88$).

Mobile Attachment was measured by the Mobile Attachment Scale [11], consisting of 10 Items with a 5-point Likert scale from 1 = 'strongly disagree' to 5 = 'strongly agree'. ($M = 2.70$, $SD = .78$).

For the measurement of *compulsive smartphone usage*, we used a scale consisting of 13 Items with a 7-point Likert scale from 1 = 'strongly disagree' to 7 = 'strongly agree' [12] ($M = 2.80$, $SD = 1.02$).

To assess *FoMO* we used the Fear of Missing Out Scale [13]. It consists of ten items on a 5-point Likert scale from 1 = 'strongly disagree' to 5 = 'strongly agree' ($M = 2.65$, $SD = .84$).

To conclude, *nomophobia* was measured with the Nomophobia Questionnaire (NMP-Q) [19] with 20 Items on a 7-point Likert scale from 1 = 'strongly disagree' to 7 = 'strongly agree'. The 20 items are summed up into one single score, which consequently ranges from 20 to 140. Based on the score, participants can be classified regarding their nomophobia: 20 = complete absence of nomophobia; 21–59 = mild level of nomophobia; 60–99 = moderate level of nomophobia; 100–140 = severe nomophobia. In our survey, the participants reach an average score of ($M = 61.86$, $SD = 24.18$), which is a moderate level of nomophobia.

4   Results

To answer the two research questions, multiple linear regressions were conducted in order to analyze the prediction of nomophobia and the willingness for smartphone separation.

In RQ1, we meant to examine if and to what extent the factors FoMO, mobile attachment, compulsive smartphone usage, frequency of smartphone usage and well-being significantly predict nomophobia. A significant regression equation was found (F (5, 214) = 111.79, $p < .001$), with an R^2 of .85 (adjusted $R^2 = .72$). Participants' predicted nomophobia is equal to .46 + .11 (compulsive smartphone usage) − .08 (well-being) + .26 (FoMO) + .57 (mobile attachment) .04 (frequency of smartphone usage). Well-being ($p = .04$), FoMO ($p < .001$), and mobile attachment ($p < 001$) were significant predictors. Compulsive usage was a near-significant predictor ($p = .06$).

RQ2 asked for the predictors of willingness for smartphone separation. A significant regression equation was found ($F(6, 213) = 12.63$, $p < .001$), with an R^2 of .51 (adjusted $R^2 = .26$). Participants' predicted willingness for smartphone separation is equal to $3.85 + .10$ (compulsive smartphone usage) $+ .11$ (well-being) $+ .12$ (FoMO) $- .19$ (mobile attachment) $- .07$ (frequency of smartphone usage) $- .44$ (nomophobia). Only nomophobia was a significant predictor ($p < .001$). Well-being ($p = .06$) and mobile attachment ($p = .10$) were near-significant predictors.

As nomophobia was the only significant predictor for the willingness for smartphone separation, we conducted an additional exploratory regression analysis including the four sub-factors of nomophobia: not being able to communicate, losing connectedness, not being able to access information and giving up convenience. We wanted to examine which sub-factor significantly predicts the willingness for smartphone separation. A significant regression equation was found ($F(4, 215) = 16.46, p < .001$), with an R^2 of .48 (adjusted $R^2 = .23$). Participants' predicted willingness for smartphone separation was equal to $4.95 - .24$ (not being able to communicate) $- .14$ (losing connectedness) $- .09$ (not being able to access information) $- .10$ (giving up convenience). Only 'not being able to communicate' was a significant predictor ($p = .01$).

5 Discussion and Outlook

We intended to analyze the underlying factors of nomophobia and the willingness to separate from one's smartphone. Regarding nomophobia, there were several significant predictors. Higher levels of FoMO and mobile attachment lead to higher levels of nomophobia. From a theoretical standpoint, both FoMO and mobile attachment are closely linked to nomophobia. The fear of missing out on social events can be a relevant factor in developing a fear to be without one's smartphone. Additionally, high intensity of the attachment formed with the technological device predicts nomophobia, as users do not want to lose their digital companion. Nomophobia was also negatively predicted by well-being. It seems like smartphone usage does not only lead to negative emotions in users [12], but an overall good mood decreases the fear of not being in touch with the smartphone. Compulsive usage and frequency of usage were not statistically significant.

Research question 2 focused on the underlying factors of the willingness to separate from one's smartphone. Our analysis showed, that only nomophobia was a significant predictor. Whereas this relationship is rather obvious, it is interesting to note that no other predictors could be found. To gain further insights on the role of nomophobia, we looked at the four sub-factors that nomophobia consists of. Only the first sub-factor 'not being able to communicate' was a significant predictor in this analysis, which was negatively associated. This result showed, that it is the most basic function of the smartphone, namely the enablement of communication with friends and family, which predicts the (un-)willingness to separate from one's smartphone. This relationship might be even of increased importance in times of a global health crisis like we are experiencing now with the new-found Covid-19 virus. Direct contact is restricted in numerous countries; therefore, many people rely on communication devices to stay in touch with their social surroundings.

Some experimental limitations can be discussed. We did not assess the entirety of possible factors, as a voluntary participation in an online survey should not be too extensive. Due to this, we had to exclude possible factors like stress induced by the phone. We argue for further research in this field of study, to broaden the knowledge which factors predict the willingness to participate in a digital detox. It would be interesting to examine the typical predispositions of users limiting their smartphone usage, e.g. by looking at personality factors. Experiments like the present study help us understand the close connectedness users establish with their smartphone as a digital companion.

References

1. Adelhardt, Z., Markus, S., Eberle, T.: Teenagers' reaction on the long-lasting separation from smartphones, anxiety and fear of missing out. In: Proceedings of the 9th International Conference on Social Media and Society, pp. 212–216 (2018)
2. Anrijs, S., et al.: MobileDNA: relating physiological stress measurements to smartphone usage to assess the effect of a digital detox. In: Stephanidis, C. (ed.) HCI 2018. CCIS, vol. 851, pp. 356–363. Springer, Cham (2018). https://doi.org/10.1007/978-3-319-92279-9_48
3. Bianchi, A., Phillips, J.G.: Psychological predictors of problem mobile phone use. CyberPsychol. Behav. 8(1), 39–51 (2005)
4. Bodford, J.E., Kwan, V.S., Sobota, D.S.: Fatal attractions: attachment to smartphones predicts anthropomorphic beliefs and dangerous behaviors. Cyberpsychol. Behav. Soc. Netw. 20(5), 320–326 (2017)
5. Carolus, A., Binder, J.F., Muench, R., Schmidt, C., Schneider, F., Buglass, S.L.: Smartphones as digital companions: characterizing the relationship between users and their phones. New Media Soc. 21(4), 914–938 (2019)
6. Cheever, N.A., Rosen, L.D., Carrier, L.M., Chavez, A.: Out of sight is not out of mind: the impact of restricting wireless mobile device use on anxiety levels among low, moderate and high users. Comput. Hum. Behav. 37, 290–297 (2014)
7. Clayton, R.B., Leshner, G., Almond, A.: The extended iSelf: the impact of iPhone separation on cognition, emotion, and physiology. J. Comput.-Mediat. Commun. 20(2), 119–135 (2015)
8. Diener, E., et al.: New well-being measures: short scales to assess flourishing and positive and negative feelings. Soc. Indic. Res. 97(2), 143–156 (2010)
9. Duke, É., Montag, C.: Smartphone addiction, daily interruptions and self-reported productivity. Addict. Behav. Rep. 6, 90–95 (2017)
10. Elhai, J.D., Levine, J.C., Dvorak, R.D., Hall, B.J.: Fear of missing out, need for touch, anxiety and depression are related to problematic smartphone use. Comput. Hum. Behav. 63, 509–516 (2016)
11. Konok, V., Pogány, Á., Miklósi, Á.: Mobile attachment: separation from the mobile phone induces physiological and behavioural stress and attentional bias to separation-related stimuli. Comput. Hum. Behav. 71, 228–239 (2017)
12. Lee, Y.K., Chang, C.T., Lin, Y., Cheng, Z.H.: The dark side of smartphone usage: psychological traits, compulsive behavior and technostress. Comput. Hum. Behav. 31, 373–383 (2014)
13. Przybylski, A.K., Murayama, K., DeHaan, C.R., Gladwell, V.: Motivational, emotional, and behavioral correlates of fear of missing out. Comput. Hum. Behav. 29(4), 1841–1848 (2013)
14. Schmidt, C., Muench, R., Schneider, F., Breitenbach, S., Carolus, A.: Generation "always on" turned off. Effects of smartphone separation on anxiety mediated by the fear of missing out. In: Stephanidis, C. (ed.) HCI 2018. CCIS, vol. 851, pp. 436–443. Springer, Cham (2018). https://doi.org/10.1007/978-3-319-92279-9_58

15. Sharma, N., Sharma, P., Sharma, N., Wavare, R.R.: Rising concern of nomophobia amongst Indian medical students. Int. J. Res. Med. Sci. **3**(3), 705–707 (2015)
16. Statista. https://www.statista.com/statistics/1045353/mobile-device-daily-usage-time-in-the-us/. Accessed 27 Mar 2020
17. Weller, J.A., Shackleford, C., Dieckmann, N., Slovic, P.: Possession attachment predicts cell phone use while driving. Health Psychol. **32**(4), 379 (2013)
18. Wolniewicz, C.A., Tiamiyu, M.F., Weeks, J.W., Elhai, J.D.: Problematic smartphone use and relations with negative affect, fear of missing out, and fear of negative and positive evaluation. Psychiatry Res. **262**, 618–623 (2018)
19. Yildirim, C., Correia, A.P.: Exploring the dimensions of nomophobia: development and validation of a self-reported questionnaire. Comput. Hum. Behav. **49**, 130–137 (2015)

User Attitudes Towards Facebook: Perception and Reassurance of Trust (Estonian Case Study)

Triin Oper[✉] and Sonia Sousa

Tallinn University, Narva Road 25, 10120 Tallinn, Estonia
opertriin@gmail.com

Abstract. Privacy and security breaches have gained more attention and people's trust in different platforms has been affected negatively. In light of the rise of data and security breaches, trust has become important to both experts and users. We are generating more data than ever before but how this data is being used or handled is unclear. The goal of this research is to understand Estonian Facebook users' usage behavior and perception of trust in Facebook. Knowing how users perceive trust and its effect on their usage behavior, designers can create platforms that are trustworthy and thereby, user friendly.

Keywords: Trust perception · Privacy · Information disclosure · Online social networks

1 Introduction

In recent years, there has been a lot of news about privacy and security breaches on different online social network (OSN) platforms. The most notorious being the case of Cambridge Analytica, which affected millions of Facebook users whose data was being harvested without their consent and used for political purposes. This led to a lack of trust among the users, while others have decided to leave the platform altogether and/or move to an alternative platform [1].

Previous research has shown that people find it important to have control over who sees their personal information on Facebook but are more likely to disclose information on Facebook than in general [2]. Higher levels of perceived privacy and control over information flow increase trust in Facebook [3]. In addition, higher trust in Facebook leads to more information sharing, whereas awareness of the possible consequences of sharing information on Facebook leads to more protective self-disclosure behavior [4].

Facebook is a social media platform used by 79% of Estonians [5] but in recent years Facebook has faced a lot of criticism over how they collect and handle users' data. This led to Facebook admitting failure in providing secure data storage and promising to make changes in how they collect and utilize user data [6, 7]. These privacy concerns affect the trust of Facebook users in a negative way, however, trust is essential for any online social network to function. Decreased trust in Facebook has resulted in movements like #DeleteFacebook and giving competitive social media platforms a chance to gain new users [8].

© Springer Nature Switzerland AG 2020
C. Stephanidis and M. Antona (Eds.): HCII 2020, CCIS 1226, pp. 224–230, 2020.
https://doi.org/10.1007/978-3-030-50732-9_30

The purpose of this study is to understand Estonian Facebook users' usage behavior and perception of trust in Facebook, and based on that design a trust reassurance mechanism as a proof of concept. The results of the study confirm that trust in Facebook among Estonians is very low and they would like to have more control over their data. Experts designed a solution that would provide Facebook users with tools to control and manage their personal information. The users would have the opportunity to obtain more information about what data is being collected about them, how is it used and who has access to it.

The remainder of this paper is organized as follows. We first discuss the related work on privacy, control over data and trust in Sect. 2. Next, we will give an overview of the research methodology and results in Sect. 3. Finally, we summarize our findings and conclude in Sect. 4.

2   Privacy, Control and Trust

Privacy is individual's right to determine how, when, and to what extent information about them will be disclosed to another person or to an organization [9]. As we are creating more data than ever before [10], privacy and data protection have become more and more important. With the increased amount of data comes the risk of malevolent attacks. Since 2005, there have been 9071 data breaches that have been made public [11] but the amount can be several times higher. The scale of the breaches varies greatly, as both individuals and major corporations and their vast pools of data can be targeted.

The number of breach incidents in social media in 2018 was six, however, the number of records breached was 2,56 billion which accounted for more than a half of all the records breached in the first half of 2018 [12]. While the number of incidents has declined, the amount of records that get compromised has increased. A few examples of largest social media privacy breaches:

- In 2012, 171 million VKontakte users' accounts were obtained by a hacker [13]
- In 2018, personal profile data of 52,5 million Google+ users was exposed [14]
- In 2018, two major scandals hit Facebook: in the first half of the year up to 87 million users' personal data was shared with Cambridge Analytica [15] and in the second half of the year, hackers gained access to 14 million users' highly sensitive data that could be used to facilitate identity theft [16].

2.1   Control over Information

To be able to enact one's privacy preferences, the user needs to have control over who can access the information they have disclosed. Recent research has shown that if given the choice, users prefer to share less information than more [17] and this decision reflects on users privacy concerns. Some research suggests that rather than having privacy defined through the disclosure of certain types of information, it should focus on having control over who knows what about the user [18] and having "personal control over the collection, use, and disclosure of one's personally identifiable info" [19].

As personal information disclosed on social networks can reveal a lot about users' identities, the degree of control over that information should be as high as possible. For that, systems should support the user's ability to control, edit, manage, and delete information about them and decide when, how, and to what extent that information is communicated to others [20]. Control over the access of personal data allows users to "stipulate the information they project and who can get hold of it" [21].

The more the user perceives to have control over who has access to their information, the less concerned they are about privacy [22], therefore, to lessen the privacy concerns, more control functions should be offered to users - both for the disclosed information and who has access to it. However, privacy related behaviors are more likely to be influenced by users' concerns about the amount of information being accessed rather than disclosing it themselves [22].

In the case of Facebook, right now users can control who can see their disclosed information regarding other users, however, regarding third party applications on Facebook, the options are more limited. Some applications require information about the user (e.g. email address, date of birth, name and profile picture) to be accessible, which might lead to lower perceived control. Simply informing the users about what information is being shared with third party applications without changing the amount of disclosed information can increase the level of perceived control [23].

2.2   Trust

Trust in platforms depends on factors such as users' personality, knowledge based on users' prior experiences, institutional assurances from providers, calculative assurances from providers, and cognitive assurances from third parties [24, 25]. Effective privacy practices are considered essential to create and maintain users' trust [19]. A common way to positively influence users' trust is enforcing privacy policies which demonstrate the users that a platform is competent and has the will to secure any disclosed personal information. The more users trust the platform the more loyal they are by "increased purchases, openness to trying new products, and willingness to participate in programs that use additional personal information" [26].

According to Mayer [27], the extent to which an organisation, in this case Facebook, is trusted depends on perceived trustworthiness, which consists of three factors: ability, benevolence, and integrity. Ability means that the organisation or service provider has the domain specific skills and knowledge to be taken seriously. Benevolence is the degree to which a platform is concerned about the users and not just profits. Integrity is subjective - if and to what extent the platform abides by ethical and moral principles.

After the Cambridge Analytica scandal, trust in Facebook dropped 66% with only 28% of users believing that Facebook is committed to protecting the privacy of users' personal information [1]. The reason for lack of trust - users are concerned if and how their personal information is being kept private. For a user to trust a platform, there has to be motivational incentive which can be affected by propensity to trust, perception of risk, benefits of engaging in the relationship and the availability of other options that may achieve similar results [28].

Without trust, users won't interact with each other, and will stop disclosing and diffusing information that is essential for any social network to operate. To trust a certain OSN, users need to trust other users of that platform [29]. As the profiles of users should be attributed to people known in the real world, they are attributed the same value of trust as the owner of the profile [30]. To facilitate and maintain trust, OSNs need to have specific processes to not only verify that the person behind a profile is that person but also make sure that once the profile is verified, the profile will be used by that person and not someone else.

3 Research Methodology and Results

This research is composed of two parts: a survey and design session. A survey was designed based on previous research done on user behavior on online social networks, trust in technology and the methods used to measure it. For the concept design session, six experts were invited to help design an initial concept of what could be a "trust foster mechanism" that would reassure both control and trust when using online social networks. Those experts had a combined expertise in user experience, user interface and graphic design, web and application development.

3.1 Survey

A total of 198 responses were obtained and used for data analysis except when comparing attitudes regarding gender - one of the respondents preferred not to reveal their gender. Out of 198 respondents, 154 were women and 43 were men. Data was collected about the following: demographics, usage patterns, information disclosure behavior, trust in Facebook (including risk perception, benevolence, competence and general trust), awareness about data breaches, patterns and behavior change compared to the previous year and finally, privacy preferences.

The survey showed that the most popular activities on Facebook are communicating with people, visiting Facebook groups and reading the news. 71.7% out of all respondents communicate with people very often, 31.3% of respondents report to visit Facebook groups often and 29.8% of respondents read the news often. After the Cambridge Analytica scandal, most of the respondents reported to be less active on Facebook - for those, who didn't say the scandal directly affected their Facebook usage, 62,9% said they were less active than the previous year and for those, whose usage was affected 61,5% were less active. Surprisingly, 18% of the respondents whose usage was affected, are now more active on Facebook.

Looking at information disclosure, men are more inclined to disclose information with 46,5% of male respondents having high disclosure levels. Women, on the other hand, are more private with their information with 45,8% of them disclosing little information. Overall trust perception towards Facebook among respondents was rather low - 86,4% of respondents have either very poor or below par trust in Facebook. Over half of the respondents had very poor trust perception towards Facebook, regardless of their usage patterns or privacy and disclosure behavior.

The higher the levels of trust, the more people spend time on Facebook. 8,3% of the people who spend more than 4 h a day on Facebook perceive good levels of trust in the platform. Only 2,9% of the ones who spend less than an hour there, have the same level of trust in Facebook. Same tendencies apply to using Facebook's different possibilities, functionalities and features. People with low or medium activity have lower levels of trust compared to the ones with high activity.

3.2   Concept Design

The aim of this research step was to develop a paper prototype as a proof of concept by a group of design experts. To achieve this, the data gathered from the survey about Estonians' Facebook usage was combined with literature review results and presented to experts. This way, the experts had sufficient information to understand the character of the user in more detail. The design session consisted of five stages: debriefing the survey results, defining user needs and articulating problem statement, drafting the design concept vision, agreeing on a specific vision that reassures users' trust and finally, paper prototyping to consolidate the problem solutions.

One bottleneck brought out by the experts was the public image and general reputation of Facebook. The fact that Facebook has been sharing user data without their consent is acknowledged by many and people are more aware of the risks. To rebuild trust, Facebook should be more transparent in different processes - e.g. design, engineering and finances. One aspect of trust is reciprocity - users should gain something extra besides features for sharing their data. Another important topic is general trustworthiness of Facebook and its content. There is a need for users to be reassured that the information they see on Facebook is not dubious, and if something can be considered ambiguous it will not be spreaded.

Combining different possibilities that arose from the design concept drafting stage, the experts decided that a dashboard presenting information disclosed by the user and data collected about user behavior would be the best solution. Most prevailing concept was to visualise as much as possible in a simple way so that the user would have some overview by just seeing the dashboard. One way to do this is by using different data visualization techniques to draw attention to the most basic information which is data collected and shared with third party service providers. The user should also be provided with different filters to break it down - period, type and parties that have access to the information.

In addition to visualizing the data, the dashboard should include a short report about the information presented in the graphs and a possibility to further review the specifics of the shared data. This means specifying when and how was this data collected, who has access to it, when was the access granted, how is this data being used by anyone who has access to it, etc.. For the users to comprehend the vast amounts of data, it should be categorised, giving the user easy access to specific data they are interested in. It is important not to overwhelm the user, on the contrary, provide them with a simple comprehensive overview of the data they want to review.

4 Conclusion

In the past seven years, six big social networks have encountered massive privacy breaches which have an impact on users' perception of trust and also their usage. The more control users have over their information and data, the more they can trust the social network. Trust, in turn, determines whether or not users will remain loyal to a social network and will keep using it. There are several frameworks that help designers to create services that are perceived trustworthy, but Facebook has faced criticism about their design approaches. This can be solved by designing ethically, meaning that at all times the user is kept in mind.

The results of the study confirm that trust in Facebook among Estonians is very low and they would like to have more control over their data. Design experts designed a solution that would provide Facebook users with tools to control and manage their personal information. The users would have the opportunity to obtain more information about which data is being collected about them, how is it used and who has access to it. It gives users control over their information which will ultimately increase the level of trust in the platform. Knowing how users perceive trust and its effect on their usage behavior, designers can design platforms that are trustworthy and hence, user friendly.

References

1. Weisbaum, H.: Trust in Facebook has dropped by 66 percent since the Cambridge Analytica scandal, April 2018. https://nbcnews.to/2vJnYZX. Accessed 17 Mar 2020
2. Christofides, E., Muise, A., Desmarais, S.: Information disclosure and control on Facebook: are they two sides of the same coin or two different processes? Cyberpsychol. Behav. 12(3), 341–345 (2009)
3. Dhami, A., Agarwal, N., Chakraborty, T.K., Singh, B.P., Minj, J.: Impact of trust, security and privacy concerns in social networking: an exploratory study to understand the pattern of information revelation in Facebook. In: 2013 IEEE 3rd International Advance Computing Conference (IACC), pp. 465–469. IEEE, February 2013
4. Christofides, E., Muise, A., Desmarais, S.: Hey mom, what's on your Facebook? Comparing Facebook disclosure and privacy in adolescents and adults. Soc. Psychol. Personal. Sci. 3(1), 48–54 (2012)
5. Universal McCann: Wave 9. The Meaning of Moments. Glen Parker, New York (2017)
6. Lomas, N.: How Facebook has reacted since the data misuse scandal broke, April 2018. https://tcrn.ch/327pql5. Accessed 17 Mar 2020
7. Ivanova, I.: 8 promises from Facebook after Cambridge Analytica, April 2018. https://cbsn.ws/32hl1w0. Accessed 17 Mar 2020
8. Kokoszka, P.: #DeleteFacebook: Facebook alternatives to get your social media fix, July 2018. http://bit.ly/38M1JRC. Accessed 17 Mar 2020
9. Buchanan, T., Paine, C., Joinson, A.N., Reips, U.D.: Development of measures of online privacy concern and protection for use on the Internet. J. Am. Soc. Inf. Sci. Technol. 58(2), 157–165 (2007)
10. Data Never Sleeps 6.0 (2018). http://bit.ly/3d46QiF. Accessed 17 Mar 2020
11. Data Breaches (2019). https://www.privacyrights.org/data-breaches. Accessed 17 Mar 2020
12. Gemalto: Data privacy and new regulations take center stage (2019). https://breachlevelindex.com/request-report. Accessed 17 Mar 2020

13. Whittaker, Z.: 171 million VK.com accounts stolen by hackers, June 2016. https://zd.net/2IPZPnM. Accessed 17 Mar 2020

14. MacMillan, D., McMillan, R.: Google exposed user data, feared repercussions of disclosing to public, October 2018. https://on.wsj.com/2SHCdYg. Accessed 17 Mar 2020

15. Price, R.: Hackers stole millions of Facebook users' highly sensitive data—and the FBI has asked it not to say who might be behind it, October 2018. http://bit.ly/2WwK4KL. Accessed 17 Mar 2020

16. Price, R.: Facebook endured a staggering number of scandals and controversies in 2018 - here they all are, December 2018. http://bit.ly/38U8bW1. Accessed 17 Mar 2020

17. Wathieu, L., Friedman, A.A.: An empirical approach to understanding privacy valuation. In: HBS Marketing Research Paper, (07-075) (2007)

18. Livingstone, S.: Children's privacy online: experimenting with boundaries within and beyond the family (2006)

19. Cavoukian, A.: Privacy by design in law, policy and practice. A white paper for regulators, decision-makers and policy-makers (2011)

20. Hansen, M.: Marrying transparency tools with user-controlled identity management. In: Fischer-Hübner, S., Duquenoy, P., Zuccato, A., Martucci, L. (eds.) Privacy and Identity 2007. ITIFIP, vol. 262, pp. 199–220. Springer, Boston, MA (2008). https://doi.org/10.1007/978-0-387-79026-8_14

21. Borking, J.J., Raab, C.D.: Laws, PETs and other technologies for privacy protection. J. Inf. Law Technol. 1, 1–14 (2001)

22. Hoadley, C.M., Xu, H., Lee, J.J., Rosson, M.B.: Privacy as information access and illusory control: the case of the Facebook News Feed privacy outcry. Electron. Commer. Res. Appl. 9(1), 50–60 (2010)

23. Wang, N., Xu, H., Grossklags, J.: Third-party apps on Facebook: privacy and the illusion of control. In: Proceedings of the 5th ACM Symposium on Computer Human Interaction for Management of Information Technology, p. 4. ACM, December 2011

24. Gefen, D., Karahanna, E., Straub, D.W.: Trust and TAM in online shopping: an integrated model. MIS Q. 27(1), 51–90 (2003)

25. Kim, D., Benbasat, I.: Trust-related arguments in internet stores: a framework for evaluation. J. Electron. Commer. Res. 4(2), 49–64 (2003)

26. Lauer, T.W., Deng, X.: Building online trust through privacy practices. Int. J. Inf. Secur. 6 (5), 323–331 (2007)

27. Schoorman, F.D., Mayer, R.C., Davis, J.H.: An integrative model of organizational trust: past, present, and future (2007)

28. Flechais, I., Riegelsberger, J., Sasse, M.A.: Divide and conquer: the role of trust and assurance in the design of secure socio-technical systems. In: Proceedings of the 2005 Workshop on New Security Paradigms, pp. 33–41. ACM, September 2005

29. Sherchan, W., Nepal, S., Paris, C.: A survey of trust in social networks. ACM Comput. Surv. (CSUR) 45(4), 1–33 (2013)

30. Strufe, T.: Safebook: a privacy-preserving online social network leveraging on real-life trust. IEEE Commun. Mag. 47, 95–101 (2009)

Problematic Use of the Internet - Using Machine Learning in a Prevention Programme

Eryka Probierz[1,2]([ID]) and Adam Gałuszka[1] [ID]

[1] Silesian University of Technology, 44-100 Gliwice, Poland
erykaprobierz@gmail.com
[2] University of Silesia, 40-007 Katowice, Poland

Abstract. The aim of the study is to use machine learning methods in building a prevention program for Problematic Use of the Internet. On the basis of the collected database, a multi-stage analysis was performed to construct a model for selecting the users of the prevention program in order to best match the content that will be included in it. The results were based on three decision tree models. The use of such a matching mechanism in a prevention programme is likely to increase its effectiveness and reach a wider audience. Additionally, the problematic use of the Internet itself is a heterogeneous phenomenon and proper identification of the most addictive elements and work on them has a chance to increase the effectiveness of prevention.

Keywords: Problematic Internet Use · Prevention programme · Decision trees

1 Introduction

Over the years, a great many constructions have been created to describe the excessive or inappropriate use of technology such as the Internet. There is talk of its compulsive use, its dependence on the Internet or net-holism [1]. The lack of clarity in defining this phenomenon is the result of many independent studies, as well as an attempt to provide a clear answer to the need to describe and explain the phenomenon, which began in the 1990s [2]. However, regardless of the name of the phenomenon, there is a growing group of people struggling with the consequences of excessive Internet use [3]. The increase in the number of people in need of help in this area has made it necessary for psychologists, pedagogues or practitioners' psychotherapists, as well as scientists - researchers.

1.1 Contribution

In this work a set of psychological tools designed to measure different aspects of PUI level is used to build an expert system for selection of personalized preventic program. On the basis of data statistical analysis, it is proposed to model the expert system as a set of three decision trees being one of machine learning approaches [4, 5]. The first tree automatically classifies the PUI risk level, the second one determines the duration of the prophylactic programme, the third one determines type of prevention program.

© Springer Nature Switzerland AG 2020
C. Stephanidis and M. Antona (Eds.): HCII 2020, CCIS 1226, pp. 231–238, 2020.
https://doi.org/10.1007/978-3-030-50732-9_31

2 Theoretical Background

Problematic Use of the Internet is a complex phenomenon, the occurrence of which is connected with the preceding factors supporting the development of inappropriate forms of Internet use [6, 7, 17]. The PUI phenomenon is defined as a set of non-adaptive beliefs and their behavioral consequences relating to the Internet and having a real impact on the quality of an individual's functioning. The mechanism of formation of Problematic Internet Use assumes, apart from obvious having access to the Internet, the occurrence of certain situational factors and specific psychopathology leading to non-adaptive beliefs about the Internet. Among situational factors, stressful situations, unplanned, sudden changes in lifestyle play an important role. Among psychopathologies, depression, anxiety, and addictions are the most common. Non-adaptive beliefs combined with social factors lead to Generalized Problematic Use of the Internet [8]. Based on the PUI construction, a scale was created of a generalized PUI, which in its second edition has been translated into Polish (own translation) and used in this study [8, 9]. This scale consists of four subscales. One of them is preference social contacts online. This may be due to the belief that this kind of communication is safer or more effective [10]. Another subscale is insufficient self-regulation, i.e. reduced ability to control time spent on the Internet. It consists of two components: cognitive engagement, often compared to the phenomenon of immersion, and compulsive use of the Internet. The third subscale is mood regulation, a strategy in which a person experiencing unpleasant, in his or her opinion, emotions tries to react on the Internet. The last one subscribes to the PUI (e.g. reduction of family or collegial relations or negligence at work). Referring to the diathesis-stress model one can assume that one of the PUI predecessors may be the personality of the network user [11, 13].

3 Method

3.1 Participants

A heterogeneous sample of 523 Polish Internet users over a period of 9 months (March 2018 to November 2018) was obtained. The data was collected using an online survey, which was constructed on the google portal of the survey. Link to the survey was sent to people interested in using social networking sites, e-mailing list and Internet forums. The data was collected and analyzed anonymously. The invitation to participate was posted in the form of a post to which one could respond, and additionally encouraged to send the obtained link to further friends.

3.2 Questionnaires

Socio-demographic survey. The survey was used to investigate the relationship between basic socio-demographic data and Problematic Internet Use. The survey included questions about gender, age, romance (Yes/No), marital status (free, informal, marital, divorced, widower), education (primary, lower secondary, basic, secondary and higher), professional status (work, unemployed, studies, studies and works), place of residence (village, small town, medium town, big town). Another element included questions about the time of using the Internet daily and weekly, the most frequently chosen device for browsing the Internet, the place where the network is most frequently used and the purpose of using the Internet.

GPIUS2 – Generalized Problematic Internet Use Scale 2 [7]. The scale consists of 15 items that measure five constructions. There are 3 questions for each structure. The scale measures preference for online social interaction, mood regulation, cognitive preoccupation, compulsive Internet use and negative outcomes. Each question can be answered by selecting from a 7-point scale, starting with 1 - strongly disagree and ending with 7 - Strongly agree. The maximum score possible on the scale is 105 and the minimum is 15.

DASS-21 Depression, Anxiety and Stress Scale – 21 [12]. This tool consists of three subscales, each of which consists of 7 questions. Subscribers to depression, anxiety and stress, respectively. The answer can be given by selecting from 4 possible options, starting with 0 - Did not apply to me at all and ending with 3 - Applied to me very much, or most of the time. In order to calculate the overall score you need to sum up the results of the individual scales and then add the results multiplied by two to each other, which allows you to obtain a scale with a minimum score of 0 and a maximum score of 42.

3.3 Obtained Data

Based on the data obtained, 304 women and 212 men participated in the study. 195 people were in informal relationships, 233 were single, 79 were married and 9 were divorced. 116 people lived in a big city, 164 in a medium-sized town, 154 in a small town and 82 in a village. 263 people worked, 143 studied, 85 worked and studied, and 15 people were unemployed.

4 Results

The aim of the study was to obtain a representative set of data allowing to build a procedure to determine the intensity and type of Problematic Use of the Internet. This type of grouping allows to adjust the prophylactic program, both in terms of duration and types of materials provided to participants [11]. The first stage of the examination was to determine the duration of the prophylactic programme for a given person. To accomplish this task, the stages of classification of the obtained data were specified. The first stage divided the study group into three risk groups: low risk, medium risk and high risk. This division was made on the basis of the results of the sum for the scale of Problematic Internet Use. Due to the large research group, it was decided to determine the normality on the basis of the values of the bias and curtosis for GPIUS2 sum. The results obtained allowed to state that the distribution has the features of normal distribution.

Low risk group: from 15 points to medium − standard deviation.
Medium risk group: from medium − standard deviation to medium + standard deviation.
High risk group: medium to medium + standard deviation up to 105 points.
On the basis of the presented division, 85 persons with low risk of PIU, 348 persons with medium risk of PIU and 83 persons with high risk of PIU. Then, in order to determine the duration of the prophylactic programme, the data obtained from the DASS-21 questionnaire were used to distinguish three subscale: depression, anxiety and stress [14–16].

For this purpose, for each group (low, middle, high risk) an arithmetic mean value + half of the subscale standard deviation (depression, anxiety, stress) was calculated. Persons who obtained values greater than the sum of the mean and half of the standard deviation for a given risk group were redirected to the higher risk group.

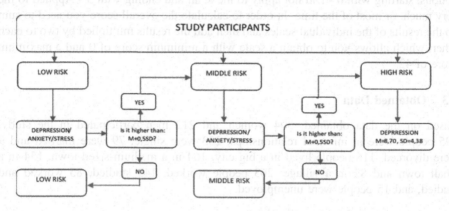

Fig. 1. Decision tree 1: automated classification of PUI risk level

Based on the method used (Fig. 1), a division into three groups was obtained (Fig. 2). The duration of the prophylactic programme was assigned to each degree of risk. The duration is 1 week for low risk individuals, 2 weeks for medium risk individuals and 4 weeks for high risk individuals.

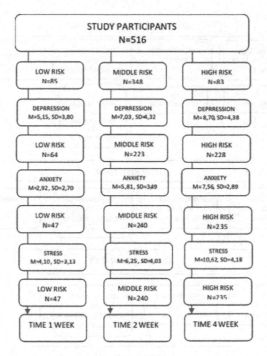

Fig. 2. Decision tree 2: duration of the prophylactic programme

The next stage of the study was to determine the type of prophylactic programme. Three specialist programmes and one general programme were specified. Specialized programs are social and communication skills program (referring to GPIUS2: preference for online social interaction), emotions and affects (referring to GPIUS: mood regulation) and time control and procrastination (referring to GPIUS2: negative consequences, cognitive preoccupation, compulsive Internet use). Anyone can be eligible for the specialist programme, whether they are in a low, medium or high risk group. Qualification for a given specialist programme is determined by the result for a given subscale, which corresponds to the specialist programme. If a person for the awarded subscale obtains a score higher than the average plus standard deviation - he or she is qualified to the program. It is possible to qualify for more programmes. Full data is presented on Fig. 3. The general program is applied when the examined person cannot be assigned to a specialized program. The number in parentheses is given for each program when it occurred together with another program.

The decision models presented allow, on the basis of data provided by a person joining a prevention programme, to decide on the duration of the programme and the type of programme.

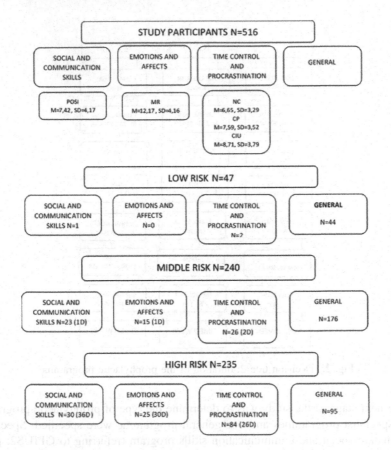

Fig. 3. Decision tree 3: type of prevention program

5 Discussion and Conclusion

The aim of the article was to specify the methods allowing to simplify the process of qualification for the prevention programme [18, 19]. The development of such methods will allow for a better adjustment of the programme and increase the effectiveness of the programme in participants [20–22]. Based on the data obtained, two schemes of conduct were distinguished. One scheme concerns the duration of the prevention programme and depends on the results in the following scales: depression, anxiety and stress. The next scheme is designed to decide whether a specialized or general program will be adjusted to the participant. Which program will be selected is determined by the data obtained from the subscale of the Generalized Problematic Use of the Internet. To sum up, three program lengths are listed: weekly, bi-weekly and monthly, and four types of programs: specialized: social and communication skills, emotions and affects, time control and procrastination and general program. The next stage of the research will be to check the effectiveness of both length and type of programme models compared to those chosen by the participants themselves. The creation of selection methods is to personalize the prophylactic program and increase its strength.

Acknowledgements. The work of Eryka Probierz was supported in part by the European Union through the European Social Fund as a scholarship under Grant POWR.03.02.00-00-I029 and Non-competition project of the Polish National Agency for Academic Exchange "International scholarship exchange of PhD candidates and academic staff", project No. POWR.03.03.00-IP.08-00-P13/18, implemented under Measure: 3.3 Internationalisation of Polish higher education, OP KED for first author.

The work of Adam Galuszka was supported by the SUT under Grant 02/060/BK_20/0007 (BK-276/RAU3/2020) the subsidy for maintaining and developing the research potential, in 2020.

References

1. Greenfield, D.: Psychological characteristics of compulsive Internet use: a preliminary analysis. CyberPsychol. Behav. **2**(5), 403–412 (1999)
2. Caplan, S.E.: Problematic Internet use and psychosocial well-being: development of a theory-based cognitive–behavioral measurement instrument. Comput. Hum. Behav. **18**(5), 553–575 (2002)
3. Davis, R.A.: A cognitive-behavioral model of pathological Internet use. Comput. Hum. Behav. **17**(2), 187–195 (2001)
4. Caplan, S.E.: A social skill account of problematic Internet use. J. Commun. **55**(4), 721–736 (2005)
5. Murthy, S.K.: Automatic Construction of Decision Trees from Data: A Multi-Disciplinary Survey. Data Min. Knowl. Disc. **2**, 345–389 (1998). https://doi.org/10.1023/A:100974463 0224
6. Kocev, D., Vens, C., Struyf, J., Džeroski, S.: Ensembles of multi-objective decision trees. In: Kok, J.N., Koronacki, J., Mantaras, R.L., Matwin, S., Mladenič, D., Skowron, A. (eds.) ECML 2007. LNCS (LNAI), vol. 4701, pp. 624–631. Springer, Heidelberg (2007). https://doi.org/10.1007/978-3-540-74958-5_61
7. Davis, R.A., Flett, G., Besser, A.: Validation of a new scale for measuring problematic Internet use: implications for pre-employment screening. CyberPsychol. Behav. **5**(4), 331–345 (2002)
8. Caplan, S.E.: Theory and measurement of generalized problematic Internet use: a two-step approach. Comput. Hum. Behav. **26**(5), 1089–1097 (2010)
9. Pontes, H.M., Caplan, S.E., Griffiths, M.D.: Psychometric validation of the generalized problematic Internet use scale 2 in a Portuguese sample. Comput. Hum. Behav. **63**, 823–833 (2016)
10. Spada, M.M.: An overview of problematic Internet use. Addict. Behav. **39**(1), 3–6 (2014)
11. Shapira, N., Goldsmith, T., Keck, P., Khosla, U., McElroy, S.: Psychiatric features of individuals with problematic Internet use. J. Affect. Disord. **57**(1–3), 267–272 (2000)
12. Makara-Studzińska, M., Petkowicz, B., Urbańska, A., Petkowicz, J.: Polish Translation of the DASS-21 [Measurement instrument]. http://www2.psy.unsw.edu.au/dass/Polish/Polish.htm
13. Ceyhan, A., Ceyhan, E.: Loneliness, depression, and computer self-efficacy as predictors of problematic Internet use. CyberPsychol. Behav. **11**(6), 699–701 (2008)

14. Gámez-Guadix, M., Orue, I., Smith, P., Calvete, E.: Longitudinal and reciprocal relations of cyberbullying with depression, substance use, and problematic Internet use among adolescents. J. Adolesc. Health **53**(4), 446–452 (2013)
15. Park, S., Hong, K., Park, E., Ha, K., Yoo, H.: The association between problematic Internet use and depression, suicidal ideation and bipolar disorder symptoms in Korean adolescents. Aust. N. Z. J. Psychiatry **47**(2), 153–159 (2012)
16. Caplan, S.: Relations among loneliness, social anxiety, and problematic Internet use. CyberPsychol. Behav. **10**(2), 234–242 (2007)
17. Aboujaoude, E.: Problematic Internet use: an overview. World Psychiatry **9**(2), 85–90 (2010)
18. Kormas, G., Critselis, E., Janikian, M., Kafetzis, D., Tsitsika, A.: Risk factors and psychosocial characteristics of potential problematic and problematic Internet use among adolescents: a cross-sectional study. BMC Public Health **11**(1), 95 (2011). https://doi.org/10.1186/1471-2458-11-595
19. Moreau, A., Laconi, S., Delfour, M., Chabrol, H.: Psychopathological profiles of adolescent and young adult problematic Facebook users. Comput. Hum. Behav. **44**, 64–69 (2015)
20. Shaw, M., Black, D.W.: Internet addiction. CNS Drugs **22**(5), 353–365 (2008). https://doi.org/10.2165/00023210-200822050-00001
21. Probierz, E., Sikora, W., Gałuszka, A., Gałuszka, A.: Predictive algorithms in social sciences – problematic Internet use example. In: Gruca, A., Czachórski, T., Deorowicz, S., Harężlak, K., Piotrowska, A. (eds.) ICMMI 2019. AISC, vol. 1061, pp. 89–98. Springer, Cham (2020). https://doi.org/10.1007/978-3-030-31964-9_9
22. Gałuszka, A., Probierz, E.: Problematyczne używanie internetu a cechy osobowości i wczesne nieadaptacyjne schematy użytkowników sieci. Annales Universitatis Paedagogicae Cracoviensis. Studia de Cultura. Cyberpsychologia. Nowe strategie badania mediów i ich użytkowników **10**(4), 40–50 (2018)

Influence of Ad Congruence and Social Cues on the Probability of Choosing a Restaurant

Aline Simonetti$^{(\boxtimes)}$, Shobhit Kakaria, and Enrique Bigné

University of Valencia, 46022 Valencia, Spain
{aline.simonetti,shobhit.kakaria,enrique.bigne}@uv.es

Abstract. Information processing of digital content includes conscious and unconscious processes, memory, attitudes, and emotions and moods. Build up into the Heuristic-Systematic Model, that states that persuasion can occur through a systematic or heuristic way, this research explores the effect of social media (SM) ratings and the ad content embedded in the SM website. Online ratings (part of the user-generated content (UGC) in SM platforms) are often heuristics cues. Subtle forms of congruence, such as the matching category between a restaurant advertiser and the third-party ad, as well as UGC, could have an impact on consumers' attitudes towards the former. However, research on how SM platforms and advertising embedded on them are processed is scarce. This study investigates whether congruence between the advertiser and the ad and the UGC have an impact on the probability of going to the restaurant. We conducted a within-subjects 2 × 2 design online study with 295 participants manipulating ad congruence (congruent × incongruent) and valence of the ratings (positive × negative) to measure the probability of going to the restaurant. Each participant was exposed to four restaurants in a TripAdvisor layout with UGC. The results show that ad congruence had no statistically significant effect; however, the valence of the UGC had a main effect, in which a positive valence led to an average of 72% probability of going to the restaurant and negative valence to 42%. We concluded that the UGC is strong enough to overcome any effect of ad congruence in this study.

Keywords: Social media · Advertising · UGC · Restaurant

1 Introduction

Information processing of digital content is acknowledged as being part of the subfield marketing discipline "consumer behaviour", which includes conscious and unconscious processes, memory, attitudes, and emotions and moods [1]. One model of information processing of ad content is the Heuristic-Systematic Model (HSM) [2] proposing that persuasion can occur through a systematic or heuristic way. In social media platforms, the UGC is often classified as heuristics cues. In advertising, ad congruence defines which ad should be placed in the media, with the aim of increasing attention to the ad by making it relevant to the user. However, the results of ad congruence studies are mixed [3–6]. Subtle forms of congruence, such as the matching category between a restaurant advertiser and the third-party ad embedded alongside it,

© Springer Nature Switzerland AG 2020
C. Stephanidis and M. Antona (Eds.): HCII 2020, CCIS 1226, pp. 239–245, 2020.
https://doi.org/10.1007/978-3-030-50732-9_32

as well as UGC, could have an impact on consumers' attitudes towards the former. Despite it, research on the interaction of the UGC and embedded ads is scarce in social media platforms. This study investigates whether congruence between the advertiser and the third-party ad and the UGC (ratings of the restaurant) have an impact on the probability of going to the advertised restaurant.

A search in the literature shows that two models of information processing of ad content frequently used by marketing researchers are the Elaboration Likelihood Model, formalised by Petty and Cacioppo [7], and the HSM [2]. Within the HSM, a heuristic processing means that cues with little information can be used to reach a decision. In TripAdvisor, for example, consumers process the overall rating of a restaurant in a heuristic manner, since that rating can be considered as a simple and concise cue [8]. These star ratings have become highly relevant as firms are witnessing first-hand the significant impact of a well-managed star rating in driving sales [8]. We posit that because of the nature of heuristic processing, consumers may form their impressions about the service according to the overall rating provided by other consumers, having this heuristic cue as a source of impact in their decisions. In fact, a TripAdvisor survey with consumers registered in the platform revealed that among the Spanish respondents, 91% take into consideration the online reviews of the restaurant [9]. Therefore, our first research question is:

RQ1: Does the valence of the UGC affect the probability of going to an advertised restaurant?

Past research demonstrated that congruence affects perceptions towards the ad [10–12], that ultimately may influence the purchase decision of the advertised product [10, 12, 13]. Karmarkar [14] developed two experiments using a target object and a display set with other objects that either matched or mismatched the category of the target. The second study was incentive-compatible and replicated the findings of the first study. They showed that the purchase intention of the target differs between the two conditions, in which participants in the group of the displayed matched products reported significant more intention to purchase the target item than those of the mismatched group. Moreover, more the perceived similarity and liking of the objects, higher the purchase intent. The explanation given for these findings is that the matched displays options might support or reinforce the purchase decision of the target object; whereas a mismatched set might induce the feeling of opportunity cost by reminding the consumer that the money could be spent in another type of product. Therefore, our second research question is:

RQ2: Does the congruence of the embedded ad affect the probability of going to an advertised restaurant?

We answered both research questions in an online behavioural study using TripAdvisor stimuli.

2   Method

In this study, we refer to congruence as the relationship between the categories of both the social media content and the ad embedded on it. A congruent condition in TripAdvisor in our study means that the third-party ad has the same type of food as the main advertiser, i.e. if the advertiser is a pizza restaurant, the embedded ad is also from a competitor of the same segment (a pizza restaurant). An incongruent condition means both categories are not the same (e.g., the embedded ad could be of a sushi restaurant).

2.1 Design

A within-subjects (WS) in a 2 × 2 design with ad congruence (congruent × incongruent) and valence of the ratings (positive: 4.5 stars × negative: 1.5 stars) as the independent variables (IV), type of restaurant as a covariate, and the probability of going to the restaurant as the dependent variable. We decided to use the continuous metric of the probability of going to the restaurant instead of an intention to go scale because it was found that the former captures better the real behaviour [15].

We used the same upper part layout TripAdvisor uses when displayed in a desktop. We decided for not including any comments as they would be a significant source of confounding due to their subjective nature. There were four different types of restaurant (pasta, pizza, paella, steak) and four stimuli: (1) positive valence and ad congruent (PV_AC); (2) negative valence and ad congruent (NV_AC); (3) positive valence and ad incongruent (PV_AI); and (4) negative valence and ad incongruent (NV_AI). Each participant saw four stimuli (one of each condition linked to one different restaurant per condition). There were four groups of participants in order to cover all the 16 stimuli (four types of restaurant × four conditions) (Table 1). The presentation order was randomised across participants.

Table 1. List of the four groups and conditions.

	Restaurant 1	Restaurant 2	Restaurant 3	Restaurant 4
Group 1	PV_AC	NV_AC	PV_AI	NV_AI
Group 2	NV_AC	PV_AC	NV_AI	PV_AI
Group 3	PV_AI	NV_AI	PV_AC	NV_AC
Group 4	NV_AI	PV_AI	NV_AC	PV_AC

2.2 Participants

The experiment was conducted in Spain. Spain was chosen due to its representative size and increasing potential in the restaurant market [16]. 295 participants living in Spain (57% female; age range: 18–67, mean age: 33,3; 62% workers, 27% students, and 11% unemployed; 93% users of TripAdvisor restaurant platform) answered an online survey via the online platform ClickWorker. The participants were monetarily compensated for completing the experiment. The data were collected in January 2020.

2.3 Procedure and Task

The participants received an email from an online survey platform inviting them to complete the survey designed using the SurveyMonkey platform.

The participants saw a screen with the first TripAdvisor stimulus. When they decide to proceed to the next part, they rated the probability of going to the restaurant they just saw using a slider bar ranging from 0 to 100%. After it, the second TripAdvisor stimulus appeared, and the task was the same until the last question for the fourth restaurant was answered. The order of presentation of the four stimuli was randomised across participants. Then three control questions came in sequence (liking of the presented foods, frequency of eating in restaurants, frequency of using TripAdvisor when eating in restaurants). Finally, they answered some demographic questions (e.g., gender, age) and a manipulation check question (i.e., a question asking for the purpose of the experiment). The experiment was conducted in Spanish.

2.4 Pre-test

We conducted an online pre-test with 32 participants (mean age 27.7) to verify whether the chosen ads are perceived as congruent or incongruent. Participants rated pairs of images using a slider bar ranging from 0 to 100 (0 = not congruent at all, 50 = neutral, and 100 = very congruent). A pair was composed by a picture of the advertised restaurant combined with either its congruent ad or its incongruent ad. Therefore, each participant rated eight pairs in total (4 restaurants × 2 types of ad for each). The order of presentation was randomised across participants.

2.5 Analyses

The data were analysed using SPSS 26.0 statistical software.

3 Results

3.1 Pre-test

A within-subjects ANOVA showed that the manipulation in ad congruence was valid, as the two ad categories differed between them $(F(1, 31) = 297,726, p = .000)$. The four ads chosen as congruent ads had a mean congruence of $M = 79.164$ $(SD = 17.046)$, and the four ads chosen as incongruent ads had a mean congruence of $M = 18.047$ $(SD = 16.009)$. We also looked to the means of congruence level for each stimulus in separate. All the four congruent stimuli had means above 50 (using a 95% C.I.), and all the four incongruent stimuli had means below 50 (95% C.I.).

3.2 Online Study

In the online study, participants faced four TripAdvisor stimuli each one linked to one of the four conditions (PV_AC, NV_AC, PV_AI, NV_AI), and answered the probability of going to each restaurant. A within-subject ANOVA (repeated measures) with the probability of going as the dependent variable (continuous variable) resulted in a significant main effect of valence. Positive ratings of the UGC led to a higher probability of going to the restaurant $(F(1, 294) = 235.581, p = .000)$, answering our RQ1.

In average, participants indicated a 71% probability of going to the restaurant (SD = 18.20) when in the positive valence condition and 43% in the negative one (SD = 26.38). For RQ2, the analysis resulted in a null-effect of congruence. There was neither a main effect of congruence nor an interaction effect of valence and congruence in the DV.

4 Conclusion

The present study addressed whether the congruence of the ad could have an impact on the TripAdvisor advertiser. More specifically, we sought to observe if the user would change the probability of going to the restaurant depending on the type of the third-party embedded ad. We found that congruence does not affect this probability; however, the valence of the UGC has a main effect on it, addressing the other question of this study. Positive evaluations of the restaurant made by other people increase the probability of the user going to that restaurant compared to the same restaurant with negative evaluations. It is relevant to mention that the participants did not have access to any comment of customers, but only to the average ratings of the place, which means that participants relied on a simple heuristic cue. The valence of the heuristic cue (i.e., ratings) had a main effect on the probability of going to the restaurant, in which a positive valence led to higher values than negative valence. We also searched for a possible interaction between the heuristic cue and the congruence of the ad, and it turned that this interaction is non-significant. We concluded that the UGC is strong enough to overcome any effect of ad congruence in our study. Since all the ads were from direct competitors (i.e., other restaurants), it does not matter if the ad shows a competitor of the same category or not, because both do not influence on the consumers' probability of going to the restaurant. Thus, an ad of a direct competitor does not harm the advertiser (main restaurant); however, the negative valence of the UGC does.

5 Implications, Limitations, and Future Directions

This research demonstrated the importance of UGC in social media for business. The valence of the ratings affected the four tested restaurant types in the same way. Considering this strong effect, businesses do not need to seek only to manage good pictures of their places or to be concerned with the third-party ad that is shown in their advertisement in TripAdvisor. More importantly, they should consider that the content created by the users of the social media platform has a direct and powerful impact on the decisions of future customers. Therefore, to promote actions that can generate a positive impact on the business in social media may also be considered in the marketing strategy plans.

However, this study has limitations that can be overcome in future researches. The participants made their decisions considering a hypothetical situation. To improve internal validity, an incentive-compatible task could be used. The layout of the TripAdvisor stimulus reflected only the desktop version of the platform layout.

Therefore, the mobile version should be tested to confirm if the findings apply to other page designs. We tested only one form of congruence, one type of ad (static and small size) and used only the TripAdvisor platform. To improve external validity, more forms of congruence and ads could be verified in TripAdvisor as well as in other service platforms (e.g., Booking.com). An interesting future direction would be to explore the reasons behind the behavioural findings by applying neurophysiological tools. As an example, eye-tracking could be used to explore how visual attention is distributed across the stimulus.

Acknowledgements. The authors gratefully acknowledge the financial support of Rhumbo (European Union's Horizon 2020 research and innovation program under the Marie Skłodowska-Curie Grant Agreement No. 813234).

References

1. MacInnis, D.J., Folkes, V.S.: The disciplinary status of consumer behavior: a sociology of science perspective on key controversies. J. Consum. Res. **36**(6), 899–914 (2010)
2. Chaiken, S.: Heuristic versus systematic information processing and the use of source versus message cues in persuasion. J. Pers. Soc. Psychol. **39**(5) (1980)
3. Moore, R.S., Stammerjohan, C.A., Coulter, R.A.: Banner advertiser-web site context congruity and color effects on attention and attitudess. J. Advert. **34**(2), 71–84 (2005)
4. Wang, A.: Advertising engagement: a driver of message involvement on message effects. J. Advert. Res. **46**(4), 355–368 (2006)
5. Moorman, M., Neijens, P.C., Smit, E.G.: The effects of magazine-induced psychological responses and thematic congruence on memory and attitude toward the ad in a real-life setting. J. Advert. **31**(4), 27–40 (2002)
6. Rieger, D., Bartz, F., Bente, G.: Reintegrating the Ad: effects of context congruency banner advertising in hybrid media. J. Media Psychol. **27**(2), 64–77 (2015)
7. Petty, R.E., Cacioppo, J.T.: The elaboration likelihood model of persuasion. In: Communication and Persuasion. SSSOC, pp. 1–24. Springer, New York (1986). https://doi.org/10.1007/978-1-4612-4964-1_1
8. Yoon, Y., Kim, A.J., Kim, J., Choi, J.: The effects of eWOM characteristics on consumer ratings: evidence from TripAdvisor.com. Int. J. Advert. **38**(5), 684–703 (2019)
9. TripAdvisor LCC: Influences on Diner Decision-Making (2018). https://www.tripadvisor.com/ForRestaurants/r3227. Accessed 15 Dec 2019
10. Chun, K.Y., Song, J.H., Hollenbeck, C.R., Lee, J.H.: Are contextual advertisements effective? The moderating role of complexity in banner advertising. Int. J. Advert. **33**(2), 351–371 (2014)
11. Dahlén, M., Rosengren, S., Törn, F., Öhman, N.: Could placing ads wrong be right? Advertising effects of thematic incongruence. J. Advert. **37**(3), 57–67 (2008)
12. Segev, S., Wang, W., Fernandes, J.: The effects of ad-context congruency on responses to advertising in blogs: exploring the role of issue involvement. Int. J. Advert. **33**(1), 17–36 (2014)
13. Kim, S., Choi, S.M.: An examination of effects of credibility and congruency on consumer responses to banner advertisements. J. Internet Commer. **11**(2), 139–160 (2012)

14. Karmarkar, U.R.: The impact of 'display-set' options on decision-making. J. Behav. Decis. Mak. **30**(3), 744–753 (2017)
15. Wright, M., Macrae, M.: Bias and variability in purchase intention scales. J. Acad. Mark. Sci. **35**(4), 617–624 (2007). https://doi.org/10.1007/s11747-007-0049-x
16. TripAdvisor LLC: The 2019 TripAdvisor and TheFork Economic Impact Study | TripAdvisor For Restaurants (2019). https://www.tripadvisor.com/ForRestaurants/r8927. Accessed 15 Dec 2019

The Framing Effect of Questions in Community Question-Answering Sites

Qian Wu[✉], Dion Hoe-Lian Goh, and Chei Sian Lee

Wee Kim Wee School of Communication and Information, Nanyang
Technological University, 31 Nanyang Link, Singapore 637718, Singapore
Qian003@e.ntu.edu.sg, {ASHLGoh,LeeCS}@ntu.edu.sg

Abstract. In Community Question-Answering (CQA) sites, the question is often the starting point for information exchange, eliciting a series of responses that result in a response network (RN) whose nodes are the postings, while edges represent the responses between postings. This argument is supported by framing theory which posits that different message forms, their "frames", lead to different user responses.

This research investigated how question frames influenced their resulting RNs. Question frames were operationalized as conversational and informational frames. Social network analysis was conducted to explore the RNs of different question frames for both Science, Technology, Engineering and Mathematics (STEM) and non-STEM topics.

Interestingly, most STEM conversational questions had postings that directly responded to the question, whereas informational questions attracted more comments on response postings. However, no significant differences were found in the non-STEM topics. Our research suggests that users should appropriately frame questions to generate desired responses from the community.

Keywords: Community Question-Answering · Framing theory · Response behavior · Centrality · Social network analysis

1 Introduction

Community Question-Answering (CQA) sites refer to virtual communities where users ask and respond to questions online. In these sites, the question is often the starting point for information exchange that elicits a series of responses [3]. Further, these responses result in a response network (RN) whose nodes are the postings, while edges represent the responses between postings.

As such, the manner in which a question is phrased can affect the RNs obtained. This argument is supported by the framing theory which posits that the same content framed in different ways leads to different recipient responses [1]. Likewise, question frames emphasize on different perspectives of the same problem and thus guide responders to concentrate on the different aspects of the problem [8]. Specifically, question frames could influence the responses by narrowing down the scope of problems [5]. In addition, question frames would further influence asker-responder relationships. For instance,

© Springer Nature Switzerland AG 2020
C. Stephanidis and M. Antona (Eds.): HCII 2020, CCIS 1226, pp. 246–252, 2020.
https://doi.org/10.1007/978-3-030-50732-9_33

questions with more openness could lead to better asker-responder relationships than "closed" questions (e.g. yes/no question) [19]. Put succinctly, question frames affect both individual responses and response relationships between postings. In the research, we operationalized question frames as informational frames for information-seeking, and conversational frames for generating discussions [9].

Beyond question frames, RNs in virtual communities are influenced by different types of content [6]. For example, it has been suggested that political topics can generate more responses than mathematics topics [11]. Similarly, there are more factual and technical contributions in science topics than those related to people and relationships topics [22]. Hence, this present research classified topics into two types – Science, Technology, Engineering and Mathematics (STEM) and non-STEM topics. This classification is in line with the findings that the two topics show types different use behaviors of electronic resources [12].

Taken together, our overarching research question is:

How do different question frames influence the RNs in CQA sites of STEM and non-STEM topics?

To investigate this research question, the structural centrality, which evaluates the importance of the questions in their RNs, was measured. Given that the RN comprises both postings and response relationships, content analysis was used to classify questions frames. Finally, the structural centrality and graphs of relationships were investigated with social network analysis (SNA).

2 Theoretical Framework

Framing theory suggests that the way that a message is constructed would bring about the specific interpretations by recipients [10]. Specifically, the way that the message is constructed is called a "frame" and the effect of a frame on the cognitive behavior is termed the "framing effect" [8]. This theory was widely cited in studies of collective action to generate expected responses from the publics [15]. For example, the "gain/loss frame" emphasizes the expected gains/losses of recipients will affect their decision-making process [16]. Similarly, in a survey of friendship, the people mentioned in responses varied among different question frames [4]. These findings suggests that questions would guide recipients to focus on the different perspectives of the same problem, and hence, further influence follow-up responses [8]. Hence, we propose that question frames in the CQA process, which is a collective action of information seeking and sharing, would lead to different RNs.

Previous studies have divided questions into two types of frames [9]. First, the informational frame refers to questions intended for information seeking. This type of frame would typically receive the needed information for askers with fewer responses, and thus, has higher information efficiency in information seeking [22]. Next, the conversational frame focuses on organizing discussions among users. It is suggested that this type of frame is mostly used by "discussion persons" and elicits more responses than the informational frame [2]. In sum, informational frames aim to meet the information needs of askers, while conversational frames aim to foster interactions between members of a community.

3 Framing Effect on RNs

Studies concerning the framing effect in collective action suggested that the process of framing was strongly influenced by the context (e.g. [1]). In line with these studies, we further investigated whether the framing effect of questions varied among different contexts. Previous studies indicated that users' preferences for electronic resources differed between the STEM and non-STEM domain [12]. This finding suggested that users' behaviors, including their responses, might differ between these two domains. Further, research has shown that the amount of responses and users' relationships varied between STEM and non-STEM topics in CQA sites [11, 22].

Currently, there are two types of networks in studies concerning virtual communities: (1) the user network whose nodes represent users and edges represent followed relationship, and (2) posting network whose nodes represent postings and edges represent responses. In particular, the former was mostly used in prior CQA studies and users' relationships have been extensively discussed (e.g. [2, 9]). These studies aimed to detect the experts or authorities among users [11, 22]. The latter network could better investigate the responses and information exchange relationships of postings. Thus, we constructed posting networks to investigate the framing effect of questions on RNs.

4 Data Collection and Analysis

Stack Exchange (SE) is a commonly used platform in CQA studies, and it comprises a range of STEM and non-STEM communities. In our work, the mathematics (MA) community was selected to represent STEM topics, while the English Language & Usage (EL) community was chosen to represent non-STEM topics. The two communities were established on similar dates and have similar numbers of visits each day. In terms of the sample size, previous works recommended that a minimum number of 100 questions should be used to construct the RNs [7]. Therefore, the 100 questions with most votes in the two communities were obtained via the application programming interface (API) provided by the SE website. The time range was set from 2010, the establishment date of the two sites, to September 31, 2019.

Analysis of data was two-fold. First, content analysis was used to classify question postings to the two frames. Previous studies of frame classification suggested that different frames were distinguished by their semantic grammar, including subject pronouns, verbs or conjunctions used in the sentences [20]. Considering that subject pronouns were usually omitted in informal questions – a phenomenon termed "conversational deletion" in linguistics [18] – we classified the two frames with verbs and conjunctions used in the sentence. In particular, informational frames were distinguished by verbs and conjunctions of "how to/can/long/much/many/do", "what is/are", while conversational frames were distinguished by conjunctions of "why", "is there any" and "or". Examples of informational frames include "What are imaginary numbers?", "What is the result of $\infty-\infty$?", and "How did 7 come to be an abbreviation for 'and' in Old English?". Examples of conversational frames include questions such as "Is there a word for a person with only one head?", "Why do English writers avoid explicit numerals?", and "Why does this innovative method of subtraction from a third grader always work?".

Next, the structural centrality of RNs was examined in SNA analysis. Here, structural centrality refers to the importance of the node in a network [17]. Three types of postings were included in the RNs: (1) question postings, (2) follow-up postings of questions, which is termed "direct responses", and comprises the answer postings and the comment postings to the question, and (3) comment postings of answer postings, which is termed "indirect responses". Furthermore, the indices of structural centrality used in this research were (1) degree centrality which counts the number of direct responses to a question, (2) betweenness centrality which calculates the frequency of a question that is between two other posting nodes, with higher betweenness centrality indicating fewer indirect responses of questions, and (3) eigenvector centrality which counts both direct and indirect responses to a question [21]. In addition, the RN graphs were drawn with the Gephi 0.9.2. Finally, SPSS v26 was used for the individual t-test of the differences between the two question frames.

5 Results

A total of 13,649 posts were downloaded. Of these, there were 96 question postings, 1,769 answer postings and 7,350 comment postings for STEM topics. At the same time, 100 question postings, 1,005 answer postings and 3,329 comment postings for non-STEM topics were obtained. In total, there were 196 question postings, comprising 52 STEM questions and 33 non-STEM questions with informational frames, as well as 44 posts STEM questions and 67 non-STEM questions with conversational frames.

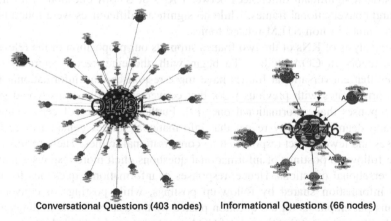

Conversational Questions (403 nodes)   Informational Questions (66 nodes)

Fig. 1. Networks of informational/conversational questions

First, to explore the differences of RNs between informational and conversational frames at the network level, the graphs of RNs belonging to the two frame types were constructed. Figure 1 shows the RNs of question frames. Here, nodes with larger size represent the postings of higher degree, and the links represent the response between the two postings. The relative importance of the questions in the RN can be reflected by the size of other nodes, with generally smaller sizes indicating higher importance of the question. It is clear that the RN of informational frames are more dispersed with larger size of other nodes (indicating less importance), and fewer amounts of responses than the that of conversational frames.

Further, to examine the framing effect of questions on RNs between two topics, the individual t-test was conducted. In the STEM-related topics, results showed that conversational frames had significantly higher degree centrality than informational frames ($t = 4.459$; $p = 0.000 < 0.001$), which meant that there were more direct responses in conversational questions. Betweenness centrality of conversational questions were higher than informational questions ($t = 2.093$; $p = 0.041 < 0.05$), which indicated that there were more comments to the follow-up postings of informational questions. As for eigenvector centrality, the means of conversational questions were higher than that of informational questions ($t = 3.214$; $p = 0.023 < 0.05$). Hence, RNs of conversational questions had more responses in total than informational questions. However, there was no significant difference in degree centrality ($t = 1.134$; $p = 0.260 > 0.05$), betweenness centrality ($t = 0.814$; $p = 0.418 > 0.05$) and eigenvector centrality ($t = 0.939$; $p = 0.350 > 0.05$) between the two frames in the non-STEM topics.

6 Discussion and Conclusion

In this research, we found differences between RNs across the two frames. Further, we uncovered differences in structural centrality between the two topics. These results demonstrated significant differences between RNs of STEM questions with informational and conversational frames, while no significant differences were found between the two frames in non-STEM-related topics.

The analysis of RNs of the two frames supports our proposition of the relevance of framing theory in CQA studies. To begin with, the eigenvector centrality of RNs indicates that conversational frames have more responses than informational frames, which corroborates with previous work that conversational questions would generate more responses than informational ones [9]. Further, measures of betweenness centrality and degree centrality reveal that informational frames generate more indirect responses and fewer direct responses than conversational frames. These results indicate that the follow-up postings of informational questions elicit more responses than those of conversational questions. Hence, responses of informational questions focus more on the information shared by follow-up postings, while postings of conversational questions put emphasis on the question posted by the askers. These findings are supported by the argument that the role of CQA answerers can be divided into two types – the "answer person" who provides informative responses with shorter threads and "discussion person" who establishes interactive relationships with longer threads [23]. Given that CQA users can distinguish the two types question frames [9], it is reasonable that informational frames would attract more answer persons, while conversational frames would attract more discussion persons.

It is interesting that the framing effect varies between the STEM and non-STEM topics. One possible explanation might be the different social norms in the communities of the two topics. Previous studies suggested that norms of CQA sites influence the amount of responses [22]. At the same time, non-STEM sites provide more social support than STEM sites, which lead to higher homophily among users [2, 13]. In online discussions, higher homophily leads to fewer responses with different opinions [14]. Hence, there were fewer responses to conversational questions in the non-STEM site, which further resulted in smaller differences between RNs of the two question types.

Importantly, our research provides a new perspective in CQA studies. It has been suggested that CQA studies could be divided into user-centered studies and content-centered studies, with the latter mainly focusing on the quality evaluation of postings. This research provides a new perspective in content-centered studies by focusing on question frames and indicating that the same problem with different frames would lead to different RNs. Furthermore, though previous studies have highlighted that responses might vary between factual/technological questions and opinion/discussion questions [22], little work has been done in revealing the mechanism of this effect. Here, framing theory gives a plausible explanation to how question types influence the responses. In addition, the framing effect further advances the understanding in how askers organize their expected RNs in the collective knowledge context. These findings, in return, support framing theory in collective actions studies with a new context.

The understanding of the framing effect of questions can better facilitate askers to generate questions to meet their information needs. In regards to information seeker, they can phrase their statements with the informational frame and generate RNs with fewer responses with the specific solution [9]. As for those who prefer multiple opinions or ideas, conversational frames are more appropriate to generate discussions.

Given that question frames affect both direct and indirect responses, we suggest an evolvement analysis of RNs to better understand the framing effect on different responses. The limitation of the research is the explanation of framing effect between the two topics (STEM and non-STEM). Given that the difference between topics might due to the differences among users [12], a survey could be conducted to investigate this possibility. Moreover, question frames might not only influence the RNs, but also the quality of responses [9]. Thus, qualitative analysis is suggested in future work to examine the information quality of the responses elicited by the two frames.

References

1. Ackland, R., O'Neil, M.: Online collective identity: the case of the environmental movement. Soc. Netw. 33(3), 177–190 (2011)
2. Adamic, L.A., Zhang, J., Bakshy, E., Ackerman, M.S.: Knowledge sharing and Yahoo Answers: everyone knows something. In: Proceedings of WWW 2008, pp. 665–674. ACM (2008)
3. Bighash, L., Oh, P., Fulk, J., Monge, P.: The value of questions in organizing: reconceptualizing contributions to online public information goods. Commun. Theory 28(1), 1–21 (2018)

4. Campbell, K.E., Lee, B.A.: Name generators in surveys of personal networks. Soc. Netw. **13**(3), 203–221 (1991)
5. Ciardelli, I.: Questions as information types. Synthese **195**(1), 321–365 (2016). https://doi.org/10.1007/s11229-016-1221-y
6. Cui, Y., Wise, A.F.: Identifying content-related threads in MOOC discussion forums. In: Proceedings of the Second (2015) ACM Conference on Learning @ Scale - L@S 2015, pp. 299–303. ACM Press (2015)
7. Efron, M., Winget, M.: Questions are content: a taxonomy of questions in a microblogging environment. Proc. Am. Soc. Inf. Sci. Technol. **47**(1), 1–10 (2010)
8. Goffman, E.: Frame Analysis: An Essay on the Organization of Experience. Northeastern University Press, Boston (1975)
9. Maxwell Harper, F., Moy, D., Konstan, J.A.: Facts or friends?: Distinguishing informational and conversational questions in social Q&A sites. In: Proceedings of the 27th International Conference on Human Factors in Computing Systems, pp. 759–768. ACM Press (2009)
10. Ivaturi, K., Chua, C.: Framing norms in online communities. Inf. Manag. **56**(1), 15–27 (2019)
11. Jurczyk, P., Agichtein, E.: Discovering authorities in question answer communities by using link analysis. In: Proceedings of the Sixteenth ACM Conference on Information and Knowledge Management, p. 919. ACM Press (2007)
12. Krueger, S.: STEM and non-STEM library users have increased their use of e-books. Evid. Based Libr. Inf. Pract. **12**(2), 178–180 (2017)
13. Ladhari, R., Massa, E., Skandrani, H.: YouTube vloggers' popularity and influence: the roles of homophily, emotional attachment, and expertise. J. Retail. Consum. Serv. **54**, 102027 (2020)
14. Lai, M., Tambuscio, M., Patti, V., Ruffo, G., Rosso, P.: Stance polarity in political debates: a diachronic perspective of network homophily and conversations on Twitter. Data Knowl. Eng. **124**, 101738 (2019)
15. Malinick, T.E., Tindall, D.B., Diani, M.: Network centrality and social movement media coverage: a two-mode network analytic approach. Soc. Netw. **35**(2), 148–158 (2013)
16. van Merode, F., Nieboer, A., Maarse, H., Lieverdink, H.: Analyzing the dynamics in multilateral negotiations. Soc. Netw. **26**(2), 141–154 (2004)
17. Newman, M.: Networks. Oxford University Press, Oxford, New York (2018)
18. Thrasher, R.H.: Shouldn't Ignore These Strings: A Study of Conversational Deletion. Xerox University Microfilms (1974)
19. Van Quaquebeke, N., Felps, W.: Respectful inquiry: a motivational account of leading through asking questions and listening. Acad. Manag. Rev. **43**(1), 5–27 (2018)
20. Vicari, S.: Measuring collective action frames: a linguistic approach to frame analysis. Poetics **38**(5), 504–525 (2010)
21. Wasserman, S., Faust, K.: Social Network Analysis: Methods and Applications (Structural Analysis in the Social Sciences). Cambridge University Press, New York (1995)
22. Welser, H., Gleave, E., Barash, V., Smith, M., Meckes, J.: Whither the experts? Social affordances and the cultivation of experts in community Q&A systems, pp. 450–455 (2009)
23. Welser, H.T., Gleave, E., Fisher, D., Smith, M.A.: Visualizing the signatures of social roles in online discussion groups. J. Soc. Struct. **8**(2), 1–32 (2007)

Latent Profile Analysis of Generation Z and Millennials by Their Smartphone Usage Pattern

Yeon Ji Yang, Hyesun Hwang, Muzi Xiang, and Kee Ok Kim[✉]

Department of Consumer Science, Sungkyunkwan University, Seoul, Korea
kokim@skku.edu

Abstract. This study aims to classify Generation Z and Millennials according to their smartphone usage patterns and provide insights into the digital generation. We developed a scale to measure the patterns of smartphone usage following an extensive literature review and classified the smartphone usage pattern of Generation Z and Millennials using a latent profile analysis. Differences among groups according to socio-economic characteristics and smartphone related issues were analyzed. The indicators of the pattern of smartphone usage composed of the degree of involvement in actively producing information, passive searching of information, bonding and linking social connections, enjoying entertainment, and playing digital skills. Latent profile analysis produced five distinctive groups according to the degree of involvement in these activities. From this study, it is evident that the digital generations differ in their pattern of smartphone usage. This study provides practical implications for smartphone industry professionals and those interested in the younger generation's digital transformation.

Keywords: Generation Z · Millennials · Digital generation · Digital usage pattern · Latent profile analysis

1 Introduction

Smartphones have greatly impacted daily lives following the development of mobile networks. Smartphone users acquire information and communicate with the world, independent of time and location. Furthermore, people actively participate in society and acquire knowledge and information by accessing online networks through a small, and always-on hand-held device. These changes have led to the emergence of generations with new lifestyles and patterns of use associated with digitized attributes.

In the industrial age before the digital era, the same generation had similar values and behaviors because they shared passively similar external experiences such as historical, cultural, political, and social events. Thus, previous generation research has distinguished generations from the cohort perspective according to birth year. However, it is now important to consider how individuals utilize and encounter information and communication technologies in their daily lives, to understand the generations emerging in radical technology developments exceeding the age cohort analysis according to the birth year.

© Springer Nature Switzerland AG 2020
C. Stephanidis and M. Antona (Eds.): HCII 2020, CCIS 1226, pp. 253–260, 2020.
https://doi.org/10.1007/978-3-030-50732-9_34

In this study, the digital generation that frequently utilizes and encounters information and communication technologies is investigated by classifying them into Generation Z and Millennials according to their smartphone usage pattern and examined the differences among the groups according to socio-economic characteristics and smartphone-related issues.

2 Smartphone Usage Pattern

Smartphones are used daily in areas such as schedule management, information search, shopping, learning, games, and social media. Therefore, the use of smartphones exceeds simply using digital devices. It is broadly related to thinking procedures and values pursued. Consequently, to understand how smartphones embed into lives, we develop a fine scale that analyzes patterns of usage adapted from [1–5].

This study examines the types of smartphone utilization from aspects including smartphone literacy, the range of content exchange, and smartphone use motivation and subsequently categorize smartphone users according to their smartphone usage patterns.

3 Methods

3.1 Data and Analysis

The data was collected through a survey of 364 adult smartphone users aged 20 to 39 years. The data was analyzed using SPSS 23.0 and R 3.5.0, according to the following steps. First, frequency analysis was conducted to check the input error of the data and the general characteristics of the survey subjects. Second, to verify the scale, Cronbach's α and exploratory factor analysis (EFA) were examined using SPSS 23.0, and confirmatory factor analysis (CFA) was performed using R 3.5.0. Third, latent profile analysis (LPA) was conducted using R 3.5.0, to categorize consumers according to their smartphone usage patterns. Finally, a crosstabulation analysis was conducted to examine the differences between the groups.

4 Results

4.1 Verification of Scale

The scale used in this study was adapted from existing studies. A validation of the scale was conducted in three stages.

First, Cronbach's α was computed to assess consistency in the measurement questions and questions with lower internal consistency were deleted.

Second, an EFA was conducted to investigate the structure among variables to ensure the validity of the scale. The first factor was the ability to actively share and produce information with an open relationship and called it "creating and sharing information". The second factor is "information search" used to obtain information and search for information immediately. The third factor called "digital literacy", consists of the measurement questions of technology literacy. The fourth factor comprises questions of measuring limited exchanges with acquaintances and is called the "social connection". The questions about smartphone usage regarding rest and entertainment are grouped into the fifth factor called "entertainment".

Finally, confirmatory factor analysis was conducted to investigate the reliability and validity of the measured questions purified by EFA.

4.2   Latent Profile Analysis

LPA determines the optimized number of clusters using statistical criteria. This study considers three statistical criteria.

First, Akaike information criterion (AIC) [6] and Bayesian information criterion (BIC) [7] were considered. The fit of the model increases with decreasing AIC and BIC values [8]. Second, we consider the parametric bootstrapped likelihood ratio test (BLRT) [9]. This is used to verify the model comparison between k and k-1, and determines if the model is suitable and if the p value is significant. Third, the quality of classification can be determined by entropy [10]. The closer the entropy value to 1, the better the fit of the model. Generally, entropy values above 0.8 indicate a better fit of the model [8].

The index of suitability by cluster is shown in Table 1. From Table 1, the most suitable number of clusters is six. However, the six clusters showed a small group of cases consisting of 84, 108, 49, 23, 29, and 53 cases. Thus, the final clusters were determined to be five, which did not differ much in their suitability.

Table 1. Index of suitability

Model	Classes	AIC	BIC	BLRT	Entropy
1	1	3967.473	4005.937		1
1	2	3742.38	3803.923	0.01	0.7694188
1	3	3710.178	3794.8	0.01	0.6662596
1	4	3698.088	3805.789	0.01	0.6536302
1	5	3613.191	3743.97	0.01	0.800835
1	6	3577.36	3731.217	0.01	0.8137325
6	1	3705.904	3782.832		1
6	2	3518.85	3676.554	0.01	0.8194312

The smartphone usage patterns by cluster are shown in Table 2. Cluster 1, named "digital pioneer", had the highest usage scores for all five factors, especially indicating high digital capability. Cluster 2, named "active information explorer", consisted of users with high scores for three usage types, including searching for new information and knowledge, social connection, and entertainment. Cluster 3, named "relationship-oriented", had a high usage score only for information-sharing activities to maintain relationships with friends and acquaintances. Cluster 4, named "information creator &

sharer", consisted of smartphone users whose smartphone usage was focused on creating and sharing information. In Cluster 5, the usage scores for all factors were low except for the information search factor, and was named "passive information seekers".

Table 2. Smartphone usage pattern

Group	Smartphone usage factor				
	Creating & sharing information	Information search	Digital literacy	Social connection	Entertainment
Digital pioneer (n = 51)	HIGH	HIGH	HIGH	HIGH	HIGH
Active information explorer (n = 108)	LOW	HIGH	MIDDLE	HIGH	HIGH
Relationship-oriented (n = 101)	MIDDLE	MIDDLE	MIDDLE	HIGH	MIDDLE
Information creator & sharer (n = 53)	MIDDLE	LOW	LOW	MIDDLE	LOW
Passive information seeker (n = 33)	LOW	MIDDLE	LOW	LOW	LOW

4.3 Socioeconomic Characteristics

The socioeconomic characteristics of each cluster is shown in Table 3. The noticeable difference in gender is that the proportion of female users in the digital pioneer group is higher than that of male users, while the proportion of male users in the information creator and sharer group is higher than that of female users. Regarding monthly expenditure, the proportion of high expenditure group was greater in the information creator and sharer group than in the other groups.

4.4 Smartphone-Related Issues

The differences in smartphone-related issues among groups are shown in Table 4. There were differences in the smartphone replacement cycle, frequently used social media, and information channel for purchase.

The relationship-oriented, and passive information seeker groups recorded the shortest and longest replacement cycles respectively. The "active information explorer" group used YouTube and community sites more than other groups. The "digital

Table 3. Socioeconomic characteristics by clusters

Frequency (%)

		Total	Digital pioneer	Active information explorer	Relationship oriented	Information creator & sharer	Passive information seeker	χ^2
Sex	Male	167 (48.3)	15 (29.4)	47 (43.5)	54 (53.5)	35 (66.0)	16 (48.5)	16.033**
	Female	179 (51.7)	36 (70.6)	61 (56.5)	47 (46.5)	18 (34.0)	17 (51.5)	
Age	20–25	171 (49.4)	46 (42.6)	51 (50.5)	28 (54.9)	18 (54.5)	28 (52.8)	3.267
	26–39	175 (50.6)	62 (57.4)	50 (49.5)	23 (45.1)	15 (45.5)	25 (47.2)	
Education	High school	25 (7.2)	4 (7.8)	7 (6.5)	8 (7.9)	3 (5.7)	3 (9.1)	8.629
	University student	98 (28.3)	13 (25.5)	28 (25.9)	28 (27.7)	18 (34.0)	11 (33.3)	
	University graduate	202 (58.4)	30 (58.8)	67 (62.0)	59 (58.4)	28 (52.8)	18 (54.5)	
	Graduate school	21 (6.1)	4 (7.8)	6 (5.6)	6 (5.9)	4 (7.5)	1 (3.0)	
Monthly income (Unit = 1,000 Won)	<1000	110 (31.8)	19 (37.3)	35 (32.4)	25 (24.8)	16 (30.2)	15 (45.5)	13.686
	1000 ≤, <3000	140 (40.5)	18 (35.3)	48 (44.4)	43 (42.6)	19 (35.8)	12 (36.4)	
	3000 ≤, <4000	45 (13.0)	5 (9.8)	16 (14.8)	15 (14.9)	6 (11.3)	3 (9.1)	
	4000 ≤	51 (14.7)	9 (17.6)	9 (8.3)	18 (17.8)	12 (22.6)	3 (9.1)	
Monthly expenditure (Unit = 1,000 Won)	Less than 500	128 (37.0)	17 (33.3)	40 (37.0)	33 (32.7)	19 (35.8)	19 (57.6)	40.053***
	500 ≤, <1000	90 (26.0)	10 (19.8)	36 (33.3)	30 (29.7)	9 (17.0)	5 (15.2)	
	1000 ≤, <2000	75 (21.7)	18 (35.3)	24 (22.2)	20 (19.8)	6 (11.3)	7 (21.2)	
	2000 ≤	53 (15.3)	6 (11.8)	8 (7.4)	18 (17.8)	19 (35.8)	2 (6.1)	

**p < .01, ***p < .001

pioneer" group used Facebook more than the other groups. The "passive information seeker" group used Kakao Story more often than other groups.

The "digital pioneer" group mainly used social media when searching for product information. The "relationship oriented" appeared to search for products on price comparison sites. Furthermore the "information creator & sharer" group mainly searched for product information from online reviews and online communities. The "passive information seeker" searched for product information on online portal sites or manufacturers' official websites.

Table 4. Smartphone related issues by cluster

Frequency (%)

		Total	Digital pioneer	Active information explorer	Relationship oriented	Information creator & sharer	Passive information seeker	$\chi 2$
Smartphone use period	Less than 6 mths	66 (19.1)	10 (19.6)	22 (20.4)	18 (17.8)	10 (18.9)	6 (18.2)	15.18
	6 mths–1 yr	73 (21.1)	12 (23.5)	26 (24.1)	20 (19.8)	8 (15.1)	7 (21.2)	
	1–1.5 yrs	68 (19.7)	9 (17.6)	21 (19.4)	27 (26.7)	10 (18.9)	1 (3.0)	
	1.5–2 yrs	45 (13.0)	8 (15.7)	10 (9.3)	13 (12.9)	7 (13.2)	7 (21.2)	
	More than 2 yrs	94 (27.2)	12 (23.5)	29 (26.9)	23 (22.8)	18 (34.0)	12 (36.4)	
Smartphone replacement period	Less than 2 yrs	92 (26.6)	13 (25.5)	21 (19.4)	36 (35.6)	17 (32.1)	5 (15.2)	27.285**
	2–2.5 yrs	133 (38.4)	24 (47.1)	50 (46.3)	36 (35.6)	12 (22.6)	11 (33.3)	
	2.5–3 yrs	61 (17.6)	6 (11.8)	22 (20.4)	18 (17.8)	9 (17.0)	6 (18.2)	
	More than 3 yrs	60 (17.3)	8 (15.7)	15 (13.9)	11 (10.9)	15 (28.3)	11 (33.3)	
Considerations for smartphone purchases	Design	106 (30.6)	21 (41.2)	32 (29.6)	26 (25.7)	19 (35.8)	8 (24.2)	23.72
	Size and convenience	27 (7.8)	1 (2.0)	9 (8.3)	9 (8.9)	5 (9.4)	3 (9.1)	
	Function	72 (20.8)	9 (17.6)	20 (18.5)	28 (27.7)	11 (20.8)	4 (12.1)	
	Price	81 (23.4)	8 (15.7)	27 (25.0)	20 (19.8)	14 (26.4)	12 (36.4)	
	Manufacturer	47 (13.6)	10 (19.6)	13 (12.0)	14 (13.9)	4 (7.5)	6 (18.2)	
	Operating system	13 (3.8)	2 (3.9)	7 (6.5)	4 (4.0)	0 (0.0)	0 (0.0)	
Most frequently used social media	YouTube	96 (27.7)	6 (11.8)	39 (36.1)	26 (25.7)	15 (28.3)	10 (30.3)	45.462**
	Instagram	107 (30.9)	19 (37.3)	30 (27.8)	36 (35.6)	15 (28.3)	7 (21.2)	
	Facebook	64 (18.5)	16 (31.4)	18 (16.7)	20 (19.8)	7 (13.2)	3 (9.1)	
	Community sites	31 (9.0)	4 (7.8)	15 (13.9)	6 (5.9)	3 (5.7)	3 (9.1)	
	Kakao story	23 (6.6)	1 (2.0)	2 (1.9)	7 (6.9)	6 (11.3)	7 (21.2)	
	Others	25 (7.2)	5 (9.8)	4 (3.7)	6 (5.9)	7 (13.2)	3 (9.1)	
Product information search	Price comparison site	60 (17.3)	7 (13.7)	22 (20.4)	22 (21.8)	6 (11.3)	3 (9.1)	34.907*
	Social media	66 (19.1)	16 (31.4)	18 (16.7)	19 (18.8)	7 (13.2)	6 (18.2)	
	Reviews	78 (22.5)	12 (23.5)	15 (13.9)	26 (25.7)	17 (32.1)	8 (24.2)	
	Online portal site	31 (9.0)	1 (2.0)	18 (16.7)	2 (2.0)	5 (9.4)	5 (15.2)	
	Online community	98 (28.3)	14 (27.5)	30 (27.8)	28 (27.7)	17 (32.1)	9 (27.3)	
	Official site	13 (3.8)	1 (2.0)	5 (4.6)	4 (4.0)	1 (1.9)	2 (6.1)	

**p < .01, ***p < .001

5   Conclusion

To understand the digital generation, in this study, we partitioned the digital generation according to their smartphone usage patterns and examined the demographic differences and smartphone use among the classes.

The results of this study are as follows:

First, factors influencing smartphone usage patterns were extracted from existing studies and classified into five sub-components: creating and sharing information, information search, digital literacy, social connection, and entertainment.

Second, an LPA was conducted according to the smartphone usage pattern. The patterns were classified into five types. The "digital pioneer" is a group of smartphone users who are familiar with new digital technologies and actively participate in various activities. Although "active information explorer" often use smartphones to obtain information, they rarely create or share information. The "relationship oriented" is a group that shares information limited to friends and acquaintances. The "information creator and sharer" generates and exchanges content such as searching for information from online channels. Lastly, the "passive information seeker" is a group that shows lower scores for smartphone activity compared to other groups.

Third, differences in characteristics of socio-economics and smartphone-related issues were investigated. The "digital pioneer" group had a large proportion of women and people using Facebook as their main social media site. The "active information explorer" group used YouTube frequently among the social media sites. The "relationship-oriented" group showed shorter smartphone replacement cycles, and used Instagram frequently. The "information creator and sharer" group had the highest proportion of males and monthly expenditure. The group of "passive information seekers" were the consumer type with the lowest monthly expenditure and shortest smartphone replacement cycle. They frequently use Kakao Story, where only Kakao Talk friends can communicate and share personal content.

From this study, the current digital generation can be categorized according to different smartphone usage patterns. Additionally, smartphone users who pursue different purposes of smartphone use have different characteristics. To adequately understand the digital generation, it is necessary to examine how digital devices are utilized daily and how the patterns of use of digital devices affect lives.

References

1. Kim, N.I., Lee, S.B.: The effect of public lifestyle on motivation and behavior using social media. Korean J. Advert. Publ. Relat. 13(2), 306–341 (2011)
2. Kim, E., Jeong, I., Bae, Y.: Interaction on the Internet and social trust on differing effects of limited or open interactions. Korean J. Broadcast. Telecommun. 26(5), 44–77 (2012)
3. Kim, Y.: The effect of the need for cognition and self-esteem on SNS usage of senior consumers. Int. Telecommun. Policy Rev. 26(1), 81–112 (2019)
4. Lim, I.T., Lee, S.M.: The influence of smart-phone literacy in elementary school students' mothers upon children's smart-phone overuse. Korean J. Child Educ. 24(1), 285–302 (2015)

5. Wang, Y., Fesenmaier, D.R.: Towards understanding members' general participation in and active contribution to an online travel community. Tourism Manag. **25**(6), 709–722 (2004)

6. Akaike, H.: A new look at the statistical model identification. IEEE Trans. Autom. Control **19**(6), 716–723 (1974)

7. Schwarz, G.: Estimating the dimension of a model. Ann. Stat. **6**(2), 461–464 (1978)

8. No, U., Lee, E., Lee, H., Hong, S.: Classification of student's school violence during middle school: applying multilevel latent profile models to test individual and school effects. Surv. Res. **18**(2), 67–98 (2017)

9. McLachlan, G.J., Peel, D.: Finite Mixture Models. Wiley, New York (2000)

10. Ramaswamy, V., DeSarbo, W.S., Reibstein, D.J., Robinson, W.T.: An empirical pooling approach for estimating marketing mix elasticities with PIMS data. Mark. Sci. **12**(1), 103–124 (1993)

Interacting with Cultural Heritage

Magical Pond: Exploring How Ambient and Tangible Art Can Promote Social Interaction at Work

Araceli Patricia Alcarraz Gomez, Ann-Charlott Beatrice Karlsen,
Bjørn Arild Lunde, and Susanne Koch Stigberg$^{(\boxtimes)}$

IT Department, Østfold University College, Halden, Norway
{araceli.p.gomez,ann.c.karlsen,bjorn.a.lunde,
susanne.k.stigberg}@hiof.no

Abstract. Social interactions between employees are beneficial for employees' well-being and a company's productivity. We are interested in how interactive technology can be designed to create a more enjoyable work environment and support social interactions at work. Using a four-step design process (research, ideate, prototype and test) and rapid prototyping, we created a prototype implementing elements of both ambient and tangible user interfaces to engage employees during coffee breaks. We created a concept of a magical pond to increase the ludic design and playfulness of the prototype. Glass crystals, ambient lighting and fairy wings cause an anticipated contrast to the normal work environment. Here, we present our design process and prototype to inspire future work in the field.

Keywords: Ambient technology · Tangible user interface · Social interaction

1 Introduction

Forming friendships and social interaction can be crucial for employees' engagement and productivity at work. In a world, where people work 40 h a week, they spend potentially more time at work, than at home with your family. Having healthy relationships with coworkers is therefore in everyone's best interest [1]. Stress is another factor, that can have an impact not only regarding productivity at work, but also a person's mental and emotional health while outside of work [3]. We are interested in if and how interactive ambient technology can be designed to reduce stress and create a more enjoyable work environment. To explore this research question, we have designed an interactive artifact as an example of pervasive technology using tangible and ambient interface elements. This poster paper presents our design process, as well as the final prototype. In Sect. 2, we list related work that inspired our process. We discuss chosen methods in Sect. 3 and present the final prototype in detail in Sect. 4. We conclude the poster paper with a discussion about future work.

C. Stephanidis and M. Antona (Eds.): HCII 2020, CCIS 1226, pp. 263–269, 2020.
https://doi.org/10.1007/978-3-030-50732-9_35

2   Related Work

We found three projects [4, 6, 7] from our literature review, that inspired the design of our prototype. Mood squeezer [4] is a design project with the purpose of drawing workers out of their offices and into the common lunch area. The main objective was to engage and create social interaction at the workplace. The project had three elements, 1) a station with colored balls to squeeze 2) floor tiles with colored lights 3) a website with the same colored "lights" as the floor tiles. When a ball was squeezed, the ball's color would light up as a spot in the floor tiles, and on the website. The colors were not mapped in any obvious, since colors have different meaning to different people. The study showed that the prototype encouraged social interaction. It worked as an ice breaker among the workers and the artifact also created curiosity and playfulness among several of the workers. Some created games or challenges involving the artifact, they developed a sense of ownership over the artifact and would often pridefully demonstrated it to visitors. This resulted in the artifact being placed at the office for a longer period, than what was planned.

The project described in "Building Mood, Building Community: Usage Patterns of an Interactive Art Installation" [7] had the aim to explore interaction around mood, the paper explains how interactive art installation could possibly improve and contribute to change the environment from "serious workplace" to more playful and creative space for social awareness and connectedness within workplace settings. The interactive art installation called mood.cloud is an artifact shaped like a cloud consisting of many LED lights, and an ipad available for the participants to use. The cloud was placed above the participants, while the ipad was in their reach, under the cloud. On the ipad the participants were able to select an image relating to their mood and that would display colors on the mood.cloud. The paper concluded that participants felt that they contributed to something bigger, connectedness and foster feelings as they became encouraged to interpret, appropriate, and be aware of others around them by interacting with a big visual interactive artifact that is placed in an open space. Because the artifact is big and visual, it provides an experience that differs from the usual everyday experience, supporting people's curiosity and interaction.

The "Wall Relief" [6] is an installation put in an office setting to see if tangible and interactive media could improve efficiency and reduce stress at work. Even though the product developed in this paper is largely focused on the health aspect of the work environment, they still include research regarding engagement and well-being in the workplace. The "Wall Relief", is inspired by martial art; Thai Chi. The idea is to convert the stress relieving properties from Thai Chi into an interactive media device that can be placed in the office. The authors designed the "Wall Relief" to be a mobile device instead of a stationary installation to the wall, which is useful if you want to test in different environments. The prototype consisted of an aluminum frame with laser engravings, spray paint and seven panels to display images. A Kinect was used to capture movements and display the corresponding images.

All three projects are ludic experiences supporting people's curiosity, playfulness and social interaction. The threshold to engage with them is low and the effects are visible for everyone. These insights will guide the continuing design process of our prototype.

3   Method

Using a four-step design process (research, ideate, prototype and test) [8] and rapid prototyping techniques [2], we created a prototype using elements of both ambient and tangible user interfaces to engage employees during coffee breaks. The workplace is a faculty corridor at a university college, including kitchen, meeting areas and offices for lecturers. During the research phase we conducted a literature review presented in chapter 2 and a series of interviews with four lecturers to understand how and where they socialize at work. During the ideation phase we created individual mood boards and sketches. The goal was to create an interactive art installation from another world, feeling like fantasy as a contrast to the traditional office environment. To explore how users can interact with our sketches we wrote scenarios and storyboards. In a final group meeting, we decided on a shared concept with updated sketches and storyboards. In the prototyping phase we used several iterations of rapid prototyping to explore different materials, look & feel and interactions. Prototyping materials included micro: bit[1], Arduino Uno[2], NeoPixels[3] and servo motors. Laser cutting and 3D printing were used to create the physical prototypes. During this phase, we had to downsize our concept to create an achievable prototype. The prototype is described in more detail in chapter 4. For user testing, we installed the prototype in the common area near the kitchen for a week. During this time, we had two sessions of observations, there we sit in a sofa nearby the prototype and noted down how people engaged with the prototype. Afterwards, we interviewed them regarding their experiences with the prototype. In chapter 5 we sum up our findings from the user testing and provide some thoughts for future work.

4   The Prototype

The prototyping phase conveyed our design exploration. We performed several iterations of rapid prototyping to transform our ideas from the initial design concept into the final prototype. In the following, we describe our design concept, the look & feel and implementation of the prototype [5].

4.1   Design Concept

Our aim was to create a non-utilitarian interactive technology that provides an aesthetic experience and invokes spontaneous and playful behavior through collaborative exploration and investigation. The prototype is composed of several concepts and ideas that have been merged into one design. The interactive art installation should give users the possibility to explore, be intrigued and collaborate. It should include:

---

[1] https://microbit.org.

[2] https://www.arduino.cc.

[3] https://www.adafruit.com/category/168.

- tangible objects for users to manipulate
- sensor input to enable embodied interactions
- ambient environment that can be seen simultaneous by several people
- cooperative actions to encourage social interactions
- hidden features and rewards for playfulness

For our prototype we decided to focus on exploring the tangible objects and the ambient environment (Fig. 1).

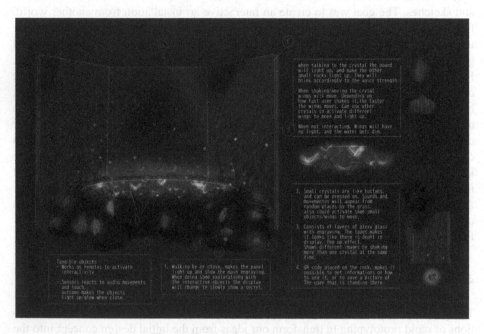

Fig. 1. Final design concept sketches

4.2 Look and Feel

The prototype consists of four parts: a background display, a pond, wings and crystals to create an ambient installation and tangible objects that enable people to control the installation.

Ambient Background. The background display was made out of 3 sheets of engraved plexiglass, laser cut boxes as a base for the plexiglass and integrated NeoPixel stripes that light up the engravings. We programmed the led-stripes to shift color to create the desired mood for the prototype.

The Pond. We created a pond from Styrofoam with a plexiglass top and integrated led stripes. Similar to the background, the NeoPixel stripes were programmed to change color, giving the illusion that there was movement in the pond.

Wings and Crystals. These are the tangible interaction elements of the prototype. The wings were made by laser cut and engraved plexiglass and connected to servo motors and Neopixels, making them light up and flutter. All wings have different colored lights. Moreover, we created two crystals, that users could play with and thereby control the wings. Both wings and crystal were controlled using Micro:bits, to enable communication between them. The crystals reacted on movement, so users could take them, turn them upside down or shake to explore the installation. One crystal controlled the lights of the wings and the other crystal controlled the movement. So, when shaking one crystal, the wings would light up and shaking the other crystal made the wings start to flutter. Furthermore, both duration and intensity of the shaking matters. If both crystals were shaken once, two wings would light up and two wings would shake, two shakes made four wings light up and flutter, three shakes would make all of the wings light up and flutter. The interaction was timed, stopping the wings' actions after a while (Fig. 2).

Fig. 2. High-fidelity prototype

4.3 Implementation

As described earlier, we relied heavily on laser cutting techniques to create the elements. We designed the shapes and patterns using Adobe Illustrator and then fabricated them using the laser cutter. We had to iterate this process several times to create the right design that would stand out in the chosen workplace environment. To create the interactive elements we used Micro:bits, Arduino Uno, Neopixel LED stripes, and servo motors. In total, we used four Micro:bits: one in each crystal, one for controlling the servo motors and one for controlling the lights of the wings. The Micro:bits communicated using built-in radio functionality. Arduino Uno was implemented to control the lighting of the ambient environment (background and pond). In Fig. 3 you see the wiring diagram for our prototype. We had to use a 5 V external power supply for the neopixel stripes and servo motors connected to the micro:bit.

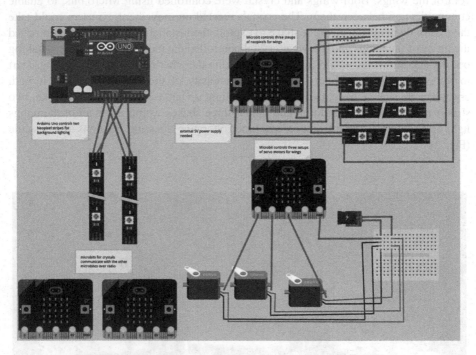

Fig. 3. Wiring diagram using Fritzing (https://fritzing.org/home/)

5 Initial Findings and Future Work

We placed the prototype in the common area of the IT department at Østfold University for initial testing. We were interested in how the employees reacted to the installation and what kind of engagement the prototype would invoke. We had two 2-h observation sessions, there we sat in a sofa nearby the prototype and noted down how people engaged with the prototype. In total, 25 employees engaged with our prototype. Afterwards, we interviewed them shortly about their experiences with the prototype. These are our initial findings:

- **Stress.** Exploring the prototype took a couple of minutes for the employees. Stressed or busy just ignored it.
- **Playfulness.** Employees expressed joy and amusement while interacting with the installation. One person jumped back of surprise, others started laughing. Most of them stated that they were uncertain as to what would happen next and that they were searching for more surprises. Several of them came back to play with it again.

- **Social interaction.** Many of the employees that used the prototype, called for colleagues to demonstrate the interaction or asked them to try it out themselves.

The initial findings support the previous literature that interactive ambient art supports people's curiosity, playfulness and social interaction. However not all employees engaged with the prototype and many of them asked for more hidden features and functionalities. It would be interesting to explore how the prototype needs to be changed to attract also stressed people to help them calm down. Furthermore, it would be interesting to see how employees could enhance the prototype to add new hidden features to it. During the initial testing we observed employees how they explored, collaborated and investigated the prototype while expressing amusement and joy. Some even showed frustration and confusion. It would be interesting to see how the playfulness of the prototype changes over time.

References

1. Admin: The importance of social relationships at work, https://www.servicefutures.com/the-importance-of-social-relationships-at-work. Accessed 19 Mar 2020
2. Beaudouin-Lafon, M., Mackay, W.E.: Prototyping tools and techniques. In: Human-Computer Interaction, pp. 137–160. CRC Press, Boca Raton (2009)
3. Colligan, T.W., Higgins, E.M.: Workplace stress: etiology and consequences. J. Workplace Behav. Health **21**(2), 89–97 (2006)
4. Gallacher, S., et al.: Mood squeezer: lightening up the workplace through playful and lightweight interactions. In: Proceedings of the 18th ACM Conference on Computer Supported Cooperative Work & Social Computing, pp. 891–902 (2015)
5. Houde, S., Hill, C.: Chapter 16 - what do prototypes prototype? In: Helander, M.G., et al. (eds.) Handbook of Human-Computer Interaction, 2nd edn, pp. 367–381. North-Holland, Amsterdam (1997). https://doi.org/10.1016/B978-044481862-1.50082-0
6. Profita, H., et al.: Wall relief: a health-oriented interactive installation for the workplace environment. In: Proceedings of the Ninth International Conference on Tangible, Embedded, and Embodied Interaction, pp. 607–611 (2015)
7. Scolere, L.M., et al.: Building mood, building community: usage patterns of an interactive art installation. In: Proceedings of the 19th International Conference on Supporting Group Work, pp. 201–212 (2016)
8. Sharp, H., et al.: Interaction Design: Beyond Human-Computer Interaction. Wiley, Hoboken (2019)

Quantifying Museum Visitor Attention Using Bluetooth Proximity Beacons

Jonathan D. L. Casano$^{(\boxtimes)}$, Jenilyn L. Agapito, Abigail Moreno,
and Ma. Mercedes T. Rodrigo

Ateneo de Manila University, 1108 Quezon City, Metro Manila, Philippines
jcasano@ateneo.edu.com,
{jcasano, jagapito, mrodrigo}@ateneo.edu,
abigail.moreno@obf.ateneo.edu

Abstract. This paper shows initial work on utilizing Bluetooth Low-Energy (BLE) beacons to uncover patterns in visitor paths and to determine the concentration of visitor attention within the Ateneo Art Gallery (AAG), the Philippines' first museum of modern art. Participants carried phones instrumented with an application that logged distance estimates from BLE beacons deployed around the museum. The logs were then analyzed to produce scarf plots that visually represent paths taken. The results show the potential of BLE beacons for indoor location tracking. Aggregated visualization of similar scarf plots showed four notable patterns that provide insights on the museum areas that draw attention. The assumed usual route (pattern 1: Start at 1st floor, go to 2nd floor then visit 3rd floor) was confirmed and an uncommon visiting pattern was discovered (pattern 2: Start at 3rd floor, go to 2nd floor, then visit 1st floor). It was also found that some visitors do not get to explore the entire museum (pattern 3: Some visitors only went to the 1st and 2nd floors. Pattern 4: Some visitors only went to the 2nd and 3rd floors). These insights can be used to make decisions regarding exhibit arrangement or museum layout design.

Keywords: Museum visitorship · BLE beacons · Indoor location tracking

1 Introduction

Museums commonly make use of surveys, feedback forms [1], and manual tracking of time spent [2] to measure visitor engagement. Though straightforward and easy to execute, these methods do not provide precise information about the paths that the visitors traverse within a museum. These paths, when tracked, can provide insights about which areas are visited, giving museums an indication of where visitors choose to focus their attention [3]. Understanding such behaviors may help museum curators design more engaging exhibits arrangements for their visitors. Thus, researchers are beginning to explore how technologies such as Bluetooth Low-Energy (BLE) beacons may be utilized to track positions in an enclosed area.

Recent work on indoor positioning focuses on two radio technologies, namely, Wireless Fidelity (WiFi) and Bluetooth Low-Energy (BLE) to ascertain the location of a target smart device [4]. The low cost and efficient nature of BLE beacons provided enough motivation for several research groups to create preliminary wayfinding systems based on BLE beacons [5].

© Springer Nature Switzerland AG 2020
C. Stephanidis and M. Antona (Eds.): HCII 2020, CCIS 1226, pp. 270–277, 2020.
https://doi.org/10.1007/978-3-030-50732-9_36

In this study, we used BLE beacons to determine visitors' position within the Ateneo Art Gallery (AAG), the Philippines' first museum of modern art. This undertaking serves as a proof of concept on (a) the use and possible limitations of BLE technologies to track visitors paths in a multi-floor museum such as AAG; (b) measurement of visitor interest and attention in exhibits within AAG; and (c) ways by which the analyzed data might be used to influence museum exhibit layout and design.

2 Review of Related Literature

Museum engagement is important for a variety of reasons. First, better engagement with exhibits in a museum has been shown to optimize overall visitor experience [6] and increase the visitors' perceived value of the exhibits [7]. Conversely, unengaging museum experiences cause future visitorship decline [8]. Second, engagement may be used as basis for the design of systems in museums [9] and as justification to rearrange the exhibits [10]. Lastly, in the context of learning, high engagement during visits to STEM-themed museums have positively influenced learning rate [11]. Hence, museums are taking interest towards understanding visitor engagement.

Respondents are often asked questions to determine their perceived quality of experience through feedback forms, from which engagement may be approximated [1, 2]. Though easy to execute, these methods do not capture information relevant to engagement such as visitor paths [3]. To address this, some museums provide their visitors with phones that are ready to respond to visual markers located near the exhibits, such as printed pictures or Quick Response (QR) codes [11].

As museums try to find more elegant ways of tracking visitor paths, technologies such as BLE beacons are becoming a device of interest. BLE beacons emit radio signals that may be detected by a smartphone. This allows the unobtrusive tracking of stationary and ranging location while the visitor is roaming around. BLE beacons are easily deployed and re-positioned as needed and are power-efficient as well as low cost [12]. Hence, research has focused on descriptive analyses where proximity data was used mainly to determine and visualize visitor attention [3, 13]. A common disadvantage reported is the BLE beacons' unstable and fluctuating signal strength [14].

As a continuation of previous work, the authors' deployed BLE beacons inside The Mind Museum, a world-class science museum in the Philippines. An app was created that allowed visitors to activate augmented-reality content using their phones once they are near an exhibit [15]. This followed a Notify-to-Interact framework [16] where each exhibit would trigger participation from the visitor and engagement is measured by how much the visitor interacts with the notification. This current work wishes to leverage on BLE beacons to explore the possibility of quantifying attention and interest while requiring the least amount of participation from museum visitors.

3   Unity Application and RadBeacons

The phones for data collection were instrumented with an application made in Unity. A Unity plugin [17] allowed the conversion of radio signals from the BLE beacons into Received Signal Strength Indicator values (RSSI) from which an estimated distance ($d_{estimate}$) may be calculated using the power regression formula [18] in Eq. 1. In the formula, TxPower refers to the beacon's transmission strength and RSSI is the received beacon strength from a particular distance. The constant values in the formula converts $d_{estimate}$ to meters.

$$d_{estimate} = 10 \frac{TxPower - RSSI}{10x2} \tag{1}$$

These distances were recorded in a csv file together with their timestamp information, beacon names, and floor numbers. The RadBeacons used, had their transmission strength and advertising rate set to maximum in order to mitigate inaccurate distance readings near spaces with corners, thick walls and inclined floors [19].

4   Testing Methods

The deployment and testing were conducted at the Ateneo Art Gallery (AAG) which has three (3) floors: the 1st and 3rd floors consist mainly of paintings and artifacts while the 2nd floor had artifacts and an interactive exhibit.

The research team worked with the AAG's Museum Education Officer (MEO) to determine strategic areas within the museum where thirty (30) RadBeacons can be unobtrusively deployed. The placements are shown in Fig. 1.

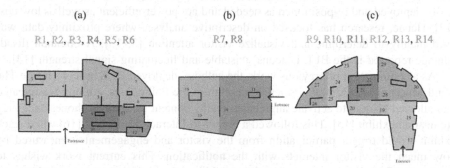

(a)　　　　　　　　　　(b)　　　　　　　　　　(c)

R1, R2, R3, R4, R5, R6　　　　　R7, R8　　　　R9, R10, R11, R12, R13, R14

Fig. 1. Orthogonal view of the floor maps showing the beacon placements numbered 1 to 30, as well as, beacon groupings (regions) labelled R1 to R14 in the (a) first floor, (b) second floor and (c) third floor of the AAG.

There were two (2) recruitment efforts undertaken. First was an onsite approach. The testing team was positioned at the Information Area by the entrance and exit doors of the AAG. When a visitor entered the museum, the team approached and invited them to participate. Willing visitors were briefed about the goal of the study and the extent of their participation. They were asked to sign an informed consent form and were asked to complete a short demographics questionnaire to collect information about their age, gender, and whether or not it was their first time in the AAG. After the briefing, each participant was given a mobile phone instrumented with the Unity app. They were instructed to bring the phone with them as they walked around the museum. They were also asked to leave an ID in exchange for the phone given to them to ensure that they will return it upon exit.

The second approach was the recruitment of senior high school (SHS) students from the STEM track of an all-girls private school in Pasig City. Two batches were scheduled to visit the Ateneo Laboratory for the Learning Sciences on different dates and part of their itinerary was a visit to the AAG. Since the SHS students were minors, informed consent from their parents/guardians were likewise sought before their trip. During actual testing, same procedure as discussed previously was followed. The research protocol and questionnaires were approved by the Ateneo University Research Ethics Office.

5 Analysis

5.1 Participant Profile

A total of sixty-six (66) participants were involved in the experiment, majority of which were first time visitors to the AAG (Table 1). The research team conducted three (3) sessions of testing – the first with the randomly invited museum goers while the second and third, with the two different batches of senior high school (SHS) students.

Table 1. Profile of the participants.

	Session 1			Session 2			Session 3		
Gender	M	F	Others	M	F	Others	M	F	Others
N	9	8	0	0	21	3	1	24	0
Total N	17			24			25		
First time in the AAG?	Yes = 71%			Yes = 75%			Yes = 80%		
	No = 29%			No = 25%			No = 20%		

Two respondents' csv files – one from each the first and third sessions – were corrupted and were not included in the analysis. Additionally, the 2nd floor of the AAG was closed for renovation during the second and third testing sessions. Hence, the succeeding sections consider the data only of the first session respondents.

5.2 Data Cleaning

In this study, we used a scarf plot to visualize multiple beacon distance readings over the course of a respondent's visit. The X-axis represents the time of the respondent's visit from start to finish, and the Y-axis lists the 30 beacons (labelled 0–29), or 14 regions (labelled 0–13). The colors represent the average distance reading for a beacon or region at a particular time slice. The darker the color. the closer the distance reading of the beacon is at that particular point. For example, in Fig. 2(d), at column labelled 'start', the respondent is closest to region 0 (1st floor near entrance).To generate the scarf plots, we preformed several iterations of data cleaning.

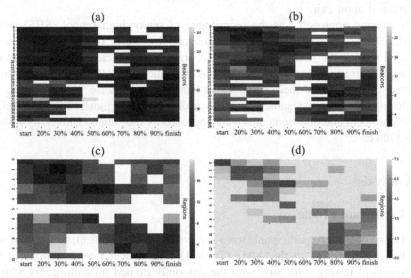

Fig. 2. Respondent #9's scarf plots after each data cleaning step – (a) Scarf plot generated from raw data gathered; (b) Scarf plot after removing erroneous floor readings; (c) Scarf plot after grouping the beacons into regions; and (d) Scarf plot after incorporating Immediate, Near, and Far distances and enforcing 7.5 m as the maximum plottable value.

First, because BLE signals can pass through walls and across floors, readings from beacons located on a different floor were being retrieved incorrectly. To address this, the respondent's current distance from a nearby beacon was compared with its next recorded distance. If the difference is greater than 10 m, the second reading is filtered out of the logs. Next, the beacon distances were categorized as Immediate (1–2 m), Near (2–4 m), or Far (>= 4 m) and the maximum plottable value for the scarf plot was set to 7.5 m. This reduces the noise in the plots by minimizing the possible distances to represent.

Finally, the beacon distance readings were grouped into regions based on proximity to each other in order to soften the scarf plot's gradient and highlight the concentration of the respondent's attention and path during the visit. Figure 2 shows the evolution of the scarf plots generated for one respondent after each of the data cleaning steps.

5.3   Analysis of Visitor Paths

As previously mentioned, the analysis that follows considers the 17 participants from the 1st session during when the 2nd floor was still accessible. However, two (2) visitors had either a corrupted log or a scarf plot that was still too noisy to categorize despite going through data cleaning.

To normalize the differences in time and duration of visit, the total time was divided into 10 equal parts. Similar looking scarf plots were aggregated, from which four types of user paths were observed as seen in Fig. 3.

Figure 3 offers some insights on visitor path and attention. First, the most popular path among the respondents is starting from the 1st floor going up to the 3rd (9/15 or 53%) (Fig. 3(d)). There were visitors who opted to start from the 3rd floor down to the 1st (2/15 or 13%) (Fig. 3(c)). We also note that there were visitors who did not get to see the entire museum (4/15 or 26%) (Fig. 3(a) and 3(b)).

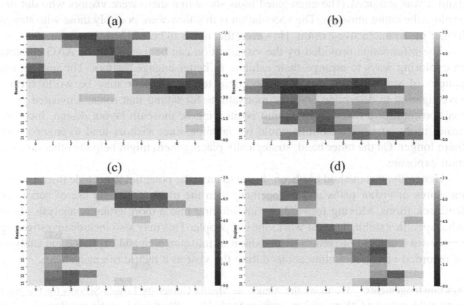

Fig. 3. Aggregated scarf plots of respondents' data group according to path similarity. (a) Respondents who visited just the 1st and 2nd floors of the AAG (2/15 or 13%). (b) Respondents who visited just the 2nd and 3rd floors (3/15 or 17%). (c) Respondents who opted to start their visit from the 3rd floor down to the 1st floor (2 /15 or 13%). (d) Respondents who opted to start their visit from the 1st floor up to the 3rd floor (9/15 or 53%).

We also observe that the darkest colors are seen in the 2nd floor (Regions 6 and 7, Beacons 12 to 15). Finally, the aggregated scarf plots, regardless of the path taken, were able to record close distance readings towards the very end of the visit at region 0. This was the time the visitors returned to the entrance on the 1st floor to return the phone.

6 Conclusions and Future Work

The use of BLE beacons for museum visitor tracking appears promising. They are power-efficient and low cost, hence, a feasible option for these kinds of undertaking. Their size allows them to be inconspicuously positioned in museum areas. The Unity app developed was able to unobtrusively capture indoor location data on the visitors' paths while inside the AAG. A limitation of the RadBeacons used is that their signals can pass through walls and across floors. This can be addressed by performing data cleaning steps as explored in this study.

Visualization and analysis of the data showed more concrete representations of patterns indicative of the paths the visitors took while in the museum. It reaffirmed the assumed common pattern of starting from the 1st floor to the 3rd floor. A rather uncommon route of starting from the 3rd floor going to the 1st floor was discovered. A notable finding is that the respondents appear to have spent more time in the 2nd floor where an interactive exhibit was stationed. The aggregated plots show that there were visitors who did not explore the entire museum. The speculation is that they were possibly those who stayed longer in the interactive exhibit. However, this needs to be verified.

The information provided by the visualization can be useful for the AAG curators in exploring ways to arrange their exhibits to better engage visitors. The uncommon pattern of starting from the 3rd floor going to the 1st floor may be worth further investigation to determine possible motivations for taking that route. Unvisited areas may prompt for a redesign in exhibit positioning or museum layout design. Incorporating more interactive exhibits could be valuable since visitors tend to engage with them longer. On the other hand, strategically placing them might help the other areas to gain exposure.

Generally, this method has been shown to have the potential to provide finer grained measures of visitor paths and engagement than the more traditional use of survey or feedback forms. Moving forward, we are looking into a more granular analysis about what specific exhibits interest what kinds of people. This may also include investigating the visitors' tendency to return to an exhibit or museum area and exploring the analysis of recorded verbal communications during the visit as a metric of engagement.

Acknowledgements. We thank the Ateneo de Manila University Loyola Schools for the grant entitled "Ateneo Art Gallery Visitor Tracking Study Using Bluetooth Low-Energy Beacons". We also wish to express our thanks to the Ateneo Art Gallery Museum Education Office and its Administrators, specifically Ms. Estela Bagos (AAG Museum Education Officer) and Ms. Victoria Herrera (AAG Director and Chief Curator) for allowing the conduct of this experiment within the museum. Lastly, we thank the participants who willingly volunteered to participate in the study.

References

1. Martella, C., Miraglia, A., Cattani, M., Van Steen, M.: Leveraging proximity sensing to mine the behavior of museum visitors. In: 2016 IEEE International Conference on Pervasive Computing and Communications (PerCom), pp. 1–9. IEEE (2016)

2. Yoshimura, Y., Krebs, A., Ratti, C.: Noninvasive bluetooth monitoring of visitors' length of stay at the louvre. IEEE Pervasive Comput. **16**(2), 26–34 (2017)
3. Rashed, M.G., Suzuki, R., Yonezawa, T., Lam, A., Kobayashi, Y., Kuno, Y.: Tracking visitors in a real museum for behavioral analysis. In: 2016 Joint 8th International Conference on Soft Computing and Intelligent Systems (SCIS) and 17th International Symposium on Advanced Intelligent Systems (ISIS), pp. 80–85. IEEE (2016)
4. Chang, Y.J., Wang, T.Y.: Comparing picture and video prompting in autonomous indoor wayfinding for individuals with cognitive impairments. Pers. Ubiquit. Comput. **14**(8), 737–747 (2010)
5. Chang, Y.J., Chen, Y.R., Chang, C.Y., Wang, T.Y.: Video prompting and indoor wayfinding based on bluetooth beacons: a case study in supported employment for people with severe mental illness. In: 2009 WRI International Conference on Communications and Mobile Computing, vol. 3, pp. 137–141. IEEE (2009)
6. Taheri, B., Jafari, A., O'Gorman, K.: Keeping your audience: presenting a visitor engagement scale. Tour. Manag. **42**, 321–329 (2014)
7. Black, G.: Transforming Museums in the Twenty-First Century. Routledge, Abingdon (2012)
8. Chamberlin, M.: A study of young adult programming at american historic house museums. Doctoral dissertation, The University of the Arts (2018)
9. Ali, S., Koleva, B., Bedwell, B., Benford, S.: Deepening visitor engagement with museum exhibits through hand-crafted visual markers. In: Proceedings of the 2018 Designing Interactive Systems Conference, pp. 523–534 (2018)
10. Rashed, M.G., Suzuki, R., Yonezawa, T., Lam, A., Kobayashi, Y., Kuno, Y.: Robustly tracking people with lidars in a crowded museum for behavioral analysis. IEICE Trans. Fundam. Electron. Commun. Comput. Sci. **100**(11), 2458–2469 (2017)
11. Cesário, V., Radeta, M., Matos, S., Nisi, V.: The ocean game: assessing children's engagement and learning in a museum setting using a treasure-hunt game. In: Extended Abstracts Publication of the Annual Symposium on Computer-Human Interaction in Play, pp. 99–109 (2017)
12. Jeon, K.E., She, J., Soonsawad, P., Ng, P.C.: Ble beacons for internet of things applications: survey, challenges, and opportunities. IEEE Internet Things J. **5**(2), 811–828 (2018)
13. Vavoula, G., Tseliou, M.A., Tsiviltidou, Z.: Bluetooth low energy beacon-based positioning for multimedia guides in heritage buildings: a case study. In: World Conference on Mobile and Contextual Learning, pp. 102–109 (2019)
14. Spachos, P., Plataniotis, K.N.: BLE Beacons for Indoor Positioning at an Interactive IoT-Based Smart Museum (2020). arXiv preprint arXiv:2001.07686
15. Vidal Jr., E.C.E., Ty, J.F., Caluya, N.R., Rodrigo, M.M.T.: MAGIS: mobile augmented-reality games for instructional support. Interact. Learn. Environ. **27**(7), 895–907 (2019)
16. Ng, P.C., She, J., Park, S.: Notify-and-interact: a beacon-smartphone interaction for user engagement in galleries. In: 2017 IEEE International Conference on Multimedia and Expo (ICME), pp. 1069–1074. IEEE (2017)
17. Pitman, T.: BluetoothLE for iOS, tvOS and Android, Shaltamic LLC (2014). Unity Asset Store   https://assetstore.unity.com/packages/tools/network/bluetooth-le-for-ios-tvos-and-android-26661
18. Al Qathrady, M., Helmy, A.: Improving BLE distance estimation and classification using TX power and machine learning: a comparative analysis. In: Proceedings of the 20th ACM International Conference on Modelling, Analysis and Simulation of Wireless and Mobile Systems, pp. 79–83 (2017)
19. Iqbal, Z., et al.: Accurate real time localization tracking in a clinical environment using bluetooth low energy and deep learning. PloS one **13**(10), e0205392 (2018)

The Museum Guidance System
in Gamification Design

Zi-Ru Chen[✉]

Southern Taiwan University of Science and Technology, No. 1, Nan-Tai Street,
Yungkang Dist., Tainan 710, Taiwan R.O.C.
zrchen@stust.edu.tw

Abstract. Gamification is the application of game-oriented design approaches or game-inspired mechanics to otherwise non-game contexts. Mobile guiding system is the design process of information interactions. It is the integration of information design, interaction design, and sensorial design. The e-learning system of mobile guide is able to be loaded gamification concepts and let mobile learning interestingly, diversely, and validly. The problem of the research was if a guided system is combined the concept of gamification design into museum guide services for non-commercial purposes, it also provided the same benefits to the promotion of museum learning and knowledge, integrating mobile devices as navigation media. It would improve more users to participate in a museum and use the guide system actively, and then arise their interest and achievement. The research method was adopted prototyping implementation and user test. The result was to establish a preliminary model for developing a museum mobile guide system of gamification design.

Keywords: Gamification · Museum learning · Multimedia guided system

1 Introduction

1.1 The Museum Learning and Guiding System

Nowadays, museums play the role of social education. It has a wealth of collections and related materials, and stimulates and encourages people to learn through educational programs, exhibitions, activities, etc. [1]. Lord et al. [2] believed that informal education is the most successful in affective learning, which can change audience's attitude and interest, audience's use of guide, and affect their visiting experience and willingness to come again. Guide is frequently used by visitors in museums. Many museums and researchers like to explore what kind of guide method can improve learning motivation and effectiveness of visitors. In terms of guide device, currently, digital guide of personalized mobile is widely used. Such mobile guide can display multimedia, wireless communication and database technology with mobile device, and replace traditional printed material and guide manual [3]. The mobile device is characterized by high portability and powerful computer functions. When combined with the easy-to-use mobile guide, it may interact with the display content, allowing visitors

C. Stephanidis and M. Antona (Eds.): HCII 2020, CCIS 1226, pp. 278–285, 2020.
https://doi.org/10.1007/978-3-030-50732-9_37

to select their favorite exhibits at any time and at any place, and meeting different needs for experience activities.

1.2 Gamification Design Applied in Guide Service

Previous research was pointed out that games can make people happy, make complicated things simple, and also change human behavior. Games can not only be used for entertainment or learning, but to change people's living habits, business behaviors, political and social activities, etc. Therefore, the design concept and application of "gamification" have received wide attention in recent years. The word "gamification" is generally defined as applying elements such as game thinking, game mechanism and design structure to non-game social activities and services [4]. Gamification is a phenomenon. Deterding et al. [4] explained that gamification is the use of game elements to perform certain activities with specific purposes in non-game situations. In 2015, New Media Consortium put forward some examples of gamification applied to museums, and believed that this trend could enhance visitors' viewing experience. It also pointed out that how to enhance the creative experience process is a major challenge for such guide design in the future [5]. The game system can stimulate users' emotions, promote better feeling and connection between people and technology interfaces [6]. Besides, the integrated use of interactive technology and interactive design also involves the management of aesthetic experience [7].

2 Problem and Objective

In recent years, museum education has gained active development. In light of the guide design in most museums, this study found that museum guides are mostly printed in writing, and multimedia video broadcasting and personnel on-the-spot interpretation and other ways are provided to convey exhibit information. However, most of the exhibits in the museum are of rich historical significance and profound knowledge background. If a museum provides different guide services and information content for different visitors, it will impose an excessive burden on manpower and material costs. In addition, traditional guide method can by no means achieve the best presentation and explanation effect for in-depth and detailed expertise of each exhibit. Also, professional but important exhibit information is often hard to understand, thereby depriving visitors of the motivations for further information, and preventing them from understanding the connotation of important cultural relics. Therefore, this study took the "Wood-frame Construction of Eastern Architecture Exhibition" of Ancient Machinery Research Center in Southern Taiwan University of Science and Technology as an example (refer to Fig. 1) to explore new possibility of museum guide planning and design through game-based design thinking, and guide the public to re-recognize the museum learning mode.

Fig. 1. The interior of "wood-frame construction of eastern architecture exhibition".

3   Methodology and Steps

This study adopted prototyping implementation and user testing methods. Through literature reviews, this study obtained the game elements, and made the prototype based on guide content planning, game elements and rules, system interface design, and prototyping of game guide system. Finally, the user testing was carried out to confirm feasibility of the prototype and explore the learning effect of application of game and augmented reality in museum guide.

3.1   The Arrangement of the Mode and Factors of Gamification

Based on the previous reviews, this study took 6 game elements proposed by Zichermann and Linder [8], including points, levels, trophies/badges/achievements, virtual goods, leaderboards and virtual gifts as the analysis basis to extract elements that attract people in the game, and applied to the game-based design of the mobile application. The study proposed design specifications or criteria of the game-based mobile application program. Please refer to Table 1 for the gamification design framework.

Table 1. The design framework of gamification factors.

Game elements		
Category	Game mechanics	Game dynamics
Personal	Points	Reward
	Levels	Status
	Trophies/badges/achievements	Achievement
	Virtual goods	Self expression
Social	Leaderboards	Competition
	Virtual gifts	Altruism

3.2   The Implementation of a Prototype for the Museum Guide System

Exhibition Themes Selection. Above Fig. 1 shows the interior of "Wood-frame Construction of Eastern Architecture Exhibition". There are various exhibits and display plans in the exhibition hall. In this study, 8 main exhibition themes were sorted out and used as exhibition contents of subsequent game-based guide plan.

Please refer to description in Table 2 for eight exhibition themes and the guide plan.

Table 2. The introduction and game plan of eight selected exhibition themes.

No.	Display form	Exhibition theme	Game element and rule planning
1	Display planes	*Timeline Wall*	Multiple-choice game
2	Display planes	*Moving Track*	Multiple-choice game
3	1:3 physical models	*Dougong Group*	Drag-moving game
4	Physical models	*Calibration Instrument*	Drag-moving game
5	A 1:3 physical model	*Wooden Construction*	Silhouette-match game
6	1:6 DIY models	*Dougong Instruction*	Silhouette-match assembling game
7	Display planes	*Song Dynasty Costume*	Pairs-matching game
8	A 1:6 physical model	*Timing Tower*	Story-driven game

The Design of User Interface and Flow. According to the framework of game elements and rules, the interface flow and usability design were carried out to plan. Refer to Fig. 2 for part of the interface design. In terms of usability process design, as the museum guide discussed in this study focused on the interaction between visitors and exhibits, the "augmented reality" technology was adopted to achieve virtual-real integration. The guide experience was divided into "virtual scenes" and "real scenes". "Virtual scenes" refer to the guide information and game interactive content of exhibits provided in the application program, while "real scenes" refer to the contents of exhibits in the physical environment. The whole experience of guide/game was carried out simultaneously/alternately between virtual scenes and real scenes, so as to reach "creating innovative museum guide design and achieve "gamifying museum guide experience" proposed by this study, as seen in Fig. 3.

start page   lead story   task list   illustration   exhibit intro   interaction with AR   game mode

Fig. 2. The interface design of the museum guide system

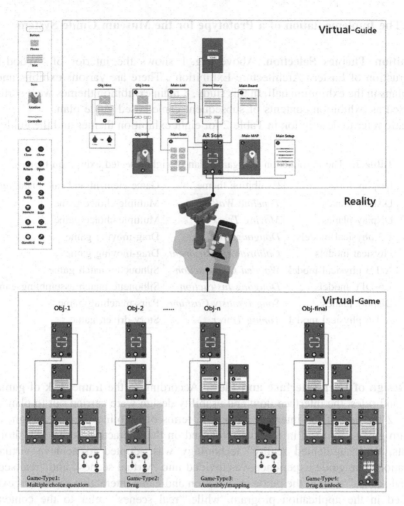

Fig. 3. User interface flow of the museum guide in gamification design

Prototype System Implementation. The system software in this study was developed by using a game engine, Unity. Unity is a cross-platform game development engine, with a hierarchical, comprehensive development environment, including visual editing, detailed attribute editor and dynamic game preview functions. It is also used to make games or develop game prototypes. Thus, it meets the needs of this study. The version adopted in this research is Unity 2018.2. 5f1. As for the selection of hardware devices for guide, considering of making more people get involved, smartphones are chosen as the platform for development.

4 User Testing

After the system is built, it is tested and used in the exhibition hall of "Wood-frame Construction of Eastern Architecture Exhibition" of Ancient Machinery Research Center, Southern Taiwan University of Science and Technology to ensure smooth implementation of the system, as shown in Fig. 4.

Fig. 4. User testing of museum guide system in the exhibition

4.1 Participant Background

This study intended to explore whether the mobile application featuring gamification design in museum guide is helpful to the learning results of audience. It tested the feasibility of guide system and observed testers' system usage behavior. The total number of samples is 40, all of whom are college students aged 18 to 30 (15 males and 25 females). They were familiar with the user interface design and process in the mobile application program, but did not know the relevant knowledge of wooden buildings. The study hoped to know whether the subjects can successfully complete the exhibition experience through the guide App developed in this study.

4.2 The Analysis of System Usage Behavior

Visiting Time of Each Exhibit. The test results show that the average visiting time is 27 min 4 s. For the visiting time of 8 exhibits, please refer to Table 3. The average visiting time of 5 exhibits is about 3 min, namely "Moving Track", "Dougong Group", "Calibration Instrument", "Song Dynasty Costume" and "Timing Tower". Among all the exhibits, the one with the shortest visiting time is "Timeline Wall". Most of the subjects passed through the game checkpoint of the exhibit in a very short time. The game was simple for most of the subjects, but some subjects deemed that there were too many words in this guide interface and they may sometimes ignore the important information.

The one with the most visiting time is No. 6. When visiting the exhibits of "Dougong Instruction", as the game design was interaction between hands-on and exhibits, the subjects need to assemble the scattered Dougong components by observing the Dougong structure. Thus, they spent much time on this exhibit. Most

Table 3. Table captions should be placed above the tables.

Exhibit no.	Shortest time of visit	Longest time of visit	Avg. time of visit	SD.
1	00:00	05:24	01:43	01:17
2	00:23	04:56	02:09	01:08
3	00:43	07:14	02:10	01:23
4	00:27	08:26	02:54	01:47
5	01:30	13:57	04:17	02:34
6	01:04	16:11	07:01	03:41
7	12:11	09:05	03:38	02:00
8	00:00	07:04	03:13	01:31

subjects believed that such guide method was the most interesting, and they can understand the Dougong structure through the hands-on assembly process.

Game Rule and Achieving Level. Each exhibit task in the guide system is a level. Subjects may obtain one key and up to 100 points when they beat a level, and 10 points will be deducted if they fail. If a subject beats a game task at the first time, he may get a golden key, and get a silver key when he didn't beat the task at the first time. Only one of the two keys can be obtained at each level. According to the experimental results, many subjects pointed out the detection problem of image recognition resulted in the low passing rate. The average passing number of 8 exhibits is 4.475, exceeding half of the exhibit task. It can be known that the mobile guide application developed based on the gamification and augmented reality is not difficult for most subjects to master the system and game tasks in a short time.

5   Discussion and Conclusion

According to the user tests, the study suggested on the application of gamification in the interface of museum guide system, and on the design of game content. In terms of application of gamification to the interface of the guide system, the experimental results showed that as subjects needed to use smart mobile phones for testing, they should be focused on both the mobile phones and the exhibits, and failed to carefully read the text introduction on the guide system. It was suggested that the text be presented in the form of voice or animation, which would make it easier for visitors to get involved in the situation when experiencing the exhibition.

In terms of game content design, the subjects preferred the game content with high feedback, such as the game level design of "Dougong Instruction" and "Song Dynasty Costume". The interactive modes of hands-on operation and pairing make subjects felt fun in the guide process. Subjects pointed out that the question-and-answer mode and the way of finding components were boring. It was suggested that the user-friendly interactive mode with high feedback should be provided, so that visitors can have a good interactive experience when visiting the exhibition.

This study hoped to adopted prototyping to develop a guide application program that applies gamification concepts and augmented reality, and to obtain a preliminary design model of gamification for museum guide. Then, this study validated the feasibility of such model through user tests, and the display medium is an interface of mobile device. The preliminary result shows that the application of gamification in museum guide can extend the time of visiting exhibitions in a museum, and has significant effects on museum learning through questionnaires and interviews. It can be seen that gamification has a positive impact on the application of museum guide, and the related research may also be carried out in an in-depth manner.

References

1. Hooper-Greenhill, E.: The educational role of the museum, London and New York
2. Lord, B., Lord, G.D.: The Manual of Museum Management. The Stationery Office, London (1997)
3. Yu, S.C.: Interaction design of personal digital mobile guide example of the exhibition "Emperor Chien-lung Grand Cultural Enterprise" in National Palace Museum. Museum, Master's thesis, Yuan Ze University (2003)
4. Deterding, S., Khaled, R., Nacke, L., Dixon, D.: Gamification: toward a definition. In: Gamification Workshop, CHI 2011 (2011)
5. Johnson, L., Adams Becker, S., Estrada, V., Freeman, A.: NMC horizon report: 2015 higher education edition. The New Media Consortium, Austin, Texas (2015)
6. Roy, M., Hemmert, F., Wettach, R.: Living interfaces: the intimate door lock. In: Proceedings of the Third International Conference on Tangible and Embedded Interaction, pp. 45–46. ACM, New York (2009)
7. Locher, P., Overbeeke, K., Wensveen, S.: Aesthetic interaction: a framework. Des. Issues 26, 70–79 (2010)
8. Zichermann, G., Linder, J.: The Gamification Revolution: How Leaders Leverage Game Mechanics to Crush the Competition. McGraw-Hill Education, New York (2013)

Explore the Usability of the Cultural Museum Website – An Example of Pazeh Cultural Museum

Hsiu Ching Laura Hsieh[✉]

Department of Creative Design, National Yunlin University of Science
and Technology, Douliu, Taiwan
laurarun@gmail.com

Abstract. The aim of this research is to Construct the Pazeh Cultural museum website and explore the usability of the Pazeh Cultural museum website. The method of this research is explained as following. 1) Field investigation and data collection. 2) Construction of information structure of Pazeh Cultural Mobile Museum website. 3) Transform the information structure into an interface prototype. 4) Recruit users for testing. 5) Apply the system usability scale (SUS) and open questionnaire to evaluate usability. 6) Statistics and Analysis the system usability scale (SUS) Finally, according to the research results, suggestions are proposed for the future design and development of Pazeh cultural museum website.

Keywords: Usability · Pazeh cultural museum

1 Introduction

The advancement in technology has greatly accelerated the rise of internet and thus the prevalence of websites which have become the main tool of searching and learning for the users. The Pazeh Tribe in Liyutan Village, Sanyi, Miaoli County has many unique culture and ecological resources, but the local museum has not effectively promoted Pazeh culture. Digital mobile museum website is the most economical way of promotion in which there is no boundary for the dissemination of information while achieving cultural promotion is also possible. The objective of the research is for the establishment of Pazeh Cultural Mobile Museum website, integrating the historical information and natural resources of the Pazeh Tribe. Through interactive web pages and recording Pazeh culture digitally, not only the participation of users would be increased but also the awareness for preserving Pazeh culture in the Pazeh people and the public would be stimulated. The aim of this research: (1) Construct a digital mobile museum website. (2) Discuss the usability of the digital mobile museum website.

© Springer Nature Switzerland AG 2020
C. Stephanidis and M. Antona (Eds.): HCII 2020, CCIS 1226, pp. 286–290, 2020.
https://doi.org/10.1007/978-3-030-50732-9_38

2   Literature Review

The literature information of the research is: Digital mobile museum website, Usability and Interface design, Interactive web design, and Pazeh Culture, all of which will be explained one by one below.

2.1   Digital Mobile Museum Website

With the rise of internet, physical museum is transforming toward digitalization. Visitors to museums in the past have been restricted by the duration of the exhibition and the space of the museum. Museums have only the initial function of exhibition without providing further exploration service to the people. Digitalization differentiates the museum website from the physical museum in that the website can present all relevant information of the exhibition in a digital fashion to the public [2]. Digital mobile museum solves the restrictions of the physical museum and becomes an extension of the physical museum through integrating resources by means of digital technology.

2.2   Usability and Interface Design

Usability is having in the center the users who can instinctively and efficiently use the product, interface, or system. In 1993, the scholar Nielsen defined usability as the function a user can easily use a system, and he also set the 5 standards of usability evaluation as easy to learn, easy to remember, usage efficacy, few operation errors, and user satisfaction [8]. In 1994, the scholar Preece [9] further defined usability as the degree of ease, effectiveness, efficiency, and security of the system used and the attitude of the users for operating the system. Interface is a medium that can facilitate communications between people or between people and the system [7]. In order to have the interface be suitable for people so that communications between people and system, between people, testing the usability must be undertaken when constructing the interface.

2.3   Interactive Web Design

Interactive web page is a user-oriented website that is logically different from the regular information-oriented web page. Interactive web pages transmits graphics, texts, and information to the users in multiple ways Interactive web page preference provides new experience to the users. Clicking on buttons and the mouse, animations and other ways topple the experience of operating the website by the users. More attention to the content of the website by the users will thus happen.

2.4   Pazeh Culture

Pazeh is one of the Pingpu Tribes in Taiwan and is distributed in Liyutan Village in Sanyi of Miaoli County, Taiwan [13]. The subject of the research is the Pazeh people in Liyutan Village in Sanyi, Miaoli County. After undergoing field investigation and exploring literatures, four categories of Symbols, Heroes, Rituals, and Values are classified according to the Cultural Onion Mode by Hofsted in 2010 [3]. The four categories are introduced in the following:

The Pazeh in the Liyutan village have unique and diverse cultural characteristics, The following classifies the Pazeh symbol as five items: 1). Attractions and Monument: The Liyutan village is surrounded by monuments and buildings such as Longteng Bridge and Liyutan Reservoir. 2). Ecological resources: The Liyutan village is rich in natural resources. Such as Leopard Cat, Sus Scrofa Taiwanus, Muntiacus Reevesi, Ring-cupped Oak and Letterwood. 3). Hunting: The Pazeh people fished in the Doroko River with hunting equipment such as Harpoon, Eel cage, Gobies cage, and Crab cage. 4). Clothing: Including ritual clothing, social class symbol jewelry, daily clothing. The social class is distinguished by the complexity of textile technology. 5). Food: The Pazeh people live on fishing, so their diet consists mostly of fish processing such as Gobies, Fish rice cake, Mitten crab [10, 11].

Liyutan Elementary School is where the Pazeh new year's festivities and rituals are held annually after the establishment of Taiwan Pazeh Cultural Association in 1999 [12], inviting all Pazehs to come celebrate together. Gong dance starts the festivities and playing the gongs signifies the beginning of the New Year. 'Zou Biao' is the marathon for men [4, 5]. The men who crossed the finish line would win a satin flag that represents manhood and courage and the respect of the whole village. During the festivities, singing of the Aiyen song commemorates the ancestors and offer gratitude to the heaven [6]. At the conclusion of the festivity, people are invited to have Pazeh style meal and to dance around in the plaza.

The Liyutan Village is itself a wall-less museum. Personally participating in the Pazeh new year's festivities, reading the old books, listening to Pazeh songs are undoubtedly more astounding than visiting a museum. Through Pazeh Cultural Mobile Museum website, the public can gain the understanding of Pazeh's rich culture and natural resources on line. The website will also compile all the rituals, sites, culture, and natural resources in the website so that the public will have a more comprehensive knowledge of the Pazeh Tribe without having to step into Liyutan Village and the goal of promoting Pazeh culture will be achieved.

3   Method

The research is to explore the usability of the digital mobile museum website. There was a need to have the feedback of the testing users, so 15 heavy internet student users between ages 18–15 were chosen to undergo testing. There are six steps in this research. 1) Field investigation and data collection. 2) Construction of information structure of Pazeh Cultural Mobile Museum website. 3) Transform the information structure into an interface prototype. 4) Recruit users for testing. 5) Apply the system usability scale (SUS) and open questionnaire to evaluate usability. 6) Statistics and Analysis the system usability scale (SUS).

4 Results

Statistics and Analysis the system usability scale (SUS). The first phase questionnaire results. Please see the Table 1 below.

Table 1. The first phase questionnaire results

Subject/question	Q1	Q2	Q3	Q4	Q5	Q6	Q7	Q8	Q9	Q10	SUS score	SUS gradescale
S1	4	2	5	1	5	1	5	1	5	1	95	A
S2	3	2	5	1	4	1	5	2	5	2	85	B
S3	3	2	4	1	3	3	5	2	5	2	75	C
S4	3	2	5	1	4	2	5	1	5	1	87.5	B
S5	5	2	4	2	4	2	5	1	4	2	82.5	B
S6	3	2	5	1	4	2	5	2	5	1	85	B
S7	4	1	5	2	5	1	5	1	5	1	95	A
S8	3	1	5	1	5	2	5	1	5	1	92.5	A
S9	3	1	5	1	3	2	5	1	5	1	87.5	B
S10	3	1	4	1	3	3	5	1	5	1	82.5	B
S11	2	1	4	1	3	2	5	1	4	2	77.5	C
S12	2	1	5	2	5	2	5	1	4	1	85	B
S13	3	1	5	1	4	2	5	2	5	2	85	B
S14	4	2	4	1	4	2	4	2	5	2	80	B
S15	2	1	4	1	4	2	5	1	4	1	82.5	B

The research explored the usability of the Pazeh Cultural Mobile Museum by deploying the system usability scale (SUS). The average score of SUS is 70 [1]. The average score of the website is 85.16, above the average. SUS has five levels Of the 15 users who underwent the testing, 3 gave an A rating, 10 B's, and 2 C's; all 15 are within acceptable range, meaning that the usability of the Pazeh Cultural Mobile Museum website has reached average goal. In the first 4 questions of the open answer part, the questions ranged from the ecology of the Pazeh Tribe, culture, fishing and rituals. The goal of the questions was to test the degree of understanding the website by the testing users. Out of the 15 testing users, 11 answered all correctly, and the rest of the 4 missed one question, meaning that the Pazeh Cultural Mobile Museum is easy to understand and is able to provide knowledge to users.

5 Discussion and Conclusion

According to the testing results, the acceptance rate in terms of the illustrations and interactive structure of the Pazeh Cultural Mobile Museum website is quite high among the users who also prefer easy intuitive operation. Interactive website can better attract users to browse the web pages more closely, and the users can gain more information on the Pazeh culture. Intuitive clicking also increases the operation efficiency of the website and reduces mistakes thus enhancing the acceptance rate by the users.

The Pazeh Cultural Mobile Museum website is different from other mobile museums in that it changes the impression in the public of the information-oriented digital mobile museums and is more able to attract users to visit the Pazeh Cultural Mobile Museum website plus achieving the goal of inspiring the public awareness on preserving Pazeh culture. The research explored the usability of the Pazeh Cultural Mobile Museum. During the process of creation, some sticking points were discovered. The recommendations from the testing users are provided for future development of the Pazeh Cultural Mobile Museum website as reference.

References

1. Bangor, A., Kortum, P.T., Miller, J.T.: An empirical evaluation of the system usability scale. Int. J. Hum.-Comput. Interact. **24**(6), 574–594 (2008)
2. Chen, P., Hsiang, J., Chiang, T., Hong, J.: Discussion of digital museums. Museology Q. **16** (3), 15–37 (2002)
3. Hofstede, G., Hofstede, G.J., Minkov, M.: Cultures and Organizations - Software of the Mind. McGraw-Hill, Maidenhead (2010)
4. Lin, H.: Distribution and Population of PingPu. Council of Indigenous Peoples, Executive Yuan, Taipei (2003)
5. Lin, H.: The Pazeh ethnography survey. Council of Indigenous Peoples, Executive Yuan, Taipei (2007)
6. Li, R.G., Lin, C.T.: Pazih Texts and Songs. Institute of Linguistics, Academia sinica, Taipei (2002)
7. Marcus, A.: Dare we define user-interface design? Assoc. Comput. Mach. **9**(5), 19–24 (2002)
8. Nielsen, J.: Usability Engineering. Morgan Kaufmann Publishers Inc., San Francisco (1993)
9. Preece, J., Rogers, Y., Sharp, H., Benyon, D., Holland, S., Carey, T.: Human Computer Interaction. Addison-Wesley Longman Ltd., Essex (1994)
10. Pan, D.H.: The History of Pingpu Pazeh: A Hero in the History of Taiwan's Development. MC Publishing Inc., Taipei (2002)
11. Li, N., Lu, W.: Digitizing Project on the Formosa Aborigines Collection of National Taiwan Museum (VIII) (Research Grant NSC100-2631-H115-001). National Science Council, Executive Yuan, Taipei (2016)
12. Tian, H.: The ethnic certification movement of Pazeh. National Chengchi University Ethnology Department thesis, Taipei (2016)
13. Zhang, S.F.: Miaoli Liyutan Pazeh history paleography compilation. Culture and Tourism Bureau, Miaoli County, Miaoli (2007)

Embodied Interaction for the Exploration of Image Collections in Mixed Reality (MR) for Museums and Other Exhibition Spaces

Kathrin Koebel(✉) ⓘ and Doris Agotai

Institute for Interactive Technologies IIT, University of Applied Sciences and Arts
Northwestern Switzerland FHNW, Windisch, Switzerland
{kathrin.koebel,doris.agotai}@fhnw.ch
http://www.fhnw.ch/iit

Abstract. Although museums and archives dispose of extensive cultural heritage data, suitable interfaces for exploration of these collections are lacking. We describe an applied research based on an archive of historic photographs. Our main objective is to engage the general audience in the exploration of this data and thus facilitate discovery and insight. Embodied interaction [1] promises much potential for this endeavour and is highly suitable for museums and exhibition spaces when implemented with vision based technology as no contact with hardware is required. In addition, MR output is attractive for surrounding audiences. To test this assertion, an immersive interactive MR exploration space was developed applying embodied concepts, where the user's position and movement in the interaction space combined with in-air gestures are used for application control of the super-positioned collection data space. A user study was conducted to measure differences in user engagement, exploration behaviour and discovery between this embodied interaction concept and traditional WIMP interaction. With embodied interaction, a significantly higher degree of exploration of the collection space was measured and users discovered slightly more novelties and connections. Additionally, a higher sense of immersion, fresh perspective on the contents and increased interest in the collection were reported. Hedonic qualities (e.g. stimulation, aesthetic appeal, reward factor) scored significantly higher while pragmatic qualities such as perceived usability were lower.

Keywords: Embodied interaction · Natural user interaction · Human computer interaction · Data exploration · Cultural heritage · Mixed reality · User engagement · User experience

1 Introduction

Museums and archives possess significant amounts of cultural heritage data that often remain unused or merely receive little attention. One reason for this is

© Springer Nature Switzerland AG 2020
C. Stephanidis and M. Antona (Eds.): HCII 2020, CCIS 1226, pp. 291–299, 2020.
https://doi.org/10.1007/978-3-030-50732-9_39

the lack of suitable interfaces for exploration. Real value is created by making this data accessible to the public through suitable interfaces for exploration and discovery. In this paper, we describe an applied research based on the Ringier Bildarchiv (RBA), a large database of historical photographs. Our main objective is to engage the general audience (i.e. non-expert users) in the *exploration* of this data and thus facilitate *discovery and insight* while also providing a great *user experience*. In the context of museums, immersive visualisation combined with embodied interaction [1] is offering promising prospects for that purpose when implemented with vision based technology, where no contact between user and hardware devices is required. And in comparison to other immersive technologies such as virtual reality, MR output is highly visible and attractive for surrounding museum visitors. An additional benefit of this method notably for large databases lies in its ability to rapidly offer an overall impression of the contents.

The RBA containing more than 7 million analog press photos is Switzerland's largest picture archive. The images document people and events in the country's recent history (1930–2000) and cover a wide range of public and private life matters – from politics to sport and culture to everyday life. In the course of digitalisation, the analog archive originally collected and curated by a prominent publishing house was handed over to the state archive. Since 2015, sections of the collection are accessible to the public at the "Schauarchiv" (engl. archive exhibition) of Stadtmuseum Aarau where – under professional supervision and instruction on proper dealings with these historic contents – users can browse through the original archive boxes. In addition, selected portions of the RBA have been digitised and systematically stored in a database and public access is offered via a web interface [2]. Transforming this ordinary online collection into an interactive exploration space for museum visitors offers an interesting use case for this research.

2   Theory and Related Work

Idreos et al. define data exploration as "efficiently extracting knowledge from data *even if we do not know exactly what we are looking for*" and explain that some key facets to achieve this objective are advanced data visualization and alternative exploration interfaces that help users navigate the underlying data space [3]. In this research we focus on the latter. Interactive immersive technologies provide such an alternative interface that stimulates user engagement and cognition. Already in the 60s, Sutherland illustrated in his visionary essay "The ultimate display" how technology can augment human cognition and take advantage of a broader range of senses and capabilities than tradition interfaces [4].

Interactive immersive technologies offer multiple benefits for engaging users in the data exploration task: *Direct manipulation* has been lauded for the reduction of information processing distance between the user's intentions and the facilities provided by the system. This reduces physical as well as mental work and lets users accomplish their goals with less effort [5]. In regards to data exploration, LaViola et al. claim mounting evidence that direct interaction offered by immersive environments provides benefits for perception and interpretation of data. They argue that such direct manipulation interactions are more fluid and more efficient in comparison to non-immersive data displays with traditional WIMP interaction [6]. Additionally, affordances offered by the established relation between input and output vocabularies not only promise a faster learning curve but also contributes to the *sense of immersion*. Cummings further argues that greater immersion produces a stronger sense of presence which leads then to a higher engagement in the system or experience [7].

The theory of *embodied interaction* unites immersion into the virtual environment with direct, natural user interaction and adds a phenomenological motivation for exploring psychological and social aspects of human-computer interaction. Dourish defines embodied interaction as "interaction with computer systems that occupy our world, a world of physical and social reality and that exploit this fact in how they interact with us" [1]. Embodiment super-positions abstract data spaces with concrete, tangible interaction spaces and by doing so, harnesses the potential of mental processes that are embedded into the body [8]. And since the human experience is shaped by the physical world, it's not surprising that we are most engaged and effective when acting physically. Embodiement is further closely coupled to topics such as proprioception and spatial memory, that describe how we perceive and understand our bodies and our environment. Concerning the latter, embodiment and the phenomenological movement emerged amongst other influences from Uexküll's concept of "Umwelt". This theory originating from the field of biosemiotics maps out the spheres of perception of an individual [9] and is primarily concerned with the user's natural environment, not the technology involved. Weiser who coined the term "calm computing" anyhow campaigns that technology should be invisible and not intruding the user's consciousness [10]. This is particularly true for the given use case, where the user's focus should be guided on the content and not on the technology itself. And Elmqvist et al. offer some guidelines for "fluid interactions" where they emphasise, inter alia, the importance of ensuring that continued exploration is always possible and users never reach dead ends [11].

While many museums offer online collections to explore their databases, data exploration by the means of interactive immersive environments are still rare in practice in the cultural heritage domain. Nonetheless, an interesting example is mARChive. This interactive 360-degree data landscape offers an intuitive platform to engage with a collection of 100'000 objects of Melbourne's Museum Victoria [12]. Also noteworthy, from a related domain, is Müller et al.'s zoomable UI, a physically-based data exploration approach – inspired by the search process of a rummage table – to interact with data by deforming the surface of an elastic display [13]. An example showing that embodied interaction leads to higher user engagement is "Be the data", which pursues the objective of educating non-STEM students about data analytics using an embodied approach. Findings indicate that this method provides the necessary engagement to enable students to quickly learn about high-dimensional data and analysis processes despite minimal prior knowledge [14]. And for gestural interfaces, Minority Report is a prime example. Yet before being scientific advisor on the film, Underkoffler developed Oblong g-speak, a spatial operating environment offering gesture control and multi-user collaboration for big data analytics [15]. One of it's applications particularly relevant for this research is "Exo", a visualisation tool for exploring nearly 2300 exoplanets identified by NASA's Kepler mission [16].

3   Methods, Process and Materials

With the goal of animating non-expert users to explore the contents of the RBA archive in mind, we investigated various visualisation and interaction possibilities, including embodied interaction, and technological capabilities for recognizing user input in MR. We examined the spheres of perception and their reciprocal effect for the given use case (see Fig. 1). With respect to the museum use case interaction concepts, that do not require direct contact between user and hardware, and render output in a way that is relevant not only for the main user but also for the broader audience, were favoured.

Fig. 1. Umwelten

We specified interaction patterns required to reach the goal. Following Shneiderman's principle "overview first, zoom and filter, then details on demand" [17] the application should allow interaction with the archive (or a subset) as a whole as well as allowing to zoom in on items of interest and provide additional details on selected objects. In addition, we defined levels of involvement ranging from 0 to 3 (no active participation to high user involvement) for a potential solution.

Applying design thinking we developed a set of concept ideas inspired by research on state of the art and technology. Concept evaluation considered factors such as dimensions of meaning, determinants regarding usability and user experience, feasibility and relevance for the use case. Selected concepts employing embodied interaction aspects were further developed by the means of rapid prototyping and resulted in the installation prototype described in Sect. 4.

To examine the effect of embodiment on the exploration task and single out this one factor – namely the form of interaction – for examination from all other conditions that may have an effect [20], we designed a study that compares embodied interaction with WIMP interaction. To test the hypothesis, that *embodied interaction stimulates users more to explore, make discoveries and gain insight from information spaces than WIMP interaction*, we've built two prototypes that differ solely in the way how users interact. In one scenario, we use traditional WIMP interaction (i.e. mouse input). In the other scenario, we've applied the concept of embodied interaction by which the user's body movement and position in the room as well as in-air gestures are used for application control. The installation contained two sets of 120 photos each, that were randomly selected from the RBA photo database and the setup is shown in Fig. 2.

We've conducted a user study (n = 16) where the form of interaction was the only independent variable in the study design. For dependent variables we

Table 1. Research questions for user study

Q1	*Which form of interaction animates users more to explore the image collection?*
Q2	*Does the form of interaction affect how much insight is gained, how many discoveries are made, and if connections are recognized between objects?*
Q3	*Which form of interaction leads to a higher user engagement and a better UX?*

defined metrics derived from user behaviour, performance and self declaration targeted to the 3 research questions (see Table 1). The test procedure comprised a pre-questionnaire (demographics, technical affinity, interest in application domain). Then for each scenario, first the features offered by the given prototype were demonstrated and there was time for learning the novel forms of interaction before doing the actual exploration task, followed by an evaluation of performance by means of questionnaire with open questions and ratings on 5-point Likert scales regarding immersion, fatigue as well as the two standardized evaluation scales UES-SF [18] and UEQ [19]. In addition, user behaviour was logged during the use of the application. The procedure ended with comparative and open questions and took about 60 min. in total. The participants (ages 21–71, ø 41, 10 male, 6 female) were of diverse occupational backgrounds. 80% indicated some interest in museums, 5 stated to have experienced immersive technologies previously and 7 tried in-air gestures once before (e.g. Nitendo Wii, Microsoft HoloLens). Only 2 declared occasional use of this form of interaction.

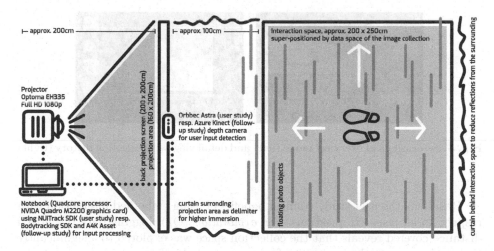

Fig. 2. Setup of the installation

4   Results

We've developed an immersive interactive MR exploration space offering overview, detail view and selection history as key features for exploring the contents of the image collection. In *overview mode* (see Fig. 3, left) objects are floating around freely. This fluid visualisation rendered on a large display should engage museum visitors to interact with the application and animate explorative behaviour. By physically moving around the interaction space, the user virtually moves through the depths of the super-positioned collection data space. Items that are further away from the user are rendered with lower brightness to increase depth perception. The application allows to zoom in on items of interest in an embodied manner by simply approaching them. By selecting an object – executed through an in-air click gesture – the application switches into *detail view mode* (see Fig. 3, right), where additional information for the selected item such as description, location, year and photographer is provided. In addition, a *selection history* is offered in this mode to return to previously selected objects for the purpose of comparison. Furthermore, the MR setup ensures that the application offers an attractive experience not only for the interactor, but also for others in vicinity who act as mere observers.

The software is implemented with Unity and the user's gestures and movement are tracked through a depth camera (see Fig. 2). Although this computer vision based technology is less precise in recognising gesture input than body-attached sensors, it's more suitable for use in public settings such as museums.

Fig. 3. Screenshots of overview mode (left) and detail view with selection history (right)

Results of the user study confirm benefits of using embodied interaction with respect to all research questions. For *exploration* (Q1), logging data on virtual distance covered reveals that the collection space was explored to a significantly higher degree and the majority of users gauged this form of interaction to be more animating for the exploration task. Also UEQ's stimulation score is considerably higher and attains the benchmark 'excellent'. Concerning *discovery* (Q2) evaluation of user performance showed slightly more discoveries of novelties and correlations, plus UEQ's novelty score is significantly higher. Besides, there was a stronger agreement on obtaining a fresh perspective on the contents. In regards to *user engagement and user experience* (Q3) UES-SF's reward factor and aesthetic appeal scores were considerably higher and a higher sense of immersion was reported. There was no considerable difference in UES-SF's overall user engagement score (3.79 vs. 3.71, on scale from 1 to 5), yet UES-SF's perceived usability is significantly weaker. Overall, while scores for hedonic qualities were significantly higher (UEQ-HQ 1.67 vs. 1.18, on scale from -3 to +3), pragmatic qualities were considerably lower (UEQ-PQ 0.82 vs. 1.46). The primary reason for this were inaccuracies in gesture recognition. Although UEQ values above 0.8 are considered positive, this points to explicit potential for improvement.

Fig. 4. Participants interacting with the installation during the user study

For this reason the depth camera was subsequently replaced with a higher quality device and a qualitative follow-up usability study (n = 5) using the new hardware was conducted [21]. Results showed some improvement in UES-SF's perceived usability score (3.60). There was no major change in the UEQ-PQ score, yet an increase was noticed in the UEQ's overall attractiveness score (1.60), which demonstrates the interconnection of usability and overall user experience.

5 Discussion and Outlook

Both scenarios received rather high scores compared to UEQ benchmark data. It was particularly surprising, that even the WIMP interaction scenario received considerable positive ratings in particular by the older segment of participants who had in general more difficulties with gesture input. Several participants of this cohort mentioned that controlling gesture input absorbed their full attention. A reason for this could be that some research unveils spatial interaction problems as an early indicator for age-related dementia [22]. While gesture input has many benefits such as the natural characteristics of direct mapping of user movements, a drawback for all demographics is the need for clear delimiters to indicate initialisation and determination of gestures. Otherwise normal human motions may be interpreted as gestures while not intended as such. This concerns only in-air gestures, whereas the proposed embodied depth movement provides a continuous input and is therefore not affected by this issue.

In addition to the form of interaction also the personal interest in the application domain in general, and specific topics covered by the archive in particular, affects to what degree test users engage with the presented data. Differences in the overall interest in the application domain were taken into account and compensated for in the test design, however the personal emotional reference made with particular photographs such as emotions evoked by memories about a past incident are highly subjective and unpredictable.

Further research questions include investigation of the connection between spatial awareness, immersion and exploration, the impact of emotional references to the photograph's content on explorative behaviour and how a shared experience and gamification approaches could increase the level of involvement and thus engage users even more in the exploration of historic photographic artifacts.

References

1. Dourish, P.: Where the Action Is: The Foundations of Embodied Interaction. MIT Press, Cambridge (2001)
2. Stadtmuseum Aarau: Sammlungsbereiche Ringier Bildarchiv RBA. http://emp-web-57.zetcom.ch/eMP/eMuseumPlus. Accessed 24 Feb 2020
3. Idreos, S., Papaemmanouil, O., Chaudhuri, S.: Overview of data exploration techniques. In: Proceedings of the 2015 ACM SIGMOD International Conference on Management of Data, pp. 277–281 (2015)
4. Sutherland, I.: The ultimate display. In: Proceedings of IFIP Congress, vol. 65, pp. 506–508 (1965)
5. Hutchins, E.L., Hollan, J.D., Norman, D.A.: Direct manipulation interfaces. Hum. Comput. Interact. 1(4), 311–338 (1985)
6. LaViola, J.J., Forsberg, A.S., Laidlaw, D.H., Van Dam, A.: Virtual reality-based interactive scientific visualization environments. In: Liere, R., Adriaansen, T., Zudilova-Seinstra, E. (eds.) Trends in Interactive Visualization, pp. 225–250. Springer, London (2009). https://doi.org/10.1007/978-1-84800-269-2_10
7. Cummings, J.J., Bailenson, J.N.: How immersive is enough? A meta-analysis of the effect of immersive technology on user presence. Media Psychol. 19(2), 272–309 (2016)
8. Storch, M., Cantieni, B., Hüther, G., Tschacher, W.: Embodiment. Die Wechselwirkung von Körper und Psyche verstehen und nutzen, 2nd ed. Huber, Bern (2010)
9. von Uexküll, J.: Bedeutungslehre. Bios, Abhandlungen zur theoretischen Biologie und ihrer Geschichte sowie zur Philosophie der organischen Naturwissenschaften, Bd. 10. J.A. Barth, Leipzig (1940)
10. Weiser, M.: The world is not a desktop. ACM Interact. 1, 7–8 (1994)
11. Elmqvist, N., Moere, A.V., Jetter, H.C., Cernea, D., Reiterer, H., Jankun-Kelly, T.J.: Fluid interaction for information visualization. Inf. Vis. 10(4), 327–340 (2011)
12. Shaw, J., Kenderdine, S., Hart, T.: mARChive (2014). http://www.icinema.unsw.edu.au/projects/marchive/project-overview. Accessed 4 Mar 2020
13. Müller, M., Keck, M., Gründer, T., Hube, N., Groh, R.: A zoomable product browser for elastic displays. In: Proceedings xCoAx 2017, 5th Conference on Computation, Communication, Aesthetics & X, Lisbon, Portugal (2017)
14. Chen, X., et al.: Be the data: embodied visual analytics. IEEE Trans. Learn. Technol. 11(1), 81–95 (2017)
15. Underkoffler, J.S., Parent, K.T., Kramer, K.H.: System and method for gesture based control system. US Patent 7,598,942 (2009)

16. Thorp, J.: Exo: a visualization of Kepler's exoplanet candidates (2012). https://vimeo.com/41655330. Accessed 4 Mar 2020
17. Shneiderman, B.: The eyes have it: a task by data typetaxonomy for information visualizations. In: Proceedings 1996 IEEE Symposium on Visual Languages, pp. 336–343. IEEE (1996)
18. O'Brien, H.L., Cairns, P., Hall, M.: A practical approach to measuring user engagement with the refined user engagement scale (UES) and new UES short form. Int. J. Hum. Comput. Stud. **112**, 28–39 (2018)
19. Laugwitz, B., Held, T., Schrepp, M.: Construction and evaluation of a user experience questionnaire. In: Holzinger, Andreas (ed.) USAB 2008. LNCS, vol. 5298, pp. 63–76. Springer, Heidelberg (2008). https://doi.org/10.1007/978-3-540-89350-9_6
20. Flick, U.: Sozialforschung. Methoden und Anwendungen. Rowohlts Enzyklopädie, Hamburg (2009)
21. Nielsen, J.: How many test users in a usability study. Nielsen Norman Group (2012)
22. Verghese, J., Lipton, R., Ayers, E.: Spatial navigation and risk of cognitive impairment: a prospective cohort study. Alzheimer's Dementia **13**(9), 985–992 (2017)

Participatory Management for Cultural Heritage: Social Media and Chinese Urban Landscape

Xiaoxu Liang[✉][iD]

Polytechnic University of Turin, Viale Mattioli, 39, 10125 Turin, Italy
Xiaoxu.liang@polito.it

Abstract. Community participation plays a core role in sustainable urban development and inclusive cultural heritage management [1, 2]. Despite the broad attention on the World Heritage Property management in China, little research has been done on systematically reviewing the practices of community participation within Chinese cultural heritage, nor defining the role of social media played in it. To fill this research gap, this paper aims to explore how social media can contribute to community engagement and further influence sustainable cultural heritage management by providing a systematic literature review. Based on the evolving definition of community participation from the Historic Urban Landscape approach, this work starts with a review on the conceptualization of community participation. This article continues with a discussion on the role of the community played in participatory management. Following that, the argument is mainly concerning that social media is one of the vital tools to engage a wider range of audiences in conservation practices. To conclude, online urban heritage practices offer a platform for local citizens, especially grassroots, to collaborate with heritage institutions and professionals. Social media practices, such as mapping, may have a wider resonance when they combine broader communication and collaboration methods.

Keywords: Holistic urban heritage conservation · Digital community participate · Social media

1 Introduction

Along with the launching process of the Historic Urban Landscape Approach, the World Heritage Center is endeavoring to involve a variety of stakeholders in heritage identification, protection, and preservation as a worldwide strategic policy [3, 4]. Community engagement is identified as a bond which can contribute to rebuilding the relationship for the past, present, and future in the cultural heritage assets and socio-economic values [5].

Different regions have their own localized concepts of heritage conservation which are not supposed to be aligned with the globalized notion [6]. It is worth mentioning that the focus of heritage conservation in China during the last decades is gradually transiting from the materiality to sustainable development with greater emphasis on community participation [7, 8]. Indeed, China is undertaking effective actions to adhere

© Springer Nature Switzerland AG 2020
C. Stephanidis and M. Antona (Eds.): HCII 2020, CCIS 1226, pp. 300–307, 2020.
https://doi.org/10.1007/978-3-030-50732-9_40

to wider international standards with better consideration of the notion of authenticity, collective memory, identity and the sense of place [9, 10]. Besides the traditional participatory management discussion, how the Information and Communication Technologies (ICT) encourage and enable new forms of engagement with heritage in different cultural contexts have raised the interest of relevant scholars [11–13].

2 Conceptualization of Community Participation

2.1 Community Engagement as an Effective Tool of Historic Urban Landscape Approach

The HUL approach stands out as a "bottom-up" expression of social values and social choice [1], which can better recognize cultural diversity and the dynamic nature of urban heritage in the context of rapid globalization. Although the discussion[1] and approval[2] of HUL implementation in Chinese context occurred slightly laggard, it significantly evokes a wide discussion on the regional level and emphasized on a sustainable development of the local community by concerning the priority on the improvement of living conditions and sharing benefits from urban heritage conservation [8].

The 'community engagement tools' are listed as one of the expanded conservational instruments by the HUL approach [3] in the attempt to educate and empower diverse stakeholders to identify key values of their cultural heritage and promote sustainable urban development [14]. Aline with it, the role of local community played in urban regeneration in China is gradually shifting from a passive agent to an important character in obtaining alternative solutions [15]. Meanwhile, an extensive legislative and regulatory system related to urban heritage has been endowed for strengthening the soft power [16]. A well-known pioneer example in China is the restoration project in Tianzifang, Shanghai [8]. During the decision process of this project, the local government and developers effectively involved the local community and successfully avoided the massive relocation. As an extent, the 2015 international forum *City and Society*[3] organized by UNESCO discussed on themes concerning "Community, Space, and Governance" aiming to enhance the effectiveness of engagement [17].

Nevertheless, how to apply the western born "doctrinal" approach to worldwide societies and how to define operational principles to ensure urban conservation models

---

[1] It refers to the International Conference in Shanghai on 'Historic Urban Landscape' on 9-10 December 2014, hosted by the World Heritage Institute of Training and Research for the Asia and the Pacific Region under the auspices of UNESCO, WHITRAP Shanghai.

[2] It refers to the 'Shanghai Agenda' for the Implementation of UNESCO Recommendation on Historic Urban Landscape (HUL) In China: First edition on 10 December 2014; revised on 10 January 2015.

[3] The conference was hosted by Tongji University, organized by World Heritage Institute of Training and Research for the Asia and the Pacific Region under the auspices of UNESCO, WHITRAP Shanghai.

that respect the values, traditions, and environments of different cultural contexts still needs further examination in practice.

2.2 Discussion on Community Engagement

Modern approaches to urban conservation and heritage planning are promoting heritage as living, to be integrated into planning processes and contribute to the quality of life of their communities [5].

Following the supplement of "community" in *Global Strategy of World Heritage*[4], a series of conference discussions and declarations started to focus on the role of community in heritage protection. Ten years later, the conference *World Heritage and Sustainable Development: The Role of Local Communities* highlighted the guarantee of local communities' benefit. In 2015, *the Policy on the Integration of a Sustainable Development Perspective into the Processes of the World Heritage Convention*[5], known as Kyoto Vision, further emphasizes sustainable that development of world heritage has to involve local communities and consider their benefit. Since then, the participation of community stakeholders has become one of the core measures of heritage protection. The "core community" that created living heritage and sustains the original function of heritage is seen as an inseparable part of heritage [18].

At the same time, in China, the top-down process has given rising to a range of new actors and stakeholders in heritage-making and negotiating the AHD. while "citizens and communities are experiencing, performing, and documenting heritage" in a more bottom-up way [7].

3   The Role of Community

Identifying the core community which should be admitted to engaging in local decision-making with first priority, is a common concern of both China and the West [5, 18]. This should be considered or defined precisely while partnering with author-ities, experts and economic actors, as well as the question of the broader communities as facilitators are [5]. Furthermore, Poulios highlighted that the "core community" in the living heritage approach is a different concept from the "local community" of the values-based approach [18]. In China, community identification is directly linked with the institutional division which is known as the Hukou system[6] [8]. In identifying actors, as well as their relationships, within the stakeholders' map in heritage protec-tion, Maags demonstrates in detail the competition among participants, including both the state and non-state ones, for the voices and power in Chinese cities [19].

Undoubtedly, citizens are attached to local history and cultural identity. Thus, various of active participatory methods are conducted aiming to raise awareness and building capacities of local communities and share both benefits and responsibilities

---

[4] 31st session of the World Heritage Committee, Christchurch, New-Zealand, 23 June–2 July 2007.

[5] 39th session of the World Heritage Committee, Bonn, Germany, 28 June–8 July 2015.

[6] China's Hukou system is a family registration program that serves as a domestic passport, in which the migrants are gully involved in both local decisions and welfare benefits.

from the heritage conservation process [20, 21]. Meanwhile, the "popular action" as a roman model has been introduced to China. Beyond this, multi-active participatory methods were utilized in this cultural revitalization so as to cultural heritage protection process [22]. In 2009, 22 sites in south-west of China were selected to take part in the World Bank Guizhou Cultural and Natural Heritage Protection and Development Project[7]. Cultural mapping was used in River County to involve ethnic minority communities. In Gate Tower old city, an eco-museum approach encouraged residents to create an exhibition of their ethnical culture with the help of the Chinese National Ethnology Museum [22].

Integrating heritage conservation in sustainable urban development through community collaboration and empowerment is essential [4, 8, 23]. As an inclusive and holistic approach, HUL is highly relevant to the arise awareness of civic engagement and its broad applicability in international practice [1]. However, an obvious challenge to address it in China is the indistinction between private and public which is clearly different from the western state-civil society relationships [8]. which means, the notion of civic engagement still needs to be particularly well distinguished in the Chinese context.

4 New Forms of Community Engagement in the Digital Era: Social Media and Heritage

4.1 Communities Online

In the recent few years, there is emerging attention on applying digital platforms to engaging the local communities in the urban renewal process to better protection and promotion of cultural heritage values [24]. On one hand, urban landscapes can epitomize the nexus between cultural and historic cities, recording human interaction with built environments beyond space, time and societies [3]. On the other hand, digital community participation can improve conservation and preservation techniques, enrich archives with interactive media, augment participatory experiences, and beyond [25, 26]. Harrison argued that the ways to catch up on the corporeal influence of the affective qualities of heritage in the daily practices need to be further explored [27]. While Svensson offers a great answer that social media can enable and strengthen people's affective engagement with heritage [28].

The internet as a social media could be a key community-based platform for sustainable living heritage conservation [12]. New online communities have emerged, which is formed with specific cultural practices, or centered around affinities based on place and heritage [11, 12]. It fosters an open culture wherein anyone who is so motivated can become involved in the cultural heritage protection [13]. Although social

---

[7] World Bank began to assist in cultural heritage conservation in China since 1990s. The investing approach shifted in 2000 from developing tourism to integrate cultural heritage in local economic development and sustainable tourism.

media cannot represent the opinion of the whole civic society, it offers an open-participatory platform to a broader range of agents to reach across scales and connect with mass audiences [12, 13], which is crucial for collaborative planning and conservation.

4.2 Digital Ways to Participate in Heritage Conservation

Digital technologies of communication have changed the ways of participating, interacting, and organizing in planning practices and facilitated the engagement of civic organizations [24, 29]. In this digital era, obviously, the power to represent the city is no longer concentrated in the elites controlling popular media but is distributed by common smartphone users [30]. Online information seeking and interactive civic messaging is influencing community engagement stronger than traditional printings, broadcast media and face-to-face communication [31]. In addition, it is not only established individuals and organizations that make use of the Internet and social media, but there have also emerged new online communities that are gathered on activities based on cultural heritage [32]. Besides enabling strangers to share experiences with places, historical events, and cultural practices, social media also strengthens the relation of existing communities by helping them 'remember, experience, and perhaps re-imagine their own heritage' [28]. Despite that, some researchers concern that the new media platform has mainly been used for dissemination of information, rendering it an elitist rather than a democratic tool [11, 13].

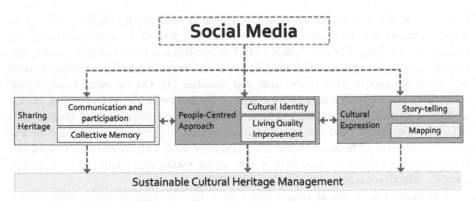

Fig. 1. The contribution of social media to sustainable cultural heritage management (Produced by the author).

At the aspect of application approaches, various digital products can improve our understandings of people-centered heritage and foster the public to take part in heritage conservation (see Fig. 1). Nowadays, people have the chance to create their own digital heritage landscapes, museums, and archives [33]. Furthermore, in the case of the Carpano museum, Spacca and her colleagues examined that Augmented Reality (AR) applications can promote industrial and other kinds of cultural heritage without space and time constraints [26]. Meanwhile, social media apps, such as Facebook, can be used to contribute to making collective community memory visible by story-telling practices [34]. Location-based mobile games are utilized in Palazzo Madama Museum to foster young visitors to a larger extent motivation to explore museums and facilitate their meaning-making process [25].

To make cultural heritage conservation a far more inclusive process is immense. The challenges are complex and far different in most cultural contexts [35]. In the recent ten years, the incipient collaborative planning and public participation through the functions of the internet in China have had an increasingly vital influence [9, 10]. On one hand, the Chinese government has tried several times to employ the use of Information and Communication Technologies for provoking better citizen engagement with the aim of creating a positive impact on cultural heritage conservation. Digital application and online communication have gradually become an important method of public consultation and supervision during the construction phase of renewal planning in Dashilar [36]. On the other hand, experts and civic groups utilized social media spontaneously to criticize the large-scale relocation in the regeneration projects of Beijing's bell and drum tower neighborhood which is proposed by the local government [4]. By using social media, these groups of activists were able to contest official propositions for the area and, based on scientific arguments, suggest better ways to care for current everyday life and alternative forms of memories that matter to its inhabitants [4, 10].

5 Conclusion

UNESCO's Recommendation on the Historic Urban Landscape marks a brand-new integrated approach to the conservation of Chinese cultural heritage. It highlighted the importance of community engagement and offers a series of participatory tools at the international level, which required deep civic engagement to identify the key values of concerned heritage objects. Social media is one of the vital tools to engage a wider range of audience in conservation practices. It can not only promote in the educational level by rendering heritage and relevant information more accessible, but also involve citizens in further documentation by crowdsourcing. Storytelling and Mapping are the current main research practices of social media to enable a greater awareness of cultural diversity.

While in the Chinese context, online urban heritage practices are considered to have more impact considering the speed of broadcast and involved quantity. Social media offers a platform for local citizens to collaborate with heritage institutions and professionals. A wider utilization of social media in the decision-making process of Chinese heritage conservation can potentially contribute to a more effective on-line community engagement.

References

1. Pereira Roders, A., Bandarin, F. (eds.): Reshaping Urban Conservation. CHC, vol. 2. Springer, Singapore (2019). https://doi.org/10.1007/978-981-10-8887-2

2. Settis, S.: We the Citizens, English translation of chapter 7 of Paesaggio, Costituzione, cemento: la battaglia per l'ambiente contro il degrado civile (Einaudi, 2010). Calif. Ital. Stud. **2** (2011)
3. Bandarin, F., van Oers, R.: The Historic Urban Landscape: Managing Heritage in an Urban Century. Wiley, Chichester (2012)
4. Bideau, F.G., Yan, H.: Historic urban landscape in Beijing: the Gulou project and its contested memories. In: Maags, C., Svensson, M. (eds.) Chinese Heritage in the Making, pp. 93–118. Amsterdam University Press (2018)
5. Court, S., Wijesuriya, G.: People-centred approaches to the conservation of cultural heritage: living heritage. In: Chitty, G. (ed.) Heritage, Conservation and Communities: Engagement, Participation and Capacity Building, pp. 34–50. Routledge, Newyork (2017)
6. Harrison, R.: Understanding the Politics of Heritage. Manchester University Press, Manchester (2009)
7. Svensson, M., Maags, C.: Mapping the Chinese heritage regime: ruptures, governmentality, and agency. In: Svensson, M., Maags, C. (eds.) Chinese Heritage in the Making: Experiences, Negotiations and Contestations, pp. 11–38. Amsterdam University Press (2018)
8. Verdini, G., Frassoldati, F., Nolf, C.: Reframing China's heritage conservation discourse. Learning by testing civic engagement tools in a historic rural village. Int. J. Heritage Stud. **23**, 317–334 (2017)
9. Cheng, Y.: Collaborative planning in the network: Consensus seeking in urban planning issues on the Internet—the case of China. Plann. Theory **12**, 351–368 (2013)
10. Deng, Z., Lin, Y., Zhao, M., Wang, S.: Collaborative planning in the new media age: the Dafo Temple controversy. China. Cities. **45**, 41–50 (2015)
11. Giaccardi, E.: Heritage and Social Media: Understanding Heritage in a Participatory Culture. Routledge, London (2012)
12. Ginzarly, M., Pereira Roders, A., Teller, J.: Mapping historic urban landscape values through social media. J. Cult. Heritage **36**, 1–11 (2019)
13. Kitchin, R., Dodge, M.: Code/Space: Software and Everyday Life. MIT Press, Cambridge (2011)
14. van Oers, R., Roders, A.P.: Road map for application of the HUL approach in China. J. Cult. Heritage Manage. Sustain. Dev. **3**, 4–17 (2013)
15. Li, J., Krishnamurthy, S., Pereira Roders, A., van Wesemael, P.: Community participation in cultural heritage management: a systematic literature review comparing Chinese and international practices. Cities **96**, 102476 (2020)
16. Whitehand, J.W.R., Gu, K., Whitehand, S.M.: Fringe belts and socioeconomic change in China. Environ. Plann. B Plann. Des. **38**, 41–60 (2011)
17. WHITRAP: Report for the 39 Session of the World Heritage Committee. WHITRAP, Bonn, Germany (2015)
18. Poulios, I.: Discussing strategy in heritage conservation: living heritage approach as an example of strategic innovation. J. Cult. Heritage Man Sust. Dev. **4**, 16–34 (2014)
19. Maags, C.: Creating a race to the top: hierarchies and competition within the Chinese ICH transmitters system. In: Maags, C., Svensson, M. (eds.) Chinese Heritage in the Making, pp. 121–144. Amsterdam University Press (2018)
20. Borona, G., Ndiema, E.: Merging research, conservation and community engagement. J. Cult. Heritage Manage. Sustain. Dev. **4**, 184–195 (2014)
21. Ferreira, T.C.: Bridging planned conservation and community empowerment: Portuguese case studies. J. Cult. Heritage Manage. Sustain. Dev. **8**, 179–193 (2018)

22. Nitzky, W.: Community Empowerment at the periphery? Participatory approaches to heritage protection in Guizhou, China. In: Blumenfield, T., Silverman, H. (eds.) Cultural Heritage Politics in China, pp. 205–235. Springer, New York (2013). https://doi.org/10.1007/978-1-4614-6874-5_11

23. MacRae, G.: Universal heritage meets local livelihoods: 'awkward engagements' at the world cultural heritage listing in Bali. Int. J. Heritage Stud. **23**, 846–859 (2017)

24. De Filippi, F.D., Coscia, C., Guido, R.: from smart-cities to smart-communities: how can we evaluate the impacts of innovation and inclusive processes in urban context? IJEPR **8**, 24–44 (2019)

25. Rubino, I., Barberis, C., Xhembulla, J., Malnati, G.: Integrating a location-based mobile game in the museum visit: evaluating visitors' behaviour and learning. JOCCH **8**, 1–18 (2015)

26. Spacca, S., Dellapiana, E., Sanna, A.: Promoting industrial cultural heritage by augmented reality: application and assessment. Open Cybern. Syst. J. **12**, 61–71 (2018)

27. Harrison, R.: Heritage: Critical Approaches. Routledge, New York (2012)

28. Svensson, M.: Heritage 2.0: maintaining affective engagements with the local heritage in Taishun. In: Svensson, M., Maags, C. (eds.) Chinese Heritage in the Making, pp. 269–292. Amsterdam University Press (2018)

29. Lin, Y., Zhang, X., Geertman, S.: Toward smart governance and social sustainability for Chinese migrant communities. J. Clean. Prod. **107**, 389–399 (2015)

30. Castells, M.: Communication Power. OUP, Oxford (2013)

31. Shah, D.V., Cho, J., Eveland, W.P., Kwak, N.: Information and expression in a digital age: modeling internet effects on civic participation. Commun. Res. **32**, 531–565 (2005)

32. Volland, N.M.: Taking urban conservation online: Chinese civic action groups and the internet. In: Online Society in China: Creating, Celebrating, and Instrumentalising the Online Carnival, pp. 184–199 (2011)

33. Aigner, A.: Heritage-making 'from below': the politics of exhibiting architectural heritage on the Internet – a case study. Int. J. Heritage Stud. **22**, 181–199 (2016)

34. van der Hoeven, A.: Historic urban landscapes on social media: the contributions of online narrative practices to urban heritage conservation. City Cult. Soc. **17**, 61–68 (2019)

35. Riva Sanseverino, E., Riva Sanseverino, R., Anello, E.: A cross-reading approach to smart city: a European perspective of Chinese smart cities. Smart Cities **1**, 26–52 (2018)

36. Fu, Z., Bu, Y.: Constructing the Research Model of Beijing Neighborhood Through the Living Lab Method. In: Rau, P.-L.P. (ed.) CCD 2016. LNCS, vol. 9741, pp. 527–539. Springer, Cham (2016). https://doi.org/10.1007/978-3-319-40093-8_52

Discussion on Aesthetic Design in Chinese Painting Based on Cross-Cultural Design

Yuting Pan[✉] and Wei Yu

East China University of Science and Technology, Shanghai, China
1312644998@qq.com

Abstract. This article was based on the study of traditional Chinese painting aesthetics and Western cultural active factors. The author deconstructs and extracts cultural elements and features in order to explore and innovate the methods of modern cross-cultural design. The author aiming at the current situation of traditional aesthetics in Chinese paintings which has vague identification and weak influence in modern international cultural exchanges. Therefore, this study combines qualitative analysis, literature research method and flow charts method to analyze the value of traditional Chinese painting elements, and summarizes the methodology of modern cross-cultural design based on traditional Chinese painting aesthetics. Standing on the universal view, the author views the modern design innovation of traditional art from the perspective of history and culture. At the same time, according to the process of cross-cultural design, the flow chart of modern cross-cultural product design that based on traditional Chinese painting value system is simulated.

Keywords: Cross-cultural design · Chinese painting aesthetic · Globalization

1 Introduction

1.1 A Subsection Sample

The contemporary world is in the context of the common development and interplay of multi-culture: on the one hand, the impact of globalization is unstoppable spreading all over the world, on the other hand, cultural diversity and inverse pluralism are intertwined, diversified regional culture of sustainable development also affects the process of globalization, which making the social background of cross-cultural design more complicated; the global economy is growing with a solid and rapid pace, also the business needs of continuous development in multiple directions and channels provide economic soil for cross-cultural design; furthermore, technological innovation is accelerating at constant speed. While reducing the production cost of many local traditional cultural products, it also increases the possibility of cultural display methods, the possibility of restoring and renewing complex handicraft, and the possibility of cross-cultural integral design.

C. Stephanidis and M. Antona (Eds.): HCII 2020, CCIS 1226, pp. 308–316, 2020.
https://doi.org/10.1007/978-3-030-50732-9_41

2 Modern "Chinese Style" Based on Traditional Chinese Painting Aesthetics

"Cathay" and "Orientalism" are far from Chinese traditional aesthetics in fact. The understanding and alienation of "Chinese style" in the international market often make the "Chinese style" expressed by many products become a European style, rather than a parody of Chinese art as some sinologists usually think [1]. Meanwhile, many local Chinese designers make great efforts to maintain and trace back the Chinese traditional aesthetics, which makes the "Chinese style" products become closed art creation only belonging to Chinese people. However, design, like historical narrative, requires both grand narrative and "local knowledge". It requires both a central perspective and multiple ways of understanding and expression [2]. The "Chinese style" advocated in this paper is inspired by the above two design styles, which are mixed into a more complex situation: In the new era, based on the aesthetic features of traditional Chinese painting, the cross-cultural design of modern Chinese style transforms the traditional aesthetics viewpoint and values into the international language in the world, and displays the thought core of Chinese culture by universal approaches of material layer.

2.1 Deconstructing the Traditional Aesthetic Characteristics of Chinese Painting

Chinese Painting are Numerous in Its Classification: According to the artistic technique of expression, Chinese painting can be subdivided into wash painting, heavy colored, meticulous brushwork, freehand brushwork, line drawing, etc. According to the theme, Chinese painting also can be divided into figure painting, landscape painting, flower and bird painting, etc. Chinese painting contains traditional philosophy and aesthetic concepts of the Chinese nation in terms of theme, conception, individual characteristic and expression techniques. This study emphatically lists several elements that are widely used in modern cross-cultural design, discusses and analyzes the values and spiritual world of traditional Chinese painting in modern design according to specific cases.

Wash Painting. Traditional Chinese painting grasps the romantic artistic personality (in literature and art), requires brushwork to be flat, round, reserved, emphasized and changed. The ink law requires that "Chinese ink presenting five colors: focal, thick, heavy, light and clear". The traditional wash painting originated from Tang Dynasty, formed in the Five Dynasties, flourished in the song, Yuan Dynasty. The birth and development processes of wash painting are deeply influenced by the prosperous literati thinking under the historical background of these dynasties. Literati advocate grace, therefore the style of their painting pursues the beauty of simplicity and elegance. The spirit of wash painting is not only the atmospheric spirit of freehand brushwork, but also the understanding of life. The atmosphere of wash painting is not only natural atmosphere, but also humanistic atmosphere.

Color. The color application history of the Chinese nation can be traced back to a few thousand years ago. At 1800 years ago, in the Wei and Jin Dynasties, "six methods of painting" was put forward by Xie He. Among them "Employing the best color with its category" laid a relatively complete and effective theoretical foundation for the later application of traditional Chinese painting, and had a long-term and profound impact on later painters. The "category" of Chinese painting is a broad concept, which has a meaning of "similar". The application of color is not only based on the intrinsic color of objects, but also should be combined with different objects, environments, scenes, artistic conception, taking the "red ink bamboo" painted by Zheng Banqiao as the example, which also shows that in the specific creation process of traditional Chinese painting, painters have subjective energy and free space, so in traditional Chinese color aesthetics, the emotions and personalities of literate painters are preserved.

Rudimental Aesthetic Law. The "manage location" in the "six methods of painting" is the early artist's understanding of the composition of Chinese painting. Chinese painting lay stress on the integrity. Symmetry, contrast and proportion relationship in structure are all for the sake of achieving overall harmony. The so-called "place intention before painting" refers to that Chinese painting usually attaches great importance to the transmission of artistic conception, which makes the common patterns of Chinese painting diverse and flexible. In the specific application process, it can be used alone or mixed with several patterns. The composition pays attention to the contrast nothingness and essence, and stresses that "Sparse places can make horses gallop. Dense places cannot even be penetrated by the wind". There is real in the virtual, also virtual in the real. Furthermore, as a common form of vivid and freehand composition in Chinese painting, "Space Reservation" reflects the profound and exquisite artistic conception of the picture by means of emptiness to express reality [3]. Traditional oriental aesthetic taste and social perception can be seen in Chinese painting through different directions.

2.2   Present Situation of Design Based on Traditional Chinese Painting Aesthetic

Whether it is global historical view or globalization, its concept, objective facts and trends are all western topics, which are all based on the worldwide structure with the West as the center of value system and economical interests. In fact, nonwestern cultural system are facing constantly marginalization. Therefore, although Chinese painting is the pithiness of Chinese culture, but in the mixed and complex background of the new era, its influence is constantly decreasing, its form and technique have not been significantly updated, and its position can not be stable and developed. In the exploration and practice of combining traditional aesthetics of traditional Chinese painting and modern design, art creators are facing enormous pressure and challenges while creating new cultural symbols on the basis of traditional culture.

(1) It is difficult to extract and innovate the cultural elements of traditional Chinese painting: language is a medium which would lost. In the process of extracting and converting the classical aesthetics elements of traditional Chinese painting into the universal language, certain information contained would be lost. At the same time, with the coming of the fifth generation information communication era and the highly commercialized era, the way of information communication in the

commodity design processes is more direct, and the purpose of communication is closer to the direct exchange of information, which is contrary to the implicit beauty concepts of "Words empty as the wind are best left unsaid." and "endless artistic conception" in traditional Chinese aesthetics. These trend leads to the more direct information extraction through modern means, the more intensive the modern perspective is, the more distorted the core of traditional Chinese painting is.

(2) It is difficult for traditional Chinese painting to be transformed into modern design language: there are too many elements in Chinese painting. The system of traditional Chinese painting is complicated, which derive the kinds of branches in dynastic changes. Also, there is no unified representative image of Chinese painting, it is difficult to be summarized, which leads to the understanding of Chinese painting even for many people of its own nation is often presentative and incomplete. At the same time, even though Chinese painting has been regarded as the treasure of traditional art for thousands of years, it also faces the barrier of transformation in the process of converting such art works into commercial design in the contemporary age.

(3) The resonance of traditional Chinese painting is weakening: Chinese traditional aesthetics has a unique sense of mystery after thousands of years of history. However, because of the different ideologies, ideological concepts, social systems, theoretical structures and even knowledge cognitions in various developing stages, the implied meaning of many elements and function of many patterns are constantly weakening, which also causes differences and difficulties in understanding, and it is difficult to resonate.

(4) Traditional Chinese painting elements face obstacles of cultural understanding differences in the process of joining the international market: in the way of Chinese painting elements entering the international market, facing different cultures and different thinking systems in the global market, the understanding and acceptance of Chinese painting elements are different.

3 The Design Process Based on Traditional Chinese Painting Aesthetic

3.1 Deconstructing the Traditional Aesthetic Characteristics of Chinese Painting

After the middle of the 20th century, the British historian Geoffrey baleclough first proposed the concept of global historical perspective. He believed that western historiography should be reoriented, focusing on the study of differences, interactions and influences among different countries, regions and civilizations. At the same time, it should be paid attention to the "cross-cultural interaction", which means "while considering the unique ways of different ethnic groups to organize their own society, the world history also pays special attention to the various ways of cross-cultural communication among ethnic groups" [4, 5]. The global view of history is often used as a research method and narrative mode of history, sociology and other fields. Even though the concept of "anti western" or "anti globalization" is becoming more popular. In this paper, author attempts to apply the global perspective of history to the modern design process. Under the background that traditional art such as Chinese painting itself has become an remote art system for most people, author tries to use the past resources into the present application, and discusses the path based on the combination of traditional Chinese painting elements and modern design.

In this paper, flow charts method are used as the main research method: Through the construction of cross-cultural design scene and the establishment of modern design flow chart based on traditional Chinese painting, the author analyzes each stage and each link of the process respectively. Potential risks can be identified, we can find out the factors that lead to the risk, and carry out mining and analysis according to the design process based on Chinese painting.

3.2   Modern Design Model Based on Traditional Chinese Painting Aesthetics

How to combine Chinese painting aesthetics with Chinese design, countless designers have done many times of exploration, including many outstanding cases. According to the theoretical research of cross-cultural design and the analysis of the investigation process of traditional cultural creative product design, the author refers to the Xie Shihai's design process model in the research of cross-cultural product design [6], focuses on the cognitive analysis process of traditional culture, dissects the market environment of the target population and the creator population. Then, This paper proposes the model of modern innovative design process based on traditional Chinese painting (see Fig. 1):

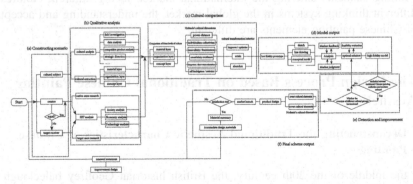

Fig. 1. The model of modern innovative design process based on traditional Chinese painting

(a)   Constructing scenario: First, the stage of constructing a cultural scenario consists of three parts: Creators, cultural subject and target receivers. Among them, the creator population refers to the group who applies cultural resources and realizes it in the form of modern design; the cultural subject in this paper refers to the multi-dimensional cultural group based on traditional Chinese painting; the target receiver refers to the market group that the creator population need to face and consider in their creation. The relationship among the three parts also determines the different categories of design: in the context of the unity of the creator population and the cultural subject, when the creator is consistent with the target receiver, the situation have been constructed is the cultural and creative design circumstances for the local propagation of the aesthetic culture of traditional Chinese painting; when the creator is inconsistent with the target receiver, it is the cross culture for the multi-cultural market design scenario. When the target receiver includes the cultural groups of different ethnic groups, it is a complex multi-cultural integration design. It is not only the first step of modern design based on traditional culture, but also an essential part of cultural and creative design to make clear the research object and design purpose. For example, the multimedia electronic "The Picture of the Bian River on Qingming Day" of China Pavilion of Shanghai World Expo 2010 is a good case of cross-cultural integration design for mixed target receivers. The source of the material is Zhang Zeduan's work in the Northern Song Dynasty. It uses digital technology and animation making, and adopts sound and photoelectric technology. The bold hypothesis makes the picture vivid and imaginal. It can not only help native groups increase the understanding of the item and comprehend the cultural value behind it, but also make the target receivers of different nations reduce the understanding deviation of cultural differences and contact the traditional Chinese cultural products in an intuitive way.

(b) Qualitative analysis: after determining the scenario components and design objectives, cross-cultural design process needs to collect and study the data of cultural subject, such as field investigation, historical data analysis, competitive product analysis, strategic direction, analyzes and summarizes the feasible design objectives, which are conform to the cultural idea and market trend. At the same time, according to whether the target receivers is unified with the creators, the social, economic and technical background of the target receivers should be separately identified and analyzed; the characteristics of the target receivers, the market capacity of the target receivers, the pain spots of the consumer should be analyzed; stimulates and understands the behavior path of the consumer's using process. Take Dunhuang cultural creativities as an example, the series are mostly extracted from traditional art such as Dunhuang murals. In recent years, the propulsion of "one belt, one road" has made Dunhuang culture back to vitality and become a cultural exchange calling card with national and local characteristics. Under the background of this policy, the purpose of design is closer to cultural output. Aiming at this phenomena, LKK design team comprehensively combed Dunhuang culture through professional design process, and extracted Dunhuang art through multi-dimensional comprehensive design research, the unique highlighted color, the pattern with religious significance, and the characteristic architectural texture, animal and plant materials are used to create the exclusive super symbol and the visual identification system of Dunhuang Cultural Creation brand.

(c) Cultural comparison: cultural comparison is the core of successful transformation. This paper regards the cultural subjects of the target receivers as the comparative culture. Through the comparative study of the cultural subject and the comparative culture in the three layers, it analyzes the cultural differences from the layers of material layer, organization layer and concept layer, combines the cultural characteristics and advantages that should be retained by the comparative subject culture of society, economy and technology, so as to improve and optimize the parts that in contradiction with the organizational level and concept level of the comparative culture, in order to spread the advanced traditional thinking of the main culture and realize "cultural identity". According to Hofstede's cultural dimension theory put forward by Hofstede, a famous sociologist and psychologist in the Netherlands, cross-cultural design can be carried out from six dimensions: power-distance, individualism-collectivism, masculinity/feminization, uncertainty avoidance, long-term and short-term orientation, self indulgence/restraint, so as to avoid the design error caused by the difference of ideas in design [11]. For example, web design, promotion of the same product by the same company, typesetting and information emphasis will be great different in different countries.

(d) Model output: the essence of product model outputting is to simulate and explore the final scheme. In this stage, low fidelity prototype design is carried out, such as sketch, line drawing labeling, conceptual model, then the creators make a market judgment based on the qualitative analysis of the main culture subject, the target receivers, comparative culture, and make comparisons between them. According to the functions, economic cost, existing technology and other factors of the product, the relatively optimal solution is selected. After the feasibility evaluation, it finally outputs the high fidelity model which can be operated and demonstrated. In the context of this article, modern cross-cultural design needs to take advantage of the pattern and function of the material layer, the straightaway behavior mode and popular language of the organization layer, the core value system of the concept layer to form the conceptual model of cross-cultural product design.

(e) Detection and improvement: after outputting the model, the creators need to put the product model on the market, test the satisfaction of users, observe the data, verify the objectives, collect information, summarize materials, continuously find problems and continuously improve the final scheme to achieve the expected design objectives. In the context of this article, the test of products should focus on whether the traditional Chinese painting aesthetics and modern culture are mutually exclusive, and whether different cultural groups are exclusive in the concept layer in cross-cultural design. This part also makes the detection and improvement steps particularly important.

(f) Final scheme output: the product basically realizes the unification of the functions and values of both cross-cultural design and modern design based on traditional culture in this stage, summarizes and induces the product design process, which would accumulates the data information for subsequent product improvement or redesign.

4 The Design Process Based on Traditional Chinese Painting Aesthetic

There is a fundamental difference between Chinese painting and modern design based on traditional Chinese painting aesthetics: Chinese painting is the expression of subjective will; while the design based on traditional Chinese painting is the fusion design that can be mass produced with the purpose of promoting and disseminating the national culture, which absorbs the nutrients of traditional art, fully considers the balance between the target groups and the main cultural groups. The innovation of this paper lies in: firstly, based on the global perspective, this paper combines traditional Chinese painting, globalization and Hofstede's theory of cultural dimension, looking on cross-cultural design from the historical perspective and art design. Secondly, in the process of extracting the aesthetic elements of traditional Chinese painting, the article focuses on describing the application of its humanistic spirit. The author believes that in the practice of cross-cultural design, designers should not ignore the emotional connotation of the ideological layer. Thirdly, this paper constructs an orderly and simple flow chart model for cross-cultural design of traditional Chinese painting aesthetic elements, which is based on certain well-known successful cases of modern design of traditional Chinese aesthetics, so as to help dismantle the steps of cross-cultural design and understand them.

During the investigation and writing of this article, the author believes that the oriental traditional culture gene (such as Chinese painting aesthetics, etc.) which is full of verve and subjective sensibility, and the Western cultural active factors which emphasize rationality and objectivity, in a sense, like the Taiji diagram which is regarded as the origin of Chinese philosophy, are the Yin and Yang sides of the overall cultural life of human beings. The two sides of the unified Taiji maps of global civilization can interact harmoniously and interactively, and have become a powerful dual core engine or fusion power source to promote the sustainable progress and Harmonious Co prosperity of the future community of human destiny. To explore the complementary mechanism of the organic integration of the two individuals, and try to find the balance between traditional oriental culture and modern western design, it can create a outstanding new design culture and new achievements of human civilization in the future, which is also the basic intention and main purpose of this paper.

References

1. Hugh, H.: Chinese Style: Chinese Elements Lost in the West for 800 Years, 1st edn. Peking University Press, Britain (2017)
2. Wu, X.: Do we really need a global historical view?. Acad. Res. **05**(1), 23–26,147 (2005)
3. Zhang, X., Hao, Y.: From Chinese painting pattern to Western plane composition. J. Beijing Inst. Graph. Commun. **06**(4), 20–23 (2006)
4. Yu, M.: Interaction: a new paradigm for the development of human civilization. Hong Kong Macao J. **46**(6), 17–23, 93 (2019)
5. Barraclough, G.: History in a Changing World, p. 10. University of Oklahoma Press, Norman (1955)

6. Bentley, J., Ziegler, H.: New Global History: The Inheritance and Exchange of Civilization (Before 1000 A.D.). Peking University Press, Beijing (2014)
7. Xie, S., Research on cross-cultural product design. Nanjing University of Aeronautics and Astronautics (2012)

Towards the User Interface of Augmented Reality-Based Public Art

Heehyeon Park[1] and Gapyuel Seo[2(✉)]

[1] Hanseo University, Seosan 31962, South Korea
hpark@hanseo.ac.kr
[2] Hongik University, Sejong 30016, South Korea
gapseo@hongik.ac.kr

Abstract. Many people would agree that the rapid development of digital technology has brought about significant changes in human life as a whole. These changes are meant to promote many new and exciting aspects of life, to benefit society. In this respect, the changes seen in the venue of public art is no exception. It has been shown that various types of public art using digital media have recently appeared, which are considered an exciting new form of media and art expression. Recently, there have been many attempts to create Mural Art utilizing augmented reality technology. Augmented reality technology provides a sense of coexistence between the physical and virtual worlds, attracting the attention of the public and the author. In this study, the interface of an AR Mural Art was defined as a visual image that mediates between real and virtual art forms, and through this, the interactivity and user experience of AR Mural Art were examined through an actual case production. As a result of experiments through actual production cases in Seosan City in Korea. We classify three key elements of interface design for identifying the user experience and interactivity of AR Mural Art. First, the light intensity is identified according to the place and location as it is used in the art. Second, the art form is analyzed as a material feature of public art. Third, the physical distance and location of viewers and the actual public art itself are identified and reviewed.

Keywords: AR (Augmented Reality) · Public art · Public Mural Art

1 Introduction

The advances of digital technology have brought about significant changes in human life in politics, economy, society, culture, and arts, and offer new ways for artists to express their ideas to society in general. In particular, the diversification of expression styles with the emergence of new technologies has laid the foundation for new art forms today that did not exist in the past. For example, as digital media developed, interactivity became important in the arts field as an ultimate tool for artistic expression in modern times. The interaction between the work and the audience has been strengthened through sensory changes through various media. This change in the appreciation and acceptance of art changes the relationship between the artwork and the audience by understanding and interpreting the work in an active participatory, and modifies the artist's

© Springer Nature Switzerland AG 2020
C. Stephanidis and M. Antona (Eds.): HCII 2020, CCIS 1226, pp. 317–323, 2020.
https://doi.org/10.1007/978-3-030-50732-9_42

communicative way beyond the passive attitude of the audience [1]. In particular, the augmented reality technology that breaks down the boundary between the real world and the virtual world provides the feeling of coexistence between the physical world and the virtual world, attracting the attention of the public and the artist.

In this paper, we examined changes in augmented reality technology and public art, and examined the user experience and characteristics of the user interface required in the process. We discussed the characteristics of augmented reality technology and described the process of making it into a new form of expression in public art. We implemented it by applying it to an augmented reality application called the "Seosan Original City Story." This project is a smartphone application that is used to augmented the use of reality technology to create public art and video that can be also linked to a mobile device. Additionally, we investigated the utility of public art expressed in the field of an augmented reality, and suggested the elements necessary for the use of UI/UX production through the production process.

2   Augmented Reality and Public Mural Art

2.1   Features of Augmented Reality

Today, the feature of augmented reality is utilized to increase the effectiveness of reality by combining virtual objects on the real world environment. By definition, augmented reality is also described as "a computer graphic technique that synthesizes virtual objects or information into an environment that actually exists and looks like an object in the real environment [2]". In this way, when digital artifacts are filled in the physical space of reality, the personality of the physical space changes. Therefore, fundamentally speaking, augmented reality uses real-time information accompanied by various sensory organs, including vision and hearing, to enrich the experience of reality for the audience experiencing this type of art form.

According to the method of augmented reality, there are many methods of generating a virtual object using an image such as a marker, and a markerless method of generating a virtual object using Global Positioning System (GPS) information instead of the actual marker. The method of using the marker is a method of registering and using the marker in advance, to match the position of creation of the virtual object and the coordinates in space. This method recognizes a marker through the use of digital equipment, in order that a virtual object is superimposed on the marker. By registering the marker image in advance, you can easily create a virtual object in the real space to implement augmented reality. In this way, Unity provides an augmented reality developer kit called Vuforia, which is helpful in making it easier for developers to implement augmented reality.

Generally speaking, the marker image is identifiable and any photograph or graphic image can be registered as long as there is sufficient singularity to distinguish it from the background image. In this way, it is different from recognizing a QR code composed of a certain pattern. And this is an advantage that the registered image can be used as a tool for message delivery, while maintaining the function of producing augmented reality content. In addition, a natural causal relationship between the audience and the artwork is formed in the process of finding an image, and can be sent to a carrying device such as on a smartphone or tablet. Of course, the user can configure the natural interaction to occur in the process of moving from side to side to look around the various faces of the virtual object, which is shown and implemented in the screen.

2.2 Public Mural Art

Public art generally refers to works that are installed and displayed in a place open to the general public, and includes installation art in a designated place or design for the place itself. The feature of public art is expressed in various ways such as with urban environmental sculptures, murals, street furniture, floor pavement, and transportation facilities. In other words, public art is aimed at the wide public and is characterized by being able to contain and deliver a variety of messages, including social and political messages to its viewing audiences. Among these factors, public art expressed on the wall is the most popular form of public art [3]. Mural art is used as an important cultural art content that creates exciting and pleasant places to visit and congregate for the public, in urban environments and urban landscapes. Well-made murals go beyond the sights of a simple street art, and bring vitality to the city through the enjoyment and response of the citizens viewing this type of art form.

Fundamentally, mural Art is a painting drawn on the interior and exterior walls of natural or artificial structures such as ancient cave paintings, palaces, temples, churches, caves, and tombs. In this context, the murals depicted on urban structures or architectures are being reborn as works of art installed on the street using various techniques and materials. Murals used as a public art form must exist on the wall and exist as a vibrant urban mural, only if the spirit of the community or community consciousness is premised to communicate with the emotions of the local community. In addition, mural art is an important element of place, which is a concept that encompasses not only the spatial characteristics of the place but also the social and political context of the areas and regions where they are painted and showcased [4]. Materials that represent murals are being diversified from a variety of pigments such as paint, paint, ink, spray lacquer, and natural materials such as stone, metal, soil, wood, and textiles to the use of advanced systems such as LED lighting and beam projectors. Augmented reality technology is also being used as a tool for expressing the message and meaning of Public Mural Art. From the process of selecting a marker in which augmented reality is implemented, the process of interacting with a virtual object through this marker, and in the process, you can feel new experiences and emotions, and the interaction with public art is revealed as well as appreciated.

In the case of augmented reality, it provides users with a new experience in an environment that consists of a mixture of real presence and representation represented by virtual objects. This process uses user experience (UX) which is provided to users in public art with augmented reality, which is also provided through a user interface (UI). The change in interactivity due to the development of digital media has led to the development of the interface between the audience and the work, and thus various interactions are possible. Basically, augmented reality is one of the ways in which the change of the interface is clearly revealed, and it is inducing an active action by the audience holding their display device and approaching the real object and looking into the monitor. Such a view through a portable or mobile device is also a way of life that is happening every day in modern society, and this use of art mirrors society in that respect.

2.3   Interactivity of Public Art and UI/UX

Interactivity in art refers to the action in which the viewer interacts with the work provided by the artist in the process of contact with the work or a wide meaning including the time and space in which the work exists. Generally speaking, the characteristic of interactivity is that the meaning of the viewer becomes more important by including the audience in the process of actively participating in the process of creation and completion of the work, rather than fixing the position of the listener to the position of the passive receiver [5]. Interactivity is not just that the audience is the object of communication about the artwork by reacting to the interaction with the work. The spectator's reaction within the elements of the artwork has become more important because the viewer can change the meaning and concept of the artwork in the process of showing the artwork. Interactivity as a tool is not just that which is used by the audience, but is also the object of communication as used in reference regarding the artwork. The spectator's reaction within the elements of the work has become more important, because the viewer can change the meaning and concept of the artwork in the process of the artwork being shown to the world. In other words, the reaction of the viewer has an important position as an element of the work, and helps the author dictate where to move next to showcase the artwork in this venue and medium.

The various experiential elements that viewers feel while interacting with the work become an important element constituting the concept of the work itself. This means that the meaning and concept of the work are revealed in the interaction between the artist's intention and the subjectivity of the audience reacting to it. Interactivity is more emphasized in modern art as the idea and theory of digital technology develops. Public art incorporating augmented reality technology allows viewers to feel a new space-time, because they can enjoy the virtual world through the screen of the mobile device and the work located in the real space at the same time. In addition, there is a feature that the interaction effect can be enhanced through this process. The user interface drives the interaction of public art and augmented reality content. Here, the interface in public art based on augmented reality is the boundary between the real world artwork and the virtual world image displayed on the screen, and it is a significant factor for the viewer to immerse in the work and lead the optimal interaction.

In this study, we intend to define the boundary between the visual image of public art and the visual image displayed through the screen as the interface of AR Mural Art. The interface is to drive interaction with public art and image markers, which act as a medium for images seen through the screen. The term User Interface is widely utilized in the field where digital media is used, but the interface of public art has a different characteristic from the general interface production. Most public art is often produced outside, not indoors, and usually has a large size and various materials.

3 Design Approaches

In this paper, we implemented an interface design for interactivity by using the process of creating the "Seosan Original City Story" smartphone application.

In this case, we selected six Public Mural Art produced by local public artists and produced animations to explain the concept and intention of the work through interviews with artists. This project is an application designed to connect public art and motion graphics to mobile devices by applying augmented reality technology, as a collaboration work between Seosan Culture City Project Team and Hanseo University. The effects of public art expressed in augmented reality were examined, and important elements were identified during effective UI/UX production in the process. The production process consisted of 5 stages. First, the public art wall was determined in the selection stage. Second, the video production stage that fits the concept and intention of the artist was identified. Third, image recognition and augmented reality linkage using Unity and Vuforia programs was chosen. Fourth, we reviewed the augmented reality interlocking application production stage. Fifth, it was conducted as a verification stage of effectiveness through resident interviews and questionnaires (Fig. 1).

First, in the public art selection stage, the artwork of six teams was selected through the utilization of a young artist competition. Second, in the video production stage, we tried to deviate from the concept and intention of the artist as little as possible. In addition, related information such as the author's name, the title of the work, and the subject was included to be searched. Third, in the image recognition stage through the Unity program, we made use of the Vuforia program to recognize the public mural art image as a marker. During this process, there was a lot of trial and error and difficulty when recognizing other prints or advertisement images that were actually also considered as markers. The reason was that large-scale works in the outdoor environments had to recognize as images. Some works had a strange proportion to be displayed on one screen, and some work had a short distance between buildings, and the entire work could not be captured on the screen. Therefore, each of the six works used different materials. Various mixed materials such as paint, acrylic, iron, glass, stainless steel, and tiles were used. Depending on the material, it was revealed that in some cases there was a material that reflects light heavily, and the shadow between the wall and the installation created a large and dark shadow. To solve these problems, only a part of the work linked with augmented reality was utilized, and some images of buildings had to be cut out of the final visual to create the desired result.

After producing the Seosan original city story (Seosan1city) application, we completed the were resident's interview. Based on the results of the interview, we suggested three elements necessary for the user experience and immersive interaction of the outdoor AR Mural Art.

Interface Considering Light Intensity

The light intensity of the location is a very important factor in realizing augmented reality. It is necessary to select the image of the time zone used by the most people and adjust the image recognition accuracy in consideration of the light intensity of the place, including the consideration of the intensity of sunlight and weather.

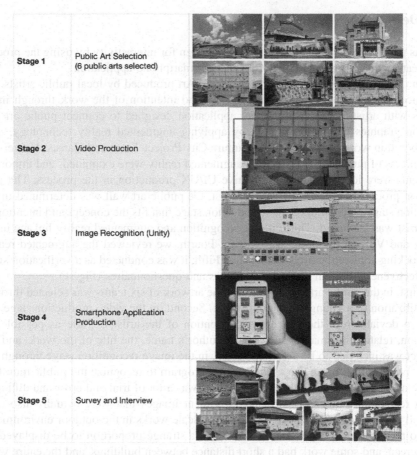

Stage 1	Public Art Selection (6 public arts selected)
Stage 2	Video Production
Stage 3	Image Recognition (Unity)
Stage 4	Smartphone Application Production
Stage 5	Survey and Interview

Fig. 1. Process of creating the "Seosan Original City Story" smartphone application

Interface Considering Material

We should consider whether it is a material that reflects light, such as glass or stainless steel, and whether there are any places with dark shadows that will affect the art. Even in the case of this case, there was a difficulty in the case of materials with reflectivity or transparency that had to be tried and tested several times to produce the most beneficial results.

Interface Considering Physical Distance and Location

The distance between the spectator and the artwork served as a very important factor for a highly immersive interaction. In this process, there are some tasks in which interface creation is difficult, due to the narrow gap between the buildings. In some cases, the distance is too close to be recognized by the screen, or the length of the work is too long to be captured by one screen. Also, it is necessary to consider the physical distance and location even if the work is installed too high for the eye level viewing of an audience.

4   Conclusion and Future Work

In this study, we presented the utility and utilization of public art using a form of augmented reality. In addition, we implemented an application that links motion graphic content related to public artworks of art, by utilizing an augmented reality image recognition. Besides this, we implemented an application that links motion graphic content related to public artworks of art, by utilizing augmented reality image recognition. We suggested three main elements for user interface and user experience for immersive user interaction through the AR application. First, we reviewed the light intensity according to the place and location. Second, we analyzed AR as a material feature of public art. Third, we considered and analyzed the physical distance and location of viewers and actual public art. As future work, we plan to conduct more in-depth research on user interfaces and user experiences in various public art showcases where augmented reality is already being utilized.

References

1. Lee, J.: A study on the usability of augmented reality technology as a tool for media arts in contemporary arts. Munhak Kwa Eoneo Hakhoi **41**(4), 363–400 (2019)
2. Wikipedia. https://ko.wikipedia.org/wiki/증강현실. Accessed 5 Jan 2020
3. Xiao, C., Lee, S.W.: A study on the application plan of murals in the sustainable urban regeneration as public AR. J. Korean Soc. Des. Cult. **25**(4), 255–270 (2019)
4. Issue Maker. https://blog.naver.com/issue7177. Accessed 07 Oct 2019
5. Choi, M.: The stature of media art in contemporary art: evolution of materiality and interactivity, p. 13 (2015)

Displaying Art in Virtual Environments

Helping Artists Achieve Their Vision

Tobias Piechota$^{(\boxtimes)}$, Marcel Schmittchen, and Christopher Lentzsch

Ruhr-University of Bochum, 44780 Bochum, Germany
{tobias.piechota, marcel.schmittchen,
christopher.lentzsch}@ruhr-uni-bochum.de

Abstract. In this paper, we explore the possibilities posed by the use of the Crytek game engine to display art in interactive virtual environments. Enabling artists, among others, to enhance their creative process by viewing virtual models of unfinished art pieces and allowing to create and experience a virtual presentation of the art pieces. Furthermore, we will present our approach during the phases of our project and the results of a showcase event with artists in which we presented our prototype.

Keywords: 3D-models · Art · CryEngine · Game engine · Interactivity · Presentation · Virtual environments · Virtual exhibitions

1 Introduction

Displaying art always poses a challenge to artists, galleries and museums. The way an object is presented shapes the way the object is perceived—from static billboards to videos and animations many forms are used [1, 2]. All forms come with their own set of strengths and limitations. Thus, the presentation of an artwork is always a compromise between the artist's vision, the respective possibilities, and limitations of the used form and the location of the presentation.

Digital models can be used to facilitate such decisions. Digital models of art pieces like jewelry, sculptures or statues are already often created early in order to instruct manufacturers. Placing such models in a virtual showcase enables the artists and other stakeholders to experiment with different conditions. Using game engines to create virtual museums and enhance the visitor's experience has already been explored [3]. Our approach focuses on the support of the decision process during the creation and the planning of real-world exhibitions.

© Springer Nature Switzerland AG 2020
C. Stephanidis and M. Antona (Eds.): HCII 2020, CCIS 1226, pp. 324–328, 2020.
https://doi.org/10.1007/978-3-030-50732-9_43

2   Approaching the Project

The artist showed us an early physical prototype of the art piece and stated clearly how the object should be presented. To accomplish her vision, we employed the Crytek game engine (CryEngine[1]) [4, 5]. Game Engines are built to enable interactivity between the player and the game. We considered this an important aspect as it enhances the possibilities of engagement with the artwork and thus helps to find new ideas and consider new aspects.

We structured the project into the following steps (see Fig. 1). First, we created a digital environment in which the artwork can be presented. Step 2: The available digital version of the art piece already made by the artist needed to be adopted to be compatible with the used engine. Step 3: The digital art piece can be imported into the engine. When all the required pieces are in one place the interactive features can be defined and implemented until the application is finally ready to be presented.

3   Implementation of the Prototype

The first step we have taken was to create a so-called map based on the artists' vision and wishes. Our map, in particular, should contain a naturalistic landscape. To achieve that, we used the CryEngine's given toolsets.

First, we designed the terrain with a hilltop in the middle surrounded by other hills. Then a material and a texture layer were added to the ground, in our case, green grass. Since the material and the texture layers are flat, we had to add the actual grass, among other flowers, using the vegetation-editor toolset. Adding vegetation like that increases performance costs, which is why we decided to only add this kind of vegetation to the center of the map, where the art piece would be located. We also added some trees on the surrounding hills of the map.

Since the game engine will render the artist's work in realtime, we were able to add the ability to change lighting conditions during the presentation; thus a script was implemented that would change the sun's position and time of day when running the application. The idea was to present the artwork with different lighting conditions to further showcase the object under different conditions. An example of how the application looks during the night-time setting can be seen in Fig. 2.

The ability to move the camera using default input methods like keyboard and mouse or a game controller was also present.

A change of lighting conditions or the ability to move the viewport freely has not been requested by the artist. However, we added these features to enable further perspectives the artist would benefit from during her decision process. The artwork was given to us as a rough digital model – which has only been created as a blueprint for the manufacturer. We colorized it to make it appealing to the recipient before importing it into our application. We did this using Blender[2], a tool that enabled us to modify the

---

[1] A game engine by Crytek GmbH, https://www.cryengine.com/.

[2] 3D-Modelling Tool by The Blender Foundation, https://www.blender.org/.

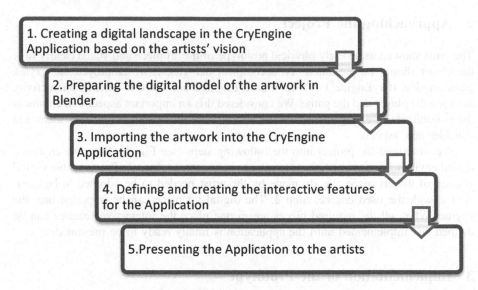

1. Creating a digital landscape in the CryEngine Application based on the artists' vision

2. Preparing the digital model of the artwork in Blender

3. Importing the artwork into the CryEngine Application

4. Defining and creating the interactive features for the Application

5. Presenting the Application to the artists

Fig. 1. Structure of the project

Fig. 2. A view of the artwork from a distance during night-time settings

artwork i.e. the piece colorization based on the artist's vision. After that, the following step was to use a Plugin called CryBlend[3] to prepare the Object for importing it into the CryEngine. Thus, the model was imported into the application and the result can be seen in Fig. 3.

---

[3] Blender-Plugin by the CryBlend Team, https://www.cryblend.weebly.com/.

Fig. 3. A piece of art as seen in the application during day-time settings

As requested by the artist, the model was placed in the middle of the map to be the centerpiece of attention. Additionally, we implemented the ability to rotate the object. Since the application already featured the possibility to move the view, it was possible to engage with the displayed art piece from every desired point of view.

4 Showcasing the Prototype

The presentation of the early prototype was held at the University of Applied Sciences in Bochum. In addition to the artists from the University in Düsseldorf, other researchers from different disciplines such as CAD, electrical engineering and art were present.

While explaining the technical aspects of the application, we showcased features like the dynamic lighting and controllable viewport. We invited the original artist to experience the application for herself using a standard game controller to move in the digital environment.

The initial verbal feedback was very positive. A majority of the attendants have told us that they have never seen such an approach to presenting art before. The interactive element has left a clear impact as different artists approached us, wanting to try the application for themselves.

5 Conclusion and Outlook

Though the application is considered to be a prototype in its earliest stages of development, based on the attendants' reactions we conclude that our approach can support artists in their line of work. Our approach employed a standard game controller to be used to control the viewport, but other, more intuitive, methods could be explored in the future. By giving the artist more intuitive and interactive tools they could plan their artworks and the realization of their vision more profoundly.

The rising availability of consumer-grade AR and VR solutions [6] allows for further engagement with the virtual objects – such as pre-production presentations (even for groups) or displaying/testing different variants or stages of art pieces as augmented layers. The use of stereoscopic 3D can also be employed in real-world art exhibitions, as it holds the potential to further enhance the engagement with the artwork on display.

The presentation mode could allow artists not only to present their artwork in new ways not possible in the real world i.e. free from constraints like time and space or gravity. Even virtual art exhibitions online could be possible; Enhancing not only the possibilities but also the reach for artists worldwide. Also, the application could be used to plan exhibitions in more detail. Envisioned looks and perspectives could be tried by the artist in the applications early to be later realized in the real world.

References

1. Wojciechowski, R., Walczak, K., White, M., Cellary, W.: Building virtual and augmented reality museum exhibitions. In: Proceedings of the Ninth International Conference on 3D Web Technology - Web3D 2004 [Internet], p. 135. ACM Press, Monterey (2004). http://portal.acm.org/citation.cfm?doid=985040.985060. Accessed 30 Jan 2020
2. Greenberg, R., Ferguson, B.W., Nairne, S.: Thinking About Exhibitions [Internet]. 1st edn. Routledge (2005). https://www.taylorfrancis.com/books/9780203991534. Accessed 29 Jan 2020
3. Urban, R., Marty, P.F., Twidale, M.B.: A second life for your museum: 3D multi-user virtual environments and museums. In: Archives & Museum Informatics, Toronto, p. 28 (2007)
4. Crytek GmbH. CRYENGINE V Manual [Internet]. CRYENGINE V Manual. https://docs.cryengine.com/display/CEMANUAL/CRYENGINE+V+Manual
5. Tracy, S., Reindell, P.: CryENGINE 3 Game Development: Beginner's Guide. Packt Publishing Ltd., Birmingham (2012)
6. Alkhamisi, A.O., Monowar, M.M.: Rise of augmented reality: current and future application areas. Int. J. Internet Distrib. Syst. 01(04), 25–34 (2013)

Experience Communication Design
of Intangible Cultural Heritage Shanghai Style
Lacquerware Brand Based on H5 Game

Siqi Wang and Rongrong Fu[✉]

East China University of Science and Technology, No. 130, Meilong Road,
Xuhui District, Shanghai, People's Republic of China
elkwang@126.com, muxin789@126.com

Abstract. The lacquer craft of Shanghai Style Lacquerware has been listed as
the intangible cultural heritage of Shanghai since 2013. However, Shanghai
Style Lacquerware falls into a solid storage protection barrier at the present
stage. As the influential non-material culture, it wins certain market recognition
but lacks a perpetual attraction to the young audience. Based on this problem,
this paper conducts propagation and promotion for Shanghai Style Lacquerware
in the form of H5 game, and carries out design and research from the angle of
experience communication. It is expected that this study could further expand
the core user group and promote the appeal of the brand, as well as provide a
fundamental design paradigm and effective reference for the transmission of
intangible cultural heritage.

Keywords: Shanghai Style Lacquerware · H5 game · Experience
communication · Interaction design

1 Introduction

In the information time, the implementation of the digital brand strategy can
undoubtedly promote the communication and innovation of intangible cultural heritage
brand and allow the traditional culture noticed by the public constantly. It is also
possible to change its solid-state storage protection mode and maximize the cultural
value and economic benefits. Shanghai style lacquerware has been included as the
intangible cultural heritage since 2013. However, its development and operation are an
extensive situation with the silence of the cultural connotations and spiritual values.
The main problems are as follows: (1) the brand communication content is single, out
of the context of modern media, and failed to arouse the excitement of the audience;
(2) the rigid communication model as well as the narrow channels led the lack of brand
authenticity and participation; (3) The audience base is weak, which is unable to form a
social culture cluster effect and achieve cultural scale benefits.

With the advent of convergence media in the digital age, "experience" may become
the key word for future brand communication and even economic life. HTML5, as the
core language of the World Wide Web with many advantages, provides a new idea for
improving the brand cultivation and dissemination of Shanghai style lacquerware brand

© Springer Nature Switzerland AG 2020
C. Stephanidis and M. Antona (Eds.): HCII 2020, CCIS 1226, pp. 329–335, 2020.
https://doi.org/10.1007/978-3-030-50732-9_44

in this study. With H5, the cross-terminal light application, applied as the connection of traditional culture and the mobile social circle of the audience, immersive experience communication can effectively elevate the reputation and public awareness of the brand.

2 Research on Experience Communication Based on H5 Game

For brands, the essence of "experience" is to use the Internet as the core and sharing as the mechanism, so that the audience can obtain a sense of self-identity at each "experience" touchpoint and value chain. Brand communication is no longer a passive process of persuasion. It is essential for Shanghai style lacquer brand to create a kind of flow experience for the audience through the Internet channels, which can improve the effectiveness of communication and drive the audience's positive emotions.

2.1 Analysis of the Target Audience

The current audience of Shanghai Lacquerware are mainly middle-aged and elderly groups (with a certain understanding of lacquerware craftsmanship) and children (participating in extracurricular activities of the Lacquerware Museum). The potential target audience is still mainly the youth group of post-95 s and post-85 s. They frequently use mobile social media such as WeChat and have the highly active and topical WeChat Moments. Additionally, their media content acceptance is much higher. At the same time, as the main people who promote the fast-paced life of the city, they live under working pressure and desire to realize themselves. They suffer from unban loneliness and conformity, and they have sharing desires. They also have a "Buddha-like" yearning for a slow and beautiful life, which is the creative basis of Shanghai lacquerware H5 experience game.

2.2 Selection of the Disseminating Carrier

The brand needs to build virtual scenes for providing immersive brand experience in the audience's mobile social circle, which is required to grasp the audience's living habits and media usage preferences. The WeChat H5 game is a very suitable carrier. Based on WeChat's large and stable user group as well as multiple functions such as social, interaction, entertainment and data collection, information can be accurately delivered in a short period of time. Utilizing the simplicity and interactivity of H5, the efficiency of brand communication can be improved by creating the interactive experience and multi-integrated sensory stimulation. Meanwhile, H5 game provides a platform for timely dialogue between users and the brand, even among users, inspiring participants to create personalized experience works and share them to meet self-display psychology, which is an opportunity for brand secondary communication and topic creation.

3   Research on H5 Experience Game Design

3.1   Design Principles

Principle of Consistency. The vision, function, internal and external forms of expression of H5 game should be unified with the theme, so that users can clearly perceive the brand content conveyed by the game. It is essential for the elements of game interface to be coordinated. A well-defined sensory system can improve users' comfort and memory. From the functional level, consistent interaction methods, interactive buttons and information feedback in the task flow increase the predictability of the game, which would make users to feel the game is easy to learn, actionable and efficient.

Principle of Basic Simulation. The game is based on handicraft technology experience. Therefore, lacquerware models, technical steps and the work scene should be based on the real lacquerware production process. Reasonable simplification and beautification on the basis of the actual process, which accords with the general cognition of users as well as gives a fresh "Easter Egg", can improve the user experience. Meanwhile, immersive scene and reasonable guidance of visual flow are realized through multi-sensory, R technology, etc. When users enter the game, they can quickly perceive the role of "craftsman" and clear game tasks.

Principle of Information Feedback. Users can get immediate and accurate information feedback in the game task flow, which is a necessary condition for deepening the immersive experience. Feedback enables users to perceive their complete control of the game and the rate of the task flow, and make timely adjustments and modifications.

3.2   Design Scheme and Technical Method

Based on the above-mentioned research on user needs, the "Budda-like" lacquerware making game "Four Seasons of Peach Blossom Land" is defined as a personalized decompression game. The game guides users to follow simplified lacquer making steps and achieve personalized creations with smooth interactive gesture experience. Create a four-season craftsman workshop scene is created to bring users a vivid atmosphere. Users can complete the personalized work and experience a short and focused "slow life" alone with season changes of "Spring Flowers", "Summer Rain", "Autumn Moon" and "Winter Snow" within several minutes. After the completion of the work, the work reference score, friend list ranking, AR360 degree display, sharing and other functions are provided to meet users' desire for challenge and self-expression. The three design principles proposed above were followed during the specific design process (Fig. 1).

Consistency. The game design is highly consistent with the brand theme in terms of element selection, color selection, interface design, etc. In order to bring users a sense of relaxation and healing experience, lightsome buttons like bubbles are used in the control elements, and the soothing color system with low saturation is applied. The

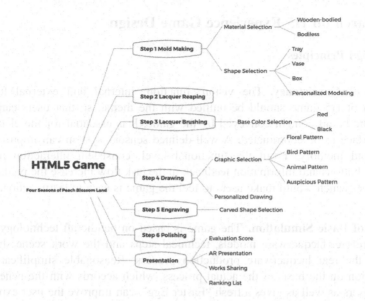

Fig. 1. Information architecture

interface composition consists of the lacquer making model, design navigation bar and virtual seasons background.

Compared with language symbols, visual and auditory symbols are more able to break the screen boundary between users and the brand, which can achieve the emotional resonance and integration. In addition to the healing dynamic visual effect, several natural and soothing auditory elements such as birdsong, soughing of the wind in forest trees, wheat wave, raindrop, aeolian bell, etc. are also added to the scene construction according to the changes of seasons and day-night.

Basic Simulation. The empathy engagement and realism not only require the integration of multi-sensory, but also the consistent interaction form which affects the users' real-time emotional experience. A variety of light interaction including multi-contact control, gravity sensing, image rendering, camera shooting and other interactive gestures are applied for users to complete the lacquer production process.

As the H5 game is a three-dimensional light experience process, AR technology has become a better option to optimize the sense of substitution. In the process of making lacquerware, users can use AR technology to view and adjust their works 360° at any time. When users share their works in Moments, their friends can also view lacquerware works by scanning QR code link with AR technology. Through a series of real simulations, when the brand culture tone highly matches the users' emotional experience, users' perception and evaluation of the brand can be effectively improved.

Information Feedback. The information feedback that this H5 game design focuses on includes immediate information feedback and result information feedback. The home page includes the unshaped wooden tire on the workbench with the background of spring cherry blossoms. After clicking to start the game, there are no lengthy game descriptions and game rules. User can immediately get inside the game character of "artisan", when they find that simple gestures can be used to turn the workbench and shape the wooden tire molding easily.

In the game task flow, the simple and easy-to-use interaction can make the lacquerware accurately formed to meet the user's psychological anticipation, which means for users there's a lot of room to express their creativity; In addition to providing necessary model and pattern selection, in the process of body modeling, drawing and engraving, users are allowed to personalize their lacquer. The high controllability can stimulate the user's desire of self-creation. Aside from experiencing the beauty of traditional lacquerware, users can also complete personalized and modern graffiti lacquerwares, which can express their emotions and instant inspiration.

In the feedback of result information, when users finally complete the lacquer work, the reference score and friends ranking list are also provided in addition to generating the work display poster and AR display. As a determinant of the experience communication effectiveness, the creation of shared value includes not only the users' confidence in sharing, but also the possibility of activating the sharing interaction between users. The setting of ranking list can promote the enthusiasm of game competition and challenge among users and friends, enhance the game's interest and user's curiosity, and motivate users to play twice and continue to create shared value. The greater the shared value of brand are created, the more active the sharing interaction is, and the longer the sharing path is, the more profound the brand meaning is created. Effective brand topic building and experience participation can also enhance the brand association, forming users' emotional cognition of brand (Fig. 2).

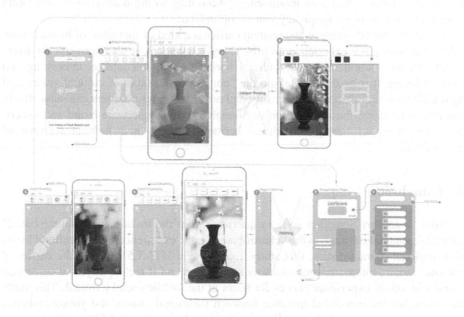

Fig. 2. Interface design

3.3 Game Prototype Test

In the prototype test stage, it mainly evaluates users' acceptance and experience of the game. In this study, college students, office workers and other young groups with high wechat activity were selected as the first participants. The feedback questionnaire includes five aspects: userexperience, task completion, communication form, topic sharing and the final brand communication effect.

The result shows that most participants "feel relaxed and comfortable" "willing to share when completing excellent works" "didn't know much about lacquerware before playing this game" and are able to memorize the working steps. These positive answers show that this game has a relatively high user acceptance and experience. On the other hand, some participants concerned about whether it took too much time and was difficult to complete the work. In the subsequent optimization of design, more consideration should be given to the operability of interaction (especially the first step, which participants thought was the most difficult), adjusting the difficulty of the game, etc.

3.4 Game Launch

At this stage, the WeChat official account of Shanghai style lacquerware brand with solid audience base has not been established. It is difficult to achieve effective cognitive transformation of potential audience based on the push of WeChat public account platform. Therefore, the first point-to-point spread of H5 experience game is launched as the news feed advertisement. The accurate and effective brand communication can be achieved with the process of "launch testing - precise advertising delivery - continuous promotion - real-time monitoring". According to big data analysis and cloud computing, the delivery frequency can be optimized.

Secondly, the H5 game as the content carrier is a kind of metaphor of brand image. While the immersive experience arouses users' excitement, it also converts the traditional and educational intangible cultural heritage handicraft into an interesting and modern image. It is essential to avoid the "compulsory" output of cultural values and rigid content to maintain users' curiosity and novelty. Therefore, users can subjectively and actively receive the information of Shanghai style lacquerware brand and experience the beauty of intangible cultural heritage through their familiar recreational interaction.

4 Conclusion

In order to convert Shanghai style lacquerware from the traditional "resource-based" intangible cultural heritage to the "charm-based" and "experience-based" cultural brand with regional characteristics, this study takes wechat HTML5 game as the carrier of communication, integrates multi-sensory stimulation and R technology, and constructs brand immersion experience scenes for users in the mobile social terminal. This study has shortened the emotional distance between traditional brands and young audience and effectively improved the public awareness and reputation of Shanghai style lacquerware brand.

References

1. Csiksczentmihalyi, M., Kolo, C., Baur, T.: Flow: the psychology of optimal experience. J. Aust. Occup. Ther. J. **51**(1), 3–12 (2014)
2. Zhao, K.: "Experience spread": new design fulcrum of brand communication in the internet + times. J Art Des. **6**, 85–87 (2017)
3. Sun, H.Y., Ding, S., Deng, Y.N., et al.: Research on the experience communication of social networking services. J. Art Des. **9**, 86–88 (2011)
4. Zhou, Y., Xu, T., Zhu, Z., Wang, Z.: Learning in doing: a model of design and assessment for using new interaction in educational game. In: Zaphiris, P., Ioannou, A. (eds.) LCT 2018. LNCS, vol. 10925, pp. 225–236. Springer, Cham (2018). https://doi.org/10.1007/978-3-319-91152-6_18
5. Zhou, T., Li, H., Liu, Y.: The effect of flow experience on mobile SNS user's loyalty. J Ind. Manage. Data Syst. **110**(6), 930–946 (2010)
6. Harmat, L., de Manzano, O., Theorell, T., et al.: Physiological correlates of the flow experience during computer game playing. J. Int. J. Psychophysiol. **97**(1), 1–7 (2015)
7. Sang, J., Mei, T., Xu, Y.Q., et al.: Interaction in design for mobile visual search. J. IEEE Trans. Multimedia **15**(7), 1665–1676 (2013)

Human-Vehicle Interaction

Prevalence of Driving Schedule Habits and Fatigue Among Occupational Heavy Truck Drivers

Junmin Du[1], Weiyu Sun[2], Xin Zhang[3($\boxtimes$)], Huimin Hu[3], Yang Liu[4], and Haoshu Gu[1]

[1] Beihang University, Beijing, China
[2] Hefei Hualing Co. Ltd., Hefei, China
[3] China National Institute of Standardization, Beijing, China
zhangx@cnis.ac.cn
[4] Beijing Foton Daimler Automotive Co. Ltd., Beijing, China

Abstract. During the cab design phase, a thorough understanding of the driver's driving habits is a necessary foundation for the cab's human-machine interface design and a guarantee of a good driving experience. However, in the domestic heavy truck cab design currently, the driver's driving habits are not considered enough, which leads to poor cab design, worse user experience and road safety risk. This study investigated the prevalence of driving schedule habits, fatigue and the associated truck cab design factors influencing fatigue of occupational heavy truck drivers. The results show that 66% of the drivers usually drove more than 4 h without taking a break. About 19% of the drivers felt obvious fatigue before the single driving completed. The single driving duration in the night was significantly longer than in the daytime. A feature of "abler people do more work" was generalized, which meant the later the fatigue appeared, the longer the driving went. The primary reasons for cab design that influencing driving fatigue was seat belt and seat. The findings suggest that working conditions created significant features to occupational heavy truck driver group. The driver's fatigue management and driving time interval management require targeted optimization. Policymakers to set up policy guidelines to match driving features and enforce compliance with heavy truck driving and rest time, and for cab designers to improve the cab ergonomics to make compliance with drivers' anthropometry characteristics.

Keywords: Heavy truck driver · Driving schedule habit · Fatigue · Investigation

1 Introduction

Road traffic accidents caused by truck have a large percentage. According to the data collected by Traffic Management Bureau of the Public Security Ministry of China, 50.4 thousand road traffic accidents, 25.0 thousand people died, and 46.8 thousand people injury caused by truck in the year 2016, which accounted for 30.5%, 48.23% and 27.81% of the total number of vehicle accidents respectively. The amount of truck

© Springer Nature Switzerland AG 2020
C. Stephanidis and M. Antona (Eds.): HCII 2020, CCIS 1226, pp. 339–348, 2020.
https://doi.org/10.1007/978-3-030-50732-9_45

accidents is much higher than that of truck ownership. The consequences of heavy truck accidents are more serious. The per-vehicle fatality and injury rates for heavy trucks are much higher than for all types of vehicles (Daniel et al. 2004).

Such a high rate of accidents involvement may be committed for a variety of reasons. Fatigue in trucking is an important issue. It was found that the risk of involvement in an accident increases with the number of hours and the time at which the drivers are at the wheel (Hamblin 1987; Lin et al. 1993). Prolonged driving time, time of day and rotation of shifts exposed truck drivers on the effects of fatigue and circadian rhythms (Fatigue 1977; Adams and Guppy 2003; Perttula et al, 2011; Wang and Pei 2014; Meng et al. 2015). Fatigue and circadian effects on driving performance, such as vigilance, attention, reaction, are well-established (Fatigue 1977; Wang and Pei 2014). Fatigue is one of the significant risk factors of extremely serious road accidents in China (Liu et al. 2018). Unable to choose the time of breaks or use clock time to regulate fatigue makes the risk of fatigue higher (Perttula et al. 2011; Snyder 2017). There exists a time-dependent effect for rest breaks for truck drivers (Chen 2014). Driving at night increases the crash risks caused by sleepiness. Amount of long-haul drivers reported having problems in staying alert, even worse having dozed off while driving (Häkkänen and Summala 2000; Zhang and Chan 2014; Zwahlen et al. 2016).

Besides the road safety risk related to truck drivers, the other prevalent risk among truck drivers is an occupational injury. A high incidence of spinal disorders, including neck and back pain, was observed in occupational drivers (Okunribido et al. 2006; Okunribido 2016; Massaccesi et al. 2003). Fatigue on feet or other parts of the body was also found to be prevalent among truck drivers (Du et al. 2017). The pain or fatigue may turn into chronic occupational musculoskeletal injuries after a long period of accumulation. The factors that contribute to causing occupational injuries are diverse. The pains might be caused by prolonged sitting, poor postures, exposure to whole-body vibration and other non-driving factors such as heavy lifting, poor diet or other psychosocial factors (Robb and Mansfield 2007). Postural stress from twisting of the torso and frequent handling of loads, appear to be the main contributors to low back pain (Okunribido 2016). It also contributed significantly to all self-reported pains, aches or discomforts in the trunk or neck regions (Massaccesi et al. 2003).

For a long time, the situation that truck driving causes a large number of accidents and driver health problems has not been improved significantly, although it is well-established that fatigue is correlated with driving time and regulations that limit the driving time of the truck driver is also established by some countries. For instance, in US federal motor carrier safety administration interstate suggested a 14-h driving window, 11-h driving limit, 30-min break, 60/70-h duty limit, and 34-h restart rules (FMCSA 2015). In China, the regulation on the implementation of the road traffic safety law requires: driving the vehicle continuously should not for more than 4 h without parking or having a rest period of fewer than 20 min (SCOC 2017). However, how well the truck drivers obey the regulations and manage their driving time is unclear. The lack of data in the driver feature field, particularly data relating occupational heavy truck driver's driving habit, is one of the crucial cruxes. Meanwhile, the understanding of the driving situation is also the foundation for human-machine interface design of truck cab as bad cab design results in fatigue on long-running.

The study presented in this paper is based on the above considerations. The features of Chinese occupational heavy truck driver user group, driving schedule habits, and fatigue feeling caused by cab design were collected through questionnaires. The results were helpful for understanding Chinese occupational heavy truck driver group features and needs, providing implications for the fatigue management and education of occupational drivers, and indicating references for human-machine interface design of the truck cab design.

2 Materials and Methods

The data used in this study were collected from occupational heavy truck drivers in Beijing metropolis through a questionnaire survey. The survey was conducted in Daxing district and Changping district, Beijing. The survey was conducted in the lounges of two locations, which one was located in a logistics company, the other one was in a heavy truck service area. At these two locations in the Beijing metropolis, heavy truck usage is very high. At each selected location, trained interviewers stayed in the lounge and approached drivers who were having a rest there. The participants were required occupational, had driving heavy truck experience in the past year, and the truck-mounted weight should be at least 8 tons. The purpose of the study was explained to the driver prior to the interview to obtain their consent. Of the 100 drivers approached, 100 took part in the survey, for a response rate of 100%. All the drivers approached were willing to take part in the survey. The questionnaire was written on-site. Total of 100 questionnaires copies was issued, and 100 valid questionnaires were returned. The questionnaires were all completed and 100% effective.

The primary topics in the questionnaire were as follows.

- Truck driver group baseline data, including gender, age, height, weight, truckload capacity.
- Driving schedule habits, including driving frequency, driving mileage in the past year, driving time (daytime/nighttime/both), the single continuous driving time (without break), the total driving time within 24 h (excluding rest time), fatigue appear time.
- Device in cab that reported causing fatigue, including seat belt (tightness, fix position), seat (height adjustment range, back and forth adjustment range, angle adjustment range, seat depth, width, back, headrest, lumbar support, seat hardness), pedals (control force of accelerator pedal, brake pedal, clutch pedal, the space between the accelerator pedal and the brake pedal), handles (the control force of handbrake and shift lever, the size of shift lever handle), steering wheel (outer diameter, grip diameter, height adjustment range, angle, feedback force, the block on the view field of the instrument panel), and others (mirror adjustment, blind spot area, entertainment system switch/adjustment button, air conditioning system switch/adjustment button, car lighting switch, glove box, first step height of stairs, distance between steps).

Data from the questionnaire were analyzed using Excel and SPSS. Statistical methods such as Student's t-test and Pearson's correlation coefficient test were used.

3 Results

Of the 100 truck drivers who participated in the survey, all of them were males. Considering no female driver was met during the survey period in the lounges carried out the survey, it indicated that the males had an absolute advantage in quantity among the occupational truck drivers. The Mean and Standard Deviation of the drivers' age was 34.6 ± 7.6 years old. The participants' height was 172.14 ± 4.86 cm and the weight was 77.32 ± 9.22 kg, which was among the middle-heavy and moderately weighted range in Chinese adults (GB10000-88 1988). The truck-mounted weight was 22.92 ± 8.78 tons. Majority of the drivers drove every day (88%). High as 99% of the drivers drove above 5,000 km in the past year, and nearly one-third of the drivers drove above 45,000 km in the past year.

Of the 100 truck drivers in the survey, 34% of them driving usually in the daytime, 23% driving usually in nighttime, 43% driving usually both in daytime and nighttime. Daytime meant that the natural light was well illuminated, and the driver could see the road conditions and traffic signals without using the lights. While nighttime meant the driver needed to use the lights to see the road conditions and traffic signals. In August during the day of the survey in Beijing, daytime was about from 5 am to 7:30 pm and the rest was nighttime. Within a 24-h period, the average single driving duration in the daytime was 4.12 ± 1.12 h, in the night was 5.00 ± 0.85 h. The significant difference was found between these two driving times (p ≤ 0.01). The average single driving duration of drivers who drove in both daytime and night was 4.67 ± 1.71 h, which had no difference with those who drove in daytime merely, neither with those in night merely. There was a significant difference in the fatigue appear time between daytime (3.68 ± 0.91) and nighttime (4.22 ± 0.90) driving (p ≤ 0.01).

Of the 100 truck drivers in the survey, high as 66% of the drivers usually drove more than 4 h without taking a break, which meant the single driving time was longer than 4 h. For the drivers driving in the daytime, about 53% of them usually drove more than 4 h without taking a break. The percentage was up to 93% and 63% for those who drove in nighttime and both time respectively. For drivers who usually drove more than 4 h without taking a break (named group A), the duration of total driving time within a 24-h period was 7.67 ± 2.40 h. This time was 6.12 ± 2.58 h for drivers who usually drove less than 4 h (named group B). The significant difference was found between group A and group B in the duration of total driving time within a 24-h period (p ≤ 0.01). For the fatigue appear time, it was 4.32 ± 0.96 h in driver group A, and it was 3.41 ± 1.28 h in group B. Significant difference was found between the two groups in fatigue appear time (p ≤ 0.001). No significant differences were found between groups in single driving time, drivers' age, and truck-mounted weight.

About 19% of the drivers felt obvious fatigue before the single driving completed. All of these drivers usually drove more than 4 h without taking a break. Among them, 8 drivers usually drove in daytime, 3 drivers in the nighttime, 8 in both. The Comparison of the two driver groups was made, one group (named group C) was the 19% drivers who felt obvious fatigue before the single driving completed, the second group was the other 81% drivers (named group C) who did not feel obvious fatigue before the single driving completed. The single driving time without a break of group C was

5.74 ± 0.99 h, and group D was 4.28 ± 1.32 h. Significant differences were found between the two groups in single driving time (p ≤ 0.001). There were no significant differences in fatigue appear time, the duration of total driving time within a 24-h period, and drivers' age.

Of the 100 truck drivers in the survey, 67% (named group E) of them reported fatigue appearance time was when driving continuously for more than 4 h, and the other 33% (named group F) reported less than 4 h. There was a significant difference in the single driving duration between group E (4.94 ± 1.25 h) and group F (3.75 ± 1.32 h) (p ≤ 0.001). Meanwhile, there was a significant difference in the duration of total driving time within a 24-hperiod between group E (7.70 ± 2.36 h) and group F (6.00 ± 2.60 h) (p ≤ 0.001). No significant difference was found in the age and truck-mounted weight between group E and F.

4 Uncomfortable Devices that May Cause Fatigue

Uncomfortable devices in the cockpit may cause fatigue or make fatigue appear soon. The devices that the respondents reported uncomfortable and caused fatigue is shown in Fig. 1. The seat belt and the seat were the main devices causing driving fatigue or discomfort, and the percentage of respondents who choose seat belt or seat as top causes was 60% and 49% respectively.

The problem with the seat belt was a bit tight and uncomfortable for a long time driving, reported by 63% of the respondents. Even more, 16% of the respondents complained that the seat belt was very tight and had hard strangled force on the driver. Additional, about 1/3 respondents felt the upper fix position of the seat belt was too high, which made the belt strangled neck.

The problems caused by the seat were concentrated on the backache. 40% of the respondents were unsatisfied with the lumbar support, which could not fit the lumbar curve or had an inappropriate location. 24% of the respondents were unsatisfied with the seat hardness and complained the seat was too solid. 18% of the respondents were unsatisfied with the headrest, which made the neck hanging and uncomfortable while long-distance driving. 14% of the respondents complained the seat back was too concave/narrow/low/small and not fit the driver's body shape. 13% of the respondents complained the seat depth was small. Also, 4% of the respondents complained the seat width was small. 32% of the respondents reported the seat adjustable height was not enough, and 41% of the respondents reported the seat back and forth adjustment range was not enough.

In addition to seat belts and seats, a few respondents reported that fatigue or uncomfortable caused devices included accelerator pedals (11%), shift levers (8%), steering wheels (5%), brake pedals (3%), and others device (3%). The primary complains were the unfordable angle, stock and force of the pedals, exertive and unsuitable size shift levers, unsuitable outer diameter, grip diameter, force, adjustment range, the position of steering wheels.

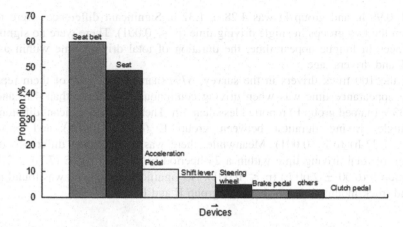

Fig. 1. Main devices causing driving fatigue or discomfort

5 Discussion

The subjects in this paper are occupational heavy truck drivers. They have many reasons for running at night and driving for a long time, such as transporting vegetables and other fresh-keeping goods, daytime urban traffic regulations limit on trucks, drivers themselves want to make more money. Driven by these internal and external factors, the heavy truck drivers tend to drive a long time. It is not easy to reverse the fact that too many accidents and health problem caused by the truck driver's long time driving. It needs the collaborative efforts of each relative component parts to make the situation better. The key contributors include at least drivers themselves, their family and community, transport companies and the traffic administration. Ergonomics occupational should also address the features when developing the human-machine interface design of the truck cab and driving fatigue management for truck drivers.

The results showed that more than half of the truck drivers (66%) drove continuously more than 4 h without break. The condition was more serious in nighttime driving. The rate of drivers driving continuously 4 more hours in the night (93%) was far more than that in the daytime (53%). Even more, the average single driving duration in the night (5.00 ± 0.85) was significant longer (p ≤ 0.01) than in daytime (4.12 ± 1.12). The 4 h of continuous driving is longer than the general half-day working period of the normal shift system. Considering the sitting posture has to be maintained by the driver at all time during driving, the working intensity of driving continuously 4 more hours is relatively heavier than sitting working in an office. Furthermore, the vigilant attention needs on driver reinforce the working intensity.

Of the 100 truck drivers in the survey, total 19% of the drivers felt obvious fatigue before the single driving completed. All of the 19% drivers usually drove more than 4 h without taking a break. So, if these drivers could take a break within 4 h driving, the rate would decrease definitely. However, compared with daytime driving, fewer drivers felt fatigued in nighttime before the single driving completed.

The individual difference was obvious in the survey. The comparing between group E and F showed that the later fatigue appearance group drove significant longer hours, no matter in the single driving duration or the duration of total driving time within a 24-h period. It could be speculated that the respondent's sensitivity to fatigue affects the total duration of their driving to a certain extent. In other words, the driver who was prone to fatigue had a relatively short driving time. Otherwise, the person had a relatively long driving time. It showed the characteristics of "abler people do more work", which meant the later the fatigue appeared, the longer the driving went. The correlation coefficient between the single continuous driving time and the fatigue appearance time was 0.495, which was a moderate correlation. The correlation coefficient between total driving time within 24 h and the fatigue appearance time was 0.346, which was a weak correlation. In other words, the fatigue appearance time was moderately related to the single continuous driving time and was less correlated with the total driving time within 24 h.

The previous studies showed that drivers might become drowsier with the deteriorated in their driving performance during the simulated prolonged driving task. However, this study shows if drivers used to drive regularly day or night time for prolonged task (more than 4 h) during their working days, their fatigue tolerance time was longer, and the night driving even has more advantages on delay fatigue appearance time. The reasons might include long-term fixed driving time schedule, habit, sleep cycle, individual difference, less interference and lower workload in the night time and so on.

Domestic occupational heavy truck drivers are mainly young and middle-aged. Their physical strength and endurance are at the highest time of their lives. However, due to differences in personal physique and human tolerance, fatigue tolerance time is different and has limits. It is an essential ability for drivers to aware his/her own endurance limitation and breaks a long time driving resolutely to have a rest, as as to avoid taking the possible risk to lead to terrible consequences. If it is difficult to reduce the total time of their long-term driving, then controlling from the perspective of a single continuous driving time might delay the occurrence of fatigue, and to some extent alleviate the series of problems caused by fatigue. Besides, learn more knowledge about fatigue is also helpful. This study is in agreement with the study by Feyer and Williamson (1995) who argued that for all drivers, the influence of circadian rhythms was evident in the occurrence of fatigue, with better management of the problem evident among drivers who were able to arrange the timing of rest to more closely coincide with periods of fatigue. The results of this experiment verified similar experiments by Feyer et al. (1997) which is concerned about the degree of driver fatigue under different time schedules. In addition, driving time (day or night) also has a significant impact on fatigue tolerance time, and nighttime fatigue tolerance is longer. Therefore, considering the factors such as external factors, time periods, and individual differences in driving time, it is an idea to actively control the long-term fatigue driving by formulating the driving and rest system and guiding and restraining from the personal and commercial perspectives. Night driving of truck drivers may require more stringent fatigue management institutions.

Traffic safety is a major issue related to not only the safety of each individual but also an important factor to family and in building social security. Driver's personal safety and physical health is the source of personal, family and social happiness. Conversely, the attitude from family and society effects drive attitude deeply. Drivers' related personnel, especially their family members, should be included in the traffic safety education. The traffic safety education is still far from perfect.

Traffic safety accidents caused by driver fatigue occur rapidly. The optimistic in the human-machine interface design of the truck cab and driving fatigue management for truck drivers not only can secure the safety of traffic participants but also care for the health of drivers. In the driving system, most of the respondents pointed out that the seat belt is the main problem causing driving fatigue. In the design of car seats, most of the current automotive industry uses the human body size data of the female group P5 and male P95 of the user group as the basis, and the user satisfaction is 90%. However, it can be seen from this study that the drivers of the truck were mainly young and middle-aged male. The size of the P5 body of this user group is larger than that of the female P5. Therefore, the size of the body of the truck driver should be used as the body size of the truck driver. The design basis, rather than the female P5 size as the design basis, results in a small seat size problem, seriously weakening driving comfort. The most important thing about design is to help curb the occurrence of traffic accidents and avoid health impairment.

Transport companies play a pivotal role in truck traffic safety. A survey found that EU occupational drivers have a serious shortage of sleep time (Philip et al. 2002). Goel (2010) has introduced a method of scheduling the driving and working hours of truck drivers in accordance with Regulation (EC) No. 561/2006. It turns out to be that reasonable industry guidelines based on sound regulatory regulations can greatly improve the prevailing problems in the industry. Drivers education and work schedules integrating notions of sleep hygiene as well as the promotion of sleep medicine could significantly improve road safety (Philip 2004). Regulations have a wide range of influence on traffic safety. Under the Chinese drivers' hours rule the driver must take 20 min of break time once the driver has driven for 4 h in a day (Order 405 2004). Obviously, more efforts focus on comprehensive regulations and rigorous monitoring methods are needed to improve the policy execution effectiveness.

In conclusion, the findings suggest that working conditions created significant features to occupational heavy truck driver group. The driver's fatigue management and driving time interval management require targeted optimization. Policymakers to set up policy guidelines to match driving features and enforce compliance with heavy truck driving and rest time, and for cab designers to improve the cab ergonomics to make compliance with drivers' anthropometry characteristics. For instance, the effort seeking to decrease the risk of fatigued driving may have to help drivers to obey the regulation. In addition, cab design should conform to human factors criterion to avoid discomfort while driving.

Acknowledgement. This research was supported by National Natural Science Foundation of China (project number 71601007), 2017NQI project (2017YFF0206601) and President Foundation of China National Institute of Standardization (project number 522018Y-5984).

References

Adams, G.J., Guppy, A.: Truck driver fatigue risk assessment and management: a multinational survey. Ergonomics **46**(8), 763–779 (2003)

Chen, C., Xie, Y.: Modeling the safety impacts of driving hours and rest breaks on truck drivers considering time-dependent covariates. J. Saf. Res. **51**, 57–63 (2003)

Mayhew, D.R., Simpson, H.M., Beirness, D.J.: Heavy trucks and road crashes. Report, Traffic Injury Research Foundation, Ottawa, Ontario, Canada (2004)

Du, J., Lu, H., Sun, W., Zhang, X., Hu, H., Liu, Y.: Investigation on driving habits of Chinese truck driver. HCI **2017**(713), 526–531 (2017)

Feyer, A.-M., Williamson, A.: Work and rest in the long-distance road transport industry in Australia. Work Stress **9**(2), 198–205 (1995)

Feyer, A.-M., Williamson, A., Friswell, R.: Balancing work and rest to combat driver fatigue: an investigation of two-up driving in Australia. Accid. Anal. Prev. **29**(4), 541–553 (1997)

FMCSA (Federal Motor Carrier Safety Administration). Interstate Truck Driver's Guide to Hours of Service (2015)

GB10000-88. Human dimensions of chinese adults. Quality and Technical Supervision Bureau (1988)

Goel, A.: Truck driver scheduling in the European Union. Transp. Sci. **44**, 429–441 (2010)

Hamblin, P.: Lorry driver's time habits in work and their involvement in traffic accidents. Ergonomics **30**(9), 1323–1333 (1987)

Häkkänen, H., Summala, H.: Sleepiness at work among commercial truck drivers. Sleep **23**(1), 49–57 (2000)

Lin, T., Jovanis, P., Yang, C.: Modeling the safety of truck driver service hours using time-dependent logistic regression. Transp. Res. Rec. **1407**, 1–10 (1993)

Liu, G., et al.: Risk factors for extremely serious road accidents: results from national Road Accident Statistical Annual Report of China. PLoS ONE **13**(8), e0201587 (2018)

Massaccesi, M., Pagnotta, A., Soccetti, A., Masali, M., Masiero, C., Greco, F.: Investigation of work-related disorders in truck drivers using RULA method. Appl. Ergon. **34**(4), 303–307 (2003)

Meng, F., et al.: Driving fatigue in occupational drivers: a survey of truck and taxi drivers. Traffic Inj. Prev. **16**(5), 474–483 (2015)

Okunribido, O.O.: An investigation of posture and manual materials handling as risk factors for low back pain in delivery drivers. Ergon. Soc. S. Afr. **28**(2), 19–27 (2016)

Okunribido, O.O., Magnusson, M., Pope, M.: Delivery drivers and low-back pain: a study of the exposures to posture demands, manual materials handling and whole-body vibration. Int. J. Ind. Ergon. **36**(3), 265–273 (2006)

Order of the State Council of the People's Republic of China (No. 405). Regulation on the Implementation of the Road Traffic Safety Law of the People's Republic of China (2004)

Perttula, P., Ojala, T., Kuosma, E.: Factors in the fatigue of heavy vehicle drivers. Psychol. Rep. **108**(2), 507–514 (2011)

Philip, P.: Sleepiness of occupational drivers. Ind. Health **43**, 30–33 (2004)

Philip, P., et al.: Work and rest sleep schedules of 227 European truck drivers. Sleep Med. **3**(6), 507–511 (2002)

Robb, M.J.M., Mansfield, N.J.: Self-reported musculoskeletal problems amongst occupational truck drivers. Ergonomics **50**(6), 814–827 (2007)

SCOC (State Council of China). Regulation on the Implementation of the Road Traffic Safety Law of the People's Republic of China (2017)

Snyder, B.H.: The tyranny of clock time? Debating fatigue in the US truck driving industry. Time Soc. 1–24 (2017)

Wang, L., Pei, Y.: The impact of continuous driving time and rest time on commercial drivers' driving performance and recovery. J. Saf. Res. **50**, 11–15 (2014)

Fatigue, W.H.: Circadian rhythm, and truck accidents. In: Mackie, R.R. (ed.) Vigilance, pp. 133–146. Springer, Boston (1977). https://doi.org/10.1007/978-1-4684-2529-1_8

Zhang, T., Chan, A.H.S.: Sleepiness and the risk of road accidents for occupational drivers: a systematic review and meta-analysis of retrospective studies. Saf. Sci. **70**, 180–188 (2014)

Zwahlen, D., Jackowski, C., Pfäffli, M.: Sleepiness, driving, and motor vehicle accidents: a questionnaire-based survey. J. Forensic Legal Med. **44**, 183–187 (2016)

Facing Driver Frustration: Towards Real-Time In-Vehicle Frustration Estimation Based on Video Streams of the Face

Oliver Franz[1,2], Uwe Drewitz[1], and Klas Ihme[1(✉)]

[1] German Aerospace Center, Institute of Transportation Systems, Lilienthalplatz 7, 38108 Brunswick, Germany
klas.ihme@dlr.de
[2] University of Osnabrück, 49069 Osnabrück, Germany

Abstract. Drivers frequently experience frustration when facing traffic jams, red lights or badly designed in-vehicle interfaces. Frustration can lead to aggressive behaviors and negative influences on user experience. Affect-aware vehicles that recognize the driver's degree of frustration and, based on this, offer assistance to reduce the frustration or mitigate its negative effects promise remedy. As a prerequisite, this needs a real-time estimation of current degree of frustration. Consequently, here we describe the development of a classifier that can recognize whether a frustrated facial expression was shown based on video streams of the face. For demonstration of its real-time capabilities, a demonstrator of a frustration-aware vehicle including the classifier, the Frust-O-Meter, is presented. The system is integrated into a driving simulator and consists of (1) a webcam, (2) a preprocessing unit, (3) a user model, (4) an adaptation unit and (5) a user interface. In the current version, a happy song is played once a high degree of frustration is detected. The Frust-O-Meter can form the basis for the development of frustration-aware vehicles and is foreseen to be extended to more modalities as well as more user need-oriented adaption strategies in the near future.

Keywords: Affect-aware vehicles · Empathic systems · Automated facial expression analysis · Driver frustration

1 Introduction

Frustration is a negative affective state that occurs when goal-directed behavior is blocked (e.g. [1]). Because driving is normally done for a purpose (e.g. going to work, taking the kids to school or quickly driving to the super market), drivers frequently experience frustration when they face obstacles, such as traffic jams and red lights or have problems to program their in-vehicle navigation or infotainment systems due to badly designed interfaces. Frustration can lead to aggressive behaviors (e.g. [2]) and can affect driving behavior due to negative effects on cognitive processes relevant for driving [3]. In addition, negative user experience coming along with frustration impacts user interaction with technical systems in general and has a significant influence on the acceptance of technical systems [4]: The lower the quality of the user experience, the

C. Stephanidis and M. Antona (Eds.): HCII 2020, CCIS 1226, pp. 349–356, 2020.
https://doi.org/10.1007/978-3-030-50732-9_46

lower the acceptance and thus also the willingness to use and buy a technical system. However, frustrating experiences when using technical systems, especially in complex traffic, cannot always be avoided by design for every situation. Here, affect-aware vehicles that recognize the driver's degree of frustration and, based on this, offer assistance to reduce frustration or mitigate its negative effects promise remedy (e.g. [5–8]). As a prerequisite for the development of frustration-aware vehicles, a method for recognizing frustration in real-time is needed. Humans communicate emotions by changing their facial expression, so that understanding a person's facial expression can help to infer his or her current emotional state [9]. Hence, an automated recognition of a frustrated facial expression could be an important brick for developing affect-aware vehicles. Interestingly, recent studies identified facial activation patterns that correlate with the experience of frustration during driving that may be automatically classified as indicator for frustration [10, 11].

Consequently, the goal of this work is to present a facial expression classifier that is capable of determining whether or not a frustrated face was shown based on video recordings. In order to show its real-time capability, we integrated the classifier into a demonstrator, the Frust-O-Meter, which works as part of a realistic driving simulator. In the following, we describe the development and performance of the classifier, introduce the modules of the Frust-O-Meter as well as their interplay and finally discuss potential improvements of the demonstrator together with ideas for further research.

2 Facial Expression Classifier

2.1 Short Description of Data Set

The data set used for training and validation of the classifier stems from an earlier driving simulator study with 30 participants conducted to investigate facial muscle activities that are indicative for frustration. Participants had to drive through an urban street with the task to quickly deliver a parcel to a client. Obstacles, such as red traffic light, traffic jams, or construction sites occurred that blocked the participant and thus induced frustration (for details, see [10, 11]). Participants' faces were videotaped using a standard IP-cam (resolution of 1280 × 720 pixels) with 10 frames per second. The software package Emotient FACET (Imotions, Copenhagen, Denmark) was used to extract information regarding the evidence of activity of 19 facial action units (AUs[1]) frame-wise from the facial videos. Using a data-driven clustering approach based on the AU data averaged in windows of 1 s, five facial expressions were identified to predominantly occur in the data set corresponding a *frustrated* facial expression, two slightly different neutral expressions (*neutral 1* and *neutral 2*), *smiling* and *frowning* (for details, see [11]). These facial expressions were used as labels for the classifier development for this paper. Thus, the final data set contained the activity information for 19 AUs together with a label of a facial expression (neutral 1, smiling, frowning, frustrated or neutral 2) for each second from 30 participants driving roughly for 10 min (30 participants × 10 min × 60 s ∼ 18,000 data points).

---

[1] AUs can be seen as atomic units of facial behavior related to activation of facial muscles, see [12].

2.2 Classifier Set-up for Frame-to-Frame Frustration Classification

To classify the labeled data, a multi-layer perceptron (MLP) was used. This type of supervised learning method uses interconnected layers of neurons to learn and generalize over training examples. An MLP learns by adjusting the initially random weights, which are attached to each neuron in the net in order to minimize the output error. The algorithm used to adjust the weights is the backpropagation algorithm [13]. It is a way of realizing gradient descent to minimize the error of the net which allows adjusting the weights and learns to discriminate the different classes of data.

A feature vector with 19 dimensions (corresponding to the 19 AUs) was fed with a batch size of 32 into the net. Three fully connected hidden layers (32, 16 and 16 neurons) were used to project onto the output layer. The activation of the output layer (5 neurons) was calculated with a SoftMax function to generate the probabilities for each label. The argmax of the output layer returned the predicted label for each sample. The classifier was implemented in Python. The computational graph underlying the neuronal net was written with the TensorFlow package.

2.3 Evaluation Procedure

Before the training of the artificial neural network was started, 20% of the data were randomly split as hold-out set for later testing and never used during training. The remaining 80% of the data were split into 70% training and 30% validation data. In each epoch both sets were randomly shuffled before using the training data for training and the validation set to check the performance at the end of each epoch and test for potential overfitting of the net. After finishing the training, the hold-out set was used to test the performance of the net on previously unseen data. In the end, the structure and weights were saved for the usage in the demonstrator at a later point.

2.4 Classification Results

The classification result shown in Fig. 1 represents the performance of the trained net on the test set. The true labels are plotted on the y-axis against the predicted label on the x-axis. An overall accuracy of 69% was reached on the test set with the MLP. With 93%, the accuracy was highest for the frustrated facial expression, despite relatively high accuracies also for most of the other expressions (neutral 1: 70%, smiling: 71%, frowning: 79%). Solely the expression 'neutral_2' had lower accuracies (41%) and was repeatedly misclassified as frowning. As our goal was to construct a classifier for detecting the facial expression of frustration, the performance of this net was considered to be acceptable.

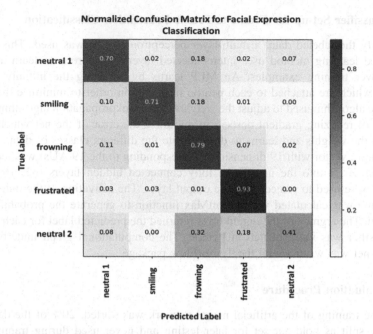

Fig. 1. Confusion matrix depicting the classification accuracy of the employed classifier.

3 Demonstrator: The Frust-O-Meter

In order to present the real-time capability of the classifier, we integrated it into a demonstrator, called the *Frust-O-Meter*. The Frust-O-Meter is currently integrated into a realistic driving simulator and consists of the five modules (1) a webcam, (2) preprocessing unit, (3) user model, (4) adaptation unit and (5) user interface (see Fig. 2 for a sketch of the architecture). The modules are detailed in the following:

- **Webcam**: The webcam is a standard Logitech C920 webcam recording with a resolution of 1920 × 1080 at a framerate of 30 fps. The camera is mounted on the dashboard to record the participants face from a frontal position. The video data is streamed to the preprocessing unit.
- **Preprocessing unit**: The purpose of the preprocessing unit is to extract the frame-wise activation of the facial AUs from the video streams and to make these available for the user model for further processing. In the current version, the commercial software package Emotient FACET (Imotions, Copenhagen, Denmark) is used in this step, which can estimate the evidence of activity for 19 AUs for each frame. Thus, a 19-dimensional vector for each frame is passed on to the user model.
- **User model**: In the user model, the preprocessed data regarding the facial activation are interpreted to gain an estimate of the user's current degree of frustration. For this, initially the model classifies the incoming AU data using the trained facial expression classifier described above with respect to the currently shown facial expression (two different neutral expressions, smiling, frowning, frustrated, see 2 Facial Expression Classifier). Following the results reported in [11] that the

frequency of showing the frustrated facial expression correlates with the subjective frustration experience, the occurrence of this facial expression is integrated over the last 20 data points in order to estimate the current degree of frustration. This means that the frustration estimate could take values between 0 (no frustrated facial expression was shown in the last 20 frames) and 20 (the frustrated facial expression was shown permanently during the last 20 data points). The result of the frustration estimation from the user model is passed on to the adaptation unit and the user interface.

– **Adaptation unit**: The idea of the adaptation unit is to select and execute an appropriate adaptation strategy that supports the user in mitigating her or his currently experience level of frustration or help to reduce the negative effects frustration has on (driving) performance. Currently, this is realized in a very simple form by randomly playing one of two happy music songs (either *Hooked on a Feeling* in the version by Blue Swede or *Have You Ever Seen the Rain* by Creedence Clearwater Revival) via loud speakers for about one minute once the frustration estimate reached a threshold value of 15 or above.

– **User interface**: Finally, the user interface has the purpose to present the frustration estimate as well as the output of the facial expression classifier to the user. In the simulator the user interface was shown on a monitor in the center console of the vehicle mock-up. The upper half of the monitor contained a display of the frustration estimate in the style of a speedometer (which explains Frust-O-Meter as name for the demonstrator), in which values above 15 are displayed in red, while the remainder is shown in white (see Fig. 2). The lower half contains smileys for the facial expressions together a time series display of the classifier output over a configurable time window.

The modules of the Frust-O-Meter work in real-time, so that user could drive through a simulated urban drive (realized in Virtual Test Drive, VIRES Simulationstechnologie, Bad Aibling, Germany) with frustrating situations, such as construction sites or red lights (cf. [2, 10, 11]). In this way, it is possible for the users to experience a real-time adaptation of a system to their current frustration level.

4 Discussion and Outlook

Here, we presented a real-time capable classifier for recognizing a frustrated facial expression from video streams and its integration into the Frust-O-Meter, a demonstrator of a frustration-aware vehicle. The Frust-O-Meter links a real-time estimation of the degree of frustration from the facial expression with a simple adaptation and a user interface to communicate the current level of frustration. The user model of the demonstrator estimates the current degree of frustration based on a temporal integration of facial expressions classified as frustrated. As classifier, we used a multi-layer perceptron that was trained on video recordings of 30 participants experiencing frustration in a driving simulator study. The adaption to the frustration of the user is currently realized by playing a happy song when a certain degree of frustration is realized.

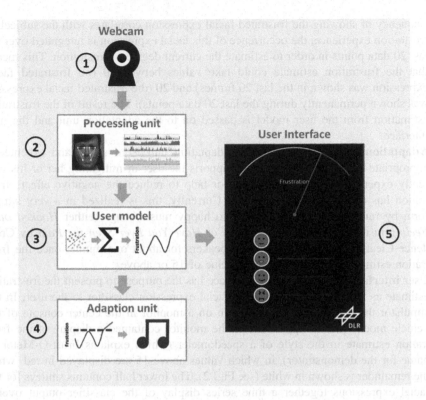

Fig. 2. Sketch of the architecture of the Frust-O-Meter.

While the Frust-O-Meter is a useful means to render possible that people experience the idea of a real-time adaption to their degree of frustration, there are a lot of challenges that need to be tackled to develop a real fully-functioning frustration-aware vehicle. For instance, affective states like frustration are multi-component processes [14, 15] that not only manifest in the facial expression, but also come along with changes in cognitive appraisals, physiology, gestures or prosody. Therefore, information from other sensors besides a webcam (e.g. electrocardiogram, infrared imaging, or mricrophone [16–19]) should be integrated into the user model to improve the frustration estimation. Surely, extending the sensor set also demands a more sophisticated preprocessing unit and user model. Moreover, the only possible adaptation was playing a happy song randomly chosen from a set compiled based on the authors' preferences. Although music has the potential to improve the drivers' mood [20], other strategies may even be better suited. Very promising seem to be empathic voice assistants that support drivers in dealing with their frustration or help to overcome the causes of frustrations (e.g. offer help when dealing with a badly designed interface) [8, 21]. In order to realize this, information about the context to derive the cause of frustration in the user model as well as suitable approaches to select and apply the best possible strategy in the adaptation unit are needed as for example described in [22]. To sum up, in spite of the delineated ideas for further research, the Frust-O-Meter is an elegant way to demonstrate a frustration-aware vehicle based on automated recognition of facial expressions from video recordings.

Acknowlegdement. The authors thank Dirk Assmann for his effort in setting up the demonstrator. In addition, we gratefully acknowledge the financial support for the project F-RELACS, which is funded by the German Federal Ministry of Education and Research (grant number: 16SV7930).

References

1. Lazarus, R.S.: Progress on a cognitive-motivational-relational theory of emotion. Am. Psychol. **46**, 819–834 (1991)
2. Lee, Y.-C.: Measuring drivers' frustration in a driving simulator. Proc. Hum. Factors Ergon. Soc. Ann. Meeting **54**, 1531–1535 (2010)
3. Jeon, M.: Towards affect-integrated driving behaviour research. Theoret. Issues Ergon. Sci. **16**, 553–585 (2015)
4. Picard, R.W., Klein, J.: Computers that recognise and respond to user emotion: theoretical and practical implications. Interact. Comput. **14**, 141–169 (2002)
5. Oehl, M., Ihme, K., Pape, A.-A., Vukelic, M., Braun, M.: Affective use cases for empathic vehicles in highly automated driving: results of an expert workshop. Accepted at HCI International 2020 (2020)
6. Stephanidis, C., et al.: Seven HCI grand challenges. Int. J. Hum.–Comput. Interact. **35**, 1229–1269 (2019)
7. Löcken, A., Ihme, K., Unni, A.: Towards designing affect-aware systems for mitigating the effects of in-vehicle frustration. In: Proceedings of the 9th International Conference on Automotive User Interfaces and Interactive Vehicular Applications Adjunct, pp. 88–93. ACM, New York (2017)
8. Oehl, M., Ihme, K., Drewitz, U., Pape, A.-A., Cornelsen, S., Schramm, M.: Towards a frustration-aware assistant for increased in-vehicle UX. In: Janssen, C.P., Donker, S.F., Chuang, L.L., Ju, W. (eds.) The 11th International Conference on Automotive User Interfaces and Interactive Vehicular Applications: Adjunct Proceedings, pp. 260–264. ACM, New York (2019)
9. Erickson, K., Schulkin, J.: Facial expressions of emotion: a cognitive neuroscience perspective. Brain Cogn. **52**, 52–60 (2003)
10. Ihme, K., Dömeland, C., Freese, M., Jipp, M.: Frustration in the face of the driver: a simulator study on facial muscle activity during frustrated driving. Interact. Stud. **19**, 488–499 (2018)
11. Ihme, K., Unni, A., Zhang, M., Rieger, J.W., Jipp, M.: Recognizing frustration of drivers from face video recordings and brain activation measurements with functional near-infrared spectroscopy. Front. Hum. Neurosci. **12**, 669 (2018)
12. Ekman, P., Friesen, W.V., Hager, J.: The Investigator's Guide for the Facial Action Coding System. A Human face, Salt Lake City (2002)
13. Rumelhart, D.E., Hinton, G.E., Williams, R.J.: Learning representations by back-propagating errors. Nature **323**, 533–536 (1986)
14. Scherer, K.R.: Emotions are emergent processes: they require a dynamic computational architecture. Philos. Trans. R. Soc. B Biol. Sci. **364**, 3459–3474 (2009)

15. Scherer, K.R.: What are emotions? And how can they be measured? So. Sci. Inf. **44**, 695–729 (2005)

16. Zepf, S., Stracke, T., Schmitt, A., van de Camp, F., Beyerer, J.: Towards real-time detection and mitigation of driver frustration using SVM. In: 2019 18th IEEE International Conference on Machine Learning and Applications (ICMLA), pp. 202–209 (2019)

17. Lotz, A., Ihme, K., Charnoz, A., Maroudis, P., Dmitriev, I., Wendemuth, A.: Behavioral factors while driving: a real-world multimodal corpus to monitor the driver's affective state. In: Calzolari, N. (ed.) LREC 2018. Eleventh International Conference on Language Resources and Evaluation. European Language Resources Association (ELRA), Paris, France (2018)

18. Zhang, M., Ihme, K., Drewitz, U.: Discriminating drivers' emotions through the dimension of power: evidence from facial infrared thermography and peripheral physiological measurements. Transp. Res. Part F Traffic Psychol. Behav. **63**, 135–143 (2019)

19. Cevher, D., Zepf, S. and Klinger, R.: Towards Multimodal Emotion Recognition in German Speech Events in Cars using Transfer Learning, https://arxiv.org/abs/1909.02764

20. van der Zwaag, M.D., et al.: The influence of music on mood and performance while driving. Ergonomics **55**, 12–22 (2012)

21. Braun, M., Schubert, J., Pfleging, B., Alt, F.: Improving Driver Emotions with Affective Strategies. MTI **3**, 21 (2019)

22. Drewitz, U., et al.: Towards user-focused vehicle automation: the architectural approach of the AutoAkzept project. Accepted at HCI International 2020 (2020)

One of by Map - Two if by See: Implications of Dissonant Affordance Structures in Human-Computer Interaction with especial Reference to the Case of Driver-Automated Vehicle Relationships

P. A. Hancock[1(✉)] and G. M. Hancock[2]

[1] University of Central Florida, Orlando, FL 32826, USA
peter.hancock@ucf.edu
[2] California State University Long Beach, Long Beach, CA 90840, USA

While disparate forms of human-computer interaction clearly present a heterogeneous landscape of possibilities, there are some commonalities across contexts, especially as they pertain to contemporary complex systems. Here, we examine the manner in which pattern-predicated, artificial intelligence (AI) is enacted in the transportation world, and how these emerging technologies are expressed in human-dominated operational worlds. We also explore how patterns and principles distilled extend beyond the world of transportation to the full gamut of human-computer interaction. Few would dispute that artificial intelligence, in its various 'narrow,' 'broad,' 'weak,' and 'strong' forms is now exerting a burgeoning impact upon the world in which we live. It is also evident that current, specialized incarnations of AI (i.e., the 'narrow' versions), operate largely upon pattern-matching capacities that are accelerated by computational powers to distill, compare, and extract such patterns at rates that exceed even the most facile human expert. This said, such systems express their own forms of 'affordance' capacity. While these AI applications are becoming ubiquitous, it is within advanced, on-road vehicles that their impact is being exerted on the general public most evidently. Therefore, we here consider the affordance structures, designed and fabricated into automated vehicles as compared to those that have evolved in human beings.

Although humans have only been around a few million years, the perception-action systems which they have inherited may be more than hundreds of millions of years old. Thus, these capacities have become well-adjusted to the environments to which they are now 'tuned.' In contrast, AI-based vehicle control is only decades old and, even within that time, have had little chance to adapt to their ecological niche. Yet, our own human-driven technological world changes the constraints of the ecosystem in which human beings now operate, and AI systems today can rapidly assimilate context-specific information to optimize their own actions. Thus, we are witnessing a confluence of merging capacities in an emerging world which, somewhat paradoxically, humans remain responsible for. Ours is a time of subtle conflict and aspirational cooperation such that necessarily there are dissonances between human and machine; and driving is a world where these dissonances are becoming ever more evident and dangerous.

© Springer Nature Switzerland AG 2020
C. Stephanidis and M. Antona (Eds.): HCII 2020, CCIS 1226, pp. 357–358, 2020.
https://doi.org/10.1007/978-3-030-50732-9_47

Technologists, especially those developers and venture capitalists that are hoping for some of the part of the estimated \$15 trillion market that is automated transportation, always tout the improvements in safety that a 'flawless' system could render. They point to the 40,000 road fatalities and the millions of associated injury crashes which haunt our highways. They are convinced, and can be convincing, that automation can 'solve' this particular societal ill. Yet one question that is rarely asked is the following. How efficient are human drivers at avoiding collision? We have the numerator in terms of crashes, as already cited. What we do not have is a realistic and valid estimate of the denominator. Without a numerical specification of the number of 'dynamic non-events' occurring on our roads, it is not possible to say whether automated vehicles are relatively better; although pragmatists can argue that any absolute reduction in numbers are a social 'good.' In general, we believe the number of non-events (indexed for example by the non-occupation of a common road area per unit time) as in the order of many trillions. Thus, humans already prove exceptionally able at this task, and any improvements must necessarily here be marginal. Thus, the vision of autopia is one that is dangerously chimerical.

What we here suggest is that the affordance structures of human and automation are necessarily incommensurate. That is, each entity 'sees' the world in differing ways. While current collision patterns represent shortfalls of human-human interaction, emerging collisions will derive from incommensurate human-automated vehicle interaction; and these we are beginning to see. However, there must then be collisions derived from shortfalls in automated vehicle-automated vehicle interaction which, because of their present frequency on the road, we are not yet really seeing. These respective collision patterns can be plotted out on a configuration by configuration basis. The fallacy is that automation to automation will rove flawless. It will not. Such systems may be able to learn at a faster rate but exploring indeterminate environmental conditions will witness such failures, whatever the enthusiasms of current roboticists. It has not escaped our attention that the same argument is generalizable to all forms of human-human, human-AI, and AI-AI interactions, as we discuss in the formal conclusions of our presented work.

Investigating User Needs for Trip Planning with Limited Availability of Automated Driving Functions

Tobias Hecht(✉) ⓘ, Maximilian Sievers, and Klaus Bengler ⓘ

Chair of Ergonomics, Technical University of Munich, Boltzmannstr. 15, 85748
Garching, Germany
t.hecht@tum.de

Abstract. The possibility to engage in so-called non-driving related activities (NDRAs) is an important benefit of automated driving. However, in the beginning, automated driving functions will be limited to certain sections of a drive, e.g., to highways or less complex city infrastructure. In order to efficiently engage in NDRAs, planning of a trip with regard to the availability of automated driving will become important. Yet, there are no approaches to incorporate the user in the trip planning process. Thus, we have performed scenario-based design approach and a participatory design workshop to derive user require-ments for a trip planning human-machine interface (HMI). Amongst others, participants required having the ability to configure general travel profiles, e.g., on-time arrival or maximization of uninterrupted automated driving time. Moreover, the system should provide the user with a comparison of key data on various route options, such as an overview of available levels of driving automation and arrival times. Within this work, a low-fidelity prototype for such an HMI was developed based on derived requirements. For future development, this prototype needs further improvement and evaluation.

Keywords: Automated driving · Non-driving related activities · Human-machine interface

1 Motivation

The introduction of SAE International Levels of Automation (LoAs) 3 and 4 will allow users in the near future to legally engage in non-driving related activities (NDRAs) [1]. The engagement in NDRAs has been shown to be the second most important advantage for future users of automated driving cars [2]. Furthermore, activity engagement can influence the rating of a trip [3] and the acceptance of an automated driving function [4]. Numerous studies have already researched desired activities. Popular activities are watching videos, reading books/newspapers/magazines, as well as using smartphones [5, 6]. Upon introduction, automated driving functions will only be available on certain parts of a drive, e.g., on highways or less complex city infrastructure, allowing drivers to engage in NDRAs for a limited amount of time. Yet, interrupting an activity has been shown to have negative effects [7]. Planned and uncritical requests to intervene (RtIs) are likely to occur more often than the highly researched time-critical take-over

© Springer Nature Switzerland AG 2020
C. Stephanidis and M. Antona (Eds.): HCII 2020, CCIS 1226, pp. 359–366, 2020.
https://doi.org/10.1007/978-3-030-50732-9_48

situations [8]. Thus, the users of automated driving functions can be supported in their activity planning and interruption management by displaying the remaining time until an upcoming RtI or an overview of the trip and its automated driving parts. This can be done by using map-based information on infrastructure and car-2-x communication. Researchers have already proven advantages of such predictive HMI elements for the users' acceptance [9], the usability evaluation [9], and with regard to the NDRA engagement [10]. Furthermore, aspects that affect the participation in NDRAs during a trip been studied [11]. Different activities were found to require different time budgets and are interruptible to varying degrees [11, 12]. Furthermore, Hecht et al. [13] have proven different preferences regarding the minimum automated driving time. Besides the research on the support of users in phases of (automated) driving, the authors are not aware of any studies focusing on user interfaces for trip planning that helps the users to determine the route best suited to their current needs. Unlike in today's navigation systems, the availability of automated driving functions will be an important factor for future trip planning. Thus, we have implemented a scenario-based design (SBD) approach and conducted a participatory design (PD) workshop with the aim of answering the following research questions:

1. What requirements do users have when it comes to determining the route best suited to their current needs (i.e., NDRA engagement)?
2. How could a human-machine interface (HMI) that addresses these user requirements look like?

The cumulative result is a low-fidelity prototype of a trip planner with special regards to needs resulting from desired activity engagement for automated driving functions with restricted availability.

2   Method

In order to shed light on this relatively unexplored topic, we have implemented a user-oriented design approach for user-friendly interactive systems (closely linked to ISO 9241-210 [14]). This iterative process includes the *description of context of use,* the *specification of user requirements,* the *developments of design solutions,* and an *evaluation phase.* Within this paper, only the first three steps will be described, but further need for evaluation is described in the discussion section of this paper.

With this paper, we focus on an HMI solution for trip planning before starting the ride. For this work, we assume an automated driving function to be limited to certain sections of a drive. The developed HMI solution can potentially be used regardless of the exact capabilities of future automated driving systems. Furthermore, the HMI concept can be implemented in an app to plan the trip before entering the car (and thus help to adjust the starting time of a drive according to trip options), or as an integrated part of the car's navigation system, thus allowing for an interaction via the central information display (touch screen). The presented HMI solution was designed to be part of the latter.

After the description of use (see Sect. 1), user requirements must be specified. According to Rosson et al. [15], a PD workshop attended by potential users of the system is a valuable option to do so. In addition to this PD workshop, a scenario-based design approach (including personas) was implemented to help approach the topic and generate additional requirements and design ideas. Based on the requirements, a low-fidelity prototype was developed with the wireframe tool Balsamiq [16].

The PD workshop took place at the Technical University of Munich and participants were three laypersons and two usability experts from the chair of ergonomics, aged 18 to 30. The workshop started with a getting-to-know game, followed by an introductory presentation by the workshop leader. The introduction was followed by a game to further dive into the topic. The challenge of this game was to fit as many NDRAs with given durations in a trip of automated and manual driving periods. After the game, a brainstorming section was implemented. The participants were split into two groups, each assigned one persona, a fictional character. Each group received a description of their character, as well as descriptions of their typical drives. The drives included a fictional car equipped with an automated driving function limited to certain areas and (traffic) conditions. No trip planner was available. Due to changing circumstances concerning the ability to drive automated, both personas experienced difficulties while engaging in their chosen activities. Based on these scenarios, participants were asked to derive user requirements for the trip planner. After a presentation of the requirements to the other group, a dot voting was performed. The most important requirements were used by the participants to develop first ideas for HMI solutions.

3   Results

As described in the previous section, the goal of both SBD and PD workshop was to derive requirements with regard to a trip planning HMI. All demands gathered through different parts of the workshop and the SBD phase can be seen in Table 1, separated into desired user inputs and system responsibilities. In general, users wished to take part in the trip planning process, but also highlight the importance of configurable travel profiles to quickly start a trip. These profiles, e.g., for commuting or leisure, should include the users' general priorities regarding automated driving times and their tendency to accept interruptions through RtIs. Also, participants wished to state a minimum useful duration of individual automated driving segments. Moreover, user required to be supported in the choice of a route by an abstract visualization of available automated driving sections.

Based on the user requirements and HMI best practice recommendations, especially Nielsen's heuristics [17] and the Gestalt principles [15], a low-fidelity prototype was designed using the wireframe tool Balsamiq. The resolution for the wireframes was set to 1280 × 640 (as in the Volkswagen 15″ navigation system *Discover Premium* [18]). In the following, four screens of this prototype are described. These include the home screen, a screen for standard travel profile settings, a visualization of route options, and an overview of chosen trip settings.

The home screen (see Fig. 1) prominently displays favorite destinations (R4) for a currently logged-in person and the possibility to enter a new destination. Also recently travelled destinations are displayed. Introducing personal settings allows to adapt to

Table 1. Derived user requirements based on SBD and PD workshop.

User inputs: The user would like to …	System responsibilities: The system should …
R1) … configure the **general priorities for the current trip**, e.g., on-time arrival or maximization of uninterrupted automated driving sections	R7) … provide the user with a comparison of **key data on the various route options**, such as the arrival times or an overview of the available LoAs
R2) … set a **minimum continuous span of time** that a trip segment offering a certain automation level must last for it to be accounted for in the route planning process	R8) … provide the user with a **reliable prediction on the available levels** of driving automation throughout the tri
R3) … set the **uninterrupted completion** of an important NDRA as an absolute priority irrespective of the consequences on travel time	R9) … take **real-time data** into account to improve the accuracy of the predicted travel times and the available LoAs on various route options, such as data on traffic congestion, route closures or weather conditions
R4) … choose from a customizable selection of **standard destinations** with preconfigured trip priority settings	R10) … adapt its general route planning behavior to match the **user's overall, long-term preferences**
R5) … choose from a **customizable selection of standard travel priority settings** when selecting a destination	R11) … adapt its trip-specific route planning behavior to best suit the **user's current priorities,** NDRA requests as well as mental and physical state
R6) … invest **as little time as possible** in planning the trip while still finding the route that best suits their needs	R12) … proactively **warn the user** about unusual circumstances **affecting travel time or NDRA possibilities**
	R13) … always **await the user's consent before changing the route** during a trip, unless the user has given the system explicit permission to continuously optimize the route for a certain priority, such as achieving the shortest possible travel time

long-term preferences (R10) and to choose from standard travel profiles (R5). Travel profiles enable the users to invest as little time as possible in planning the trip while still finding the route that best suits their needs (R6). Through pressing the menu button, one third of the current screen is overlaid with the main menu. It includes the options to change the current user, change visualization options and check for map updates. Furthermore, new travel profiles can be created and existing profiles can be edited and deleted (R5). In the travel profile settings, users can adjust their preferences regarding interruptions and total (automated) driving time with sliders (R1; see Fig. 2). Furthermore, the minimum useful duration of individual automated driving segments can be set (R2).

After having chosen a favorite, recently travelled or new destination on the home screen, the user is forwarded to an overview of the planned trip (see Fig. 3). Based on the currently activated travel profile, the system suggests a route and displays its main characteristics (R11). Users have the option to switch to another predefined travel

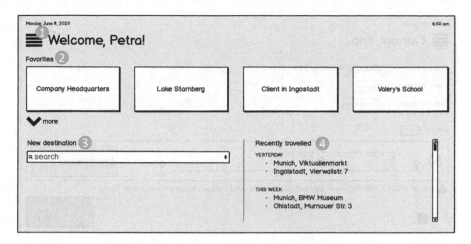

Fig. 1. Home screen with main menu (1), favorite trips (2), search box for new destinations (3), and recently travelled destinations (4).

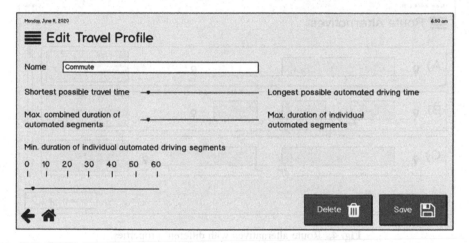

Fig. 2. Travel profile settings and editing options.

profile (R1; possibly influencing the system's route suggestions), see what other route alternatives there are, and define *do not disturb* segments through clicking on the respective automated driving section (R3). During these sections, the system will use all its options to guarantee the displayed automated driving times. *Do not disturb* sections are also highlighted in the overview. In case users want to edit the route suggested by the system, they are forwarded to an overview of different route alternatives where also available automated driving sections and key data like total trip duration, as well as manual and automated driving time are visualized (R7, see Fig. 4). There is also the option to switch to a map-based overview (as known from e.g., Google Maps).

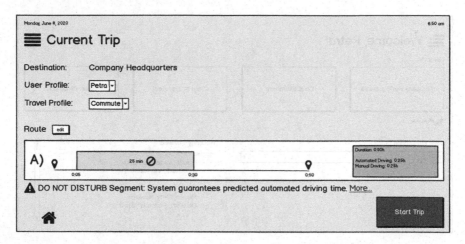

Fig. 3. Current trip overview with *do not disturb* segment.

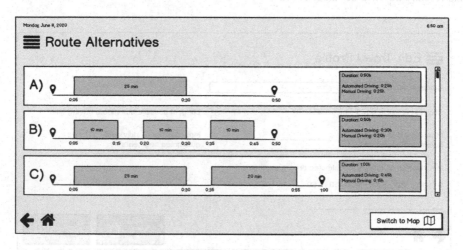

Fig. 4. Route alternatives with different properties.

4   Discussion and Future Work

This work aims at the development of an HMI for trip planning with a SAE Level 3 or Level 4 automated driving function that is limited to certain sections of a route. In order to derive requirements for such an HMI, an SBD approach and a PD workshop were implemented and a low-fidelity prototype developed. Derived user requirements highlight the importance of being able to adjust personal preferences by defining travel profiles and thus easily influence the system's route suggestions according to the current user specific needs. Users would like to invest as little time as possible while still finding the route best suited to their current needs. Based on these requirements, a low-fidelity prototype was developed. According to ISO 9241-210 [14], the prototype must now be evaluated by a larger sample of future users regarding acceptance and usability. This can be achieved by applying typical user-centered software development tools and processes. Based on this future evaluation, a further, more advanced prototype will be developed.

However, challenges for the implementation of the developed HMI (and the underlying idea) can be found in the uncertainty of future automated driving functions. Up to now, exact abilities to drive automated and system limits (and their predictability) are unclear. Maybe, the trip planner would have to be expanded with a certainty symbol (for automated driving durations). Furthermore, the abilities of the respective automated driving functions most likely influence the developed trip planner's usefulness. A system with a very limited availability probably benefits more from detailed route planning than one that is already more sophisticated. Moreover, Level 2 has not been integrated in this early stage prototype but should be in the future.

In conclusion, the potential of a trip planner needs to be (re)evaluated once Level 3 or 4 driving automation has advanced to the point that it is legally available on the market. Until then, a more sophisticated prototype should be developed to further assess acceptance of the concept and improve the system's usability.

References

1. SAE International: J3016. Taxonomy and Definitions for Terms Related to Driving Automation Systems for On-Road Motor Vehicles (2018)
2. König, M., Neumayr, L.: Users' resistance towards radical innovations. The case of the self-driving car. Transp. Res. Part F Traff. Psychol. Behav. (2017). https://doi.org/10.1016/j.trf.2016.10.013
3. Susilo, Y., Lyons, G., Jain, J., Atkins, S.: Rail passengers' time use and utility assessment. Transp. Res. Rec. (2013). https://doi.org/10.3141/2323-12
4. Naujoks, F., Wiedemann, K., Schoemig, N.: The importance of interruption management for usefulness and acceptance of automated driving. In: Proceedings of the 9th International Conference on Automotive User Interfaces and Interactive Vehicular Applications, Oldenburg, Germany (2017). https://doi.org/10.1145/3122986.3123000
5. Pfleging, B., Rang, M., Broy, N.: Investigating user needs for non-driving-related activities during automated driving. In: Alt, F. (ed.) Proceedings of the 15th International Conference on Mobile and Ubiquitous Multimedia (MUM). International Conference on Mobile and Ubiquitous Multimedia (MUM), Rovaniemi, Finland, 12–15 December 2016, pp. 91–99. The Association for Computing Machinery, Inc, New York (2016). https://doi.org/10.1145/3012709.3012735
6. Hecht, T., Feldhütter, A., Draeger, K., Bengler, K.: What do you do? An analysis of non-driving related activities during a 60 minutes conditionally automated highway drive. In: Ahram, T., Taiar, R., Colson, S., Choplin, A. (eds.) Human Interaction and Emerging Technologies. Proceedings of the 1st International Conference on Human Interaction and Emerging Technologies (IHIET 2019). Human Interaction and Emerging Technologies (IHIET 2019), Nice, 22–24 August 2019, pp. 28–34. Springer, Cham (2020). https://doi.org/10.1007/978-3-030-25629-6_5
7. Janssen, C.P., Iqbal, S.T., Kun, A.L., Donker, S.F.: Interrupted by my car? Implications of interruption and interleaving research for automated vehicles. Int. J. Hum Comput Stud. (2019). https://doi.org/10.1016/j.ijhcs.2019.07.004

8. Holländer, K., Pfleging, B.: Preparing drivers for planned control transitions in automated cars. In: Abdennadher, S., Alt, F. (eds.) MUM 2018. 17th International Conference on Mobile and Ubiquitous Multimedia. Proceedings, Cairo, Egypt, 25–28 November 2018. The 17th International Conference, Cairo, Egypt, 25–28 November 2018, pp. 83–92. The Association for Computing Machinery, Inc., New York (2018). https://doi.org/10.1145/3282894.3282928

9. Richardson, N.T., Flohr, L., Michel, B.: Takeover requests in highly automated truck driving. How do the amount and type of additional information influence the driver–automation interaction? MTI (2018). https://doi.org/10.3390/mti2040068

10. Wandtner, B., Schömig, N., Schmidt, G.: Secondary task engagement and disengagement in the context of highly automated driving. Transp. Res. Part F Traff. Psychol. Behav. (2018). https://doi.org/10.1016/j.trf.2018.06.001

11. Hecht, T., Darlagiannis, E., Bengler, K.: Non-driving related activities in automated driving – an online survey investigating user needs. In: Ahram, T., Karwowski, W., Pickl, S., Taiar, R. (eds.) IHSED 2019. AISC, vol. 1026, pp. 182–188. Springer, Cham (2020). https://doi.org/10.1007/978-3-030-27928-8_28

12. Naujoks, F., Purucker, C., Neukum, A.: Secondary task engagement and vehicle automation – comparing the effects of different automation levels in an on-road experiment. Transp. Res. Part F Traff. Psychol. Behav. (2016). https://doi.org/10.1016/j.trf.2016.01.011

13. Hecht, T., Kratzert, S., Bengler, K.: The effects of a predictive HMI and different transition frequencies on acceptance, workload, usability, and gaze behavior during urban automated driving. Information (2020). https://doi.org/10.3390/info11020073

14. DIN Deutsches Institut für Normung e.V.: Ergonomics of human-system interaction - Part 210: Human-centred design for interactive systems (DIN EN ISO 9241-210) (2010)

15. Rosson, M.B., Carroll, J.M., Hill, N.: Usability Engineering. Scenario-Based Development of Human-Computer Interaction. Morgan Kaufmann, San Francisco (2002)

16. Balsamiq Wireframes Home. Balsamiq Studios, LLC (2020)

17. Nielsen, J., Molich, R.: Heuristic evaluation of user interfaces. In: Chew, J.C., Carrasco, J.C., Carrasco Chew, J. (eds.) Empowering People. CHI '90 Conference Proceedings. The SIGCHI Conference, Seattle, Washington, United States, 1–5 Apr 1990, pp. 249–256. Addison-Wesley, Reading (1992). https://doi.org/10.1145/97243.97281

18. Volkswagen: Discover Premium (2020). https://webspecial.volkswagen.de/vwinfotainment/de/de/index/infotainment-systeme#/?detail=0e6ebf85-4c68-4218-82ad-a64eadf8e3c4. Accessed 18 Mar 2020

Calculation and Validation of Driver's Readiness for Regaining Control from Autonomous Driving

Woojin Kim$^{(\boxtimes)}$ ⓘ, Hyun Suk Kim ⓘ, Seung-Jun Lee ⓘ, and Daesub Yoon ⓘ

Electronics and Telecommunications Research Institute, 218 Gajeong-ro, Daejeon 34129, Korea
wjinkim@etri.re.kr

Abstract. In level 3 automated driving, if the vehicle fails to drive automatically or the operational design domain (ODD) ends, the human driver must control the vehicle i.e., be a fallback-ready user. So far, human drivers have had little experience of taking over vehicle control during driving and there is a lack of research on how they react in this situation. Consequently, there has been a research need to know how much the driver is ready to take-over the control authority, in order to predict and compensate the risk of the transition to manual driving from the out of the control loop. In this paper, we propose the concept of the driver's readiness (DR). To calculate the DR, we propose to use various human factors, such as workload, situation awareness, attention, activeness and so on. In order to validate our proposed algorithm, the heuristic experiments have been performed. We have drawn our real-time DR calculation algorithm and validated with subjective observations from 30 participants. The results of regression analysis show that the subjective observations and DR calculations have linear relationships.

Keywords: Automated driving · Transition of control · Human factors · Heuristic experiments · Driver monitoring systems · Time budget · Driver's readiness

1 Introduction

The driver's role in the automatic driving system depends on the automatic driving phase. In Society of Automotive Engineering (SAE) J3016, the level of automated driving has been changed from manual driving (level 0) to total driving automation (level 5). The driver's role is highlighted from level 0 to level 3, and above level 4, the driver's involvement is removed [1]. Therefore, level 3 is conditional automation and the route to the destination consists of stages where the driver operates manually and stages where the automatic driving system (ADS) automatically operates.

The operation of the manual driving stage is performed by the driver, while that of the automatic operation stage is performed by the ADS installed in the vehicle. If the automatic driving stage is completed, or if it is difficult to be driven by ADS, the driver should take over the control of the driving.

© Springer Nature Switzerland AG 2020
C. Stephanidis and M. Antona (Eds.): HCII 2020, CCIS 1226, pp. 367–373, 2020.
https://doi.org/10.1007/978-3-030-50732-9_49

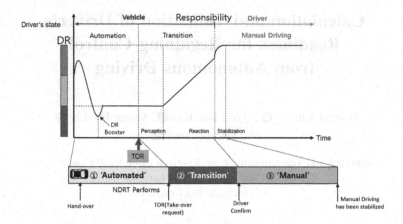

Fig. 1. Concept of control transition from automated driving to manual driving [5]

The scope of this paper is focused on the SAE Level 3. If there is insufficient operational information or automated driving is not available anymore during automated operation at SAE Level 3, the automated driving system must provide the driver with an alarming message, as known as take-over request (TOR). When the driver percepts the TOR message, he or she should react to regain the vehicle control authority from the ADS [2–4].

In order to evaluate and more likely predict the take-over performance, we need to know how much the driver is ready to take-over the control authority. We call this driver's readiness (DR) and this metric is applicable to manage the risk of the transition to manual driving and prevent driving from out-of-control. Figure 1 shows the control transition process and corresponding DR progress.

When regaining control from automated to manual, DR is an index which indicates how much the driver is ready for driving as follows:

- DR is quantization of continuous value 0–1, where
  - low (0–0.3): hard to regain control
  - medium (0.3–0.7): can regain control with some additional effort, and
  - high (0.7–1): can regain control with few additional effort.
- DR can be calculated in real-time manner.
- The representative DR of the control transition will be decided by estimating DR at the moment of take-over request (TOR).

To calculate the DR, we propose to use various human factors, such as workload, situation awareness, attention, activeness and so on. Those factors can be obtained by sensors and questionnaires directly and indirectly.

In order to validate our proposed algorithm, the heuristic experiments have been performed. We have drawn our real-time DR calculation algorithm and validated with subjective observations from 30 participants. The results show that subjective observations and DR calculation have linear relationships with p-value under 0.01.

The rest of this paper is organized as follows: in Sect. 2, the related human factors are introduced. The proposed algorithm is addressed in Sect. 3 and the heuristic experiments and their results are described in Sect. 4. Then the conclusion follows in Sect. 5.

2 Human Factors for DR

In this work, we have organized the main parameters of the readiness into four categories as shown in Fig. 2.

Each category is driver characteristics, mental parameters, physical parameters, and environmental parameters. In our driving readiness algorithm, which will be described in the next section, we have tried to apply the human factors in the above four categories evenly.

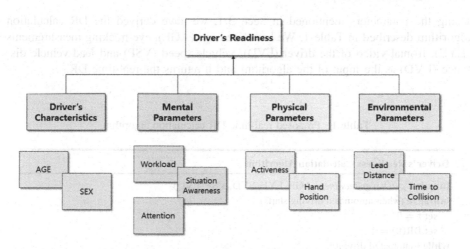

Fig. 2. Categories of human factors related to DR

3 DR Calculation

3.1 Parameters for DR Calculation

For the driver's characteristics, we have considered the age of the drivers. For the mental parameters, we have introduced the predicted response time (PRT) by adopting a cognitive framework. In order to calculate PRT, auditory notification time, visual attention shifting time, perception time of driving situation, and decision making time has been included in order. Each cognitive response time can be obtained by eye-tracking measurements. Attention (ATT) has also been used as an important parameter, which indicates whether the driver look forward or not and can be obtained from eye-tracking measurements.

For the physical parameters, we have introduced the predicted reaction time (PAT) by adopting the activeness of the driver. The activeness has binary states of *active* and *inactive*, where active state indicates the existence of driver's movement while inactive state indicates low movement level. Since moderate movement makes the driver's next movement more explosive, it is strongly related to the driver's reaction to the TOR. The activeness can be obtained from the frontal camera of the driver.

Finally, since there is a difference in the ability to regain the control depending on the surrounding driving situation, the environmental parameter is considered for calculating DR. In this work, we have adopted time-to-collision (TTC) as the environmental parameter. If TTC is larger than the sum of PRT and PAT, the surrounding situation does not affect DR, however, else DR should be lowered to raise an alarm to the driver. TTC can be estimated by using the relative speed of the vehicle and distance to the lead vehicle.

3.2 Algorithm Description

Using the parameters mentioned in Sect. 3.1, we have derived the DR calculation algorithm described in Table 1. We have used age (AGE), eye-tracking measurements (EYE), frontal video of the driver (FVD), vehicle speed (VSP) and lead-vehicle distance (LVD) as the input of the algorithm and it returns the real-time DR.

Table 1. Proposed real-time DR calculation algorithm

Driver's Readiness Calculation Algorithm
function *getDriverReadiness*(AGE, EYE, FVD, VSP, LVD)
initialize (when automated driving starts)
set t = 0
set DR(0) = 1
while (automated driving)
get AGE, EYE, FVD, VSP, LVD (from the monitoring system)
compute a = a(AGE)
compute a' = a'(AGE)
compute PRT = PRT(EYE)
compute ATT = ATT(EYE)
compute PAT = PAT(FVD)
compute TTC = TTC(VSP, LVD)
compute as
if (TTC − (PRT + PAT) > threshold)
$d = 1 - \frac{\epsilon}{e^{-a'(PRT+PAT)}}$
else
d = 0
end
if (ATT == 1)
Compute $DR(t + T) = 1 - e^{-a'T} + DR(t)e^{-a'T}$
else
Compute $DR(t + T) = DR(t)e^{-aT} + d(1 - e^{-aT})$
end
update t ← t + T
end

4   DR Validation

4.1   Heuristic Experiments

Setup for an Experimental Environment. In order to analyze human factors in Level 3 automated driving, we have collected various kinds of measurements categorized to *Driver*, *Vehicle* and *Environment* (DVE). To obtain the DVE measurements relevant to control transition of a vehicle from ADS, we have constructed a driving simulator as shown in Fig. 3. The simulator provides vehicular information such as speed and environmental information like lead-vehicle distance. The eye-related are measured by the eye-tracker. There are also the motion sensors and physiological sensors which are used to measure the driver's behaviors and internal status. The provisions with the visual and auditory channels are performed by the tablet deployed on the center fascia, while the provisions with the haptic channel are performed by the vibration motor installed under the driving seat.

In order to validate the DR calculation algorithm, 30 participants have been recruited and three sessions of the control regaining have been performed for each participant. Both the objective measurements (from sensors) and subjective measurements (from questionnaires) have been collected.

Experimental Procedure. Before the experiment starts, the participant performs pre-questionnaires. The experiment starts with a 3 min' autopilot with non-driving related tasks (NDRTs) [6] and information provision until the vehicle gives TOR. The participant recognizes the TOR sign and then he or she begins with manual driving by pushing a transition button. After sufficient manual driving, the simulator stops driving. During the driving, all the measurements are collected and saved in the server. After the experiment ends, the participant performs post-questionnaires such as NASA-TLX [7].

While the experiments are designed to be focused on the internal factors such as *Driver* and *Vehicle* and the external factors, *i.e. Environment*, such as unexpected events after transition of control and the road condition such as curvature.

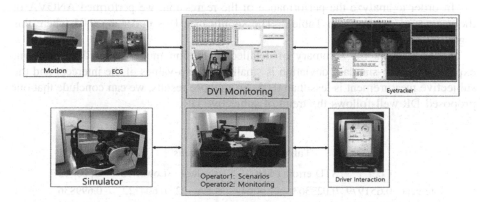

Fig. 3. Setup for the heuristic experiments

4.2   Results

In order to validate the correspondence of our proposed algorithm with participants' subjective questionnaires, we have performed the regression analysis. Figure 4 shows the calibrated fitting results of the regression. The blue dots indicate the heuristic experimental data and the red ones the predicted values from the regression model with R-squared value is 0.465.

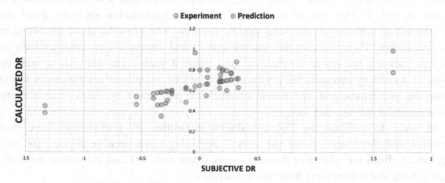

Fig. 4. The calibrated fit plot of the calculated DR with respect to the subjective questionnaires (Color figure online)

Table 2. ANOVA of the regression

	df	SS	MS	F	Significance F
Regression	1	0.255885	0.255885	15.62667	**0.000477**
Residual	28	0.458497	0.016375		
Total	29	0.714383			

In order to analyze the performance of the regression, we performed ANOVA of the regression as shown in Table 2. The significance F is under the 0.05 where this regression model is usable.

Table 3 shows the summary of detailed regression model using data from our experiments. The standard deviation is small and the p-values of the intercept and the subjective measurement is less than 0.05. From those results, we can conclude that our proposed DR well-follows the trend of subjective DR.

Table 3. Regression results

	Coef	STD error	t Stat	p-values	Lower 95%	Upper 95%
Intercept	0.651979	0.023363	27.90647	**5.59e−22**	0.604122	0.699836
DR_Calc	0.200433	0.050703	3.953058	**0.000477**	0.096572	0.304294

5 Conclusions

In order to evaluate and predict the take-over performance, we have defined and proposed to use the metric driver's readiness (DR). Especially in this work, the DR calculation algorithm and its validation have been presented. Human factors are adopted as the main parameters of the DR and the heuristic experiments are designed and performed to evaluate the consistency of our proposed algorithm.

Statistical regression analysis has been performed with experimental data (the objectively calculated DR and the subjectively surveyed DR) and the results support that our proposed DR well-follows the trend of subjective DR.

Acknowledgement.   This research was supported by a grant (20TLRP-B131486-04) from Transportation and Logistics R&D Program funded by Ministry of Land, Infrastructure and Transport of Korean government.

References

1. Taxonomy and definition for terms related to on-road motor vehicle automated driving systems in SAE J3016 (2014). revised in 2016
2. Kim, H., Kim, W., Kim, J., Lee, S., Yoon, D.: Design of driver readiness evaluation system in automated driving environment. In: ICTC 2018 (2018)
3. Kim, W., Kim, H., Lee, S., Kim, J., Yoon, D.: Sensor selection frameworks for practical DSM in level 3 automated vehicles. In: ICTC 2018 (2018)
4. Kim, J., Kim, H., Kim, W., Yoon, D.: Take-over performance analysis depending on the drivers' non-driving secondary tasks in automated vehicles. In: ICTC 2018 (2018)
5. Kim, J., Kim, W., Kim, H., Yoon, D.: Effectiveness of subjective measurement of drivers' status in automated driving. In: VTC 2018 (2018)
6. Kim, H., Kim, W., Kim, J., Lee, S., Yoon, D.: An analysis of transition characteristics of driver control authority according to NDRT type. FAST-zero 19 (2019)
7. Hart, S., Staveland, L.:: Development of NASA-TLX (Task Load Index): results of empirical and theoretical research. In: Advances in Psychology, vol. 52, pp. 139–183. North-Holland (1988)
8. Kim, H., Kim, W., Kim, J., Yoon, D.: A study on the control authority transition characteristics by driver information. In: CSCI-ISSC 2019 (2019)
9. Kim, H., Kim, W., Kim, J., Lee, S., Yoon, D.: A study on the effects of providing situation awareness information for the control authority transition of automated vehicle. In: ICTC 2019 (2019)
10. Kim, W., Kim, J., Kim, H., Lee, S., Yoon, D.: A study on the driver's response performance according to modality of planned TOR in automated driving. In: ICTC 2019 (2019)

Requirements for an Autonomous Taxi and a Resulting Interior Concept

Manuel Kipp[1]([✉]), Ingrid Bubb[1], Johannes Schwiebacher[1],
Ferdinand Schockenhoff[2], Adrian Koenig[2], and Klaus Bengler[1]

[1] Institute of Ergonomics, Technical University of Munich,
Boltzmannstr. 15, 85748 Garching b. München, Germany
{manuel.kipp, i.bubb, johannes.schwiebacher,
bengler}@tum.de
[2] Institute of Automotive Technology, Technical University of Munich,
Boltzmannstr. 15, 85748 Garching b. München, Germany
{schockenhoff, adrian.koenig}@ftm.mw.tum.de

Abstract. Due to a variety of possible activities, which passengers are able to follow in a self-driving vehicle, we are convinced that the flexibility of mobility as a service allows offering different theme-taxis. Within the project UNI-CARagil (founded by the Federal Ministry of Education and Research of Germany), we develop a concept for theme taxis. Since the aspired vehicle concept regarded in the project opts for an optimal interior-space, a taxi for work purpose is suggested.

In this paper, we present the requirements for the fully automated driverless taxi and a resulting interior concept. The focus of the requirement specification are the fundamental needs of the passengers to safely enter and leave the vehicle and the possibilities to use time during a ride efficiently. Another main aspect of the requirements is the well-being of the passengers during their entire stay in the vehicle.

Keywords: Autonomous taxi · Interior concept · User requirements

1 Introduction

Autonomous electric vehicles will play a key role in coping with increasing mobility requirements and advancing urbanization. Following a user centered approach in order to meet the needs of the users of self-driving vehicles, new concepts for the development of modular architectures for fully automated and driverless vehicle concepts are being introduced as part of the UNICARagil project.

UNICARagil, funded by the Federal Ministry of Education and Research of Germany (BMBF), is a project with eight German universities and six industrial partners that deals with new challenges of mobility [1].

The above-mentioned challenges include autonomous driving, connected vehicles, shared mobility and electrification of vehicles. The research focus of the project is on automation, safety, security, verification & validation and modularization [1]. Dynamic

C. Stephanidis and M. Antona (Eds.): HCII 2020, CCIS 1226, pp. 374–381, 2020.
https://doi.org/10.1007/978-3-030-50732-9_50

modules are used in the vehicles being built as part of the project, which can be steered up to 90°. Those modules should enable a high agility and permit new manoeuvers.

Further, within the scope of the project UNICARagil, we will have two different vehicle sizes in which we will demonstrate four different fundamental use cases. Therefore, we develop a modular, scalable vehicle platform with matching car body. Only the interior changes according to the different use case. For the small vehicle platform, we consider an "autoTAXI" that can be ordered on demand as well as used as ride sharing and an "autoELF" which demonstrate a car for private use. The large vehicles demonstrate an "autoSHUTTLE" which can be used as an addition to public transport and an "autoCARGO" as a delivery vehicle.

The Technical University of Munich (TUM) is responsible for the body and interior of the autoTAXI. As part of the development process, we are focusing on a door concept and interior design including the necessary human machine interfaces (HMI), which will hopefully increase passenger comfort.

2 Requirements for an Autonomous Taxi

Herzberger et al. [2] asked for expectations and needs of the user for the different use cases in the project UNICARagil. They found that persons expect to do tasks such as reading, relaxing, using the mobile phone, working, doing sightseeing or sleep which accord to other authors opinion [2–4]. Considering these different user needs, we find that the introduction of theme-taxis in the future is a solution for these diverse requirements. As a result, within the project we put our focus on an interior, which enables the passenger to work while driving. Important for us is the possibility to store documents, a computer or a tablet and two comfortable, full seats.

Diels et al. [5] define a conceptual framework for the passenger experience in driving a highly automated vehicle. According to this framework, we try to outline rough requirements for the entry, interior package as well as for the human machine interface.

2.1 Geometric Considerations

Considering that only 1–3 persons drive normally with a taxi as well as studies, which prove that motion sickness is less if sitting in the direction of travel, our preferred direction of seat is in the way of the route [6, 7]. Additionally, a good field of view can reduce motion sickness, therefor this will be an another requirement to achieve [8]. As Diels et al. [5] state one mayor factor for the experience of comfort in an automated vehicle is the usability of the automobile. In their definition, this includes among other aspects accessibility and ease of use.

According to this, one of our requirements is to ensure an easy way to ingress and egress. In typical light vehicles, people usually have to adopt extreme positions in order to place themselves in the vehicle [9], so we define as one requirement that upright entry/exit positions are possible in our vehicle concept comparable. Additionally, grips should support person to enter and get of the car.

One crucial factor is the sill height to ingress and egress. Within the UNICARagil project, we integrate the energy systems (battery) into the platform floor. This influences the sill height, which immediately affects the way to enter the car. Further, the interior concept effect the way to ingress or egress the car as well. To fulfil our requirement of an upright access, we define that during the ingress and egress our roof height should be at least 1800 mm, With the digital human model (DHM) RAMSIS™ we investigate, how this roof height affect different entry positions of large persons, i.e. the 95th percentile.

Two different sizes of vehicle should be possible by the modular approach of the project UNICARagil [1], therefore we have first external restrictions of the interior dimension in length and width. To achieve still a good sitting position with a good field of view and less interferences with other passengers, we define that the sitting height should be comparable to a chair or couch height (H30 $\sim$ 400 mm) and adjustable for different anthropometric sizes. To ensure tasks such as reading and working are possible, the chairs should include armrest as well as tables adaptable to user needs. As Yang et al. [10] report persons engage different posture for different non-driving-related-tasks. So at least two different posture should be possible with suggested seats. Wasser et al. [11] state, that the user need to have control and autonomy over the interior space. Therefore, within our interior concept, we will try to develop a concept that is easy adaptable to different user needs. This includes next to flexible positioning of the seats, different possibilities to store luggage.

Regarding described premises, we can define the geometric boundaries of the interior more precisely. Therefore, we work with RAMSIS™ to define critical dimensions as for example the height of the interior including sitting persons of different anthropometric typologies. Here the leg length of the very tall man with the 95th percentile is decisive for the interpretation of the length of the interior and that of the very small woman with the 5th percentile for the seat height. Further, we use the DHM RAMSIS™ to consider different possible sitting position within the vehicle platform.

2.2   Requirements for the Human-Machine-Interfaces (HMI)

Diels et al. [5] describe *"peace of mind"* as major factor for the experience of comfort in an autonomous vehicle. They think the *peace of mind* can be influenced by the use of different HMI systems. Wasser et al. [11] term different functions an HMI for autonomous cars should support at least such as booking, access system, ride information and route control. This accords to König [12] who thinks feedback of vehicle behaviour in general is necessary for the passengers. Next to this, there is still a need for known functions such as climate control and interior lighting.

2.3   Thermal Comfort Requirements

Thermal comfort is an important requirement for the well-being of the occupants and should be considered. The term thermal comfort is described in the DIN EN ISO 7730 which refers to the sensation of mind compared to the current thermal environment [13]. Various human factors such as physical activity, metabolic rate, clothing, gender and age as well as environmental parameters such as temperature, humidity, airflow and radiation influence the thermal sensation.

Particularly against the background of electromobility and autonomous driving, the focus is on new air conditioning concepts that show new possible dynamics, be efficient and meet the requirements of future vehicles with a novel interior design.

3 The Concept of the Interior Results from the Presented Requirements

Considering that the door, the interior as well as the HMI concept influence each other, we develop the overall concept iteratively. In this paper, we want to present the current state in our development process.

3.1 Interior Topology

We think the user will order the taxi depending on their needs and therefore ask for different theme-taxis. In the project, we want to demonstrate how the interior of the taxi can be designed. In order to meet described requirements, the UNICARagil project selects a 2 + 2 seater with a vis-à-vis arrangement for the taxi. Our focus is on two main seats in the direction of the vehicles route. Occupants can adopt different postures for different activities at these seats. The seats are adjustable around the range of 400 mm for different anthropometric sizes and include armrest adjustable as well according to anthropometric requirements. Tables for work are mounted in the armrests as folding tables. Stowed away, they do not present a barrier during the boarding process.

If necessary, four people can use the vehicle in this arrangement. The additional two people sit in the opposite to the travel direction and their seats offer no functions to enable work. These seats are foldable seats, so that when not in use this space can be utilized freely, e.g. for luggage. A symmetrical seat shell design makes it possible to change the seating arrangement of the main seats and folding seats in relation to the direction of travel so that a flexible interior concept can be implemented.

In this project, a new concept of the cabin's air conditioning is considered which aims the improvement of thermal comfort combined with reduced energy consumption.

Local and global thermal comfort phenomena are manifold and still subject to ongoing research in the future. At the institute of ergonomics (LfE) studies were conducted that evaluate the influence of local conditioning on the overall comfort to evaluate an overhead air conditioning concept [14]. It was shown, that local thermal sensation in one body part could have a significant impact on the global thermal comfort. The strongest effect for cooling was noted at the head and upper body while the extremities are preferred for heating. Every passenger inside the taxi has to be able to have climate conditions that meet his/her expectations of a comfortable thermal environment. To achieve this, the autonomous taxi has to be divided into four zones with an overhead system for each passenger. The requirement is that the user can set a target interior temperature between 18 and 24 °C. In addition to the HVAC-system, a surface heating system is to be integrated into the vehicle floor to warm up the leg area.

3.2   Door Concept

The most important requirements for the door kinematics are to open and close automatically, to swing up as little as possible, to take up as little packaging space as possible and to be able to open manually in an emergency. Considering different known door kinematics (such as swivel door, scissor door, wing doors, sliding door etc.) none fulfil these requirements completely. The consideration of pros and cons of the different kinematic principles leads to a combination of the swing and sliding kinematics for the taxi in the UNICARagil project. A two-part swing-slide door combines the advantages of the two principles with a slight increase in weight. The doors should first swing outwards through a 4-joint in order to reach the final position via rails on the door side. The total door opening width of 1500 mm is achieved from two door sides, each 750 mm wide.

As described, we require for the ingress and egress a high clearance height of the interior. However, this is in direct contradiction to other design criteria, such as the appearance or the drag coefficient. The interior height of the taxi in UNICARagil is therefore 1450 mm (defined by the head clearance of large sitting persons). However, this does not allow an upright front entry and exit with a purely lateral door opening. For this reason, an opening of a part of the roof in a lifting movement is part of the overall concept of the doors. In the width of the doors and with a third of the roof width, the roof on both sides of the vehicle is lifted by 400 mm. The resulting weakening of the torsional stiffness of the body structure and the load paths over the body structure is absorbed by two constructive ideas. On the one hand, the central beam of the structure in the roof is designed to be very torsional stiff over a wide shear area, and on the other hand, the roof closes the body structure in the closed state, with the roof opening structure complementing the body structure by means of a locking system.

3.3   Interior HMI

According to the different user needs, we develop first ideas of interfaces considering two information perspectives: direct and mobile.

The central display is a screen that has about 10 in. diagonal, mounted close to the seat individually for each main seat. Here the passengers can control functions of the vehicle interior, such as lighting or climate. Furthermore, passengers can use onboard entertainment functions (e.g. Radio or newspaper) or an interactive map to inform about nearby sights or other POIs (e.g. ATM) during their trip. The mobile interface is an application for a private mobile device that is used primarily for organizing the journey, such as calling the taxi or making payments. The private smartphone can also be used to identify a passenger for boarding via an app.

4   Discussion and Outlook

The concept ideas presented in this article are based only on the results of various expert workshops and literature. However, in order to be able to assess the passenger comfort and to detail the proposed concepts, users are required to evaluate these rough concepts [15]. The aim is to evaluate the concept of the autoTAXI at different levels.

First, we will test virtual results with a mock-up that is currently being set up. Augmented reality (AR) is used to offer the opportunity to complement the physical mock-ups with virtual designs. By using AR, we want to evaluate concept ideas for the interior and to check anthropometric packaging considerations. In addition, questions such as the good placement of necessary handholds or placement of luggage should be answered with this mock-up. Still, several questions especially concerning the HMI design are not answered jet and need further investigations. It is important to know the applicability of HMI in the interior and the access conditions of autoTAXI.

When the real vehicle is assembled, further physical tests with a user group are performed to compare the results with the mock-up. As people no longer drive the vehicle independently, but act as passengers, the role of the user changes. Due to the vis-à-vis seating arrangement and the different trajectories of the vehicle, the user experience has to be evaluate for the driving experience and motion sickness. In addition, we need to evaluate the user experience in terms of interior and entry requirements, the use of HMI as well as to answer the question of whether this taxi concept is comfortable and applicable for the passenger.

Since the financial resources of the project are limited, not all concept ideas will be integrated in the driving prototype. Therefore, these constraints must be taken into account in the development as well as evaluation process. For example, as one crucial factor we will not be able to develop a car seat according to our requirements. Nevertheless, even this limited prototype offers the possibility to evaluate the user experience and to develop requirements for the interior development process of autonomous vehicles according to the results.

5 Conclusion

As in this paper discussed, we demonstrate first requirements and concept ideas for an autonomous taxi. Within the project UNICARagil, we will develop a theme-taxi designed for work purpose with a 2 + 2 seater vis-à-vis concept. Through different interfaces, user will achieve different information and control functions of the vehicle interior. We introduce a door concept in which passenger can ingress and egress in upright positions. Nevertheless, all these ideas are on virtual basis and depending on the development process of the UNICARagil project.

Further investigation to the user needs and experience have to be performed. An evaluation of the described concept ideas with a user group is needed.

In order to evaluate these first virtual results, a mock-up of the taxi is set up. This will be used to test not only the concept ideas for the interior, but also the entry for the vehicle. The mock-up can also be used to investigate the experience and benefits of the interior and access concept. To answer the question how the trajectories of the vehicle and the 2 + 2 seater vis-à-vis concept influence the perception of comfort and driving experience, we would like to conduct tests on the real vehicle. In conclusion, Fig. 1 tries to illustrate the current status as well as the further steps still need to be done.

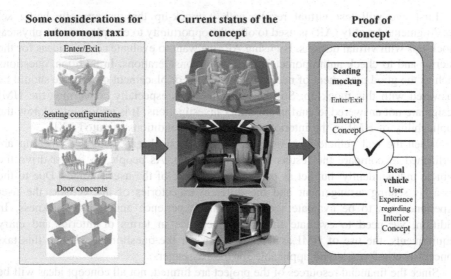

Fig. 1. Summary of the current status in the development process of the autoTAXI.

Acknowledgments. This research is accomplished within the project "UNICARagil" (FKZ EM2ADIS002). We acknowledge the financial support for the project by the Federal Ministry of Education and Research of Germany (BMBF).

References

1. Woopen, T., et al.: UNICARagil - Disruptive modulare Architektur für agile, automatisierte Fahrzeugkonzepte. RWTH Aachen University, Aachen (2018)
2. Herzberger, N., Schwalm, M., Reske, M., Woopen, T., Eckstein, L.: Mobilitätskonzepte der Zukunft - Ergebnisse einer Befragung von 619 Personen in Deutschland im Rahmen des Projekts UNICARagil. RWTH Aachen University (2019)
3. Becker, T., Hermann, F., Duwe, D., Stegmüller, S., Röckle, F., Unger, N.: Enabling the Value of Time. Implications for the interior design of autonomous vehicles. https://www. muse.iao.fraunhofer.de/content/dam/iao/muse/de/documents/projekte/180611_EVoT_ study_report_EN_final.pdf
4. Pfleging, B., Rang, M., Broy, N.: Investigating user needs for non-driving-related activities during automated driving. In: Häkkila, J., Ojala, T. (eds.) The 15th International Conference, pp. 91–99 (2016)
5. Diels, C., et al.: Designing for comfort in shared and automated vehicles (SAV): a conceptual framework (2017)
6. Bohrmann, D.: Probandenstudie - Vom Fahrer zum Passagier. ATZ Extra **24**, 36–39 (2019)
7. Lokhandwala, M., Cai, H.: Dynamic ride sharing using traditional taxis and shared autonomous taxi. A case study of NYC. Transp. Res. Part C Emerg. Technol. **97**, 45–60 (2018)
8. Turner, M., Griffin, M.J.: Motion sickness in public road transport. The relative importance of motion, vision and individual differences. Br. J. Psychol. **90**, 519–530 (1999)

9. Lu, J.-M., Tada, M., Endo, Y., Mochimaru, M.: Ingress and egress motion strategies of elderly and young passengers for the rear seat of minivans with sliding doors. Appl. Ergon. 53(Pt A), 228–240 (2016)

10. Yang, Y., Klinkner, J.N., Bengler, K.: How will the driver sit in an automated vehicle? – the qualitative and quantitative descriptions of non-driving postures (NDPs) when non-driving-related-tasks (NDRTs) are conducted. In: Bagnara, S., Tartaglia, R., Albolino, S., Alexander, T., Fujita, Y. (eds.) IEA 2018. AISC, vol. 823, pp. 409–420. Springer, Cham (2019). https://doi.org/10.1007/978-3-319-96074-6_44

11. Wasser, J., Diels, C., Baxendale, A., Tovey, M.: Driverless pods: from technology demonstrators to desirable mobility solutions. In: Stanton, Neville A. (ed.) AHFE 2017. AISC, vol. 597, pp. 538–550. Springer, Cham (2018). https://doi.org/10.1007/978-3-319-60441-1_53

12. König, W.: Nutzergerechte Entwicklung der Mensch-Maschine- Interaktion von Fahreras-sistenzsystemen. In: Winner, H., Hakuli, S., Lotz, F., Singer, C. (eds.) Handbuch Fahrerassistenzsysteme. A, pp. 621–632. Springer, Wiesbaden (2015). https://doi.org/10.1007/978-3-658-05734-3_33

13. DIN EN ISO 7730:2006-05, Ergonomie der thermischen Umgebung - Analytische Bestimmung und Interpretation der thermischen Behaglichkeit durch Berechnung des PMV- und des PPD-Indexes und Kriterien der lokalen thermischen Behaglichkeit (ISO_7730:2005); Deutsche Fassung EN_ISO_7730:2005. Beuth Verlag GmbH, Berlin

14. Stuke, P.: Vertical interior cooling system for passenger cars: Trials and evaluation of feasibility, thermal comfort and energy efficiency. München (2016)

15. Wasser, J., Diels, C., Baxendale, A., Tovey, M.: Ergonomic evaluation of a driverless pod design. Proc. Hum. Factors Ergon. Soc. Ann. Meeting 62, 1389–1393 (2018)

Impact of Visual Embodiment on Trust for a Self-driving Car Virtual Agent: A Survey Study and Design Recommendations

Clarisse Lawson-Guidigbe[1], Nicolas Louveton[2],
Kahina Amokrane-Ferka[3], Benoît LeBlanc[1],
and Jean-Marc Andre[1(✉)]

[1] IMS UMR CNRS 5218, ENSC-Bordeaux INP, Bordeaux, France
clarisse.lawson-guidigbe@irt-systemx.fr,
jean-marc.andre@ensc.fr
[2] CERCA, Université de Poitiers, Université François Rabelais de Tours,
CNRS, Poitiers, France
[3] IRT SYSTEMX, Paris, France

Abstract. Designing trust-based in-car interfaces is critical for the adoption of self-driving cars. Indeed, latest studies revealed that a vast majority of drivers are not willing to trust this technology.

Although previous research showed that visually embodying a robot can have a positive impact on the interaction with a user, the influence of this visual representation on user trust is less understood.

In this study, we assessed the trustworthiness of different models of visual embodiment such as abstract, human, animal, mechanical, etc., using a survey and a trust scale. For those reasons, we considered a virtual assistant designed to support trust in automated driving and particularly in critical situations. This assistant role is to take full control of the driving task whenever the driver activates the self-driving mode, and provide a trustworthy experience.

We first selected a range of visual embodiment models based on a design space for robot visual embodiment and visual representations for each of these models. Then we used a card sorting procedure (19 selected participants) in order to select the most significant visual representations for each model. Finally, we conducted a survey (146 participants) to evaluate the impact of the selected models of visual embodiment on user trust and user preferences.

With our results, we attempt to provide an answer for the question of the best visual embodiment to instill trust in a virtual agent capacity to handle critical driving situations. We present possible guidelines for real-world implementation and we discuss further directions for a more ecological evaluation.

Keywords: Visual embodiment · Trust · Virtual agent · Self-driving car · HRI

1 Introduction

In the past decade, we have witnessed the birth of a new kind of technology: virtual assistants. They provide a new way of interacting with more and more complex machines and are meant to support the user in his daily activities. In the context of

© Springer Nature Switzerland AG 2020
C. Stephanidis and M. Antona (Eds.): HCII 2020, CCIS 1226, pp. 382–389, 2020.
https://doi.org/10.1007/978-3-030-50732-9_51

automated driving, the virtual assistant is the spokesperson of the automated car. He acts as a mediator between the car and the driver and embodies the car intelligence [1]. Among the different concepts presented by car manufacturers we can find invisible characters only present by their voice (YUI from Toyota) [2], or cartoon characters represented on a screen (Hana concept from Honda), or abstract representations (Dragon Drive concept from Nuance). We lack scientific publications that support those design choices especially in regards to trust since different studies [9, 19–22] showed that a large majority of people do not trust highly automated cars.

In our study we assess trustworthiness of various visual embodiment models for virtual assistant. We needed first to select a range of representative images for our models. For this purpose, we conducted to a picture sorting procedure. Once our visual representation sample was defined we ran an online survey to actually assess trustworthiness.

2 Related Work

2.1 Visual Embodiment and Trust

Researchers have been investigating the visual representation of virtual assistants from varying perspectives. Some of them focus on the question of the importance of a visual embodiment [14, 15, 17]. Their results showed that visual embodiment is important for a pleasant interaction especially when the user's visual attention is not required. However the realism of the embodiment might be of little importance. Others focus on the advantages of designing a humanlike face for a virtual assistant [13, 16, 18] but also the most important features to implement on the face. For example Disalvo & al. found in [11] that to project a high level of humanness a robot face should have a mouth, a nose, and eyelids. In [10], the authors found that the faces ranked as least friendly (without pupils or mouth, with eyelids) were also the ones ranked as less trustworthy. Similarly, Li et al. showed in their study [3] that a robot's visual embodiment has an impact on user's likeability and the found a significant correlation between likeability and trust in the robots.

2.2 Design Space for Virtual Assistants

It is worth noting that all the research work presented above focus on the "Humanlike" visual embodiment. However, the design space is much larger and there are many other models of visual embodiment to choose from. In [5], Haake & Gulz suggested a 3 dimensional design space for visual embodiment including basic model, graphical style and physical properties. The basic model refers to the constitution of the visual embodiment which can follow the form of a human, an animal, a fantasy concept, an inanimate object or a combination of these. The graphical style which can be naturalistic or stylized refers to the degree of details used in the visual design. Considering this design space, the possibilities are countless and the question of which one is most trustworthy depending on the role of the virtual assistant remains. In our study, we focus on the dimension of basic model for a virtual assistant in a highly automated car.

We hypothesized that depending on the assistant visual embodiment model, user trust level in the automated system will be different. Hence some visual embodiment models might instill higher levels of trust than others.

3   Research Methodology

Our study articulates two procedures. The first one is a picture sorting procedure meant to help us select images that represented the most each of the predefined virtual assistant models We then incorporated these selected visuals in our survey.

3.1   Picture Sorting Procedure

Picture sorting [6], one of the many card sorting techniques, is used to study user's mental models and how they categorize different type of images.

19 participants [4] (11 male, 8 female, mean age = 28,10) recruited from IRT SystemX and from a student house (Paris, France) took part in the card sorting procedure.

We collected 82 pictures from the website Pinterest based on ten (10) predefined models: "Human Naturalistic", "Human stylized", "Animal Naturalistic", "Animal stylized", "Human Mechanical", "Animal Mechanical", "Mini Mechanical", "Abstract", "Inanimate", "Fantasy". Those models were formed based on the first 2 dimensions of the design space proposed in [5].

All models labels were in French during the experiment (translated here). Many other possibilities of models can be identified but for this experiment we chose to focus on only 10.

Pictures were printed and placed on a large table. Models labels were also placed on a table next to the pictures. (see setting in Fig. 1 and Fig. 2)

Fig. 1. Picture sorting setting (before)   **Fig. 2.** Picture sorting setting (after)

Firstly, we red to the participants the definition of every label and answered their questions to make sure they understood what each label meant. Then we asked them to sort the pictures by label following two rules:

– A picture can be placed in more than one group. If that's the case participant can put the picture in a group and use additional post-it to specify the other group(s) where the image might also be classified.
– In the case where a picture cannot be placed in any of the predefined groups, the participant can put it in a separate "Non categorized" group.

At the end of the process, we ask the participant to explain his sorting and especially the pictures that were not sorted. Then we asked for their age and professional background before they leave.

3.2 Picture Sorting Results

Each participant sorting results were saved in an excel file and analyzed using the spread rate of each image in predefined groups [7]. Two criteria were used for selection. A model is selected if it has at least 4 representative pictures. A picture is representative if it have been placed in the same group by at least 70% of participants.

Using these criteria, we were able to select 5 of the predefined models and for each of them 4 pictures (Fig. 3).

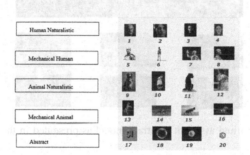

Fig. 3. Virtual assistant models and representative pictures selected by picture sorting.

3.3 Survey Procedure

Participants were invited to this online study via a link shared on social Media like Facebook, Whaller and different mailing lists (universities, student associations and professional associations). 146 participants (88 female, Mean age = 36.92 SD = 14.04 ranging from 19 to 72) completed the online survey. 124 (82.87%) participants had a driver's license.

When they clicked on the link they were forwarded to a hosted (at Université de Poitiers) version of LimeSurvey, the survey tool that we used for this study.

On the first page participants red general information about the study procedure and gave their informed consent and data assessment agreement. The survey consisted of five parts:

(1) An introduction with questions on driving habits and virtual assistant's usage;
(2) A short text instructing participants to imagine sitting in a highly automated car with a virtual assistant handling the driving task when automated mode is

activated. We asked a few questions on participant behavior in manual mode and once automated mode is activated;

(3) Participants are now instructed to imagine a critical driving situation in automated mode -with the virtual assistant in charge of the driving task- (shifting manoeuver in busy traffic to give passage to an ambulance coming from behind). Then they are presented with each of the 5 visual embodiment models (one model at a time and each model represented by 4 different images; example of abstract model in Fig. 4) selected in the picture sorting procedure. For each model they are asked to fill a 16 items questionnaire (on a scale of 0 to 10) that assessed perceived anthropomorphism, liking and self-reported trust towards the model.

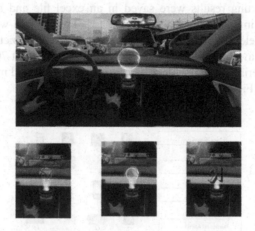

Fig. 4. Virtual assistant Abstract model as presented in the survey

We used a translated version of the questionnaire developed and used in a simulator study by Waytz et al. (2014) in [8]. The order in which models were presented was automatically randomized by Limesurvey.

(4) Here participants can choose the best and worst assistant between the ones presented in part (3).

(5) Participants are asked to fill their personal information as age, gender, education level, country of residence, professional activity.

3.4 Preliminary Survey Results

Nine items in the questionnaires assessed self-reported trust towards each model. The items were averaged to form a single composite ($\alpha = 0.97$), namely the trust score.

Our results (Table 1) based on this trust score are showing that the Mechanical Human category followed by the Human and Abstract ones were ranked with the highest scores in trust. Conversely, Animal and Mechanical Animal are appearing to be the least appropriate to elicit trust with virtual assistant in autonomous car (Table 2).

Table 1. Median ranks and other non-parametrical statistics

	Human	Animal	Mechanical hum	Mechanical animal	Abstract
Median	5.611	4.444	5.833	5.000	5.278
Minimum	0.000	0.000	0.000	0.000	0.000
Maximum	10.000	10.000	10.000	10.000	10.000
25th percentile	4.111	2.278	4.444	2.889	3.778
50th percentile	5.611	4.444	5.833	5.000	5.278
75th percentile	7.333	5.972	7.528	6.444	7.111

Table 2. Paired **Samples** Wilcoxon signed-rank test. Hypothesis is measurement one greater than measurement two.

		W	p
Mechanical human	Mechanical animal	5728.500	<.001
Mechanical human	Animal	6478.500	<.001
Human	Animal	5660.000	<.001
Human	Mechanical animal	4852.500	<.001
Abstract	Animal	5303.000	<.001
Abstract	Mechanical animal	4651.000	<.001
Mechanical human	Human	4360.500	<.001
Human	Abstract	3567.500	0.503
Mechanical animal	Animal	3812.000	0.002

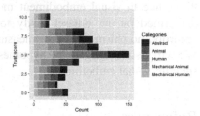

Fig. 5. Trust score across conditions

Figure 5 show on one hand the distribution of trust score in our study; and on the other hand, it shows how many times each model has been ranked on that particular score. First, trust score distribution shows a frequent scoring between five (the middle of the scale) and eight. This seems to indicate that participants had a relatively positive attitude towards trusting the proposed models (median is generally above five, except for animal model). Very high scores in trust (nine or ten) were rather rare; a non-negligible part of our results shows that a lack of trust may also occur (scores between zero and four). Indeed, looking at model categories, our findings are pointing out that the Animal and Mechanical-Animal categories are more represented in low trust score. Conversely, Human, Mechanical-Human and Abstract are categories the most represented in higher trust scores (third quartile above 7).

4   General Discussion

The objective of this study was to investigate the impact of virtual assistant's visual embodiment model on user trust in a highly automated car. We measured trust through an online trust questionnaire assessing a range of visual embodiment models, selected in a prior picture sorting procedure.

Our preliminary results are pointing to the Mechanical Human model followed by the Human and Abstract to be the most suitable embodiment models for representing a virtual assistant in an autonomous driving context; while Animal and Mechanical Animal models must be avoided.

Of course, this study by its methodology cannot answer all questions we may raise on virtual assistant assessment. Especially, on-line studies may induce many uncontrolled factors such as (the screen size, participant reading & understanding, doing the survey alone or with someone's help). Furthermore, participants had to rely on a static picture which might have influence their answers. Seeing a virtual assistant in movement might be very different. For a better ecological validity, future studies might replicate this experiment in a controlled environment like a driving simulator or even a real car with a real-life automated driving experience.

Despite these limitations we have been able through this study to demonstrate a difference in visual embodiment models in regards to trust. Further analysis will be performed on our dataset firstly to identify the impact of the different models on anthropomorphism and liking measures but also correlations between these 3 measures. We will also investigate the hypothesis of potential user profiles related to preference of specific visual embodiment.

References

1. Nuance: Automotive Assistants, Anthropomorphism and autonomous vehicles (2017). http://engage.nuance.com/wp-autonomous-driving
2. Okamoto, S., Sano, S.: Anthropomorphic AI agent mediated multimodal interactions in vehicles, pp. 110–114 (2017). https://doi.org/10.1145/3131726.3131736. Author, F., Author, S.: Title of a proceedings paper. In: Editor, F., Editor, S. (eds.) CONFERENCE 2016, LNCS, vol. 9999, pp. 1–13. Springer, Heidelberg (2016)
3. Dingjun, L., Rau, P.-L., Li, Y.: A cross-cultural study: effect of robot appearance and task. Int. J. Soc. Robot. **2**, 175–186 (2010). https://doi.org/10.1007/s12369-010-0056-9
4. Nielsen, J.: Card Sorting: How Many Users to Test. Alertbox Column (2004). http://www.useit.com/alertbox/20040719.html
5. Haake, M., Gulz, A.A.: Look at the roles of look & roles in embodied pedagogical agents – a user preference perspective. Int. J. Artif. Intell. Educ. **19**(1), 39–71 (2009)
6. Lobinger, K., Brantner, C.: Picture-sorting techniques. card sorting and Q-sort as alternative and complementary approaches in visual social research. In: Pauwels, L., Mannay, D. (eds.) The Sage Handbook of Visual Research Methods, 2nd Revised and Expanded Edition, pp. 309–321. Sage, London (2020)
7. Paul, C.L.: Analyzing card-sorting data using graph visualization. J. Usab. Stud. **9**(3), 87–104 (2014)
8. Waytz, A., Heafner, J., Epley, N.: The mind in the machine: anthropomorphism increases trust in an autonomous vehicle. J. Exp. Soc. Psychol. **52**, 113–117 (2014). https://doi.org/10.1016/j.jesp.2014.01.005
9. Lazányi, K., Maráczi, G.: Dispositional trust—Do we trust autonomous cars? In: 2017 IEEE 15th International Symposium on Intelligent Systems and Informatics (SISY), Subotica, pp. 000135–000140 (2017)

10. Kalegina, A., Schroeder, G., Allchin, A., Berlin, K., Cakmak, M.: Characterizing the design space of rendered robot faces. In: Proceedings of the 2018 ACM/IEEE International Conference on Human-Robot Interaction - HRI 2018, pp. 96–104 (2018). https://doi.org/10.1145/3171221.3171286
11. Disalvo, C., Gemperle, F., Forlizzi, J., Kiesler, S.: All robots are not created equal: the design and perception of humanoid robot heads. In: Proceedings 4th Conference on Designing Interactive Systems: Processes, Practices, Methods, and Techniques, pp. 321–326 (2002). https://doi.org/10.1145/778712.778756
12. Klamer, T., Allouch, S.: Acceptance and use of a zoomorphic robot in a domestic setting. In: Proceedings of EMCSR, pp. 553–558 (2010)
13. Edsinger, A.: Designing a humanoid robot face to fulfill a social contract (2000)
14. Reinhardt, J., Hillen, L., Wolf, K.: Embedding conversational agents into AR: invisible or with a realistic human body? In Proceedings of the Fourteenth International Conference on Tangible, Embedded, and Embodied Interaction (TEI 2020). Association for Computing Machinery, New York, NY, USA, pp. 299–310. https://doi.org/10.1145/3374920.3374956
15. Yee, N., Bailenson, J.N., Rickertsen, K.: A meta-analysis of the impact of the inclusion and realism of human-like faces on user experiences in interfaces. In: Proceedings of CHI 2007, San Jose, CA, USA, pp. 1–10 (2007)
16. Blow, M., Dautenhahn, K., Appleby, A., Nehaniv, C., Lee, D.: The art of designing robot faces: dimensions for human-robot interaction, 331–332 (2006). https://doi.org/10.1145/1121241.1121301
17. Kim, K., Bölling, L., Haesler, S., Bailenson, J., Bruder, G., Welch, G.: Does a digital assistant need a body? the influence of visual embodiment and social behavior on the perception of intelligent virtual agents in AR, 105–114 (2018). https://doi.org/10.1109/ISMAR.2018.00039
18. Breazeal, C.L.: Designing Sociable Robots. MIT Press, Cambridge (2002)
19. http://newsroom.aaa.com/2017/03/americans-feel-unsafe-sharing-road-fully-self-driving-cars/
20. Hooft van Huysduynen, H., Terken, J., Eggen, B.: Why disable the autopilot?, pp. 247–257 (2018). https://doi.org/10.1145/3239060.3239063
21. https://newsroom.aaa.com/2019/03/americans-fear-self-driving-cars-survey/
22. Fradrich, E., Cyganski, R., Wolf, I., Lenz, B.: User perspectives on autonomous driving. a use-case-driven study in Germany, (Arbeitsberichte des Geogtraphischen Instituts der Humboldt-Universität Berlin, Heft 187) (2016)

Improving the Detection of User Uncertainty in Automated Overtaking Maneuvers by Combining Contextual, Physiological and Individualized User Data

Alexander Trende[1]([✉]), Franziska Hartwich[2], Cornelia Schmidt[2], and Martin Fränzle[1,3]

[1] OFFIS e.V, Escherweg 2, 26121 Oldenburg, Germany
alexander.trende@offis.de
[2] Cognitive and Engineering Psychology, Chemnitz University of Technology, Wilhelm-Raabe-Straße 43, 09120 Chemnitz, Germany
[3] University of Oldenburg, Ammerländer Heerstraße 114-118, 26129 Oldenburg, Germany

Abstract. Highly automated driving will be a novel experience for many users and may cause uncertainty and discomfort for them [1]. An efficient real-time detection of user uncertainty during automated driving may trigger adaptation strategies, which could enhance the driving experience and subsequently the acceptance of highly automated driving [2]. In this study, we compared three different models to classify a user's uncertainty regarding an automated vehicle's capabilities and traffic safety during overtaking maneuvers based on experimental data from a driving-simulator study. By combining physiological, contextual and user-specific data, we trained three different deep neural networks to classify user uncertainty during overtaking maneuvers on different sets of input features. We evaluated the models based on metrics like the classification accuracy and F1 Scores. For a purely context-based model, we used features such as the Time-Headway and Time-To-Collision of cars on the opposing lane. We demonstrate how the addition of user heart rate and related physiological features can improve the classification accuracy compared to a purely context-based uncertainty model. The third model included user-specific features to account for inter-user differences regarding uncertainty in highly automated vehicles. We argue that a combination of physiological, contextual and user-specific information is important for an effectual uncertainty detection that accounts for inter-user differences.

Keywords: Human-computer-interaction · Autonomous driving · Human modelling · Machine learning

1 Introduction

Switching from being the driver to purely being a passenger in highly automated vehicles will be a huge step for many users. A pleasant and comfortable driving experience has to be provided to make this step acceptable. This study is part of the

© Springer Nature Switzerland AG 2020
C. Stephanidis and M. Antona (Eds.): HCII 2020, CCIS 1226, pp. 390–397, 2020.
https://doi.org/10.1007/978-3-030-50732-9_52

AutoAkzept [2] project, which aims at investigating and developing an adaptive automation for highly automated vehicles to reduce subjective user uncertainty about the vehicle's performance during usage. For this purpose, it is necessary to detect user uncertainty during the ride so that the automation's behavior can be adapted in order to provide a more pleasant driving experience [3]. Several researchers focused on the investigation of passenger comfort or discomfort detection respectively [4–6]. Although there is a difference between discomfort and uncertainty, we argue that a similar methodological approach can be used to measure both. [7] Investigated the possibility of measuring discomfort using physiological parameters like heart rate or galvanic skin conductance. Based on results from a driving-simulator study with 40 participants, the researchers concluded that heart rate is a viable measure for discomfort detection in simulated automated driving. Similarly, the authors of [8] used physiological indicators like electrocardiogram, electromymogram and skin conductance to measure stress during real world driving tasks. [9] Builds upon contextual information recorded via a front facing camera on the vehicle hood to build a model that can classify user discomfort. Data was collected in an on-road study with 19 participants in an urban environment. The researchers used distances and Time-To-Collisions to other traffic participants like pedestrians and cars as features for their model. A logistic regression model was fitted and several sets of features for the training process were compared. The researchers found that the addition of contextual features to a model with just vehicle dynamic data improves the performance of the discomfort detection. [10] Trained a Long Short-Term Memory network to model the risk perception of drivers based on contextual features like the state of the participant's vehicle (e.g. accelerations or steering) or the state of other traffic participants or the infrastructure. Based on the above-mentioned research and further studies, we conclude that the combination of contextual and physiological features for the classification of uncertainty seems to be promising.

In this study, we investigated whether the combination of contextual, physiological and user-specific features can improve the uncertainty detection in highly automated overtaking maneuvers based on data recorded in a driving s study presented in [11].

2 Methods and Materials

2.1 Data Acquisition

A driving simulator study with 50 participants (28 female, 22 male) was carried out to collect training data for the investigated models. The participants were aged from 20 to 43 years ($M = 25.9$, $SD = 4.7$) and held a valid driver's license. The study took place in a fixed-base driving simulator with a fully equipped vehicle interior and a 180° horizontal field of view, including a rear-view mirror and two side mirrors. Highly automated driving was performed along a 7 km long test track, which included a 4 km long urban road section with a speed limit of 50 km/h and a 3 km long rural road section with a speed limit of 100 km/h. Along this route, each participant experienced three different overtaking maneuvers, whereof two took place in the 50 km/h and one in the 100 km/h part of the track. During these maneuvers, the participants' vehicle had to change onto the oncoming lane in order to bypass an obstacle on its own lane (a bus at a bus stop, a parking truck, a construction zone). Highly automated driving along the test track was prerecorded based on a dynamic driving style and replayed identically for all participants.

During driving, the participants were wearing a Microsoft Band 2 smart band to record their heart rate (HR) and interbeat interval (IBI) [7] with a frequency of 10 Hz. In addition, they gave continuous feedback on their perceived uncertainty about the vehicle's performance during driving via a manual input device. Therefore, they held an ACD pro 10 handset control with a lever that had to be pressed gradually in accordance with the extent of their currently perceived uncertainty throughout the entire drive [1]. Stronger pressing of the lever corresponded to stronger uncertainty. The handset control signal was recorded simultaneously with driving data with a frequency of 60 Hz and transformed into a continuous scale of 0 (lever not pressed = certain) to 100 (lever fully pressed = uncertain). Participants exercised this procedure during a training session before driving along the test track. They received a monetary compensation for their participation after the study. For more information about the study, see [11] (Fig. 1).

Fig. 1. Image of the driving simulator inside. The participants experienced an autonomous 7 km long drive through urban and rural environments. The pictured participant wears a Microsoft Band 2 smart band for heart rate measurement and holds a handset control for reporting her subjective discomfort [1].

2.2 Modelling

For this study, we just focused on the overtaking situations during the drive. We extracted data for each overtaking maneuver and participant, which resulted in a dataset consisting of 150000 data points (3000 data points per overtaking maneuver for 50 participants) per feature. To generate training labels for our classifier, we applied a threshold of 10 (on a scale of 0 to 100) for the recorded handset control values. We found that this threshold helps to avoid labeling random and unintended handset presses incorrectly. Values below the threshold were labelled as not uncertain ("0") and above as uncertain ("1"). Overall, the distribution of labels was roughly 3:1 ("0":"1"). This leads to a baseline accuracy of around 75% for the proposed binary classification models. The investigated models only differed in the amount of features that have been used (s. Figure 2). The first model contained solely contextual features like the vehicle's speed, acceleration and Time-To-Collison to other traffic participants. The second model adjoined the two physiological features of heartrate and interbeat interval. For the third model, we added another feature we called "individual uncertainty proneness" to account for differences in user preferences regarding their subjective uncertainty and risk perception during the usage of automated vehicles. The "individual uncertainty proneness" parameter was calculated based on the handset control values for each participant based on data from a second drive that has not been used for the models' training process. We calculated the sum of handset control values along this drive for each user and separated the resulting distribution into three groups (low, medium, high uncertainty proneness). These values can be understood as a probability that the participant has a general tendency towards a low, medium or high uncertainty in an automated drive. All features were standardized before the model training.

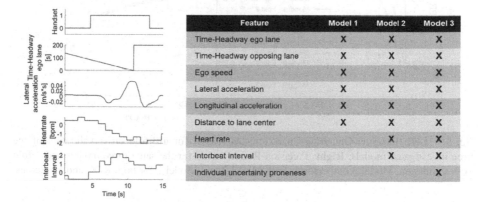

Fig. 2. Left: Plots for the uncertainty value and four example features for one overtaking maneuver during the experiment. **Right:** Overview of features used in each of the three models.

Deep neural networks (DNN) were chosen as models for this application. The DNN contained two hidden layers with 30 rectifier neurons each. Training and test data was shuffled before each training epoch. A 3-fold cross-validation was used for the training process. After the training, a "Receiver-Operating-Characteristics" (ROC) and "Precision-Recall" analysis was performed for each model and fold. The best classifier threshold was calculated based on the F1 Score. The accuracy, F1 Score, Precision, Recall/True-positive rate (TPR) and True-negative rate (TNR) were calculated after applying the best classifier threshold.

3 Results

3.1 Model Evaluation

The best models were chosen based on the Precision-Recall curves and the corresponding F1 Scores (s. Figure 3). Model 1, which utilizes just the context-related features has a mean accuracy of 75% and TPR of 73% over the three folds (s. Table 1). This means that 27% of the data points labelled as "1" were falsely classified as "0". Furthermore, the model just matches the accuracy for a random classifier given the class distribution of the dataset. By adding physiological features, namely heartrate and interbeat interval, Model 2 is able to classify 80% of the uncertain events correctly and reaches an F1 Score of 0.65. This increase is mainly achieved through a higher precision of the classifier. By including the "individual uncertainty proneness" parameter, the best model, with respect to all metrics, could be trained. It has an accuracy of around 85%, an F1 Score of 0.72 and the overall highest TNR of 87%.

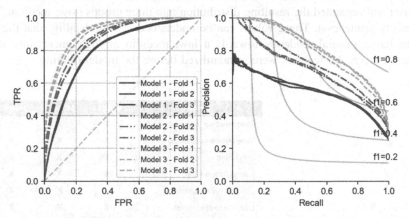

Fig. 3. Left: Receiver-Operating-Characteristics (ROC) for a 3-fold cross validation of the three investigated models. **Right**: Precision-Recall curves for the same three models and 3-fold cross validation. Model 3 outperforms both Model 2 and Model 1 for both ROC and F1 Scores.

Since the overtaking maneuvers were the same for all participants, Model 1 had to learn to classify uncertainty for every participant merely based on a combination of contextual features like a low Time-Headway to the obstacle to overtake or the participant's vehicle's lateral acceleration. This leads to false positives due to differences between participants and their thresholds for subjective uncertainty for the given maneuver. In this study, a few participants did not press the handset control during some of the overtaking maneuvers at all. Reasons could be a high threshold for their subjective uncertainty regarding the presented automation or a misunderstanding of the experimental instructions. Model 1 will also classify the data points of these subjects as positive, thus producing false positives. In theory, the addition of the physiological features can improve the performance of the classifier by increasing the TNR. If a participant does not perceive a driving situation as uncertain, the physiological features

Table 1. Overview over the results of the model evaluations. Model 3 outperforms the other two models for all metrics. The classification thresholds were calculated based on the F1 Scores of the Precision-Recall curves. The means for all metrics were then calculated given this classification threshold.

Metric	Model 1	Model 2	Model 3
Accuracy	0.75	0.80	0.85
Area-Under-Curve	0.80	0.87	0.92
Area precision-recall	0.74	0.82	0.89
Precision	0.49	0.58	0.67
Recall/True-positive rate	0.73	0.75	0.77
True-negative rate	0.75	0.82	0.87
F1 score	0.59	0.65	0.72

should reflect this. This seems to work for Model 2 to some extent since it classifies more of the negative data points correctly, thus reducing false positives. By adding the "individual uncertainty proneness" to Model 3, the model includes an indicator stating whether the participant is generally sensitive to uncertainty in automated driving, leading to further reduction of false positives for participants with a high threshold for their subjective uncertainty.

4   Discussion

In this study, we compared three different models to detect subjective uncertainty in overtaking maneuvers based on data recorded in a driving simulator study. The model that includes not just physiological and contextual information but also a feature that describes a user's overall tendency to feel uncertain during the usage of automated vehicles performed best for all calculated metrics. The study's data showed that the subjective uncertainty varied widely between subjects during the study. A model using just contextual information may not be able to account for this variation. We argue that considering user-specific information like this "individual uncertainty proneness" or demographic features, like age or gender have to be considered for a useful model. These parameters could be learnt over time during usage of an autonomous vehicle or may be determined by a questionnaire. It has to be emphasized that the cross-validation used in the present study used data from all participants of the study. So far, it was not possible to build a model that can reliably detect uncertainty for a user whose data was not used in the model's training process. Furthermore, it is important to note that the driving-simulator setting can have a great effect on the subjective uncertainty. Some or most of the participants may feel low or even no uncertainty in these simulated environments.

We plan to improve and expand the proposed model in future research. Since we so far just used data from overtaking maneuvers, it would be useful to extend the model in a way that it can classify uncertainty in more diverse traffic situations. This may make the addition of more contextual features necessary. Additionally, we want to incorporate more physiological features like pupil dilation, galvanic skin conductance or seating position assessed pressure seats [7]. As mentioned above, we hypothesize that more user information may help to account for inter-user differences. We plan to use questionnaires featuring demographic items in upcoming studies to add theses as features for our model. Furthermore, a natural extension of the model would be to incorporate more temporal information. The subjective uncertainty is just classified based on the features for the current time point. Adding features that carry temporal information like moving means, gradients or even memory-based model architectures like Long Short-Term Memory networks [12] could improve the classification accuracy even further.

We expect these additions to improve the proposed model for uncertainty detection further subsequently leading to more reliable and trustworthy human-centered adaptive automated driving.

Acknowledgment. This work was supported by the German Federal Ministry of Transport and Digital Infrastructure in the funding program Automated and Connected Driving, AutoAkzept and by the DFG-grants "Learning from Humans – Building for Humans" and "Dynamic Conflict Resolution and Integrated Causal Methods" (project numbers 433 524 510 and 433 524 788).

Supported by:

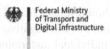

Federal Ministry of Transport and Digital Infrastructure

on the basic of a decision by the German Bundestag

References

1. Hartwich, F., Beggiato, M., Krems, J.F.: Driving comfort, enjoyment and acceptance of automated driving–effects of drivers' age and driving style familiarity. Ergonomics **61**(8), 1017–1032 (2018)
2. Drewitz, U., et al.: Automation ohne Unsicherheit: Vorstellung des Förderprojekts AUTOAKZEPT zur Erhöhung der Akzeptanz automatisierten Fahrens (2019)
3. Drewitz, U., et al.: Towards user-focused vehicle automation: the architectural approach of the AutoAkzept project. Accepted for HCII2020 (2020)
4. Siebert, F.W., Oehl, M., Höger, R., Pfister, H.-R.: Discomfort in automated driving – the disco-scale. In: Stephanidis, C. (ed.) HCI 2013. CCIS, vol. 374, pp. 337–341. Springer, Heidelberg (2013). https://doi.org/10.1007/978-3-642-39476-8_69
5. Bellem, H., Thiel, B., Schrauf, M., Krems, J.F.: Comfort in automated driving: an analysis of preferences for different automated driving styles and their dependence on personality traits. Transp. Res. Part F Traffic Psychol. Behav. **55**, 90–100 (2018)
6. Rossner, P., Bullinger, A.C.: How do you want to be driven? investigation of different highly-automated driving styles on a highway scenario. In: Stanton, N. (ed.) AHFE 2019. AISC, vol. 964, pp. 36–43. Springer, Cham (2020). https://doi.org/10.1007/978-3-030-20503-4_4
7. Beggiato, M., Hartwich, F., Krems, J.: Using smartbands, pupillometry and body motion to detect discomfort in automated driving. Front. Hum. Neurosci. **12**, 338 (2018)
8. Healey, J.A., Picard, R.W.: Detecting stress during real-world driving tasks using physiological sensors. IEEE Trans. Intell. Transp. Syst. **6**(2), 156–166 (2005)

9. Telpaz, A., Baltaxe, M., Hecht, R.M., Cohen-Lazry, G., Degani, A., Kamhi, G.: An approach for measurement of passenger comfort: real-time classification based on in-cabin and exterior data. In: 2018 21st International Conference on Intelligent Transportation Systems (ITSC), November 2018, pp. 223–229. IEEE (2018)
10. Ping, P., Sheng, Y., Qin, W., Miyajima, C., Takeda, K.: Modeling driver risk perception on city roads using deep learning. IEEE Access 6, 68850–68866 (2018)
11. Hartwich, F., Schmidt, C., Gräfing, D., Krems, J.: In the passenger seat: differences in the perception of human vs. automated vehicle control and resulting HMI demands of users. Accepted for HCII2020 (2020)
12. Hochreiter, S., Schmidhuber, J.: Long short-term memory. Neural Comput. 9(8), 1735–1780 (1997)

Theorization Human-Computer Interaction in the All-Digital Car: Mediatized Driver Experiences

Sarah Viktoria Christiane von Hören[1,2(✉)]

[1] Hanover University of Music, Drama and Media, Hanover, Germany
[2] Bosch SoftTec GmbH, Phoenixstraße 3, 31137 Hildesheim, Germany
`sarah.vonhoeren@bosch-softtec.com`

Abstract. It is a common behavior to enrich the automotive driving experience with various media services and applications. However, the effects of this habit are examined mostly from a safety perspective; there is a lack of scientific tools and methods to examine the joint media and driving experience. Therefore, to address Human-Computer Interaction (HCI) while driving from an experience perspective, the model of Mediatized Driver Experiences (MDX) is introduced. It offers a new framework to classify driving and media experiences. In focus are not (only) negative conjunctions (such as distractions), it is rather a holistic approach to the joint experience of the driving and media situation. Therefore, findings from both vehicle safety and communication science were incorporated to develop the MDX model. The model addresses the formation of subjective experiences through influencing factors including the driver as well as the driving, media and social situation. Enjoyment, agency and perceived safety form the subjective experience, hence, the MDX core. Each dimension underlies processes of self-regulation, cognitive processes and affective effects of the driver. The measured core dimensions are then used to classify and aggregate the individual experiences on a higher level.

Keywords: In-car media experiences · Media and driving framework · In-car user experience

1 Introduction

People have an extensive media use in their daily lives (especially millennials [1]), which is now extended into the vehicle. When looking at how people are spending their time while driving, one can see that it is quite the common behavior to enrich the driving experience with media services and applications. Thus, modern In-Vehicle Infotainment Systems (IVIS) bring new opportunities for media use into the car – it becomes the "all-digital car".

Because the nature of these situations are driving situations, it is always primarily about the driver in a traffic situation. Consequently, behavior and its consequences are often analyzed from a safety perspective. In current research, this often results in the analysis of dual-task scenarios, with focus on distraction and workload or the systems that enable media usage (smartphones and IVIS) [2]. Precisely because this behavior is

© Springer Nature Switzerland AG 2020
C. Stephanidis and M. Antona (Eds.): HCII 2020, CCIS 1226, pp. 398–407, 2020.
https://doi.org/10.1007/978-3-030-50732-9_53

using media – listening to music, podcasts, writing messages, receiving information about the news and using other various applications – the effects of this behavior should also be examined from an experience and media effect perspective.

To focus on the experience and its effects is quite common in the research of media effects in communication science [3]. Media effects refer to "the consequences of media use experienced by the individual message recipient or audience member" [4]. However, despite the ubiquity of people using media via the high complex multimodal IVIS or via the smartphone, little is known about the media situation [5] and thus, even less about the experiences. To conclude, there is a lack of scientific tools and methods to examine the joint media and driving experience [6, 7].

With the proposed model of *Mediatized Driver Experiences* (MDX) this gap shall be closed. The model is designed as well from findings from vehicle and road safety research, traffic psychology, but also from communication science. Therefore, it addresses the Human-Computer Interaction, but from an experience point of view that results from the interdisciplinary integration with communication science.

This article first highlights the relevance of the theorization of HCI in the all-digital car and discusses current research findings that are relevant for the analysis of media and driving situations. Then, the MDX framework is introduced and the individual dimensions are presented. Finally, an empirical outlook is given, as well as a conclusion emphasizing potentials and limitations.

2 Relevance of a Theorization of HCI in the All-Digital Car

General research on media usage while driving is sparse, but research focusing on smartphone usage or IVIS is vast. Smartphone usage while driving is one of the main topics in road safety literature [8]. In the context of research regarding smartphone usage while driving, the phenomenon "texting while driving" has a high significance [9, 10] and consequently gets a lot of research attention. The behavior, using the smartphone and texting while steering a vehicle, has been investigated and shown to be very risky in many studies [11–16].

Looking at this from a media usage perspective, and thus from a communication science view, one can address the general, daily media use of people. In daily media behavior, current research refers to online vigilance [17] and research reading being permanently online and permanently connected (POPC) [18]. The core idea is that people have a POPC-mindset, meaning they are permanently connected with social networks, and thus other people. Obviously, the POPC-mindset does not exclude driving situations, even though online vigilance has so far not been transferred inside the vehicle to a great extent. Nevertheless, being socially connected to others while driving has been subject of studies [9]. Thus, using media while driving is also a POPC phenomenon. The driver wants to fulfill his communication and media needs which for him enriches the driving experience.

At the same time, IVIS are evolving. Original Equipment Manufacturers (OEMs) either integrate software to enable smartphone content on the head unit (e.g. Apple CarPlay, Android Auto, MirrorLink, mySPIN) or integrate apps directly into their head units, without the smartphone being the source of the content (e.g. TripAdvisor,

Spotify, Alexa). These built-in systems offer the users an allegedly safe way [5] to interact with their media or to text while driving. Drivers use these systems for accessing their apps, some of them driving related (e.g. navigation) and many for recreational purposes (e.g. listening to audiobooks, podcasts or for digital communication) [5].

However, in most research functionalities that enable media usage while driving are not seen as experiences with specific effects, they are examined either from a user experience (UX) or from a safety perspective. While looking at UX and safety is very important, there is still a deficit in research for the combined driving and media experience. UX research focusses on design patterns [19] or the fulfilling of individual needs for the user [20]. Safety is often examined with dual-task research, for example using the Lane Change Test [21] and workload research like the Nasa Task Load Index [22]. However, the outputs of these tests and scales say nothing about the joint media and driving experience and what people subjectively experience.

While modern smartphones have penetrated all markets worldwide, there are still many vehicles without advanced IVIS. From the history of automotive infotainment, it can be seen that HCI in the car has always been influenced by upcoming new technologies customers first get used to in the world outside the car [7]. Consequently, if the car does not offer these functions, the drivers just use their smartphones handheld or in a cradle.

If a driver engages in a second, driving unrelated task, evidence shows that it results in inattention and thus higher accident risk for the driver [23, 24]. However, research indicates [25] that drivers engage in adjustment strategies, which makes them feel safe. In a systematic review, Oviedo-Trespalacios et al. [25] conclude that research on how drivers can perform their secondary tasks interactively while driving and even adjust their driving behavior is sparse, however, it is still a common behavior in the vehicle.

When looking at adjustment strategies, one should also consider the research regarding the "optimism bias" [26], which shows that risk evaluation is highly subjective – and that people cannot objectively estimate their own risky driving behavior. As an example, while drivers assume that writing messages while driving reduces safety, there is no correlation with the fact that they would write few messages while driving – rather the opposite [8].

Otherwise, there is research that indicates that people use interactive media for cognitive balance while driving [27]. Boredom, resulting from less demanding driving situations, can lead to inattention and a depletion of cognitive resources. Steinberger et al. [27] (similar to the research of Takayama and Nass [28]) found that playful intervention (interactive media) out of boredom reduces unsafe coping mechanisms such as speeding and at the same time promotes anticipatory driving. People perform tasks best when they are adequately engaged with the task [27]. However, digital entertainment content as an adjustment strategy seems to be challenging, because it does not react to changes in cognitive, manual or visual factors [27].

Consequently, there is the need for a paradigm change regarding the research of media and driving behavior. We cannot only focus on the negative conjunctions (safety research), but should also focus on the experience people undergo when using media and driving at the same time. This change can be offered by the interdisciplinary theorization of HCI in the all-digital car, developing a new framework for media and driving situations.

To sum up, using media while driving is not just something automotive companies offer, it is a behavior the users demand [11] (see POPC-mindset). If the vehicle does not offer a "good" solution [7], they will just use what they have already in their pocket. Therefore, OEMs should design their experiences in the best possible way.

3 Mediatized Driver Experiences – The Framework

Taking into account all the above arguments, the core dimensions of the MDX are the drivers' *enjoyment*, *agency* and *perceived safety* – as these dimensions seem to be the most important ones for driving and media experiences. The Mediatized Driver Experience framework attempts to gain deep insights in the world of experience of driving and media usage. This paragraph elaborates the framework in detail.

The framework uses the core dimensions as well as external influencing factors, which could fundamentally impact the media and driving experience. Consequently, the model of Mediatized Driver Experience is introduced (see Fig. 1). At the core of the model are subjective experiences, which are constructed primarily from driving and media situations. The MDX core dimensions together result in the subjective experience of a person driving a vehicle while interacting with a digital system. The dimensions formed can always be located in the four independent, predictive dimensions: *driving, media* and *social situation, driver*.

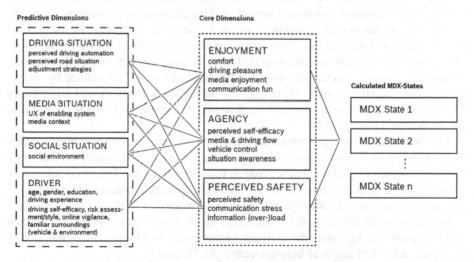

Fig. 1. The proposed model of Mediatized Driver Experiences

Putting the active driver at the core, the model also takes cognitive processes and affective effects into consideration. Each dimension underlies the driver's self-regulation processes [29]. The driver has a decisive influence on the dimensions. These are not done to the person, i.e. there is not just a reaction, but also decisions that lead to a common world of experiences. The cognitive processes enable the experience and affective processes, which make the experiences unique to the driver. Affective processes refer to the emotions, which arise from driving, the outer environment and the media content. The following paragraphs will explain the integral parts of the model in detail. The independent predictors are depicted on the left hand and the subjective experience in the middle of Fig. 1.

3.1   Core Dimensions

As stated before, the proposed model is highly subjective. Hence, the subjective experiences of the driver are at the center of MDX. Three dimensions, that each are composed of subjective variables from the four independent influencing predictors (driving, media and social situation & driver), build the core. The dimensions are derived from empirical research, theories and models from vehicle and road safety research, traffic psychology, but also from communication science.

The first dimension is **enjoyment** – enjoyment caused as well by the driving and media situation. Enjoyment is at the center, because the enjoyment experience is central for most recreational experiences. On the one hand, entertainment can originate from driving itself. This is a matter of comfort [30] and driving pleasure [31, 32]. On the other hand, enjoyment can also be created by media entertainment [33, 34], which focuses on the (positive) emotions that manifest themselves during reception by the recipients [35, 36]. Further, the entertainment effect is to be considered, that can arise through communication, i.e. through social interaction. In conclusion, enjoyment consists of (dis-)comfort, media enjoyment, driving pleasure and communication fun.

The second dimension is **agency**, which is particular important in the driving context, but is also derived from interactive media research. Agency [37–40] describes the experience of competence and responsibility; the immersion in the media reception and driving situation. Agency, in other words "the ability to act", is defined by action- and situation-related variables. Therefore, this dimension holds perceived self-efficacy [41] (to feel effective), media and driving flow [42, 43], media and vehicle control [26] and situational awareness [44].

The third dimension is **perceived safety**, which is – from an objective perspective – the most important variable. Designing engaging experiences in the safety critical space of the car requires a careful balance between fun and safety [45]. Perceived safety [26, 46] includes the actual feeling of safety, the stress through communication and outer environment and unsafety through informational (over-)load [47].

When using the MDX model empirically, the measured core dimensions are then used to classify and aggregate the individual experiences on a higher level (right side of Fig. 1, see Sect. 4 "Empirical Measurements: An Outlook").

3.2   External Influencing Factors – Predictive Dimensions

As mentioned before, the model also considers external influencing factors. The first group of predictors deals with the context variables that relate to the **driving situation**. Three factors are of interest for these dimensions in order to assess the driving situation from the driver's point of view. Here, "perceived driving automation" is of interest, which deals with the extent to which the driver relies on the safety and driving mechanisms of the car. In addition, the perceived difficulty of the driving situation "perceived road situation" is included and finally, whether the driver actively changes his driving situation by using adjustment strategies.

The second dimension is about the **media situation**, i.e. the content component, but also about how the content is technically implemented and communicated (e.g. UX [48]). The question arises as to what extent problems arise due to poor usability or to what amount usability positively influences the experience.

The **social situation** dimension is about the physical (and to some extent digital) social environment during the experience. Thus, it is assumed that the presence of other people can influence the experience. This is crucial for the driving and media situation, as it is assumed that this can fundamentally change the situation (e.g. choice of content or talking passengers). The model will therefore include whether the social situation influences the MDX experience.

The **driver** dimension is about the person who is at the center of the experience and the predispositions that this person brings to the situation. The socio-demographic dimensions of age, driving experience, gender and education are included here, as well as attitudes towards driving risks and driving itself (e.g. driving self-efficacy or risk style [49]). Also the individual POPC-mindset (online vigilance) is of interest.

These external influencing factors are surely not exclusive. Because the driving situation is influenced by numerous factors (as are the individual dispositions), this selection makes no claim to absolute completeness. The factors were selected according to their theoretical fit.

4 Empirical Measurements: An Outlook

The MDX-model does not only measure the dependent (core) and independent (predictive) dimensions. It has another layer, which consist of aggregated and classified dimensions. The output of the model of Mediatized Driver Experiences (s. Fig. 1) is on the right side, the so-called "MDX-States". These states are based on the empirical measurements of the core dimensions. For this purpose a multidimensional scale has been developed that will be introduced in future literature. The dimensions will be analyzed via explorative cluster analysis to see how the experiences are structured. Therefore the number of MDX states is not defined yet, as well as the variables that will define the states in the future.

The first study was conducted end of 2019. A large number of diverse participants (1024 drivers from Germany) took part in a quantitative online survey. They were asked about a specific driving and media situation within the last week. All the relevant core dimensions were queried. Therefore, each dimension was operationalized with a suitable or slightly adapted scale. The results will be integrated into the further development of MDX and the research of media usage while driving.

5 Conclusion

It was found that there are not enough scientific methods to investigate media experiences in the all-digital car. At the same time, there is an increasing relevance to examine exactly those experiences. This is to be filled from the perspective of both traffic psychology and communication science. The newly formed MDX model anticipates to close this gap.

However, limitations are to be found in the fact that the model is still in its infancy and can therefore change in the future and that it has not yet been tested with an IVIS. Despite, it shows great potential for interdisciplinary work and the reconstruction of media and driving experiences.

In conclusion: The presented model can be empirically measured for any driving and media situation. It is not exclusive for a specific media or driving context, and thus can help to investigate the multitude of media and driving situations. The framework anticipates to classify these experiences in a later state. MDX will help to better understand media use in vehicles and contribute to the examination and improvement of in-car media experiences.

References

1. Lee, M., Kwahk, J., Han, S.H., et al.: Developing personas & use cases with user survey data: a study on the millennials' media usage. J. Retail. Consum. Serv. **54**, 102051 (2020). https://doi.org/10.1016/j.jretconser.2020.102051
2. Vollrath, M., Huemer, A.K., Hummel, T.: Ablenkung durch Informations- und Kommunikationssysteme. Gesamtverband der Deutschen Versicherungswirtschaft: Forschungsbericht, Nr. 26. GDV, Berlin (2015)
3. Valkenburg, P.M., Peter, J., Walther, J.B.: Media effects: theory and research. Annu. Rev. Psychol. **67**, 315–338 (2016). https://doi.org/10.1146/annurev-psych-122414-033608
4. Allen, M. (ed): The SAGE Encyclopedia of Communication Research Methods, vol. 2455, p. 91320. SAGE Publications, Thousand Oaks (2017)
5. Strayer, D.L., Cooper, J.M., Goethe, R.M., et al.: Assessing the visual and cognitive demands of in-vehicle information systems. Cogn. Res. Princ. Implic. **4**(1), 18 (2019). https://doi.org/10.1186/s41235-019-0166-3
6. Bengler, K.: Driver and driving experience in cars. In: Meixner, G., Müller, C. (eds.) Automotive User Interfaces, vol. 5, pp. 79–94. Springer, Cham (2017). https://doi.org/10.1007/978-3-319-49448-7_3
7. Meixner, G., Häcker, C., Decker, B., et al.: Retrospective and future automotive infotainment systems—100 years of user interface evolution. In: Meixner, G., Müller, C. (eds.) Automotive User Interfaces, pp. 3–53. Springer, Cham (2017). https://doi.org/10.1007/978-3-319-49448-7_1
8. Musicant, O., Lotan, T., Albert, G.: Do we really need to use our smartphones while driving? Accid. Anal. Prev. **85**, 13–21 (2015). https://doi.org/10.1016/j.aap.2015.08.023

9. Alnizami, H., Alvarez, I., Gilbert, J.E.: Socializing under the influence of distracted driving: a study of the effects of in-vehicle and outside-of-the-vehicle communication while driving. In: Stanton, N.A., Landry, S., Di Bucchianico, G., et al. (eds.) Advances in Human Aspects of Transportation, vol. 484, pp. 243–255. Springer, Cham (2017). https://doi.org/10.1007/978-3-319-41682-3_21

10. Benson, T., McLaughlin, M., Giles, M.: The factors underlying the decision to text while driving. Transp. Res. Part F Traffic Psychol. Behav. **35**, 85–100 (2015). https://doi.org/10.1016/j.trf.2015.10.013

11. Caird, J.K., Johnston, K.A., Willness, C.R., et al.: A meta-analysis of the effects of texting on driving. Accid. Anal. Prev. **71**, 311–318 (2014). https://doi.org/10.1016/j.aap.2014.06.005

12. Hayashi, Y., Russo, C.T., Wirth, O.: Texting while driving as impulsive choice: a behavioral economic analysis. Accid. Anal. Prev. **83**, 182–189 (2015). https://doi.org/10.1016/j.aap.2015.07.025

13. Ortiz, C., Ortiz-Peregrina, S., Castro, J.J., et al.: Driver distraction by smartphone use (WhatsApp) in different age groups. Accid. Anal. Prev. **117**, 239–249 (2018). https://doi.org/10.1016/j.aap.2018.04.018

14. Oviedo-Trespalacios, O.: Getting away with texting: behavioural adaptation of drivers engaging in visual-manual tasks while driving. Transp. Res. Part A Policy Pract. **116**, 112–121 (2018). https://doi.org/10.1016/j.tra.2018.05.006

15. Preece, C., Watson, A., Kaye, S.-A., et al.: Understanding the psychological precursors of young drivers' willingness to speed and text while driving. Accid. Anal. Prev. **117**, 196–204 (2018). https://doi.org/10.1016/j.aap.2018.04.015

16. Vollrath, M., Huemer, A.K., Teller, C., et al.: Do German drivers use their smartphones safely?-not really! Accid. Anal. Prev. **96**, 29–38 (2016). https://doi.org/10.1016/j.aap.2016.06.003

17. Klimmt, C., Hefner, D., Reinecke, L., et al.: The permanently online and permanently connected mind: mapping the cognitive structures behind mobile internet use. In: Vorderer, P., Hefner, D., Reinecke, L., et al. (eds.) Permanently Online, Permanently Connected: Living and Communicating in a POPC World, pp. 18–28. Routledge, New York (2018)

18. Vorderer, P., Hefner, D., Reinecke, L., et al. (eds.): Permanently Online, Permanently Connected: Living and Communicating in a POPC World. Routledge, New York (2018)

19. Mirnig, A., Kaiser, T., Lupp, A., et al.: Automotive user experience design patterns: an approach and pattern examples. Int. J. Adv. Intell. Syst. **9**, 275–286 (2016)

20. Riener, A., Geisler, S., van Laack, A., et al. In: 7th Workshop "Automotive HMI": Safety Meets User Experience (UX). Gesellschaft für Informatik e.V (2018)

21. Huemer, A.K., Vollrath, M.: Learning the lane change task: comparing different training regimes in semi-paced and continuous secondary tasks. Appl. Ergon. **43**(5), 940–947 (2012). https://doi.org/10.1016/j.apergo.2012.01.002

22. Hart, S.G., Staveland, L.E.: Development of NASA-TLX (Task Load Index): results of empirical and theoretical research. In: Human Mental Workload, vol 52, pp 139–183. Elsevier (1988)

23. Collet, C., Guillot, A., Petit, C.: Phoning while driving I: a review of epidemiological, psychological, behavioural and physiological studies. Ergonomics **53**(5), 589–601 (2010). https://doi.org/10.1080/00140131003672023

24. Collet, C., Guillot, A., Petit, C.: Phoning while driving II: a review of driving conditions influence. Ergonomics **53**(5), 602–616 (2010). https://doi.org/10.1080/00140131003769092

25. Oviedo-Trespalacios, O., Haque, M.M., King, M., et al.: Understanding the impacts of mobile phone distraction on driving performance: a systematic review. Transp. Res. Part C Emerg. Technol. **72**, 360–380 (2016). https://doi.org/10.1016/j.trc.2016.10.006

26. DeJoy, D.M.: The optimism bias and traffic accident risk perception. Accid. Anal. Prev. **21** (4), 333–340 (1989). https://doi.org/10.1016/0001-4575(89)90024-9
27. Steinberger, F., Schroeter, R., Watling, C.N.: From road distraction to safe driving: evaluating the effects of boredom and gamification on driving behaviour, physiological arousal, and subjective experience. Comput. Hum. Behav. **75**, 714–726 (2017). https://doi.org/10.1016/j.chb.2017.06.019
28. Takayama, L., Nass, C.: Assessing the effectiveness of interactive media in improving drowsy driver safety. Hum. Factors **50**(5), 772–781 (2008). https://doi.org/10.1518/001872008X312341
29. Früh, W.: Der aktive Rezipient—neu besehen. In: Früh, W. (ed.) Medienwirkungen: Das dynamisch-transaktionale Modell, pp. 237–258. VS Verlag für Sozialwissenschaften, Wiesbaden (1991)
30. Engelbrecht, A.: Fahrkomfort und Fahrspaß bei Einsatz von Fahrerassistenzsystemen. Grin Verlag GmbH, Norderstedt (2013)
31. Hagman, O.: Driving pleasure: a key concept in Swedish car culture. Mobilities **5**(1), 25–39 (2010). https://doi.org/10.1080/17450100903435037
32. Högberg, J., Hamari, J., Wästlund, E.: Gameful experience questionnaire (GAMEFUL-QUEST): an instrument for measuring the perceived gamefulness of system use. User Model User Adap. Inter. **27**(2), 215 (2019). https://doi.org/10.1007/s11257-019-09223-w
33. Klimmt, C., Hartmann, T., Frey, A.: Effectance and control as determinants of video game enjoyment. Cyberpsychol. Behav. **10**(6), 845–847 (2007). https://doi.org/10.1089/cpb.2007.9942
34. Hartmann, T.: Die Selektion unterhaltsamer Medienangebote am Beispiel von Computer-spielen. Zugl.: Hannover, Hochsch. für Musik und Theater, Dissertation, 2005, Halem (2006)
35. Bilandzic, H., Schramm, H., Matthes, J.: Medienrezeptionsforschung. UTB, vol 4003. UVK-Verl.-Ges; UTB, Konstanz, Stuttgart (2015)
36. Schweiger, W.: Theorien der Mediennutzung: Eine Einführung. Vollst. zugl.: München, Univ., Habil.-Schr., 1. Aufl. Lehrbuch. VS Verl. für Sozialwiss, Wiesbaden (2007)
37. Schlütz, D.: Bildschirmspiele und ihre Faszination. Zuwendungsmotive, Gratifikationen und Erleben interaktiver Medienangebote. Reinhard Fischer, München (2002)
38. Klimmt, C.: Computerspielen als Handlung: Dimensionen und Determinanten des Erlebens interaktiver Unterhaltungsangebote. Unterhaltungsforschung (2006)
39. Laurel, B.: Computers as Theatre. Addison-Wesley, Reading (1991)
40. Murray, J.H.: Hamlet on the Holodeck: The Future of Narrative in Cyberspace. MIT Press, Cambridge (1997)
41. Klimmt, C., Hartmann, T.: Effectance, self-efficacy, and the motivation to play video games. playing video games: motives, responses, and consequences, pp. 133–145 (2006)
42. Csikszentmihalyi, M. Das Flow-Erlebnis: Jenseits von Angst und Langeweile: im Tun aufgehen, 4. Aufl. Konzepte der Humanwissenschaften: Psychologie (1992)
43. Sherry, J.L.: Flow and media enjoyment. Commun. Theor. **14**(4), 328–347 (2004). https://doi.org/10.1111/j.1468-2885.2004.tb00318.x
44. Stanton, N.A., Salmon, P.M., Walker, G.H., et al.: State-of-science: situation awareness in individuals, teams and systems. Ergonomics **60**(4), 449–466 (2017). https://doi.org/10.1080/00140139.2017.1278796
45. Steinberger, F., Schroeter, R., Babiac, D.: Engaged drivers-safe drivers: gathering real-time data from mobile and wearable devices for safe-driving apps. In: Meixner, G., Müller, C. (eds.) Automotive User Interfaces, vol. 24, pp. 55–76. Springer, Cham (2017). https://doi.org/10.1007/978-3-319-49448-7_2
46. Svenson, O., Fischhoff, B., MacGregor, D.: Perceived driving safety and seatbelt usage. Accid. Anal. Prev. **17**(2), 119–133 (1985). https://doi.org/10.1016/0001-4575(85)90015-6

47. Eppler, M.J., Mengis, J.: The concept of information overload: a review of literature from organization science, accounting, marketing, MIS, and related disciplines. Inform. Soc. **20**(5), 325–344 (2004). https://doi.org/10.1080/01972240490507974
48. Diefenbach, S., Hassenzahl, M.: Psychologie in der nutzerzentrierten Produktgestaltung. Springer, Heidelberg (2017)
49. Vollrath, M., Krems, J.F.: Verkehrspsychologie: Ein Lehrbuch für Psychologen, Ingenieure und Informatiker, 1st edn. Kohlhammer Standards Psychologie, Kohlhammer (2011)

"Light On": A Voice Controlled Vehicle-Light System Based on Translating Drives' Voice into Computer Commands to Reduce Operation Workload of Drivers

Yuan Yin[✉]

Imperial College, London, UK
y.yin19@ic.ac.uk

Abstract. Driving, including manual controlling and decision making, asks a huge operation workload for drivers. Even a small distribution can lead to serious traffic accidents. The wrong use of vehicle lights and the misunderstanding of vehicle lights are some of the causes of traffic accidents. Therefore, this study tries to promote a voice controlled vehicle-light system which could translate people's voice into computer commands and reduce the operation workload of people. To be specific, this study presents an interface - "Light On", a semi-autonomous vehicle-light system based on Voice User Interface (VUI) and the screen in the vehicle to reduce traffic accidents caused by the incorrect use of vehicle lights. The vehicle lights can be switched on and off automatically based on GPS. Voice is used to give etiquette vehicle-light commands and cancel the wrong commands detected by system. Graphical User Interface (GUI) on screen and VUI will provide feedback of vehicle-light using condition. The study also involves a small-scale prototype-evaluation experiment to evaluate the feasibility of the system. The results are promising as they revealed that "Light On" has the potential to be accepted by drivers and put forward some future semi-autonomous vehicle-light-design suggestions. Furthermore, the results can offer preliminary support in what might be a bigger in the program of work. Also, the VUI can transfer information among vehicles. This may be a potential new communication way for drivers besides vehicle light and gesture.

Keywords: Vehicle light system · Voice user interface · Semi-autonomous controlling · Traffic accident

1 Introduction

Since traffic accidents are one of the top 10 causes of death worldwide [1], researchers are detecting the causes of traffic accidents and trying to find measures to reduce traffic accidents. Some researchers have found that driving including hand controlling and decision making. These ask a huge operation workload for drivers and therefore, even a small distribution can lead to serious traffic accidents [2]. Also, some researchers found that the incorrect use of vehicle lights and the misunderstanding of vehicle lights are some of the main causes of accidents [3]. Therefore, it is necessary to promote a

© Springer Nature Switzerland AG 2020
C. Stephanidis and M. Antona (Eds.): HCII 2020, CCIS 1226, pp. 408–416, 2020.
https://doi.org/10.1007/978-3-030-50732-9_54

vehicle-light system, which is easier to control, to reduce the operation workload of drivers and in this way reducing traffic accidents [4, 5].

2 Literature Review

Now there are some existing methods promoted to reduce traffic accidents by reducing workload. Some researchers focused on how to reduce the workload of drivers [6–8]. Based on the fact that 90% of traffic accidents are caused by human mistakes, autonomous vehicles are promoted as a way to solve the problem [6, 7]. However, such a system mainly relies on the intensity of illumination to detect if the front light is required [8]. Therefore, the current self-driving vehicle-light system cannot control vehicle-light etiquette such as alternating high and low beams to signal "Thank you" to other road users. Also, different with vehicle-light regulation, vehicle-light etiquette is unpredictable. Therefore, it is not easy to be learned by autonomous vehicles and preset. Thus, it may be not a good idea to use a self-driving system to solve this problem in recent decades. Some researchers promoted the design on vehicle-light. Some specialists designed the new layout of the LED sealed light [9]. Some researchers studied the suitable luminance of vehicle lighting simulations [10]. More research focused on how to improve the existing vehicle light. For example, Huang, et al. refined the light-emitting diode of automotive headlight [11]; Hung refined the digital micro-mirror device of the automotive headlight [12].

It can be seen that the existing research mainly focused on the autonomous vehicles or improve the vehicle light itself. As for autonomous vehicles, although it can reduce operation workload, a survey showed that there were still more than 50% of people who refused to use autonomous vehicles [3]. Therefore, more interventions need to be considered to increase this low acceptance. As for the improvement of vehicle light, this measure did not change the vehicle-light operation behavior and could not reduce the workload of drivers.

Therefore, an easier and more accepted measure should be promoted. Thus, the paper tried to present a voice controlled vehicle-light system that could translate people's voice into computer commands and reduce the operation workload of people. To be specific, "Light On" is presented to reduce traffic accidents caused by incorrect use of vehicle lights. It is a semi-autonomous vehicle-light system based on VUI and is more easily to be accepted.

3 "Light On" Design Process

3.1 User Research

We interviewed 30 drivers aged 24–41 years in China to understand their thoughts about the reason for traffic accidents; the problems they meet in driving; the vehicle-light using process; their opinion on voice controlled vehicles and vehicle-light. The preliminary research data are summarized as follows:

- Expert drivers use more etiquette vehicle-lights like "thanks" or "please go first" than young drivers. In other words, using etiquette vehicle-lights is a workload for young drivers if they are forced to operate.
- Drivers lose some vehicle-light operation sometimes like using Left/Right turn signal before changing the lines.
- Turning right or turning left can be predicted through traffic lights, GPS or experience. However, if there are emergent conditions happened, the vehicle-light operation will increase the workload of drivers.
- When drivers follow the instruction of GPS, they will sometimes meet the condition: they need to recognize where they need to go from GPS, observe traffic conditions in a crossroad and operate vehicle-light at the same time. This is a high workload condition for drivers. If drivers are distracted or they are the green-hand drivers, this condition will happen more easily.
- Some drivers think what they should only do is to control the steering wheel like a driving game to reduce the driving workload.
- Drivers can accept VUI to control their vehicles.
- Drivers think answering whether operating this command is a better form than giving command directly.
- The acceptance rate is higher in younger drivers (less than 30 years old) than that of older drivers (more than 30 years old).
- Drivers hope the manual operation can co-exist with VUI.

3.2   Analysis of Requirements

We further summarized the opportunity points of the design requirements as:

- VUI command should be given in the form of question answering. However, it should also have the function to control the vehicle light through voice command.
- The command could control vehicle-light operations in traffic rules and etiquette vehicle lights.
- The vehicle light can be controlled by VUI and manual. For example, when the driver manually operates the vehicle light, the voice controlled vehicle light will not operate again.
- The vehicle light can be automatically operated when some emergency happened.
- The automatically vehicle light operation should connect with GPS and the vehicle light could change based on the GPS guideline.
- The vehicle light can be switched off manually or through VUI.

3.3   Design of the System

The interactive design "Light On" was selected to satisfy the needs. Interfaces are mainly constituted by four parts: Vehicle light information about which light is used, An overview of the vehicle light using condition, GPS guideline and Map (Fig. 1).

Vehicle light information about which light is used will give direct information about which light is now switched on. If the vehicle light operation is an etiquette operation, the name of the etiquette will be shown (Fig. 2). Besides, if the operation is based on the traffic roles, the direction of the vehicle in the interface will change. An overview of the vehicle light using condition shows the whole vehicle-light using condition. This is used to give an overview for drivers about which vehicle light has been switched on. The GPS guideline includes a word instruction about the next driving direction. Also, the direction icon is used to reduce the operation workload. A Map is used to give drivers a driving distance in a graphic way.

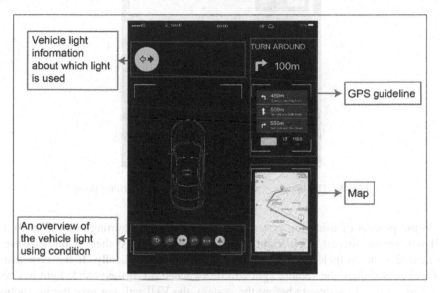

Fig. 1. The composition of main interfaces: vehicle light information about which light is used, an overview of the vehicle light using condition, GPS guideline and map

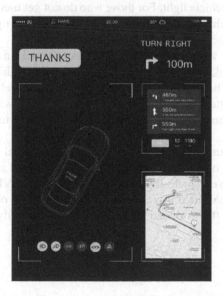

Fig. 2. The interface of an etiquette (Thanks) vehicle light operation

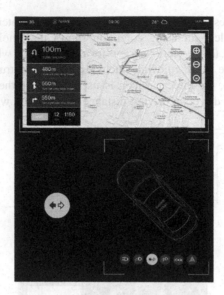

Fig. 3. The interface when the vehicle nears a turning point

In the process of using the system, when drivers near a turning point (Fig. 3), the VUI will remind drivers "Left/Right turn signal switch on". If there is no response in the next 2 s, the vehicle light will be switched on automatically. If the response is "Cancel or No" then, the vehicle light will be switched off. If the vehicle light has been switched on or off by drivers before the system, the VUI will not give the instruction.

Added VUI in current driving behavior will be a better choice compared with replacing current vehicle light operations. For those who get used to VUI, they can rely on VUI to control the vehicle light. For those who do not get used to VUI, the VUI will be a monitor about vehicle light using which will give the operation suggestion if people forget to give the operation.

When the etiquette vehicle light is needed (take "Thanks as an example), drivers only need to say "Thanks" which is a voice response to the other vehicle drivers who provide convenience. Then, the VUI will have some etiquette vehicle light operation. If a driver receive etiquette vehicle light from others, the VUI will also tell the drivers "the vehicle saying thanks to you" to help his or her understand what the car light represent.

Compared with manually operate, voice is a more natural response in etiquette. Therefore, the etiquette operation can be more easily controlled and drivers do not need to remember the relative vehicle light characters. Therefore, VUI can reduce driving workload. Also, VUI can help drivers detect the meaning of other drivers. This is a method that can reduce the workload to recognizing the other drivers' information from vehicle light.

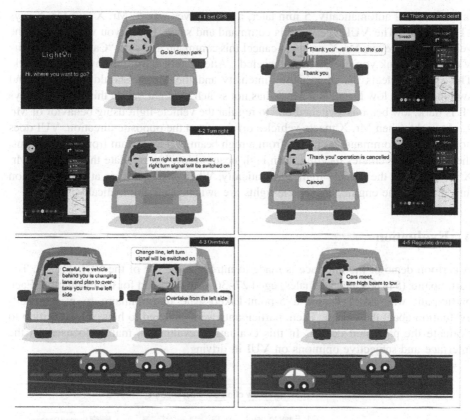

Fig. 4. The scenario of how VUI is used in driving. Figure 4-1. How to set GPS; Fig. 4-2. How VUI automatically operate vehicle light; Fig. 4-3. How drivers give instruction (like overtaking) which is not based on GPS and how the information is delivered to other vehicles; Fig. 4-4. How to cancel a command; Fig. 4-5. How to regular driving

3.4   Scenario of VUI

Figure 4 shows how the VUI can be implemented in the form of a graphic. A male driver Mr. X, 24 years old, plans to drive to "Park A". When he enters his vehicle, Mr. X touches the screen. The screen shows the "Welcome page" and ask where he want to go. Mr. X says "Go to Green Park". Guided by GPS, Mr. X plans to turn right in 100 meters. The screen says "Turn right at the next corner, right turn signal is switched on" and the right turn signal is switched on automatically in 2 s. After turning, the right turn signal is switched off automatically. Later, Driver B drives in front of Mr. X and Mr. X wants to change the lane. Therefore, Mr. X says, "Overtake from the left side". When hearing the command, the vehicle switches on left turn signal" and the turning signal vehicle light is shown in the screen interface. At the same time, a message is sent to the screen of Driver B and the VUI for Driver B says "Careful, the vehicle behind you is changing lane and plan to overtake you from the left side". The Driver B receives this information and keeps his speed to avoid traffic accidents. After overtaking, the signal is switched off automatically. 5 min later, a driver gives way to Mr. X and Mr. X says "Thank you". The VUI receives this command and says "Thank you will show to the vehicles". However, Mr. X wants to cancel this command and says "Cancel". Then, the VUI says "Thank you operation is canceled". After a long drive, the day becomes dark. The system detects the illumination intensity and the Mr. X should switch on and switches on the low beam. But Mr. X has not switch the light on. At this time VUI says "It is dark, low beam is switched on" to regular the vehicle-light using behavior of Mr. X. At night, when Mr. X meets vehicles driving from the opposite direction, VUI does not detect the command to change from a high beam to a low beam from Mr. X. Thus, the VUI says "vehicles meeting, turn high beam to low" to regulate the action of Mr. X and changes the vehicle light automatically. When Mr. X arrives at his destination and turns off the engine, all vehicle-lights are switched off automatically.

4   Evaluation

A cartoon demo of the interface is made to introduce the use of the VUI (Fig. 4). Ten participants (5 males and 5 females) aged 27–36 were recruited for the evaluation. Each participant was asked to fill a 5-point-Likert-scale questionnaire to give a self-evaluation about the design. Then, participants were gathered to have a focus group to evaluate the promoted design. In this evaluation, evaluate is mainly focused on the interface and subjective opinions on VUI in driving.

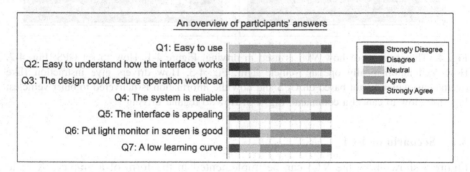

Fig. 5. Results of the 5-point-Likert-scale questionnaire of 10 participants

Figure 5 shows an overview of participants' answers from the questionnaire. From this overview, it can be seen that nearly all participants thought the VUI could be easy to use (Q1). However, some participants mentioned that the interfaces which have similar functions have a different layout on different pages. This will confuse users. Most of the participants think the design is attractive (Q5) but some participants also pointed out that it is strange to speak in the whole driving. Although some participants thought that the interface was hard to understand, many of them agree that the interface was clear (Q2). Most of the participants agreed that the system was easy to learn (Q7). However, many participants were also dubious about whether the VUI can be a reliable way to give out commands (Q4). Putting the light condition to the screen has triggered a discussion (Q6). More participants believed this will be helpful while some people refute it. Some participants thought the system will reduce the workload when driving while some participants challenged this statement (Q3).

Drivers were satisfied with the creative design of the prototype. However, they also found some problems in the design besides what has been mentioned before. Such as (a) drivers may communicate with passengers. Therefore, how does the system distinguish whether the sentence is the command or communication? (b) Not all vehicles involve screens. If the system could be downloaded in a phone, it will be better. However, if the screen of the phone can include all functions that have been promoted needs to be discussed. (c) Drivers need to use voice to give instructions and they need extra attention to what VUI said. Therefore, if VUI could reduce the operation workload is uncertain. More researches need to be done to proof it. (d) Some drivers have less trust in VUI because they do not know the wrong rate of it. However, they added that if the principle of the VUI could be explained then the trust will increase. (e) The color of the interface is not supported by some participants because they think black is not a good choice by day.

In the future design, we will modify the design based on feedback questions: (i) The background color will be changed based on the illumination and the layout of interfaces which include similar functional parts will be rearranged; (ii) A system which could detect whether drivers are communicating with passengers or giving a command will be added; (iii) Methods which could increase the reliability of VUI and design will be considered, like show professional inductions about the system in waiting page; (iv) The phone terminal will be considered as the carrier of the design. After the improvement of the design, more evaluation will be conducted, including whether VUI is a nature interaction in driving and test whether VUI can reduce operation workload in field study.

5 Conclusion

The research promoted "Light on" - a concept for an interactive vehicle-light system which is controlled by VUI. This design helps drivers control the vehicle light by speaking instead of manual operation and reduces the workload of drivers and increasing driver's efficiency. Also, the design helps drivers feel more relax when driving because they only need to judge if the operation is right instead of giving out operations. To be specific, the advantages of this system is (i) the vehicle light could be controlled by both manual and VUI. (ii) The VUI can control vehicle lights which are set based on traffic regulation and etiquette vehicle lights. (iii) The VUI can be used as a monitor and correct the wrong vehicle light using.

The contribution of this study is that (a) the VUI can transfer information among vehicles. This may be a potential new communication way for drivers beside vehicle light and gesture; (b) this study has the potential to be accepted by drivers and put forward some future semi-autonomous vehicle-light-design suggestions; (c) the results of the experiment can offer preliminary results in what might be a much bigger program of this work.

References

1. World Health Organisation: The top 10 causes of death, City (2018)
2. 深度:一一揭开,无人驾驶汽车的优点、缺点和不容忽视的问题. City (2019)
3. Christensen, J.: Wrong on red: the constitutional case against red-light cameras. Wash. Univ. J. Law Policy **32**, 443–466 (2010)
4. Patten, C.J., Kircher, A., Östlund, J., Nilsson, L., Svenson, O.: Driver experience and cognitive workload in different traffic environments. Accid. Anal. Prev. **38**(5), 887–894 (2006)
5. Rasmussen, J.: Cognitive Control and Human Error Mechanisms. Wiley, London (1987)
6. Wu, Z., Pan, G.: Smart Car Space: An Application. In: SmartShadow: Models and Methods for Pervasive Computing. Advanced Topics in Science and Technology in China. Springer, Heidelberg (2013). https://doi.org/10.1007/978-3-642-36382-5_6
7. Hancock, P.A., Verwey, W.B.: Fatigue, workload and adaptive driver systems. Accid. Anal. Prev. **29**(4), 495–506 (1997)
8. Anderson, R.E.J.S.S.C.R.: Social impacts of computing: codes of professional ethics. Soc. Sci. Comput. Rev. **10**(4), 453–469 (1992)
9. Huang, N.H.: Low profile round LED sealed light with spider design. Google Patents (2008)
10. Ekrias, A., Eloholma, M., Halonen, L., Song, X.-J., Zhang, X., Wen, Y.J.: Road lighting and headlights: luminance measurements and automobile lighting simulations. Build. Environ. **43**(4), 530–536 (2008)
11. Huang, M.-S., Hung, C.-C., Fang, Y.-C., Lai, W.-C., Chen, Y.-L.J.O.: Optical design and optimization of light emitting diode automotive head light with digital micromirror device light emitting diode. Optik **121**(10), 944–952 (2010)
12. Hung, C.-C., et al.: Optical design of automotive headlight system incorporating digital micromirror device. Appl. Opt. **49**(22), 4182–4187 (2010)

Design and Evaluation of an In-Vehicle Communication System

Xin Zhou[✉]

Tsinghua University, Beijing, China
zhoux18@mails.tsinghua.edu.cn

Abstract. In this research, we proposed the in-vehicle communication system with the help of augmenting reality. A driving simulation environment was built to support the testing. The participants engaged in two tasks parallelly: one driving task (primary task) and one spoken task (secondary task). The participants should take the primary task with high priority and finish the secondary task using the spare effect. The primary task was a common car following task. The scenario was set at high-way and the speed was 75 km/h on a two lanes straight road. The participant should follow the leading vehicle with an appropriate distance. To evaluate their driving performance, the average speed, the average departure from the road, and the average acceleration were chosen and compared between two conditions. There was no significant difference between two conditions.

Keywords: Driving simulator · Driving safety · In-vehicle communication

1 Introduction

Despite expert warnings, many drivers throughout the world use cell phones or talking to other passengers while driving. Studies clearly indicate that this type of behavior has a negative effect on drivers' ability to drive safely.

While video calling using mobile phones remains a potential distraction for today's drivers, in this paper we turn our attention to see whether having conversations with the passengers replaced by video calling using augmented reality (AR) displays could improve the user experience without raising the risk level.

AR displays project images into the user's visual scene in such a way that those images appear to be part of the natural scene. AR devices, such as HoloLens, have the potential to reduce driver distractions by presenting visual information close to the driver's visual focus, while also allowing the driver to continue to view the driving environment. However, HoloLens is a powerful computer and we can expect drivers to use it as such, even engaging in video calls. It is not known how distracting this is.

Therefore, in this paper we assess the effects of a video call on the screen, simulating AR effect, and contrast this to the case of a speech-only conversation. We conducted a study in which participants controlled a simulated vehicle and at the same time engaged in a secondary task to do word guessing. Based on prior work with video calling while driving, our hypothesis is that on straight roads drivers' visual attention to the road ahead will be reduced when they can see the passenger compared to the case when they can only hear them (Reason might be owing to nonverbal cues such as facial expressions, gestures, and posture that are not available when conversing by looking through the rear mirror).

2   Methodology

2.1   Tasks

The participants engaged in two tasks parallelly: the driving task and a spoken task. We define the driving task as the primary task and the spoken task is a secondary task. The driver should take the primary task with high priority and finish the secondary task using the spare effort. We take the common car following as the driving task. The scenario was set at high-way and the speed was 75 km/h on a three lanes straight road. The driver must follow a blue passenger car with an appropriate distance. Apart from the lead vehicle there was no other traffic. During the experiment procedure, the leading car may change lane suddenly due to the road crone set on the road. The participants must follow the leading car to change lane and manage to avoid the crash accident. As a result, if the participant was devoted to the secondary task, he would miss the sudden behavior of the front car and got involved in an accident.

As the participant performed the primary task, he also engaged in a spoken task. The driver and passenger would play a serious of games of guessing the words. The game was designed for two players. One player was given a target word and he should describe the meaning of the word without directly saying this word. The driver should guess the word. The purpose of this game was to offer the driver with the feeling of talking with the passengers.

The spoken task was carried on with two different ways: traditional method and visible method. The traditional method is just the talking between the passenger and driver that the driver can only hear the passenger and make response merely basing on the vocal information. The visible method enables the driver to make use of his optical channel by indirectly seeing the passenger's facial expression and gesture through AR device. We adopted the WeChat video call to transfer the real-time picture of the passenger to the driver. The position of the video call was the top right corner of the driving scenario. Although we first wanted to use the HoloLens to offer the AR experience, the HoloLens 1 generation no longer supports the Skype. As an alternative, we use WeChat video talk as a compromise. Actually, the experience of these two methods is similar considering that we only conduct the driving task through driving simulator. The simulator can only provide 2D image while the true driving scenario should be 3D. For each participant the same experimenter acted as the passenger sitting behind the driver.

2.2   Design

We conducted a one-factor within-subjects experiment in which we compare two conditions. In the speech-only condition the driver can only hear the passenger(experimenter). In the video-call condition the driver could see the passenger(experimenter) additionally. In both conditions the passenger can see the driving scenario and the state of the driver, just like the true experience when he is sitting behind the driver. We counterbalanced the presentation order of the two conditions. The items of guessing game were the same for each participant.

2.3   Participants

Six student participants took part in the experiment to test the proposed demo. They are all the students from the course HCI. Each participant would receive a gift for taking part in the experiment.

2.4   Driving Scenario Building

The driving scenario was built with SimVista, the built-in develop kit of SimCreator. The total length of the road is 20 km. The speed of the leading car is set at 75 km/h. We design two different roads with different setting of the road crone. The detailed information of setting is shown in Table 1.

Table 1. The configuration of the road crone (position)

	1st crone	2nd crone	3rd crone	4th crone	5th crone
Road 1	3 km	8 km	11 km	17 km	18 km
Road 2	1 km	6 km	12 km	15 km	18 km

2.5   Objective Measurement

We collected several results including the driving performance, the eye movement, and the performance of the game. The detailed description is shown as follows:

1) Percent dwell time on different AOIs (Area of interest).
   We have three AOIs: road ahead, video call interface, and speed dashboard. A higher percent of dwell time indicates more visual resource being devoted to the specific area. This can directly show the participant's visual resource allocation.
2) Standard deviation of lane position, as defined in SAE J2944. Increased SDLP can indicate worse driving performance.
3) Number of missed words in the game. Missed words can indicate the performance of the game.

2.6   Subjective Measurement

1) The usability questionnaire.
2) NASA TLX.

3   Results

3.1   Design of the In-Vehicle Communication System

The purpose of designing the in-vehicle communication system arouses from my personal experience. Traditionally, when we talk to acquaintance, we tend to look at him/her. We can conduct eye communication to better understand his/her intention and make judgement about his/her emotional state. When we want to have a talk with the driver, we can no longer see him/her directly. As an alternative, we can only hear, and the communication is quite eccentric. As a result, we want to design a system that can improve the quality of communication even when we are driving a car.

Traditionally, we hold the view that when you are driving a car, you must concentrate all your effort on the driving task. However, that is the merely the regulation or imagination. The truth is that the driver may make a phone call or operate his cellphone to check the notification. If we only count on the imagination that all the drivers will obey the rules and regulations, we are just escape from the problem. We should not compromise and be a coward. A question is raised naturally: Can we help to solve the problem that the driver wants to refer to other information that may shift his visual attention? Or could we help weaken the influence of visual attention shift? When we check the existing technology, augmented reality is the best option.

Following this path, we put forward our solution to help enrich the in-vehicle communication. The first thing we need to clarify is that the comparison is between AR-based display and traditional dashboard-based display. We should not make the assumption that all the driver will obey the traffic rules and refuse using cell phones while driving. We aim to lower the effect of the multimedia information on the driving performance.

The design of the communication system is simple, we need two cameras to capture both the driver and the passenger's image. The real-time image of the passenger is shown through a window fixed at the right top corner of the driving scenario. The driver can switch quickly between the road and the video call interface. All the glance and fixation behavior will be record by the SMI head-wear eye tracker.

The primary task is a simple car following task. The secondary task is a word guessing game. By setting the word guessing task we want to simulate the communication environment for the driver.

3.2   Test Results

We invite six users to test out prototype. The whole procedure lasted for about 45 min. Each participant will try the two conditions and fill a questionnaire to report their feelings about the system. The analysis about the test results will be carried on from two aspects: the objective measurement and the subjective measurement.

Objective Measurement

Eye Tracker Data

The analysis of eye tracker data is carried on with the software BeGaze. The segment of the AOI (area of interest) is shown in Fig. 1.

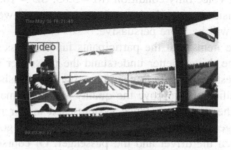

Fig. 1. The segment of AOI (Color figure online)

Figure 1 was capture by the head-wear eye tracker. The red rectangle is the area of video call interface, the green rectangle is the area of road and the yellow rectangle is the area of speed dashboard.

First, we collected some parameter of the drivers' eye movement on the three areas.

We also visualize the time allocation on the three areas. The dwell time on the three areas is shown in Fig. 2. The overall data of the fixation and glance support the hypothesis that the driver utilize the in-vehicle communication system quite frequent. The total dwell time on the road is about 35% and the total dwell time on the video interface is about 29%.

DWELL TIME

■speed ■road ■video ■other

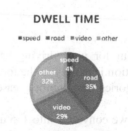

Fig. 2. The dwell time on three AOIs

The number of glance and fixation on the road is far more than the video call interface. The finding supports the driver still gather most of their attention on the driving task. We still need to investigate the fixation and glance behavior from a minor aspect. Thus, we calculate the average fixation duration and the average pupil size.

Driving Performance

The drivers' performance of the secondary task can show the quality and efficiency of the communication. We use the number of missed words as the indicator.

We first conduct the Shapiro-Wilk normality test for both conditions. The result shows the data pass the normality test.

We then conduct the paired t-test on the performance of the two conditions for each participant. The participants" performance under two conditions show margin significant. The performance under video call condition (M = 2.83, SD = 3.37) is better than the performance under voice only condition (M = 5.83, SD = 18.97), t (5) = −2.1958, p-value = 0.079. Consider we only have 6 participants, if we could recruit more participants the result will be more persuasive.

By referring to the items that the participants fail to guess within 60 s, we find video call can help the driver better understand the passenger's expression through their expression and gesture. The finding supports our hypothesis that the introduction of video call will significantly improve the quality and performance of the talking.

Considering that the driver assistance system used in our research is actually a feedback of video images, our original intention is to provide a good user experience in communication between the driver and the passenger. Of course, the premise of the function realization is that the system can not affect the driver's normal driving safety behavior. Therefore, we mainly researched and demonstrated it during the experiment.

Our experimental data is mainly based on the single factor analysis of the driver assistance system. Therefore, Welch and Brown analyzed the speed and off-center line data, and the significance value is much larger than 0.05, so it can be obtained. It is concluded that there is no significant difference in the driver's behavior in the presence or absence of the driving assistance system. The above two data mainly reflect the stability of the vehicle speed and driving route.

The analysis results of the above experimental data are very important for our next work. We have confirmed through experimental design and data analysis that the video assisted driving system in our study does not affect the driver's driving activities, and further explains our company. The research done has certain research value.

Subjective Measurement

User Experience Evaluation

Learning and using, is it helpful for your driving behavior and so on. The main acquisition of the above information is mainly in the form of questionnaires, which are mainly divided into four categories: availability, ease of use, easy learning, and satisfaction.

In the data processing stage, we convert it into 1–5 unequal scores according to the answer options, which agrees that the score is up to 5 points, and so on.

The obtained visualization results give us a certain understanding of the user experience. The figure shows the specific scores of the six subjects in each category. It can be seen that in terms of usability, the ratio is 3:3, that is, half of the people think it is more useful, and the other half means that it does not help. In terms of ease of learning and use, all the scores of the participants are larger than the average value, indicating that everyone agrees with the easy learning and use characteristics of the system in this study, and does not consume a lot of time for the participants to deeply study the system. Understand that simple communication can be easily used. In terms of satisfaction, only one participant score was lower than the average. Most of the participants were satisfied with the system, mainly in the stability of the system and the comfort during driving.

NASA TLX Subjective Evaluation
In fact, the psychological load level of users when using products also directly affects the user's subjective satisfaction. In order to increase the reliability of the experimental questionnaire, we completed the NASA TLX scale after each group of participants participated in the experiment. The user scores the behavior of participating in the experiment according to the above six dimensions.

The mental load of the six subjects in the experiment was: 70.67, 82.67, 84.67, 80.00, 52.33, 64.33. From the experimental results, the brain load score is still relatively high overall, indicating that during the experiment, our auxiliary system did not consume a lot of energy of the subjects, and this result is also related to our previous driving behavior of the participants. The results of the data analysis are consistent.

4   Discussion

This research has carried out the following research work and achieved corresponding research results:

1) Through the literature research, this study comprehensively combed the application scenarios of the car driving assistance system, and finally determined the communication problem between the driver and the passenger through the realization of the video visualization function. As we all know, in the driving process, the driver is mainly used to drive my vehicle safely. According to our investigation of the driver's driving habits, most people will unconsciously turn their attention to the dialogue when they communicate with other people. This is because of an instinct, especially when making some interesting conversations, you will unconsciously want to observe the communicator's facial expressions, and such frequent movements may pose a threat to safe driving. On the one hand, this study realizes the interaction between the driver and the passenger through the video screen line projected on the windshield during normal driving. On the other hand, through the analysis and processing of the experimental data, we have drawn a very important conclusion, that is, In the case of using the system, the driver does not affect the normal driving because of watching the video screen. On the contrary, he can improve the driver's driving comfort and safety, especially the research is related to deaf and some people. Special people who need gesture communication provide convenience for information exchange.

2) This study verified its effectiveness and reliability through experiments. The experiment evaluated the degree of access to the driver's communication information in both assisted and unassisted driving situations. The main results are as follows:

a) When there is an auxiliary system, the number of guessing games completed by the participants is significantly higher than that of the experimental subjects without the assisted driving conditions. (Or, to complete the same number of guessing games, the participants who have the auxiliary system spend less time) This also shows that in the process of communication, many expressions and actions play a key factor, if only text is used Communication can sometimes have a certain impact on understanding.

b) In both cases, there was no significant difference between the participants in avoiding obstacles during driving and maintaining the speed of the vehicle. In other words, after we joined a video assistant system, the driver would not Watching the picture in the video affects normal driving, because during the use, any driver will not always stare at the video feedback system, its presence is more similar to the dashboard of our car, or like the driving mirror You won't always pay attention to all of its dynamics, but you will maintain a certain frequency to see the information it feeds back with glasses, and our implementation goal is exactly the same, verifying its security and reliability through comparison.

3) This study can be installed in all existing models. The video assist system used in the experiment has no requirements for the type of the car, and its construction process is relatively simple, and the cost is relatively low. Through the investigation of most of the models on the market, all vehicles do not have similar auxiliary tools for car interior communication, and this research provides a new idea for car auxiliary systems, we can carry out functional on the existing basis. Development, for example, for the auxiliary system of public transportation such as taxis, we can add hand movement capture, facial feature capture, etc. This is mainly because during the public transportation driving process, the driver's own safety is very important. In the absence of the assisted driving system, the driver can only rely on the rearview mirror in the cab to observe the rear, and it also has many blind spots, such as only seeing the face, unable to see the hand movements of the rear person, and Our system can only conduct a risk assessment in time by analyzing facial features and hand movements. If there are some dangerous behaviors such as robbery or attacking the driver, a voice prompt will be given to inform the driver of the potential risk factors and let the driver Drivers can have a correct approach, this is just one of them that can be developed Function, there are many related functions can be developed for use in our support system, based on the result, this study follow safe driving some related studies provide some valuable reference.

References

1. McEvoy, S.P., Stevenson, M.R., McCartt, A.T., Woodward, M., Haworth, C., Palamara, P., et al.: Role of mobile phones in motor vehicle crashes resulting in hospital attendance: a case-crossover study. BMJ **331**(7514), 428 (2005). bmj.38537.397512.55v1

2. Isa, K.A.M., et al.: Mobile phone usage behaviour while driving among educated young adults in the urban university. Procedia Soc. Behav. Sci. **36**, 414–420 (2012). ISSN 1877-0428
3. Papantoniou, P., Papadimitriou, E., Yannis, G.: Review of driving performance parameters critical for distracted driving research. Transp. Res. Procedia **25**, 1796–1805 (2017)

Transport, Safety and Crisis Management

The Evolution of "GOJEK" as an Indonesian Urban Mobile Ride Hailing Model Study Case: Public and Government Regulatory Responses on Urban Mobile Ride Hailing

Ajree D. Malawani[✉][iD], Salahudin Salahudin[✉], Zuly Qodir[✉][iD],
Mohammad Jafar Loilatu[✉], and Achmad Nurmandi[✉][iD]

Department of Government Affairs and Administration,
Jusuf Kalla School of Government, Universitas Muhammadiyah Yogyakarta,
Indonesia JL. Brawijaya, Bantul, Yogyakarta, Indonesia
ajreedmalawani@gmail.com, nurmandi_achmad@umy.ac.id

Abstract. The emergence of mobile-based transportation and transaction is rapidly gaining popularity, particularly among urbanized areas. Thus, paper sought to illustration the evolution of GoJek as a form of public transportation through the lens of statutory law, government policies, and other public documents that are related to what GoJek has become today. Other relevant topics related to the emergence of GoJek such as transportation, MSME and economic matters are also discussed. The setting/context for this study will be Indonesian policies and the characters such as ride-hailing companies and the public. Law and regulations from January 2010 until December of 2019 were gathered using text mining. Collected data were then analysed with the help of a qualitative data analysis software called NVivo. Finding shows that GoJek has become the most prominent ride-haling in Indonesia, and the positive sympathy from the public helped in pressing the government for its legalisation. It was also found out that GoJek has also helped MSME and in boosting the national economy. In 2018, GoJek, thorough its GoFood service, has recorded an unprecedented 500 million orders. Also, GoJek has been emphasizing on the importance of self-regulation among professional services and co-regulation among industries. Compared to a direct regulation, a co-regulatory approach is more effective and flexible and offers better chances of protecting the welfare of the consumers as it employs a dialogue process between stakeholders where the results deviate from the common state command-and-control regulation.

Keywords: GoJek · Ojek · Mobile-based app · MSME · Economy

1 Introduction

The World Population Review data published on February 17, 2020, Indonesia's capital Jakarta has a population of approximately 10,770,487 in 2016 from 9,607,787 in the 2010 census. Jakarta's population is estimated at 3.45% of Indonesia's total population, with 272697127 being the total population of the country. Based on

C. Stephanidis and M. Antona (Eds.): HCII 2020, CCIS 1226, pp. 429–438, 2020.
https://doi.org/10.1007/978-3-030-50732-9_56

satellite navigation data, Jakarta has the worst traffic congestion in the world, with an average of 33,000 stop-and-go a year. The authorities have recognized the importance of transportation in the functioning of a city, so the government aims to increase transport trips from 23% to 60% by 2030. The existence of private cars will remain and continue to increase, and this challenges the authorities as to how to manage and integrate their existence into a comprehensive urban transit system (Gerber et al. 2018). This challenge led Nadiem Makarim to create a ride-hailing platform called "GoJek" in 2010. The term GoJek originated from the word Ojek, referred to unlicensed motor-cycle taxis that are prominent in Indonesia. In 2015, GoJek launched an application that allows transport passengers to book a ride; this resulted in brawls between GoJek drivers against traditional Ojek drivers and conventional taxi drivers and operators.

Currently, the GoJek Company has seventeen services namely: GoRide, GoCar, GoBluebird, GoSend, GoBox, GoMassage, GoClean, GoFood, GShop, GoMart, GoMEd, GoTix, GoPlay, GoPulsa, GoPoints, GoNearby, and GoBills. GoJek provides a simple, user-friendly, and "human-sounding" mobile application. The application exploited the attractive aspects of motorcycle-based mobility with the ease of cashless and traceable digital transactions, offering its riders more convenient, safer, and fixed-rate rides, which spared them from regular price-haggling nuisance. For the convenience of GoJek drivers, the company-built majority of its worker pool, equipping the non-descript 'man on the street' with a beloved corporate identity and a bright new look (Lee 2018). The sense of the concrete components and visions that make up a physical GoJek show how the economy of the internet network is becoming material and reality. GoJek has been dubbed the 'super-app', a software application that com-bines diverse technical knowledge to a greater extent than the sum of its parts; hence, it incorporates the technology of a mobile phone, motor vehicles, and other necessities such as helmets, hats, and face masks, to provide services as requested by the end-user (Jesse 2015).

GOJEK is a unique phenomenon of human-computer interaction research in a specific environment. This paper will describe and analyze the evolution of GoJek as a ride-hailing service from pro and contra perspective up to this service got legitimation from Government. This study focuses on how should work be assessed for the quality or effectiveness of Gojek; government policies generally lack clear qualitative, and quantitative criteria for HCI research assessment (Lazar and Barbosa 2019).

2   Previous Studies

Transportation can in the form of private vehicles and public transportations that includes bus, train, and taxicabs, among others. Taxicabs are one of the transportation modes that are very much popular in most urbanised areas; it can provide point-to-point services in twenty-four hours within seven days (Diaz Olvera and Pochet 2019; Ge et al. 2017; Li and Hou 2019; Long et al. 2017; Silalahi et al. 2017). Presumably, taxicabs move from one point to another as per request by its consumer, or the end-user. The fact that it does not need to follow a route, stop to a station, nor look for another passenger once it is already being booked, it can efficiently meet the needs of the service consumer (Hu et al. 2019). It is identified to be more efficient compared to other transportation modes such as bus and train due to its door-to-door service (Liu et al. 2020; Suatmadi et al. 2019).

The emergence of mobile-based ride-hailing taxis also led to the birth of mobile-based motorcycle taxis (Long et al. 2017). Motorcycle taxis are known in developing countries, particularly in Asia (Long et al. 2017; Salanova Grau et al. 2018). Nonetheless, transportation is one of the important factors which needs to be addressed in a developing community (Imandasari et al. 2019; Saffan and Rizki 2018). One of the alternatives to addressed transportation is the emergence of mobile-based taxis due to its efficient accessibility (Imandasari et al. 1255) and convenience (Rachman et al. 2020). In Indonesia, online taxis (hereafter referred to and locally known as *Ojek*) has part of public transpiration, an innovative counterpart of traditional motorcycles that begun its online services in 2015 (Purnawan and Musliadi 2019; Suhartoyo et al. 2018) and later added car and other services.

The so-called "sharing economy" is overshadowed by technologically facilitated commercial exchanges. Hence, the terms "crowd-based capitalism" or "platform capitalism" were preferred (Fraiberger and Sundararajan 2015). In particular, the platform economy is fueled by wealthy venture capitalists seeking to increase their private fortunes by finding new ways of extracting value from socially produced wealth. What makes them capitalist is that these infrastructures are privately owned and operated to extract profits by becoming the ground on which transactions take place. Among the existing taxi capitalism, the medallion capitalism, where a quota of licenses will be adopted, is referable to platform capitalism, like Uber, where quota is not set, among other necessary regulations (Tucker 2018).

In coordinated structures or networks in sharing economy, participants carry out sharing activities in the form of renting, loan, selling, selling and transfers of products, resources, space, money, and transport solution (Holbrook and Schindler 2003). In view of sharing economy as a central structure and a term that is significantly disputed, the sharing economy lies in three fundamental core issues: (1) the access economy, (2) the economy of the network, and (3) community-based economy (Acquier et al. 2017). The suggested importance of credibility in peer economy indicates that a possible distinguishing feature of sharing economy is a systemic process of integration with more ephemeral and less intensive shared economy types that impact a more ephemeral, lower-intense, and systemic process with integration and value development (Arcidiacono et al. 2018) (Table 1).

We identify success factors of the digital-sharing economy to these populations, identify shortcomings, and propose mitigation strategies based on prior research related to trust, social capital, and theories of collective efficacy. Information interfaces and presentation: Four principles of the sharing economy platforms allow people within and across communities to connect with individuals to provide and benefit from basic skills and services such as babysitting and housecleaning, or physical resources such as housing and transportation. Utilizing the idle hours of those individuals with appropriate resources helps sharing economy function (Frenken 2017; Scholz 2016; Frenken and Schor 2017). Sharing economy activities fall into four broad categories: recirculation of goods, increased utilization of durable assets, exchange of services, and sharing of productive assets (Daunoriene et al. 2015)

Table 1. Previous studies on sharing economy

Authors	Form	Regulation
(Holbrook and Schindler 2003)	Collaborative consumption, in the form of renting, lending, trading, bartering, and swapping of goods, services, transportation solutions, space, or money	Sharing activities
(Acquier et al. 2017)	Three foundational cores: (1) Access economy, (2) Platform economy, and (3) Community-based economy	Platform
(Arcidiacono et al. 2018)	Peer economies bring us to forms of sociality with value creation	
(Avital et al. 2015)	Beyond just transgressing against local laws, sharing economy companies struggle to protect their consumers in countries where governance is weak and these companies are not able to vet their sharers (drivers, renters, etc.)	Consumer protection
(Böcker and Meelen 2017)	The sharing economy here is a particularly interesting case, because in contrast to many other sustainable innovations, certain sharing economy sectors are scaling up very rapidly. Synthesising from previous sharing economy studies, and in line with a sustainability approach, economic, environmental and social motivations are considered	Contract law
(Bradley and Pargman 2017)	to democratise access to low-cost bicycling and repair, to use under-utilised assets while simultaneously building a culture of trust and generosity, and to democratise access to information beyond the money-based economy	
(Breidbach and Brodie 2017)	The concept and practice of a "sharing economy" and "collaborative consumption"	collaborative consumption
(Cherry and Pidgeon 2018)	as a more sustainable form of consumption; as an economic opportunity; and as a pathway to a decentralised, equitable and sustainable economy	
(Codagnone et al. 2017)	the 'collaborative economy', 'crowd-employment or crowd-working', the 'gig economy', the 'on-demand economy', etc	crowd working
(Constantiou et al. 2017)	Four Models of Sharing Economy Platforms Sharing economy platforms combine organizational and market mechanisms in innovative ways to gain competitive advantages over incumbents. We call the resulting four sharing economy models "Franchiser," "Principal," "Chaperone" and "Gardener."	crowd working
(Pazaitis et al. 2017)	With this new opportunity for increased "cooperativism," we're moving toward a true sharing or collaborative economy - one that is not controlled by a few large intermediary operators, but that is governed by and for the people	crowd working or "cooperativism"

3 Research Method

This study uses content and historical analysis to examine the impact of media narratives on current ride-hailing policies in Indonesia. The setting/context for this study will be Indonesian policies and the characters such as ride-hailing companies and the public. Law and regulations from January 2010 until December of 2019 were gathered using text mining. To collect the documents via agent automatically is important for text mining. In this study, the data were analyzed by using Nvivo 12 Plus. Research findings revealed that there is a potential conflict between HCI and public policy on the GoJek evolution story. The HCI community can inform policymakers by providing expertise and taking part in the development of policy related to mobile ride-hailing services (Lazar and Barbosa 2019).

4 Findings

4.1 Evolution of Gojek

The journey of GoJek began in 2010 as a motorcycle ride-hailing call centre in Indonesia. The homegrown mobile application was then launched in 2015 with only three services: GoRide, GoSend, and GoMart. Since then, the mobile application has evolved into a Super Application, a multi-services platform with around 17 services today. GoJek is now a leading technology group of platforms serving millions of users in Southeast Asia. In the GoEcosystem, GoFood claims to have increased the number of orders in 2018 with an unprecedented 500 million orders. Amongst many, these are the top five most popular menus, namely chicken, pasta, noodles, fried foods, and cake. The total transaction value of GoFood (GoFood's/GTV's gross transaction value) exceeds $2 billion in 2018, which implies a cumulative distance of 624,971,059 miles, or 1,625,8 times the duration of Earth to Moon. GoJek claims that GoFood is Southeast Asia's biggest food-supply-service. The success of GoJek in its Food delivery services is being sought to disrupt by GrabFood, a food delivery service under another mobile-based ride-hailing company called Grab. Currently, GrabFood covers 80% of the micro, small, and medium-sized enterprises (MSME) companies.

4.2 GoJek Economics

Based on the research conducted by Google, the Temasek and Bain Company e-Conomy SEA2019 ride-hailing (online food and transport services) in the ASEAN region has a market share of only $3 billion (gross merchandise value/GMV). This market value hit $12.7 billion in 2019 and is expected to hit $40 billion in 2015. As of the GMV trip to Indonesia, it hit around US$ 980 million in 2015, grew up to $5.7 billion in 2019, and expected to increase up to $18 billion in 2025, highest among countries within Southeast Asian Region. In Indonesia, there are two major mobile-based companies that offer food delivery services, GoJek and Grab. The market share of food services exceeded $400 million in 2015, while electronic transport values $2.5 billion. In 2019, GMV foodservice grew to $5.2 billion, while online transport amounted to $7.5 billion. The global online food supply company, which is expected to be $20 billion in 2025, is estimated to equal GMV online transport.

Among the mobile-based taxis in Indonesia, GoJek has gained popularity. An online survey conducted in the previous year shows that 85.22% of the respondents use GoJek, 66,24% uses Tomb, while 50% uses Uber (Katadata.go.id). The low percentile of Uber can be traced to its services that are limited to transportation. Mobile-based transportation is extensively used as a public transport mode, as opposed to traditional motorcycle taxis and conventional taxis, because of its fixed rates. The Application also helps customers to be driven to the passenger's location and to drive fairly easily in contrast to the use of public buses or conventional taxis.

The study by the Demographic Institute, Faculty of Economics and Business, University of Indonesia in 2018 found that GoJek contributes up to $2,861,999,150.40 per year to the Indonesian economy with its GoCar, GoLife, and GoFood services (https://ldfebui.org). The contribution was generated from the difference in incomes between partners and owners of SMEs before and after GoJek was established. Under GoRide services (motorcycle), GoJek records $1,068,393,348.00 a year, while $551,770,691.50 for GoCar. Other services being offered by GoJek, such as GoLife, has generated $77,897,038.80. The revenue generated from the partnership of GoFood and MSME generated $1,168,455,582.00, highest among other revenues the government has generated from GoJek (https://ldfebui.org)

Law No. 22/2009 and Government Regulation Number 74/2014 regulates ride-hailing vehicles as they are defined to be a non-fixed route public transportation. In Indonesia, the maximum number of vehicles is determined by the local government together with the Ministry of Transportation, so as the release of the license to operate. Transportation fair is determined by the service in accordance with the price set by the Ministry of Transportation. This law does not cover mobile-based taxis and the unfair competition between conventional and mobile-based taxis. Provisions under transportation laws and economy law created work opportunities for the registered freelance drivers of ride-hailing taxis in Indonesia. In 2010, GoJek (one of the mobile-based ride-hailing services in Indonesia) started as non-mobile-based ride transport with only 20 motorbikes. After five years, GoJek finally launched its mobile application in 2015, which can be used by the end-user to order a vehicle. Upon ordering, the desired destination must be indicated, and the price fair for that destination will be visible to the end-user. This feature is a transformation from the conventional negotiation between the service provider and the end-user to a non-compelling transaction. Also in 2015, the Ministry of transportation issued memorandum UM.3012/1/21/Phb/2015 that prohibits the operation of mobile-based ride-hailing taxis as the requisites to operate as public transport were not satisfied by the operators. The prohibition emanated from the unsatisfied public transportation provisions under Law No. 22/2009.

This was also aggravated by the demonstration of conventional taxi operators and drivers citing the lack of legal basis of online-based taxis to operate. Despite the prohibition made by the Indonesian government, other mobile applications that offer transportation services emerged and started its operations, such as Grab and Uber, in 2016. Mobile-based taxis faced criticism due to the lack of legal basis, and these criticisms were upheld by the government and issued a memorandum prohibiting the operation of the said taxis. As a reply to the action made by the Ministry of

Transportation, online-based taxis appealed to the government. As a result, the Indonesian President issued a pronouncement through his spoke-person that further regulation must be passed to further accept online-based taxis. Hence, online-based taxis have already championed the public and had been getting positive sympathy.

The call from the President and the resentment from the people forced the government to issue another policy through Transportation Ministerial Decree No. 32 of 2016 to facilitate online-based taxis. Provisions under the said law amend the Law No. 22/2, which does not cover the online-based public transportation industry. Thus, on October 1, 2016, legalized online-based taxis are thereby legalized. The authorization of online-based taxis from the Ministry of Transportation did not please the industry of conventional taxis. Additionally, Transportation Ministerial Decree No. 32 of 2016 was ratified as the Supreme Court revoked some provisions under it. The ratification was made under Transportation Ministerial Decree No. 26/2017. In 2017, another amendment was made regarding the non-route passenger transportation services under Transportation Ministerial Decree No. 108/2017. This law acknowledges the existence of online-based taxis as public transportation. Provisions under the said law do not, however, include the legalization of motorcycles as a form of public transportation. When it comes to online-based motorcycles, it is still illegal since two-wheeled vehicles are not considered a form of public transportation. However, in March 2019, statutory law legalizing the online-based motorcycle as a form of public transportation has been put into law (Fig. 1).

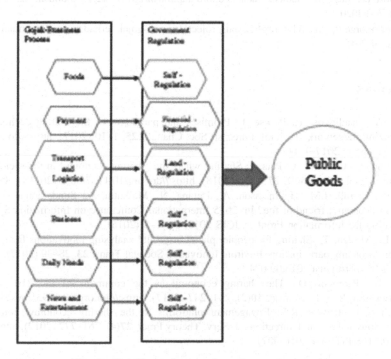

Fig. 1. Gojek's business and regulatory responses

5 Conclusion

Over the years, GoJek has been emphasizing on the importance of self-regulation among professional services and co-regulation among industries. This study looks at the theory of co-regulation as a framework of analysis as it could be a more effective approach in governing a mobile-based platform economy. Compared to a direct regulation, a co-regulatory approach is more effective and flexible and offers better chances of protecting the welfare of the consumers as it employs a dialogue process between stakeholders where the results deviate from the common state command-and-control regulation. However, self-regulation and co-regulation maintain blurred boundaries.

Self-regulation of Gojek's business commonly refers to a group of experts in a specific field who develops the rule and codes of conduct which regulate or guide the behaviour, actions, and standards of those within the group such as codes of practice, accreditation arrangements, and adoption of standards. On the other hand, co-regulation refers to specific and definite government participation in the regulatory framework. The specific types of instruments or mechanisms, such as codes of practices, voluntary agreements, and dispute resolution procedures that may be created under a self-regulatory regime, are similar under a co-regulatory framework. It is the degree of government involvement and legislative backing that determines the difference between the two.

Data Source. https://databoks.katadata.co.id/datapublish/2019/10/23/. Publish: 23/10/2019. Akses: 17/03/2020
https://doi.org/https://ldfebui.org/special-project/dampak-gojek-terhadap-perekonomian-indonesia-di-2018/

References

Acquier, A., Daudigeos, T., Pinkse, J.: Promises and paradoxes of the sharing economy: an organizing framework. Technol. Forecast. Soc. Chang. **125**, 1–10 (2017). https://doi.org/10.1016/j.techfore.2017.07.006

Arcidiacono, D., Gandini, A., Pais, I.: Sharing what? the 'sharing economy' in the sociological debate. Sociol. Rev. **66**(2), 275–288 (2018). https://doi.org/10.1177/0038026118758529

Avital, M., Carroll, J.M., Hjalmarsson, A., Levina, N., Malhotra, A., Sundararajan, A.: The sharing economy: friend or foe? In: 2015 International Conference on Information Systems: Exploring the Information Frontier, ICIS 2015, pp. 1–8 (2015)

Böcker, L., Meelen, T.: Sharing for people, planet or profit? analysing motivations for intended sharing economy participation. Environ. Innovation Societal Trans. **23**, 28–39 (2017). https://doi.org/10.1016/j.eist.2016.09.004

Bradley, K., Pargman, D.: The sharing economy as the commons of the 21st century. Cambridge J. Reg. Econ. Soc. **10**(2), 231–247 (2017). https://doi.org/10.1093/cjres/rsx001

Breidbach, C.F., Brodie, R.J.: Engagement platforms in the sharing economy: conceptual foundations and research directions. J. Serv. Theory Pract. **27**(4), 761–777 (2017). https://doi.org/10.1108/JSTP-04-2016-0071

Cherry, C.E., Pidgeon, N.F.: Is sharing the solution? exploring public acceptability of the sharing economy. J. Cleaner Prod. **195**, 939–948 (2018). https://doi.org/10.1016/j.jclepro.2018.05.278

Codagnone, C., Biagi, F., Abadie, F.: The passions and the interests: unpacking the "sharing economy". SSRN Electron. J. (2017). https://doi.org/10.2139/ssrn.2793901

Constantiou, I., Marton, A., Tuunainen, V.K.: Four models of sharing economy platforms. MIS Q. Executive **16**(4), 236–251 (2017)

Daunorienė, A., Drakšaitė, A., Snieška, V., Valodkienė, G.: Evaluating sustainability of sharing economy business models. Procedia Soc. Behav. Sci. **213**, 836–841 (2015). https://doi.org/10.1016/j.sbspro.2015.11.486

Diaz Olvera, L., Plat, D., Pochet, P.: Looking for the obvious: motorcycle taxi services in Sub-Saharan African cities. J. Transp. Geogr., 102476 (2019). https://doi.org/10.1016/j.jtrangeo.2019.102476

Fraiberger, S.P., Sundararajan, A.: Peer-to-peer rental markets in the sharing economy. SSRN Electron. J., 1–39 (2015). https://doi.org/10.2139/ssrn.2574337

Frenken, K.: Sustainability perspectives on the sharing economy. Environ. Innovation Societal Trans. **23**(May), 1–2 (2017). https://doi.org/10.1016/j.eist.2017.04.004

Frenken, K., Schor, J.: Putting the sharing economy into perspective. Environ. Innovation Societal Trans. **23**, 3–10 (2017). https://doi.org/10.1016/j.eist.2017.01.003

Ge, W., Shao, D., Xue, M., Zhu, H., Cheng, J.: Urban taxi ridership analysis in the emerging metropolis: case study in Shanghai. Transp. Res. Procedia **25**, 4916–4927 (2017). https://doi.org/10.1016/j.trpro.2017.05.368

Gerber, P., Caruso, G., Cornelis, E., de Chardon, C.M.: A multi-scale fine-grained LUTI model to simulate land-use scenarios in Luxembourg. J. Transp. Land Use **11**(1), 255–272 (2018). https://doi.org/10.5198/jtlu.2018.1187

Government Regulation Number 74/2014: Road Traffic and Transportation (2014)

Holbrook, M.B., Schindler, R.M.: Nostalgic bonding: exploring the role of nostalgia in the consumption experience. J. Consum. Behav. **3**, 107–127 (2003). https://doi.org/10.1002/cb.127

Hu, B., Xia, X., Sun, H., Dong, X.: Understanding the imbalance of the taxi market: from the high-quality customer's perspective. Physica A Stat. Mech. Appl. **535**, 122297 (2019). https://doi.org/10.1016/j.physa.2019.122297

Imandasari, T., Sadewo, M.G., Windarto, A.P., Wanto, A., Lingga Wijaya, H.O., Kurniawan, R.: Analysis of the selection factor of online transportation in the VIKOR Method in Pematangsiantar City. J. Phys: Conf. Ser. **1255**(1) (2019). https://doi.org/10.1088/1742-6596/1255/1/012008

Jesse, R.: Teacher quality policy when supply matters. Am. Econ. Rev. **105**(1), 100–130 (2015). https://doi.org/10.1257/aer.20121242

Law No. 22/2009: Road Traffic and Transportation (2009)

Lazar, J., Barbosa, S.D.J.: Introduction to human-computer interaction. In: Conference on Human Factors in Computing Systems - Proceedings (2019). https://doi.org/10.1145/3290607.3298804

Lee, D.: How ojek became gojek: disruptive technologies and the infrastructure of urban citizenship in Indonesia. Int. J. Urban Reg. Res. **1**(1) (2018)

Li, J., Hou, L.: A reflection on the taxi reform in China: innovation vs tradition. Comput. Law Secur. Rev. **35**(3), 251–262 (2019). https://doi.org/10.1016/j.clsr.2019.02.005

Liu, Q., Ding, C., Chen, P.: A panel analysis of the effect of the urban environment on the spatiotemporal pattern of taxi demand. Travel Behav. Soc. **18**, 29–36 (2020). https://doi.org/10.1016/j.tbs.2019.09.003

Long, J., Szeto, W.Y., Du, J., Wong, R.C.P.: A dynamic taxi traffic assignment model: a two-level continuum transportation system approach. Transp. Res. Part B Methodological **100**, 222–254 (2017). https://doi.org/10.1016/j.trb.2017.02.005

Pazaitis, A., De Filippi, P., Kostakis, V.: Blockchain and value systems in the sharing economy: the illustrative case of backfeed. Technol. Forecast. Soc. Chang. **125**, 105–115 (2017). https://doi.org/10.1016/j.techfore.2017.05.025

Purnawan, P., Musliadi, M.: The potential of problems on operational go-jek and grab bike. J. Phys. Conf. Ser. **1402**(2) (2019). https://doi.org/10.1088/1742-6596/1402/2/022026

Rachman, H.O., Chotib, Kurniawan, K.R.: Impact of online taxi bikes presence on Margonda Street, Depok. IOP Conf. Ser. Earth Environ. Sci. **436**, 012007 (2020). https://doi.org/10.1088/1755-1315/436/1/012007

Saffan, A.F., Rizki, M.: Exploring the role of online "Ojek" in public transport trips: case of Jakarta metropolitan area rail users. IOP Conf. Ser. Earth Environ. Sci. **158**(1). https://doi.org/10.1088/1755-1315/158/1/012024

Salanova Grau, J.M., Estrada, M., Tzenos, P., Aifandopoulou, G.: Agent-based simulation framework for the taxi sector modeling. Procedia Comput. Sci. **130**, 294–301 (2018). https://doi.org/10.1016/j.procs.2018.04.042

Scholz, T.: Platform cooperatism: challenging the corporate sharing economy. Rosa Luxemburg Stiftung, New Your Office (Magazine Article), pp. 1–26 (2016)

Silalahi, S.L.B., Handayani, P.W., Munajat, Q.: Service quality analysis for online transportation services: case study of GO-JEK. Procedia Comput. Sci. **124**, 487–495 (2017). https://doi.org/10.1016/j.procs.2017.12.181

Suatmadi, A.Y., Creutzig, F., Otto, I.M.: On-demand motorcycle taxis improve mobility, not sustainability. Case Stud. Transp. Policy **7**(2), 218–229 (2019). https://doi.org/10.1016/j.cstp.2019.04.005

Suhartoyo, S., Sonhaji, S., Azhar, M., Suharso, P.: Legal aspects of PT. Gojek Indonesia in the partnership agreement dealing with the public transport standards. In: E3S Web of Conferences, vol. 68, pp. 1–8 (2018). https://doi.org/10.1051/e3sconf/20186802008

Transportation Ministerial Decree No. 108/2017: Provisions under this decree legalises mobile-based taxis as a form of public transportation (2017)

Transportation Ministerial Decree No. 26/2017: Operation of People with Transport Vehicles not in General Motor Route (2017)

Transportation Ministerial Decree No. 32 of 2016: Transparent Legal Umbrella Taxi Application (2016)

Tucker, E.: Uber and the unmaking and remaking of taxi capitalisms: law and the "sharing economy", pp. 357–392 (2018). https://doi.org/10.2307/j.ctv5vdczv.15

UM.3012/1/21/Phb/2015: Notification Letter Number UM.3012/1/21/Phb/2015 (2015)

Aid Demand Aggregation Using Technology During Disaster Relief

Charmie Kapoor[✉], Divyanka Kapoor, Nishu Lahoti,
and Trevor Cobb Storm

Graduate School of Design and Harvard John A. Paulson School of Engineering
and Applied Sciences, Harvard University, Cambridge, USA
charmiekapoor@mde.harvard.edu

Abstract. The humanitarian aid industry's supply chain is fragmented into a variety of segments which link individuals, companies, intergovernmental organizations, local government agencies, and aid workers. In this multifaceted network, the contributions meant ultimately for impacted people may not reach their intended destination or worse, the contributions may not be useful in the crisis zone. We believe an opportunity exists to enable transparency in the humanitarian aid supply chain. Our solution ensures equipping the on-the-ground relief agencies with technology that helps them understand and forecast the demand of impacted people in their region and link the heads of these agencies to an integrated supply network.

Keywords: Aid relief · Data aggregation · Wearable sensor · Aid relief · Climate · Government · Collaboration · Relief organizations

1 Introduction

The total amount of humanitarian aid given each year can reach upwards of 27 billion dollars. Shortly after crises such as hurricanes, floods, or sectarian violence impact a region, aid organizations, usually in the form of nonprofits and governments, supply clothing, food, and medical supplies to support impacted people. In 2018 alone, 2.3 million people across the globe received humanitarian assistance; in years to come, humanitarian aid experts fear the number of people impacted by humanitarian crises will logarithmically increase as climate change sparks more fast-onset natural disasters, and political upheavals leave whole populations at risk[1]. Subsequently, the dollar amount given in humanitarian aid is set to increase.

Yet various case studies have shown that humanitarian aid can be rife with waste and inefficiencies. The industry's supply chain is fragmented into a variety of segments which link individuals, companies, intergovernmental organizations, local government agencies, and aid workers[2]. In this multifaceted network, the contributions meant ultimately for impacted people may not reach their intended destination or worse, the

---

[1] Source: https://interactive.unocha.org/publication/globalhumanitarianoverview/.

[2] Source: https://www.brookings.edu/book/delivering-aid-differently/.

© Springer Nature Switzerland AG 2020
C. Stephanidis and M. Antona (Eds.): HCII 2020, CCIS 1226, pp. 439–448, 2020.
https://doi.org/10.1007/978-3-030-50732-9_57

contributions may not be useful in the crisis zone. In some cases excess contributions are destroyed. Sometimes these supplies go directly to landfill, or in dire situations, doused in gasoline and burned, resulting in a negative impact on the region's environmental ecosystem[3].

We believe an opportunity exists to enable transparency in the humanitarian aid supply chain. If we can equip on-the-ground relief agencies with technology that helps them understand the demand of impacted people in their region and link the heads of these agencies to an integrated supply network, we believe that more of the 27 billion dollars contributed annually towards humanitarian disasters can be used more effectively. The industry's network of actors is complex. A product that enables more seamless coordination of activities and transactions could fill a latent demand across the various agencies involved in supporting humans in need.

2 Dissecting the Problem

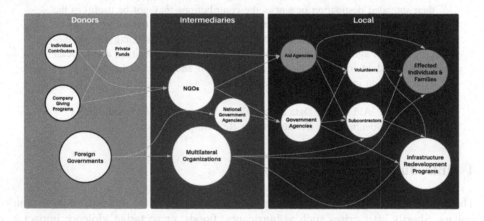

It is estimated that 25% of global humanitarian aid meets the full transparency requirements set out by the United Nations. In 2016, a network of aid agencies at the World Humanitarian Summit agreed on four components to transparent financing of humanitarian disasters[4]:

- Publishing timely, transparent, harmonized, and open data on humanitarian funding within two years.
- Utilizing data analysis to explain the impact of activities conducted by various organizations.
- Using digital platforms and open data standards to ensure accountability in decision making.

---

[3] Source: https://www.cbsnews.com/news/best-intentions-when-disaster-relief-brings-anything-but-relief/.

[4] Source: https://fts.unocha.org/sites/default/files/improving-humanitarian-transparency-with-the-iati-and-the-un-ocha-fts.pdf.

- Supporting access and publishing of data to ensure trackability of funding.

We believe that a majority of aid organizations struggle to meet these standards due to an inability to aggregate information for data analysis and digital platforms. Without systems that span the entire supply chain - starting from the donor network passing through the intermediate agencies, ultimately reaching people impacted by humanitarian disasters - transparency may be near impossible. Thus a system which could aggregate demand directly from impacted users could create a "ground-up" feedback loop at critical points in the supply chain. This aggregate information could inform upstream players in the supply chain on the funding amounts and the type of aid that would be the most impactful to combat humanitarian crises.

We utilized a systems map to segment humanitarian aid relief. This exercise helped us understand where new technologies could be inserted into the supply chain to make the greatest improvements in transparency. The questions that guided our thinking were:

1. Which segment of the supply chain has the best real-time information on the people and regions impacted by the humanitarian crises?
2. Which segment of the supply chain struggles the most with coordinating information and supplies?

Ultimately, we chose to focus on the local level of the disaster. Specifically, we chose to focus on local agencies that engage directly with affected individuals. These agencies are responsible for aggregating demand of materials and requesting, or purchasing, supplies to serve anywhere from 5,000 to 100,000 people directly impacted by crises. If we could better solve for coordination challenges experienced by relief agencies, we believe their improved efficiency could have ripple effects across the entire aid relief supply chain.

2.1 Fast Onset Disasters

To further focus our project, we segmented our research on a certain type of humanitarian crises: fast-onset, natural disasters. We uncovered that anywhere between 25 million and 1 billion people will become "environmental migrants" by 2050, or humans displaced after their homes are gradually destroyed by ecological change[5]. This prediction revolves mostly around slow-onset natural disasters, events such as the erosion of Miami's coastline, which will force whole populations to eventually leave their homes. We asked ourselves the following question:

---

[5] Source: https://www.climateforesight.eu/migrations/environmental-migrants-up-to-1-billion-by-2050/.

- If potentially 1 billion people will be impacted by natural disasters in 2050, what advances in technology and science could be piloted today in order to get ahead of the market curve?

Our design thinking process ultimately led us to fast-onset natural disasters, or events such as hurricanes, earthquakes, and floods which have a material impact in 2019 and could be aided by advances in technology.

Fast-onset natural disasters are projected to displace up to 14 million people every year[6]. Comprising meteorological hazards such as flooding, mudslides, or windstorms, as well as geophysical hazards such as tsunamis, earthquakes or volcanic eruptions, cannot be predicted with certainty and thus pose a unique set of challenges for the delivery of humanitarian aid.

Although the impacts can be varied, there are characteristics shared by all of these disasters. We started to ideate how interventions aimed at one particular type of disaster in a specific geography could be designed. We ultimately focused on floods in India, using the 2018 floods in the southern province Kerala as a precedent. However, our intention was to build a product suite that has core elements that are translatable between geographies and types of fast-onset natural disasters.

2.2 Humanitarian Supply Aid Chain

Many factors contribute to coordination difficulties in disaster relief, such as the inherently chaotic post-disaster relief environment, the large number of actors involved in disaster relief, and the lack of sufficient resources. Aid agencies often do not even attempt to collaborate, finding coordinating resources and actions amongst the variety of groups on-the-ground too difficult. As such, there have been few coordination success stories, such that "coordination has continued to be the fundamental weaknesses of humanitarian action."[7]

The core of these coordination challenges happens in the "Recovery" phase of natural disasters, or the phase following the immediate response to the event, during which governments, militaries, and locals are focused on saving lives[8]. In the Recovery phase, aid agencies staff full teams and deploy operations on the ground to support ailing communities. We decided that focusing on this phase of humanitarian disasters would present the opportunity to impact the supply chain through the utilization of new technologies. It is in the Recovery phase that intra-organizational challenges arise and improved means of collaboration could help more efficiently route funds and resources.

---

[6] Source: https://reliefweb.int/report/world/sudden-onset-disasters-make-14-million-people-homeless-every-year.

[7] Source: https://www.academia.edu/9116986/Coordination_in_humanitarian_relief_chains_Practices_challenges_and_opportunities.

[8] Source: https://disasterphilanthropy.org/issue-insight/the-disaster-life-cycle/.

While attempting to understand why aid resources go misplaced during the recovery phase, we came to understand that aid-related waste and mismanagement happens at local distribution points. Often these local distribution points can be town centers converted into disaster management operations sites. In many fast-onset natural disasters, these sites are often temporary shelters, or settlements that are hosting affected individuals and families for a short-to-medium timeframe while disaster zones are cleared. In the case of the 2018 Kerala Floods, temporary shelters were set up for three weeks while towns and villages were cleared of rubble from the damage. Our research revealed that the operational systems of shelters, and thus their internal supply chain management systems, were often underdeveloped. We thus sought to understand what types of innovative solutions could help heads of shelter more adequately manage aid supplies.

3 Emerging Technology and Humanitarian Aid

There are many precedents for the application of emerging technologies in the humanitarian aid sector. Fueled by grants from the United Nations pulse lab and innovation network, or started by aid organizations to address their own challenges, the landscape is vibrant, and we didn't have to look far to find inspiration. The Harvard Humanitarian Initiative has published extensively in the field, and have both in-development prototypes and active projects that leverage drones, big data, and sensors to address a wide range of challenges across the aid supply chain.

One visionary project funded by the United Nations helped to shape our thinking. The World Food Programme (WFP) helps feed 80 million people around the globe, but since 2009 the organization has shifted from delivering food to transferring money to people who need food. They believe that this approach could feed more people, improve local economies, and increase transparency, and early reports are promising.

The WFP has directed resources to thousands of Syrian refugees, in what is one of the largest blockchain based financial implementations for a charitable cause in history. Instead of shipping food they give refugees cryptocurrency vouchers to redeem at local markets. Using eye-scanning technology to verify the recipients identity, they are eliminating the potential for fraud, and increasing transparency while stimulating the local economy[9]. The project, called Building Blocks, has had the following impact in the last year:

1. More than 100,000 refugees served on a monthly basis.
2. The UN saved more than 40,000 USD per month in bank transfer costs.
3. Tens of millions of USD of aid has been delivered through the blockchain.

This project in particular was a source of inspiration for our intervention. As we look towards the future, we believe blockchain will become more embedded in the humanitarian aid supply chain, solving many of the underlying challenges with financial transparency and accountability. Similarly, the use of eye-scanning and biometric identification to assist with fund distribution demonstrates the potential of aid delivery at the intersection of two emerging fields. We built upon these concepts to develop an intervention we believe has the potential to transform the way aid supply chains are managed in post-disaster scenarios. The following sections will provide a deep-dive into this proposed intervention.

4 Innovations Framework

Two frameworks guided the core of our solution development process: design thinking and world building. We utilized techniques from the former - such as discussing precedents, drawing features in timeboxes, and asking "how might we" questions - to orient ourselves around a particular problem space. In addition, we built out personas across the entire humanitarian aid supply chain to understand what types of interventions would be useful for each stakeholder group. Ultimately, this user-centric design thinking process helped our team understand that the primary users in our system map were local heads of distribution, either at temporary shelters or local community centers, who could directly benefit from on-the-ground demand being aggregated and organized.

In order to project how our solution could be impactful over time, we also engaged in world building exercises. We often tried to imagine how the nascent technology of today - blockchain, virtual reality, peer-to-peer mesh networks - would become the commoditized technology of tomorrow. By posing the following question, "What will the world look like in 2050?" we pushed ourselves to anticipate how different technologies will evolve to impact humanity. Understanding the evolution of everything, from distributed ledgers to collaboration technology, helped us choose a technology type and ultimate intervention that not only will push the boundaries of today's

---

[9] Source: https://www.coindesk.com/united-nations-sends-aid-to-10000-syrian-refugees-using-ethereum-blockchain.

technology, but also specifically anticipate the needs of people impacted by fast-onset natural disasters.

Finally, we researched the total number of potential users in the market, different pricing tiers at which we could sell our product, and what revenue figures would be required in the next 1, 2, and 5 year time horizons to build and sustain a successful business. Although our project may not have the economic upside of many of our peers, we believe the potential impact on human lives and the potential value to society is considerable. In the following section these frameworks will be apparent throughout various facets of our intervention.

5   The Technology and Demand Aggregation

The foundational layer of our solution is a biometric sensor that can be distributed to individuals impacted by fast-onset natural disasters. Upon entrance into a temporary settlement, or check-in at a local distribution site, the biometric sensor can be distributed to each affected individual. This sensor acts as both a passive and an active information device, providing key data points to the heads of shelter. It actively collects pulse, temperature, blood sugar, and hydration levels at increments throughout the day. Additionally, if tapped three times, it sends out an emergency SOS signal to the shelter heads. The purpose of this technology is to provide a link between the affected people and the heads of distribution.

If the key metrics collected from the sensors can be aggregated, the information can be used to organize supply chains and purchase orders for the temporary settlement. For example, aggregate blood sugar information can indicate if sufficient food is being distributed. Hydration levels can indicate if water is readily available. Temperature can provide insight on the amount of clothing or bedding needed. And finally, an SOS function can connect impacted people with shelter heads in the case of emergencies or imminent danger in these vulnerable environments.

Biometric sensors can offer an interface point between the distributors and the distributees. Aggregation of the individual-level data and a focus on the aggregate demand can help shelter heads resource plan in the Recovery phase. And, most importantly, anonymization of this information can ensure that affected individuals receive the care they need without their personal data being compromised.

5.1   Spatial Dashboard

The information aggregated from each individual would ultimately be represented in a spatial dashboard. This dashboard would provide a detailed breakdown of the shelter's food, water, and medical supplies. Additionally, it summarizes macro-level vital information on people throughout the camp. A supply tracking diagram can show when certain supplies are expected to arrive in the camp, helping the shelter heads monitor existing supply and demand of resources. And finally, smart forecasting can help the shelter heads plan in advance for additional supplies, contacting upstream partners for food, equipment, and clothing well before a crisis hits the settlement.

This dashboard is immediately utilized as a desktop and mobile phone application. In the medium term, we believe the dashboard could be represented in an AR/VR application, viewed through technologies such as the Microsoft Hololens or Facebook Oculus. In the long-term, we believe that media technology will advance to the point where this dashboard could be projected onto a physical space through a small lapel-clip. Ultimately, the purpose is that this dashboard should be readily available for use for a shelter head that is on-the-go, or constantly working face-to-face directly with individuals in dire need of physical and mental support.

Detailed Breakdown

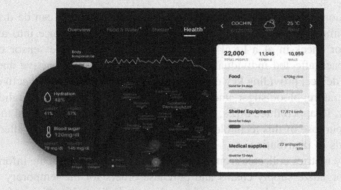

Supply Tracking

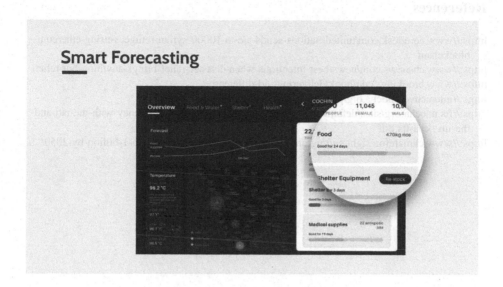

6 Conclusion

We leveraged the Business Model Canvas to identify key stakeholders, and visually map our solution. We empathized with our target users through design-thinking tactics, and pushed these methods further to rapidly prototype and sketch solutions that would address the primary "customer pains".

We will continue testing our product suite in real world settings: with residents of temporary shelters, with shelter heads, and alongside aid-relief organizations. Our initial literature review and interviews with domain experts helped us understand the problem, and conducting a user-test in the real world will help us:

- Identify challenges or threats to product usability outside the product development process
- Gain holistic consumer feedback from various stakeholders that interact with the product
- Refine and improve the product before initial in-field testing

Additionally, we hope to collaborate with the Harvard Humanitarian Initiative and experts from the Harvard Medical School to continue to examine possible areas for improvement and potential growth vectors.

References

https://www.coindesk.com/united-nations-sends-aid-to-10000-syrian-refugees-using-ethereum-blockchain
https://www.cbsnews.com/news/best-intentions-when-disaster-relief-brings-anything-but-relief/
https://www.brookings.edu/book/delivering-aid-differently/
https://interactive.unocha.org/publication/globalhumanitarianoverview/
https://fts.unocha.org/sites/default/files/improving-humanitarian-transparency-with-the-iati-and-the-un-ocha-fts.pdf
https://www.climateforesight.eu/migrations/environmental-migrants-up-to-1-billion-by-2050/

Flow-Based ROS2 Programming Environment for Control Drone

Kay Okada and Eiichi Hayakawa$^{(\boxtimes)}$

Takushoku University, 815-1, Tatemachi, Hachioji City, Tokyo 193-0985, Japan
r78415@st.takushoku-u.ac.jp,
hayakawa@cs.takushoku-u.ac.jp

Abstract. This study describes a flow-based programming environment for drone programming. With the increasing demand for drones in recent years, end- users have also had the opportunities to program the operation of the drones. However, it is difficult for the end-user to read and program the source code, so the traditional text-based programming is inefficient. On the other hand, a framework for controlling drones such as Robot Operating System 2 (ROS2) has appeared, and libraries have been enriched. However, the API is complicated, and the programming cost still high.

In contrast, this system provides end-users with a flow-based programming interface using node-red. In the flow-based programming interface, functions abstracted by nodes, and programs can be created by connecting them with a line. This user interface allows the end-user to quickly create a program while visually confirming what he is doing. In drone programming, it is necessary to be able to easily switch between an actual drone and a simulator for an execution test. It was using a simulation environment that can operate the drone controlled on ROS2.

Keywords: ROS2 · Drone · GUI programming · Node-red · Programming environment

1 Introduction

1.1 Background

In recent years, drones are widely used for home delivery and aerial photography. The enhanced drone programming kit allows end-users to program and fly the drone. Also, in robot development, programming using the control framework Robot Operating System (ROS) or ROS2 has become popular. ROS is software that provides tools such as libraries to support the creation of robot applications and is currently support on many drones or robots.

1.2 Related Work

Similar research on existing GUI drone programming systems includes research aimed at teaching students [1]. We will develop an environment that can control drones by using an environment that can be programmed by combining blocks called Blockly [2].

© Springer Nature Switzerland AG 2020
C. Stephanidis and M. Antona (Eds.): HCII 2020, CCIS 1226, pp. 449–453, 2020.
https://doi.org/10.1007/978-3-030-50732-9_58

In a system for programming by combining blocks, a block of the program corresponds to one block. The interface that connects Blocks has few functions of blocks and is not suitable for the ROS programming model. In this study, while controlling the drone with a GUI, the drone is restricted to fly more safely.

1.3 Problems

ROS programming is complicated. The ROS programming, which is mainly composed of text-based programs such as Python and C++, is complicated for end-users, and it is difficult to understand what they are doing. As a result, the current situation is that the efficiency of making flight programming has deteriorated. Also, there is not always an environment where drones can fly safely, which is a challenge in existing research. Therefore, we need an environment to switch between the real machine and the simulator without rewriting the program. Research Objective.

2 Research Objective

2.1 Objective

This research aims to simplify drone programming by replacing text-based ROS2 program with GUI.

2.2 Expected Effect

When programming with ROS2, which is composed of text-based programs, it is not straightforward for users to understand what they are doing. On the other hand, by replacing it with a GUI base, end-users can program while visually checking what they are doing. As a result, the end-user can program drone movement in an easy-to-understand environment.

Besides, we expect that it will be possible to perform programming according to the situation by making it possible to switch between the actual machine and the simulator without performing operations such as rewriting the program.

3 Design

3.1 Topic Communication in ROS

There is a program model of ROS called "topic communication". A communication source program and a communication destination program distribute and subscribe to data on a bulletin board called a topic, respectively, to control data.

For example, it is assumed that there is a program for transmitting a drone camera video and a program for displaying a video. The transmission program distributes the video to the topic, and the display program displays the video of the drone by subscribing to the topic.

In this research, we will construct an environment that enables topic communication by GUI operation.

3.2 GUI Programming Environment

As a visual programming method, there is a programming interface called a flow base. In flow-based programming interfaces, functions are abstracted in the form of nodes, and programs can be created by connecting them with lines.

The feature of this programming method is that the flow of data between nodes can be confirmed. In addition, I thought that it might be close to the ROS model because the program was created by communication between components.

In this research, we will implement the environment using "node-red" which is one of the platforms that can perform flow-based programming on the web.

3.3 System Configuration

Figure 1 shows the architecture of the system implemented in this research.

Broadly speaking, there are two components, node-red [3] and ROS2. User programming is performed by node-red and drone control is performed by ROS2.

The user connects the nodes on the browser and performs programming. The created program is sent to ROS2 through the function of reflecting topics. Finally, the drone subscribes to the topic delivered in ROS2 and performs the specified action.

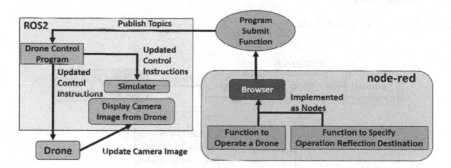

Fig. 1. System configuration

3.4 Design of Node-Red

Implement the function to operate the drone as a node in node-red. For example, takeoff and forward functions. These nodes are designed so that the user can input as an argument on how long the movement should be performed.

In addition, we will implement nodes to distribute user-programmed content to ROS2 topics.

In ROS2, topics can be distributed using CLI with Terminal. Therefore, in this node, the function to perform CLI input is described in Node.js. By changing the distribution node and changing the connection destination, the design is made so that the switching between the simulator and the actual machine can be performed seamlessly.

Figure 2 shows an example of coding the flight programming of a drone using a GUI.

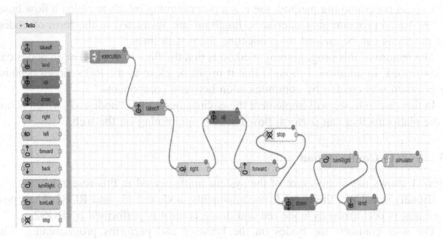

Fig. 2. Drone programming example on node-red

3.5 Virtual Node

Figure 3 shows a virtual node.

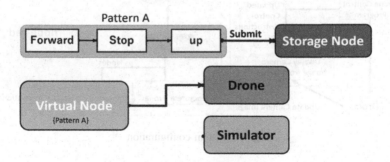

Fig. 3. Virtual node

It is implementing a storage node that can temporarily save programmed drone movements. The programs sent to the storage node can be saved as a single motion with a name. By using a virtual node for using the program saved with this name, the drone can make the saved movement.

The movement of "forward, stop, up" is stored in the "storage node," and then the user can connect the "virtual node" to the drone or simulator to perform the movement "forward, stop, up". Also, as shown in Fig. 4, this virtual node can be directly connected to a node that controls the movement of the drone.

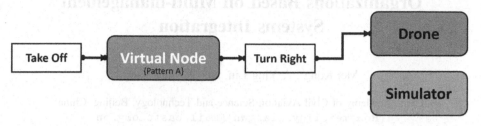

Fig. 4. Example of using virtual node

4 Conclusion

With this design, it became possible to create a flight program while checking the movement of the drone using the GUI. Also, since switching between the simulator and the actual machine can be performed only by switching the nodes, it is possible to cope with a situation in which the actual machine cannot be flown.

In this research, we implemented a one-way drone instruction using a GUI. However, in an actual environment, it is necessary to capture data such as various sensor values. It needs to be able to subscribe to topics delivered from drones, not only topic distribution to drones.

References

1. Tilley, E., Gray, J.: A visual block programming language for the control of drones. In: Tilley, E., Gray, J. (eds.) ACM SE 2017: Proceedings of the SouthEast Conference, pp. 208–211 (2017)
2. Blockly A JavaScript library for building visual programming editors. https://developers.google.com/blockly/
3. Node-red: Low-code programming for event-driven applications. https://github.com/node-red/node-red

Research on Safety Risk Management Programme, Procedures and Standards in Aircraft Design and Manufacture Organizations Based on Multi-management Systems Integration

Mei Rong[✉], Ying Liu, and Weihua Jiang

China Academy of Civil Aviation Science and Technology, Beijing, China
{Rongmei, liuy, jiangwh}@mail.castc.org.cn

Abstract. This paper studies the theoretical background and methods of SMS and other management systems of aircraft design and manufacturing organizations, analyzes the similarities and differences between SMS, DAS, QS and CAS. And the SRM programme is developed based on multi-system integration and the requirements of ICAO Annex 19. This paper also constructs the document system of SRM based on the programme, including procedures of system and work analysis, hazards identification, risk assessment and control, and safety risk assessment standards. This study is of great practice value for construction and implementation of SRM in aircraft design and manufacturing organizations, and will promote the integration of multiple management systems in these organizations.

Keywords: Safety risk management programme · Management systems integration · Safety risk management procedures and standards

1 Introduction

ICAO Annex 19 safety management (Second Edition) requires that organizations responsible for the type design or manufacture of aircraft, engines or propellers in accordance with Annex 8 shall implement Safety Management System (SMS). According to this requirement, civil aviation administrations of all countries are working on formulating relevant regulations. Civil aviation administration of China (CAAC) has issued AC-398-AA-2018-01 *The Construction Guideline on Safety Management System (SMS) in Civil Aviation Products Design and Manufacturing Organizations* in September 2018 to start the construction of SMS for aircraft design and manufacturing organizations.

As the core of SMS, safety risk management (SRM) is the most important and challenging work of SMS construction in design and manufacturing organizations. Although these organizations in China have not established and implemented SRM systematically before, the Design Assurance System (DAS), Production Quality System (QS) and Continuous Airworthiness System (CAS) implemented in these

C. Stephanidis and M. Antona (Eds.): HCII 2020, CCIS 1226, pp. 454–462, 2020.
https://doi.org/10.1007/978-3-030-50732-9_59

organizations have ensured that the products meet minimum safety level requirement in compliance with airworthiness regulations. Therefore, the SRM programme of design and manufacturing organizations couldn't be separated from the original work. It needs to integrate the multiple management systems to ensure the reasonable cost and to achieve the purposes of the prevention management.

2 Basic Concepts of Safety Risk Management

According to Annex 19, safety risk management (SRM) is the core component of SMS, and it is composed of hazard identification, hazard analysis, risk assessment and risk control. Annex 19 also emphasizes that hazard identification shall be based on a combination of reactive and proactive safety data collection methods. Therefore, the most important basic work of SRM is collecting safety data in various ways during the whole life cycle of aircraft design, manufacturing and operation. And the ultimate purpose of SRM is to optimize aircraft design and production, improve product reliability and safety, and improve service quality for operators.

3 Comparative Analysis of Management Systems of Aircraft Design and Manufacturing Organizations

At present, the airworthiness management systems established and operated by aircraft design and manufacturing organizations in China mainly include Design Assurance System (DAS), Production Quality System (QS) and Continuous Airworthiness System (CAS). The relationship between these management systems is summarized in Table 1 from the aspects of product life cycle, purpose, realized SMS related functions, etc.

It can be seen that the DAS, QS and CAS have realized some functions of SMS based on the analysis above. For example, DAS ensures the ability to identify hazards in the design, QS ensures the consistency of manufacturing and design, and CAS emphasizes the collection, analysis and evaluation of continuous airworthiness information. However, the existing systems and processes are benchmark safety risk control (based on airworthiness regulations and operational regulations). SMS is not only concerned about benchmark safety, but also about how to achieve acceptable safety level of operation through risk management process, which is generally above the benchmark safety level.

At the same time, the SMS of aircraft design and manufacturing organizations involves two aspects. One is to analyze the safety mechanism of the product itself to ensure the safety level of the product operation. The existing management system has played an important role in ensuring the benchmark safety. The other is to analyze the impact of the organizational factors (involving the responsibility division, existing management system, etc.) on product safety. SMS is an important system to ensure the continuous and effective of the existing management system in this aspect.

Table 1. Relationship between SMS and other systems

System	Life cycle	Purpose	Realized SMS related functions
DAS	Concept design ~ test verification	Airworthiness. Ensure product design complies with regulations	Ensure the ability to identify various safety related issues in the design. Design and certify products in accordance with airworthiness regulations and achieve the product safety level required by airworthiness regulations
QS	Test verification ~ operation	Airworthiness. Ensure manufacturing is consistent with product design	Ensure the consistent of manufacturing and design. Produce products that meet the safety level required by airworthiness regulations
CAS	Test verification ~ operation	Airworthiness. Identify and correct unairworthiness and unsafe conditions during continuous operation	Determine the actual airworthiness risk level through comprehensive collection, analysis and evaluation of the information that is not conducive to the continuous airworthiness, and decide whether to take necessary measures to ensure that the product complies with the airworthiness regulations

4   SRM Programme of Aircraft Design and Manufacturing Organizations

As shown in Fig. 1, this paper studies and establishes the SRM programme of aircraft design and manufacturing organizations in China based on the integration of multiple management systems and the requirements of risk management work. The programme includes system analysis/change analysis, hazard identification, risk analysis and assessment, risk control, continuous information collection and monitoring, etc. The programme can help identify, assess, mitigate and prevent safety related issues.

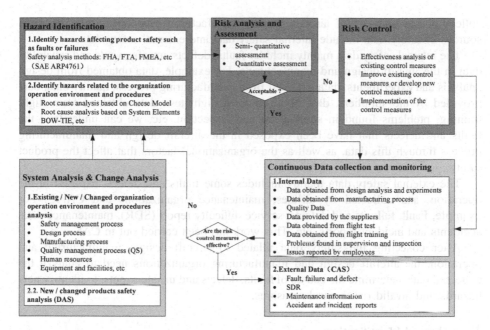

Fig. 1. Safety risk management programme of aircraft design and manufacture organizations

4.1 System Analysis/Change Analysis

Generally, the triggers of SRM include regular system and work analysis, new changes, and identification of new hazards or invalid risk control measures through data analysis.

The scope of safety management includes organization and products in aircraft design and manufacturing organizations. So, system analysis/change analysis can be divided into two parts, existing/new/changed organization operation environment and procedures analysis, and new/changed products analysis.

The existing/new/changed organization operation environment and procedures include analysis of safety policies, safety management process, design process, manufacturing process, quality management process, human resources, equipment and facilities, etc. And the internal audit of the quality management process has been included in QS. The new/improved product analysis has been implemented as product safety analysis and assessment in DAS to ensure the benchmark product safety.

The common system and work analysis methods include SHEL model, work flow chart, what if and so on. Brainstorm meetings attended by managers, operators and other employees can also be used.

4.2 Continuous Data Collection and Monitoring

Extensive collection of safety data is the basis of safety risk management. The possible hazard in product life cycle can be identified comprehensively through the data collection and analysis of aircraft design, manufacturing and operation. The main sources of safety data include internal safety data and external safety data.

The internal safety data mainly includes faults, defects, unsafe events and reliability data in the aircraft design and manufacturing. For example, data obtained from design analysis and experiments, data obtained from manufacturing process, quality data, data provided by the suppliers, data obtained from flight test, data obtained from flight training, problems found in supervision and inspection, etc. we can understand the faults and defects that have been exposed in the aircraft design and manufacturing process through this data, as well as the organizational factors that affect the product safety.

The external safety data mainly includes some faults and defects exposed in the operation, and collected by airlines, maintenance organizations and CAAC. For example, Fault, failures and defects, service difficulty report (SDR), maintenance data, accidents and incident reports, etc. This work has been carried out in CAS.

After collecting the safety data related to aircraft design, manufacturing and operation, the aircraft design and manufacturing organizations need to analyze the collected data, determine the causes of faults, defects and unsafe events, to identify new hazards and invalid risk control measures.

4.3 Hazard Identification

Hazard identification is the procedure of identifying a condition or an object that likely to cause or lead to potential accidents or incidents during the process of product design, manufacture and operation etc.

Hazard identification is based on system analysis/change analysis, and continuous data collection and monitoring. The system analysis/change analysis is a form of proactive hazard identification. That is, the potential risks can be found by proactively analyzing the organizational change, human resource change and product modification before the occurrences and to implement the precautionary management. The mode of continuous data collection and monitoring which incorporates the methods of passive, proactive and predictive data collection, can support the analysis of chain of events, to determine the cause of faults, defects and safety occurrence, and to identify the potential hazards.

The hazards of aircraft design and manufacturing organizations can be divided into two categories. The first category is the inherent unsafe factors of the product itself, such as design defects, material defects, technology defects, etc. The other category refers to the organizational factors that may cause unsafe factors in aircraft design and manufacturing, such as defects of policies, procedures, responsibilities, human resources, equipment and facilities, supervision and inspection, etc.

The first category hazard identification has been ensured by DAS. The main analysis methods include functional hazard assessment (FHA), failure modes and effects analysis (FMEA), fault tree analysis (FTA), common cause analysis (CCA) and so on, that recommended in SAR ARP4761 Guidelines and Methods for Conducting the Safety Assessment Process on Civil Airborne Systems and Equipment.

The second category hazard analysis methods mainly include SHEL model, swiss cheese model, management oversight risk tree analysis (MORT), fishbone diagram, etc.

4.4   Risk Analysis and Assessment

After identifying the hazard, the aircraft design and manufacturing organizations should analyze the root causes, the function mechanism of the hazard, and the potential consequences of the hazard in depth, which is the basis of the risk assessment.

Generally, risk can be synthetically assessed from two aspects, one is the severity of the consequences of the hazard, the other is the probability that it will occur. Then the organizations should determine the risk level of the hazard, whether the risk is acceptable, as well as the priorities of the risk management. As for the acceptable hazards, there is no need to develop the risk control measures, but it is important to collect and monitor its relevant data continuously. As for the unacceptable hazards or unacceptable hazards after the mitigation measures, the organizations should develop the control measures in accordance with their risk levels.

4.5   Risk Control

The aircraft design and manufacturing organizations should determine the effectiveness of the existing risk control measures implemented on the hazard before develop new control measures. If these measures are ineffective, the organizations should analyze the cause and develop new measures. If there are no existing measures, the organizations should develop the practical measures based on the causes of hazard and the risk level of it. The risk control measurements should be implemented after it is developed.

Through continuous data collection and monitoring, the aircraft design and manufacturing organizations could judge whether the safety risk have been reduced to an acceptable level (Acceptable Level of Safety Performance ALoSP). If the measures are effective, the risk management process is completed. But the organizations still need to monitor the data related to the hazard. And if the measures are proved ineffective, the organizations should identify these measures, and adjust it or develop the new measures.

5   Safety Risk Management Policies, Procedures and Standards in Aircraft Design and Manufacture Organizations

In accordance with the safety risk management programme, the aircraft design and manufacturing organizations should consider to share the documents with other systems, or refer to the necessary documents of other systems, when they develop the safety risk management procedures and standards. The directory created by this paper on safety risk management policies, procedures and standards is shown in Table 2.

From Table 2, we can see the integration of multi-management systems mainly manifested in the following aspects.

(1) Risk management policy and risk assessment standard are shared in SMS and QS.

Table 2. Directory of safety risk management policies, procedures and standards

Document name	Document categories	Whether existing in SMS individually	Share the documents with other systems	Need to refer to related documents in other systems
Risk management policy	Policy	No	Production Quality System (QS)	
System and work analysis procedure	Procedure	Yes		
Hazard identification procedure	Procedure	Yes		(1) The procedures associated with safety analysis and assessment in Design Assurance System (DAS) (2) The procedures associated with data collection in Continuous Airworthiness System (CAS)
Risk analysis and assessment procedure	Procedure	Yes		
Risk assessment standard	Standard	No	Production Quality System (QS)	
Risk control procedure	Procedure	Yes		

(2) Hazard Identification Procedure refers to the procedures associated with safety analysis and assessment in Design Assurance System (DAS), and the procedures associated with data collection in Continuous Airworthiness System (CAS).

6 Conclusion

This paper studies the Safety Risk Management (SRM) programme of aircraft design and manufacturing organizations to ensure the coordinated operation of SMS with DAS, QS and CAS. The programme is not to discuss from the perspective of aircraft design and manufacturing organizations in isolation, but focuses on systematically collecting various types of safety data during the whole life cycle of aircraft. And through comprehensive analysis of safety information, the problems or defects in design and manufacturing can be found. This programme is not only to focus on the collection and analysis of safety data afterwards, but also lay more emphasis on the identification, analysis, evaluation and control of hazards in advance. Based on meeting the minimum safety requirements of airworthiness regulations, the concept of Acceptable Level of Safety Performance (ALoSP) is introduced. It is no longer limited to the identification of product safety problems caused by faults or failures, but more focused on the inefficient organizational structure, communication, invalid technical activities and safety culture. The results of this paper are of great practice value for integration and promotion of multiple management systems in aircraft design and manufacturing organizations and to implement the proactive safety risk management.

References

1. ICAO: Annex 19 Safety Management. International Civil Aviation Organization, Montreal, Canada, July 2016
2. ICAO: Annex 8 Airworthiness of Aircraft. International Civil Aviation Organization, Montreal, Canada, July 2018
3. CAAC: CCAR 21 Certification Procedures for Products and Parts. Civil Aviation Administration of China, Beijing, China, May 2017
4. ICAO.Doc.9859 Safety Management Manual. International Civil Aviation Organization, Montreal, Canada (2018)
5. Li, S., He, P., Lu, Y., Li, J.: Difference analysis between safety management system and airworthiness management system in civil aircraft design and manufacture organization. In: The 5th International Symposium on Knowledge Acquisition and Modeling, London, UK, June 2015, pp. 15–20 (2015)
6. Wolf, H.: The emerging role of safety management systems in aerospace. In: IEEE Aerospace Conference Proceedings, March 2012, pp. 1–11 (2012)
7. Stolzer, A.J., Halford, C.D., Goglia, J.J.: Implementing Safety Management Systems in Aviation. Ashgate Publications (2011)
8. Stolzer, A.J.: Collegiate aviation maintenance programs: focus on quality or safety? J. Aviat. Aerosp. Educ. Res. 9(2), 3 (2000)
9. CAAC: AC-21-AA-2013-19 The Requirements for Continuous Airworthiness System of Type Certificate Holder. Civil Aviation Administration of China, Beijing, China, September 2013
10. IAQG: AS9100D Quality Management System-Requirements for Aviation, Space, and Defense organization. International Aerospace Quality Group, September 2016
11. AIA: NAS9927 Safety Management System Practice for Design and Manufacturing. Aerospace Industries Association of America (2016)
12. Sun, Y., Zhang, Y., Li, J.: Study on programme of risk management in aircraft design and manufacture organization. J. Saf. Sci. Technol. 12(8), 132–137 (2012)
13. Yi, W.E.I., Xin-feng, C.H.E.N.: Research of safety risk evaluation for service difficulty report. J. Civ. Aviat. Univ. China 2(5), 42–46 (2011)
14. Werfelman, L.: A New Way to Measure. https://flightsafety.org/asw-article/a-new-way-to-measure/, September 2018
15. FSF: NTSB Urges Changes in Aircraft Design Assessments. https://flightsafety.org/ntsb-urges-changes-in-aircraft-design-assessments/, September 2019

16. Chen, J.: Research on Integrated Reengineering of Quality Management System and Safety Management System for Civil Aircraft Test. Shanghai Jiao tong University, June 2014
17. SAE: ARP4761 Guidelines and Methods for Conducting the Safety Assessment Process on Civil Airborne Systems and Equipment. Society of Automotive Engineers, December 1996
18. Ericson, C.A.: Hazard Analysis Technique for System Safety. Wiley, Fredericksburg (2005)

Using Block-Based Programming and Sunburst Branching to Plan and Generate Crisis Training Simulations

Dashley K. Rouwendal van Schijndel[1(✉)], Audun Stolpe[2], and Jo E. Hannay[2]

[1] Department of Technology Systems, University of Oslo,
Pb. 70, 2027 Kjeller, Norway
`d.k.rouwendal@its.uio.no`
[2] Department of Applied Research in IT, Norwegian Computing Center,
Pb. 114 Blindern, 0314 Oslo, Norway
{`audun.stolpe,jo.hannay`}`@nr.no`

Abstract. Simulation-based exercises for crisis response are difficult to plan. We suggest an intuitive planning interface where exercise managers can use block-based programming to create machine-readable training vignettes. An answer set programming module interprets these vignettes and generates all possible actions and causal relations, which are then visualised for the exercise manager in a sunburst diagram. This allows exercise managers to create training vignettes using visual techniques and to see the possible results and causal relations of the trainees' actions. This facilitates using exercise results to adjust further vignette design.

Keywords: Simulation-based training · Block-based programming · Answer set programming · Visual planning

1 Introduction

Simulation-based crisis response exercises and training within military and civilian organisations are often complex, and it has proven difficult to design exercises with clear learning objectives and targeted building and assessment of skills; see for example, [4,11,14]. To improve on this situation, an *Exercise Management & Simulation* architecture (ExManSim) was proposed, where the organisational and technical challenges concerning structured planning, execution and analysis of exercises are explicitly addressed [5].

Existing systems for simulation-based training often focus on what objects and interactions should be present in simulations, rather than on what skills should be stimulated and measured [5,6]. In contrast, a central point in the ExManSim architecture is to offer skill-stimulating events as basic building blocks, so that exercise managers can compose simulations in terms of learning effects, rather than merely in terms of objects and their interactions.

This demands tool support that abstracts away details, so that the exercise manager (trainer) can compose training vignettes (a series of events) designed to

© Springer Nature Switzerland AG 2020
C. Stephanidis and M. Antona (Eds.): HCII 2020, CCIS 1226, pp. 463–471, 2020.
https://doi.org/10.1007/978-3-030-50732-9_60

stimulate the desired skills. ExManSim focuses on decision-making skills, such as situational awareness, resource coordination and collaboration; e.g., [2]. We propose to use block-based programming; a visual programming methodology for composing computer programs from blocks that represent predefined functionality. Here, we will use blocks designed to compose events into vignettes.

After the exercise manager has composed a vignette using block-based programming, the vignette object information is exported to an answer set programming (ASP) module. ASP allows for the creation of knowledge representation models that can be stored in machine-readable formats. In our system, ASP runs behind the scenes and uses the object information and basic predefined vignette parameters to calculate valid possible sequences of events and their possible outcomes. This stored information is then used to implement a simulation semi-automatically on a virtual simulation platform.

In time, data collected from the trainees' actions and interactions within the vignettes will be used with ASP to create new block-based designs for follow-up vignettes that focus on training aspects that need special attention. In this manner, the system supports deliberate practice [3] and adaptive thinking [12,13] in order to maximise learning.

2   Planning at Several Levels of Abstraction

Based on workshops with crisis response practitioners and researchers, we are designing ExManSim to facilitate planning at several levels of abstraction. Referring to Fig. 1, think of a use case where an exercise manager at a National Disaster Training Centre (NDTC) designs an abstract exercise template consisting of a "crisis with two dependent events". Then, handing this template over to a National Fire Training Centre, a template "fire in indoor industrial space" is designed by the exercise manager there. The NDTC also hands over its abstract template to a "Hazardous Materials Safety Agency". There, the NDTC's template is refined to a "handling of pressurised substance in indoor industrial space" template. Then, for different industries and organisations, a fire exercise manager consultant designs concrete vignettes (the lowest level in Fig. 1. Here, one for "bin fire in airplane hangar", "fuel puddle in garage", and "stove fire in industrial kitchen", etc. Likewise, a pressurised material exercise manager consultant designs concrete vignettes; for example "pressure tank in factory".

3   Vignette Design Using Block-Based Programming

Human beings are more efficient at processing visual information than textual representation; for pointers, see [10]. Block-based programming is a popular visual method to compose computer programs. People who have no prior skills in computer programming can easily compose programs from predefined pieces (blocks) of functionality. These blocks are presented visually in menus and can be specialised for various uses in actual programs. Blocks are then assembled in

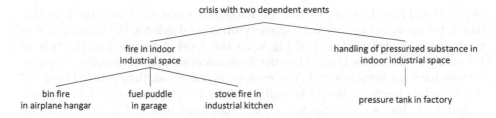

Fig. 1. Levels of abstraction for vignettes

a graphical workspace to form a computer program. This technique is now used in various products; such as Micro:bit[1] and Tynker[2].

Block-based programming reduces the rate of syntax-errors and increases efficiency for individuals who are non-frequent programmers [7]. It makes programming easier, since the coding options are available visually as in show in Fig. 2. It is easier to create a system via recognition (since the blocks appear in a selection menu) rather then by recall [9].

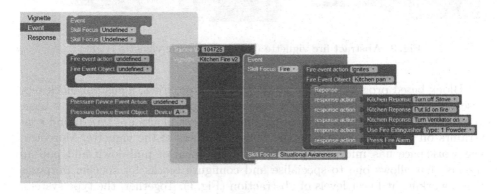

Fig. 2. Recognition-based vignette construction

Block-based programming is designed to visualise abstract syntax constructions. We hold that a block-based visual programming language will also provide crisis management personnel, who may have little or no simulation-technical skills, with an intuitive tool for designing training vignettes. We use the generic Blockly code library[3] that allows one to create customised block languages.

In the example in Fig. 3, the exercise manager has been tasked to design training for a stove fire in industrial kitchen (bottom level of Fig. 1) and has been handed a template for fire in indoor industrial space (middle level of Fig. 1) by

---

[1] https://microbit.org/.
[2] https://www.tynker.com/.
[3] https://developers.google.com/blockly.

the National Fire Training Centre. He is therefore presented with the template blocks for fire in indoor industrial space training pre-loaded in the vignette design work space; see leftmost part of Fig. 3. At this level of abstraction, the type of fire and the skill to be trained has not been selected, and the possible response actions have not been selected. The exercise manager can then proceed to detail the template blocks with blocks and variables for the particular fire response training; in this case, a stove fire. In the rightmost part of Fig. 3, the exercise manager selects blocks for a pan fire which ignites as the first crisis event. The skill to be trained is situational awareness. Concrete responses are added as blocks to the response template block and includes the option for the trainee to turn off the stove, put a lid on fire (pan), turn the ventilator on and/or use a powder-based fire extinguisher.

Fig. 3. Abstract fire vignette (left), defined fire vignette (right)

Block-based programming serves a dual purpose. First, a custom block representation of a vignette acts as a grammar. It presents the user with a basic vocabulary in the form of elementary blocks. These blocks are typed, and constraints on the types determine the well-formedness of the vignette. Moreover, the workspace has information devices in the form of pull-down and pop-up menus that allows one to specialise and configure blocks for specific purposes when working at lower levels of abstraction (Fig. 1). Together, the type system, the constraints and the information devices represent an approach to syntax learning based on direct recognition rather than recall.

Secondly, block-based programming offers a feature to convert composite blocks into custom code or text. We exploit this by wiring each block to a piece of ASP code. The vignette grammar ensures that these code snippets are compositional and add up to a logical description in ASP of the initial situation of the training exercise. In turn, this description is fed as input to a causal theory, also encoded in ASP, that encodes the interaction between the objects as well as the effects of actions in the training domain. The reason for this is described in more detail in the next section.

4   ASP and Model Output Visualisation

The block design space is hooked into an ASP representation of the salient causal relations in the training domain. Then, ASP will compute the coherent plays, if any, that the selected set of blocks and properties support. In fact, the computation of the vignette provides two different reasoning services. One is *validation*: not all block puzzles yield playable vignettes even if they are syntactically correct. For instance, the vignette designer may decide to include a wet chemical extinguisher if the vignette involves a fire in kitchen grease, since wet chemical extinguishers are designed for that. He may also decide to include a foam extinguisher, which is not appropriate for grease fires, to allow the trainee to make mistakes. However, if the designer does not select at least one effective extinguisher, then the vignette is not successfully playable. Such a vignette with an unattainable goal is *invalid* and will be rejected by the ASP computation. The second reasoning service is to *deduce* or *generate* the different ways in which the initial situation can evolve according to the causal theory. If presented in a suitably friendly format, the vignette designer can gain a sense of the depth and training value of his current block layout and can revise it when necessary.

The details of the answer set programming module itself is not the focus of this paper. Rather, the focus is the visual user interface of the vignette design space. The challenge from a user interface point of view is that the number of ways a situation can develop from even a simple causal theory is usually too large to be conveniently represented by a traditional rooted top-down or bottom-up tree widget. More often than not, certainly for most interesting vignettes, this is going to be a very bushy tree with a high branching factor. Our experiments with decision trees and other tree-like structures indicate that the user will have to scroll through very large visualisations to get an overview of the possible outcomes; in particular to view the leaf nodes, where the success or failure of a course of action is recorded.

In order to be useful to the designer, the plays or models generated by ASP should be visualised in a manner that more effectively conveys the training potential of the vignette. As a minimal requirement, the visualisation should display all the choice points; that is, all the different courses of action a trainee may opt for and all the outcomes of the different plays; distinguishing successful from unsuccessful ones in a single window frame.

An evolution diagram frequently used in biology for representing phylogenetic trees [8] is the sunburst diagram.[4] A phylogenetic tree represents evolutionary relationships among organisms. The pattern of branching in a phylogenetic tree reflects how species or other groups evolved from a series of common ancestors, which means that the branching factor is usually considerable. A sunburst diagram (also known as a ring chart, multi-level pie chart, belt chart and radial treemap) shows hierarchies through a series of rings, that are sliced for each category node. Each ring corresponds to a level in the hierarchy, with the central circle representing the root node and the hierarchy moving outwards from it. The growth in size of the number of rings is constant, irrespective of the branching factor, since a single ring encodes all parent-child relationships in that level of the tree. Also, due to its concentric 360° nature, the sunburst diagram maximizes the use of space within a single frame.

---

[4] https://datavizcatalogue.com/methods/sunburst_diagram.html.

Figure 4 shows a trimmed down excerpt of some ways in which the kitchen fire vignette evolves, according to the ASP encoding of a causal theory relating, stoves, pans, grease, fans, extinguishers, and so on.

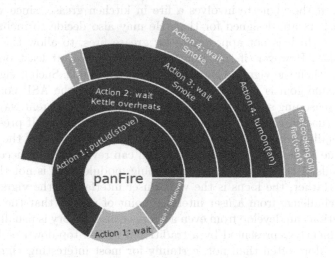

Fig. 4. Reduced example of a sunburst diagram for the kitchen fire vignette.

The particular sunburst diagram in Fig. 4 is from the Plotly open source graphing libraries.[5] It has several attractive features that makes it a good fit for our purposes. Not only is it capable of representing, for most realistic cases, sufficiently large number of choice points, branches and outcomes in a single window pane, it also adjusts the centre of the diagram interactively. That is, when the user clicks on a segment other than the centre, the sunburst chart can rearrange itself to make that segment the new centre. Thus, irrespective of the size of the data set, scrolling is never needed for exploration.

Finally, note that the sunburst representation of vignettes can be made to support both of the reasoning services mentioned above; that is both exploration and validation. Using a colouring scheme that labels permitted states and actions in green and prohibited ones in red (cf. [1]), an invalid vignette is one with an entirely red outer rim. This colouring scheme offers a way of designating a vignette as invalid, while still developing available of information about it. The point at which a story or play becomes red, for instance, is valuable information for debugging the Blockly layout of the vignette. This is ongoing research.

5   The Feedback Loop

A further purpose of the ExManSim architecture is that after a training has been completed by a trainee, the system can reset and the vignette design can be

---

[5] https://plot.ly/graphing-libraries/.

adjusted according to the trainees' performance. The trainees can then undergo the training once more with the vignette adapted to their new skill levels.

The data collection that takes place during training will give valuable insight of what the future focus of the trainees' training should be. In an example of the kitchen fire, it may be that the trainees are not sufficiently knowledgeable about different types of fire extinguishers, and therefore in the next training round there could be more focus on this particular facet of training. The premise is that you can automate this training adaptive system via the ASP module.

A topic that we are actively researching at the time of writing, is to use the green/red colouring scheme that was mentioned toward the end of the previous section for scoring plays. The green/red feature, a version of which we have already implemented, is a kind of *deontic overlay* that is grafted onto the causal theory. It describes sufficient conditions for classifying actions as either green (acceptable, legal) or red. The ASP engine propagates these conditions over complex states and transitions, based on the rules in the causal theory. In itself, this is not a new idea, but derives from (cf. [1]). What *is* novel, to the best of our knowledge, is the idea of using the deontic overlay for scoring plays. In the simplest case, this is matter of subtracting the sum total of red states and actions from the green ones to obtain a crude measure of the overall quality of the course of action pursued in that play.

The scores will be used for solution optimisation and dynamic assignment of difficulty levels, and will be applied in repeated rounds of training. This will give an effective record of the progress a trainee is making and give insight to the effectiveness of the various parts of the training overall. This addresses a basic challenge in simulation-based training.

6   Final Remarks

To summarise the process that ExManSim supports: Exercise regulatory bodies provide basic requirements and exercise templates. Domain-specific exercise managers are directed to a block-based vignette design tool where abstract block-based vignettes that represent the above exercise templates have already been created. The exercise manager specifies domain-specific block-based details as desired in the block-based template vignette. When this is completed, the block-based vignette design is passed in machine-readable format to an answer set programming module, which creates an outline of all the possible actions a trainee can take in the vignette. Scoring methods are built into the system to help assess a trainee's performance. The exercise manager will then get a visual overview of the answer set model in a sunburst diagram, where he can decide whether to accept the generated model or go back and adjust the vignette design. When the vignette is accepted, the virtual training scene and vignette is generated in a simulation, and the virtual training can take place. The data from the training is collected, and after the training has ended, the design and training cycle can repeat, but now with specific recommendations which can be applied to the vignette design for greater customisation toward the needs of the trainee.

We postulate that this feedback loop of training, performance analysis and retraining at the exercise manager's control through an easy-to-use, block-based vignette design methodology and real-time visualisation of the trainees possible actions, will allow for a form of simulation-based training that creates greater training efficiency, feedback and record keeping.

References

1. Craven, R., Sergot, M.: Agent strands in the action language nC+. J. Appl. Logic **6**(2), 172–191 (2008). Selected papers from the 8th International Workshop on Deontic Logic in Computer Science
2. Endsley, M.R.: Theoretical underpinnings of situation awareness: a critical review. In: Endsley, M.R., Garland, D.J. (eds.) Situation Awareness Analysis and Measurement, pp. 13–32. Lawrence Erlbaum Associates Publishers, Mahwah (2000)
3. Ericsson, K.A.: The influence of experience and deliberate practice on the development of superior expert performance. In: Ericsson, K.A., Charness, N., Feltovich, P.J., Hoffman, R.R. (eds.) The Cambridge Handbook of Expertise and Expert Performance, pp. 683–703. Cambridge University Press, Cambridge (2006)
4. Grunnan, T., Fridheim, H.: Planning and conducting crisis management exercises for decision-making: the do's and don'ts. Eur. J. Decis. Process. **5**, 79–95 (2017)
5. Hannay, J.E., Kikke, Y.: Structured crisis training with mixed reality simulations. In: Proceedings of 16th International Conference Information Systems for Crisis Response and Management (ISCRAM), pp. 1310–1319 (2019)
6. Hannay, J.E., van den Berg, T.W.: The NATO MSG-136 reference architecture for M&S as a service. In: Proceedings of NATO Modelling and Simulation Group Symposium on M&S Technologies and Standards for Enabling Alliance Interoperability and Pervasive M&S Applications (STO-MP-MSG-149). NATO Science and Technology Organization (2017). paper 13
7. Holwerda, R., Hermans, F.: A usability analysis of blocks-based programming editors using cognitive dimensions. In: Proceedings of 2018 IEEE Symposium on Visual Languages and Human-Centric Computing (VL/HCC). IEEE Computer Society (2018)
8. Letunic, I., Bork, P.: Interactive tree of life (iTOL): an online tool for phylogenetic tree display and annotation. Bioinformatics Adv. Access **23**(1), 127–128 (2006)
9. Monig, J., Ohshima, Y., Maloney, J.: Blocks at your fingertips: blurring the line between blocks and text in GP. In: Proceedings of 2015 IEEE Blocks and Beyond Workshop. IEEE (2015)
10. Moody, D.L.: The "physics" of notations: toward a scientific basis for constructing visual notations in software engineering. IEEE Trans. Softw. Eng. **35**(6), 756–779 (2009)
11. Pollestad, B., Steinnes, T.: Øvelse gjør mester? Master's thesis, University of Stavanger, Department of Media and Social Sciences (2012). in Norwegian
12. Pulakos, E.D., Arad, S., Donovan, M.A., Plamondon, K.E.: Adaptibility in the work place: development of a taxonomy of adaptive performance. J. Appl. Psychol. **85**(4), 612–624 (2000)

13. Shadrick, S.B., Lussier, J.W.: Training complex cognitive skills: a theme-based approach to the development of battlefield skills. In: Ericsson, K.A. (ed.) Development of Professional Expertise, pp. 286–311. Cambridge University Press, Cambridge (2009)
14. Skarpaas, I., Kristiansen, S.T.: Simulatortrening for ny praksis: Hvordan simulatortrening kan brukes til å utvikle hærens operative evne. Tech. rep. Work Research Institute (2010). in Norwegian

Development of Simple and Inexpensive Pedestrian Simulator in General Traffic Conditions

Taisei Sasaki$^{(\boxtimes)}$ ⓘ and Mitsuhiko Karashima$^{(\boxtimes)}$ ⓘ

Tokai University, Tokyo, Japan
taiseisasaki16@gmail.com, mitsuk@tokai-u.jp

Abstract. This research proposed the simple and relatively inexpensive pedestrian simulator that consisted of three large monitors, a self-propelled treadmill, and the three-dimensional simulator application and that could investigate the pedestrian behavior under general traffic conditions.

In order to confirm the validity of the proposed simulator, the accuracy of the participants' senses of distances and speeds on the simulator was compared with in the real world through experiments. The participants were required to reproduce the distances and the speeds through walking respectively on the simulator and in the real world.

The results of the experiments revealed that the senses of distances on the simulator was the same as the senses in the real world, and that the sense of 80% slower speed than usual walking speed on the simulator was also the same. The results, however, revealed that the senses of usual walking speed and 130% faster speed on the simulator were slightly slower than the senses in the real world though the participants on the proposed simulator could correspond to the change of the walking speed more precisely than in the real world. These suggested that the proposed simulator was valid practically for investigating pedestrian behavior.

Keywords: Pedestrian simulator · Pedestrian behavior · General traffic condition

1 Introduction

Experimental research of investigating the pedestrian behavior must assure the safety of the participants. Many researches had been conducted under the limited traffic conditions of the real world, such as no other vehicles, to ensure the safety (Kamiyama [1], Lu [2], Haga [3], Schildbach [4]). The pedestrian simulator would be effective to ensure the safety regardless of any traffic conditions. There are the pedestrian simulators but most of them are large-scale or expensive simulators (Feldstein [5]) or under the limited conditions such as pedestrian crossing (Sween [6], Byington [7], O'Neil [8]). With referring to the process of developing the driving simulator for bicycle (Mizoguchi [9]), this research proposed the simple and relatively inexpensive pedestrian simulator consisting of three large monitors, a self-propelled treadmill, and the three-dimensional

© Springer Nature Switzerland AG 2020
C. Stephanidis and M. Antona (Eds.): HCII 2020, CCIS 1226, pp. 472–479, 2020.
https://doi.org/10.1007/978-3-030-50732-9_61

simulator application in order to investigate the pedestrian behavior under general traffic conditions.

2 Proposed Simulator

2.1 Design

The proposed simulator is consisted of the following components as shown in Fig. 1.

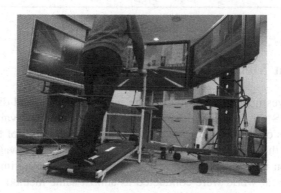

Fig. 1. Proposed simulator

Components. The proposed simulator was consisted of the components as follows; a self-propelled treadmill, a digital tachometer, a PC, three-dimensional simulator application, and three monitors. Users walk on the self-propelled treadmill which is mainly consisted of spindle, belt, and handle. The tachometer measures the revolution speed of self-propelled treadmill and sends the speed to the PC. In the PC, the three-dimensional simulator application converts the speeds' unit into "km/h" and simulates the three-dimensional city map from the 3D model data of the city to display the three-dimensional street of the city. Users can walk on the simulated street of the city with the three two-dimensional monitors. The monitors are arranged on the half circle as shown in Fig. 2. Users can manipulate the direction with the mouse.

Hatada [10] revealed that it was necessary to satisfy the following factors in order to reproduce the three-dimensional space with two-dimensional monitor; users could recognize the absolute distance and the relative distance, and, perceive the spread space. And Hatada [10] was also revealed that the large size of the monitor and the large viewing angle of the monitor were effective to increase sense of immersion.

In the proposed simulator, the recognition of the absolute distance and the relative distance are satisfied by using 3D model in our developed application, and the perception of the spread space" is satisfied by using three large monitors where the users can move head and eyeball without limitation. Accordingly, it would be expected that the proposed simulator could reproduce the three-dimensional space with three two-dimensional monitors.

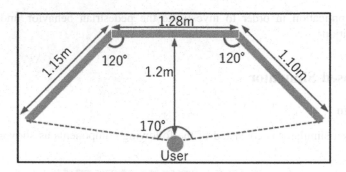

Fig. 2. Monitors' arrangement

3 Experiment Method

Mizoguchi [9] investigated on differences the senses of speeds and distances between real world and DS through experiments in order to confirm the validity of the DS. Three experiments on this research were conducted with reference of Mizoguchi [9] in order to compare the accuracy of the senses of side distances, forward distances, and speeds between on the simulator and in the world. Both the experiments on the simulator and in the real world were conducted as almost same method.

As results of the experiments, it was revealed that the senses of speeds were slower on the DS than in the real world, and the differences of the senses between DS and real world were enlarged as the velocity of the bicycle increased. In addition, the senses of distances on the DS did not matched to real world.

In this research the experiments were conducted as almost same method of Mizoguchi's experiments in order to confirm the validity of the proposed simulator.

3.1 Side Distances Experiments

Participants. Eleven university students (9 males and 2 females, aged from 19 to 22 years old), who could walk healthily, participated in the experiment. This study has been approved by the research ethics committee of Tokai University (No. 19189).

Experimental Procedures. The explanation of the experiment was provided to the participants and they provided the informed consent to the experimenter. The participants were required to walk straight 30 m as shown in Fig. 3. After the participants finished walking, they were required to answer the side distance from themselves to the inverted triangle marker (L_1 in Fig. 3) when they passed right beside the marker. The participants were required to walk three times for three kinds of length of L_1 (0.6, 1.0, 2.0 m). The order of L_1 was fixed through the participants (1.0, 0.6, 2.0 m).

The participants did this set of three times walking both on the simulator and in the real world, and the order of the experimental environments was fixed in the order of the real world and the simulator through the participants.

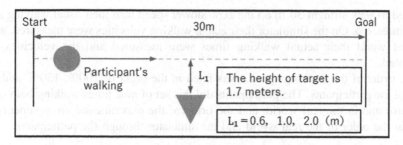

Fig. 3. Layout chart of the side distances experiments

3.2 Forward Distances Experiments

Participants. Participants were the same as "3.1 Side Distances Experiments".

Experimental Procedures. The participants were required to walk straight and stop at the position where they felt the distance between themselves and the triangle marker was the same as the target distance (L_2 in Fig. 4). After participants stopped walking, the experimenter measured the distance between themselves and the triangle marker. The participants were required to walk four times for four kinds of length of L_2 (5, 10, 15, 20 m). The order of L_2 was fixed through the participants (10, 15, 20, 5 m).

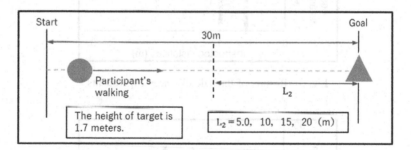

Fig. 4. Layout chart of the forward distances experiments

The participants did this set of four times walking both on the simulator and in the real world, and the order of the experimental environments was fixed in the order of the real world and the simulator through the participants.

3.3 Speeds Experiments

Participants. Participants were the same as "3.1 Side Distances Experiments".

Experimental Procedures. The participants were required to walk straight 30 m on their usual walking speed (100%) three times. They were also required to walk straight 30 m on the 30% faster speed than their usual walking speed three times. They were required to walk straight 30 m on the 20% slower speed than their usual walking speed three times, too. On the simulator their actual walking velocities were measured, and in the real world their actual walking times were measured and the velocities were calculated.

The order of the walking speeds was fixed in the order of 100%, 130%, and 80% through the participants. The participants did this set of nine times walking both on the simulator and in the real world, and the order of the experimental environments was fixed in the order of the real world and the simulator through the participants.

4   Results and Discussions

4.1   Senses of Distances

From the results of the distances experiments, as Fig. 5 and Fig. 6 shows, it was revealed that there were no significant differences between the proposed simulator and the real world as shown Table 1.

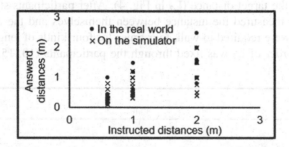

Fig. 5. Results of the side distances experiments

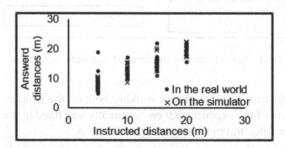

Fig. 6. Results of the forward distances experiments

Table 1. ANOVA for the distance experiments between the proposed simulator and the real world

Side		Forward	
Distances	F (1, 10)	Distances	F (1, 10)
0.6 m	0.100	5 m	0.230
1 m	1.804	10 m	0.042
2 m	2.985	15 m	0.010
		20 m	0.965

The results revealed that the proposed simulator, which considered the factors given Hatada [10] to reproduce the real world on large plain monitor, could reproduce the senses of distances in the real world.

4.2 Senses of Speeds

Figure 7 shows the results of the speed experiments without abnormal values. On 80% speed, there is no significant difference by ANOVA between the proposed simulator and the real world. On 100% and 130%, however, there are significant differences. In addition, F value suggested that the differences tended to be enlarged as the speed increased.

80%: F (1, 10) = 0.899, p > 0.05
100%: F (1, 10) = 5.302, p < 0.05
130%: F (1, 10) = 9.523, p < 0.05

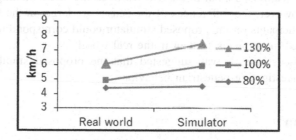

Fig. 7. Results of the speeds experiments

In Kuriyagawa [11], the experiments about DS for cars with spherical screen conducted. The results revealed that the drivers on DS increased the velocity more than the instructed velocity as the angles of screen decreased. Namely DS needed horizontal 50° and vertical 35° viewing angles at least in order to control the same velocity as the instructed velocity. The viewing angle of the proposed simulator had 170° angles horizontally but around 17° angles vertically. This narrow vertical angle might affect these differences of the senses of speed.

The precision of the correspondence to the change of the walking speed was also analyzed. The walking velocity on 130% speed divided by the velocity on 100% speed was compared to 1.3 statistically and the velocity on 80% speed divided by the velocity on 100% speed was also compared to 0.8. Table 2 shows the summary of the statistical analysis results.

Table 2. Results of one sample t test for a mean

	In the real world		On the simulator	
	From 100% to 130%	From 100% to 80%	From 100% to 130%	From 100% to 80%
Sample mean	1.361	0.892	1.321	0.805
t value	0.9534	4.3446	0.2721	0.0765
P value	0.3629	0.0015	0.7911	0.9405

The results revealed that the participants on the proposed simulator could correspond to the change of the walking speed more precisely than in the real world. The higher precision on the simulator might be caused as it was difficult for the participants to walk physically on the instructed velocity (80%) due to feeling it unnatural. On the other hand, the participants on the simulator could walk on the instructed velocity with support from the treadmill's handle.

As results of three kinds of experiments, it was revealed that the senses of distances on the proposed simulator were the same as in the real world. The senses of speeds on the simulator were almost similar to the real world on the usual walking speed and the slower speed, however, the differences of the senses are large on the faster speed. In addition, the participants on the proposed simulator could correspond to the change of the walking speed more precisely than in the real world.

From the discussions, it was suggested that the proposed simulator was valid practically for investigating pedestrian behavior.

5   Conclusion

This research proposed the simple and relatively inexpensive pedestrian simulator that consisted of three large monitors, a self-propelled treadmill and the three-dimensional simulator application.

In order to confirm the validity of the proposed simulator, the accuracy of the participants' senses of distances and speeds on the simulator was compared with in the real world through experiments. The results of the experiments revealed that the senses of distances on the simulator was the same as the senses in the real world, and that the sense of 80% slower speed than usual walking speed on the simulator was also the same. The results, however, revealed that the senses of usual walking speed and 130% faster speed on the simulator were slightly slower than the senses in the real world though the participants on the proposed simulator could correspond to the change of the walking speed more precisely than in the real world. These suggested that the proposed simulator was valid practically for investigating pedestrian behavior.

References

1. Kamiyama, T., Karashima, M., Nishiguchi, H.: Proposal of new map application for distracted walking when using smartphone map application. In: Bagnara, S., Tartaglia, R., Albolino, S., Alexander, T., Fujita, Y. (eds.) IEA 2018. AISC, vol. 819, pp. 337–346. Springer, Cham (2019). https://doi.org/10.1007/978-3-319-96089-0_36
2. Lu, J.-M., Lo, Y.-C.: Can interventions based on user interface design help reduce the risks associated with smartphone use while walking? In: Bagnara, S., Tartaglia, R., Albolino, S., Alexander, T., Fujita, Y. (eds.) IEA 2018. AISC, vol. 819, pp. 268–273. Springer, Cham (2019). https://doi.org/10.1007/978-3-319-96089-0_29
3. Haga, S., Sano, A., Sekine, Y., Sato, H., Yamaguchi, S., Masuda, K.: Effects of using a smart phone on pedestrians' attention and walking. Procedia Manuf. 3, 2574–2580 (2015). https://doi.org/10.1016/j.promfg.2015.07.564
4. Schildbach, B., Ruzio, E.: Investigating selection and reading performance on a mobile phone while walking. In: Proceedings of the 12th International Conference on Human Computer Interaction with Mobile Devices and Services, pp. 93–102 (2010). https://doi.org/10.1145/1851600.1851619
5. Feldstein, I., Rukzio, E.: Investigating selection and reading performance on a mobile phone while walking. In: Proceedings of the 12th International Conference on Human Computer Interaction with Mobile Devices and Services, pp. 93–102 (2010). https://doi.org/10.1504/ijhfms.2018.096128
6. Sween, R., Deb, S., Carruth, D., Waddell, D., Furuichi, M.: Development of an effective pedestrian simulator for research. In: Proceedings of the AHFE 2016 International Conference on Human Factors in Transportation, pp. 183–191 (2016). https://doi.org/10.1007/978-3-319-41682-3_16
7. Byngton, K.W., Schwebel, D.C.: Effects of mobile internet use on college student pedestrian injury risk. Accid. Anal. Prev. 51, 78–83 (2013)
8. O'Neal, E.E., Jiang, Y., Brown, K., Kearney, J.K., Plumert, J.M.: How does crossing roads with friends impact risk taking in young adolescents and adults? J. Pediatr. Psychol. 44, 726–735 (2019). https://doi.org/10.1093/jpepsy/jsz020
9. Mizoguchi, R., Yamanaka, H.: An analysis on the performance of bicycle simulator with wide screen from the viewpoint of real perception reappearance. Jpn. Soc. Civ. Eng. D3 71 (5), I_737–I_742 (2015). https://doi.org/10.2208/jscejipm.71.i_737. (in Japanese)
10. Hatada, T.: Artificial reality and visual space perception. Jpn. Hum. Factors Ergon. Soc. 29(3), 129–134 (1993). https://doi.org/10.5100/jje.29.129. (in Japanese)
11. Kuriyagawa, Y., Kageyama, I.: Study on using driving simulator to measure characteristics of drivers. J. Coll. Ind. Technol. Nihon Univ. 42(2), 11–18 (2009). (in Japanese)

Implementation of a Learning Assistance Framework for Prolonged Evacuation Life in an Era of Massive Natural Disasters

Satoshi Togawa[1(✉)], Akiko Kondo[2], and Kazuhide Kanenishi[3]

[1] Education Center for Information Processing, Shikoku University,
123-1 Furukawa Ojin-cho, Tokushima 771-1192, Japan
doors@shikoku-u.ac.jp
[2] Faculty of Management and Information Science, Shikoku University,
123-1 Furukawa Ojin-cho, Tokushima 771-1192, Japan
[3] Research Center for Higher Education, Tokushima University,
1-1 Minami-Josanjima, Tokushima 770-8502, Japan

Abstract. In this research, we have implemented of a learning assistance framework for evacuated students. As natural disasters intensify due to climate change, evacuation timespans are becoming prolonged. This is not an exception for learners like university students. Current e-learning environments assume the existence of a stable Internet connection. However, the Internet may not be sufficiently accessible in evacuation centers for e-learning. In unstable communication environments such as makeshift Wi-Fi networks used in evacuation centers, it is difficult to conduct e-learning. Thus, a mechanism that can allow students to engage in e-learning in evacuation situations is required. In this paper, we describe the detail of implementation the learning assistance framework for evacuated learners and show the results of our experimental use of the framework.

Keywords: e-Learning · Disaster reduction for learners · Client-side virtualization · High latency internet

1 Introduction

The threat of natural disasters such as torrential rain and massive floods is increasing year by year. Typhoon No. 15 (Faxai), which occurred in September 2019, landed in the Kanto region in Japan with the strongest force ever observed. Faxai caused severe rains and substantial floods in a short period of time, which disrupted the road network in the area. This effect caused a large-scale blackout in Chiba Prefecture in Kanto region for about three weeks. The disconnection of the mobile phone network and other communication networks continued longer than the large-scale power outages. Typhoon No.19 (Hagibis), which landed in Japan in October, caused record heavy rain in the Kanto Koshin and Tohoku regions. Because of this heavy rain, levee breaches occurred extensively and simultaneously at 140 locations in 71 rivers, and the ensuing massive flood caused 93 casualties. Climate change makes tropical cyclones more and more violent, and the damage is clearly getting bigger. The report of World

© Springer Nature Switzerland AG 2020
C. Stephanidis and M. Antona (Eds.): HCII 2020, CCIS 1226, pp. 480–485, 2020.
https://doi.org/10.1007/978-3-030-50732-9_62

Meteorological Organization describes average temperatures for the past ten years (the 2010 to 2019 period) as almost certain to be the highest on record. Furthermore, 2019 is on course to be the second warmest year on record [1].

About one and a half months after the massive flooding by Typhoon Hagibis, approximately 600 people from 245 households was stayed at the evacuation center in Nagano City in the affected area. Nagano City Hall has continued the operation of the evacuation center until the end of 2019. In Fukushima and Miyagi prefectures, evacuation centers continue to operate in the same way as Nagano City. In addition, in the Great East Japan Earthquake that occurred in 2011, more than 20,000 victims even continue to live in 73 evacuation centers seven months after the disaster. In natural disasters caused by climate change and disasters caused by huge earthquakes and tsunamis, it is inevitable that the evacuation period will be prolonged.

As the phases of evacuation life change, the proportion of daily life activities, such as resuming studying, gradually increases. This "daily life under non-daily life conditions" will continue until they leave the evacuation center. Generally, shared Wi-Fi service is installed at the evacuation center. However, these communication environments have high latency and communication is interrupted. The current e-learning environments can always communicate and are built on the assumption of a high-speed and low-latency communication environment that is not suitable for use in these low-quality communication environments. We must therefore construct an e-learning environment that assumes a low-latency communication environment with unstable connection conditions in a disaster situation.

In this study, we implemented an asynchronous learning assistance framework for disaster situations. A virtual network technology separated from the Internet is used to design and implement an environment where learning can continue even if the PC or smartphone used by the learner is not connected to the Internet. There are constructed by mainly two functions of this learning assistance framework. it's are internal learning management module and learning history synchronizing module. It is built a virtual environment inside and incorporate these modules the PC or smartphone used by the learners. When a learner tries to connect to the college LMS they normally use, the framework reconnects that connection to the internal learning management module. This allows learners to use the internal learning management module as if they were using a university's LMS. If the communication status recovers even partially, the learning synchronizing module synchronizes the locally accumulated learning history to the university's LMS. Therefore, this learning assistance framework behaves as if a stable Internet connection is maintained even if the connection is lost. We aim to support the continuous use of e-learning in "daily life under non-daily life conditions" from the middle to the end of evacuation shelter life. In addition, we explain the design of a learning assistance framework for disaster situations, and that the experimental results of the execution environment are implemented as a prototype, according to effectiveness.

We first describe the current state of our proposed learning assistance framework for evacuated students. Second, we review related studies, addressing the benefits of using the learning assistance framework to support evacuated students. Third, we present the detail of the implement for the proposed assistance framework. Finally, we describe the results achieved with the experimental use of the prototype, and we present the effectiveness of tutoring based on the assistance framework.

2   Learning Assistance Framework for Evacuated Students

2.1   Outline of Learning Assistance Framework for Evacuated Learners

In this section, we describe the e-learning assistance framework for students who have been evacuated from crises such as natural disasters [2]. This research focuses on providing e-learning services for disaster risk management to ensure service continuity. Cloud infrastructure allows e-learning service providers to ensure that their systems are robust against disasters. However, learners who use such services are not necessarily provided with a sufficient usage environment in the event of a disaster. In general, power supplies and communication infrastructure such as Wi-Fi are unstable in evacuation centers during disasters. The critical point for ensuring that e-learning environments can be used in disaster situations is maintaining the learner's side of the environment. Generally, when e-learning services are designed, it is assumed that a stable communication environment exists between the service provider and the learner.

However, this assumption does not hold when a disaster occurs. When using students use a laptop or smartphone to connect with an e-learning service, they may find it difficult to continue learning smoothly unless a stable communication environment is provided. As abnormal weather due to climate change occurs more frequently, evacuation periods will last longer, and the magnitude of disasters will worsen. It is thus important to identify the best e-learning environment for prolonged evacuations.

Figure 1 shows the proposed learning assistance framework for evacuated learners. This framework works as a buffer against poor communication situation when e-learning environments are used during evacuation. Makeshift Wi-Fi networks may be set up at evacuation centers with the aim of obtaining information about the disaster and creating a channel for communication. As such Wi-Fi environments may be unstable, we aim to create a personalized e-learning service for evacuated learners that they can use on their own laptops. This e-learning service would be a component of the full e-learning service provided by the learner's university.

The personalized e-learning service stores lecture content from the learner's classes in a personalized version of the system on the learner's laptop. The students' learning history and question-and-answer history with their tutors are stored in the personalized e-learning service so that e-learning is not affected by communication problems caused by makeshift Wi-Fi environments or other issues.

Students' learning history accumulated in their personalized e-learning service is synchronized with the university's e-learning service. Question-and-answer sessions with tutors and students' discussion history with their classmates will also be monitored and synchronized with the university's e-learning service using a learning history synchronization agent. With these mechanisms, learners who have been evacuated can continue studying through e-learning.

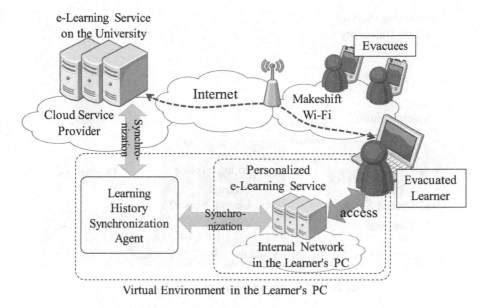

Fig. 1. Learning assistance framework for evacuated learners

2.2   Implementation of Learning Assistance Framework Prototype

In this section, we describe the implementation of our learning assistance framework prototype for evacuated learners. Figure 2 shows the architecture of this prototype. This framework is designed to ensure that each student can engage in e-learning using only their own laptop. In this implementation, Windows 10, which is a typical operating system for general users, was used for the evacuated learners. A personalized e-learning service and learning history synchronization agent were built in Linux using an Ubuntu server [3] installed on a container based virtual machine in a Windows 10 environment.

In this prototype, the priority was to ensure that the designed framework worked as expected. For this reason, the environment used by evacuees was assumed to be as general as possible. This implementation is different from previous implementation [4] and realizes container-based virtualization. Although building an environment using virtual machines runs the risk of lowering system performance. The purpose of this implementation was to prove the validity of the design and to improve system performance. By using containers, which are lightweight virtualization methods, the performance of virtualization systems can be expected to improve.

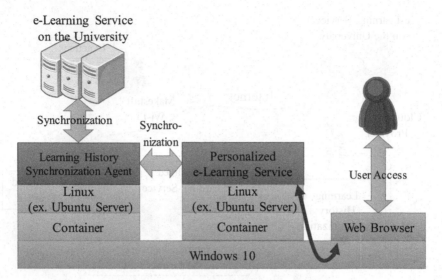

Fig. 2. Architecture of prototype implementation

3 Experimental Use and Results

In this section, we describe the results of the experimental use of our prototypical system. The proposed framework was tested to confirm its effectiveness. Table 1 shows the specifications for an evacuated learner's laptop. Table 2 shows the specifications for the container-based virtual machine on the learner's laptop.

Table 1. Specification of evacuated learner's PC

CPU specification	Intel Core i7-855U 1.80 GHz Quad Core
System memory capacity	16.0 Gbytes
SSD capacity	256 Gbytes
Operating system	Windows 10 Pro version 1903

Table 2. Definition of container-based VM Specification on the Learner's PC

CPU core limitation	Single core
System memory capacity	4.0 Gbytes
SSD capacity	10 Gbytes
Operating system	Ubuntu server 19.10 64bit edition

An Ubuntu server was installed in the container-based virtual machine environment on the learner's laptop. Moodle, a typical LMS, and the MariaDB community server [5] required for its operation were installed on the same container-based virtual machine. In addition, a virtual network was established using the laptop and configured to connect to the Internet via NAT. When the learner used their internal LMS, access was as good as using the university LMS.

Evacuated students' learning history is stored in the internal MariaDB. In order to synchronize students' learning history between their personal LMS and that of the university, differences in the history databases of the two LMSs are extracted. Since this difference extraction is performed on a virtual machine, it requires approximately two times the processing time as when it is performed on a real machine. The previous implementation which is implemented by host-based virtualization required four times the processing time of the real machine environment to extract the differences. It is thought that the overhead of the difference extraction processing was reduced as a result of changing the host-based virtualization to the container-based virtualization.

4 Conclusions

In this paper, we proposed the design of a learning assistance framework for students in situations of prolonged evacuation. In particular, it was described the implementation of the proposed learning assistance framework using container-based virtualization. We described the risks of the exacerbation of natural disasters caused by climate change and the effects of prolonged evacuation on evacuees' learning. We then proposed a learning assistance framework that can help students avoid these issues and clarified its design. We built a prototypical system based on the proposed framework and described the results of our experimental use of the system.

In addition to the learning assistance framework for Windows environments, we plan to implement a highly versatile framework for other environments. We also intend to make the learning history synchronization process faster.

Acknowledgements.   This work was supported by JSPS KAKENHI Grant Numbers 18K02922.

References

1. World Meteorological Organization: WMO confirms 2019 as second hottest year on record, Press Release Number 01/15/2020. https://public.wmo.int/en/media/press-release/wmo-confirms-2019-second-hottest-year-record
2. Togawa, S., Kanenishi, K.: Adaptive risk management framework for e-learning environment using multiple crisis alert. In: Proceedings of 13th International Technology Education and Development Conference (INTED 2019), pp. 9789–9794 (2019)
3. Ubuntu Official Web Site. https://ubuntu.com/
4. Togawa, S., Kondo, A., Kanenishi, K.: Design of a learning assistance framework for prolonged evacuation life in an era of massive natural disasters. In: Proceedings of 14th International Technology Education and Development Conference (INTED 2020) (2020, in Press). 5 pages
5. MariaDB Official Web Site. https://mariadb.com/

System Safety, Risk Management, and Human Performance Improvement

Hiroshi Ujita$^{(\boxtimes)}$ and Naoko Matsuo

Institute for Environmental and Safety Studies, 38-7 Takamatsu 2-chome,
Toshima-ku, Tokyo 171-0042, Japan
kanan@insess.com

Abstract. System safety concept is the most important philosophy for improving the safety of the huge complex system. Every engineer knows well and always considers about "The local optimization would make the entire worst of the system", and therefore understands importance of the system safety concept that well balanced design and operation are required. At present, the existing huge complex systems have been reduced in hardware risk through hardware countermeasures and quality assurance activities based on safety logic, so the remaining risk can be said to be events involving human factors. For this reason, risk reduction activities can be described as human performance improvement activities. Risk informed decision-making can be said a decision-making framework that improves human performance, based on the probabilistic risk assessment results. Furthermore, continuing this activity will eventually lead to the maintenance and improvement of the safety culture. In other words, what we want to emphasize here is that "system safety", "risk reduction activities", "human performance improvement activities", "risk informed decision-making", and "maintenance and improvement of safety culture" have similar purposes and contents.

Keywords: System safety · Defense in Depth · Risk reduction · Probabilistic Risk Assessment · Human performance improvement · Human characteristics

1 Introduction

System safety concept is the most important philosophy for improving the safety of the huge complex system. Every engineer knows well and always considers about "The local optimization makes the entire worst", and therefore well-balanced design and operation are required [1]. Even the total safety has been assured by the safety design based on Defense in Depth concept, operational problem would occur in the future by the chain of the fallacy of the Defense in Depth, then safety culture degradation, and finely organizational accident eventually happened. Probabilistic approach is required to the problems. In addition to this, we should answer to the question of "Safety Goal: How safe is safe enough?" to acquire the public confidence. To respond to the local optimization and operational problems and to safety goal question, PRA, Probabilistic Risk Assessment is required.

C. Stephanidis and M. Antona (Eds.): HCII 2020, CCIS 1226, pp. 486–494, 2020.
https://doi.org/10.1007/978-3-030-50732-9_63

Risk reduction measures that take HF, Human Factors into account include a cause analysis that analyzes and provides feedback on errors to prevent recurrences of the past errors, and a risk analysis (PRA and human reliability assessment) that predicts and takes countermeasures to prevent future risks. That is, the cause analysis and the PRA are two wheels to drive risk reduction and human performance improvement in the huge and complex systems.

2   History of Accident and Human Error Type

The history of accident and human error type trend is shown in Fig. 1. In the era when the plant system was not so complicated as in the present age, it was thought that technical defects are the source of the problem and accidents can be prevented by technical correspondence. As the system became more complex, it came to the limit of human ability to operate it, accidents caused by human error occurred. Its typical accident happened at TMI, Three Mile Island nuclear power plant in 1979. For this reason, individuals committing errors are considered the source of the problem, improvement of personnel capacity by appropriate selection and training of personnel, and proper interface design are considered effective for error prevention.

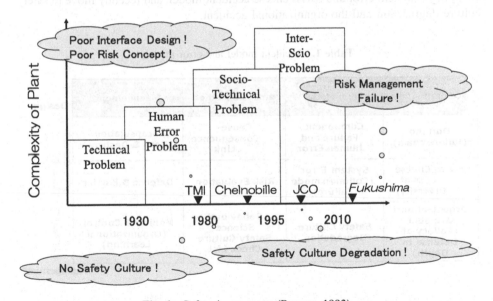

Fig. 1. Safety issue scope (Reason, 1993).

Thereafter, accidents caused by complicated interrelationships of elements such as technology, human, society, management, organization and so on occurred, and then the problem was interaction between society and technology. Furthermore, not only within the plant and enterprises but also accidents where the relationship failure with external stakeholders and organizations is a source of the problem becomes noticeable, and a framework for comprehensive problem solving including inter-organizational relationship has become to be necessary. A recent accident is a so-called organizational accident in which the form of an accident is caused by a complex factor and its influence reaches a social scale [2].

For this reason, the analytical methods, as well as type and social perceptions of error or accident, are changing with the times also. Human error and Domino accident model had initially appeared, are then has been changing to system error and Swiss cheese accident model, and recently move to safety culture degradation and the organizational accident.

3 Accident Model and Error Model

As a result, that the technology systems become huge, complex and sophisticated, safety issues are shifted to the problem of organization from human, and further from hardware, such socialization is occurring in every technical field. For this reason, the analytical methods, as well as type and social perceptions of error or accident, are changing with the times also. Table 1 shows trends of the accident model and error model [2]. Human error and Domino accident model had initially appeared, are then changing to system error and Swiss cheese accident model, and recently move to safety culture degradation and the organizational accident.

Table 1. Accident model and error model.

Accident Model	Error Model	Analysis Method	Management	
Domino (failure chain)	Component Failure and human Error	Cause-Consequence Link	Encapsulation, Seek & Destroy	**Design**
Swiss Cheese (Loss of Diversity)	System Error (Common mode Failure)	Risk Evaluation	Defense & Barrier	
Organizational Accident (Fallacy of Defense in Depth)	Safety Culture Degradation	Behavioral Science Safety Culture Check List	Monitor & Control (Organizational Learning)	**Management**

A conventional accident model is the Domino model, in which the causation of trouble and the error is analyzed, and measures are taken. In the model, slip, lapse, and mistake are used which are the classification of the unsafe act to occur by on-site work. These are categorized as the basic error type, while violation which is intentional act violating rule has become increased recently and considered as cause of social accident.

Design philosophy of the defense in depths has been established, and the accident to occur recently is caused by the excellence of the error of a variety of systems [3]. The analysis of the organization blunder is necessary for the analysis by the Swiss cheese accident model in addition to conventional error analysis.

An organization accident is a problem inside the organizations, which reaches earthshaking event for the organization as a result by the accumulation of the best intentions basically. It is an act of the good will, but becomes the error. As for the organization accident, the interdependence inside of the organization or between the organizations is accumulated by fallacy in the defense in depths, and it becomes a problem of the deterioration of the safety culture in its turn. The organizational management based on the organization analyses such as behavioral sciences will be necessary for these measures.

Swiss Cheese Model proposed by Reason, J indicates operational problem other than design problem [1]. Fallacy of the defense in depth has frequently occurred recently because plant system is safe enough as operators becomes easily not to consider system safety. And then safety culture degradation would be happened, whose incident will easily become organizational accident. Such situation requires final barrier that is Crisis Management.

4 Human Performance Improvement

Humans always make an error with a certain probability, but they are also flexible entities that can respond to ingenuity in any event. HF is a discipline that suppresses human error characteristics and extends good characteristics for understanding human characteristics and improving the environment. On the other hand, HP, Human Performance improvement is a system safety activity to reduce risk due to the human behavior in the system by understanding and optimizing human characteristics using the cause analysis and the PRA. Such activity is as part of RIDM, risk informed decision-making. HP tools are designed to take highly effective countermeasures by using tools that conform to the behavioral characteristics common to the site, rather than individual measures (e.g., describing the measures in error-related procedures).

Humans have the ability to safely and efficiently operate complex systems in a limited amount of time. Especially in large and complex plants, the working skills and abilities of the people involved are high, and safe operation is realized. However, while humans can demonstrate high abilities, they have the characteristic that misrecognition and judgment errors are easy to occur. Ergonomics and others adopt the idea that these errors are not caused by humans, but by environmental factors surrounding humans. That is, it is necessary to create an environment that can maximize its capabilities and is less prone to errors. Creating such an environment requires a good understanding of human characteristics. Therefore, improving human performance means creating an environment where human abilities can be maximized.

It describes what human characteristics are the basis for risk reduction and human performance improvement, such as;

1. Human information processing (cognition) model

2. Personal characteristics-heuristics and bias
3. Human relationship characteristics-influence
4. Group characteristics-Team behavior
5. Organizational characteristics-Organizational economics
6. Organizational characteristics-Japanese issues
7. The influence by the media

What is effective as a countermeasure based on human characteristics should be discussed; whose examples are affordance [4], heuristics and bias [5], bounded rationality [6], nudge [7], resilience [8], etc.

5 Cause Analysis

Risk reduction measures that take HF into account include a cause analysis that analyzes and provides feedback on errors to prevent recurrences of the past errors, and a risk analysis (PRA, Probabilistic Risk Assessment and human reliability assessment) that predicts and takes countermeasures to prevent future risks. This chapter describes cause analysis and the next section discusses PRA.

Since the purpose of cause analysis is to find system vulnerabilities, it is necessary to analyze the cause (root cause) of the problem, to find out where to improve it, and to take measures. The root cause is the following system vulnerability that has caused the direct cause of the trouble (human error, etc.).

- Defective hardware protection function
- Inappropriate management
- Work environment that easily induces mistakes, etc.

For this purpose, trouble cannot be prevented without considering the human characteristics and how expert think (diagnose, decision, or plan). The m-SHEL model is a model that gives an HP analysis perspective. This model describes humans and the environmental factors that surround them and is useful as an analysis guide for analysts to make analysis without overlook and plan measures that are consistent. The 4M (man, machine, media, management) model basically has the same concept.

The basic flow of root cause analysis is shown below. Of the steps 1–6, the focus of the analysis is 2–5.

1. Necessity and level of root cause analysis
2. Understanding events-documents, interviews, etc.
3. Event organization-time series analysis
4. Causal organization-why and why analysis
5. Completion of causal relationship and estimation of root cause
6. Planning of measures and evaluation of effectiveness

Certainly, it is important to master the analytical methods, but it is even more important to examine the "What is the analysis for?" This determines the level of detail of the analysis and what analysis method to use. It is not the end of the analysis, but the "planning of measures" in step 6 is the most important. That's because cause analysis is performed to take effective and versatile measures (with cost in mind).

6 Probabilistic Risk Analysis

In general, a system has functions of hardware (mechanical/electric/electronic system) and software (control system). Hazard that threatens the safety of the system lies anywhere in the lifecycle which composed of planning, concept development, design, manufacturing, operation, maintenance, and disposal phases of the system. Therefore, it is difficult to achieve high safety only by fragmentary safety technology, post-mortem analysis, engineering safety evaluation focusing on hardware, or safety evaluation focusing only on human factors during operation. In particular, huge complex systems and products sold in large volumes can cause enormous losses and tragedies in the event of an accident. To improve system safety, preventive system safety analysis is essential. It analyzes the hazard risks (thorough pre-analysis and evaluation) over the life cycle of the system and drafts control measures (safety design that removes and controls hazards) to keep the risks below target levels, derived by Safety Goal in advance.

Deterministic approach is safety assessment tool for designing the safety feature of each barrier to DiD [1]. The most severe event is assumed to represent the typical event (Design Basis Accident), while the initiating events are considered and classified by phenomena. In addition to this, one of the most important safety-related equipment failures is also assumed (Single Failure Criteria). We may guarantee the safety based on the evaluation that we can still have enough safety on that severe hypothesis. However, hypothesis based on the combination of Design Basis Accident and Single Failure Criterion failure is breakdown anymore, because the transient initiated scenario is the most severe event as predicted by Reactor Safety Study insight (1975) and as understood by TMI Accident experience (1979).

Probabilistic approach is the overall system safety assessment based on the concept of risk. It easily secured coverage of events in the process of considering the probability. Rational decisions can be done due to the presence of risk evaluation criteria of Safety Goals: a quantitative discussion on "how safe is safe enough". Furthermore, PRA has the following characteristics;

- Determination of quantitative safety trend throughout the life cycle,
- Evaluation of safety measures implemented as hardware at the initial system construction,
- Evaluation of daily operational safety from entering the commercial operation,
- Determination of inspection frequency, acceptable waiting time, time span of periodic inspection, etc. which is inherently risk-based,
- Effects by the events of large uncertainties or of difficult to predict can be quantified as an expert judge, and
- Risk assessment of external event such as Seismic or Tsunami, human reliability assessment, and common mode failure analysis, etc.

7 Safety Culture

System safety concept is the most important philosophy for improving the safety of the huge complex system. Every engineer knows well and always considers about "The local optimization would make the entire worst of the system", and therefore understands importance of the system safety concept that well balanced design and operation are required [1]. Even the total safety has been assured by the safety design based on DiD, Defense in Depth concept [2], operational problem would occur in the future by the chain that the fallacy of the DiD occurs, then safety culture would degrades, and finally organizational accident has eventually happened.

Swiss Cheese Model proposed by Reason, J indicates operational problem other than design problem [5]. Fallacy of the defense in depth has frequently occurred recently because plant system is safe enough as operators becomes easily not to consider system safety. And then safety culture degradation would be happened, whose incident will easily become organizational accident. Such situation requires final barrier that is Crisis Management.

Concept of "Soft Barrier" has been proposed here [2]. There are two types of safety barriers, one is Hard Barrier that is simply represented by Defense in Depth. The other is Soft Barrier, which maintains the hard barrier as expected condition, makes it perform as expected function. Even when the Hard Barrier does not perform its function, human activity to prevent hazardous effect and its support functions, such as manuals, rules, laws, organization, social system, etc. Soft Barrier can be further divided to two measures; one is "Software for design", such as Common mode failure treatment, Safety logic, Usability, etc. The other is "Humanware for operation", such as operator or maintenance personnel actions, Emergency Procedure, organization, management, Safety Culture, etc. Following the safety design principle of "Defense in Depth", three level safety functions should be considered for the hardware. Those are, the usual normal system, usual safety system, and emergency system including external support function. On the other hand, software for design including common mode failure treatment, safety logic, and usability should be improved together with the humanware for operation including personnel actions, emergency procedure, organization, management, and safety culture, etc.

The maintenance of a safety culture can only be achieved when the efforts of the individual engineers, the efforts of the organization itself, and external pressure on them are combined. To do so, the following four steps will be required.

1. External monitoring eyes

Corporate Socially Responsibility is necessary first, and it can be realized by externally sending out "maintaining social trust"

2. Top organizational awareness

An organization is originally created with a certain purpose (functional body), but it becomes a community over time. In order to maintain it as a functional body, the top will always remember the founder's spirit.

3. Eyes of monitoring inside the organization

Internal audit and whistleblowing (although there are opinions that this is not suitable for Japan) should be monitored by the system.

4. Personal ethics

Recently, professional ethics is being taught in educational institutions, and of course, companies, academic societies, technical societies, etc., are increasingly using ethical rules. We hope this will be the minimum qualification as engineers. The important point is to recognize the common sense of working as a member of society, not as a member of the organization.

8 Conclusion

System safety concept is the most important philosophy for improving the safety of the huge complex system. Every engineer knows well and always considers about "The local optimization would make the entire worst of the system", and therefore understands importance of the system safety concept that well balanced design and operation are required [1]. At present, the existing huge complex systems have been reduced in hardware risk through hardware countermeasures and quality assurance activities based on safety logic, so the remaining risk can be said to be an event involving human factors. For this reason, risk reduction activities can be described as human performance improvement activities. RIDM, Risk Informed Decision-Making is a decision-making framework that improves human performance. Furthermore, continuing this activity will eventually lead to the maintenance and improvement of the safety culture. In other words, what we want to emphasize here is that "system safety", "risk reduction activities", "human performance improvement activities", "RIDM", and "maintenance and improvement of safety culture" have similar purposes and contents.

Humans always make an error with a certain probability, but they are also flexible entities that can respond to ingenuity in any event. HF (human Factors) is a discipline that suppresses human error characteristics and extends good characteristics for understanding human characteristics and improving the environment. On the other hand, HP (Human Performance) improvement is a system safety activity to reduce risk due to the human behavior in the system by understanding and optimizing human characteristics using the cause analysis and the PRA. HP tools are designed to take highly effective countermeasures by using tools that conform to the behavioral characteristics common to the site, rather than individual measures (e.g., describing the measures in error-related procedures).

Risk reduction measures that take HF into account include a cause analysis that analyzes and provides feedback on errors to prevent recurrences of the past errors, and a risk analysis (PRA, Probabilistic Risk Assessment and human reliability assessment) that predicts and takes countermeasures to prevent future risks. There are two wheels to drive of the cause analysis and the PRA.

Probabilistic approach is the overall system safety assessment based on the concept of risk. It easily secured coverage of events in the process of considering the probability. Rational decisions can be done due to the presence of risk evaluation criteria of Safety Goals: a quantitative discussion on "how safe is safe enough".

References

1. Ujita, H.: Systems safety realization by PRA application. In: ASRAM 2017, Yokohama, August 2017
2. Ujita, H.: Systems safety evaluation based on system thinking. In: American Nuclear Society 2016 Winter Meeting, Las Vegas (2016)
3. IAEA: Defense in Depth in Nuclear Safety, INSAG-10. A report by the International Nuclear Safety Advisory Group (1996)
4. Norman, D.A.: The Psychology of Everyday Things. Basic Books, New York (1988)
5. Kahneman, D.: Thinking, Fast and Slow. Brockman, Inc., New York (2011)
6. Simon, H.: 'A Behavioral Model of Rational Choice', in Models of Man, Social and Rational: Mathematical Essays on Rational Human Behavior in a Social Setting. Wiley, New York (1957)
7. Thaler, R.H.: Nudge: Improving Decisions about Health, Wealth, and Happiness. Yale University Press, New Haven (2008)
8. Hollnagel, E.: Safety culture, safety management, and resilience engineering. In: ATEC Aviation Safety Forum, November 2009

Efficient Exploration of Long Data Series: A Data Event-driven HMI Concept

Bertram Wortelen[1]([⊠]), Viviane Herdel[2], Oliver Pfeiffer[3], Marie-Christin Harre[4], Marcel Saager[4], and Mathias Lanezki[1]

[1] OFFIS - Institute for Information Technology, 26121 Oldenburg, Germany
bertram.wortelen@offis.de
[2] Carl v. Ossietzky University, 26129 Oldenburg, Germany
[3] Airbus Defence and Space GmbH, 28199 Bremen, Germany
[4] Humatects GmbH, 26129 Oldenburg, Germany

Abstract. Today's easy access to data, low cost sensors and data transmission infrastructure leads to an abundance of data about complex systems in many domains like industrial process control, network intrusion detection or maritime surveillance. Analyzing this data can take a lot of effort and often cannot be fully automated. As it is hard to fully automate such analysis tasks, we present an HMI framework that supports an analyst in exploring and navigating through multiple time series of data. It is a semi-automatic approach that uses algorithms for automatically labelling low-level events in the data, but leaves the task of evaluation and interpretation to the human operator. These events are highlighted on specific time bars in the HMI framework. It enables the analyst to 1) summarize the main features of the data series, 2) filter it depending on the analysis objective, 3) identify and prioritize relevant section in the data and 4) directly jump to these sections. We present the theoretical concept of the HMI framework and demonstrate it on a process control application for hybrid energy systems.

Keywords: Data exploration · System monitoring · Time series · Event detection · Data visualization

1 Introduction

Today's easy access to data, low cost sensors and data transmission systems leads to an abundance of data in many domains like industrial process control [12], network intrusion detection [6], maritime surveillance [11] or flight data analysis [8]. Typically, the data is automatically processed as far as possible.

However, complex systems often result in complex data series, which cannot be analyzed in a fully automatic way. This is due to different reasons. For some applications, like network intrusion detection, not all kinds of anomalies are known in advance. Therefore, unsupervised algorithms are used for anomaly detection of such time series data [2], which might lead to several false alarms

© Springer Nature Switzerland AG 2020
C. Stephanidis and M. Antona (Eds.): HCII 2020, CCIS 1226, pp. 495–503, 2020.
https://doi.org/10.1007/978-3-030-50732-9_64

that need to be evaluated manually. In other applications like maritime surveillance not each correctly identified anomaly requires a reaction or response. This decision is made by a human operator who manually evaluates the identified anomaly.

Using semi-automatic data analysis algorithms for anomaly and event detection results in a human-machine system, where the human operator and the machine both monitor the system. Most of the data processing is automated by the machine, but the human operator has to evaluate the results from time to time.

Take for example an automatic process control software for a complex industrial plant, which is able to detect abnormal system behavior, but is unable to correct it or spot its root cause. In such a situation a human analyst has to manually analyze the recorded data series of the plant.

In visual analytics there are different solutions to support this task. For low-dimensional data a common and well suited approach is to use a combination of anomaly detection algorithms like Prophet [1] and visualization algorithms such as Altair [10] or others.

Depending on the dynamics of the system and the data recording frequency, the data series can become very long. Furthermore, due to the system's complexity, the analyst not only has to survey a single parameter, but rather has to analyze several parameters in context. This often takes a lot of time and effort even with support of visual analytics solutions.

We present a powerful and easy to implement HMI design concept for the aforementioned domains that can complement analysis tools used for a more detailed data analysis. The gain of this HMI design concept relies on the fact that it focuses on highlighting sections in complex time series and provides insights into which data should be analyzed in more detail. Thus it supports the human Analyst in exploring and navigating through the data, quickly recognizing automatically detected events and anomalies along a time axis, getting clues about larger event patterns and quickly estimating the severeness of the events or anomalies. The subsequent and more detailed analysis can then be performed using other tools for instance Voila [4] or Prophet/Altair.

In Sect. 2 a generic model of the operator tasks is specified including monitoring and detection tasks. Afterwards the event detection task is described. In Sect. 4 the HMI design concept is presented. It shows which parts of the user tasks are supported by this design concept. Finally, the theoretical concept is demonstrated on a process control application for hybrid energy systems.

2   Exploration of Long Data Series

This work focuses on a special class of system monitoring applications. When monitoring complex systems, a distinction can be made between real-time monitoring and retrospective exploration of system behavior. Real-time monitoring uses software that mainly shows the current status of the system. When monitoring technical systems, this is often done using mimic diagrams that represent the topology of the system with all important components. These diagrams are enriched with different sensor values for the individual components. An important goal is typically to identify critical system states as early as possible in order to be able to counteract them.

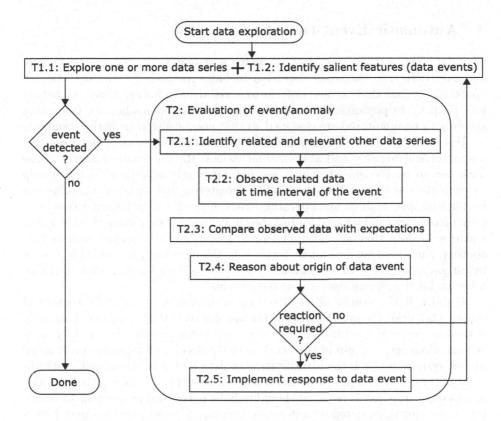

Fig. 1. Flow chart showing a prototypical data exploration task.

This time criticality often does not exist in retrospective data exploration. The goal here is to examine past system behavior in detail. An exemplary workflow can be seen in Fig. 1. It can vary in part from application to application. The main task is that the user visually explores different recorded time series of important parameters of the system and tries to discover data events like unusual patterns or salient features (task T1.1 + T1.2). Depending on the application, these can for instance point out potential problems or can be signs of performance losses that need further investigation (task T2). For this purpose, the user accesses further data series (task 2.1) that relate to the current data series and examines whether unusual behavior can also be seen in the same time range that does not match the expectations of the user (task T2.2 + T2. 3). After the causes of the abnormal system behavior have been identified (task T2.4), the user can react if necessary (task T2.5) and then continue with the data exploration.

Many monitoring applications support both types of monitoring and show current system values (e.g. in mimic diagrams), as well as time profiles for important parameters, (e.g. in line diagrams). This work focuses primarily on the second type of system monitoring: the exploration of time series data.

3 Automatic Event Detection

The data exploration task (Fig. 1) shows a strong similarity to the task of anomaly detection. Anomaly detection includes methods for the detection of "patterns in data that do not conform to a well defined notion of normal behavior" [5, p. 1]. In predominant cases this signifies that anomalies are rare, since systems to be monitored are designed so that normal behavior is the standard.

However, the data exploration task addressed in this work is not primarily about recognizing rare and abnormal situations. Rather, subtle features in the data are to be recognized, which are not inherently abnormal, but can help to evaluate the system behavior. When monitoring industrial plants, this can be for example, high or low operating costs, high or low pollutant values, etc. Other examples can be found for instance in police investigation activities, where features in data that are normally not unusual, can be unusual in a certain context. Such context-dependent features in the data can provide evidences for investigative activity. In the following we refer to data features that might be relevant for the human operator as data events.

Usually, it is a combination of several such events, or a certain pattern of events, that draw the attention of the human observer. With automated anomaly detection, unusual combinations of events are automatically detected by algorithms. However, the aim of this work is to develop an efficient, partially automated system in which the identification of data events is automated. Notwithstanding, the assessment of whether a pattern of events is an anomaly for which an operator response is required should only be performed by the human operator. This is intended to reduce automation errors due to incorrect anomaly detection and to improve understanding and awareness of system behavior among the operator.

In the following section we present a simple data visualization for time series data that is designed in order to support such partial automation.

4 Design Concept

The design concept presented in this work will primarily support the subtasks T1.1, T1.2, T2.1 and T2.2 (see Fig. 1). In the following we first present the general concept and will then illustrate it with an example.

For all important data series the design concept requires algorithms, which automatically recognize data events (e.g. increased values or strong variances) and can also quantify them if possible (Task T1.1 + 1.2). The core element of the design concept is a timeline on which these events are plotted. The timeline is divided into lanes – one lane for each data series for which events are displayed.

Recognized data events are marked and coded by a specific color on the respective lane. Each lane has its own color for it. The size of the mark depends on the intensity of the characteristic. This concept is shown in Fig. 2. Events are marked here as colored circles.

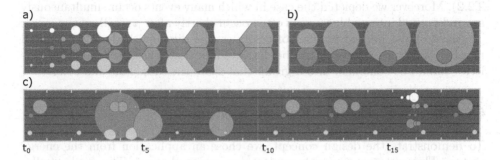

Fig. 2. Event circles on the timeline. Overlapping circles are not drawn as overlapping circles. The overlapping area is distributed between the overlapping circles. a) Increasing event sizes. b) Shape of overlapping event circles changes, based on relative size and position. c) Example with multiple sizes and positions. (Color figure online)

Figure 2a shows 5 lanes in which the intensity of the features increases from left to right. The dashed lines have only been added to highlight the lanes. With increasing intensity, the circle size can also grow beyond its own lane in order to optimally use the available space on the timeline for the visualization of the intensity. However, this can lead to overlaps, so that individual features are not recognizable. To avoid this, a simple rule for displaying overlapping parts of the circles is introduced:

If several circles overlap, the color of the circle is always shown for each point in the overlapping area, the center of which is closest to that point in relation to the radius. The boundary between two overlapping circles with the center points (x_1, y_2) and (x_2, y_2) and radii r_1 and r_2 can thus be determined and represented using the following equation of a circle:

$$\frac{(x - x_1)^2 + (y - y_1)^2}{r_1^2} = \frac{(x - x_2)^2 + (y - y_2)^2}{r_2^2}$$

This ensures that when there is overlap across several lanes, parts of each circle are always displayed in the respective feature color. In addition, no feature is disadvantaged, since each circular area is reduced in proportion to the size of the circle. Figure 2 shows the results of this rule for different overlapping circles. If overlapping event circles have the same size, the border between them becomes a straight line (Fig. 2a). Figure 2b shows the results when the sizes of overlapping circles differ. In case circles partly overlap they are drawn slightly deformed. If one circle is completely overlapped by another, it is simply drawn smaller. Figure 2c shows an example with circles of different size and relative positions on a time axis. Several events can be seen with different intensities. Patterns can be recognized on the timeline that can help to interpret the data (task T2.4). For example, it can be seen that yellow events occur at very regular intervals. If several events occur on different time series in a short period of time, this can be an indicator for possible relationships between different data series (T2.1, T2.2). Moreover we depicted the case in which many events occur simultaneously around t_{16} and intense blue events often occur shortly after a small orange event.

Since only a limited number of colors can be distinguished, only a limited number of feature categories can be displayed. In such a case, several characteristics should be combined into a group that share the same lane and color.

5   Use Case: Hybrid Energy Systems

To demonstrate the design concept, we chose an application from the energy sector. This sector is currently undergoing major changes. The study "cellular energy system" from the German Association for Electrical, Electronic & Information Technologies proposes how supply security and stability of electrical grids can be improved by combining different forms of energy in hybrid systems, described as "energy cells" [3]. A core element is the energy management of the cell itself and the ability of cells to coordinate their functionality with neighbouring cells. The application of the proposed visualization concept is demonstrated based on such a local energy management system, which is currently developed in a new district in Oldenburg in northwestern Germany. It is a hybrid energy system, which will contain a set of energy consumers and suppliers (combined heat and power (CHP) and photovoltaic (PV) plants), district heating as well as heat and power storage facilities [9]. These systems have the characteristic that electrical and thermal energy generation and storage facilities are coupled. Furthermore they have several advantages: they can increase the share of renewable energy by storing or converting excess energy, reduce carbon emission and increase their overall system efficiency. Beyond that the advancements in renewable energy technologies, operations of local heating grids and rise in prices of petroleum products are expected to make operations of hybrid energy systems more profitable in the future.

However, this adds to the complexity of managing such a system. As a result, at least two different roles are involved in the operation of such a hybrid energy system. On the one hand, this is the technical operator, who is responsible for real-time monitoring and who must ensure safe and technically flawless operation [7]. On the other hand there is the aggregator, who is responsible for the efficient, economical and ecological operation of the hybrid energy system. The proposed visualization concept will support the role of the aggregator, since the aggregator has to analyze the data series of the past system behavior in order to assess whether the way in which the system was controlled is satisfactory or whether improvements are necessary in the future.

6 Application of the Concept

Figure 3 shows a section of an early HMI prototype for the hybrid energy management system. In this application, the user can select and display a large number of data series. This can be seen in the middle area of the screenshot. It includes a variety of sensor values and external signals, such as the current market prices for electricity, as well as schedules for various technical systems. The key performance indicators (KPI) are displayed at the top: costs, CO_2 emissions and the self-supply rate of the hybrid energy system.

The lower part of the figure shows the timeline. For better illustration only four event categories are plotted on it: the three KPIs (costs - yellow, CO_2 emissions - blue, self-supply rate - green), as well as technical warnings in red (e.g. insufficient water pressure). On the right of the timeline a green area shows which section of the data is currently shown in the above diagrams. This section can be dragged larger or smaller on the timeline to show more or less data in the graphs. The area can also be moved to the left to display data from the past. If past data is displayed, the area turns blue instead of green (see Fig. 4).

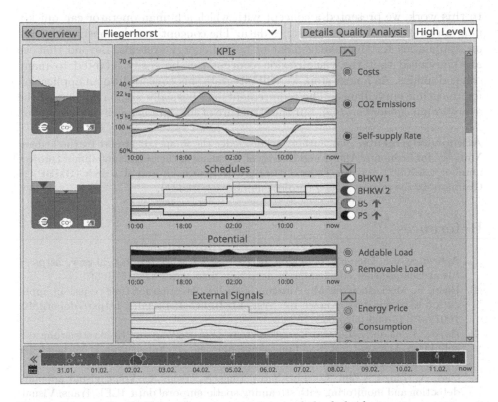

Fig. 3. Part of the HMI for the aggregator view of the hybrid energy management system (Color figure online)

Fig. 4. Timeline with the data selection window moved to past time interval. (Color figure online)

In this way, the user can navigate through the data very quickly and can have specific data displayed from events marked on the timeline (tasks 1.1 + 1.2). An initial quick assessment of the events can be made based on the size of the circles. Furthermore, recurring graphic patterns of the event circles can point out to the user known system behavior. In Fig. 3, for example, events from the categories costs and CO_2 emissions often occur shortly before midnight. This is now easy and quick for the user to detect.

7   Conclusion

In this work, we presented a concept with which a human operator can quickly gain an overview of long time series data. The concept was demonstrated using an application for the management of hybrid energy systems. Beyond that we are convinced that the visualization concept can be easily adapted to many other domains. As a next step, we will integrate this concept into an application for maritime surveillance. The requirements are basically similar to that of the energy management system, but the structure of the data is much more complex.

Acknowledgements. The authors acknowledge the financial support by the Federal Ministry for Economic Affairs and Energy of Germany in the project Intellimar (project number 03SX497) and the Federal Ministry of Education and Research (BMBF) of Germany in the project ENaQ (project number 03SBE111).

References

1. Ashrapov, I.: Anomaly detection in time series with prophet library. https://towardsdatascience.com/anomaly-detection-time-series-4c661f6f165f
2. Basu, S., Meckesheimer, M.: Automatic outlier detection for time series: an application to sensor data. Knowl. Inf. Syst. **11**(2), 137–154 (2007). https://doi.org/10.1007/s10115-006-0026-6
3. Bayer, J., et al.: Zellulares Energiesystem - Ein Beitrag zur Konkretisierung des zellularen Ansatzes mit Handlungsempfehlungen. Technical report, Verband der Elektrotechnik Elektronik und Informationstechnik e.V., May 2019
4. Cao, N., Lin, C., Zhu, Q., Lin, Y.R., Teng, X., Wen, X.: Voila: visual anomaly detection and monitoring with streaming spatiotemporal data. IEEE Trans. Visual. Comput. Graphics **24**(1), 23–33 (2017)
5. Chandola, V., Banerjee, A., Kumar, V.: Anomaly detection: a survey. ACM Comput. Surv. (CSUR) **41**(3), 1–58 (2009)

6. Davis, J.J., Clark, A.J.: Data preprocessing for anomaly based network intrusion detection: a review. Comput. Secur. **30**(6–7), 353–375 (2011)
7. Herdel, V., Wortelen, B., Lanezki, M., Lüdtke, A.: A generalized user interface concept to enable retrospective system analysis in monitoring systems. In: Proceedings of 22nd International Conference on Human-Computer Interaction (HCI International 2020) (2020)
8. Li, L., Das, S., John Hansman, R., Palacios, R., Srivastava, A.N.: Analysis of flight data using clustering techniques for detecting abnormal operations. J. Aerosp. Inf. Syst. **12**(9), 587–598 (2015)
9. Schmeling, L., Schönfeldt, P., Klement, P., Wehkamp, S., Hanke, B., Agert, C.: Development of a decision-making framework for distributed energy systems in a German district. Energies **13**(3), 552 (2020)
10. VanderPlas, J., et al.: Altair: interactive statistical visualizations for Python. J. Open Source Softw. **3**(32), 1057 (2018)
11. Voinov, S., Schwarz, E., Krause, D.: Automated processing system for SAR target detection and identification in near real time applications for maritime situational awareness. In: Maritime Knowledge Discovery and Anomaly Detection Workshop Proceedings, pp. 66–68. Publications Office of the European Union (2016)
12. Wu, W., Zheng, Y., Chen, K., Wang, X., Cao, N.: A visual analytics approach for equipment condition monitoring in smart factories of process industry. In: 2018 IEEE Pacific Visualization Symposium (PacificVis), pp. 140–149. IEEE (2018)

Construction of Airlines Safety Subculture Based on Human Factor Analysis

Yuan Zhang[✉], Yanqiu Chen, and Mingliang Chen

China Academy of Civil Aviation Science and Technology
Engineering and Technical Research Center of Civil Aviation
Safety Analysis and Preventionof Beijing, Beijing, China
zhangyuan@mail.castc.org.cn

Abstract. Airlines safety culture is composed of many elements, which can be called subculture or branch of safety culture. The human factors that lead to unsafe incidents in airlines were analyzed, mainly including violations and errors. The types and main contents of violation and error were given in detail. Furthermore, in order to avoid the occurrence of violations and errors in airlines, the construction elements and detailed contents of airlines safety culture were put forward, including compliance culture, competent culture, managers model culture, cooperation culture, safety communication culture. Finally, the construction method of safety culture was given.

Keywords: Safety culture · Human factor · Airlines · Safety

1 Introduction

With the development of civil aviation safety management theory, positive safety culture is increasingly regarded as one of the most important factors for airlines to ensure safe operation and reduce operational risks, and is also the ultimate goal of airlines safety management. Therefore, it is very important for airlines to define the content and elements of safety culture, and how to establish it.

Through literature research, most of the previous research on airlines safety culture discussed the composition and elements of safety culture as a whole [1–3]. It is relatively macro and did not consider the actual situation of the airlines. In fact, we can think it in another way. Under the overall framework of the airlines culture, there are many branches, or subcultures. Such as the just culture, the regulation culture, the reporting culture, the care culture, and so on. These subcultures constitute the airlines' overall safety culture. In view of the airlines' current situation and actual safety problems, a specific subculture is researched and established. It is very conducive to solving the actual safety problems of airlines.

According to statistics, more than 80% of civil aviation unsafe events involve human factors. It can be seen that the human factor is an important factor that restricts and affects aviation safety. Therefore, the establishment of airlines safety subculture based on human factors analysis can make the positive safety atmosphere affect every front-line employee. Through the change of safety concept and attitude of front-line

C. Stephanidis and M. Antona (Eds.): HCII 2020, CCIS 1226, pp. 504–509, 2020.
https://doi.org/10.1007/978-3-030-50732-9_65

employee, the front-line operation is gradually improved to achieve the ultimate goal of ensuring safety.

Based on the above considerations, the idea of this paper is:

First, analyze the unsafe events occurred in airlines and find out the human factors and their causes.

Then, in order to avoid the emergence of these human factors, put forward targeted airlines safety culture composition and construction methods, to achieve the goal of reducing man-made unsafe events and ultimately improving the level of safety.

2 Human Factor Analysis

Through the analysis of typical unsafe events in airlines, it is found that human factors mainly include violation and error [4–6].

There's a difference in motivation. An error is when a person tries to complete a task but fails to achieve the goal of the task by following the rules, procedures and training requirements. A violation is an active violation of a rule, procedure or training requirement at work. So the fundamental difference between an error and a violation is motivation.

2.1 Reasons for the Violation

A. Fluke psychology. It is considered that violation may not be found and punished, and may not cause unsafe events.
B. Shortcut psychology. It is considered that the standard operation procedure is too complex and unnecessary, and proper simplification steps can be done as well.
C. Self-righteous psychology. Blindly believe in their own experience and ability, work according to their own ideas and methods.
D. Curiosity psychology. Unfamiliar with new equipment, new business and new procedures, not operating according to standard operating procedures out of curiosity.
E. Profit seeking psychology. In order to improve production efficiency or because of staff shortage, ignore standard operating procedures and do not operate according to standard operating procedures.

2.2 Reasons for the Error

A. Skill based errors. Due to the improper personnel selection and training, the basic professional knowledge and operational skills of personnel can not meet the work needs.
B. Decision making errors. Mistake in decision-making and judgment caused by illness, fatigue, work pressure, time pressure and lack of personnel.
C. Cognitive errors. Incorrect information perception and inaccurate cognition caused by poor working environment and inappropriate attention distribution.

3 Safety Subculture Based on Human Factor

Aiming at the violations and errors occurring in airlines, this paper puts forward the composition of airlines safety culture, including:

3.1 Compliant Culture

A. Applicable standard operating procedures

- In view of each operating position, the standard operating procedures should be established, and not only meet the requirements of laws, regulations and standards, but also be understood and recognized by employee;
- Establish management procedures for all administrative work.

B. Comprehensive safety inspection

- Establish a perfect safety inspection system;
- Equip with experienced safety inspectors;
- Carry out daily safety inspection strictly.

C. Just safety rewards and punishments.

- Formulate a meticulous and fair system;
- Establish standard for safety rewards and punishments.

3.2 Competent Culture

A. Enough and competent personnel in all posts

- Formulate the standards for appointment and the number of personnel for each post;
- Recruit adequate and qualified personnel in accordance with the standards.

B. Training covering all staff at all stages

- Establish staff training system, including induction training, regular retraining, updating training, safety ideological education, etc.;
- Personnel are strictly assessed and those who fail to pass the assessment are prohibited from taking up their posts.

C. Allocate work reasonably, reduce fatigue and pressure

- Establish a scientific and humanized work assignment;
- Scheduling system to avoid fatigue and stress.

3.3 Manager Culture

A. Managers' understanding and commitment to safety

- Adhere to the principle of safety first in public places and documents;

- Guide the front-line employees to the correct understanding of safety gradually.

B. **Specific practices of managers to safety**

- Adhere to safety standards when there is a contradiction between operation and safety.;
- Adequate resources are invested in safety.;
- Through the practices, to demonstrate the company's attitude towards safety.

3.4 Collaborative Culture

A. **Mutual help, cooperation and reminder among employees**

- Employees supervise each other, remind each other and learn from each other, through which create a good working atmosphere.

B. **Mutual aid and collaboration among departments**

- Collaboration and resource sharing among departments.

3.5 Safety Communication Culture

A. **Internal safety information communication**

- Establish IT system or channels to make employees at all levels can get all the safety information;
- Speak freely about safety matters, such as voluntary reporting system.

B. **External safety information communication**

- Keep abreast of new technologies, new methods and new information about external operation and safety;
- The internal information will be released in appropriate ways to achieve information exchange and sharing.

4 Develop the Safety Subculture

4.1 Establishing Framework and Elements of Safety Culture

Firstly, airlines should list the elements and the specific contents of safety culture. The elements and specific contents of the safety culture should be recognized and accepted by senior management. This is an important foundation on which a safety culture can be implemented throughout the airlines.

4.2 Promoting the Safety Culture

Publicize the elements and contents of safety culture to all employees through official media. Enable all staff to understand and recognize the elements and contents of the safety culture. Take the safety culture as the basic principle of daily work gradually.

4.3 Documenting the Safety Culture

The safety culture can't just be verbal. In order to carry out the contents of safety culture into daily work, airlines should integrate the main contents of safety culture into the current system and procedure. Motivate employees to work in accordance with the principles and requirements of the safety culture in their daily work.

4.4 Resource Investment

In order to ensure the smooth construction of safety culture, airlines need to invest enough resources. This includes money, human resources, time, energy, etc. The most important of these is that the principle of safety culture should be observed when there is inconsistency in its operation.

4.5 Implementation of the Principles of Safety Culture

In order to ensure that the principles of safety culture are implemented throughout the airlines, senior management should take the lead in demonstrating them. Senior management should strictly follow the elements and specific contents of the safety culture, carry out day-to-day work. Adopt safety culture principles as a way of behaving in the airlines.

4.6 Establishing Safety Culture Construction Program

In order to ensure the orderly development of safety culture, airlines should establish safety culture construction program and carry out safety culture construction step by step in a planned way.

4.7 Safety Culture Assessment

In order to ensure the sustainable and effective of safety culture development, airlines should carry out safety culture assessment regularly. Continuously assess and improve the process of safety culture development and the suitability of safety culture.

5 Conclusion

- Airlines safety culture is composed of many sub-cultures. When analyzing and establishing safety culture, we can start from each sub-culture and establish the necessary safety culture pertinently.

- This paper analyzes the human factors that lead to unsafe incidents in airlines, and puts forward the elements and details of the construction of airlines safety culture.
- In addition to the subculture mentioned in this paper, such as learning subculture, justice subculture, information sharing subculture, can be established in the same way.

References

1. Zhao, X.N., You, X.Q.: Research and development of aviation safety culture. China Saf. Sci. J. **17**(11), 17–21 (2007)
2. Huo, Z.Q.: Discussion on safety cultural construction of civil aviation. J. Civ. Aviat. Univ. China **23**(1), 40–44 (2005)
3. Helmrich, R.L., Merritt, A.C.: Culture at Work in Aviation and Medicine National. Ashgate, Aldershot (1998)
4. Cheng, W.M., Zhou, G., Wang, G., Liu, X.S.: Psychological measurement and analysis on human unsafe behavior. China Saf. Sci. J. **19**(6), 29–34 (2009)
5. Zhang, X.Q., Wang, H., Yan, C.G.: Analysis on human factors in aviation maintenance based on DEMATEL and ANP. Saf. Environ. Eng. **21**(1), 128–133 (2014)
6. Chen, L.J., Chang, S.N.: An approach of AHP for human factors analysis in the aircraft acing accident. Procedia Eng. **17**, 63–69 (2011)

Security, Privacy and Trust

Blockchain Technology: A Bibliometric Analysis

Duaa Bukhari[1,2]($\boxtimes$)

[1] Long Island University CW Post, Brookville, NY 11548, USA
duaa.bukhari@my.liu.edu
[2] Taibah University, Medina, Saudi Arabia

Abstract. Blockchain is a decentralized transaction and data management technology. It is a relatively new technology with a wide variety of applications that may in time come to affect the whole economy and be recognized as the latest general-purpose technology. The aim of this study is to explore the literature growth and author productivity of blockchain technology research from 2008 to 2019. 9239 articles were retrieved from Scopus database and analyzed with bibliometrics approach using different perspective views. Blockchain and Blockchain Technology were used as search terms in order to run the query and obtain data. The search was performed on Title, Abstract and Keywords. The search excluded the year 2020 as we are still in the first quarter of the year. Results revealed that first publication with blockchain technology can be tracked back to 2010, and 2019 was the peak time for blockchain research. Moreover, results revealed that Chain and USA are considered to be the most productive countries producing more research, and Chinese organizations were predominant and controlling the research of the new technology. The key author was found by Scopus to be Wang, F.Y with 38 different works.

Keywords: Blockchain · Blockchain technology · Bibliometric study

1 Introduction

Blockchain is a relatively new technology with a wide variety of applications that may in time come to affect the whole economy and be recognized as the latest general-purpose technology. Blockchain has been used to create digital currency systems like Bitcoin and is starting to be used to create smart contracts [1]. As it mentioned by Swan [1], it is predicted that Blockchain based developments will lead to a large wave of disruption as it extends to other segments of the economy. However, while Blockchain has a great deal of potential, the final form of its impact that will take is still to be seen and examined [2]. Blockchain is still in the early stages of its development and acceptance, and it is just beginning to show its potential as a disruptive new technology [3]. This study aims to have an overview of the evolution of blockchain research. Specifically, the objectives of this study are: (i) to explore the growth and distribution of world literature; (ii) to identify and present the leading productive countries, organizations and key authors on the subject; (iii) to examine the distribution of publication across leading subject areas; (iv) to identify of its highly-cited publications.

© Springer Nature Switzerland AG 2020
C. Stephanidis and M. Antona (Eds.): HCII 2020, CCIS 1226, pp. 513–519, 2020.
https://doi.org/10.1007/978-3-030-50732-9_66

2 Background

Generally, a trusted third party is needed to process electronic payments between individuals. In order to solve this issue, Nakamoto offered a peer-to-peer electronic payment system based on cryptographic proof instead of trust, which is named Bitcoin [4]. Bitcoin is starting to come into its own as a digital currency, but the blockchain technology behind it could prove to be much more significant [1]. Currently, blockchain technology has become an emerging field of research and practice [5]. It is considered in the peak of inflated expectations phrase by research powerhouse Gartner Inc. in their 2016 report Hype Cycle for Emerging Technologies [6]. What is more, in their 2017 report, blockchain have moved significantly along the Hype Cycle. The reason for the interest in blockchain as mentioned [7], is its central attributes including security, anonymity and data integrity without any third-party trusted systems, and therefore it creates interesting research areas, especially from the perspective of technical challenges and limitations. It is predicted that blockchain technology to become the fifth disruptive computing paradigm after mainframes, PCs, the Internet, and mobile & social networking [1]. In 2015, Swan has defined blockchain as a single identifiable technology that is best known for underpinning the bitcoin digital currency. In other words, it is the technology that allows bitcoin to store transactions safely and publicly [1]. In 2016, blockchain has been defined by Nguyen as a digitized system of accounting records which captures in details all transactions according to a mathematical set of rules to prevent illegal interference [8]. It is considered as an open ledger where all online transactions are recorded and everyone is allowed to connect, to send or verify transactions. Another definition indicates that blockchain is a decentralized database where there is no central trusted party maintaining and storing the database, but instead it is distributed across a network and uses a consensus mechanism to verify transactions [9].

3 Methodology

As mentioned earlier, the main goal of this study is to conduct a bibliometric analysis of all blockchain technology publications in order to assess the global publications on blockchain research, using Scopus international database during 2008–2019. This study preferred Scopus database because it contains both the ISI and Scopus indexed rank papers [10]. Thus, this study contains four phases: (1) Search, (2) Result, (3) Findings, and (4) Analysis and Visualization. First, Scopus database (http://www.scopus.com) was used as a source to obtain blockchain research publications that are indexed by Scopus using significant keywords (as search terms) and limiting the search period to 2008–2019. The "TITLEABS-KEY" field tag (as shown in the search query below) was used to search literature using keywords ["Blockchain" OR "Blockchain Technology"]. Only two keywords were used to facilitate the study's goal, obtain and explore all literature that has the concept of blockchain as a technology. The search output was latter restricted to the period 2008–2019. Search Query was TITLE-ABS-KEY ("Blockchain" OR "Blockchain Technology"). Following this, the result retrieved a total number of 9,239 documents published between 2008 and 2019. The author concentrated the analysis from 2008 onwards because the blockchain was invented by Satoshi Nakamoto during that year. Subsequently, the retrieved result was interpreted with a focus on various aspects which include but not limited to, looking at literature distribution, peak time, subject area, authors, and countries. Last but not least, the results were analyzed and visualized using Excel and Scopus tools.

4   Result and Analysis

4.1   Research Growth

During the period 2008–2019, blockchain technology research has accumulated a total of 9239 global publications and registered average annual growth rate of 770 papers per year. The retrieved result from Scopus indicates that 2010 witnessed the first published paper on blockchain technology presented on a conference and published on Studies in Health Technology and Informatics Journal. However, the research growth, increased from 3877 to 9239 publications from 2018 to 2019. This high growth trend highlights that the subject witnessed fastest growth during last year. Table 1 shows the total number of published blockchain technology per year (Fig. 1).

Table 1. Blockchain research per year

Year	Number of publications
2019	5362
2018	2838
2017	806
2016	182
2015	38
2014	10
2013	2
2010	1

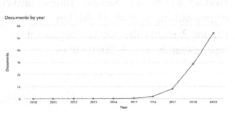

Fig. 1. Yearly publication trends of blockchain technology

4.2   Most Productive Countries in Blockchain Technology Research

The result finds that 114 countries had participated and contributed in producing blockchain research during 2010–2019, but the distribution of global research by country of publication was highly skewed. Seventy-five countries contributed 1 to 50 papers, 15 contributed 51–100 papers, 7 contributed 100 to 150 papers, 2 contributed 101–150 papers, 11 contributed 151–500 papers and 4 contributed the highest 501 to 1888. The top 10 countries global publication share varied widely from 3.27% to 20.43%. China and the USA lead the list of top 10 countries with their dominant publication shares 20.43% and 17.22% respectively, followed by India (7.02%), UK (6.42%) and six other countries (from 4.95% to 3.27%) during 2010–2019 (Table 2).

Table 2. Top ten productive countries producing blockchain research

Country	Number of publications
China	1888
United States	1591
India	649
United Kingdom	594
Germany	458
Italy	371
Australia	367
South Korea	363
Canada	338
Russian Federation	303

4.3   Contribution of Top 10 Most Productive Global Organizations

More than 520 organizations took part in global blockchain technology research during 2010–2019. The top ten organizations produced a total of 827 blockchain technology research papers during 2010–2019. The result indicates that 75.93% of the blockchain technology research was undertaken by Chinese organizations and institutions. No wonder to see also Seven Chinese universities on the top list of ten most productive organizations and show higher productivity as China dominates the research area. Figure 2 shows the top ten organizations contributed the most to blockchain technology research during 2010–2019.

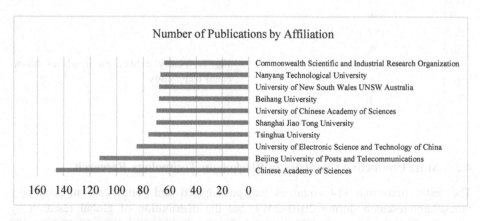

Fig. 2. Top ten leading organizations on blockchain technology research

4.4   Subject-Wise Distribution of Papers

The subject areas (as defined by Scopus database) were used as criteria for understanding the distribution of research in blockchain technology. The blockchain research were distributed in 26 subject areas. This study finds that computer science which interconnected with blockchain research accounted for the largest global publications share (78.38%) followed by engineering, mathematics, decision sciences and Business. The graph below shows the blockchain research subject areas.

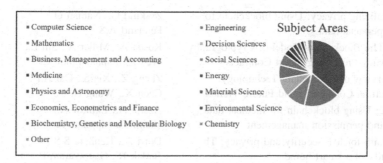

Fig. 3. Blockchain research subject-wise breakup

4.5 Highly Cited Papers and Key Authors

Wang, F.Y is highlighted in Scopus result as the key and most productive author in blockchain research with 38 different works. The most top ten productive authors in the blockchain research are shown in Fig. 3. In addition, according to the result obtained from Scopus, a total of 1333 papers were cited by others since 2016 to 2019. The paper titled Blockchains and Smart Contracts for the Internet of Things was cited the most by 905 after excluding self-citations. Table 3 shows the list of top 10 highly cited blockchain research papers (Fig. 4).

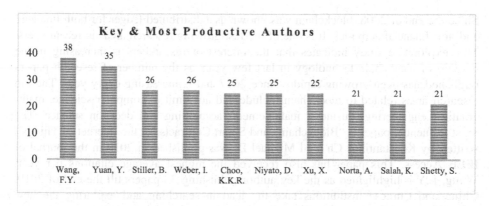

Fig. 4. Top ten key authors

Table 3. A profile of 10 highly cited papers on blockchain technology research

Document title	Authors	Cited by
Blockchains and Smart Contracts for the Internet of Things	Christidis K., Devetsikiotis M.	905
Decentralizing privacy: Using blockchain to protect personal data	Zyskind G., Nathan O., Pentland A.S.	630
Hawk: The Blockchain Model of Cryptography and Privacy-Preserving Smart Contracts	Kosba A., Miller A., Shi E., Wen Z., Papamanthou C.	524
An Overview of Blockchain Technology: Architecture, Consensus, and Future Trends	Zheng Z., Xie S., Dai H., Chen X., Wang H.	441
MedRec: Using blockchain for medical data access and permission management	Azaria A., Ekblaw A., Vieira T., Lippman A.	389
Blockchain for IoT security and privacy: The case study of a smart home	Dorri A., Kanhere S.S., Jurdak R., Gauravaram P.	382
Where is current research on Blockchain technology? - A systematic review	Yli-Huumo J., Ko D., Choi S., Park S., Smolander K.	373
Bitcoin and beyond: A technical survey on decentralized digital currencies	Tschorsch F., Scheuermann B.	366
Making smart contracts smarter	Luu L., Chu D.-H., Olickel H., Saxena P., Hobor A.	345
Bitcoin-NG: A scalable blockchain protocol	Gencer A.E., Sirer E.G., Van Renesse R.	327

5   Conclusion and Future Study

Since the end of 2008, blockchain was known as a distributed ledger for both financial and non-financial activities. It is one of the fast-growing research areas in recent years. This explorative study indicates that the interest of researchers is increasing in the domain of blockchain technology in last few years as the number of research papers published has been growing rapidly since 2017 and is increasing every year. The top research areas related to blockchain include and not limit to computer science, mathematics, engineering, business, management, accounting and decision science. The most influential paper is "Blockchains and Smart Contracts for the Internet of Things" written by Konstantinos Ch. and Michael D. was published in 2016 in the journal of IEEE Access. This paper has also received the highest average citations per year. Wang, F.Y is highlighted as the key author publishing 38 papers till the end of 2019. China and Chinese institutions take the lead in searching and exploring the new technology. This research explores diverse and relevant potential future research in blockchain technology which include a detail research study on highly cited papers with respect to the technical aspect and replication of similar research study using different literature database like Web of Science to check the similarity of this study. Further research could also apply the Lotka's law for author productivity and preform K-S test to verify the reliability.

References

1. Blockchain. O'Reilly. http://shop.oreilly.com/product/0636920037040.do. Accessed 3 Mar 2020
2. Is Blockchain a General Purpose Technology? https://papers.ssrn.com/sol3/papers.cfm?abstract_id=2932585. Accessed 10 Mar 2020
3. Pilkington, M.: Blockchain technology: principles and applications. In: Olleros, F.X., Zhegu, M. (eds.) Research Handbook on Digital Transformations. Edward Elgar Publishing, Cheltenham (2016)
4. Bitcoin: A peer-to-peer electronic cash system. http://bitcoin.org/bitcoin.pdf. Accessed 11 Mar 2020
5. Yuan, Y., Wang, F.: Blockchain: the state of the art and future trends. Acta Automatica Sinica 42(4), 481–494 (2016)
6. Trends Emerge in the Gartner Hype Cycle for Emerging Technologies (2018). https://www.gartner.com/smarterwithgartner/5-trends-emerge-in-gartner-hype-cycle-for-emerging-technologies-2018/. Accessed 19 Mar 2020
7. Yli-Huumo, J., Ko, D., Choi, S., Park, S., Smolander, K.: Where is current research on blockchain technology?—a systematic review. PloS ONE 11(10), e0163477 (2016)
8. Narayanan, A., Bonneau, J., Felten, E., Miller, A., Goldfeder, S.: Bitcoin and Cryptocurrency Technologies: A Comprehensive Introduction. Princeton University Press, USA (2016)
9. Economics of blockchain. https://papers.ssrn.com/sol3/papers.cfm?abstract_id=2744751. Accessed 18 Mar 2020
10. Oakleaf, M.: Writing information literacy assessment plans: a guide to best practice. Commun. Inf. Lit. 3(2), 4 (2009)

Effects of Recipient Information and Urgency Cues on Phishing Detection

Xinyue Cui[1,2], Yan Ge[1,2(✉)], Weina Qu[1,2(✉)], and Kan Zhang[1,2]

[1] CAS Key Laboratory of Behavioral Science, Institute of Psychology,
Beijing 100101, China
{gey, quwn}@psych.ac.cn
[2] Department of Psychology, University of Chinese Academy of Sciences,
Beijing 100101, China

Abstract. Phishing causes significant economic damage and erodes consumer trust in business communication. To better filter phishing emails, researchers have paid a substantial amount of attention to the characteristics of phishing emails. This study focused on the effects of recipient information and urgency cues on phishing detection. A total of 518 participants performed role-playing tasks in which they needed to discriminate legitimate emails and phishing emails. The results showed that the main effects of urgency cues and recipient information were significant. Under the condition of time constraints, the likelihood of replying to the phishing emails increased, and the likelihood of searching for the relevant information decreased. When recipient information was added to the phishing emails, the likelihood of replying to the phishing emails decreased, and the likelihood of deleting the phishing emails and searching the for relevant information increased. Meanwhile, the interaction effect of recipient information and time pressure was also significant. When recipient information was added to the phishing emails, the urgency cues had a significant negative effect on the detection behaviors. Under the condition of time constraints and recipient information addition, the likelihood of replying to the phishing emails increased, and the likelihood of deleting the phishing emails and searching for the relevant information decreased. These findings showed that phishing email characteristics strongly affect phishing susceptibility. A sense of urgency resulted in stress and impulsive behavior, and thus, the participants preferred quickly respond and perform less research. By exploring the mechanism underlying phishing processing, this study deepens the understanding of detecting deception and motivates more effective strategies or assistance systems to protect individuals from online fraud.

Keywords: Phishing emails · Urgency cues · Recipient information

1 Introduction

Phishing refers to the behavior of attacking end-users through computer technology and taking advantage of human psychological factors. Phishing is designed to lead consumers to counterfeit Web sites that trick them into divulging financial data such as usernames and passwords [1]. As individuals and organizations are continuing to

© Springer Nature Switzerland AG 2020
C. Stephanidis and M. Antona (Eds.): HCII 2020, CCIS 1226, pp. 520–525, 2020.
https://doi.org/10.1007/978-3-030-50732-9_67

increase their reliance on networks and the Internet [2], phishing causes significant economic damage and erodes consumer trust in business communication. Over the past few years, such attacks have increased in frequency and sophistication. The total number of phishing sites detected by the Anti-Phishing Working Group in the third quarter of 2019 was 266,387. This number is almost double the 138,328 detected in Q4 of 2018 and is at a high level not seen since late 2016 [1].

A growing body of research has begun to explore ways to shield individuals from getting phished. The solutions typically fall into one of three categories, which involve (i) educational or training interventions, (ii) new designs that can help 'nudge' users to make better decisions and (iii) work that considers individual differences in decision-making [3]. However, many interventions are unproductive because they take time and effort away from the users' primary task [3], and education and training are effective only in the short term [4]. Additionally, past experience suggests that technology does not provide adequate protection because phishers evolve with the technology and improve their baiting techniques [5]. To better filter phishing emails and alert individuals about the deception, researchers have paid a large amount of attention to the characteristics of phishing emails.

Today, attackers have shifted from sending traditional emails, hoping to deceive anyone [6], to employing more selective, targeted attacks that use relevant elements of context in order to deceive specific victims (also known as spear phishing) [6, 7]. Context can be provided in a phishing email by including information that is both specific and relevant to the victims, which could trigger their willingness to comply with a request posed by an attacker [8]. Previous studies have shown a connection between recipient information and phishing email recognition performance. A study by Holm et al. found that the number of organizational employees falling victim to phishing increased by 22.2% when the name of the employee, name of the organization the employee worked for, and name of the executive sending the email were added in the attack [8]. In addition, Bullee et al. found that those in the spear phishing group had 1.693 times higher odds of compliance than those exposed to a general phishing email [9]. Another study showed that the likelihood increased 2.62 fold when name manipulation was present compared with the control condition [10].

Phishers also use urgency cues to communicate fear, threat, and scarcity, thereby attempting to short-circuit the evaluation process and elicit compliance [11]. The sense of urgency may result in a feeling of stress and create a need to cope [12]. A time-pressured individual tends to rely more on one cue than on multiple cues [13]. Wright et al. sent two phishing emails to participants, one with a request for an urgent response and the other without. The results showed that when urgency cues were used in the email, there was a 3.19-times higher likelihood of the consumer sending his or her super code [10]. The level of attention to urgency cues is positively related to the individual's likelihood of responding to the phishing email [11], and it has a negative impact on cognitive effort [14]. Wang et al. argued that visceral triggers, including urgency cues, reduce the recipients' depth of information processing and induce recipients to make decision errors [14].

Although the topic of recipient information and urgency cues has been previously investigated, no studies known to us have specifically examined how recipient information and urgency cues might be associated with phishing email recognition performance in combination. Linking recipient information and urgency cues would help improve our understanding of the impact of phishing emails' characteristics and potentially pave the way for optimal design solutions for personnel with varying phishing susceptibility. In this article, we focused on the interaction effects of recipient information and urgency cues on phishing detection. This approach will help in the development of an improved knowledge base from which to design systems that would better meet the needs of specific types of users.

2 Methods

2.1 Participants

There were 518 valid participants in our research, ranging in age from 18 to 52 years (mean = 24.69, SD = 4.543). Of these participants, 54% were female, 68.9% claimed that they have phone phishing experience, 73.35% had mail phishing experience; and 75.29% had web phishing experience. A total of 9.46% of the subjects had lost money or private information as a result, and 13.32% of the subjects had phishing education experience.

2.2 Email Stimulus Material

In this study, 16 email screenshots were presented to participants, including 8 phishing emails. The phishing email constructed by the researchers mimicked the kinds of phishing attacks that had already been attempted on researchers or shown on antiphishing websites. Each phishing email included an email address error or an unofficial link of the sender (e.g., do-not-reply@amazon.com was modified to do-not-reply@gmail.com and https://supports.apple.com/ was modified to https://supports.opple.com/ by switching the letters "a" and "o"). To improve the involvement and immersion of the subjects, all of the emails came from authoritative companies, such as Apple, Amazon and Baidu. In addition, the content of the emails covered many topics, including order problems, account risk, system upgrades, bank consumption reminders and so on, which required the recipient to carry out an operation, such as clicking the link or replying to the email.

2.3 Design and Procedure

There were two independent variables, namely, time pressure (with or without time urgency cues) and recipient information (with or without the receiver's name), with equal numbers of emails between the phishing and legitimate conditions. All independent variables were measured within subjects, and the order of the emails was randomly assigned to the participants.

The participants registered for this experiment online, and informed consent was obtained prior to completing the survey. Their behavior was measured by performance in a roleplay task, which was previously shown to be effective [15]. The participants were told to assume the role of Zhang Wei, who works at HongHai foreign trading company and uses the email address zhangwei2012a@honghai.com. As a marketing manager, Zhang Wei receives dozens of emails every day and checks his mailbox approximately 10 times per day. The participants were asked to indicate how they would handle the 16 emails as Zhang Wei. They answered four questions after reading each email, including 'How likely are you to reply to this email?', 'How likely are you to delete this email?', 'How likely are you to search for information related to this email?' and 'How likely is this email to be a phishing email?' The participants evaluated the possibility for each question on a 5-point scale, with 1 for unlikely to 5 for very likely. Only the results of 8 phishing emails were analyzed in this paper.

3 Results

3.1 The Likelihood of Replying to the Phishing Emails

A 2 × 2 ANOVA of the likelihood of replying to the phishing emails revealed significant main effects for time urgency cues (F(1, 517) = 32.325, p < .001) and recipient information (F(1, 517) = 116.763, p < .001) as well as a significant interaction between the two (F(1, 517) = 28.983, p < .001). Overall, the likelihood of replying to the phishing emails was significantly higher in trials in which phishing emails had time urgency cues than in trials without the time urgency cues. Similarly, the likelihood of replying to the phishing emails was significantly lower in trials in which phishing emails had added recipient information than in trials in which they did not have added recipient information. As indicated by the significant interaction and as illustrated in Table 1, the participants replied with approximately the same likelihood for both levels of time urgency cues when the phishing emails had no recipient information. However, when the phishing emails contained recipient information, the participants replied to significantly more phishing emails with time urgency cues than without.

Table 1. Descriptive statistics for each condition in the email task (mean/SD)

	With recipient information			Without recipient information		
Time urgency cues	Replying	Deleting	Searching for information	Replying	Deleting	Searching for information
With	2.510 ± 1.173	2.904 ± 1.214	3.342 ± 1.236	2.821 ± 1.182	2.737 ± 1.179	2.810 ± 1.208
Without	2.092 ± 1.020	3.185 ± 1.206	3.087 ± 1.197	2.818 ± 1.251	2.577 ± 1.241	3.315 ± 1.246

3.2 The Likelihood of Deleting the Phishing Emails

In contrast to the pattern for the likelihood of replying to the phishing emails, a 2 × 2 ANOVA of the likelihood of deleting the phishing emails revealed a significant main effect for recipient information (F(1, 517) = 75.830, p < .000) but not for the time urgency cues. The interaction between the time urgency cues and the recipient information was significant (F(1, 517) = 40.356, p < .000). Overall, the likelihood of deleting the phishing emails was significantly lower in trials in which the phishing emails did not have recipient information than in trials in which the emails contained recipient information. However, when phishing emails had recipient information, the participants deleted significantly more phishing emails without time urgency cues than with. No other significant results were found.

3.3   The Likelihood of Searching for Relevant Information

For the likelihood of searching for relevant information, main effects were found for time urgency cues ($F(1, 517) = 11.038$, $p \leq .001$) and recipient information ($F(1, 517) = 10.561$, $p \leq .001$). The interaction between the two was also significant ($F(1, 517) = 100.000$, $p < .001$). As indicated by the significant interaction and as illustrated in Table 1, when the phishing emails did not contain recipient information, the likelihood of searching for relevant information was significantly higher when the phishing emails did not have time urgency cues than when they did have time urgency cues. However, when the phishing emails contained recipient information, the likelihood of searching for relevant information was significantly lower for phishing emails without time urgency cues than for those with time urgency cues.

4   Discussion

This study focused on understanding how phishing emails persuade Internet consumers to disclose sensitive information. To accomplish this goal, we conducted an email roleplay task that manipulated recipient information and urgency cues within the email. The analysis suggests that emails with urgency cues are more likely to elicit reply responses than those without. However, this effect was influenced by recipient information. These findings showed that phishing email features are implicated in affecting phishing susceptibility.

Under the condition of time constraints, the participants preferred to make a quick response to the phishing emails and to conduct less searching for information. The urgency cues made the participant feel nervous, which resulted in impulsive behavior. Unfortunately, we did not find the expected effect of recipient information. Based on previous research, recipient information may increase the response rate because it evokes the receivers' peripheral processing [10]. In contrast, we found that recipient information decreased the likelihood of response and increased the likelihood of deleting the email and searching for relevant information. This outcome could be caused by the participants' low degree of immersion and involvement, which causes the influence of the recipient's information to be reduced. With recipient information, urgency cues make the participant more likely to respond to the phishing emails than without the urgency cues. This finding suggested that recipient information makes people more engaged in finding more information and more likely to respond. Urgency cues are known to use large amounts of information processing resources [16]. Individuals focus disproportionately on urgency cues, often ignoring other elements of the email and increasing the likelihood of being phished [11].

The current study is limited in several aspects. First, most of the participants were university students, which could lead to a misunderstanding of the background of the role they were asked to play which thus decrease their degree of involvement. Second, this study employed a limited number of phishing emails, which may have increased the randomness of the experiment. Future research could expand the representative sample to be from the general population and improve the experimental materials.

In summary, this paper suggested that phishing emails' features strongly affect the processing of and response to the emails. Through an exploration of the mechanism underlying phishing processing, this study deepens our understanding of detecting deception and may motivate a more effective strategy or assistance system to protect individuals from online fraud.

References

1. Anti-Phishing Working Group. https://apwg.org/trendsreports/. Accessed 4 Nov 2019
2. Lim, V.K.G., Teo, T.S.H.: Prevalence, perceived seriousness, justification and regulation of cyberloafing in Singapore: an exploratory study. Inf. Manag. 42(8), 1081–1093 (2005)
3. Nicholson, J., Coventry, L., Briggs, P.: Can we fight social engineering attacks by social means? Assessing social salience as a means to improve phish detection. In: 13th Symposium on Usable Privacy and Security, pp. 285–298. USENIX, Santa Clara (2017)
4. Ferguson, A.J.: Fostering e-mail security awareness: the west point carronade. Educause Q. 28(1), 54–57 (2005)
5. Vishwanath, A., Harrison, B., Ng, Y.J.: Suspicion, cognition, and automaticity model of phishing susceptibility. Commun. Res. 45(8), 1146–1166 (2018)
6. Hong, J.: The state of phishing attacks. Commun. ACM 55(1), 74–81 (2012)
7. Jagatic, T.N., Johnson, N.A., Jakobsson, M., Menczer, F.: Social phishing. Commun. ACM 50(10), 94–100 (2007)
8. Holm, H., Flores, W.R., Nohlberg, M., Ekstedt, M.: An empirical investigation of the effect of recipient information in phishing attacks. In: 18th International Enterprise Distributed Object Computing Conference Workshops and Demonstrations, Ulm, Germany, pp. 357–363. IEEE (2014)
9. Bullee, J., Montoya, L., Junger, M., Hartel, P.: Spear phishing in organisations explained. Inf. Comput. Secur. 25(5), 593–613 (2017)
10. Wright, R.T., Marett, K., Thatcher, J.B.: Extending ecommerce deception to phishing. In: 35th International Conference on Information Systems, pp. 1–16. AIS eLibrary, Auckland (2014)
11. Vishwanath, A., Herath, T., Chen, R., Wang, J., Rao, H.R.: Why do people get phished? Testing individual differences in phishing vulnerability within an integrated, information processing model. Decis. Support Syst. 51(3), 576–586 (2011)
12. Ordonez, L., Benson III, L.: Decisions under time pressure: how time constraint affects risky decision making. Organ. Behav. Hum. Decis. Process. 71(2), 121–140 (1997)
13. Rothstein, H.G.: The effects of time pressure on judgement in multiple cue probability learning. Organ. Behav. Hum. Decis. Process. 37(1), 83–92 (1986)
14. Wang, J., Herath, T., Chen, R., Vishwanath, A., Rao, H.R.: Research article phishing susceptibility: an investigation into the processing of a targeted spear phishing email. IEEE Trans. Prof. Commun. 55(4), 345–362 (2012)
15. Sheng, S., Holbrook, M., Kumaraguru, P., Cranor, L.F., Downs, J.: Who falls for phish?: a demographic analysis of phishing susceptibility and effectiveness of interventions. In: The SIGCHI Conference on Human Factors in Computing Systems, Georgia, USA, pp. 373–382. ACM (2010)
16. Shah, D.V., Kwak, N., Schmierbach, M., Zubric, J.: The interplay of news frames on cognitive complexity. Hum. Commun. Res. 30(1), 102–120 (2004)

Evaluating Multiple Approaches to Impact Trust Formation: Labeling, Design, and Support Features

Benjamin Ewerz and Peter Moertl[✉] ⓘ

Virtual Vehicle Research GmbH, Inffeldgasse 21a, 8010 Graz, Austria
peter.moertl@v2c2.at

Abstract. Creating trust in wireless solutions and increasing their social acceptance are major challenges to achieve the full potential of the Internet of Things (IoT).

In the current study we investigate various methods to increase trust in wireless systems like user feedback, usability, and product labeling. This work is part of the European project SCOTT (Secure COnnected Trustable Things; https://scottproject.eu) with the goal to develop wireless solutions that are safe, trusted, and acceptable.

Participants watched three videos of three use cases and then rated the expected impact of controllability, accountability, user feedback, usability, and product labeling on their trust in the technologies. Also, two labels were evaluated: a uni-dimensional label that reflected the privacy of user data as well as a multi-dimensional label that combined the dimensions privacy, product quality, manufacturing, usability, and cost.

The results indicate that trustworthiness aspects of the system like controllability, accountability and usability have the strongest impact on positive trust formation among all the investigated methods. Furthermore, the results indicate that both the uni-dimensional and the multi-dimensional labeling conditions seemed to increase user trust at the maximum trust level and increased the participants indicated willingness to use the product. However, only the uni-dimensional label showed a positive influence on trust formation at the medium quality level.

Results of this study highlight that service and product providers have various methods at hand to help increase trust among their customers. Consumers want control over their technologies, as well as accountability of technology vendors. Furthermore, in the long term, the results suggest that customers could benefit from digital competence education that may allow them to learn to use and rely on otherwise relatively complex multi-dimensional labeling systems. Next steps for this research are suggested.

Keywords: Trust formation · Wireless systems · Labeling

© Springer Nature Switzerland AG 2020
C. Stephanidis and M. Antona (Eds.): HCII 2020, CCIS 1226, pp. 526–533, 2020.
https://doi.org/10.1007/978-3-030-50732-9_68

1 Introduction

1.1 Study Motivation

Industry currently spends considerable effort on improving system reliability and its perception of trustworthiness for the development of continuously increasing numbers of wireless and smart products. To support these efforts the Internet of Things (IOT) Security & Privacy Trust Framework[1] provides strategic principles toward developing secure IOT devices. This framework requires comprehensive disclosures concerning the product, data collection, usage and sharing. Also, recommendations are given to manufacturers to increase transparency and communication on device capability and privacy issues.

However, translating this high-level guidance into concrete measures during development is not straight-forward. Increasing communication is good, but which communication and in which form? Who is responsible for determining this information and what does success mean? These questions are investigated in the European project SCOTT ("Secure Connected Trustable Things", see https://scottproject.eu/) that intends to bring together human users, operators, engineering and management to develop new, more trustworthy wireless technology. In this paper the results of a study that investigated trust formation as part of the SCOTT project are described.

1.2 Trust

Lee and See (2004) [1] define trust as "... the attitude that an agent will help achieve an individual's goals in a situation characterized by uncertainty and vulnerability.". Based on this definition, certain conditions must be met in order to create a situation in which trust is required, namely, a level of uncertainty, risk and a certain level of interdependence, as well as the necessity to make a choice between at least two alternatives.

Trust has been defined either as an attitude, intention, belief or behavior [1]. Lee and See (2004) argue that those differences in definition can be harmonized by taking the theory of reasoned action [2] into account. In this context, trust is described as an attitude, which influences the intention of using the automated system and subsequently the actual reliance behavior. The translation from attitude, to intentions and finally to actual reliance behavior is influenced by additional factors such as context, operator state, and pre-existing knowledge (Lee & See, 2004). Lee and See (2004) describe a dynamic model of trust formation and the subsequent influence on reliance behavior.

Similarly, [3] differentiate trust prior to the interaction with a system (initial learned trust) with trust that develops during the interaction with a system (dynamically learned trust). We refer to (initial learned trust) from now on as "initially formed trust" to better reflect that this trust formation is not based on direct interaction with the system. Initially formed trust is influenced by pre-existing knowledge, expectations, and understanding of the system. The result is an initial reliance strategy that is relatively little influenced by system characteristics itself, because direct interactions with the

---

[1] https://otalliance.org/system/files/files/initiative/documents/iot_trust_framework6-22.pdf.

system have not yet commenced. Instead, initial trust formation is influenced by the information that is available about the system and the culture and attitudes that are formed. Dynamically learned trust on the other hand relies on direct system interactions and is therefore directly influenced by system characteristics under the prevalent conditions of system use and the task goals.

We believe that information that a user receives about a system should influence the initial formation of trust. Supporting the users' initial trust formation of a system is of paramount importance for manufacturers and vendors: without sufficient initially formed trust, customers may never buy a system or product. Therefore, in this paper we investigate different methods that those offering products and services can undertake to improve trust formation by offering additional trust relevant information about the product to the user.

One method to provide information of a system or a product is labeling. Labeling is already used for a variety of different products. One of the more well-known approaches to labeling are food and energy labels[2], which provide the user with information regarding a product. A similar labeling scheme may also be beneficial for the formation of user trust into new products or services, but it is unclear how such labeling could be used to positively impact trust formation. How would the effectiveness of such trust related labeling compare with other relevant information about the product or service such as user feedback, controllability or accountability? These questions are the main focus of this study.

1.3 Research Hypotheses

Offering customers additional information about the trustworthiness of their products could help increase their trust. Therefore, we hypothesize that labeling the trustworthiness of a system is expected to lead to a higher willingness to use the presented system. Additionally, it is expected that providing more and different types of trustworthiness information about a system (multi-dimensional labeling) should also show a stronger impact on positive trust formation and willingness to use a system than unidimensional labeling.

We also expect that multi-dimensional labels should have a higher reported trust formation compared to uni-dimensional labels at both medium and high levels.

User feedback that other users have given about a product or service should provide customers with valuable information about its trustworthiness. Furthermore, if this feedback is provided by an independent company, we expect this to have a bigger impact on trust formation than when it is provided by the company offering the system. This is because the information is provided by a party without self-interest.

Users should feel more inclined to trust a system if they receive feedback and are able to exert control, therefore we expect a significant influence of system control, system feedback and support features on trust formation.

---

[2] https://ec.europa.eu/info/energy-climate-change-environment/standards-tools-and-labels/products-labelling-rules-and-requirements/energy-label-and-ecodesign/about_de.

2   Method

2.1   Participants

There was a total of 32 participants (17 female) with a mean age of 25 ($M = 25.78$, $SD = 5.36$). The study took about an hour per participant. Participants received 15 Euro per person for partaking in the study, if they were recruited within the company, they received a small gift instead. The study was conducted at the Virtual Vehicle Research GmbH.

2.2   Materials

Videos

The videos used were all about three minutes long, two videos were developed by SCOTT partners, one was not part of the project.

The "Safety-Access-System", describes a system that rearranges the access to company grounds and makes it possible to regulate and monitor the behavior of drivers on company grounds.

The smartphone application "Coyero" aims to help the user by combining different functions within a single app. The video shows several examples like renting of a car via app, unlocking of a rented vehicle and the option to purchase highway tolls.

The Smart-Home learns your habits to enable it to help with daily tasks and routines, claiming to allow a lifestyle where daily tasks do not pose as much of a challenge anymore.

Labeling Systems

Two different labeling system were used within this study. Descriptions of the labeling systems can be found in Table 1 and Table 2.

Table 1. Uni-dimensional label which includes the aspect of privacy, with a range of five levels from "highest privacy label" to "lowest privacy label" (E).

Privacy setting	Collected	Transmitted	Additional service available
Highest (A)	No personal identifiable data will be collected	None	✗
High (B)	Personal identifiable data will only be collected on your device	None	✗
Medium (C)		Anonymized data	✗
Low (D)	Personal identifiable data will be collected	Personal identifiable data are transmitted but only processed by service provider	✓
Lowest (E)		Personal identifiable data are transmitted and shared with 3rd party providers	✓

Table 2. Multi-dimensional label which includes the aspects of privacy, product quality, manufacturing, usability as well as cost ranging from "highest trustworthiness" (A) to "lowest trustworthiness" (E).

Product-trustworthiness label	Usability	Producer follows certification protocols	Privacy setting	Product-quality	Cost
Highest (A)	High	✓	A	High	Highest
High (B)		✓	B		High
Medium (C)	Medium	✓	C	Medium	Medium
Low (D)	Lowest	✗	D	Low	Low
Lowest (E)		✗	E		Lowest

Questionnaires

One of the questionnaires used in this study is the Affinity for Technology Interaction (ATI) Scale. Additionally, participants answered a questionnaire consisting of two parts. The first part questions the influence of customer support, system feedback, controllability as well as user feedback on trust formation. In the second part of the questionnaire, participants are introduced to one of the two labeling systems and answer questions regarding the system they were just presented, as well as the influence the labeling system has on their trust formation towards the system they just familiarized themselves with.

Task and Procedure

Participants first read about the study intent and its process and were asked to indicate their informed consent. They were encouraged to ask questions during the study, if they had any, except during video presentation.

Before every video, participants were informed about the use case video they were about to watch, after watching the video, participants indicated their comprehension by answering questions about the video.

Every participant was offered the opportunity to re-watch a given video in case some aspect of it stayed unclear. Following the presentation of the video, participants immersed themselves into the usage of the system and were interviewed on problems they may encounter as well as privacy and data protection settings they would find acceptable in the system. After this immersion they were asked about their willingness to use the system, followed by a questionnaire that allowed participants to express their opinion about different aspects of the system and their influence on individual trust formation. The second part of the questionnaire allowed participants to rate the label they were presented and its influence on their perceived trust towards the system. Every participant saw and rated all use cases, which were pseudorandomized like the assignment to one of the labels.

3   Results

Use cases were combined for data analysis because results indicate that the answers for the uses cases did not differ significantly.

Labeling

Both labels have a significant impact on the willingness to use a system ($F(1, 28) = 4.88$, $p = .036$), but analysis with a mixed ANOVA show, that the labels do not differ significantly from each other in their influence on the willingness of participants to use a system ($F(1, 30) = 0.16$, $p = .689$). The interaction between label and time of presentation is also not significant ($F(1, 30) = 0.14$, $p = .706$).

The results show, that the labels are able to differentiate between the highest (A) and medium (C) label level, but a significant interaction shows, that only at the medium level we find a difference between the uni- ($M = 0.71$, $SD = 1.91$) and the multi-dimensional label ($M = -0.98$, $SD = 1.16$) ($F(1, 29) = 4.64$, $p = .039$).

User Feedback

User Feedback provided by an independent organization ($M = 1.52$, $SD = 1.83$) has a significantly higher influence on trust formation than user feedback provided by the company selling the system ($M = 0.58$, $SD = 1.49$), ($t(29) = -2.82$, $p = 0.0086$) as analysis with a t-test show. No provided feedback ($M = -0.92$, $SD = 2.14$) leads to significantly lower reported levels of trust than feedback provided by the company selling the system ($t(29) = 3.08$, $p = 0.005$). The same goes for user feedback provided by an independent organization, which also leads to significantly higher levels of trust than no provided user feedback ($t(29) = 3.58$, $p = 0.001$).

System Design and Support Features

In addition to user feedback and labeling, several system design and support features were investigated. Table 3 displays the results for these investigated system design and support futures concerning reported trust formation. All system aspects differ significantly from zero, which shows, that they have an impact on trust formation towards a system – which is independent from labeling. In the table we can see that there are several system aspects that have a higher impact on trust formation than labeling. The most influential being control, which stands for user control over a given system. Accountability, the accountability of a system producer towards a system user in case of problems concerning the system, also has a positive impact on trust formation. The usability of a system induces more trust than labeling, which shows, that it is also important for trust formation, to have a product that is easy to understand and use.

Table 3. Influence of user feedback, system feedback, system design and support features on trust formation. Answers ranged from "reduces trust" (−5) over "no influence" (0) to "increases trust" (+5).

Example	M	SD	p	Example	M	SD	p
Control	3.18	1.30	p < .0001	Independent Feed.[a]	1.52	1.83	p < .0001
Accountability	2.51	1.75	p < .0001	Individualization	1.49	1.35	p < .0001
Usability	2.25	1.59	p < .0001	Home installation	1.38	1.42	p < .0001
Labeling	2.21	1.38	p < .0001	Manual installation	1.16	1.13	p < .0001
System status	2.11	1.49	p < .0001	Company Feed.[a]	0.58	1.49	p = .038
Hotline	2.08	1.7	p < .0001	No Feed.[a]	−0.92	2.14	p = .023

[a]Feed. = Feedback

4 Discussion

This study shows, that while labeling has an important influence on trust formation, there are other system aspects, like control, accountability and usability which have a comparable or even bigger positive impact on trust formation. In this study, control was related to the level of control that users had over the access options of the installed systems to their device. It stands to reason that in other systems, like a system of artificial intelligence, the system aspect of control would play a comparable role for the user. This, however, indicates a need for further research because in today's rapidly advancing world, it is possible that users could be confronted with a system that they are not able to control, because they lack the ability or possibilities to do so. It is necessary to study which aspects of control are helpful to increase trust formation.

Similarly, the results indicate that perceived accountability has a notable influence on trust formation. This has an important implication for how a system vendor could increase customer trust by clarifying his responsibilities and accountability concerning system malfunctions or other use issues.

Usability was also found to impact trust formation such that a more usable system should also be easier to form trust. However, it would be interesting to further explore how additional individualization and control options may interfere with the experience of usability of a system: adding options and user choices may increase the experienced system complexity.

As expected, labeling has a significant influence on trust formation towards a system and willingness to use it. However, in contrast to our hypothesis, participants did not indicate a higher willingness to use a system with the multi-dimensional label. It is interesting to consider what could have caused this, because the multi-dimensional label contains more information than the uni-dimensional label. The ratings of the influence on trust formation by the label levels even indicate, that at a medium level, the uni-dimensional label is at an advantage in trust formation in comparison to the multi-dimensional label. These results show, that while information usually plays a very important role in trust formation, it is important to focus on the kind of information that is presented, as well as the format it is presented in.

A possible approach to explain these results is that participants in the multi-dimensional label condition were faced with a choice overload, as explained by [4]. The multi-dimensional label would offer too much information in a format that is not fitting to the unexperienced reader. This may mean, that the participants did not have a mental script [5] on how to analyze the information they were presented and therefore could not take advantage of this additional information. In this way, the multi-dimensional labels did not provide the expected advantage over uni-dimensional labels. This may indicate a need for digital competence education, to familiarize customers with (standardized) multi-dimensional labeling systems and enable them to build a mental script to take advantage of this information to form trust. We think future studies should investigate the digital competences needed for citizens to make informed decisions about complex technologies and adopt them to their interests and needs. As an immediate next step, we recommend investigating the trust formation on other user populations and increase the range of age and background knowledge of participants for future research.

Acknowledgment. SCOTT (www.scott-project.eu) has received funding from the Electronic Component Systems for European Leadership Joint Undertaking under grant agreement No 737422. This Joint Undertaking receives support from the European Union's Horizon 2020 research and innovation programme and Austria, Spain, Finland, Ireland, Sweden, Germany, Poland, Portugal, Netherlands, Belgium, Norway. The publication was written at VIRTUAL VEHICLE Research Center in Graz and partially funded by the COMET K2 – Competence Centers for Excellent Technologies Programme of the Federal Ministry for Transport, Innovation and Technology (bmvit), the Federal Ministry for Digital, Business and Enterprise (bmdw), the Austrian Research Promotion Agency (FFG), the Province of Styria and the Styrian Business Promotion Agency (SFG).

References

1. Lee, J.D., See, K.A.: Trust in automation: designing for appropriate reliance. Hum. Factors J. Hum. Factors Ergon. Soc. **46**(1), 50–80 (2004)
2. Ajzen, I.: From intentions to actions: a theory of planned behavior. In: Kuhl, J., Beckmann, J. (eds.) Action Control. SSSSP, pp. 11–39. Springer, Heidelberg (1985). https://doi.org/10.1007/978-3-642-69746-3_2
3. Hoff, K.A., Bashir, M.: Trust in automation integrating empirical evidence on factors that influence trust. Hum. Factors J. Hum. Factors Ergon. Soc. **57**(3), 407–434 (2015)
4. Lurger, B., Vogrincic-Haselbacher, C., Caks, F., Anslinger, J., Dinslaken, I., Athenstaedt, U.: Consumer decisions under high information load: how can legal rules improve search behavior and decision quality? SSRN Electron. J. (2016). SSRN 2731655
5. Light, L., Anderson, P.: Memory for scripts in young and older adults. Mem. Cogn. **11**(5), 435–444 (1983)

LINE Based Learning System for IT Security Practices Through Intrinsic Motivation

Yukio Ishihara[1](✉) and Makio Ishihara[2]

[1] Shimane University, 1060 Nishikawatsu-cho, Matsue-shi, Shimane 690-8504, Japan
iyukio@ipc.shimane-u.ac.jp
[2] Fukuoka Institute of Technology, 3-30-1 Wajiro-higashi, Higashi-ku, Fukuoka 811-0295, Japan
m-ishihara@fit.ac.jp
http://www.fit.ac.jp/~m-ishihara/Lab/

Abstract. In this study, we build a learning system on LINE app that is provided by LINE Corporation. The system incorporates three elements of Self-determination theory: autonomy, competence and relatedness in order to keep people intrinsically motivated for long. Recently the increase of phishing mails draws attention to immediate countermeasures for cybersecurity. Accessing such mails could trigger the onset of virus infection and confidential information leakage, which affects not only individuals but also the companies they work for. In reality, eliciting personal information from the recipients is sometimes not hard if they don't perform security practices as well as the mails are made deceptive and appear to be sent from well-known senders. Thus, it is necessary that people learn security practices on a daily basis and perform those all times. To provide a platform that facilitates learning in this way, we decide to build a learning system on LINE app and incorporate into it the three elements of Self-determination theory.

Keywords: Security practice · Self-determination theory · LINE app · Google Apps Script

1 Introduction

Over the last decades, the Internet and its infrastructure developed very rapidly while computers decreased their size and got smarter also connected to each other. Today, mobile devices of phones, tablets, laptops etc. gradually fit in everyday lives and support individuals' activities. It is almost agreeable that many people tend to spend much time on these devices both at home and workplaces. In addition, there seems a big shift from local platforms to clouds, on which various services are provided such as mailing, word processing, data storing etc. Thus, users need to sign in on specific webpages using their own ID and password before accessing those services.

© Springer Nature Switzerland AG 2020
C. Stephanidis and M. Antona (Eds.): HCII 2020, CCIS 1226, pp. 534–539, 2020.
https://doi.org/10.1007/978-3-030-50732-9_69

In 2018 and 2019, phishing mails seem relentless and expected to continue [1]. Some recipients fail to recognize it is phishing and type in valuable information such as their ID and password on the fake webpage. It could cause confidential information leakage affecting not only individuals but companies they work for.

In our university, e-Learning for cybersecurity is mandatory for all the staff and students, however, it's once a year. Thus, they may not follow the security practices they have learnt because their engagement may fade away as time passes after e-Learning taken yearly. In this study, we build a learning system to provide frequent and brief questions about security practices, so that all the members stay informed hopefully all times. This system is built on LINE app provided by LINE Corporation, which is one of the most successful social media apps such as Facebook, Twitter and Instagram. LINE also has the most users in Japan, and it provides a communication platform for friends, family and colleagues of their workplaces. In order for the members of our university to stay connected to our learning system for long and answer questions regularly, the learning system shouldn't be boring, a burden, an obligation, but should be somehow motivating.

To facilitate motivation, in general, the use of gamification is the mainstream. Gamification provides a basic idea that game elements and principles such as badges, medals and competition with others are incorporated into non-game areas to let people do non-game activities in more enjoyable way, hopefully leading to increasing motivation. However, there is the downside that such game elements and principles are not always promising. As known as overjustification effect, for example, providing badges and medals for people who are already intrinsically motivated may decrease their motivation. To be more specific, such people are motivated by something internal rather than external incentives.

The study of Self-determination theory examined what internal elements contribute to intrinsic motivation and it revealed three elements: autonomy, competence and relatedness [2]. "Autonomy" is a sense that people feel when they can determine what to do that they want to do, thus their decision is not influenced by anything except themselves. "Competence" is a sense that people feel when they can achieve more challenging activities because they have the confidence and mastery. "Relatedness" is a sense that people feel when they are somehow connected to other people or a community they belong to. The theory implicitly indicates that people will become intrinsically motivated and keep doing non-game activities sustainably if these three elements are appropriately taken into account in those activities.

There have been attempts to design learning platforms based on these three elements [3,4]. In the study [3], an e-learning system named Topolor 2 was built by incorporating autonomy, competence and relatedness. The evaluation of the system was conducted using questionnaires and it shows that students' perceived learning experience and learning efficiency were improved compared to other regular e-learning systems. In the study [4], it discussed how learning and game processes are related and what processes increase intrinsic motivation.

In this study, we take a similar approach to the study [3] except that we build a learning system on a social media app of LINE, which is a popular communication platform. Learning of security practices is all performed on it, which results in virtually no obstacle that prevents people from even starting to learn because no further devices or apps are required. In addition, most of the members of our university have already used LINE on their own mobile device and have been very familiar with the interface. This is why we have chosen LINE as a learning platform.

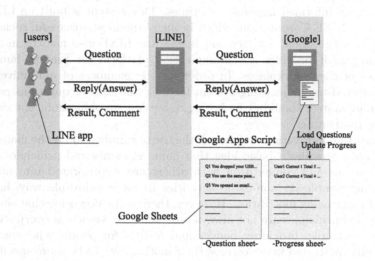

Fig. 1. Design of our learning system.

The rest of this manuscript is organized as follows. In Sect. 2, it is explained how the three elements for intrinsic motivation are incorporated into our learning system. In Sect. 3, it describes a prototype of our learning system. Finally, concluding remarks are given in Sect. 4.

2   Design of Our Learning System

Figure 1 shows the design of our learning system. This system consists of two services provided by LINE and Google. First, a set of questions are created and stored on a Google sheet. Then each of the questions is loaded by a Google Apps script and is broadcasted via a LINE official account to multiple users who use LINE app on their mobile device and have been registered as "friends" of the LINE official account. After the LINE app receives the question and displays it for the user in a conversation style, the user replies to it by tapping one of multiple options. The reply is sent back to the LINE office account, then is transferred to the Google Apps script. Afterward, the script creates a result message depending on the reply being correct. Finally, the result message is sent to the user. This is a sequence of the learning system.

To increase intrinsic motivation, in this system, the three elements: autonomy, competence and relatedness, are taken into account as follows.

◇ To fulfil autonomy, learning of security practices is set optional for the members of our university even although informing all of them of the learning by mail and web page. The members can choose to start, continue and stop learning on the system anytime. In addition, they don't have to reply to all of the questions, but whatever they want. A single question is sent at a time and every a couple of days. For privacy and security concerns, in advance, the members are informed of that they are anonymously identified on the system by unique IDs that are irrelevant to their personal information such as names.

◇ To fulfil competence, the system records how many times each of the members has chosen correct answers, and the number is sent back with the result message. Thus, this allows the members aware of their growing progress leading to increase of confidence of performing appropriate security practices.

◇ To fulfil relatedness, the members can share ideas of questions that are relevant to their daily activities or are directly connected to security issues they have experienced. Later, those questions are revised if necessary and distributed to the rest of members as new questions.

3   Prototype of Our Learning System

We built a learning system based on the design mentioned in Sect. 2. First a LINE official account and Google account were prepared. Then the LINE official account was set at bot mode. A bot was coded using Google Apps Script, which runs on Google platform and communicates with an agent, or the LINE official account. The script also accesses Google Sheets for retrieval of questions and update of users' progress.

Figure 2 shows screenshots of the conversion between the agent and an user. In (a), a question numbered as "Q8" was posted by the agent and the user replied by tapping a button "2". Afterward, the agent posted the result saying "Good choice!" because the option "2" shows a preventive action against information leakage. The result was followed by a comment of what the user should be concerned about and his/her progress statue. The progress status is represented as "C", "R" and "S" that show the number of correct answers, the ratio of "C" to the total of answers, the number of questions suggested, respectively. In (b), the conversion is the same except the result saying "A little of worry left behind." because the answer is considered to carry a potential risk of information leakage. (c) shows a conversation when the user posted any words that are not pre-defined messages. Then, the agent replied with a simple message and asked to post "QSuggestion" for how to suggest a question. (d) shows a conversation

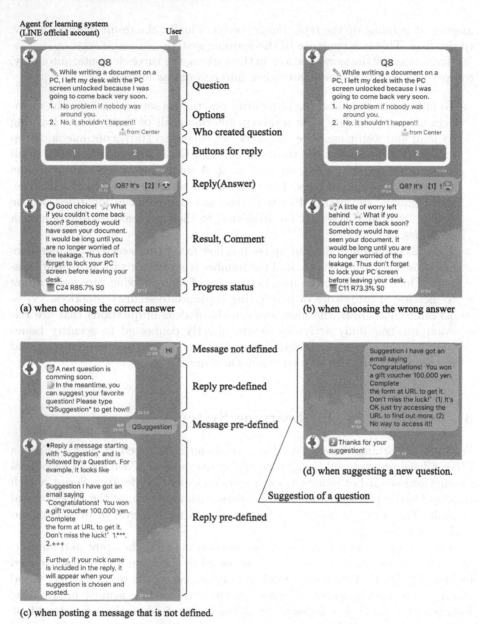

(a) when choosing the correct answer

(b) when choosing the wrong answer

(c) when posting a message that is not defined.

(d) when suggesting a new question.

Fig. 2. Prototype of our learning system.

when the user suggested a new question in a post that starts with "Suggestion". "QSuggestion" and "Suggestion" are two examples of the pre-defined messages.

In the future, we need to conduct a case study to see the effectiveness of our learning system, on which the members of our university learn security practices, and later we will investigate the effect of use of the system both on the occurrence of security incidents and on the behaviors of the members.

4   Conclusions

Recently the increase of phishing mails draws attention to immediate counter-measures for cybersecurity. Accessing such mails could trigger the onset of virus infection and confidential information leakage, which affects not only individuals but also the companies they work for. In reality, eliciting personal information from the recipients is sometimes not hard if they don't perform security practices as well as the mails are made deceptive and appear to be sent from well-known senders. Thus, it is necessary that people learn security practices on a daily basis and perform those all times. In this study, we built a learning system on LINE app, which many people use often, and we incorporated into the system three elements of Self-determination theory: autonomy, competence and relatedness in order to keep people intrinsically motivated for long.

The future work includes a case study to see the effectiveness of the system and investigation of the effect on the occurrence of security incidents and people's behaviors.

References

1. The Rising Tide of Credential Phishing: 2.4 Million Attacks Blocked by Trend Micro Cloud App Security in 2019 1H. Trend Micro Inc. https://www.trendmicro. com/vinfo/be/security/news/cybercrime-and-digital-threats/the-rising-tide-of-credential-phishing
2. Ryan, R., Deci, E.: Self-determination theory and the facilitation of intrinsic motivation, social development, and well-being. Am. Psychol. 55(1), 68–78 (2000)
3. Shi, L., Cristea, A.I.: Designing visualisation and interaction for social e-learning: a case study in topolor 2. In: Rensing, C., de Freitas, S., Ley, T., Muñoz-Merino, P.J. (eds.) EC-TEL 2014. LNCS, vol. 8719, pp. 526–529. Springer, Cham (2014). https://doi.org/10.1007/978-3-319-11200-8_57
4. Proulx, J.-N., Romero, M., Arnab, S.: Learning mechanics and game mechanics under the perspective of self-determination theory to foster motivation in digital game based learning. Simul. Gaming 48(1), 81–97 (2017)

Co-occurrence Based Security Event Analysis and Visualization for Cyber Physical Systems

HyungKwan Kim[✉], Seungoh Choi, Jeong-Han Yun, Byung-Gil Min, and Hyoung Chun Kim

The Affiliated Institute of ETRI, Daejeon, Republic of Korea
{james,sochoi,dolgam,bgmin,khche}@nsr.re.kr

Abstract. In cyber-physical systems, the control network is generally invaded by using network linkage vulnerability, which results in the malfunction of controllers. Therefore, to implement an effective monitoring system, events from security appliances such as IDS and firewall should be integrated with events from the control devices such as PLC. However, the volume of the integrated events collected on-site is large, making it impossible to monitor personnel for real-time analysis and to respond to attacks. Hence, we propose a method for event analysis and visualization based on the co-occurrence matrix and directional graph. In the analysis step, the co-occurrence between field values is calculated and saved as a matrix. In the visualization step, the field values are represented as nodes, and co-occurrences are represented as edges. In addition, the IP and Port clustering functions are implemented for successful application to complex multi-layer CPS network and long-time event analyses. This reduces graph complexity and analysis time simultaneously up to 94.3% and improves the applicability of the method. We expect that the proposed method will help monitor personnel to effectively identify and quickly respond to security threats from control systems.

Keywords: Cyber security · CPS · Event · Co-occurrence analysis

1 Introduction

Cybersecurity threats targeting critical infrastructure are increasing. For most cyber-physical systems, the final target is to cause operation failure. Therefore, generally, the attack surface is invaded to find linkage vulnerability in order to reach the target control system. In this process, various traces related to the CPS attack remain in the system on the attack route. Thus, to implement an effective monitoring system, events from security appliances such as IDS and firewall should be integrated with the events from the controller such as PLC. However, the volume of security events collected on-site is large, and the content of the events is sophisticated, making it impossible to monitor personnel for real-time analysis and to respond to attacks. Owing to this important warnings are

C. Stephanidis and M. Antona (Eds.): HCII 2020, CCIS 1226, pp. 540–548, 2020.
https://doi.org/10.1007/978-3-030-50732-9_70

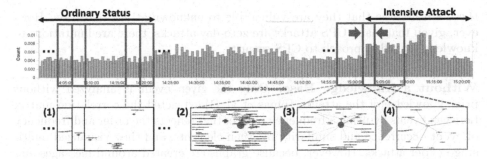

Fig. 1. Process of analyzing attack using the proposed method. (1) Because few security events are generated in the absence of an attack, they are monitored with a relatively wide time window and detailed view without clustering. (2) When an attack occurs, the number of events increases, and the visibility of the Detail View decreases. (3) The macroscopic aspects are understood by using the Clustered View, with the clustering function activated. (4) After the time window is narrowed for the time zone when the controller determines an abnormality has occurred, the Detail View is checked, and information necessary to respond to the threat is obtained.

ignored or neglected, making the system vulnerable to threats. In addition, to effectively monitor CPS security control, IT and OT security information must be integrated and analyzed. However, as security operation center (SOC) control personnel have insufficient context information on OT, the effective integrated analysis is difficult. Even if there are statistical or rule-based correlation analysis methods, it is still challenging to monitor unknown APT attacks. Therefore, we propose a practical visualization technology that can 1) quickly process a large amount of security events, 2) analyze heterogeneous events without relying on rules or engines, and 3) improve SOC control efficiency via simple parameter adjustment. Clustering is applied to existing IPs and ports in the security event to reduce computational analysis, and automatic rule-less analysis is performed based on the co-occurrence matrix. The method can be used as a highly efficient monitoring tool by utilizing the size of the time window and clustering option. Our technique can be used to recognize attacks and analyze causes (see Fig. 1). In addition, this study was conducted as a part of HAI [5] for spreading awareness about controllers in actual control system SOCs.

2 Related Work

This section discusses related research on the integrated analysis of security events, and their relevance to our approach. In the field of events correlation, there are two types of methods: knowledge-based and not knowledge-based.

Knowledge Base. The threat detection was attempted based on existing incidents or potential threats [2,3]. Those studies deploy attack models or heuristics to detect attacks, which leads to over-fitting problems. The main drawback of these studies was that they are vulnerable to unknown attack detection. However, given that many CPS attacks are zero-day attacks, there are limitations to knowledge-based approach to CPS security.

Without a Knowledge Base. Only the given event is analyzed without prior knowledge of the attack. Tomas et al. [1] extracted the correlation matrix between events by using a frequency matrix that reflects the order and frequency of event occurrence and similarity between elements, and they visualized multi-stage cyber attacks. However, because graphs are created around messages and detailed IPs and ports disappear in the similarity calculation process, its use is limited as a monitoring tool. Lee et al. [4] extracted correlated events based on the similarity between IP, Port, and Time. Major events are automatically selected, but duplicated redundant events decrease the readability of the result. In this study, an analytical method that does not rely on prior information was applied to monitor unknown attacks against CPS. In addition, information (attack starting point, contact point, IP, port of the final attack site) that can be practically used in real threat situations in a short time was analyzed in a highly visible manner in response to a large number of nodes or edges. This study aimed to develop visualization technologies.

3   Proposed Method

This section describes correlation analysis and visualization techniques that form the core of this study. First, we propose a clustering function for simplifying the graph in the preprocessing process, an analysis method based on the co-occurrence matrix, which is the core of the correlation analysis, and a method for visualizing a highly visible graph model using the co-occurrence matrix values. Figure 2 shows the workflow of the analysis technology. First, the events existing in the time window that are to be analyzed are loaded. Security events collected in the IT and OT environments are pre-normalized into six common fields (timestamp, srcIP, dstIP, srcPort, dstPort, nameEvent) for correlation analysis. (1) First, in order to reduce the computational complexity and the complexity when analyzing a large number of events, clustering is performed to ensure that the number of groups is less than a certain number of IPs and ports. (2) Next, by counting the co-occurrence between elements in each event and recording it on the matrix, the "in event" "correlation" is extracted. By performing this process on all events and analyzing the events overlaid on the co-occurrence matrix, it is possible to analyse the "correlation" between events. (3) Finally, based on the calculated co-occurrence matrix, we visualize it as a graph model, visualize event elements or relationships between elements using visualization elements of nodes and edges, and extract the attack transition processes by borrowing directional graphs. Each step is described in the following subsections.

3.1 Co-occurrence Analysis

The in-event and inter-event analyses based on co-occurrence matrix proceed as follows: First, the events collected in the time window are composed of five (key, value) tuples related to IP, Port, and Event. After extracting the unique element set ListEntity, we prepare the zero matrix corresponding to the number of elements in the set. Each row and column corresponds to an element of ListEntity. For all events, the combination of elements existing in each event is extracted, and the aerodynamics between them are accumulated in a matrix to complete the co-occurrence matrix of the entire event group. Moreover, in the case of aerodynamics, because the aerodynamics of a and b and the simultaneity of b and a are essentially the same, the redundancy of the matrix is reduced by integrating the matrix components of the lower left part into the matrix of the upper right part. Thus, correlation analysis between normalized events is automatically performed without rules or prior knowledge of attacks, and a large number of events can be matrix-compressed. This leads to the integration of a common IP, and it is also possible to associate heterogeneous IT and OT events on the same IP. In addition, the port offers an advantage in that it is possible to detect the port at which the damage is concentrated, the frequency of appearance by port, and other related parameters.

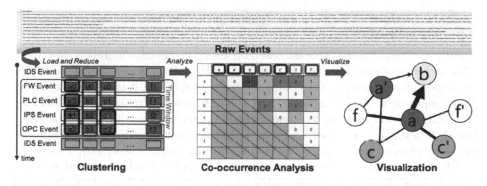

Fig. 2. A workflow of the co-occurrence-based event analysis system.

3.2 Clustering

The clustering function is to reduce the analysis complexity and computation time. The reasons why we focused on IP and Port are as follows: 1) In the case of the control system, the subnets are different for each layer, and each layer has a different criticality to control. By clustering IP, threats to the critically high layer can be generated early. 2) In the case of a port, the services or communication in the OT environment are also concentrated in the port of a specific band; it is possible to distinguish the service characteristics used by the human being per port range. Therefore, based on this, it is possible to detect uncommon threats early. The clustering method is as follows: In the event, ListIP and ListPort, which are a unique set of IP and ports, are extracted. First, the user designates the upper and lower nGroupIP and nGroupPorts of IP and Port that are considered to be appropriate. In the case of IP, masking sequentially from a narrow range of subnets ("255.255.255.255") to a wide range of subnets ("255.0.0.0") reduces the number of unique IPs; this is repeated until nGroupIP or less. In the case of Port, this section is divided into nGroupPorts based on the minimum and maximum of the Port values existing in the event, and the Port values are replaced with one of the new category values. An example is shown in the following Table 1.

Table 1. Example of clustering IP and port

	Raw set	Clustered set	nGroup
IP	192.168.0.1, 192.168.0.2, 192.168.1.1	"192.168.0.*", "192.168.1.*"	2
IP	192.168.0.1, 192.168.0.2, 192.168.1.1	"192.168.*.*"	1
Port	1, 2, ..., 100	"1–50", "51–100"	2
Port	1, 2, ..., 100	"1–100"	1

3.3 Visualization

Finally, the visualization process based on the co-occurrence matrix is described. This technology visualizes graphs centered on IP or Port. When two elements are expressed simultaneously, the complexity increases; hence, it is better to consider them separately. As the number and type of nodes increases, the burden on the controller interpreting the graph tends to increase even further. Therefore, the dashboard is composed of IP or port combinations. In the IP graph, all elements except Port are added as nodes (the port graph is reversed). That is, IP and heterogeneous security events are added as nodes. If additional information such as Zone, Region, etc. is available as a security event element, analysis and visualization from various viewpoints will be possible. Next, while traversing all the components of the co-occurrence matrix, an edge between two components is added using the corresponding value as the width of the edge. At this time, the edge is directed from src to dst and src to event. To secure visibility by reducing the number of edges between the IP and the event, the edge is created only between the potential attacker, src, and the event. The port graph is generated by applying in the same manner as described above to the port instead of the IP. In addition, the size of the node was calculated by summing all the elements related to the node on the co-occurrence matrix, and the color of the node was changed to distinguish between elements. However, in the case of IP and Port, identifying the "start point", "relay point", and "end target" of the attack is important from the perspective of preemptive response of SOC control; therefore, the same elements are distinguished based on the connected edge attributes.

4   Validation

4.1   Dataset

HAI Expansion is a dataset that adds network security equipment and operation information collector to HAI (see Fig. 3). It consists of 20,000 security events generated by network security appliances. The effectiveness of the method was verified by applying this analysis technique to a part of the dataset. In addition, the impact of clustering function on complexity and analysis time was evaluated.

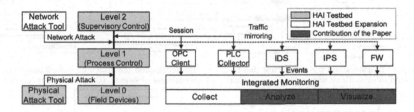

Fig. 3. HAI testbed and the contribution of the paper.

4.2   Result of Visualization

Figure 4 is the result of analyzing certain attack sections in the dataset. Specifically, it represents a "process" of setting and analyzing a time window of 600 s for an HTTP vulnerability attack section targeting an Engineering Workstation such that an unauthorized notebook connects to the control network and manages the controller. First, 1824 events that appeared for 600 s, without clustering, were analyzed (b). Due to the explosion of events, multiple IPs appeared at the same time, making it difficult to understand the threat situation. Therefore, in order to grasp the macroscopic situation, clustering was performed and analyzed (c). The first thing to note is that most security events are concentrated in the "192.168.2. *" band and the "192.168.0. *" band. In addition, it can be seen that "192.168.0. *" is the starting point of an attack with only an outcoming edge, and "192.168.2. *" serves as a relay point for an attack with an edge in both directions. The event that occurs with the highest frequency among all the events associated with the two bands is "ACL DENY", and can be first identified by the thickness of the edge. Other than that, IT events related to HTTP vulnerabilities mainly dominate, and in the "192.168.2. *" band, abnormal events occurring in OT dominate. Based on this, access to unauthorized assets would have been made in the "192.168.0. *" band, and after attacking the vulnerability with the "192.168.2. *" band, the equipment for controlling the controller existing in the subnet. After taking control, it seems to have caused unknown damage to the OT environment. Now, in order to understand the detailed damage situation in each band, the time window was reduced to 3 s, and the suspicious part was analyzed again without clustering (d). First, "192.168.0.100" and "192.168.2.10" are estimated as perpetrators and victims, respectively. In view of what happened with

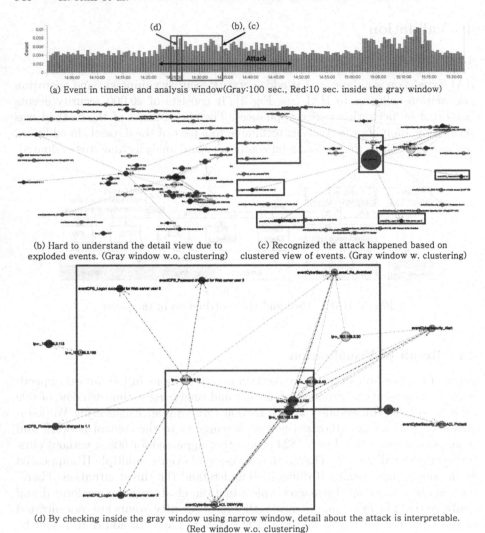

(a) Event in timeline and analysis window(Gray:100 sec., Red:10 sec. inside the gray window)

(b) Hard to understand the detail view due to exploded events. (Gray window w.o. clustering)   (c) Recognized the attack happened based on clustered view of events. (Gray window w. clustering)

(d) By checking inside the gray window using narrow window, detail about the attack is interpretable. (Red window w.o. clustering)

Fig. 4. Process of analyzing attack in adaptive way

"ACL DENY" and "http excel download", in which was common to both nodes, it is presumed that after unauthorized access, the privilege of "192.168.2.10" was seized via a vulnerability attack. In particular, after the "Password changed" and "Logon successful" events occurred on the victim node, the event suspected of attacking the controller ("Firmware version changed") occurred, indicating that there was already a significant threat to the controller. In addition, as similar patterns of attacks were conducted on "192.168.2.20" and "192.168.2.30", there is a possibility of attacks such as changing the settings of the controller in the future; therefore, preemptive action is necessary. Table 2 shows the number of nodes that change according to the size of the time window and the change in time required for calculation. When the analysis range exceeds 10 min, it is difficult to visually check the number of nodes without clustering. In the case of clustering, it is suppressed by up to dozens of about 10,000 data collected in one hour, even to the naked eye, making analysis possible. In the case of calculation time, when there was no clustering, the analysis range increased to a maximum of 18.1 s per second; however, in the case of clustering, the analysis time was reduced to an average of 1.02 s (94.3% reduced).

Table 2. Comparison on node complexity and computation time

Performance feature	Clustering	Time window				
		10	30	60	600	3600
n of Nodes	w.o.	6	25	31	110	152
n of Nodes	w.	4	8	11	13	13
Time of computation	w.o.	0.31	0.87	1.39	5.4	18.1
Time of computation	w.	0.28	0.65	0.87	0.91	1.02

5 Conclusion

In this study, CPS heterogeneous security events were automatically analyzed based on the co-occurrence matrix, and the attack transition process was visualized using a graph model. In the analysis step, the co-occurrence between field values is calculated and saved as a matrix. In the visualization step, field values are represented as nodes, and co-occurrences are represented as edges. In order to express the transition process of the attack, the attack starting point, linkage point, and final target candidates were visualized in different colors. IP and Port clustering functions are implemented for successful application to the analysis of long time range or exploded events. This reduces complexity and analysis time and improves the usability of the method. It is expected to effectively analyze the control operation and security events, and rapidly determine the attack path and the final target controller to enhance the security of the control system.

References

1. Bajtoš, T., Sokol, P., Mézešová, T.: Multi-stage cyber-attacks detection in the industrial control systems. In: Pricop, E., Fattahi, J., Dutta, N., Ibrahim, M. (eds.) Recent Developments on Industrial Control Systems Resilience. SSDC, vol. 255, pp. 151–173. Springer, Cham (2020). https://doi.org/10.1007/978-3-030-31328-9_8
2. Briesemeister, L., Cheung, S., Lindqvist, U., Valdes, A.: Detection, correlation, and visualization of attacks against critical infrastructure systems. In: 2010 Eighth International Conference on Privacy, Security and Trust, pp. 15–22. IEEE (2010)
3. Kavousi, F., Akbari, B.: Automatic learning of attack behavior patterns using Bayesian networks. In: 6th International Symposium on Telecommunications (IST), pp. 999–1004. IEEE (2012)

4. Lee, S., Chung, B., Kim, H., Lee, Y., Park, C., Yoon, H.: Real-time analysis of intrusion detection alerts via correlation. Comput. Secur. **25**(3), 169–183 (2006)
5. Shin, H.K., Lee, W., Yun, J.H., Kim, H.: Implementation of programmable CPS testbed for anomaly detection. In: 12th USENIX Workshop on Cyber Security Experimentation and Test (CSET 2019). USENIX Association, Santa Clara, August 2019. https://www.usenix.org/conference/cset19/presentation/shin

The Right to Privacy in Socio-Technical Smart Home Settings: Privacy Risks in Multi-Stakeholder Environments

Marina Konrad[✉], Sabine Koch-Sonneborn,
and Christopher Lentzsch

Ruhr-University Bochum, 44780 Bochum, Germany
{Marina.Konrad,Sabine.Koch-Sonneborn,
Christopher.Lentzsch}@ruhr-uni-bochum.de

Abstract. The multitude of users within smart home systems can lead to privacy concerns for individuals within a household. Three examples of smart home settings are conceptualized and analyzed with the framework of contextual integrity. Prominent privacy breaches are discovered. To secure the safety of PII within smart home settings we propose to develop transparency measures with manufacturers and communication with all users within a household.

Keywords: Privacy · Internet of things · Socio-technical design · Ethics

1 Introduction

Smart home settings are often pictured as single user settings set up by professionals. However, smart home users are manifold and live in shared spaces consisting of several household members [1]. End-Users set up and configure individual devices themselves and for other household members [2]. This can lead to serious privacy issues for the respective household members. We hypothesize that data protection of other household members is to be upheld less seriously because consumers often cannot honor their own values of privacy which is commonly referred to as the Privacy Paradox [3].

We discuss ethical and legal implications of privacy. Households as such are protected under legal frameworks, like the GDPR or CCPA. However, different household members are not obliged to comply with protecting each other's data under these umbrellas. Thus, we claim individuals are morally obliged to protect the privacy of all household members.

Three examples of smart home settings are conceptualized where privacy issues can occur and are analyzed using the framework of contextual integrity. Within these examples and in other smart home settings privacy is easily breached. To hinder these breaches, we propose to develop transparency measures and open communication between all household members.

© Springer Nature Switzerland AG 2020
C. Stephanidis and M. Antona (Eds.): HCII 2020, CCIS 1226, pp. 549–557, 2020.
https://doi.org/10.1007/978-3-030-50732-9_71

2 Background

Smart home devices are categorized as socio-technical infrastructures which include multiple household members [2]. These settings are especially interesting as members of a household hold a closer relationship and share different data among each other than, e.g. colleagues who share an office. Part of this setting are the smart home devices —while voice assistants are appreciated by its users, they give rise to privacy concerns [4]. This complex situation of interconnected relationships in these socio-technical settings is a special challenge to users and configurators of the smart homes.

We already see users struggling with the use and configuration of ICT which is often referred to as the privacy paradox [3]. The privacy paradox describes the dichotomy between the desire of users to keep personal information private and their use of new technologies where personal information is still disclosed. Current research has established that consumers consider privacy and security concerns more likely after purchasing an Internet of Things device [5]. Before purchasing both privacy and security concerns are not considered greatly. However, consumers value this information to be important when purchasing a device. Also, they find accessibility of information on privacy and security of IoT devices to be weak [5]. When consumers cannot uphold their own value of privacy, they likely cannot commit to protect the privacy of additional household members. This is problematic as inter alia personal data is collected, of which another household member is not aware of, is not willing to share or is not informed on privacy protection of these devices. Therefore, we conclude that technical support for the users and configurations is needed and can be provided by manufacturers to some extent, e.g., through transparency assistants and proper information.

To establish the connection between socio-technical smart home settings and potential breaches of privacy we use the framework of contextual integrity. Contextual integrity claims that personal information is always provided in context thus it may change its meaning or intent when it is used in another context. Contextual integrity asserts that privacy is violated if contextual norms of appropriateness or norms of flow are breached [6]. This is based on the idea of different societal norms and settings. People act differently in different social settings. Particularly, the content of personal information also differs. Medical history is usually shared with your physician, but not with your colleagues. Following these notions, there is no general breach of privacy or acceptance when sharing information or data but rather it matters which information, in what context and which setting is shared.

Following this idea of contexts Nissenbaum determines that flows of personal information must be appropriate [7]. Information flows are appropriate when they are legitimate according to four criteria – contexts, actors, information type and transmission principles [8]. Within this framework, context-relative informational norms are characterized. This means that contextual integrity serves to judge privacy or a breach thereof of personal information from one party to another. This transfer includes transmission, communication, transfer, distribution or dissemination of personal information [7]. Contexts thus relate to informational norms as backgrounds and introduce a multiplicity of social context [7]. The importance of contexts, as described above, is that they are recognized when personal information is shared. Actors are defined as three explicit subjects: the sender of the information, the recipient of the information and the information subject [7]. The actors distinguish the different subjects within data distribution; who the data is about, who is sharing the data and who receives it. The Actors focus on single individuals and serves to capture their relationships and roles of individuals in certain settings. Attributes or information types refer to the content of the data. The attributes also have to be recognized within their context; some specific information is appropriate in some settings but not in others. This becomes apparent when we consider the example of physician and the colleagues discussed above. Transmission principles refer to the flow of information from one individual to another. Private information is usually shared to one particular party in one particular setting. Further distribution or transmission of the information can breach the intended context of which that information was originally shared. Within the context of smart home systems, the data subject and sender of the data are important, as they are often not the same person. Transmission principles can capture the distinction between sharing information within a private space, the home, and that information to be distributed elsewhere. With analyzing four different dimensions about information distribution, we can capture the intended purpose or aim of individuals to share this information. If one of these changes contextually, or is not agreed to, privacy is violated.

3   Legal Background

Taking a legal perspective, there is a broad international consensus that the privacy of an individual needs to be protected. However, the scope of what is protected differs among different legal traditions. In comparison, data protection is defined more consistently. It refers to the protection of personally identifiable information (PII). The protection of privacy is a concept which is divided into legally manageable areas; the connecting element is the protection of personality. An essential aspect of the protection of privacy is the possibility for each individual to draw the line between privacy and publicity.

Accordingly, Article 12 of the Universal Declaration of Human Rights (UDHR) protects privacy as a universal human right. As an important international document, the UDHR is of great moral value, but not legally binding. Legally binding, on the other hand, are international treaties, such as the International Covenant on Civil and Political Rights (ICCPR). Its Article 17 is almost identical. To ease the enforcement, different systems of human rights protection have emerged at the regional level, especially in the Americas and Europe: Art. 11 of the American Convention on Human Rights explicitly states the protection of privacy ("Right to Privacy"). The European Convention on Human Rights (ECHR) states it explicitly in Art. 8—the right to respect for private and family life. The European Charter of Fundamental Rights (CFR) also guarantees self-determination, self-expression and confidentiality with the two strongly related provisions of the right to respect for private and family life, housing and communications in Art. 7 CFR and the right to protection of personal data in Art. 8 CFR. Current legislation, like the General Data Protection Regulation (GDPR) does not mention the term privacy at any point. In Art. 1 para. 2 the GDPR protects "the fundamental rights and freedoms of natural persons and in particular their right to the protection of personal data". The California Consumer Privacy Act (CCPA) covers all communications relating to natural persons and not only PII. This is a broad approach: For example, it is stated, that persons are also protected with regard to information on where they live, driving behavior, sleeping behavior and similar (Section 1798.140 (o) (1) CCPA). Its approach is very open as it regards any information that is likely to be associated with a consumer or household. Taking a broad understanding, it also refers to information about and within multi-person households—without naming the persons specifically.

4 Privacy as a Value

The importance of privacy and distribution of information to all parties affected by smart home devices in a household is high, as we claim privacy to have ethical importance and to uphold the human right to privacy as described above. The legal protection of distributing PII is not universally granted, especially in smart home settings, due to different legal frameworks. Still, we assume this protection to be important and grant an ethical argument. Based on this distinction we assume law and morality to be separate. While one is influenced by the other, laws do not reflect all societal or individual norms. The differences or similarities of law and morality are greatly discussed within the realm of philosophy of law where different authors come to different conclusions. Similarly to our claim of law and morality to be separate, H. L. A. Harts conceptualizes a separability thesis within legal positivism [9]. He assumes that morality is not necessarily captured within law. Both concepts are considered to be distinct. However, they can influence one another as they both regulate social life. Especially in the case of smart home settings, members within a household fall short of protection due to lack of definition. The individual's privacy might be legally protected, but enforcement for this protection is not always established within smart home settings. A separation between law and morality is necessary in order to account for a different claim on why privacy in these contexts ought to be protected.

If we regard privacy not only as a commodity, to be valued a certain amount of money or as something that can be sold, privacy has to be important by some other means. As privacy is distinct and differing between societies, nations, and even individuals – a value-based account is the most promising to grant its importance. The notion of human rights has been discussed as a prerequisite for a good life in recent literature [10, 11]. If we follow this notion privacy becomes one of these prerequisites to a good life. Without concerning the idea of a good life in detail, it grants a necessary foundation for human advancement and enjoyment of life. This means privacy is a necessity for human fostering. The idea of privacy is not only connected to personal autonomy which means self-determination of information about oneself, i.e. the individual right to share or not share. Privacy also concerns societal, political and social values. Privacy has instrumental value which derives from its importance to individuals, relationships and the society at large. The importance for the individual is not only dependent on the autonomy described above but is also important for moral development and personal freedoms. The concept of privacy leaves the individual to distinguish what she wants to share and want she wants to remain private, especially in connection to different contexts, and fosters the possibility to choose to express unpopular opinions and believes. While this allows both positive and negative outcomes, it grants the possibility to be open about personal information such as religion or homosexuality. Another account for the value of privacy for individuals can be found in van den Hoven [12]. Charles Fried establishes privacy to be important for trust, intimacy and friendship to foster special connection to other individuals which would not be possible without a concept of privacy [13]. Priscilla Regan claims privacy to not only be valuable for individuals but also as a common value for societies because it supports democratic political systems [14]. Privacy within a democratic system allows for possibilities for anonymous speech, the ability for secret voting and the freedom of association. It protects from intrusive government interference into the private sphere and permits the general dichotomy between private and public space [14]. This grants different individuals to be distinct within their beliefs, hobbies, interests and relationships within societies. Thus, the main values of privacy derive from other important concepts or abilities of which privacy is a prerequisite.

5   Examples

In the following we present smart home scenarios with regard to privacy that affect the inhabitants of the smart home and their relationships. We analyze how and which privacy violations can occur and how the relationship of household members is affected. We employ the concept of contextual integrity to analyze breaches of privacy within smart home settings. We use three different scenarios in the socio-technical setting of smart home households which include purchases and configuration of a new device and changes in features and privacy practices of an existing device. The following three scenarios are exemplary to deal with possible breaches of contextual integrity that occur with changes within smart home systems.

5.1   "1 + 1 = 3 Smart Speakers as an Additional Conversation Partner"

During an intimate conversation Craig's smart speaker turns on and interferes his conversation with Clara. Both of them do not know what triggered the response as none of them said the activation phrase. Clara is very uncomfortable; their conversation was private and not meant to be listened to by an outside party. She wants to know what the device listens to, what it does with the information and how it is triggered. Craig does not know. He bought the speaker because of a sale and now it is convenient to use. Craig also values his privacy and wants his conversations with Clara to be private. He is not informed on what his device records, when it listens, what data it collects and what happens with that data.

Clara and Craig look up the privacy regulations to find out that the device will constantly listen for small time periods in order to potentially be triggered. The manufacturer does not store this data. However, when the activation phrase is said the device actively listens, the data needs to be transferred to the manufacturer's server to be processed in order for the device to reply. Additionally, the history of past requests is saved. Clara and Craig decide to move their private conversations into the bedroom, a room without a smart speaker. Following their conversation, they discuss where they would like to have a smart speaker and where it is not acceptable. They place one in the kitchen—in order to look up recipes hands free—but they also decide to ban the speaker from the bedroom and bathroom.

There is a dichotomy between how Clara wants to act in their private home as a girlfriend and how she behaves when smart home devices may be recording. The context of personal space and how one acts within is of high importance for the individual's willingness to share. Parts of their conversation are further distributed which changes the transmission principle to another party than Craig. The actors within the transfer of personal information change because there is another recipient of the information. The private context within the home is breached thus contextual integrity is not present anymore.

5.2   Data Collection at the Front Door

Greg bought a smart doorbell with a video stream directly on his smart phone to keep him and his family safe. He is notified promptly once the camera's motion detection senses movement at the front door. This way he already knows at the office if his parcels were delivered and if his daughter came home from school on time. Besides that, he can also interact with the person at the front door through an intercom and tell them to wait for him or come back later. All videos are stored in the cloud for review.

One day Greg notices that is doorbell is offline and he can't access his cloud account—at this point he thinks it is a regular service outage. Later that day he receives a call from his daughter: The doorbell continuously plays a sound of laughter and a dark and distorted voice addresses her. He instructs her to unplug the WIFI and drives home immediately. His cloud account was hacked, and the hackers took over the doorbell's camera and intercom as well as all the recordings stored in the cloud. He reviews who is affected by the leak. He notices that he never before thought about the privacy of visitors and his family—he would see them at the front door after opening anyway. He also never informed them about the cloud recordings.

Greg did not make his visitors nor the other residents fully aware on the personal data being processed, the recordings being stored, the cloud server being involved. The context of approaching a door e.g. for a visiting friend has changed – it is not private anymore. The transmission principle with the distribution of the data has also changed. There is no possibility of intervention because the camera is motion activated. The location information of everyone recorded with that camera has been distributed to third parties. The recipient of the information thus has changed. Contextual integrity for visitors and the parcel delivery driver is not present and their privacy has been breached.

5.3   Anna Buys a New Vacuum

People in a shared apartment own a vacuum robot. One of the roommates, Anna, decides to upgrade to a new, better model. It has a stronger motor, it is quieter, and it is easier to navigate. It contributes to all roommates feeling more comfortable and the general cleanliness of the space. Whereas the older model was only driving around aimlessly until the battery was dead, the new model tracks its courses and generates maps of the apartment. The vacuum notifies the owner via an app if the battery is dead, it is stuck somewhere or on the status of the cleaning process. Via the app, the user can navigate the vacuum manually, start the cleaning process (even outside of the home) and generate different zones to be cleaned more extensively or not at all. A statistic is generated on the different cleaning sessions with data on specific rooms which were cleaned, the number of square meters, the time vacuumed and disruption within the cleaning process. Anna is now able to see specifically if her roommates are home, based on the interruptions. The interruptions also allow her to know which room was tidied up. Their floor plan and the statistics of the cleaning sessions are further distributed to the manufacturer to improve the functioning of the vacuum. The other roommates were not able to decide on the new model and especially its (new) privacy settings. Their data is distributed to the app and to the manufacturer.

Considering these changes, the roommates did not specifically agree their personal data to be distributed further, which introduces a change of the transmission principle from Anna or the household to the manufacturer. The context on which the data is shared has changed. They are willing to share information on their location and cleanliness of the apartment to their roommates when they are home but not to others or roommates that are not home. Contextual integrity and thus privacy have been breached.

5.4 Breaches of Contextual Integrity

These three examples help to identify prominent privacy breaches within smart home settings. The framework of contextual integrity helps to analyze if personal information is distributed appropriately. In all three examples we can examine a change in the transmission principle, context and a shift of actors. Personal information is distributed out of its intended context for individuals to another party or a familiar party outside of the home. The home as a private space has specific context which is inherently considered to be disconnected from the public. Individuals assume their personal information, i.e. habits or conversations to be private. Smart home systems can, as described above, disrupt this privacy and change the context. Even if a household member receives personal information of another household member outside of the home with smart home devices, the context will change. Additionally, the transmission principle changes. The person or entity receiving this information is not limited to other household members or visitors, but may extend to another party, the manufacturer of the device, or just by processing the data to a cloud. Thirdly, there is a shift between different actors when using smart home devices. Without smart home devices, the information subject and the sender of the information are usually the same person within a home. With the use of smart home devices, that another household member has configured, the information subject and sender of information can differ. The individual now does not privately share this information to other household members, but instead the device of another person distributes this information further. Thus, the recipient of the information changes from a household member to potentially a third party.

These changes within actors, transmission principle and context lead to PII to flow inappropriately and thus to potential breaches of privacy. The established examples focused on changes or actualities which were not communicated or discussed within the household, we think this is common in everyday life. These problems can be solved by transparency measures and joint decision making on privacy settings with all household members.

6 Discussion

In the aforementioned examples we pointed out that privacy issues in smart home context can occur easily and are introduced by different parties. Such changes are related to the change of the context which is introduced by the smart home devices cloud processing. However, the actual processing is not at the core of the problem, rather is the missing transparency for affected persons in the smart home setting. This lack of transparency can result from the lack of understanding of the actual inner workings of such devices by the original buyer and configurator; but it can also be introduced by the manufacturer through a software update or the intrusion of the system by hackers. Beside the latter, these cases do not contain a malicious intention and would not occur if transparency had been present and enabled a discussion.

Such a discussion is necessary as privacy perceptions are different and depend on the context. A special challenge in smart home environments is to not only regard the current context but to understand how this context changes through the regular use of devices, future hard- and software upgrades and how the risk of malicious incidents needs to be taken into account. Currently it is dependent on the buyer of a device to do this and to potentially include the affected persons into her considerations.

7 Conclusion and Future Work

The privacy paradox extends to the smart home and thus introduces privacy risks for all persons in the household as the context can be changed unwillingly by the introduction of smart devices—at most times through a lack of transparency and thus negotiation and awareness. To help the end-user to make informed decisions and to foster transparency we plan to develop a framework to envision such context changes. This framework should not only consist of thought-provoking scenarios but actual smart home devices and manufacturer specific illustrations and descriptions of the processing of PII. This information will be included into a card game to help envision the context changes together with other affected persons.

References

1. Wilson, C., Hargreaves, T., Hauxwell-Baldwin, R.: Smart homes and their users: a systematic analysis and key challenges. Per. Ubiquit. Comput. 19, 463–476 (2015). https://doi.org/10.1007/s00779-014-0813-0

2. Herrmann, T., Lentzsch, C., Degeling, M.: Intervention and EUD. In: Malizia, A., Valtolina, S., Morch, A., Serrano, A., Stratton, A. (eds.) IS-EUD 2019. LNCS, vol. 11553, pp. 67–82. Springer, Cham (2019). https://doi.org/10.1007/978-3-030-24781-2_5

3. Norberg, P.A., Horne, D.R., Horne, D.A.: The privacy paradox: personal information disclosure intentions versus behaviors. J. Consum. Aff. **41**, 100–126 (2007). https://doi.org/10.1111/j.1745-6606.2006.00070.x

4. Lau, J., Zimmerman, B., Schaub, F.: Alexa, are you listening? privacy perceptions, concerns and privacy-seeking behaviors with smart speakers. Proc. ACM Hum. -Comput. Interact. **2**, 1–31 (2018). https://doi.org/10.1145/3274371

5. Emami-Naeini, P., Dixon, H., Agarwal, Y., Cranor, L.F.: Exploring how privacy and security factor into iot device purchase behavior. In: Proceedings of the 2019 CHI Conference on Human Factors in Computing Systems - CHI 2019, pp. 1–12. ACM Press, Glasgow (2019). https://doi.org/10.1145/3290605.3300764

6. Nissenbaum, H.: Privacy as contextual integrity. Wash. Law Rev. **79**, 119 (2004)

7. Nissenbaum, H.F.: Privacy in Context: Technology, Policy, and the Integrity of Social Life. Stanford Law Books, Stanford, Calif (2010)

8. Martin, K., Nissenbaum, H.: Measuring privacy: an empirical test using context to expose confounding variables. Colum. Sci. Tech. L. Rev. **18**, 176 (2016)

9. Hart, H.L.A.: The Concept of Law. Oxford University Press, Oxford (2012)

10. Edmunds, M.: A Good Life: Human Rights and Encounters with Modernity. ANU Press (2013)

11. Liao, S.M.: Human rights as fundamental conditions for a good life. In: Liao, S.M. (ed.) The Right to Be Loved. Oxford University Press, Oxford (2015)

12. Van den Hoven, J.: Privacy and the varieties of informational wrongdoing. In: Computer Ethics, pp. 317–330. Routledge (2017)

13. Fried, C.: Privacy. Yale Law J. **77**, 475 (1968)

14. Regan, P.M.: Legislating privacy: technology, social values, and public policy. University of North Carolina Press, Chapel Hill (2000)

Imitation-Resistant Passive Authentication Interface for Stroke-Based Touch Screen Devices

Masashi Kudo[1(✉)] and Hayato Yamana[2(✉)]

[1] Graduate School of Fundamental Science and Engineering,
Waseda University, Shinjuku-Ku, Tokyo, Japan
kudoma34@yama.info.waseda.ac.jp
[2] Faculty of Science and Engineering, Waseda University, Shinjuku-Ku,
Tokyo, Japan
Yamana@yama.info.waseda.ac.jp

Abstract. Today's widespread use of stroke-based touchscreen devices creates numerous associated security concerns and requires efficient security measures in response. We propose an imitation-resistant passive authentication interface for stroke-based touch screen devices employing classifiers for each individual stroke, which is evaluated with respect to 26 features. For experimental validation, we collect stroke-based touchscreen data from 23 participants containing target and imitation stroke patterns using a photo-matching game in the form of an iOS application. The equal error rate (EER), depicting the rate at which false rejection and false acceptance of target and imitator strokes are equal, is assumed as an indicator of the classification accuracy. Leave-one-out cross-validation was employed to evaluate the datasets based on the mean EER. For each cross-validation, one out of the two target datasets, an imitator dataset, and the remaining 20 imitator datasets were selected as genuine data, imitator test data, and imitator training data, respectively. Our results confirm stroke imitation as a serious threat. Among the 26 stroke features evaluated in terms of their imitation tolerance, the stroke velocity was identified as the most difficult to imitate. Dividing classifiers based on the stroke direction was found to further contribute to classification accuracy.

Keywords: Passive authentication · Continuous authentication · Touch screen device · Biometrics · Imitation

1 Introduction

Stroke-based touch screen devices, such as smartphones, are widespread in the global market. Generally, touch screen devices are equipped with authentication functions, such as passwords, fingerprints and face recognition, to protect personal information. These authentication functions are susceptible to hacking by shoulder-surfing, imitation attack, and replication [1], giving rise to major security and privacy concerns.

In recent years, stroke authentication [2–6] was proposed as a novel touch screen device authentication method that boasts both high authentication accuracy and

C. Stephanidis and M. Antona (Eds.): HCII 2020, CCIS 1226, pp. 558–565, 2020.
https://doi.org/10.1007/978-3-030-50732-9_72

usability. Furthermore, to improve the security of stroke authentication, techniques to prevent illegal acquisition of touch-based information have been proposed. In 2016, Shrestha et al. [7] proposed a technique to add randomized noise to sensor data, making it difficult to obtain touch-based information on the smartphone. In the same year, Gong et al. [8] proposed a technique that makes it difficult to read screen coordinate information by applying a smartphone screen magnifier. However, these studies on stroke authentication do not account for imitation attacks by impostors through shoulder-surfing. To prevent this type of attack, we propose an imitation-resistant passive authentication interface for stroke-based touch screen devices. Moreover, we reveal stroke features that are difficult to imitate through experimental validation by 23 users.

2 Proposed Method

2.1 Overview of Proposed Method

Employing the findings of our previous study on stroke authentication [9], we propose an imitation-resistant passive authentication interface for stroke-based touch screen devices. A summary of the contributions of the previous study is provided below.

- We evaluate 26 stroke features, frequently used in the studies of stroke authentication (Table 1) in terms of their imitation tolerance and reveal features that are difficult to imitate.
- Assuming imitation attacks through shoulder-surfing, we propose a novel stroke authentication method for their prevention.
- We demonstrate the advantage gained by dividing classifiers based on stroke direction for the improvement of authentication accuracy.

Table 1. Stroke features adopted in our research

Features	Description
startX, startY, stopX, stopY	X, Y coordinates at start and end points
x20, x50, x80, y20, y50, y80	X, Y coordinates at 20%/50%/80% point
startPressure, stopPressure	Pressure at start and end points
midPressure	Pressure at middle point
maxPressure, averagePressure	Maximum and average pressure during stroke
averageVelocity	Average velocity
vel20, vel50, vel80	Velocities at 20%/50%/80% point
strokeDuration	Stroke duration
interStrokeTime	Stroke interval
lengthEE, angleEE	Distance and angle between start and end points
lengthTrj	Length of stroke trajectory
ratioTrj2EE	The ratio between lengthEE and lengthTrj
direction	Direction of stroke

2.2   Authentication System

The authentication system was built according to the proposal in our previous study [9]. An overview of the authentication system is shown in Fig. 1. The online AROW algorithm [10] was used as a classifier, and a two-stage window voting scheme [9] was adopted for the output of authentication results. The flow of this authentication system proceeds as follows:

1. A classifier is generated based on the training data.
2. For each stroke, the classifier determines whether it was drawn by the genuine user or an impostor.
3. In response to the classification result of step 2, window voting is performed for a window size of 13 strokes and outputs one voting result.
4. In response to the voting result obtained in step 3, window voting is performed for a window size 13 strokes, and the final authentication result is output.

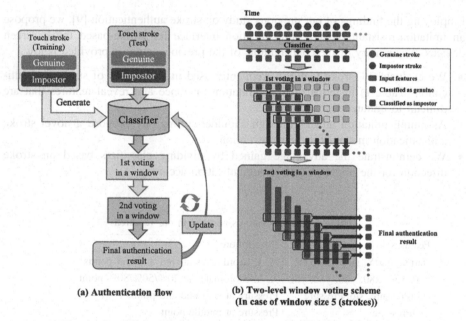

(a) Authentication flow

(b) Two-level window voting scheme
(In case of window size 5 (strokes))

Fig. 1. Overview of imitation-resistant passive authentication interface

3   Experimental Evaluation

3.1   Data Collection

We programmed an iOS application of a photo-matching game (Fig. 2) that can retrieve stroke features listed in Table 1. To verify our authentication method from the viewpoint of imitation resistance, we collected two types of stroke data: *own* and *imitation strokes. Own strokes* are obtained when users operate a smartphone as usual, whereas *imitation strokes* are the stroke operations that a user imitates by watching videos of other users' stroke operations.

We installed the aforementioned application on an iPhone 8 Plus device and collected 1,200 stroke data from each of 23 university students (13 males and 10 females). Note that we chose two people as imitation targets (hereafter, targets), recorded their stroke operations (Fig. 3), and then showed these videos to the remaining 21 students (hereafter, imitators).

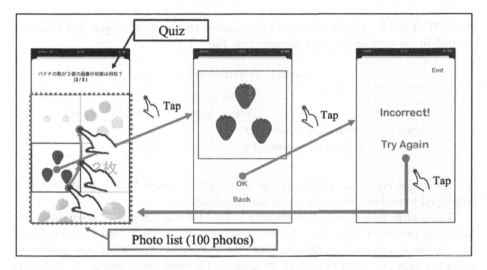

Fig. 2. Overview of photo-matching game

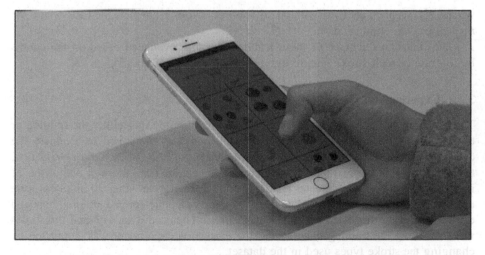

Fig. 3. Screenshot of recorded video of a target's stroke operation

3.2 Evaluation Criteria

To evaluate the classification accuracy of the authentication system, the false rejection rate (FRR) and the false acceptance rate (FAR) are calculated:

$$FRR = \frac{FN}{TP + FN} \tag{1}$$

$$FAR = \frac{FN}{FP + TN} \tag{2}$$

Here, TP, FN, FP, and TN represent classification results of the targets and imitators, defined in the confusion matrix presented in Table 2.

Table 2. Confusion matrix

		Predicted class	
		Positive (genuine)	Negative (impostor)
Actual class	Positive (genuine)	TP	FN
	Negative (impostor)	FP	TN

The equal error rate (EER) is the error rate at which FRR = FAR, and it is employed to evaluate the accuracy of user classification.

The contribution of each stroke feature to the EER was determined according to the following procedure. First, the $i(1 \leq i \leq 26)$-th feature was eliminated from the dataset used in the evaluation experiment. Then, the evaluation experiment was carried out using the same procedure as with all 26 features. The contribution rate of the *ith* feature to the EER is defined as follows:

$$E_i - E[\%] \tag{3}$$

where $E[\%]$ depicts the EER with all 26 features, and $E_i[\%]$ depicts the EER where the *ith* feature was eliminated.

The imitation tolerance of these features was thus evaluated based on the contribution rate of each stroke feature to the EER, provided by Eq. (3).

3.3 Experimental Datasets

The acquired stroke-based touchscreen data were allocated into either the training or testing dataset. The leave-one-out cross-validation was employed to evaluate the classification accuracy of the datasets based on the mean EER. In each cross-validation, the data of one of the two targets were chosen as genuine data, those of one of the 21 imitators was chosen as imposter test data, and the data of the other 20 imitators were used as imposter training data. Note that we oversampled the genuine training data and downsampled the impostor training data to obtain balanced data. Optimal thresholds were set using the training dataset, and the evaluation experiment was conducted by changing the stroke types used in the dataset.

3.4   Experimental Results

Stroke feature and authentication system evaluation results are presented.

Verification of Imitation Attacks. Table 3 presents a comparison between the datasets with and without stroke imitations. Table 3 indicates that the stroke imitation increased the EER from 0.67% to 0.75%, demonstrating that imitation attacks indeed are a serious threat for stroke authentication.

Table 3. Comparison of datasets with and without stroke imitations

No.	Training dataset				Testing dataset				EER
	Genuine		Impostor		Genuine		Impostor		[%]
	Stroke type	#Stroke	Stroke type	#Stroke	Stroke type	#Stroke	Stroke type	#Stroke	
1-1	Own (1 user)	8,000	Own (20 users)	8,000	Own (1 user)	800	Own (1 user)	800	0.67
1-2	Own (1 user)	8,000	Own (20 users)	8,000	Own (1 user)	800	Imitation (1 user)	800	0.75

Analysis of Imitation Resistance of Each Feature. The contribution of stroke features to the EER reduction is shown in Fig. 4 for the case of dataset 1-2 in Table 3. Figure 4 shows that in case of stroke imitations by impostors, "stroke velocity" contributes predominantly to the reduction of the EER. Therefore, the "stroke velocity" has a high imitation resistance, being a feature that is difficult to imitate.

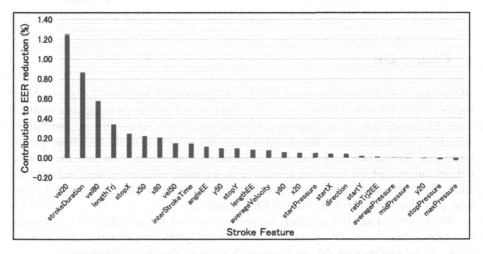

Fig. 4. Contribution of each stroke feature to EER (case of dataset 1-2)

Examination of Methods to Prevent Imitation Attacks. Further *imitation strokes* were added to the training datasets in this experiment. Table 4 presents an overview of the comparison between classifiers with and without their division according to stroke direction. Table 4 shows that inclusion of imitation strokes in the training dataset reduces the EER in cases including imitation strokes from 0.75% to 0.32%, indicating that the imitation resistance increases. Moreover, adoption classifier division according to stroke direction reduces the EER even further.

Table 4. Comparison of classifiers with and without division according to stroke direction

No.	Training dataset				Test dataset				Stroke direction	EER [%]
	Genuine		Impostor		Genuine		Impostor			
	Stroke type	#Stroke	Stroke type	#Stroke	Stroke type	#Stroke	Stroke type	#Stroke		
2-1	Own (1 user)	8,000	Own (20 users)	4,000	Own (1 user)	800	Own (1 user)	800	Irrelevant	0.54
			Imitation (20 users)	4,000						
2-2	Own (1 user)	8,000	Own (20 users)	4,000	Own (1 user)	800	Imitation (1 user)	800	Irrelevant	0.32
			Imitation (20 users)	4,000						
2-3	Own (1 user)	8,000	Own (20 users)	4,000	Own (1 user)	800	Own (1 user)	800	Separately learned for upward and downward	0.03
			Imitation (20 users)	4,000						
2-4	Own (1 user)	8,000	Own (20 users)	4,000	Own (1 user)	800	Imitation (1 user)	800	Separately learned for upward and downward	0.00
			Imitation (20 users)	4,000						

4   Conclusion

We propose an imitation-resistant passive authentication interface for stroke-based interaction with touch screen devices. By experimental validation using data acquired from 23 participants, stroke imitation was confirmed as a serious threat, and "stroke velocity" was identified as the stroke feature that is most difficult to imitate for the impostor. The inclusion of imitated stroke-based touchscreen data into the training dataset augmented the imitation resistance of the authentication system, reducing the EER. Furthermore, the adoption of classifier division according to the applied stroke direction similarly contributed to the EER reduction.

Future tasks include increasing the participant pool for validation. As generating *imitation strokes* from several users is cumbersome, generating imitation data from the stroke-based touchscreen data of the user themselves should be considered.

Acknowledgements. This research was supported by NII CRIS (Center for Robust Intelligence and Social Technology) Contract Research 2019.

References

1. Meng, W., Wong, D.S., Furnell, S., Zhou, J.: Surveying the Development of Biometric User Authentication on Mobile Phones. IEEE Commun. Surv. Tutorials **17**(3), 1268–1293 (2015)
2. Xu, H., Zhou, Y., Lyu, M.R.: Towards continuous and passive authentication via touch biometrics: an experimental study on smartphones. In: Proceedings of the Symposium on Usable Privacy and Security, pp. 187–198. Menlo Park (2014)
3. Shen, C., Zhang, Y., Cai, Z., Yu, T., Guan, X.: Touch-interaction behavior for continuous user authentication on smartphones. In: International Conference on Biometrics, pp. 157–162, Phuket (2015)
4. Miyamoto, N., Shibata, C., Kinoshita, T.: Authentication by Touch Operation on Smartphone with Support Vector Machine. Int. J. Inf. Secur. Res. **7**(2), 725–733 (2017)
5. Volaka, H.C., Alptekin, G., Basar, O.E., Isbilen, M., Incel, O.D.: Towards continuous authentication on mobile phones using deep learning models. Procedia Comput. Sci. **155**, 177–184 (2019)
6. Li, Q., Chen, H.: CDAS: a continuous dynamic authentication system. In: Proceedings of the 8th International Conference on Software and Computer Applications, pp. 447–452. ACM, Penang (2019)
7. Shrestha, P., Mohamed, M., Saxena, N.: Slogger: Smashing motion-based touchstroke logging with transparent system noise. In: Proceedings of the 9th ACM Conference on Security and Privacy in Wireless and Mobile Networks, pp. 67–77. ACM, Darmstadt (2016)
8. Gong, N.Z., Payer, M., Moazzezi, R., Frank, M.: Towards forgery-resistant touch-based biometric authentication on mobile devices. In: Proceedings of the 11th ACM Asia Conference on Computer and Communications Security, pp. 499–510. ACM, Xi'an (2016)
9. Kudo, M., Yamana, H.: Active authentication on smartphone using touch pressure. In: Proceedings of the 31th ACM symposium on User interface software and technology, pp. 96–98. ACM, Berlin (2018)
10. Crammer, K., Kulesza, A., Dredze, M.: Adaptive Regularization of Weight Vectors. Proc. Adv. Neural Inf. Process. Syst. **22**, 414–422 (2009)

Emergence of Human-Centric Information Security – Towards an Integrated Research Framework

Bin Mai[(✉)]

Texas A&M University, College Station, TX 77843, USA
binmai@tamu.edu

Abstract. In this poster, we first summarize the evolution of information security research as three stages of information security development: technology-centric, economics-centric, and the emerging trend of human-centric. We identify the main contributors and outputs of each stage. Based on this understanding, we present an integrated research framework termed Integrated Model of Human-Centric Information Security (iMOHCIS), which systematically incorporates various factors that influence human brain functions, and illustrates how human brain activities eventually lead to actual information security behaviors. This iMOHCIS framework focuses on human-centric information security at individual agent level. We then extend it to incorporate multi-agent interactions in two significant dimensions: qualitative dimension and quantitative dimension. The iMOHCIS framework and its extension capture the essence of the emerging human-centric information security, provide a comprehensive framework for understanding human elements in information security, and generate a systematic approach to identifying significant research questions related to human-centric information security. This framework also provides a foundation for human-centric information security education curriculum design.

Keywords: Information security · Human-centric · Decision making · Integrated Model

1 Emergence of Human-Centric Information Security

The evolution of information security has been at least as long as the development of information technology and information systems [1, 3]. Throughout the development history of information security, we can summarize its evolution into three stages: technology-centric information security, economics-centric information security, and the emerging human-centric information security.

1.1 Technology-Centric Information Security

Figure 1 illustrates the information security during this stage. In technology-centric information security, the focal point of interest (represented by the circle in the middle of Fig. 1) is the development of technical artifacts of information security, such as secure encryption algorithms, secure software application designs, and secure network

C. Stephanidis and M. Antona (Eds.): HCII 2020, CCIS 1226, pp. 566–572, 2020.
https://doi.org/10.1007/978-3-030-50732-9_73

communication protocols. This stage answers the question of "how can we develop technological tools to enhance information security?"

During this stage, the main contributors to information security research (represented by the arrow to the left in Fig. 1) are primarily from the technical fields of science, technology, engineering, and mathematics (STEM). And the main outputs of the research (represented by the arrow to the right in Fig. 1) are the design and development of the information security technological tools. This stage provides the foundation of information security research.

Fig. 1. Technology-centric information security.

1.2   Economics-Centric Information Security

Figure 2 illustrates the information security during this stage. In economics-centric information security, the focal point of interest is the development of incentive mechanisms of information security to optimize the information security decision maker's overall welfare, such as maximized overall expected payoffs, or minimized overall expected loss. It is very important to note that this stage does not replace the technology-centric information security, rather it expands and enhances the technical artifacts developed in the first stage. All the incentive mechanisms designed in this stage are based on a thorough understanding of the technical details of the information security technology. This stage answers the questions of "now we have the technology, how can we decide on the optimal approach to using them?"

During this stage, the main contributors to information security research are primarily traditional economists and management scientists. And the main outputs of the research are the design and development of the optimal information security incentive mechanism, such as optimal policies and regulations, or optimal information security management strategies.

It is worth pointing out that during this stage, it is "traditional economists" that are the main contributors. The term "traditional" used here refers to the main school of thoughts that individual decision makers are rational agents, who possess unbounded rationality. The proposed optimal incentive mechanisms during this stage are usually based on the assumption that the decision makers are rational.

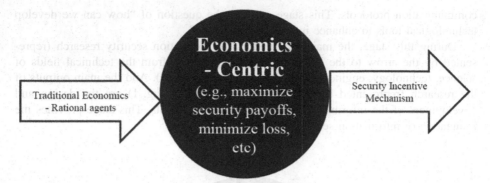

Fig. 2. Economics-centric information security.

1.3   Human-Centric Information Security

Figure 3 illustrates the information security during this emerging stage. In human-centric information security, the focal point of interests is the human decision-making during information security situations in reality. Similar to that in economic-centric stage, this stage does not replace any of the previous stages of information security; it expands and enhances the "traditional" economics to consider individual decision maker's actual behaviors in reality, while still relying on a thorough understanding of the technical details of the information security technology. This stage answers the questions of "how can we design and develop technology and incentive mechanisms that people will actually and properly use and follow in reality?"

During this stage, all factors that influence individual human being's decision making and behaviors would be incorporated in the study, and thus the main contributors to information security research will include a wide spectrum of expertise including psychology, neuroscience, behavioral economics, and sociology, etc. And the main goal of the research are the design and development of information security technical tools that users will actually use in the real world and use properly, and the information security incentives, regulations, and policies that user will actually be able to follow in reality.

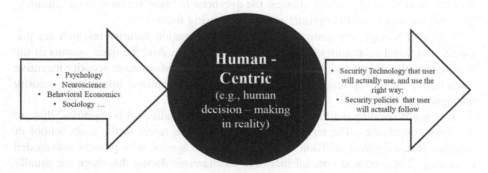

Fig. 3. Human-centric information security.

This is an emerging trend. People have recognized the limitations of the "rational agent" assumption of traditional economics, and have started investigating how actual human beings decide and behave in reality. This significant trend has profound impact on the research of information security, which is captured by what we term as "human-centric" information security.

2   An Integrated Model of Human-Centric Information Security (iMOHCIS)

With the understanding of the evolution of information security, and the emergence of human-centric information security, we now adopt Riedl and Leger's [2] (page 12) basic model of the role of the brain in IS research, systematically incorporates various factors that influence human brain functions and decision making processes, and illustrates how human brain activities result in actual information security behaviors. The result is presented as a research framework for human-centric information security. We name our framework "Integrated Model of Human-Centric Information Security (iMOHCIS)", which is illustrated in the following Fig. 4.

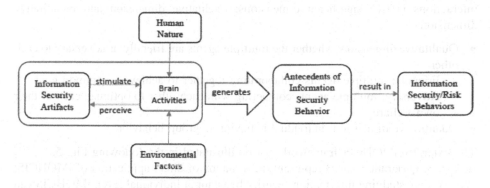

Fig. 4. An Integrated Model of Human-Centric Information Security (iMOHCIS).

The various constructs of iMOHCIS can be explained in detail in the following list:

- Information security artifacts: technology tools designed and developed to enhance information security.
  - Examples: systems, technologies, interfaces, policies, practices...
  - Based on design science, engineering, IT literature
- Brain activities: the measurement of how human brain works.
  - Examples: psychophysiological and neural signals...
  - Based on psychology, neuroscience literature
- Human nature: the innate biological characteristics shared by human groups, shaped by evolution.
  - Examples: multitasking tendencies, age, gender...

- – Based on biology, psychology, neuroscience literature
- • Environmental factors: the external factors from the individual's community environment.
  - – Examples: cognitive load of tasks, brain stimulation, cultural norms, societal influences...
  - – Based on neuroscience, sociology literature
- • Antecedents of information security behaviors: a direct stimulus that cues individual to perform a specific behavior.
  - – Examples: emotions, attitudes, intentions, biases...
  - – Based on psychology, neuroscience literature
- • Information security behaviors: the actual observed action taken by the individual.
  - – Examples: interaction time, clickstreams, decision making...
  - – Based on observed and measured outcome, experiment results.

3   Extension of Basic iMOHCIS

The iMOHCIS framework presented above focuses on human-centric information security at individual level of the agent. It can be extended to incorporate multi-agent interactions in two significant dimensions: qualitative dimension and quantitative dimension:

- • Qualitative dimension: whether the multiple agents are friendly or adversary to each other.
  - – Friendly: multiple agents collaborating together to achieve a common goal
  - – Adversary: multiple agents competing with each other to optimize each of their own welfare.
- • Quantitative dimension: individual behavior vs group behavior.

The extended iMOHCIS framework can be illustrated in the following Fig. 5.

In Fig. 5, Quadrant 1 and 3 represent the situation of direct application of iMOHCIS: when we are studying information security behavior at individual level, iMOHCIS can be directly applied, regardless of qualitative nature (i.e., friend or foe) of the individual. Quadrant 2 and 4 represent the situation of application of iMOHCIS within the context of group decisions and group behavior.

This extension of iMOHCIS allows us to investigate some significant issues resulted from the interactions in these two dimensions. For example:

- A) Qualitative dimension: how friendly agent's behaviors and adversary agent's behaviors influence each other; what type of equilibria would emerge from such interaction; how the emerged equilibria evolve under the influence of various factors.
- B) Quantitative dimension: how individual agent's behaviors and group's behaviors influence each other; how group decisions and group behaviors emerge based on individual's decision making and behaviors; how group decisions and behaviors in turn impact individual's decision and behaviors.

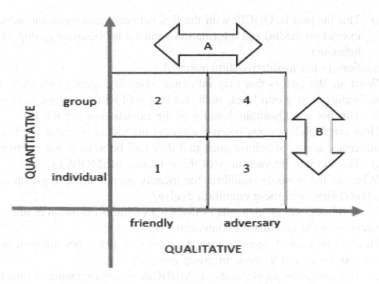

Fig. 5. Extension to iMOHCIS research framework.

4   Potential Research Topics Based on iMOHCIS

The proposed iMOHCIS framework and its extension provide a solid foundation for identifying significant research opportunities in human-centric information security. The following is a sample list of some potential significant research questions and how they are represented in iMOHCIS and its extension:

A) At individual level (Quadrant 1 and 3 of the extension):
   a) The relationships between individual's emotion states and information processing strategies
       i)   This fits into iMOHCIS with the link between brain activities (in this case, individual's information processing strategy) and antecedent of information security behavior (in this case, the emotion state of the individual)
   b) The relationships between individual's multi-tasking tendencies and behavior patterns of responding to information security warning messages
       i)   This fits into iMOHCIS with the link between human nature (multi-tasking tendency) and information security/risk behavior (security message response)
   c) The relationships between tDCS on brain regions and individual's behavior patterns of responding to information security warning messages
       i)   This fits into iMOHCIS with the link between environmental factor (tDCS) and information security/risk behavior (security message response)
B) At group level (Quadrant 2 and 4 of the extension):
   a) Compared with that at individual level, what unique elements does iMOHCIS possess at the group level?
       i)   This potentially covers all constructs and relationships of iMOHCIS
   b) The relationships between group interaction media and group interaction behavior

i) This fits into iMOHCIS with the link between environmental factor (group interaction media) and information security/risk behavior (group interaction behavior)

C) Interactions in the qualitative dimension (A):

   a) What are the factors that may influence adversary agent's behaviors, either at individual or at group level, such that they will be more prone to errors?

     i) This fits into Quadrant 3 and 4 of the extension of iMOHCIS

   b) How can friendly agents behave, either at individual or group level, to induce adversary agents to behave such that they will be more prone to errors?

     i) This fits into interaction A of the extension of iMOHCIS

   c) What are the possible equilibria for friendly agents interacting with adversary agents? How will these equilibria evolve?

     i) This integrates all elements of iMOHCIS with its extension of interaction A.

D) Interactions in the quantitative dimension (B):

   a) How do individual agent' information security behaviors differ in individual context, compared to those in group context?

     i) This integrates all elements of iMOHCIS with it extension of interaction B.

   b) How are group decisions and behaviors influenced by individual's neural characteristics?

     i) This integrates all elements of iMOHCIS with it extension of interaction B.

5 Conclusions

In this poster, we summarized the evolution of information security into three stages: technology-centric, economic-centric, and human-centric. Based on this understanding, we present an Integrated Model of Human-Centric Information Security (iMOHCIS) as the research framework for human-centric information security, and extend it in both qualitative and quantitative dimension. We are convinced that iMOHCIS and its extension capture the essence of the emerging human-centric information security, provide a comprehensive framework for understanding human-centric information security, and generate a systematic approach to identifying significant research opportunities related to information security. This framework also provides a foundation for human-centric information security education curriculum design.

References

1. Olijnyk, N.V.: A quantitative examination of the intellectual profile and evolution of information security from 1965 to 2015. Scientometrics **105**, 883–904 (2015)
2. Riedl, R., Leger, P.M.: Fundamentals of NeuroIS: Information Systems and the Brain. Springer, Berlin (2016)
3. Siponin, M.T., Oinas-Kukkonen, H.: A review of information security issues and respective research contributions. Database Adv. Inf. Syst. **38**(1), 60–80 (2007)

Neither Do I Want to Accept, nor Decline; Is There an Alternative?

Nurul Momen[1(✉)] and Sven Bock[2]

[1] Karlstad University, Karlstad, Sweden
nurul.momen@kau.se
[2] Technical University of Berlin, Berlin, Germany
sven.bock@mms.tu-berlin.de

Abstract. As we spend a considerable amount of time on various user interfaces, it often requires to provide consent for grating privileges. This article addresses the opportunity for providing conditional consent which could potentially aid the user in understanding consequences, making informed decisions, and gaining trust in data sharing. We introduce an indecisive state of mind before consenting to policies, that will enable consumers to evaluate data services before fully committing to their data sharing policies. We discuss usability, regulatory, social, individual and economic aspects for inclusion of partial commitment within the context of an user interface for consent management. Then, we look into the possibilities to integrate it within the permission granting mechanism of Android by introducing an additional button in the interface—*Maybe*. This article also presents a design for such implementation, demonstrates feasibility by showcasing a prototype built on Android platform, and elaborates on a planned user study to determine feasibility, usability, and user expectation.

Keywords: Partial commitment · Conditional consent · Data protection · Privacy

1 Introduction

The surrounding environment of today's society is being populated rapidly with pervasive systems. Consequently, users are being encountered with numerous interfaces asking for their consents about systems' data gathering practice. As it offers only binary choices (*Accept* or *Decline*) and users are conditioned to grant any access, even though they often find themselves cornered to provide consent despite having objections [3,16]. However, revoking consent requires cognitive effort, technical understanding, and consequential awareness about privacy concerns which are hard to come by from individuals [13]. The complex terms of use and data protection often cover several pages and are written in legal and complex language. It is doubtful that the majority of users read or fully understand them. In addition, privacy settings are often difficult to understand and

© Springer Nature Switzerland AG 2020
C. Stephanidis and M. Antona (Eds.): HCII 2020, CCIS 1226, pp. 573–580, 2020.
https://doi.org/10.1007/978-3-030-50732-9_74

not immediately apparent, so that laypersons are unlikely to be able to prevent the disclosure of their information. The problem here is that the privacy settings are already configured to allow the highest possible level of sharing of user data, and at best can be disabled, this is known as the opt-out process [8]. It should be noted that 'providing consent' is driven by massive incentive originated from getting access to the desired service or product. Even incentives, such as a low monetary value, tempt users to agree to the disclosure of personal information to third parties. This is due to the fact that users may not be aware of which data is requested and forwarded by them and how often [1]. Additionally, no such incentive is offered to revoke prior consent by any given user interface [15]. Thus the notion of consent in user interface suffers from two significant limitations:

'Consent' versus 'freely given consent': The General Data Protection Regulation—GDPR provides following definition: *'consent' of the data subject means any freely given, specific, informed and unambiguous indication of the data subject's wishes by which he or she, by a statement or by a clear affirmative action, signifies agreement to the processing of personal data relating to him or her* [2]. We argue that the spirit of 'freely given' is yet to be realized, due to the fact that it offers none but one option to proceed from the binary choices—*Accept* or *Decline*. Moreover, users are nudged towards pressing *accept* button to every consent interface through using privacy dark patterns [3].

Consent with indefinite validity: Currently, the user is only able to provide consent for granting privilege with unprecedented validity. We propose a third option for this contex—*Maybe*, as depicted in Fig. 1, which could enable the user to grant the requested privilege with limitation, i.e. for a certain amount of time (hours/days), or number of accesses to system resources [5,6,14]. Upon expiration of partially given consent, the user could review the app's performance in terms of resource utilization attributes and proceed to grant or revoke consent with further extended validity.

In this article, we aim at addressing the aforementioned issues. In Sect. 2, we describe our proposed solution—an alternative protocol for recording consent that offers partial consent as the third option—*Maybe*. In Sect. 3, we present a prototypical implementation and discuss the feasibility from usability, regulatory, and technical perspectives. In Sect. 4, we elaborate on a planned user experiment that focuses on identifying users' need and expectations from partial consent management within a system. This should facilitate informed decisions after understanding consequences from temporarily granted privileges. We would like to investigate whether an expiry date for consent [4] is desired and accepted by the user from convenient interaction interface. We conclude this article in Sect. 5.

2   Context of Partial Commitment

In this section we review contextual factors that support partial commitment. First, we explore the necessity for partial commitment by examining three use cases of *Maybe* button in the user interface. Our discussion is limited to the European context due to the fact that we envision to carry out user study involving users from the EU. We also discuss trust issues towards data sharing practices and psychological aspects that influence end-users' interests and therefore their behaviour.

2.1 Need and Scope in European Context

An expiry date for consent was introduced by B. Custer [4]. In [6], L. Fritsch also addressed this issue with a 'try before you buy' approach. In 2011, EU directive 2011/83/EU [12] introduced the concept of a 14-day remorse period in which consumers are entitled to return goods purchased online without any further reason. We discuss the spirit of this consumer protection directive applied to digital services which are generally regarded to sell their services in exchange for personal data as a currency [9], e.g. through service providers who capitalize on personal data through advertising [17]. In which ways could consumers reverse or restrict the transactions based on their data?

We argue that having an option to consent partially could help the user in understanding the consequences and rectifying their decisions taken earlier. After running a service with a partial consent, an evaluation of performance can facilitate intervenability, which is also emphasized by the GDPR's principle of transparency (Article 5-1a) and the right to withdraw consent (Article 7-3) [2]. We describe the following use cases to illustrate the need and scope of partial consent in users' everyday life:

Alice downloads and installs a weather app named 'Rain' on her mobile phone that runs with a conventional access control. It asks to grant several permissions as soon as she runs it for the first time. She deems it as a necessary and obvious step to proceed and grants access by pressing the button—*Allow*, as it requires from a conventional interface. Alice remains unaware of the consequences for granting access to sensitive personal information to the app— 'Rain'.

Bob - Alice's colleague, downloads the same weather app—'Rain' on his system that supports a partial consent. It asks to grant privilege as soon as he decides to install it. He deems it as worthy to check out and grants temporary privilege by pressing the button—*Maybe*, as shown in Fig. 1. After the temporary access period (set by himself—48 h), Bob receives a statistical report stating that 'Rain' accessed several APIs numerous times throughout this period. Bob uninstalls 'Rain' and gets another app named 'Cloud'. After the temporary access period, Bob finds out that it only accessed the location API thrice. He decides to keep using 'Cloud' and remains aware of the consequences for granting access to sensitive information.

Carol - a friend of Bob, decides to install another app named 'Storm' after learning about Bob's experience. After running it with partial consent—*Maybe*, she finds out that 'Storm' does not require any permission to provide a weather update. Instead, it asks for the name of a desired location for which a weather

report should be displayed. Carol shares her experience with Bob who recti-
fies his app choice too. Thus both Bob and Carol are able to make privacy-
preserving decisions applying a partial consent while using weather service
apps.

2.2 Trust and Psychological Factors

In an exploration of data narratives, people have been found to very explicitly manage their data relationships with others and organizations [18]. There
is a clearly defined need for user interfaces that support such data management
oriented feature towards relationship. We think that the ability to manage partial commitment against data receivers through choices in user interfaces will
implement such relationship management.

Trust has been found as a cornerstone in people's willingness to provide
personal data to services [11]. Trust in remote services is generally established
through brand value, social recommendations and own experience [7]. We regard
partial commitment as a strategy that enables experiential rise of consumer trust.
Privacy interactions such as comprehensive information, restrictive settings and
privacy policies have, in addition, been categorized as important for privacy-
enhancing online cues [10] that support privacy behaviors.

However, a partial commitment may have its shortcomings in contexts where
the information is shared with third parties, e.g. through social media settings [19]. In such contexts, the release of information is not easily reversible.

3   Prototype Development

This section describes our approach to implement a prototype that is able to
demonstrate partial consent in the form of a simple *Maybe* button. First, we
discuss the design process and second, we elaborate on the developed prototype.

3.1   Design

Since the introduction of Android 9.0, the user can exercise more granular control over his/her consent[1]. However, it does not offer any usage statistics or
monitoring facility to motivate rectification of consents given earlier. Our design
is focused on addressing this issue—to introduce validity to consent. Figure 1
illustrates our approach to handle permission requests through partial consent.
Besides conventional binary choices (*Accept/Decline*), it offers a third option
(*Maybe*) to the conditional statement (*Grant permission?*). Opting the third
option (*Maybe*) invokes `validity_checker()`. It determines how long the partial consent will be valid. If the user defines the validity once, it keeps the value
stored until changed explicitly. It should be noted that this design is also able
to accommodate a counter-based (API access budget) implementation.

---

[1] Permissions overview: https://developer.android.com/guide/topics/permissions/
overview; Accessed on 11 FEB 2020.

3.2 Implementation

We implemented the designed model on top of a prototype app named `A-ware`
[15]. Figure 1 shows some screenshots of it. Primarily, the prototype allows the
users to explore two lists. Installed apps are listed in the first one. The user
may carry on to discover more details about any installed app. The app details
option shows the list of permissions which are being used by that particular app.
For each of the permissions, a partial consent can be registered (as depicted
in the bottom-right screenshot). It allows the corresponding app to carry out
operations. Upon reaching expiration of the partial consent, that is calculated
from `system_timestamp`, permission is registered as revoked.

This prototype is tested on a Nokia 5 Android device running on a vendor
stock ROM (Android 7.1.1) which was rooted to achieve system privileges.

Fig. 1. Prototype implementation on Android platform: list of installed apps (image in
the left), list of permissions (image in the middle), and three privilege granting options
(image in the right).

4 Planned Experiment

Our immediate future research activity includes a user study to investigate
usability aspects of the *Maybe* button. A conception and preparation of the this
experiment is planned. This includes the introduction of a temporary release of
rights by the end user to the respective app. Our prototype, described in Sect. 4,
will go through some changes before commencing the study; e.g. consent interface during app installation. The user will encounter an interface that displays
a selection menu when the app is opened, which enables the user to grant the
requested rights for a certain time or for a certain number of accesses, so that
the app cannot access data with indefinite validity.

Is the 'Maybe' Button Desired? The aim of the study will be to find out whether the function of *Maybe* button is desired by the end users and thus could be used in their everyday life. For a preliminary evaluation, we intend to prepare an online questionnaire, which should help to evaluate whether this function is desired and potentially used, thus achieving the highest possible coverage.

Is the 'Maybe' Button Accepted? In a second step, the prototype app will be placed on user devices in which several participants are to enter certain data every day. It would be conceivable here to integrate another analogy as a cover story, in which the participants have to give daily feedback on the app. To register the feedback, a dialog box appears in which the participants can choose between *Accept*, *Maybe* and *Decline*. With the first option *Accept* the participants agree that their data will be permanently and without any limitation forwarded to the university. If the option *Maybe* is selected, another dialog box will open where the participants can choose whether the release of the data should be granted only once or for seven days. The option *Decline* prevents the release of the data, but also denies the participants the use of the portal and therefore the participation in the study.

Is the 'Maybe' Button Usable? In a third step, a similar dialog box for partial consent will be implemented in the Android operating system. It should appear as soon as an app requests permission to access data or sensor. The user would then have the possibility to decide whether to grant permanent access to the requested permission, or whether they want to allow it temporarily by registering partial consent with a *Maybe* button. This final phase of our study is to be carried out in the lab by providing a mobile device with the modified operating system in order to be able to observe and document user behavior. Participants will be invited in the laboratory to carry out a series of tasks according to predefined scenarios. The decision-making behavior of the participants will be recorded and analyzed with a view to find out more about following queries:

Annoyance threshold: How high is the annoyance about the recurring request for a right's release through partial consent?

Privacy versus convenience: Is it more important for the user to have control over their data, or does convenience prevail?

Intuitive contexts: For which life contexts and data types is the partial consent a meaningful way to protect them?

Our ongoing research will show how these considerations are valued against each other.

5   Conclusion

This article documents our exploratory effort to identify opportunities, challenges, and feasibility for including partial consent within a system. We argued that partial consent could appear in the form of a simple *Maybe* button and has the potential to address several issues concerning user's difficulty with understanding consequences and making informed decisions. We reasoned our arguments with technical, regulatory, and consumer perspectives in consideration of historic approaches to privacy negotiations and to data processing transparency.

We argue that partial consent is a worthwhile concept that reflects practice from consumer protection and that extends the spirit of the GDPR into the domain of consumer protection. This is achieved by both exploring the 'try before you buy' and the 'full refund upon product return' approaches in the market for personal data. Contrasting prior approaches, a partial consent aims at avoiding the exaggerated decision-making burden for consumers that was created by prior approaches to manage data sharing.

Our three modes of a partial consent enable trust-building between consumers and service providers. In the age of Big Data and facing the upcoming issues of trust, transparency and power in Artificial Intelligence and in smart systems, we expect the partial consent to become an important trust-building technique. Furthermore, the partial consent offers the user a possibility to go through an overview of her personal data access privileges, so that she is able to keep herself informed about data protection rights. On the other hand, it allows the service providers to introduce transparency enhancing tools to the user interface and thus enabling their system to facilitate trust-building ecosystem.

References

1. Bock, S.: My data is mine-users' handling of personal data in everyday life. In: SICHERHEIT 2018 (2018)
2. European Commission: Regulation (EU) 2016/679 of the European Parliament and of the Council of 27 April 2016 on the protection of natural persons with regard to the processing of personal data and on the free movement of such data (General Data Protection Regulation). Off J Eur Union p. L119 (2016)
3. Norwegian Consumer Council: Deceived by design, how tech companies use dark patterns to discourage us from exercising our rights to privacy. Norwegian Consumer Council Report (2018)
4. Custers, B.: Click here to consent forever: expiry dates for informed consent. Big Data Soc. 3(1), 2053951715624935 (2016)
5. Franzen, D., Aspinall, D.: Phonewrap-injecting the "how often" into mobile apps. In: IMPS@ ESSoS, pp. 11–19 (2016)
6. Fritsch, L.: Partial commitment – "Try Before You Buy" and "Buyer's Remorse" for personal data in big data & machine learning. In: Steghöfer, J.-P., Esfandiari, B. (eds.) IFIPTM 2017. IAICT, vol. 505, pp. 3–11. Springer, Cham (2017). https://doi.org/10.1007/978-3-319-59171-1_1
7. Fritsch, L., Groven, A.-K., Schulz, T.: On the internet of things, trust is relative. In: Wichert, R., Van Laerhoven, K., Gelissen, J. (eds.) AmI 2011. CCIS, vol. 277, pp. 267–273. Springer, Heidelberg (2012). https://doi.org/10.1007/978-3-642-31479-7_46
8. Fuchs, C.: Facebook, web 2.0 und ökonomische überwachung. Datenschutz und Datensicherheit-DuD 34(7), 453–458 (2010)

9. Gates, C., Matthews, P.: Data is the new currency. In: Proceedings of the 2014 New Security Paradigms Workshop, pp. 105–116 (2014)

10. Kitkowska, A., Shulman, Y., Martucci, L.A., Wästlund, E.: Psychological effects and their role in online privacy interactions: A review. IEEE Access (2020)

11. Lippert, S.K., Swiercz, P.M.: Personal data collection via the internet: the role of privacy sensitivity and technology trust. J. Int. Technol. Inf. Manag. **16**(1), 2 (2007)

12. Markou, C.: Directive 2011/83/eu on consumer rights. In: EU Regulation of E-Commerce. Edward Elgar Publishing (2017)

13. Momen, N.: Towards Measuring Apps' Privacy-Friendliness. Ph.D. thesis, Karlstads universitet (2018)

14. Momen, N., Fritsch, L.: App-generated digital identities extracted through android permission-based data access-a survey of app privacy. In: SICHERHEIT 2020 (2020)

15. Momen, N., Hatamian, M., Fritsch, L.: Did app privacy improve after the GDPR? IEEE Secur. Priv. **17**(6), 10–20 (2019)

16. Momen, N., Pulls, T., Fritsch, L., Lindskog, S.: How much privilege does an app need? investigating resource usage of android apps (short paper). In: 2017 15th Annual Conference on Privacy, Security and Trust (PST), pp. 268–2685. IEEE (2017)

17. Papadopoulos, P., Kourtellis, N., Rodriguez, P., Laoutaris, N.: If you are not paying for it, you are the product: How much do advertisers pay for your personal data. In: Proceedings of IMC (2017)

18. Vertesi, J., Kaye, J., Jarosewski, S.N., Khovanskaya, V.D., Song, J.: Data narratives: uncovering tensions in personal data management. In: Proceedings of the 19th ACM Conference on Computer-Supported Cooperative Work & Social Computing, pp. 478–490 (2016)

19. Warner, M., Kitkowska, A., Gibbs, J., Maestre, J., Blandford, A.: Evaluating'prefer not to say'around sensitive disclosures. In: The ACM Conference on Human Factors in Computing Systems (CHI), vol. 2020. Association for Computing Machinery (ACM) (2020)

Improving the Training Materials of Information Security Based on Cybersecurity Framework

Satoshi Ozaki[✉]

University of Tsukuba, 1-1-1 Tennodai, Tsukuba-shi, Ibaraki, Japan
s17301502@s.tsukuba.ac.jp

Abstract. The shortage of human resources related to information security has been a problem in Japan since the last decade. To encourage self-learning, we created training materials revised based on the guidelines of information security published by the Information-technology Promotion Agency, Japan. The materials were partly designed using a text-mining analysis based on the framework core of the cybersecurity framework published by the National Institute of Standards and Technology. In this extended abstract, we consider the accuracy of the text-mining approach and a rough design of the materials.

Keywords: Text-mining · tf-idf · Cybersecurity Framework · Self-learning

1 Introduction

Recent reports have indicated a shortage of information security staff, particularly in small and medium-sized enterprises (SMEs), which can lead to a vulnerability for supply chain attacks.

According to the "Fundamental Research for Education of Information Security Human Resources" published by the Information-technology Promotion Agency, Japan (IPA) in 2012 and its continual research published in 2014 [1], the shortage of human resources in the cybersecurity field is estimated to be approximately 81,000 people, and 61,000 people are working for companies that do not have a human resource department in this area.. In addition, the Institute of Information Security stated in its "Report on questionnaire survey on information security incidents" [2] that approximately 25% of the SMEs in Japan do not have human resources in the field of cybersecurity and that approximately 41% have only one concurrent cybersecurity information staff member. Therefore, approximately 67% of the SMEs have limited or no human resources in this field. Moreover, there have been some reports of advanced persistent threats in which attackers have attempted to attack related groups or companies that are less secure to initial attacks. One such example was reported by IPA, Japan [3]. Thus, it is important to encourage less secure communities such as SMEs to take cybersecurity more seriously.

To improve this situation, a working group for the development of human resources for cybersecurity was organized in the Cyber Security Center in Japan, which published its "Measures for Developing Cybersecurity Human Resources Inter-Group Working

© Springer Nature Switzerland AG 2020
C. Stephanidis and M. Antona (Eds.): HCII 2020, CCIS 1226, pp. 581–588, 2020.
https://doi.org/10.1007/978-3-030-50732-9_75

Report [4]" in 2018. In this report, it was reported that we require not only specialists to work in the domain of cybersecurity or general IT operations, but also experts who understand security activities and business well. In addition, numerous guidelines have been published as teaching materials for self-learning based on actual studies. Such guidelines was presented on the website of the Ministry of Economy Trade and Industry, Japan, and as of July 1,2019 [5] the number of published guidelines has reached over 150. However, it is difficult to grasp which parts of a security counter-measure activity the guidelines correspond to, and learners may encounter difficulty in finding and selecting appropriate guidelines to create a learning strategy.

2   Research Objective

We herein present a procedure for designing improved learning-materials that allow learners to fully understand the subject of security. We suggest that the framework core of the Cybersecurity Framework [6] will function as a correct mental model for learners and will lead them to organize their knowledge and improve their learning strategy. In addition, because many guidelines on information security have been previously published, we decided to revise a published document based on these guidelines.

In particular, we analyzed the published documents using a text-mining approach for each section and chapter to allow the mapping to the framework core of Cyber-security Framework 1.1 and consider the accuracy of the text-mining results compared with template coding results.

We intend to examine how much this improves the learners understanding and how much it changes their mental model, although these are treated as a future study.

3   Related Studies

Security education/training studies have been conducted from various perspectives in Japan. A study on career development in the domain of cybersecurity was conducted by Kyoko Honda [7], which focused only on the dedicated (full-time) security members and the role and occupational relationship in security-related activities. The study did not consider the effect of education or training. Another study focused on the training contents; we also found other studies that used a capture the flag (CTF) approach for practice-based training [8] and some that focused on the practice environment, because an attackable environment is required for the exercise of cybersecurity practices [9]. Son et al. studied the curriculum of universities and graduate schools for the education of experts [10]. They analyzed the curriculum based on the Cybersecurity Workforce Framework [11] defined by The National Initiative for Cybersecurity Education (NICE) under the National Institute of Standards and Technology (NIST).

As mentioned by a workshop conducted by the Cyber Security Center, experts are required to learn not only the techniques but also various learning categories (in most cases, during their non-full-time security career) to connect the security fields with management along with the knowledge of the business and security activities of both these fields. To achieve this, we need to support students in good self-directed learning.

4   Analysis for Creating Training Material

To create an improved document, we decided to revise a published document based on the core of Cybersecurity Framework 1.1. We need to clarify the correspondence between the published document and the framework core. We took a similar approach as the "Proposal to visualize the contents of information security guidelines based on the Cybersecurity Framework" [12], which is a procedure used to visualize the content of a document based on the framework core; however, in this paper, we apply it to each chapter and section of the document to try and evaluate the content and clarify the correspondence.

4.1   Existing Materials Used for Creating New Improved Materials

We created improved learning materials based on two documents: Cybersecurity Framework and Guideline of Information Security for SMEs.

The Cybersecurity Framework is a document published by the National Institute of Standards and Technology and was originally created for summarizing the security measures in a critical infrastructure. It is based on aggregating the standards, guidelines, and best practices in the cybersecurity domain, and provides a systematic and structured holistic view on various security measures. We used the version translated into Japanese published by IPA, Japan [13] for the following analysis.

"Guideline of Information Security for SMEs 3rd edition" is a document published by the IPA and was created to support SMEs' information security staff members in Japan to create a security policy and determine possible security measures.

4.2   Framework Core

The framework core has a layered structure, where each element is called either a function, category, or sub-category. Functions are the highest-level cybersecurity activities, and include *identify, protect, detect, respond,* and *recover.* Categories are the subdivisions of a function (Table 1).

4.3   Simple Text-Mining Analysis

We created a feature word vector using tf-idf for each category of the framework core using the descriptions in Cybersecurity Framework 1.1. We calculated the cosine similarity between the feature vectors of each category and each chapter and section of "Guideline of Information Security for SMEs 3rd edition." The results of the chapters with a function view integrating the value of categories in that function are shown in Table 2. We believe that the result of this text-mining shows how much the chapters and sections are similar to each category of the framework core. In this case, we can consider *identify* and *protection* as the main topics for all chapters.

Table 1. Function and category of unique identifiers (quoted from Cybersecurity Framework 1.1 [6])

Function unique identifier	Function	Category unique identifier	Category
ID	Identify	ID.AM	Asset Management
		ID.BE	Business Environment
		ID.GV	Governance
		ID.RA	Risk Assessment
		ID.RM	Risk Management Strategy
		ID.SC	Supply Chain Risk Management
PR	Protect	PR.AC	Identity Management and Access Control
		PR.AT	Awareness and Training
		PR.DS	Data Security
		PR.IP	Information Protection Processes and Procedures
		PR.MA	Maintenance
		PR.PT	Protective Technology
DE	Detect	DE.AE	Anomalies and Events
		DE.CM	Security Continuous Monitoring
		DE.DP	Detection Processes
RS	Respond	RS.RP	Response Planning
		RS.CO	Communications
		RS.AN	Analysis
		RS.MI	Mitigation
		RS.IM	Improvements
RC	Recover	RC.RP	Recovery Planning
		RC.IM	Improvements
		RC.CO	Communications

4.4 Validation of Test-Mining Analysis Compared with Template Coding Results

We evaluated the validity of the results of the text-mining of the documents, chapters, and sections using the same approach as conducted by the authors of the previous paper "Proposal to visualize the contents of information security guidelines based on the Cybersecurity Framework."

Template Coding Based on Cybersecurity Framework

To measure the validity of the text-mining results, we need to quantitatively express how they recognize the contents of the document. We used the qualitative coding method to conduct an analysis through a quantifiable approach, similar to the previous paper.

Table 2. Text mining analysis results for chapters with functional view

	Identify	Protection	Detection	Response	Recovery
Introduction for Executives	1.140	1.130	0.250	0.339	0.185
1.1. Disadvantages when they do not implement information security measures	2.605	2.756	0.689	1.645	0.756
1.2. Responsibility of executives	2.634	3.308	0.462	1.044	0.419
1.3. What executives have to do	3.660	3.140	1.003	1.625	0.789
2.1. Implement information security measures and management	1.268	0.829	0.344	0.308	0.124
2.2. Start with what you can do	1.184	1.530	0.521	0.518	0.641
2.3. Start organizational initiatives	7.694	10.026	2.638	5.453	2.288
2.4. Work in earnest	10.712	7.576	2.536	7.162	1.857
2.5. Strategies for improvement	34.700	39.219	9.182	15.055	7.560

Template coding is a procedure for defining the word group (code group) used for coding in advance. We used the sub-category of the framework core of Cybersecurity Framework 1.1 as a code group to obtain results comparable to those of the text-mining results.

The "Guideline of Information Security for SMEs 3rd edition" is analyzed herein using template coding and the results of the chapters, as shown in Table 3.

Validate the Results in Document, Chapter, and Section
We calculated the Pearson's correlation coefficient between the text-mining results and the template coding results for each chapter and section and took the averages (Table 4). We also recalculated the Pearson's correlation coefficient of the "Guideline of Information Security for SMEs 3rd edition" because the results of the previous paper are based on the second edition.

The document level analysis results show a strong correlation, the chapter level analysis results also show a rather strong correlation, and the section level analysis results show a weak correlation. Thus, we can infer that we can use the text mining results as a clue to determine which chapter (or section) is related to which category of the framework core.

Table 3. Template coding results for chapters with functional view

	Identify	Protection	Detection	Response	Recovery
Introduction for Executives	3	3	0	0	0
1.1. Disadvantages when they do not implement information security measures	7	9	0	1	2
1.2. Responsibility of executives	6	1	0	0	0
1.3. What executives have to do	6	6	0	1	0
2.1. Implement information security measures and management	1	1	0	0	0
2.2. Start with what you can do	1	4	1	0	0
2.3. Start organizational initiatives	5	3	0	0	0
2.4. Work in earnest	22	9	0	3	0
2.5. Strategies for improvement	53	27	5	2	0

Table 4. Pearson's correlation coefficient between the text-mining and the template coding

	Function layer (5 factors)	Category layer (23 factors)
Document (3rd Ed.)	0.970	0.710
Chapters average	0.862	0.543
Sections average	0.503	0.225

5   Considering the Design of Training Material and Experiment

We mapped each section and chapter of "Guideline of Information Security for SMEs 3rd edition" to the categories that seem to be related based on the information of the text-mining analysis and template coding the results of the chapters, as shown in Table 5.

During the experiment, we intended to investigate how improvements are achieved through a change in the interface and how the mental model of the learner is changed by the learning activity. Therefore, we did not change the content or architecture of the "Guideline of Information Security for SMEs" but simply showed the relationship to the categories of the framework core. For example, we plan to show lines to the related

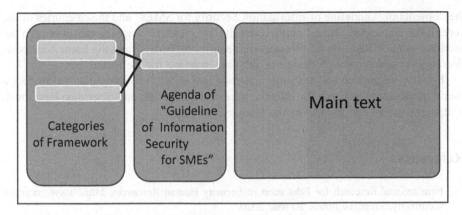

Fig. 1. Rough design of training material console

Table 5. Map chapters to categories

	Topic ID	Sub Topic ID
Introduction for Executives	ID.GV	PR.AT, PR.IP
1.1. Disadvantages when they do not implement information security measures	ID.RA	PR.AT, PR.IP
1.2. Responsibility of executives	ID.GV	ID.RA, PR.AT
1.3. What executives have to do	PR.IP, PR.AT	ID.BE, ID.SC, ID.GV
2.1. Implement information security measures and management	ID.GV	PR.AT
2.2. Start with what you can do	PR.AC	ID.RA, PR.IP, DE.CM
2.3. Start organizational initiatives	ID.GV, PR.AT	PR.IP
2.4. Work in earnest	ID.AM, ID.RA	ID.GV, PR.AT, PR.IP
2.5. Strategies for improvement	ID.AM, ID. RA, ID.SC	ID.GV, PR.AC, PR.IP

category in when the mouse is hovered over an item of the "Guideline of Information Security for SMEs" (Fig. 1).

6 Conclusion and Future Works

We analyzed the "Guideline of Information Security for SMEs" using a text-mining approach and checked the accuracy in comparison with the results of the template coding approach. Weak correlations were found even for the average sections, and it was inferred that we can use the results of text-mining as a clue for mapping between the contents of "Guideline of Information Security for SMEs" and the categories of the core of the framework. Based on these results, we created a mapping table between the sections of the "Guideline of Information Security for SMEs" and the framework core. We also presented a rough design of the user interface for the materials.

Finally, we created self-learning materials and as a future study plan to conduct a user experiment to research the effectiveness of the materials and determine how much it changes the mental models of the learners.

References

1. Fundamental Research for Education of Security Human Resources. http://www.ipa.go.jp/security/fy23/reports/jinzai/. 20 Mar 2020
2. Report of Questionnaire survey on Information Security Incidents. http://lab.iisec.ac.jp/~hiromatsu_lab/sub07.html. 20 Mar 2020
3. New type APT. https://www.ipa.go.jp/files/000024542.pdf. 20 Mar 2020
4. Measures for Developing Cybersecurity Human Resources Inter-Group Working Report. https://www.nisc.go.jp/conference/cs/pdf/jinzai-sesaku2018set.pdf. 20 Mar 2020
5. Ministry of Economy, Trade and Industry, Japan "List of security-related contents for operators" https://www.meti.go.jp/policy/netsecurity/secdoc/ope_contents.html
6. NICE Cybersecurity Framework. https://www.nist.gov/cyberframework. 20 Mar 2020
7. Hanada, K.: Research on the skill and human resources development of the information security staff IPSJ SIG Technical Repert, VoL2012 − CSEC − 58 No. 3, pp. 261–265
8. Nakaya, M., Tominaga, H.: Trial practices of offensive and defense hacking competition for game website. IPSJ Trans. CE 2018 **12**, 1–8 (2018)
9. Yukawa, M., Iguchi, N.: Implementation of fraudulent access scenario using network-based intrusion detection system on virtual machine-based network security learning system enabling offensive and defensive battle exercise. IPSJ Trans. IOTS 2018, 92–99 (2018)
10. Son, Y., Yamaguchi, Y., Shimada, H., Takakura, H.: A curriculum analysis for information security curriculum development enforcing on technical competencies. IPSJ J. **58**(5), 1163–1174
11. NICE Cybersecurity Workforce Framework. https://www.nist.gov/itl/appliedcybersecurity/nice/resources/nicecybersecurity-workforce-framework. 20 Mar 2020
12. Ozaki, S.: Proposal to visualize the contents of information security guidelines based on the Cybersecurity Framework. IPS J. **60**(12), 2196–2210
13. Translations. https://www.nist.gov/cyberframework/framework. 21 Mar 2020

Cyber Trust in the Norwegian Online Flea Market: An Ethnographic Study on Fraud

Yushan Pan[✉]

Norwegian University of Science and Technology, Trondheim, Norway
yushan.pan@ntnu.no

Abstract. This work-in-progress paper reports an ethnographic study on how cyber trust could be designed to prevent online fraud. A yearlong ethnographic study was conducted with a group of victims who were scammed in online shopping. I discuss how to re-build cyber trust by linking the various interests of actors, such as sellers, the police, the Consumer Council, the person registers authority, the national collection agency, and the classified advertisements website provider, with an anticipated safety for online shopping. Through the actor-network theory, this paper unpacks the mechanism behinds payment method of classified advertisements website and discusses cyber trust which are unsuccessful in the present case. The reason behind this is that the interests of different actors are likely not translated, which causes vulnerability and provides an opportunity for scammers. I assert that a better understanding of the social aspect of technology use will provide fruitful insights on societal changes in today's information society for better living.

Keywords: Ethnography · Safety · Online shopping · Social computing

1 Introduction

The interaction between work practice and technology has always been a central research focus within information systems, with its aim to design information systems to support human interaction in the cooperative environment. Ethnographic studies of information systems in use have demonstrated that successful information systems are inseparable from the situated activities in which they exist, and user-centred and situated design is advocated [1–3]. Such situated, worker-oriented design might involve further development, such as safety concerns in cooperation [4]. When investigating information systems in use, we see unexpected unsafe results, which points to deviations from the original design goals and objectives and the unintended consequences of using online shopping platforms such as the Norwegian online flea market.

However, in contrast to regular online stores that control unsafe purchasing on their own platforms, the online flea market, for various reasons, denies some of the responsibility for safety control outside the platform; instead, the platform suggests that both buyers and sellers use common sense, avoid prepayment, and use caution when dealing with personal information. For example, if a buyer comes across an offer that seems too good to be true, the buyer should know that it is likely a fake ad. The buyer should not prepay before asking the seller to verify his or her users on the platform

© Springer Nature Switzerland AG 2020
C. Stephanidis and M. Antona (Eds.): HCII 2020, CCIS 1226, pp. 589–596, 2020.
https://doi.org/10.1007/978-3-030-50732-9_76

through personal identification systems. Moreover, both buyers and sellers should be careful when sharing personal information; the platform suggests that if one shares only his or her first name, address, and telephone number, it would be safe enough [5].

Thus, the role of information systems as platforms has placed little focus on cooperative safety. Although empirical studies have focused on safety in technology use, most have only focused on privacy. There is still a lack of empirical studies that investigate how a safety mechanism could be designed in sociotechnical information systems for online shopping, such that information systems and work practices evolve together.

The importance of understanding this safety mechanism may become more evident if we consider the changes that have occurred within information technology in recent years. For example, in the maritime domain, safety issues were neither due to technical problems of systems nor the issues of human organisations. Safety issues occurs during the cooperation between the networked human, information systems, and interactions among humans and systems [4, 6]. This understanding of the safety mechanism deviates from safety studies in information systems. For example, safety is considered to be ethical and political [7–14], as are highly reliable human organisations [15–20]. Moreover, such a safety mechanism differs from those understandings in which safety is part of the systems and applications' attributes in systems models.

When safety issues occur during cooperation, and there is no mechanism for protecting the rights for the buyers and sellers, unsafe online purchase will happen. An example of this is if the seller has certified his or her personal ID on the platform, the buyer trusts the ads, and both sides make a deal regarding how to finalise the purchase, such as the buyer pays half of the asking price and pays the rest after receiving the item. Alternatively, perhaps the seller trusts the buyer and ships the item first. Both solutions have high risks which go beyond the current argument of ethical, privacy, and security issues in the support platform. In other words, the platform provider offers less secure information systems to the market. This paper reports an ethnographic study on the Norwegian online flea market. Through the investigation of a real case, the aim of the paper is to identify several breakdowns that occur when online fraud happens in the use of an information system provided by one of the largest online markets in Norway.

This paper is structured as follows: in Sect. 2, the research methodology, including the case, the research site, and method, is presented. Section 3 describes an ethnographic study of victims who have helped themselves find a solution to discover the scammer and convince other actors to act on the cases until, finally, they caught the scammer and requested money back. In line with my ethnographic description, in highly practical terms, Sect. 4 reflects on how to design a better information systems platform for online flea markets to provide more safe and secure experiences for both buyers and sellers. Section 5 then concludes the paper.

2   Methodology

2.1   The Case and the Research Site

The Norwegian online flea market was established in the 1990s with sections devoted to secondhand stuff. The purpose is to classify advertisements to transfer straightforward information from the seller to the buyer. In contrast to the business-to-customer model, the online flea market builds upon the integrity mechanism which leaves buyers and sellers to response their own risks a transaction. Such a flea market also differs from eBay in that there are no payment methods. This means no secure payment between sellers and buyers.

The flea market platform also does not use any third party during purchases. To secure a purchase, the two parties involved are recommended to meet in person. However, this may be inconvenient for sellers and buyers who are not in the same place. In this case, the platform suggests a few tips for both buyers and sellers to ensure the deal is protected in some way. If the buyer intends not to pay, for example, the seller could ask the platform to help with the crime case if the police were to get involved. Moreover, if the seller does not release an item after the buyer has paid for it, the buyer could ask the platform to help with the case as well.

However, if fraud occurs, no one could solve the problem until someone could help buyers. Unfortunately, in this study, the fraud had never solved, since no one could close the case. A buyer wanted to buy a mobile phone, but he decided to check the flea market, since the price is sometimes lower than when buying a brand new one. He found a phone that he wanted to buy. Then, he sent an email to the seller, as suggested by the online platform, asking the following questions: 'Why you want to sell? Do you have receipt for this phone? If we could not meet, how we could reach a deal?' Soon, the seller replied that the reason she wanted to sell the phone was because her boyfriend, who gave her the phone as a gift, betrayed her. She decided to sell the gift, since she did not need it. She presented the receipt from the phone's purchase with her name printed on the paper. However, she wanted the buyer to pay full price before she sent the phone to the buyer's address.

In this situation, the buyer checked whether the seller was recognised with a national ID before he decided whether to pay or find another option. He found that the seller was registered with a national ID, but he still had some doubt, so he replied to the seller that he would not pay but would instead choose to sign a standard contract provided by the customer council of Norway. The seller, however, did not want to sign the contract, so she proposed another solution that the buyer could pay half of the total amount immediately; otherwise, there would be no deal. Since the buyer had checked all suggested information and really wanted to buy the mobile phone, he accepted the solution. The seller then sent her bank account number to the buyer.

The buyer paid half the price to the seller, including the postage fee; then, the seller sent the tracking number of the package to the buyer. The agreement was that, when the buyer received the mobile phone, he would pay the remaining amount. All of these activities happened on Sunday. According to Norwegian Banks, a transaction cannot be made immediately, but one can register it online. This means that a person cannot see to whom he or she is transfer money – only the account number. The owner of an account would only be visible after two working days. In the meantime, if the buyer has any doubt, he or she could cancel the transaction. This is the last chance for the buyer to cancel if he or she finds the sale to be fraudulent. In this case, however, everything went smoothly, and he believed that he would receive the package on Monday or Tuesday. At the very least, he thought, he would have more information on where the package was and whom he paid.

On Monday, the buyer found out from the postal service that the package was not addressed to him; rather, the address was another city a thousand kilometre away from the buyer's address. He asked the seller what was wrong. The seller pretended she sent it to the wrong place and promised to correct it with the post office. She did correct it, but she told the buyer by email, saying that she could not take photos because her phone had dropped on the floor and was having problems taking pictures. The buyer believed her, still believing that he would receive the mobile phone. He chose to wait another two days since, in that time, if everything was correct, he would receive the package. Two days later, however, the package was dropped off at the wrong destination.

This time, he chose to ask the post office whether the package was really addressed to him. The post office confirmed that the package was addressed to no one and that it was not addressed to where the buyer lived. Then, the buyer logged on to his bank account to ask the bank to send him a receipt showing where the money went. The bank returned a paper form showing that the money was sent to a man who was living in place that was different from the seller's registered address on the online platform. It was then that the buyer was certain this must be fraud. He warned the seller via email, telling him to return the money or do the right thing to finish the deal. However, this time, there was no reply.

The buyer decided to report the case to the online platform. The online platform asked the buyer to provide all information exchanged between him and the seller. In the meantime, the platform again checked whether the seller had registered any national ID. The conclusion was sent from the online platform via their internal email systems, stating that the buyer needed to contact the customer council of Norway and the police, because, according to the law, the online platform did not have the right to further process a fraud case. The only thing the online platform could provide was a case number indicating that it was an online fraud.

The buyer later contacted the police and gave the customer council the case number provided by the online platform. The police replied that they received the case and would now investigate it. Half a year later, police notified the buyer that the online scammer was being tracked down, and a lawyer was now involved in the case. There was no clear answer regarding when the case would be closed. Police also suggested that the buyer not contact them anymore, since it was a low-priority case. If there was an update, they would notify the buyer. After a half-year investigation, however, the customer council decided to close the case, because it was impossible for the council to process it further if the seller never responded to their requests. They tried to email, post mail, and call the seller; however, since there was no reply, they needed to get back to the buyer and suggest that the buyer close the case. Nevertheless, the buyer had the right to reopen the case if there was any update from the police; in such a case, the council could then request money back from the seller.

2.2   Method

Ethnography is a suitable foundation for integrating and gathering online and offline data to obtain the 'overflowing description' [21]. Around 40% of my free time during the past year was spent online and offline, talking with the buyer, the online platform, the police, and the customer council. Moreover, I observed and listened to the conversations between the buyer and bank, police, Customer Council, and online platform. In addition, under the permission of the buyer, I read the information exchanged between the buyer and the organisation.

3   No Money Comes Back

The buyer, himself, investigated whether the seller was a scammer. He found there was a safety logo after the seller's name ('Anonymous' in this paper, although the name used online was a fake one). This means that the seller logged into the classified advertisements website with an authorised ID. Such an ID is commonly used in Norway as biometric authorisation for logging into public and financing services, such as banks, insurance companies, health information systems, and digital post, among others. The victims are affected by this logo. The reason for this is that the website says that anyone who has registered an address in Norway and with a BankID, if wanted, could log in with that BankID for verified user status [22]. This verified status builds victims' trust, even though there is no secure payment method between the buyer and seller. However, even if the ID is correct, the seller or buyer could still be a scammer.

Victims pay these scammers through bank transfers due to living in different locations and the difficulty of meeting in person. The banks have records of where the money goes, revealing, for example, the account owner, as well as the owner's registered address, email, and telephone number. To investigate how the banks could help the victims, I followed the victim I met to the bank. I discovered that the bank could not get hi money back; they could only provide a letter indicating the possible scammer. In this particular case, the letter showed a different name, a different email, a different telephone number, and a different registered address. The victim then contacted both the website and the Customer Council. This was alarming – if such personal information was different from the registered user's name on the website, was BankID verification trustworthy? Why would the website allow sellers or buyers to use a different name than the registered name associated with the BankID? Unfortunately, the website refused to disclose more information about that scammer due to its data protection policy.

Such freedom to use a different name from that associated with the BankID gives scammers the opportunity to cheat. Moreover, the lack of a payment method powered by the website makes the deal even riskier. In this case, the Customer Council confirmed the case reporting. However, they called the victim and said they could not help either. With their experience, they suggested that the victim give up, since they were unable to find the scammer.

The victim collected as much material as he could. He had materials from the Customer Council, the bank confirmation letter, the screenshots of the advertisement, and the email exchanges between the scammer and him. He then tried his last hope: the police. He sent all materials to the police and asked for help. In a postal letter, the police confirmed that they received the report and created a crime case. In that letter, the police told the victim that a notification would be sent when the investigation was finished.

However, this is not the end of the case, and money has still not been returned. The police said that the person was arrested and the case was forwarded to the national collection agency, where the victim could get his money back. However, the victim received another letter from the national collection agency, requesting that he fill out a form. In this form, the victim was promised that his account would be credited the lost money. The victim returned the form and waited for the money, but nothing happened after that. Since this is a work-in-progress paper, I am still collecting data and hope to interview the national collection agency soon.

4   The Cyber Trust

In this analysis, I address contexts of cyber trust which go beyond the purely technical issues of security design in computer systems and the interaction of those computer systems. As seen, the scammer bypassed the biometric authorisation and legally registered and verified himself on the classified advertisements website. Since the website allows the use of a nickname, rather than the real name associated with the BankID, the scammer could use a fraudulent name, email, and telephone number to cheat. This is perhaps the website's greatest flaw.

In his user experience research, Mertzum [23] argues that organisational usability is about the match between the user and the system, between the organisation and the system, and between the environment and the system. Organisational usability must be evaluated in situ. The computer systems must be used for real work. The same could apply to the organisational cyber trust. Fraud does not happen due to technical failures in online shopping. Victims do not face failures of the system; they could easily log in and see the advertainments. Victims also do not face identification and authentication problems. Instead, their trust in identification and authentication techniques causes them to believe the scammer. Such identification and authentication techniques empower the scammer as a good user. In this way, failures and errors are not about wrong passwords, wrong identification tokens, or misuse of the biometrics. The fact is that the algorithms for identification and authentication discriminate the victims during their interactions with the scammers on the website. I do not suggest that the algorithms have any technical problems. The problems are hidden in practices. Cyber trust in such practices is only about individual interaction with cybersecurity systems. More than that, it is about re-examining cybersecurity technology from a holistic point of view. Only by zooming out from a single technical issue could we see the problem in the whole information infrastructure.

5 Concluding Remarks

This article has presented an ethnographic study on cyber trust from a user's perspective. The study has analysed the problematic areas in information systems that are proposed to support a safe environment for dealing with the purchase of secondhand goods online. By analysing different actors in the information systems, their interests, and the website's interpretation of cyber trust, an outline of reconsidering cyber trust is suggested. The article asserts that cyber trust is more than technical solutions to prevent attacks and misuse of user cases in human-interface interaction. This evaluation of cyber trust must be put into real use to reveal inviable problems that are hidden in cooperation, organisation, and technical solutions in cybersecurity issues of information systems for e-commerce. To conclude, this article suggests combining both technical and social aspects of safety concerns when addressing cyber trust.

In the present case, several authorities failed to help the buyer for various reasons. The most important reason, however, was the privacy protection policy. It is understandable that the website was not able to share the scammer's personal information with the buyer. It becomes problematic that if one could use BankID to verify him or herself, should it be a problem to share information between the bank, the police, the Customer Council, and the national collection agency. It may be beyond the scope of this study to address relative laws. However, it would helpful if the website could find a payment method which builds upon the BankID and enables traceability if fraud were to occur. Such a method may be a useful tool to secure both buyers and sellers from a user's perspective. Then, cyber trust would go beyond the discussion on human-interface interaction by combining technical and social aspects of safety concerns within an infrastructure of dependency, identification and authentication, privacy, and usability. In turn, such an infrastructure could serve as a mechanism between users and security techniques from a social-technical perspective to protect all stakeholders' goals and views.

References

1. Greenbaum, J., Kyng, M.: Design at Work: Cooperative Design of Computer Systems. Lawrence Erlbaum, New Jersey (1991)
2. Suchmann, L., Blomberg, J., Orr, J.E., Trigg, R.: Reconstructing technologies as social practice. Am. Behav. Sci. 3, 392–408 (1999)
3. Aanestad, M.: The camera as an actor design-in-use of telemedicine infrastructure in surgery. Comput. Support. Coop. Work 12, 1–20 (2003)
4. Pan, Y.: From field to simulator: visualizing ethnographic outcomes to support systems developers (2018)
5. FINN.NO: Nyttige tips for en trygg handel. https://hjelpesenter.finn.no/hc/no/articles/115005831409-Nyttige-tips-for-en-trygg-handel
6. Pan, Y., Finken, S.: From offshore operation to onshore simulator: using visualized ethnographic outcomes to work with systems developers. Informatics 5, 10 (2018)
7. Abokhodair, N., Vieweg, S.: Privacy & social media in the context of the Arab gulf. In: Proceedings of the 2016 ACM Conference on Designing Interactive Systems - DIS 2016, pp. 672–683 (2016)

8. Yarosh, S., Bonsignore, E., McRoberts, S., Peyton, T.: YouthTube: youth video authorship on YouTube and Vine. In: Proceedings of the 19th ACM Conference on Computer-Supported Cooperative Work & Social Computing - CSCW 2016, pp. 1421–1435 (2016)
9. Hoyle, R., Das, S., Kapadia, A., Lee, A., Vaniea, K.: Viewing the viewers: publishers' desires and viewers' privacy concerns in social networks. In: CSCW 2017, pp. 555–566 (2017)
10. Zytko, D., Lingel, J., Birnholtx, J., Ellison, N., Hancock, J.: Online dating as pandora's box: methodological issues for the CSCW community. In: CSCW 2015, pp. 131–134 (2015)
11. Forte, A., Andalibi, N., Greenstadt, R.: Privacy, anonymity, and perceived risk in open collaboration: a study of Tor users and wikipedians. In: Proceedings of the Computer Supported Cooperative Work. Soc. Comput., pp. 1800–1811 (2017)
12. Raval, N., Dourish, P.: Standing out from the crowd: emotional labor, body labor, and temporal labor in ridesharing. In: CSCW 2016, pp. 97–107 (2016)
13. Ozcan, K., Jorgenson, D., Richard, C., Hsieh, G.: Designing for targeted responder models: exploring barriers to respond. In: CSCW 2017, pp. 916–924 (2017)
14. Wisniewski, P., Ghosh, A.K., Xu, H., Rosson, M.B., Carroll, J.M.: Parental control vs. teen self-regulation: Is there a middle ground for mobile online safety? In: Proceedings of the ACM Conference on Computer Supported Cooperative Work, CSCW, pp. 51–69 (2017)
15. Perrow, C.: A society of organizations. Theory Soc. **20**, 725–762 (1991)
16. Perrow, C.: Normal Accidents: Living with High Risk Technologies (1985)
17. Weick, K.E.: Organizational culture as a source of high reliability. Calif. Manage. Rev. **29**, 112–127 (1987)
18. Harper, R.R., Hughes, J.A., Shapiro, D.Z.: Harmonious working and CSCW: computer technology and air traffic control. In: Studies in Computer Supported Cooperative Work, pp. 225–233 (1991)
19. LaPorte, T.R., Consolini, P.M.: Working in practice but not in theory: theoretical challenges of "High-Reliability Organizations". J. Public Adm. Res. Theory. **1**, 19–48 (1991)
20. Bentley, R., Hughes, J., Randall, D., Shapiro, D.: Technological support for decision making in a safety critical environment. Saf. Sci. **19**, 149–156 (1995)
21. Sade-Beck, L.: Internet ethnography: online and offline. Int. J. Qual. Methods **3**, 45–51 (2004)
22. FINN.NO: Hvordan blir jeg en verifisert bruker? [How do I become a verified user?]. https://hjelpesenter.finn.no/hc/no/articles/202612752-Hvordan-blir-jeg-en-verifisert-bruker
23. Hertzum, M.: Three contexts for evaluating organizational usability. J. Usability Stud. **14**, 35–47 (2018)

Attention! Designing a Target Group-Oriented Risk Communication Strategy

Lara Raffel[(⊠)], Patrick Bours, and Sashidharan Komandur

Norges Teknisk Naturvitenskapelig Universitet (NTNU) Gjøvik,
Teknologiveien 22, 2815 Gjøvik, Norway
lara.raffel@gmail.com

Abstract. Online conversations through chat applications have become a universal part of human communication. But how can we be sure that the person we are chatting with is in fact the person they claim to be? This question significantly gains importance from the standpoint of safety and security when considering the chat behavior of children who are allowed access to web-enabled devices at an increasingly younger age. At the same time, the number of reported experiences with online sexual harassment and so-called grooming is unfortunately growing steadily. This paper presents insights from focus groups with school children and a resulting approach to communicating the risk of cyber grooming. The paper explores communication strategies for different stages of risk – before, during and after an incident. The way people interpret information affects the way they interact with it, which is why a user-centered design approach is employed in addition to standard guidelines of design to structure and design a communication strategy. Protecting children from sexual predators who use grooming strategies to bond with their victims is the main goal of this project.

Keywords: Chat security · Warning design · Risk communication · Grooming · Human factors · User-centered design

1 Background

1.1 AiBA

This project is conducted as part of the AiBA (Author Input Behavioral Analysis) project by the Norwegian Biometry Lab at NTNU Gjøvik. AiBA aims at identifying fake profiles in chat applications using behavioral biometrics, in particular for protecting children from sexual predators that find their victims online. For example, behavioral biometrics can reveal an adult pretending to be a teenager in order to groom children online. The algorithms analyse word usage, writing rhythm, linguistics and media input to differentiate between adults and children as well as between males and females. The system is trained with data

© Springer Nature Switzerland AG 2020
C. Stephanidis and M. Antona (Eds.): HCII 2020, CCIS 1226, pp. 597–604, 2020.
https://doi.org/10.1007/978-3-030-50732-9_77

from convicted abuse cases and chat data acquired from children using a chat prototype. It is envisioned that the algorithms will either be built into platforms and applications used by children, such as Roblox, Snapchat and Instagram, or will act as a standalone application that retrieves data from the chats. Alerting the users that such a security measurement is in place will contribute to deterring those with dishonest intentions, since there is a higher chance of being disclosed.

1.2   Online Grooming

Grooming describes behavioral patterns that are applied by sexual predators in preparation to sexually abuse a child. Colton et al. [4] describe grooming as a complex process in which the predator gains access to the chosen victim so that abuse can be initiated and maintained without being disclosed over time. However, literature shows no consensus over the specific methods that are employed by offenders [2] and empirical research has found that it is hard to recognize grooming behavior prior to abuse since it is not always clearly distinguishable from normal adult-child interactions [16]. Nevertheless, Winters et al. [16] describe that almost half of all convicted child abuse cases in the US have been preceded by what was identified as grooming behavior. Lanning [10] developed an accurate description of the process and emphasizes that grooming is a non-violent practice that aims at sexual victimization and control without using threats or physical force, as these techniques are more likely to result in cooperation from the victim's side. Lanning [9] describes the process of grooming as incremental stages, starting with identification of targets based on certain factors, followed by gathering information about the child's interests and vulnerabilities. The offender then gains access to the victim through a variety of channels, for example through clubs, sports or online. The victim is controlled by the offender by a combination of strategies such as filling emotional or physical needs, bonding, sympathy or peer pressure. The internet and its infinite number of chat platforms has opened up a new channel for child offenders to gain access to victims and provides the offenders with anonymity and a wide reach to locate victims. Goals of online sexual grooming include cyber-sexual activity, access to child pornography or arranging in-person meetings [8].

1.3   Risk Communication

Risk communication describes a set of communication measures that prepares the audience for informed decision making before, during and after an event [5]. Risk communication originates from the public health sector where it is used to communicate and educate about health risks and epidemics. The approach has also been adapted to communicate risks of natural disasters such as floods and fires, but it can also be practiced on a smaller scale, for example in the practice of warning messages and labels [11]. Lundgren et al. [11] point out that there are a vast number of approaches to risk communication that have evolved from various disciplines and that the approach should be chosen according to the context and the audience. The risk communication process usually starts with a risk assessment that evaluates who will be harmed by the hazard and what effects can be expected, as well as how long these effects last. A strategy is developed how awareness can be raised about the subject and how the audience can be educated. Information about how to take action in case of an event needs to be communicated in a clear and understandable manner. Also, a risk communication strategy should be disseminated through channels that are frequented by the target audience [11]. In addition, it is recommended to design messages according to the audiences' knowledge, interests and values [3]. Lundgren et al. [11] emphasize that the more the communicators understand the perspective of the target audience(s), the better they can choose appropriate communication methods and thus implement successful risk communication. This shows the prominent role that user research should play in risk communication and justifies the user-centred approach taken in this project.

2 Methodology

2.1 Focus Groups with Children in 7th Grade

With the goal of acquiring profound insights into the perception and knowledge about online sexual predators and grooming strategies, focus groups were designed to investigate children's chat behavior, how they react to certain messages in chats and to what extent they are aware of dangers. Two seventh grade classes with a total number of 35 pupils participated in two project days about "Chat Security". To investigate the impact of education on the subject, two focus groups were conducted before a presentation on chat security and grooming strategies was given, and four groups after, resulting in six focus groups being conducted at the school, each consisting of 5–6 children of 12 to 13 years. During preparation, it was taken into consideration that working with children results in certain challenges such as differences in children's development due to their culture and social environment [1], ensuring the children's engagement and attention [7] as well as their safety and comfort [12]. It was investigated how they think they can trust someone online and where they draw the line between appropriate and inappropriate messages. The focus groups concluded with an assessment of the concept behind the AiBA project.

The focus groups were divided into three sections. In the opening part, a brainstorming session was conducted, first on what the participants use the Internet for, and then more specifically what applications they use for chatting with other people. This data can be used to establish the most effective locations for placing information about online predators and also potential customers for the AiBA application. To challenge the children's creativity, they were then asked to come up with a username for a fictional chat. Since usernames are one of the targeting criteria of sexual predators [17], the data will be helpful to determine how children choose them. After presenting the usernames, the moderator challenged the participants by exchanging her username with one of the children's. They were asked to come up with ideas how to find out who really is behind a nickname and how to trust someone online. The second part of the focus group consisted of a made-up chat conversation that followed a simplified grooming process. The children were challenged to come up with replies or reactions to the messages which got increasingly inappropriate. After each message, the children were asked if they thought this message was written by someone of their age, an adult or if it could be both. This data will give insights about how children behave in chats and where they draw the line between appropriate and inappropriate conversations. As the last part, the AiBA project was summarised in a simple and understandable way. The children were then asked to rate how much they liked the idea of such a system by assigning a number (1 being worst and 10 being best) on a sheet of paper. They were also asked to write down a reason for their decision. After each focus group, some notes were taken on the children's overall behavior and reactions, as well as their body language and other remarks.

3   Results

The collected data was mainly of qualitative nature, showing opinions, experiences and reactions of the children. This data was analysed by applying a mix of design methods such as thematic evaluation and affinity diagramming. Exploratory statistical analyses was also used. Special attention was given to understand differences between the groups who have not received education about the subject and those who have. Already on location during the project days, it was possible to notice some immediate results. It was clear to see that there are immense individual differences in how the pupils reacted to the prompted chat messages, some being very honest, others extremely careful or evading through humour and irony. On the second day - after the presentation on chat security and online grooming - it was very striking to observe how much more careful and suspicious the children were acting. Their behavior changed and they were more direct in differentiating between appropriate and inappropriate messages. Also, the terms "sexual predator", "kidnapper" and "pedophile" were mentioned regularly, while this had not occurred on the previous day.

After an in-depth analysis, one could see that educating children about chat security and grooming can show immediate, short-term results. The children became more aware of the risk and were discussing about sexual predators several times during the focus groups if they had been educated before. The focus groups showed the popularity of using Snapchat among children of 12 and 13 years as well as their strong interest in playing online games and consuming media content. These platforms can be important partners to spread education on online grooming and could also be potential customers for the AiBA system. The children mostly chat with friends, but it is not uncommon to chat with strangers when it is about a common interest, such as gaming. The children felt confident that they could detect an adult who tries to pretend to be a teenager through the language that is used and also the content of the conversation. They rated pictures or video calls as the most reliable option to find out about someone's real identity. When creating usernames, the children unintentionally gave away personal information such as their name and age, regardless whether they had attended the presentation on chat security or not. In a fictional chat environment, those children who received education on grooming before were more self-assured to say "no", acted more confident and suspected dishonest behavior sooner than children without previous education on the topic. The overall rating of the AiBA system was more positive after the presentation, showing that the children saw more value in it than before.

The insights were further evaluated with a set of gamestorming methods as described by Gray [6], resulting in a risk assessment. The reason for a need of education are the high level of Internet access and chat usage at an increasingly younger age, meanwhile predators are using chats as a means for easy access to victims. As estimated by a recent EU study [14], children aged 12–14 years in the EU spend around 192 min online each day. Children are particularly at risk once they start conversing with strangers and give away private information, either unknowingly (i.e. through usernames), due to risk-seeking behavior (doing something "forbidden") or simply because they are not aware of the danger and engage in seemingly harmless conversations. The European Online Grooming Report [15] describes that children that are perceived by predators as particularly vulnerable are more likely to be targeted, as well as risk-taking children who are outgoing and confident online - similar to the children in the focus groups who reacted to the chat messages with humour or by being offensive. However, while it is important to take these risk factors into account, children at risk should not be stigmatised or reduced to a homogeneous group as both individual behavior and targeting tactics of online predators vary greatly. Challenges that are faced when tackling the topic are the general unawareness of the children who are active in chats and also the parent's lack of knowledge about the subject. It is sometimes treated as a taboo topic that evokes feelings of shame, it can result in victim-blaming and is seen with hindsight-bias, meaning that people claim to have "seen it coming" only after an incident, or the risk is being ignored as it seems unlikely to happen to oneself. Since children want to maintain a certain level of autonomy and privacy, a lack of parental supervision can increase the risk, as well as a lack of security measures in many chat applications. However, if the risk is not addressed, it means that ultimately more children will fall victim to sexual abuse, either through physical meetings with the predators or through online activities. Children will be exposed to sexual content and might share private pictures and information. This can result in the children being bullied, threatened or blackmailed which in turn results in psychological damage and a dependency on the relationship with the predator. In real life, consequences can be seen in a problematic relationship with the parents and peers, since the online relationship gains importance. Therefore, the goal of the risk communication is mainly preventive, aiming at children who engage in chat environments, whose safety and security as well as privacy and autonomy should be secured. Educating them about grooming will increase their caution on the web, enable them to protect themselves and give them the courage to report incidents.

As children spent a vast amount of time on the Internet, spreading information directly in the chat environments, on social media or gaming platforms is believed to be an appropriate choice of media. Furthermore, postings on social media can be used to target specific user groups that are at a higher risk. The children should be able to relate to the messengers that convey the content, therefore it is important that the messenger is close to the peer group and that the wording appeals to them. This is believed to increase the children's interest in the content and work against barriers such as ignorance and shame. Another effective way to reach the children is to conduct seminar days at schools similar to those conducted during the user research. This can provide the children with valuable background knowledge of Internet security and online behavior that can encourage them to rethink and adjust their own behavior. Building on this, the messages for precautionary advocacy can be designed, taking into account the guidelines for warning design by Sandman [13]. Thus, the messages need to be on point, raise interest, appeal to emotions and offer choice. Short, concise and understandable messages ensure that the information is interpreted in the intended way. Additionally, messages need to be interesting and appealing to the audience so that they are heeded in the first place. In combination with appealing to emotions (especially fear in proportion to the risk), chances are high that people will pay attention. Offering choices of actions to take, preferably in easy and small steps, encourages necessary changes in behavior. The main questions that need to be answered at this stage are: How does online grooming happen? What are the consequences? How can I protect myself?

The immediate response phase to a risk is triggered when the AiBA system detects suspicious behavior that indicates predatory behavior. A warning has to be sent so that the child and the parents can decide how to respond to the threat. For creating these warnings, design principles can be applied regarding the structure, understandability, noticeability and context of the messages [18]. The goal of the warning message is to make the user aware that the chat partner is showing signs of predatory behavior or grooming. The message needs to attract the users attention, so it needs to be prominently displayed and designed. Timing is crucial as sending a warning too late can result in harm to the child, while sending it too early can result in unfounded fear and false accusations. In order to justify the message and to ensure understandability, it needs to be explained how the system arrived at this conclusion, for instance by listing the suspicious characteristics of the conversation. The risk and its consequences should be explained briefly to mark the urgency of the situation and the need to take action. The warning needs to present choices and recommendations for subsequent actions in easy steps. For instance, a checklist can help the user to identify grooming behavior and if the chat partner should be blocked and reported. Since AiBA will not be infallible, the final decision to take action lies with the user.

After the immediate risk has been averted, the audience should be given options to recover and react to the incident. The focus of the recovery phase lies on providing support and counteracting apathy. The information should be sent directly to the audience so that they immediately have access to it after AiBA warned them about predatory behavior. Additionally, the information should be available on demand so that it can be reviewed at all times. Crucial points to consider are providing emotional support, indicating institutions where one can receive additional help and encouraging that grooming should be reported. Again, the information should encourage young people to draw lines and stand up for their own well-being.

4   Discussion

The short term results of the focus groups show that education about online security and grooming does seem to influence behavior and makes children more aware of risks on the web and thus more careful. The extensive use of the web and particularly chat environments by young children shows the importance of this project. Also, the high interest that the children have shown towards the topic gives hope that education measures will be received eagerly and the seriousness of this is understood very well. However, further assessment is needed to establish long term results. The importance of education on online grooming for raising awareness and preventing abuse is backed up by previous research [15]. Establishing information needs and extracting the key messages for each stage of risk communication allows for differentiated information distribution that provides the audience with relevant information when it is needed.

Work in Progress: Additional focus groups with children are planned to strengthen the results and gain additional insights. Furthermore, the communication strategy will be supplemented by a similar approach that provides information for parents, since they serve as role models and close confidants of the children. Future work will consist of refining the strategy and creating a set of tangible messages and information materials that will be evaluated and adapted based on user tests. The completed strategy will be presented in a master's thesis at NTNU and is hoped to be implemented with the completion of the AiBA system, providing children and parents with both education and practical means to protect themselves and their loved ones on the web. The interdisciplinary nature of this project is meant to encourage people working in design, risk communication and computer security to cooperate. It shows that user-centered design approach can be applied to a variety of fields outside the traditional design context. A multi-faceted risk such as online grooming needs to be managed as a collaborative approach in order to promote prevention and minimise the degree of harm.

References

1. Adler, K., Salanterä, S., Zumstein-Shaha, M.: Focus group interviews in child, youth, and parent research: an integrative literature review. Int. J. Qual. Methods **18**, 1912–1918 (2019)
2. Bennett, N., O'Donohue, W.: The construct of grooming in child sexual abuse: conceptual and measurement issues. J. Child Sex. Abuse **23**(8), 957–976 (2014)

3. Boholm, A.: Lessons of success and failure: practicing risk communication at government agencies. Saf. Sci. **118**, 158–167 (2019)
4. Colton, M., Roberts, S., Vanstone, M.: Learning lessons from men who have sexually abused children. Howard J. Crim. Justice **55**(1), 79–93 (2012)
5. Gamhewage, G.: An introduction to risk communication (2014). https://www.who.int/risk-communication/introduction-to-risk-communication.pdf?ua=1. Accessed 11 Nov 2019
6. Gray, D., Brown, S., Macanufo, J.: Gamestorming: A Playbook for Innovators, Rulebreakers, and Changemakers. O'Reilly (2010)
7. Kennedy, C., Kools, S., Krueger, R.: Methodological considerations in children's focus groups. Nurs. Res. **50**, 184–187 (2001)
8. Lanning, K.: Compliant child victim: confronting an uncomfortable reality. In: Quayle, E., Taylor, M. (eds.) Viewing child pornography on the Internet, pp. 49–60. Russell House (2005)
9. Lanning, K.: Child molesters: A behavioral analysis, 5th edn. National Center for Missing & Exploited Children (2010)
10. Lanning, K.: The evolution of grooming: concept and term. J. Interpersonal Violence **33**(1), 5–16 (2018)
11. Lundgren, R., McMakin, A.: Risk communication: A Handbook for Communicating Environmental, Safety, and Health Risks. Wiley-IEEE (2009)
12. McGarry, O.: Repositioning the research encounter: exploring power dynamics and positionality in youth research. Int. J. Soc. Res. Methodol. **19**(3), 339–354 (2016)
13. Sandman, P.: "watch out!" precaution advocacy fundamentals (2007). http://www.psandman.com/handouts/sand59a.pdf. Accessed 12 Mar 2020
14. Smahel, D., et al.: EU kids online 2020: survey results from 19 countries (2020)
15. Webster, S., et al.: European online grooming project - final report (2012)
16. Winters, G.M., Jeglic, E.L.: Stages of sexual grooming: Recognizing potentially predatory behaviors of child molesters. Deviant Behav. **38**(6), 724–733 (2017)
17. Winters, G.M., Kaylor, L.E., Jeglic, E.L.: Sexual offenders contacting children online: an examination of transcripts of sexual grooming. Journal of Sexual Aggression **23**(1), 62–76 (2017)
18. Wogalter, M.S., Conzola, V.C., Smith-Jackson, T.L.: Research-based guidelines for warning design and evaluation. Appl. Ergon. **33**(3), 219–30 (2002)

Understanding the Impact of Service Trials on Privacy Disclosure

Yayoi Suganuma[✉], Jun Narita, Masakatsu Nishigaki, and Tetsushi Ohki[ID]

Shizuoka University, Hamamatsu, Shizuoka, Japan
{suganuma,narita}@sec.inf.shizuoka.ac.jp
{nisigaki,ohki}@inf.shizuoka.ac.jp

Abstract. We have many opportunities to disclose privacy information in exchange for convenient services. In the context of privacy calculus, numerous research studies have been conducted to date on the relation between potential benefits and potential risks of privacy disclosure decisions [1,2]. However, an unresolved problem in the privacy calculus is that the intention of the privacy disclosure may vary not only between users but also in a single user. Our study hypothesized that each user always makes a decision on privacy disclosure depending on the user experience of the service in use. Therefore, we take a user-centered perspective to investigate the impact of service trials on users' privacy disclosure decisions. In this study, a task-based study scenario has designed and tested between lab members. Result of investigation, we find if the service makes users have a good impression after service trials, users tend to provide more privacy disclose.

Keywords: Privacy disclosure · User experience · User-centered perspective

1 Introduction

Privacy is becoming essential for current services. Service providers must elaborate on advertising activities such as commercials and SNS to encourage users to disclose privacy information. Service trials are one such advertising activity. Service trials can ease use of the service by providing free or half-fare.

Privacy disclosure has traditionally been well studied in the field of privacy calculus [1–5]. For example, Malhotra et al. developed a scale for internet users' information privacy concerns (IUIPC) [1]. They also showed the relationship between IUIPC and behavioral intention toward releasing personal information at the request of a marketer. Furthermore, Li et al. stated that exchange benefits, in particular perceived usefulness, have a positive effect on the intention to reveal privacy [2]. Many similar studies indicate that privacy calculus can measure user thoughts on privacy disclosure.

However, it is not easy for service providers, especially while they are developing a service, to understand the intention of a user's privacy disclosure. Moreover,

© Springer Nature Switzerland AG 2020
C. Stephanidis and M. Antona (Eds.): HCII 2020, CCIS 1226, pp. 605–612, 2020.
https://doi.org/10.1007/978-3-030-50732-9_78

we think that an unresolved problem in privacy calculus is that the intention of privacy disclosure may vary not only between users but also for a single user. The objective of our study is to understand the impact of service trials on privacy disclosure and to determine what factors during service trials affect user privacy disclosures.

In our study, we focus on user experience (UX) obtained through service trials. Additionally, we believe that if users gain a better UX through the service trials, users may disclose more privacy in return. In other words, if service providers and users obtain good consensus through service trials, users may perform appropriate privacy disclosures. In particular, we designed a task-based study scenario and tested it between lab members. The scenario consists of tasks to request users to install and try Android apps. We analyzed the behavioral intentions of privacy disclosure before and after service trials using standardized scales and semi-structured interviews.

Our main contribution is introducing the concept of service trials in the context of privacy calculus and empirically examine the effect of service trials with lab study. They reflected our participants' expectations in trial tasks for privacy disclosure and can be used as a good starting point to think about the user-centric design of trial tasks for privacy disclosure.

2   Question and Hypotheses

The research questions pertaining to our paper are as follows:

[**RQ1**] What is the impact of service trials on the privacy disclosures of users?
[**RQ2**] What types of users could be affected by service trials and by disclosing privacy?
[**RQ3**] What factors are affecting users during service trials?

We constructed hypotheses for the above questions as follows:

[**H1**] Better user experiences gained through service trials have a positive impact on the willingness to provide privacy to apps.
[**H2**] The more privacy concerns users have, the less likely users are to be affected by service trials.
[**H3**] Privacy concerns and UX are related to privacy disclosure.

Based on the user study with trial tasks and their responses in a pre-survey and post-survey, we address each of these questions.

3   Methods

We conducted a lab study to test the hypotheses described in Sect. 2. The Android app used for our study is discussed in detail along with the tasks we asked for the participants to perform.

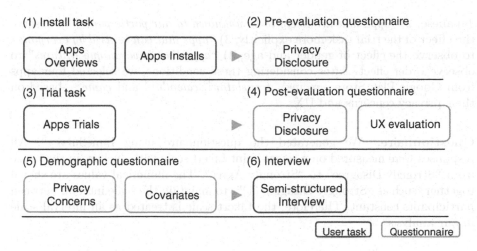

Fig. 1. Conceptual overview of our experimental study scenario

3.1 Study Design

Participants. We had 18 participants; 13 were male and 5 were female, with a mean age of 22(Std.Dev = 1.3 years). The participants who took part in our study were recruited from our university. We explained the purpose of the study, then, for all cases, participants' consent was obtained.

Scenario. Figure 1 presents the conceptual overview of our experimental study scenario. The sessions were split into two tasks, three questionnaires, and semi-structured interview:

1. **Install task:** Participants read the overviews of the apps and installed them.
2. **Pre-evaluation questionnaire:** Participants recorded their behavioral intention (BI) of privacy disclosure for each app in the questionnaire.
3. **Trial task:** Participants try each app.
4. **Post-evaluation questionnaire:** Participants recorded their BI of privacy disclosure and UX in the questionnaire.
5. **Demographic questionnaire:** Participants recorded their privacy concerns and covariates in the questionnaire.
6. **Interview:** A semi-structured interview was conducted.

During the install task, we instructed participants to read the app's features and privacy policy. We used the same questionnaire to measure the BI of privacy disclosure in pre and post evaluation.

Apps. We selected four apps from the Google Play Store during the trial task. We selected apps considering the following four conditions: 1) *"apps' overviews and privacy policy were written by Japanese"* since almost participants consist of

Japanese, 2) *"apps that are likely to be unknown to our participants"* to observe the effect of the trial task more explicitly, 3) *"apps that can be used by everyone"* to observe the effect of gender and age, 4) *"apps that have unique features"* to observe order effect. After considering these conditions, we selected four apps from Google Play Store—*recipe*[1], *translator*[2], *calendar*[3] and *game*[4]—based on their privacy concerns and UX.

Questionnaire. We generated the questionnaire using LimeSurvey[5]. All responses were measured on a seven-point Likert scale with anchors in the range from "Strongly Disagree" to "Strongly Agree". The numerical values are shown together, such as "Strongly Disagree (1)", to maintain the scale interval between participants constant. Therefore, the Likert scale is treated as an interval scale in our analysis.

3.2 Measures

Behavior Intention. For our study, we requested participants to record their BI of privacy disclosure to capture their attitude toward perusing the overview of an app and attitude toward trying the app. We use an existing scale used in the Malhotra et al.'s study [1].

User Experience. We used a standardized questionnaire as a measure of UX: User Experience Questionnaire (UEQ, [6]). The UEQ measures overall attractiveness as well as pragmatic (instrumental) and hedonic (non-instrumental) qualities of experience. The pragmatic qualities subscales include perspicuity, dependability, and efficiency. The hedonic qualities include stimulation and novelty subscales. The items are presented in the format of 26 contrasted pairs of words separated by a seven-points scale (ranging from -3 to 3) as exemplified here.

Privacy Concerns. We assumed the privacy concerns will have a negative impact on privacy disclosure. Therefore, we investigate the privacy concerns of a user using IUIPC proposed by Malhotra et al. [1].

Semi-structured Interviews. To better assess the factors that lead to the variations in consciousness before and after trying apps, we opted for semi-structured interviews. The questions in the interview were pertaining to the

---

[1] "Delish Kitchen," play.google.com/store/apps/details?id=tv.every.delishkitchen.
[2] "Microsoft Translator,"
    play.google.com/store/apps/details?id=com.microsoft.translator.
[3] "Palu - Shared Handwriting Calendar -,"
    play.google.com/store/apps/details?id=com.metamoji.palu.
[4] "Kuukiyomi 2," play.google.com/store/apps/details?id=com.fty.kuukiyomi.
[5] "LimeSurvey," https://www.limesurvey.org.

Table 1. Summary of the response for UEQ

	Increased		Unchanged		Decreased	
	M	SD	M	SD	M	SD
Recipe	1.17	0.49	−0.13	1.16	0.77	0.50
Translator	1.27	0.68	0.64	2.64	0.49	0.85
Calendar	0.78	0.49	0.38	0.48	−0.15	0.47
Game	0.72	1.06	−0.63	1.21	−0.79	0.96

impression before and after trying apps, variations in consciousness before and after trying apps, and privacy concerns on reading the overviews of the apps or trying them. An open discussion was conducted as well, where the participants explained their rationale.

4   Result and Discussion

4.1   Impact of Service Trials

With respect to our [RQ1], we analyzed the relationship between privacy disclosure and service trials. We calculated the score of pre and post evaluation BI for each participant. Then, we divided participants into three groups based on the difference between the score of pre and post-evaluation BI. The group in which the difference was positive set as the increased group. Similarly, the group with no difference was the unchanged group, and the group with the negative difference was the decreased group. We calculated the UEQ for each app in each group. Each group scored UEQ with average means of 0.98 (SD = 0.76) for increased group, 0.08 (SD = 0.95) for unchanged group, and 0.06 (SD = 1.23) for decreased group. At the group level, the average means of UEQ was significantly higher in increased group than decreased group (t(46)= 3.57, p = .00). From this result, we can see that the higher user experiences gained through service trials have a positive impact on the willingness to provide privacy to apps, and the [H1] was supported.

For the further analysis, we show the summary of the UEQ grouped by the difference in BI before and after trial in Table 1. There were significant differences in the increased group and the decreased group of *calendar* and that of *game* (p < .05). On the other hand, there were no significant differences in the increased group and the decreased group of *recipe* and that of *translator*. From the semi-structured interview of *recipe* and *translator*, some participants pointed: "Easy to use. But there are no features I want to use to provide privacy." and "I gained a good impression, but there's no need for recommendations, so there's no need for providing privacy." Thus, one possible reason could be that the factor that the trade-off between features and privacy did not meet.

Table 2. Summary of the response for privacy concerns

	Increased		Unchanged		Decreased	
	M	SD	M	SD	M	SD
Recipe	5.19	0.74	5.44	0.80	5.25	0.88
Translator	5.09	0.76	5.29	0.61	5.36	0.83
Calendar	5.36	0.83	5.66	0.61	5.34	0.61
Game	5.08	1.02	5.39	0.63	5.13	0.82

4.2 Impact of Privacy Concerns

With respect to our [RQ2], we analyzed the relationship between privacy disclosure and privacy concerns. We defined the average of the response of privacy concerns as the score of privacy concerns. Then, we calculated the score of privacy concerns for each app in each group. Table 2 shows the score of privacy concerns for each app in each group. We found that the unchanged group was the highest score of privacy concerns among the three groups. From this results, we found that participants who have high privacy concern are less likely to be affected by a service trial regardless of the app. Thus, [H2] was supported. In addition, except for *calendar*, the decreased group showed a higher score of privacy concerns than the increased group. This also implies that privacy concerns also have slightly negative impact to the privacy disclosure.

4.3 More Effective Service Trial

UEQ Subscales. With respect to our [RQ3], we identified the factor affecting participant during trial. Figure 2 shows the relationship between BI and UEQ using each UEQ subscale. As shown in Fig. 2, we can see that Attractiveness and Hedonic Quality are significantly strong effect to disclosing privacy. In contrast, Pragmatic Quality does not effect in most cases.

Interview. From Fig. 2 and the semi-structured interview, we extracted several important factors for disclosing privacy. Positive factor was the users' impression of the trials. The impression of trials is influenced by various factors such as features, usability, interface, privacy policy, and so on. On the other hand, negative factor was roughly categorized to four factors. (1) Not interested in the first place. (2) Did not mind providing privacy for the feature. (3) Permission request is displayed, but I cannot see what it is used for. (4) Too many advertisements. In our analysis on the negative factors, we excluded the factor (1) and (2) since they are unique factors for each participant. Therefore, focus on the remaining two factors. Focusing on the users who had pointed (3), it seems that the access request that the participants were not explicitly informed the purpose of use caused the distrust of the participants. Then, many participants did not allow the privacy request which cannot estimate the corresponding feature in the app. Especially in the *game*, an access request was displayed immediately after opening the app. However, after trying the app, they found that the requested privacy was not necessary for the app features. This caused significant decrease of BI. As shown in Fig. 2., we can see that Attractiveness and Pragmatic Quality are significantly small in the decreased group of the *game*. On the other hand, when explaining the purpose of use to the participants who pointed out (3), some users had changed their opinion to disclose privacy. From these results, we can say that when accessing user privacy, service providers may need to indicate the need for access to privacy, as well as specify how the information will be returned to the user.

Also, focusing on the users who had pointed (4), advertising that exceeds the functionality of the app itself will lower the user's UX and will cause discomfort for the app. If service providers reduced these factors and that eliminated factors hindering user security, users would disclose privacy naturally.

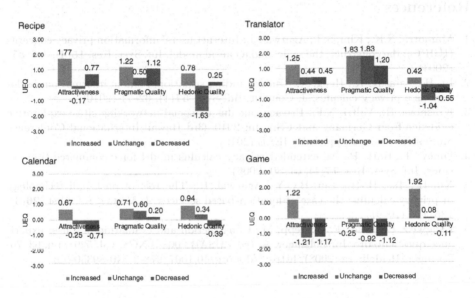

Fig. 2. Result of UEQ grouped by behavioral intention

5 Limitation

We are aware that our research may have limitations. The first is that the participants are students of computer science. Therefore they may stronger security and privacy concerns than the general user. This might cause relatively high privacy concerns scores. The second we could not measure UEQ before installing the app, we subjectively determined whether the impression had been improved. It is plausible that these limitations might have influenced the results obtained.

6   Conclusion

The present study aims to understand the impact of service trials on privacy disclosure and to determine what factors during service trials affect user privacy disclosures. The study makes two main contributions. First, if the service makes users have a good impression after service trials, users tend to provide more privacy disclose. Second, the study identifies the types of users and factors that impact privacy disclosure. Especially, we have shown that the users' privacy concerns make less likely to be affected by service trials. Also, we found that negative effects on privacy disclosure can be categorized into four. The results of this study are thus promising, and we expect the results to contribute to future studies that investigate to what extent service trials on privacy disclosure can be an enabling factor to UX.

References

1. Malhotra, N.K., Kim, S.S., Agarwal, J.: Internet users' information privacy concerns (IUIPC): the construct, the scale, and a causal model. Inf. Syst. Res. **15**(4), 336–355 (2004)
2. Li, H., Sarathy, R., Heng, X.: Understanding situational online information disclosure as a privacy calculus. J. Comput. Inf. Syst. **51**(1), 62–71 (2010)
3. Krasnova, H., Veltri, N.F.: Privacy calculus on social networking sites: explorative evidence from Germany and USA. In: 2010 43rd Hawaii International Conference on System Sciences, pp. 1–10. IEEE (2010)
4. Dinev, T., Hart, P.: An extended privacy calculus model for e-commerce transactions. Inf. Syst. Res. **17**(1), 61–80 (2006)
5. Xu, H., Teo, H.-H., Tan, B.C.Y., Agarwal, R.: The role of push-pull technology in privacy calculus: the case of location-based services. J. Manag. Inf. Syst. **26**(3), 135–174 (2009)
6. Laugwitz, B., Held, T., Schrepp, M.: Construction and evaluation of a user experience questionnaire. In: Holzinger, A. (ed.) USAB 2008. LNCS, vol. 5298, pp. 63–76. Springer, Heidelberg (2008). https://doi.org/10.1007/978-3-540-89350-9_6

PISA: A Privacy Impact Self-assessment App Using Personas to Relate App Behavior to Risks to Smartphone Users

Ludwig Toresson, Maher Shaker, Sebastian Olars, and Lothar Fritsch[✉]

Karlstad University, Karlstad, Sweden
`lothar.fritsch@KAU.se`

Abstract. We present an educative self-assessment app intended to increase awareness of app-related privacy risks. The privacy impact self-assessment (PISA) app is intended to stimulate smartphone user reflection over risks of data sharing and data extraction from their smartphones. An interactive user interface performs an end-user targeted dialogue about apps using personas with a variety of vulnerabilities. The guided dialogue about threats is intended to engage the user's reflection about own app risk. We describe the underlying model and interaction design, summarize the personas and discuss the user interfaces implemented in the app.

Keywords: Privacy risk · Privacy impact awareness · Smartphone apps · User education · User interface · Privacy personas

1 Overview and Background

We designed the Android app PISA [20] for self-assessment of app privacy impact [9,14] based on actual app statistics on Android phones [13]. PISA illustrates privacy threats and impact with the example of installed apps whose data extraction profile gets related to a selected persona's vulnerabilities, causing harmful privacy impact to the persona (see Fig. 1).

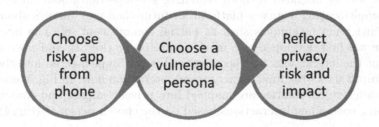

Fig. 1. High-level design of interaction flow.

© Springer Nature Switzerland AG 2020
C. Stephanidis and M. Antona (Eds.): HCII 2020, CCIS 1226, pp. 613–621, 2020.
https://doi.org/10.1007/978-3-030-50732-9_79

PISA's interactive assessment is related to a stored set of installed apps, observed app behaviors and custom-made personas [6] with expressed vulnerabilities. We engage users through a graphical, interactive dialog about the app's access to data and potential impact on the phone owner. We used app data access profiles from the KAUDROID database [4,11,15,19]. PISA is an effort to create a combined ex-ante and ex-post transparency-enhancing tool [17] intended to increase end-user awareness about data sharing practices and risks. The development is part of project ALerT - Awareness Learning Tools for Data Sharing Everywhere[1], a multi-perspective exploration of sharing awareness by gamification. An associated activity was Fromell's [10]'s *Dysconnect*, a collaborative drama-writing project for digital audio drama about algorithm's power over humans with programmed smartphone side effects. In collaboration with students at Karlstad University [12,21], a drama player for Android phones was developed that would deploy various drama-related side effects against the phone holder. ALerT investigated serious gaming for privacy education [3]: The article oversees three privacy awareness games: *Friend Inspector, Master F.I.N.D., Google Interland*. All three games are, however, concerned with privacy conduct on social networking sites. An ALerT-supervised student project experimented with gamified data sharing dilemmas in their *Dare2Share* action game [1].

2   Design

Our app engages users in a conversation about risks and impact of installed apps. PISA will ask the user to choose a persona that relates to him- or herself. The app will then query static data about the targeted app in order to display a risk to privacy related to a vulnerability the persona has expressed. Finally, a mitigation strategy can be chosen. PISA does, upon startup, randomly pick an installed app which is present in the KAUDROID data set. For this apps' specific threat profile (which is expressed in profiled identity attributes, see [14]) PISA will then offer a list of personas which have vulnerabilities for these threats. PISA users can choose a persona they are interested in. After choosing, PISA will display the potential privacy impact the app can have on the persona. Impacts are related to real-life situations. On the final step, PISA users can choose one of three options to mitigate the threat: *Uninstall, Privilege restriction, Do nothing*. This last step is intended to both stimulate self-reflection about mitigation as well as implementing a survey platform for future end user surveys about alternative mitigation techniques such as partial commitment [8]. The interaction sequence was first developed as a mock-up prototype (Fig. 2), and when consensus about the interactions had been reached it was implemented into the PISA app. Figure 3 shows the final approach and interaction flow. In Fig. 4, one example persona's vulnerabilities are mapped into privacy impact and consequences - a graphic controlling interactions based on the chosen personas (Fig. 4).

---

[1] NFR ALerT project homepage, https://www.nr.no/en/projects/alert-awareness-learning-tools-data-sharing-everywhere, accessed 2020-03-04.

Fig. 2. Mock-up 'paper' prototype for PISA.

One objectives was the implementation of a 'mobile' look-and-feel app controlled by pressing and swiping on-screen. We focused on swift interactions and small portions of information in order to enable users to quickly complete one round of assessment, with a few thumb-swiping interactions. Since the most complex interaction is the selection of a persona, we focused on a thumb-swipe controlled persona browser. Two of its screen elements are shown in Fig. 5, parts (e) and (f).

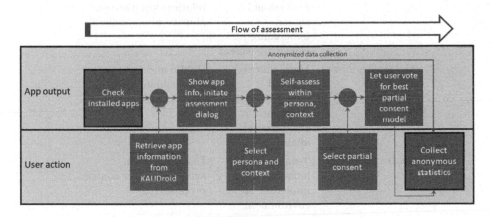

Fig. 3. Finalized interaction flow design of the PISA app.

2.1 Personas

Personas are behavioural specifications of typical users. Personas have been used to express attitudes, capabilities, and features of target users of information systems. Andrews [2] described a group of seven personas and their privacy needs in detail. These personas are designed as polyglot, urban, diverse and global-minded. Each of them has a specific vulnerability expressed through non-mainstream properties in categories such as race, sexual orientation, activism or job secrecy needs. Dupree et al. [6] surveyed security behaviours to identify five groups of personas that emerge from end-user behaviors: *Fundamentalists, Lazy Experts, Technicians, Amateurs, the Marginally Concerned*. The clustering of users via attitudes and behaviors toward security practices led to the specification of personas of varying levels of concern and with a spectrum of technological skills. From those, we created a group of five personas designed to relate to rural western Sweden. Our personas are briefly summarized in Table 1. A detailed specification is available in the PISA project report [20].

Table 1. PISA personas – key features.

Persona	Key features	Vulnerabilities
Lina Odinsson	Female e-sports celebrity, known under pseudonym	Stalking, Sabotage, Sponsor loss
Carl Göransson	Male well-off elderly citizen with beginning dementia	Exploitation, fraud, social exclusion
Markus Petersson	Male mid-life professional career, undergoing cancer treatment	Career damage, relationship distress, abusive phone sellers
Anders Andersson	Male, married regional politician with a preference for extramarital affairs	Public and private trust endangered, divorce, economic loss
Sandra Dalagren	Teen-age female homosexual in intolerant social environment	Discrimination, exclusion, risky contact proposals

Each persona is constructed into a specific life context that creates a set of specific vulnerabilities that are related to de-anonymization risk, ranging from dating to cancer treatment visits in specialized hospitals. PISA connects those to actual app's personal data extraction behaviour.

2.2 Connecting Apps Through Privacy Threats to Vulnerabilities

In our app, we connect app access to personal data to privacy threats. Those threats are effective against a persona's vulnerability. If realized, the threat will create privacy impact on the persona. Figure 4 shows how persona *Lina*'s vulnerabilities lead to privacy impact. To build and populate our model of app profiles, threats and impacts specific to personas, we pursued the following steps:

1. Creation of static app identification data from KAUDROID;
2. Creation of personas with specific privacy vulnerabilities;
3. Mapping of identification/de-anonymization threats to each persona's vulnerabilities;
4. Definition of each realized threats' privacy impact on each persona.

With the populated model, the PISA app now can follow a structured manuscript: for each app and for each persona with related vulnerabilities, PISA can show threats and resulting impact.

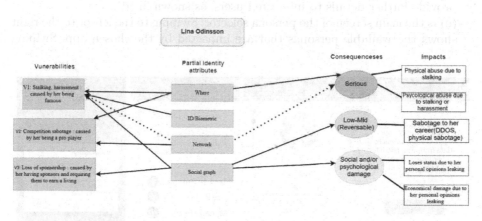

Fig. 4. Mapping of Lina Odinsson persona and her vulnerabilities to identifiable identity attributes and privacy impact.

We modeled privacy threats as identification risk based on data shared from the smartphone through apps. Our assumption is that a person being identifiable through partial identity attributes will be exposed to privacy risks. Therefore we modeled identifiability through data sharing. Using the KAUDROID data [16] (which is a database of Android app permission statistics of permissions used to access data on phones) we create a model of identity attributes collected by apps through partial identity attributes [18]. Partial Identities are constructed from sets of attributes populated from one or more permissions used [14]. For each app represented in the KAUDROID database, we populated a static record describing which identity attributes the app had accessed.

From privacy impact analysis (PIA) and data protection impact analysis (DPIA) we used several conceptualizations of privacy impact. The PRIAM method defines privacy harms in five categories: *physical harms, economic or financial harms, mental or psychological harms, harms to dignity or reputation, societal or architectural harms* [5]. A similar, but somewhat simpler conceptualization of privacy impact is offered by ENISA [7] where impact levels are described as *low, medium, high, very high* with respective criteria for their application. We defined our impact based on the descriptions in those two definitions.

2.3   Walk-Through of Interactions

A complete walk-through of the PISA user interface following the interaction plan in Fig. 3 is shown in Fig. 5. The individual steps performed are:

– Screen (a) greets the user upon start-up. Pressing the START button initiates the random selection of an app.
– Step (b) shows the chosen app, along with information about which identity attributes this app collects. Pressing the button continues.
– (c) explains the further steps. The black circles with a lowercase *i* letter provide further details to interested users, as shown in (d).
– (e) is the main screen of the persona selector. Swiping to the left or to the right shows the available personas that are impacted by the chosen app. Swiping

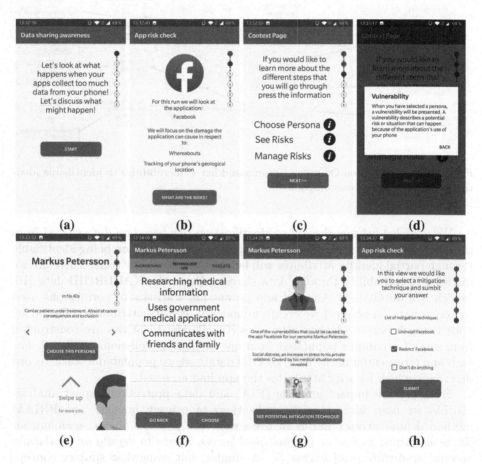

Fig. 5. PISA user interfaces: Upper row: (a) Greeting, (b) app pick, (c) instructions, (d) details Lower row: (e) persona overview, (f) persona detail, (g) vulnerability, (h) mitigation survey.

up will open the persona detail screen (f). CHOOSE will select the displayed persona.

– (f) contains three tabs that show detail information about the personas: *background, technology use, threats.* GO BACK returns to the persona selector, CHOOSE selects the displayed persona.
– (g) informs about the specific privacy impact on the chosen persona. Clicking on the button proceeds to the mitigation screen (h).
– (h) is the final step in the interaction: The choice of a mitigation action performed by selecting an option, followed by pressing the SUBMIT button.

During the interaction, users can backtrack in order to choose a different persona. After mitigation, they can play another round, or exit the PISA app.

3   Discussion and Conclusion

We built a privacy impact self-assessment app that engages a smartphone user in a reflection over own data sharing by addressing one of the installed apps through privacy threats based upon app behaviour profiles collected in KAUDROID. For this purpose we modeled five personas of Swedish people with vulnerabilities related to de-anonymization threats from the apps. We reached our goal of a swipe-friendly user interface. Informal feedback collected on the app was positive. However, some practical issues remain. Due to the limited project time, we were not able to define a larger number of personas that would relate to wider populations. A larger number of personas will require a different persona selector in order to reduce selection complexity. Our KAUDROID sample of approx. 120 apps does not cover all apps used by potential PISA users, thus interactions are restricted to the apps contained in the KAUDROID database. Finally, due to the static inclusion of KAUDROID statistics, PISA will not adapt to changing behaviours of new versions of the apps (however, this was a design decision made with the intention to avoid connection to database servers that may cause privacy issues through observable IP addresses).

In summary, we provided a graphical user interface for a guided exploration of threats, impacts and persona-based vulnerabilities created by sharing personal smartphone data with apps. Interactions which were designed for one-finger use worked well. Future prospects include an extended persona model, a wider selection of app behavioural profiles, and possible updates or on-line access to updated app information.

Acknowledgements. This article is partially funded by the ALerT project, Research Council of Norway, IKTPLUSS 2017–2021. We thank Nurul Momen and Patrick Murmann (Karlstad University) for their feedback and support.

References

1. Aasbrenn, S., et al.: Dare to share - a bachelor thesis for norwegian computing center. Technical report, Dept. of Computer Science, Norwegian University of Science and Technology (NTNU) (2019)

2. Andrews, G.: User personas for privacy and security. web pages. https://medium. com/@gusandrews/user-personas-for-privacy-and-security-a8b35ae5a63b, https://medium.com/@gusandrews/user-personas-for-privacy-and-security-a8b35ae5a63b. Accessed 27 Feb 2020

3. Bergen, E., Solberg, D.F., Sæthre, T.H., Divitini, M.: Supporting the co-design of games for privacy awareness. In: Auer, M.E., Tsiatsos, T. (eds.) ICL 2018. AISC, vol. 916, pp. 888–899. Springer, Cham (2020). https://doi.org/10.1007/978-3-030-11932-4_82

4. Carlsson, A., Pedersen, C., Persson, F., Söderlund, G.: Kaudroid: a tool that will spy on applications and how they spy on their users. Technical report, Karlstad University, Department of Mathematics and Computer Science (2018). http://urn.kb.se/resolve?urn=urn:nbn:se:kau:diva-66090

5. De, S.J., Le Métayer, D.: PRIAM: a privacy risk analysis methodology. In: Livraga, G., Torra, V., Aldini, A., Martinelli, F., Suri, N. (eds.) DPM/QASA -2016. LNCS, vol. 9963, pp. 221–229. Springer, Cham (2016). https://doi.org/10.1007/978-3-319-47072-6_15

6. Dupree, J.L., Devries, R., Berry, D.M., Lank, E.: Privacy personas: clustering users via attitudes and behaviors toward security practices. In: Proceedings of the 2016 CHI Conference on Human Factors in Computing Systems, CHI 2016, pp. 5228–5239. Association for Computing Machinery, New York (2016). https://doi.org/10.1145/2858036.2858214

7. ENISA: Guidelines for smes on the security of personal data processing. Technical report TP-05-16-090-EN-N11, European Union Agency For Network and Information Security (ENISA) (2016). https://doi.org/10.2824/867415

8. Fritsch, L.: Partial commitment – "Try Before You Buy" and "Buyer's Remorse" for personal data in big data & machine learning. In: Steghöfer, J.-P., Esfandiari, B. (eds.) IFIPTM 2017. IFIP AICT, vol. 505, pp. 3–11. Springer, Cham (2017). https://doi.org/10.1007/978-3-319-59171-1_1

9. Fritsch, L., Momen, N.: Derived partial identities generated from app permissions. In: Proceedings of the Open Identity Summit (OID) 2017. LNI, vol. 277. Gesellschaft für Informatik (2017)

10. Fromell, A.: Performing algorithmic power: 'dysconnect' as digital political dramaturgy (2019)

11. Hatamian, M., Momen, N., Fritsch, L., Rannenberg, K.: A multilateral privacy impact analysis method for android apps. In: Naldi, M., Italiano, G.F., Rannenberg, K., Medina, M., Bourka, A. (eds.) APF 2019. LNCS, vol. 11498, pp. 87–106. Springer, Cham (2019). https://doi.org/10.1007/978-3-030-21752-5_7

12. Mangafic, A.: Artistic control of side effects in playpod by scripting and game loop technology (2019)

13. Momen, N.: Towards measuring apps' privacy-friendliness (licentiate dissertation). Technical report 2018:31, Karlstad University, Department of Mathematics and Computer Science (2018). http://urn.kb.se/resolve?urn=urn:nbn:se:kau:diva-68569

14. Momen, N., Fritsch, L.: App-generated digital identities extracted through android permission-based data access-a survey of app privacy. In: Proceedings SICHERHEIT 2020, LNI. Gesellschaft für Informatik eV (2020). https://doi.org/10.18420/sicherheit2020_01

15. Momen, N., Hatamian, M., Fritsch, L.: Did app privacy improve after the gdpr? IEEE Security & Privacy 17(6), 10–20, November-December 2019. https://doi.org/10.1109/MSEC.2019.2938445

16. Momen, N., Pulls, T., Fritsch, L., Lindskog, S.: How much privilege does an app need? investigating resource usage of android apps (short paper). In: 2017 15th Annual Conference on Privacy, Security and Trust (PST), pp. 2268–2685, August 2017. https://doi.org/10.1109/PST.2017.00039, https://ieeexplore.ieee.org/document/8476943

17. Murmann, P., Fischer-Hübner, S.: Tools for achieving usable ex post transparency: a survey. IEEE Access 5, 22965–22991 (2017)

18. Pfitzmann, A., Hansen, M.: Anonymity, unlinkability, unobservability, pseudonymity, and identity management-a consolidated proposal for terminology. In: Designing privacy enhancing technologies, pp. 1–9. Technische Universität Dresden, 10 August 2010

19. Sundberg, S., Blomqvist, A., Bromander, A.: Kaudroid-project report: Visualizing how android apps utilize permissions. report, Karlstad University (2019). http://kau.diva-portal.org/smash/record.jsf?pid=diva2:1282064

20. Toresson, L., Olars, S., Shaker, M.: Privacy impact self-assessment app. Technical report, Karlstad University, Department of Mathematics and Computer Science (2020). http://urn.kb.se/resolve?urn=urn:nbn:se:kau:diva-76317

21. Wahlberg, M., Larsson, D., Steinvall, D., Mangafic, A.: Playpod: Multi-medial enhancement of audio theatre on android smartphones. Technical report, Karlstad University (2019). http://urn.kb.se/resolve?urn=urn:nbn:se:kau:diva-70812

Human Error in Information Security: Exploring the Role of Interruptions and Multitasking in Action Slips

Craig Williams[1], Helen M. Hodgetts[1,2], Candice Morey[1],
Bill Macken[1], Dylan M. Jones[1], Qiyuan Zhang[1],
and Phillip L. Morgan[1(✉)]

[1] School of Psychology, Cardiff University, Cardiff CF10 3AT, UK
{williamscl31,hodgettshl,moreyc,macken,jonesdm,
zhangq47,morganphil}@cardiff.ac.uk
[2] Department of Applied Psychology, Cardiff Metropolitan University,
Cardiff CF5 2YB, UK

Abstract. Breaches of cyber-security often arise unintentionally from the human user such as when switching between subtasks or external interruptions, disrupting the flow of work and leading to action slips in the execution of a task procedure [1, 2]. There has been little research into the perceived effects of task interruption and switching on computer-based tasks when such action slips can potentially compromise information security. Semi-structured interviews were conducted on nine university employees who regularly handle sensitive information, designed to identify which features of information-sensitive computer-based tasks are the most susceptible to disruption. Potential sources of human error in were identified with task interruption judged to be more likely than multitasking as a source of error. The interview findings will serve as the basis of experimental investigations into how disruptions in the flow of a task procedure can cause action slips that may compromise the handling of sensitive data. Well-informed empirical work in the area of Cyberpsychology is critical to understanding the processes involved, and to guiding potential solutions rooted in human-machine interface design and human computer interaction.

Keywords: Cyber security · Information security · Human error · Interruption · Cyberpsychology

1 Introduction

Interventions to improve information security have largely involved technological safeguards (e.g., improved firewalls and anti-virus software), but there is also increasing acknowledgement of the role of the human user in interacting with and maintaining the effectiveness of these defense mechanisms [3]. Even when adequate training has been provided, omissions, inaccuracies, and other mistakes can arise from temporary lapses of attention [1, 2]. Such slips can contribute to breaches in information security. Although information-sensitive settings have received little scrutiny, it seems likely that such errors are more common in the presence of workplace stressors such as workload, interruption/distraction or fatigue [4, 5] sometimes arising indirectly as a result of poor work organization or low staffing levels [6]. This study is concerned with understanding how the particular requirements of handling sensitive data, both in terms of the types of task undertaken and the stressors that are at play, contribute to errors and delays.

The suggestion that settings that constitute high attentional load—high cognitive demand, multiple overlapping tasks, unexpected task interruptions—could leave the worker vulnerable to action slips or time costs, is also supported by the cognitive psychology literature. In laboratory studies, performance deficits (e.g., increased reaction time and/or error rates) are reliably documented when alternating between two tasks relative to performing the same two tasks individually [7]. Such effects are typically attributed to an attention bottleneck [8]. The execution of one task is significantly slowed by the temporal proximity of another because the cognitive system is incapable of planning and responding to two tasks at the same time. It seems reasonable to expect that in settings involving information security such loads may be high due to multitasking and that these will lead to effects on efficiency and accuracy that will have material consequences.

The effects of switching between tasks can be distinguished from those involving task interruption. This involves the temporary suspension and subsequent resumption of a primary task in order to attend to an unexpected secondary activity. Interruptions are commonplace in the modern work environment which is attended by a plethora of emails, phone calls, text messages and face-to-face interruptions that are likely to break up the flow of an ongoing task. This can result in a time cost in resuming the primary task [9–11], and/or forgetting to execute an action after interruption [2, 12–14]. The Memory for Goals model of interruption [15] interprets these effects in terms of activation and decay, such that a goal will diminish in activation when suspended by an interruption, either to the extent that it is forgotten, or that a time cost is incurred to reactivate the suspended goal. Even in cases when a user attempts to defer an interruption to a more convenient time, the very action of momentarily engaging with the interrupter for a few seconds (e.g., by telling a colleague that they will be able to help at a later point), can be enough to derail their train of thought, causing procedural errors [1] and/or a time cost at resumption [9, 10].

There has been little experimental work examining the effects of multitasking and interruption with a focus on information security. One study demonstrated how users are more prone to cyber vulnerabilities (e.g., less accurate in sorting between legitimate and phishing emails) when multitasking (completing an online survey simultaneously on the other half of the computer screen [16]). Another study required participants to make a security judgment about which applications to install on a phone, and found that malicious applications were more likely downloaded when multitasking [17]. In addition to a tendency to be less cautious with potentially malevolent cyber material, it is conceivable that multitasking and interruptions could contribute to another risky cyber behavior: accidental disclosure of secure information. Many jobs now involve information that has limitations on circulation (within and/or outside the organization), whether it is company material under embargo, internal memos or emails, or the demographic, financial, or occupational health details of employees. Privacy breaches are always a possibility, for example, in information omission, commission, or the mis-timing of disclosure, such as violating an embargo. Given what we know about attention and human information processing, it is likely that action slips with material security consequences are more likely when employees are multitasking and when interruptions occur [2, 12].

The literature indicates that human error is by far the weakest link in cyber security, whether due to a lack of knowledge about secure policies and procedures ('mistakes') or due to unintentional errors in the execution of routine procedures ('action slips'). Prevailing theories of attention predict that suspending a task at crucial moments when goals and plans must be coordinated for impending action will necessarily result in slower task performance and more frequent errors. While increasing awareness and understanding of potential vulnerabilities in the cyber domain might improve workflows, investigating the types of action slips that can lead to a breach in security and ways in which they can be minimized is imperative. We therefore interviewed employees who regularly work with sensitive information to gain insight into the work-tasks they usually perform, and their view of how multitasking and interruptions affect their performance at work. The knowledge gained from these interviews can in due course be applied to the design of novel laboratory studies aimed at quantifying the costs of workflow disruption in terms of time and accuracy.

The aims of the study were to 1) identify information-sensitive computer-based tasks that are the most susceptible to disruption; 2) understand the characteristics of task interruption and/or multitasking in the context of information-sensitive computer-based tasks, and 3) from the perspective of individuals working with sensitive information, understand how task interruption and/or multitasking may affect performance.

2   Method

Nine employees of a large UK university were each interviewed separately. To be included in this sample, participants needed to handle sensitive information when performing computer-based tasks as part of their work role (e.g., Professional Services staff working in areas such as IT, finance, research administration and/or governance, human resources). They were given £10 for their participation and completed the study before or after work or during unpaid breaks. Interviews were semi-structured, with two interviewers present, and typically lasted about 45 min. Transcribed interviews were subjected to a thematic analysis, with the qualitative data coded following the systematic process highlighted by [18].

3   Results

3.1   Computer-Based Primary Task

The first theme to emerge was that of the everyday computer-based tasks in which that participants engaged, with subthemes regarding the type and nature of the task. In all cases, the most common task that involved the handling of sensitive data was either entering information into a database, or responding to emails that contained sensitive information. The type of sensitive information dealt with commonly involved either health/well-being (e.g., occupational health reports, counselling referrals), financial (e.g., student hardship, staff payroll), or demographic details of staff/students (e.g., date of birth, addresses, passport number). Participants described in depth the nature of the tasks carried out, detailing the precise steps to be performed (e.g., entering information, comparing, verifying, saving, attaching, sending, advising), and in many cases it emerged that there were clear procedural steps that had to be undertaken to complete the task. Regarding the cognitive processes engaged in completing the task, all nine participants mentioned memory (e.g., a mental list of checks to be done, or remembering details from one database to be able to cross reference with another), and five specifically mentioned procedural memory (e.g., having to consciously remember the order of steps in a particular procedure). Also frequently-mentioned was attention (e.g., vigilance for error, or attention switching between different sources of information), judgment, problem solving, and decision making.

The second theme concerned the factors that could hinder performance when completing the computer-based task. Seven participants talked about task interruption as an environmental constraint, with face-to-face interruptions being the main source (most often colleagues, but sometimes other walk-in enquiries). Participants described how interruptions can be completely unpredictable in terms of their occurrence (e.g., happening when in the middle of something), and their duration (e.g., distraction could be momentary, or could take time away from the main task for a long period). Three participants mentioned background sound as a constraint (particularly in an open-plan office), and five participants said that high workload and the associated time pressure could impact their performance.

The third theme evolved around the types of errors that could arise during the handling of sensitive information. Data-input errors were most likely to occur, such as typographical errors (e.g., a wrong number in financial details), misspelling of names, error in date-of-birth format (British vs American), or inputting information into the wrong table/column. Some participants mentioned that procedural omissions could be made, for example, after arranging a student appointment, forgetting to log that information into the database; forgetting to file a paper copy; or forgetting to add an email attachment. Errors could also take the form of an unintended distribution of sensitive information. For example, one participant reported inputting information into templates, but sometimes not removing all the previous student's details so that their details are unintentionally sent out to others. Another participant described how there are different levels of disclosure for different people (e.g., counsellors, academic staff, students' parents) and how distribution could be directed incorrectly and without adequate consent for that sharing. Three participants mentioned email-based errors that could result in revealing sensitive information to unauthorized recipients (e.g., forgetting to remove information in the email trace when forwarding, or sending to an unintended recipient with a similar email address).

3.2   Understanding Characteristics and Effects of Task Interruptions

Participants were next asked specifically whether their performance on the computer-based task was ever affected by the need to multitask or was on occasion interrupted.

Although participants did report multitasking (e.g., switching between different sources of information to complete a task), all reported that their performance was more negatively affected by interruption. Interruptions were perceived as being unpredictable, often out of their control, frequently associated with their own sense of urgency, and, as one participant put it "takes me out of the loop of what I was doing". In contrast, multitasking was perceived as self-initiated and necessary for task completion. Questions then followed that aimed to understand in greater depth the characteristics and effects of interruptions when performing an information-sensitive computer-based task.

The majority of participants reported that the initiating source of an interruption was most often auditory (six cited face-to-face interruptions as most likely, and two mentioned phone calls). Only one participant rated email interruption as being most distracting. When elaborating on interruption source, participants reported that by its nature face-to-face interruption was almost impossible to ignore and needed immediate acknowledgement so as not to appear rude (they were perceived as being urgent). Even if this interaction was only momentary (e.g., a quick query, or to schedule a more convenient time to engage properly), the temporary stopping of their prior task led them to lose track of their place in the task or lose the thread of what they had been doing. Phone interruptions were viewed as needing to take priority over any computer-based event, although one participant noted that their response to the telephone was not as immediate as that to a colleague interrupting in person. In contrast, emails could more easily be deferred so that ongoing tasks were not disrupted, and some participants reported turning off notifications and only checking emails periodically. While the initiating source of interruptions were auditory, the majority of participants (8 out of 9) reported that the actual interrupting task needing to be carried out was almost always computer-based (e.g., looking up information on a database).

Participants were asked to rate the frequency of interruptions occurring during a busy and quiet working period on a 5-point scale (1 = Never, 2 = Rarely, 3 = Sometimes, 4 = Quite Often, 5 = Almost Always). Interruptions during busy work periods were judged to occur 'quite often' (mean rating = 4.00, SD = 0.87), but only 'sometimes/rarely' during quieter times (mean = 2.39, SD = 1.11). Using a 5-point scale to attempt to quantify the effects of interruption, it was clear that participants felt that interruptions were sometimes – quite often disruptive to their ongoing task (mean = 3.56, SD = 0.68), and could sometimes have a negative impact (mean = 3.17, SD = 0.70).

Participants were asked to provide an example of when they felt an interruption had contributed to a negative outcome. Various errors occurred after being interrupted such as inputting the wrong details, inputting information into the wrong part of a table, or omitting an item/section of information due to loss of concentration. One participant recounted being distracted while sending an email, and put multiple addresses into 'cc' rather than in the blind field so that individual identities were revealed to others on the list. Another participant had intended to remove 'cc' on an email but was interrupted and forgot to do so when they returned to the email, and subsequently confidentiality was compromised.

In addition to errors, participants described the time costs of interruption. This could comprise the extra time taken retracing previous actions in order to pick up the thread of what they had been doing, or in terms of unnecessary repetition (e.g., one participant reported duplicating processes unintentionally as they had forgotten they had already been done). If an error has been made in programming for example, it can take time to locate and rectify that error before being able to continue. As a further negative effect, some participants commented that interruptions increased workload and stress especially at busy times.

4 Discussion

4.1 Summary of Findings

The computer-based tasks that the University employees most often performed when handling sensitive data were responding to emails and inputting/retrieving information from databases. These all required a number of task steps and would tend to place demands on memory (particularly procedural memory) and attention (e.g., switching between sources to gather information). Users engaged in both multitasking and task interruptions on a frequent basis, but while multitasking was accepted as 'part of the job', interruptions were regarded as unwelcome and disruptive. The cost of interruption was either in terms of time (e.g., rechecking when resuming the task), or errors, due to not checking when resuming the task (e.g. inputting/typing errors, or failing to execute an intended action, particularly checking procedures). When checks were not made, this could result in sensitive information being logged incorrectly or distributed to an unintended or unauthorized recipient. Face-to-face questions were seen as more urgent and therefore more likely to interrupt the ongoing task than emails that could be more easily deferred. When deferring face-to-face interruptions, participants reported that the flow of their task had been disrupted. The quantitative data analysis demonstrated that interruptions were perceived as being frequent, disruptive, and as having a negative impact on performance.

4.2 Recommendations

While the current interviews provided information regarding the nature, characteristics and effect of interruptions on performance, well-designed empirical work is essential to better understanding the processes involved. Interruptions were frequently mentioned as being disruptive to procedural tasks—characterized by the requirement to complete several steps, sometimes in a particular order—with participants reporting losing track of what they had already done and what they were about to do. As the basis for assessing action slips in the handling of sensitive information, we recommend using a procedural task and particularly one that mimics the inputting of data. Participants frequently mentioned that slips could occur in the sending of emails, and so in our lab we have recently developed a procedural task that is based around this ecologically valid task context.

Auditory-initiated interruptions (face to face or telephone) were viewed as 'more interrupting' than their visually-initiated counterparts (such as emails), due to a sense of perceived urgency and social etiquette in responding to another person. Future research could assess whether the auditory modality is more attention-grabbing than the visual modality within a laboratory setting. Moreover, it would be useful to further investigate the utility of deferring an interruption. The interviews revealed that interruptions do not need to be long to be perceived as disruptive, although it may be modulated by the overall long-term level of demand.

The information gleaned from these interviews can help form the basis of experimental tasks to investigate how disruptions in the flow of a task procedure can cause action slips that may compromise the handling of sensitive data. Well-informed empirical work is critical to improving understanding of cognitive processes and subsequently to inform interruption handling strategies. Furthermore, such research can contribute to technological solutions rooted in human-machine interface design that will be critical to supporting users within dynamic and multitasking environments, and ultimately to reduce the incidence of unintentional security breaches.

Acknowledgements. This research was funded by the UK National Cyber Security Centre.

References

1. Altmann, E.M., Trafton, J.G., Hambrick, D.Z.: Momentary interruptions can derail the train of thought. J. Exp. Psychol. Gen. **143**, 215–226 (2014)
2. Li, S.Y.W., Blandford, A., Cairns, P., Young, R.M.: The effect of interruptions on postcompletion and other procedural errors: An account based on the activation-based goal memory model. J. Exp. Psychol. Appl. **14**, 314–328 (2008)
3. Nobles, C.: Botching human factors in cybersecurity in business organizations. HOLISTICA–J. Bus. Public Adm. **9**(3), 71–88 (2018)
4. Kraemer, S., Carayon, P.: Human errors and violations in computer and information security: the viewpoint of network administrators and security specialists. Appl. Ergon. **38**, 143–154 (2007)
5. Reason, J.: Human Error. Cambridge University Press, Cambridge (1990)
6. Liginlal, D., Sim, I. Khansa, L., Fearn, P.: Human error and privacy breaches in healthcare organizations: causes and management strategies. In: AMCIS Proceedings. Paper 406 (2009)
7. Rogers, R.D., Monsell, S.: Costs of a predictable switch between simple cognitive tasks. J. Exp. Psychol. Gen. **124**, 207–231 (1995)
8. Pashler, H.: Attentional limitations in doing two tasks at the same time. Curr. Dir. Psychol. Sci. **1**, 44–48 (1992)
9. Hodgetts, H.M., Jones, D.M.: Contextual cues aid recovery from interruption: the role of associative activation. J. Exp. Psychol. Learn. Mem. Cogn. **35**, 1120–1132 (2006)
10. Hodgetts, H.M., Jones, D.M.: Interruption of the tower of London task: support for a goal activation approach. J. Exp. Psychol. Gen. **135**, 103–115 (2006)
11. Monk, C., Trafton, J.G., Boehm-Davis, D.A.: The effect of interruption duration and demand on resuming suspended goals. J. Exp. Psychol. Appl. **14**, 299–313 (2008)
12. Morgan, P.L., Patrick, J., Waldron, S., King, S., Patrick, T.: Improving memory after interruption: exploiting soft constraints and manipulating information access cost. J. Exp. Psychol. Appl. **15**, 291–306 (2009)
13. Morgan, P., Patrick, J.: Paying the price works: Increasing goal-state access cost improves problem solving and mitigates the effect of interruption. Q. J. Exp. Psychol. **66**, 160–178 (2012)

14. Morgan, P., Patrick, J., Tiley, L.: Improving the effectiveness of an interruption lag by inducing a memory-based strategy. Acta Physiol. (Oxf) **142**, 87–96 (2013)
15. Altmann, E.M., Trafton, J.G.: Memory for goals: An activation-based model. Cogn. Sci. **26**, 39–83 (2002)
16. Zhang, H., Singh, S., Li, X., Dahbura, A., Xie, M.: Multitasking and monetary incentive in a realistic phishing study. In: Proceedings of British HCI. BCS Learning and Development Ltd, Belfast, UK (2018)
17. Liu, Q., McLaughlin, A.C., Watson, B., Enck, W., Davis, A.: Multitasking increases stress and insecure behavior on mobile devices. In: Proceedings of the Human Factors and Ergonomics Society 59th Annual Meeting, pp. 1110–1114 (2015)
18. Braun, V., Clark, V.: Using thematic analysis in psychology. Qual. Res. Psychol. **3**, 77–101 (2006)

A Study on Biometric Authentication and Liveness Detection Using Finger Elastic Deformation

Yu Yoshitani[✉] and Nobuyuki Nishiuchi

Graduate School of Systems Design, Tokyo Metropolitan University,
6-6 Asahigaoka, Hino, Tokyo, Japan
yoshitani-yu@ed.tmu.ac.jp, nnishiuc@tmu.ac.jp

Abstract. One of the most used biometric modalities is known as fingerprint, and has been widely used in daily life. However, it is not sufficiently recognized that there is a vulnerability of spoofing in the fingerprint authentication. There is a possibility of making a forged fingerprint by using residual fingerprint. In order to prevent the spoofing, it is required to add another information for authentication or use a completely different approach.

In the current research, we focused on the finger elastic deformation as another information for authentication. In order to get the information of the finger elastic deformation, continuous images of the fingerprint are captured while the finger is pressed onto the device. The device for capturing continuous images and measuring pressing force. For the verification of our proposed method, three forged fingers were made with different blending ratio which allow to login the fingerprint authentication of iPhone 7.

Keywords: Biometrics · Personal authentication · Liveness detection · Spoofing · Forged finger · Finger elastic deformation

1 Introduction

In the information society in recent years, it is important to authenticate an individual. Biometrics has attracted attention as one of the methods for authenticating individuals. One of the most used biometric modalities is known as fingerprint, and has been widely used in daily life. However, it is not sufficiently recognized that there is a vulnerability of spoofing in the fingerprint authentication [1, 2]. There is a possibility of making a forged fingerprint by using residual fingerprint. In order to prevent the spoofing, it is required to add another information for authentication or use a completely different approach [3–5].

There have been many studies on the liveness detection in fingerprint authentication. Yamagishi [6] suggested a fingerprint authentication which used fingerprint and artificial pattern in order to prevent the spoofing. By attaching the artificial pattern on the user's nail, it is possible to use both upper side and underside of finger for the authentication. However, it should be considered that users could feel uncomfortable or inconvenient to use the artificial pattern.

C. Stephanidis and M. Antona (Eds.): HCII 2020, CCIS 1226, pp. 630–635, 2020.
https://doi.org/10.1007/978-3-030-50732-9_81

In the current research, we focused on the finger elastic deformation as another information for authentication. In order to get the information of the finger elastic deformation, continuous images of the fingerprint are captured while the finger is pressed onto the device. The device for capturing continuous images and measuring pressing force. For the verification of our proposed method, three forged fingers were made with different blending ratio which allow to login the fingerprint authentication of iPhone 7.

2 Authentication Device

Figure 1 shows the device configuration of our proposed authentication. A finger is pressed on the upper surface of the acrylic block (3 cm × 3 cm × 7 cm, slope angle: 45°). At that time, the elastic deformation of the fingerprint is illuminated by the LED lighting (CosSystem, TE-12DSA-DKD-944233) from the lower surface of the acrylic block and is captured by the high-speed camera (Photoron, FAST SYSTEM MC 2.1). Simultaneously, the pressing force of the finger is measured by the load cell (Kyowa, DPM-911B). The image and the pressing force were synchronized by using the data logger (Graphtech, midi LOGGAR GL900). Through these experimental devices, obtained continuous images and the pressing force are shown in Fig. 2.

Fig. 1. Device configuration for capturing continuous images and measuring pressing force

Due to verify the proposed method, three types of forged finger with different gelatin blending ratio were created (Fig. 2). A small amount of milk powder was mixed to color the forged finger in white. Three forged fingers were confirmed in advance that they were able to login the fingerprint authentication of iPhone 7 (Fig. 3).

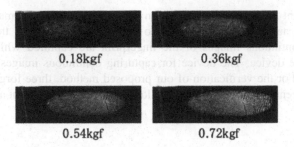

0.18kgf   0.36kgf

0.54kgf   0.72kgf

Fig. 2. Continuous images of fingerprint while finger is pressed to device

Fig. 3. Forged fingers (Gelatin:Water = 1:2 [left], 1:3 [center], 1:4 [right])

3   Authentication Algorithm

For the image processing of the fingerprint images, OpenCV4 was used. The details of the authentication algorithm are summarized below;

- Step1) Data acquisition: The continuous images (eleven images) and the pressing force was inputted.
- Step2) Smoothing processing: Smoothing processing is performed to remove noise from fingerprint images. Bilateral Filter is used for smoothing.
- Step3) Trimming: The fingerprint area is trimmed by the fixed-size window.
- Step4) Binary processing: Adaptive thresholding processing is performed.
- Step5) Getting the number of pixels in the fingerprint area: The number of pixels (fingerprint ridge) of fingerprint area was counted at even pressing force intervals from the continuous images as personal data.
- Step6) Verification: The average of correlation coefficient and Euclidean distance are used.
- Step7) Evaluation: Equal error rate (EER) based on the false acceptance rate (FAR) and false rejection rate (FRR) is calculated.

4   Validation Experiment

4.1   Experimental Methodology

Ten subjects (21 to 24 years old) participated in the experiment. In the validation experiment, the following two trials were conducted using data collected six times from ten subjects.

Genuine Trial. Five comparisons were conducted for ten subjects (a total of 50 comparisons). The reference data was compared the probe data of the genuine subject.

Impostor Trial. Fifty four comparisons were conducted for ten subjects (a total of 540 comparisons). The reference data was compared the probe data of each impostor.

4.2   Experimental Results and Discussion

Personal authentication

Correlation Coefficient
No significant difference was recognized between the genuine trial and the impostor trial in the verification results using correlation coefficient. Even if the total number of pixels was different in each subject, the correlation coefficient was high because the transition shape of the number of pixels was similar. Therefore, proposed method using correlation cocfficient for the verification wasn't suitable for the personal authentication.

Euclidean Distance
The EER verified Euclidean distance was 35%. Generally, the EER of fingerprint authentication is less than 0.1%, so the EER of proposed personal authentication wasn't sufficient. It was suggested that Euclidean distance of the total number of pixels wasn't either effective for personal authentication.

Liveness detection

Correlation Coefficient
Figure 4 shows the comparison between the alive finger (subject A) and the three forged fingers on the transition of the number of pixels in fingerprint area. No significant difference was found between the genuine trial (alive finger × alive finger) and the impostor trial (alive finger × forged finger) in the verification results using correlation coefficient. Therefore, proposed method using correlation coefficient for the verification wasn't suitable for the liveness detection.

Euclidean Distance
The EER verified Euclidean distance was 30%. The EER of proposed liveness detection wasn't sufficient.

Differential Value of Personal Data
As shown in Fig. 4, the shape of the transition is similar between the alive finger and the forged fingers except the range from 0.04 to 0.20 kgf. Therefore, the differential value (the change in the number of pixels per pressing force) was calculated by using

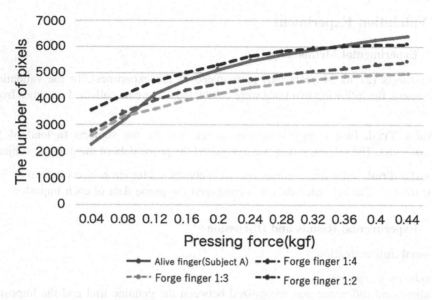

Fig. 4. The number of pixels of fingerprint area at even pressing force intervals for forged finger and alive finger

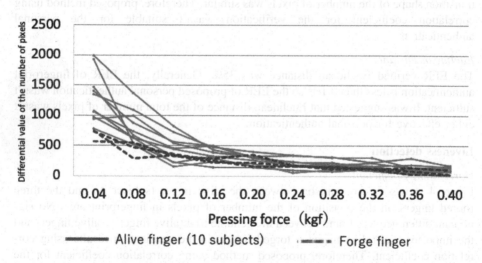

Fig. 5. Differential value of the number of pixels in the fingerprint area for forged finger and alive finger

the data of Fig. 4. Calculation result is shown in Fig. 5. When the threshold value is set to 700 pixels at 0.04 kgf and 0.08 kgf in Fig. 5, the accuracy rate of the detection whether alive finger or forged finger was 100%. Therefore, proposed method using differential value of personal data was suitable for the liveness detection.

5 Conclusion

In this study, we verified the effectiveness of the personal authentication and liveness detection using the finger elastic deformation. In order to get the information of the finger elastic deformation, continuous images of the fingerprint were captured while the finger was pressed onto the device, and pressing force was simultaneously measured. For the verification of our proposed method, three forged fingers were made. As a result of the experiment and analysis, we confirmed that it was difficult to identify the subject by using the finger elastic deformation, however, it was possible to make a distinction between alive finger and forged finger by using the differential value of the number of pixels.

References

1. Matsumoto, T., Matsumoto, H., Yamada, K., Hoshino, S.: Impact of artificial 'gummy' fingers on fingerprint systems. In: Proceedings of the SPIE 4677, Optical Security and Counterfeit Deterrence Techniques IV, pp. 275–289 (2002)
2. Schuckers, S.A.C.: Spoofing and anti-spoofing measures. Inform Secur. Tech Rep 7(4), 56–62 (2002)
3. Galbally, J., Alonso-Fernandez, F., Fierrez, J., Ortega-Garcia, J.: A high performance fingerprint liveness detection method based on quality related features. Future Gener. Comput. Syst. 28(1), 311–321 (2012)
4. Galbally, J., et al.: An evaluation of direct and indirect attacks using fake fingers generated from ISO templates. Pattern Recogn. Lett. 31, 725–732 (2010)
5. Tan, B., Schuckers, S.: Liveness detection for fingerprint scanners based on the statistics of wavelet signal processing. In: CVPRW 2006 (2006)
6. Yamagishi, M., Nishiuchi, N.: Hybrid fingerprint authentication using artifact-metrics. Int. J. Biomet. 1(2), 160–172 (2008)

Product and Service Design

A Study on Oral Health Care System Designing for the Middle-Aged Based on SAPAD-PCA

Shanshan Chen and Yajun Li[✉]

Nanjing University of Science and Technology, Nanjing 210094, China
lyj5088@163.com

Abstract. *Objective:* In this paper, we paid attention to the oral health care for the middle-aged, reorganized and consolidated the resource of all related parties, and improved the experience of the oral treatment to the middle-aged. As a result, we could improve the level of their oral health. *Methods:* We analyzed the mapping of activities, objects and meanings with the theory framework of Semiotics Approach of Product Architecture Design (SAPAD). Then we obtained the meaning clusters through the method of cluster analysis. We introduced the method of Principal Component Analysis (PCA) to analyze the meaning clusters quantitatively and calculate information contribution rates so that we could get the core meaning clusters. *Result:* We finished the mapping of meanings and objects by analyzing the relationships between them which were behind those core meaning clusters. Then we achieved the user's key behaviors and found their real needs. With this step, we succeed in the improvement of experience about the oral health care service system for the middle-aged. *Conclusion:* We studied the treatment process of oral treatment for the middle-aged by combining the SAPAD framework and PCA method, which we researched about users' behaviors deeply and found their key needs by the quantitative method. So we could think about problems and solve them more objectively and comprehensively. From the aspect of methods, we had perfected the SAPAD framework and had some creation. Finally, we made use of the SAPAD-PCA model to the oral health care service system for the middle-aged and provided a new solution to the improvement of their oral health.

Keywords: Oral health care system for the middle-aged · SAPAD · PCA · Service design

1 Introduction

According to "The Fourth National Oral Health Epidemiological Survey Report", it is said that the rate of calculus in middle-aged reached 96.7% and the rate of gingival bleeding reached 87.4%, which is compared with a decade ago [1]. That is to say, the condition of oral health of middle-aged should be improved. Researchers all over the world have studied the improvement of the oral health of middle-aged from the mainly two aspects. On one hand, in the aspect of treatment and nursing, many scholars have studied how to improve the oral health of middle-aged and old people. Herrmann Gianna et al. [2] focused on reducing dry mouth to improve the oral health of the middle-aged. Bidinotto Augusto Bacelo et al. [3] tried to improve the overall health of

© Springer Nature Switzerland AG 2020
C. Stephanidis and M. Antona (Eds.): HCII 2020, CCIS 1226, pp. 639–653, 2020.
https://doi.org/10.1007/978-3-030-50732-9_82

the elderly by preventing tooth loss and properly handing the concerns about chewing and tooth appearance. Ehtesham H et al. [4] thought that the intelligent system for differential diagnosis of oral medicine using the artificial intelligence (AI) capabilities could help specialists in achieving differential diagnosis in a wide range of oral diseases. Neel Shimpi et al. [5] thought that the existing electronic dental record (ERG) user interface (UI) design greatly affected the efficiency of dental providers. So they redesigned the EDR UI from the results would increase both the quality and utility of clinical documentation to improve it. Suebnukan Siriwan et al. [6] formulated recommendations for the design of clinical information technology that would help to improve the acquisition of clinical required by oral surgeons at all levels of expertise in their clinical decision-making. Tynan Anna et al. [7] thought that the status of oral health of patients in residential aged care facilities (RACFs) through the approach that integrated oral health program incorporating OHTs and tele-dentistry. Aro Taru et al. [8] thought it is the main problem that nurses are uncertain to oral health care behavior during the daily care of the middle-aged. So it should strengthen the oral health education and enhance the confidence during the oral health care work in basic education and in-service education. Ju X et al. [9] demonstrated that a context-specific oral health literacy intervention was partially successful in improving oral health literacy and oral health literacy-related outcomes in this vulnerable population, but only after multiple imputation MI. Richie Kohli et al. [10] found that nursing staff can be aware of the poor oral health of residents and be improved their ability of daily oral health care service through the innovation training. The researchers believed that the oral health can be integrated into daily routines which could improve oral and system health and reduce inequities in oral health care for older adults in this way.

On the other hand, in the aspect of improving the awareness of oral self-protection of the middle-aged, Astrom Anne et al. [11] used the method of a prospective cohort design to improve the awareness of oral health awareness of middle-aged so that improve the resistance of oral diseases. Ordell S et al. [12] did some experiments with middle-aged and elderly, which demonstrated smoking cessation in dental clinics is effective for them. Kang Jing et al. [13] did some longitudinal study in an English ageing population, which has demonstrated that poor cognitive function at early stage was associated with poorer oral health and higher risk of tooth loss in later life. The gradient relationship suggested that an improvement in cognitive function could potentially improve oral health and reduce the risk of tooth loss in the ageing population. Guo Jing et al. [14] found that although the tooth less and denture restoration status recorded in the survey was improved, which compared with the results 10 years ago, more efforts needed to be made on strengthening oral health promotion, particular for elderly people and those living in rural areas. Wang Chun Xiao et al. [15] found that the oral health behaviors of the middle-aged and elderly could be improved, for example, educating patients to develop tooth brushing and flossing habits.

However, they didn't study how to improve the service experience of oral care for the middle-aged and elderly from the perspective of users systematically. Semiotics Approach of Product Architecture Design (SAPAD) [16] framework is created by professor Hu Fei and Sato together. The model is based on the theory of product semiotics, which is aim to solve the practical problems with the user-centered thought. Now the framework has been used in many fields to solve practical problems. Hu F and

Zhou K et al. [17] solved the problem about the community rehabilitation service design under the mode of combining medical care with nursing care for the elderly by using the SAPAD framework. Wang Y et al. [18] improved the umbrella design which is used by drivers with the SAPAD framework. But the above researches were subjective within the SAPAD framework to solve the practical problems. So we tried to perfect the SAPAD framework by combining with the method of Principle Component analysis (PCA) [19], which combined quantitative analysis with qualitative analysis.

2 Describe the Principle of the SAPAD-PCA

2.1 The Construction About Meaning Clusters of the SAPAD Framework

Firstly, we analyzed the users' behaviors with the SAPAD framework and decomposed them into some small parts that included tasks and subtasks. Secondly, we displayed all the objects (include related person and items) contained subtasks gradually and obtained the mapping of activities and objects. Thirdly, we made all the tasks match with the 6 meaning layers, which contain the physical layer, syntactic layer, empirical layer, semantic layer, pragmatic layer and social layer, and obtained the mapping of activities and meanings. Lastly, we obtained the meaning clusters by cluster analysis with the tasks that had been classified as the 6 meaning layers at last step.

2.2 Make Sure the Core Meaning Clusters with the PCA Method

Principal Component Analysis (PCA), also called matrix data analysis, changes the related variables into some uncorrelated comprehensive index variables by means of variable transformation [20]. As a result, it could make the dimension of data be reduced and simplify problems. We analyzed the meaning that had been obtained by clusters the cluster analysis before by the PCA method, which made every meaning cluster as the evaluation index, and invited experts to score that were used as samples to compose the data matrix. Then we reduced the dimension of it. By calculating the main components' rate of information contribution, we got the core meaning clusters. Here is the specific calculating process in details:

Suppose there are n samples here. And each sample has m evaluation indexes. They make up $m \times n$ data matrix: $X = (x_{ij})_{n \times m}$. Now we need to calculate the average and variance of each index. Here is some about formulas:

$$\bar{x}_j = \frac{1}{n} \sum_{i=1}^{n} x_{ij}, (i = 1, 2, \ldots n; j = 1, 2, \ldots m) \tag{1}$$

$$s_j^2 = \frac{1}{n-1} \sum_{i=i}^{n} (x_{ij} - \bar{x}_j)^2, (i = 1, 2, \ldots n; j = 1, 2, \ldots m) \tag{2}$$

Standardize each index value x_{ij}. Here is the formula:

$$\widetilde{x}_{ij} = \frac{x_{ij} - \overline{x}_j}{s_j}, (i = 1, 2, \ldots n; j = 1, 2, \ldots m) \qquad (3)$$

Calculate the correlation matrix: $R = (r_{ij})_{m \times m}$, Here is the formula:

$$r_{ij} = \frac{\sum_{k=1}^{n} \widetilde{x}_{ki} . \widetilde{x}_{kj}}{n - 1}, (i, j = 1, 2, \ldots, m) \qquad (4)$$

$r_{ij} = 1$, $r_{ij} = r_{ji}$, r_{ij} is the i th and the j th index's correlation coefficient.
Then find the eigenvalue (λ) of the relation coefficient matrix (R).

$$|\lambda I - R| = 0 \qquad (5)$$

The eigenvalue $\lambda_1 \geq \lambda_2 \geq \ldots \geq \lambda_m \geq 0$.
Calculate the information contribution rate of eigenvalue λ_i. Here is the formula:

$$b_j = \frac{\lambda_j}{\sum_{k=1}^{m} \lambda_k} (j = 1, 2, \ldots, m) \qquad (6)$$

Find the maximum contribution rate $(b_j)_{max}$, which the corresponding strong correlation index is defined as the core meaning cluster.

2.3   Make Sure the New Function Service Module

Finally, we finished the construction that based on meanings and objects through the mapping of the core meaning clusters and objects. Then we found users' key activities through the related items. Thus the user's truly needs could be mined. So we reconstructed the function models of the target product by analyzing users' needs. It is very important for the SAPAD framework that find the core meaning clusters and reconstruct the users' activities through it. As a result, the product functions can be optimized.

Here is the process about SAPAD-PCA frame in details (Fig. 1):

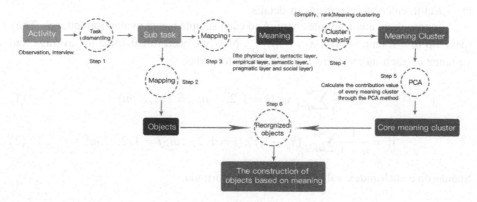

Fig. 1. SAPAD-PCA flow chart

3 The Practical Case About the Oral Health Care System of the Middle-Aged with SAPAD-PAD Frame

3.1 Make Sure Behavior Route of the Middle-Aged

We researched three special hospitals such as the Eight One Hospital of PLA, Nanjing Stomatological Hospital, Jiangsu Stomatological Hospital and so on. And we finally studied deeply with one of patients, A who took the treatment of periodontal disease, from the five.

The patient A, male and 56 years old, is a teacher in a high school. He lives in a residential quarters called Zhuyuan, Xuanwu District in Nanjing. Perhaps being influenced by the working pressure, environment problems and other factors, he often suffered from periodontal disease and went to hospital for treatment irregularly.

We tracked the route of patient A's treatment with the method of nonparticipant observation and interviewed with him deeply. So we understood the whole process from inflammation of the gums to the end of treatment and then depicted his treatment route (as shown in Fig. 2).

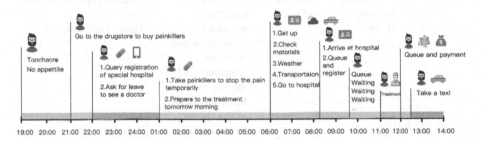

Fig. 2. Picture of A's treatment route

3.2 Construct the Oral Health Care Service System for the Middle-Aged

The Analysis to the Mapping of Activities, Subtasks and Objects. According to the A's treatment route, we divided each activities into tasks and subtasks and matched them with the related items. By mapping from activities to objects, we obtained six behavior modules: inflammation of gingiva and blood retention, choose a hospital to registration, go to hospital, take the number and wait at hospital, enter the clinic and have a treatment, end of treatment and so on. The Table 1 is about the behavior module of the selection of a hospital for registration. The module could be divided into the two task modules: there're still numbers on the line and none on the line. The module that there're still numbers contains three subtasks: search hospitals' information, search doctors' information and have an appointment with a doctor. The module about none number online contains three situations: delay but still choose special hospitals, choose community hospitals and go to the special hospital for offline registration. The module, delay but still choose special hospitals, could be divided into three subtasks: delay, go to the community hospital for registration and stop pain temporary and reselect the time and hang the number of the special hospital again. The module, choose the community hospital, contains two subtasks: hang the number offline and queue in the community hospital and hang the number. The module, go to the special hospital and hang the number offline, contains three subtasks: still choose to special hospital and hang the number, maybe there are some left and maybe or not.

Table 1. Mapping analysis from activity to object

Activities	Surroundings	Task	Subtask	Related items
Choose to hospital for registration	Home	There're some number online	Search hospitals' information	Patient/cellphone
				Patient/cellphone
			Search doctors' information	Patient/cellphone
			Have an appointment with a doctor	
	Home Community Hospital Home	None on the line (1)	Delay	Patient/cellphone
			Go to the community hospital for registration and stop pain temporary and reselect the time	Patient/cellphone/visiting card
			Hang the number of the special hospital again	Patient/cellphone
	Special hospital	None on the line (2)	Hang the number offline	Patient/cellphone/visiting card
			Queue in the community hospital and hang the number	Patient/visiting car/registration form
	Special hospital	None on the line (3)	Still choose to special hospital and hang the number	Patient/cellphone
				Patient/cellphone/visiting card/registration form
			Maybe there are some left	Patient/cellphone/visiting card
			Maybe or not	

The Analysis About Mapping of Activities, Objects and Meanings. We found the meanings behind the user's activities and divided them into six mapping layers [21]: the physical layer, syntactic layer, empirical layer, semantic layer, pragmatic layer and social layer, which formed the mapping of activities and meanings. According to the user's six behavior modules, we classified the twenty-eight subtasks as six meaning maps. Then we got the twenty-eight meanings that matched with the physical layer, twenty-two meanings that matched with syntactic layer, twenty-two meanings that matched with empirical layer, twenty-two meanings that matched with semantic layer and eighteen meanings that matched with pragmatic layer. Table 2 is the mapping analysis from activities to meanings about the module of choosing hospital to register.

The Cluster Analysis and Meaning Clusters. Clustering is the process that the data is classified into different classes or clusters. There's a strong correlation among the data in the same cluster. And there's no correlation among the data in different clusters [21]. We had the cluster analysis to the meanings of empirical layer, semantic layer, pragmatic layer within the principle of cluster analysis. The correlation of meanings is classified into four levels from 0 to 3, which 0 represents no correlation, 1 represents sick correlation, 2 represents correlation and 3 represents strong correlation. That is to say the sub-meanings in the same meaning cluster have a strong correlation and those in different meaning cluster only have sick correlation.

The semantic layer is the user's semantic experience. Here the semantic layer is the experience during the whole process of the treatment. We got six meaning clusters through the cluster analysis: (1) Pain and worried; (2) too much information to choose; (3) Too difficult to have a treatment timely; (4) Bad traffic; (5) Noisy medical environment; (6) High price and so on.

The empirical layer is that users understand the functions and process the information based on their previous experience and knowledge. We got seven meaning clusters through the cluster analysis: (1) Access to information efficiently by cellphone; (2) Community hospitals can make up for special hospitals; (3) Special hospitals are more professional; (4) Only be delayed if no number in special hospitals; (5) Fast by self-service process; (6) More convenient by car; (7) Medical insurance can make sure the lower price and so on.

The pragmatic layer is the purpose of symbols and the communication effects of groups in the Semiotics theory [22]. Here the pragmatic layer is users' expectations to products. We got five meaning clusters through the cluster analysis: (1) Want to get accurate and efficient information; (2) Hope the time as little as possible during the queuing and driving; (3) Hope be cured well; (4) Hope a good treatment experience; (5) Hope a favorable price and so on. As shown in the Table 3.

The PCA and the Core Meaning Clusters. We used the statistical method of the PCA method to analyzed the core meanings that obtained by the cluster analysis and let the six meaning clusters about the semantic layer as the indexes. The six meaning clusters is that: pain and worried (A_1), too much information to choose (A_2), too difficult to have a treatment timely (A_3), bad traffic (A_4), noisy medical environment (A_5), high price (A_6). We invited five experts to score for each meaning cluster, which let the scores as samples. The indexed are classified into five levels from 1 to 5, which 1 represents not important at all, 2 represents not important, 3 represents not sure, 4 represents important, 5 represents very important. We obtained the date matrix which shown as Table 4.

Table 2. Mapping analysis from activity to meaning

Activities	Tasks	Subtasks	Meanings				
			Physical layer	Syntactic layer	Empirical layer	Semantic layer	Pragmatic layer/social layer
Choose to hospital for registration	There're some number online	Search hospitals' information	Patient/cellphone	Unfamiliar with hospitals	It's convenient to get the information of hospital on the Internet	Search the information is Inefficient and time wasted	Eager to recommend hospitals
		Search doctors' information	Patient/cellphone	Unfamiliar with doctors	It's convenient to get the information of doctor on the Internet	Blind and aimless	Eager to be recommended hospitals
		Have an appointment with a doctor	Patient/cell-phone	Check numbers online	It's convenient to hang the number online	Convenient and quick	Eager to be recommended doctors
	None on the line (1)	Delay	Patient/cell-phone	No number in the special hospital	Delay and have some numbers	Too little numbers, feeling boredom	Eager to be treated as quickly as possible
		Go to the community hospital for registration and stop pain temporary and reselect the time	Patient/cell-phone/visiting card	Community provided treatment	Can be treated in community hospital anytime	Convenient to go to the community hospital	Special hospital is better than the community
		Hang the number of the special hospital again	Patient/cell-phone	Hang the number later	Delay and the special hospital would have some numbers	Pain	Eager to register as quickly as possible
	None on the line (2)	Hang the number offline	Patient/cell-phone/visiting card	Can be treated in community hospital	No number in the special hospital and go to the community hospital	Convenient to go to community hospital	
		Queue in the community hospital and hang the number	Patient/visiting car/registration form	Can be treated in community hospital anytime	There're some numbers in the community hospital	Convenient to see the doctor in community hospital	Hope to be cured by the community hospital
	None on the line (3)	Still choose to special hospital and hang the number	Patient/cell-phone	Hang the number offline	The special doctor is more professional		
		Maybe there are some left	Patient/cellphone/visiting card/registration form	Hang the number offline	Left some numbers that have been missed offline	Happy to register successfully	Eager to be treated
		Maybe or not	Patient/cellphone/visiting card	Hang the number offline	Maybe no number offline	Boredom to fail to register	Eager to be treated

We standardized the data matrix by using the formula (3) and calculated it to get the correlation coefficient matrix R with the formula (4). Then we calculated the eigenvalue λ of coefficient matrix R with formula (5) and put the eigenvalue λ into formula (6) to get characteristic value λ's the information contribution rate and relation of indexes. Shown as Tables 5 and 6.

Table 3. The cluster analysis of meanings about the semantic level

	Worried	Pained	Convenient and quick 1	Convenient and quick 2	Search the information is inefficient and time wasted Blind and aimless	Convenient to go to the community hospital 1	Convenient to go to the community hospital 2	Convenient to see the doctor in community hospital	Too little numbers, feeling boredom	Boredom to fail to register	Happy to register successfully	Terrible transportation	Noisy medical environment	High price
Worried	3	2	2	2	0	0	0	0	0	0	0	0	0	0
Pained	2	3	2	2	0	0	0	0	0	0	0	0	0	0
Convenient and quick 1	2	2	3	3	0	2	2	2	0	0	0	0	0	0
Convenient and quick 2	2	2	3	3	1	2	2	2	0	0	0	0	0	0
Search the information is inefficient and time wasted Blind and aimless	0	0	0	1	3	1	1	0	0	0	0	0	0	0
Convenient to go to the community hospital 1	0	0	2	2	1	3	3	3	1	1	1	0	0	0
Convenient to go to the community hospital 2	0	0	2	2	1	3	3	3	1	1	1	0	0	0
Convenient to see the doctor in community hospital	0	0	2	2	0	3	3	3	1	1	2	0	0	0
Too little numbers, feeling boredom	0	0	0	0	0	1	1	1	3	3	2	0	0	0
Boredom to fail to register	0	0	0	0	0	1	1	1	3	3	3	0	0	0
Happy to register successfully	0	0	0	0	0	1	1	2	2	3	3	0	0	0
Terrible transportation	0	0	0	0	0	0	0	0	0	0	0	3	0	0
Noisy medical environment	0	0	0	0	0	0	0	0	0	0	0	0	3	0
High price	0	0	0	0	0	0	0	0	0	0	0	0	0	3

We found that b_1 is the maximum of the information contribution rate after calculating and three of them, A_1, A_2 and A_3 had the high load, were strong positive correlation, which the three indexes were pain and worried, too much information to choose and too difficult to have a treatment timely. It was the reason that users were worried about too difficult to hang the number in special hospitals and too high of the time cost so that they eager to have a treatment timely. And users' real needs had never been understood so that they couldn't get the useful information effectively and they should spend large amount of time to query. This is why the index that too much information is difficult to choose also had a lot weight. With the same process, we could get the information contribution for the all layers that included empirical layer and pragmatic layer. Then we obtained their meaning clusters with high load: pick up

Table 4. The data matrix of semantic layer

	A_1	A_2	A_3	A_4	A_5	A_6
P_1	5	5	5	2	3	5
P_2	4	3	4	2	3	3
P_3	3	2	3	2	2	4
P_4	4	2	3	3	2	4
P_5	5	4	5	2	2	5

Table 5. The correlation coefficient matrix of semantic layer

Index	A_1	A_2	A_3	A_4	A_5	A_6
A_1	1.0000	0.871	0.896	−0.134	0.327	0.643
A_2	0.871	1.000	0.959	−0.514	0.560	0.642
A_3	0.896	0.959	1.000	−0.559	0.456	0.598
A_4	−0.134	−0.514	−0.559	1.000	−0.408	0.134
A_5	0.327	0.560	0.456	−0.408	1.000	−0.218
A_6	0.643	0.642	0.598	0.134	−0.218	1.000

Table 6. The information contribution rate and relation of indexes

		A_1	A_2	A_3	A_4	A_5	A_6
b_1	61.868%	0.886	0.993	0.984	−0.543	0.507	0.648
b_2	22.917%	0.274	−0.024	0.000	0.513	−0.754	−0.684

information effectively by mobile phones, fast by self-service process, hope the time as little as possible during the queuing and driving, hope a favorable price and so on.

The Mapping Analysis from Core Meaning Clusters to Objects. We had get the meaning clusters with high load by using the statistical method PCA, which were having a treatment timely, pain and worried, too much information to choose, pick up information effectively by mobile phones, fast by self-service process, hope the time as little as possible during the queuing and driving, hope a favorable price and so on. We concluded them into three meaning clusters as the core meaning cluster, which were convenient and timely medical treatment, relieve pain and cheaper price.

Through the mapping analysis from meanings to activities, we found that the core meaning cluster about convenient and timely medical treatment contained seven key activities: register conveniently, quick access number, convenient transportation, suitable registration, recommend suitable hospital, recommend the best route and transparency for hospital and doctor information. The core meaning cluster about relieving pain contained five key activities: give preventive suggestions timely, give medical guidance, provide relaxed and considerable services, care about the health of teeth and humanized design of environment. The core meaning cluster about cheaper price contained six key activities: enjoy the medical insurance, reasonable charges, provide price comparison service, provide insurance service, provide reimbursement service and reimbursement program. Shown as the Fig. 3.

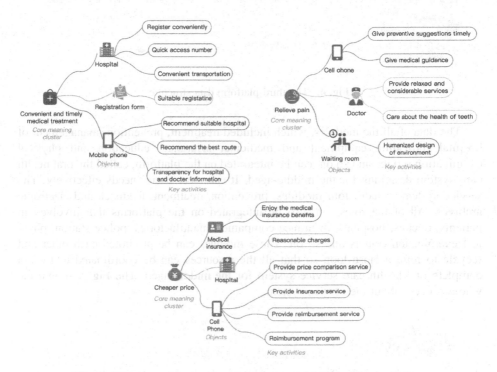

Fig. 3. Mapping with core meaning clusters, objects and key activities

The Oral Health Care Service Design of Middle-Aged Based on Behaviors, Meanings and Objects. We cleared the meaning and objective about the oral health care service system of the middle-aged with the construction of relationship of meanings. Then we obtained seven main key activities, included medical service, prevention and monitoring, hospital management, equipment and medical supplies, insurance service, health education and physical examination service and so on, that were concluded with the eighteen key behaviors. So we found that none of them, which were hospitals, government and patients, could not meet all needs that involved seven main key behaviors. As a result, we need a third platform that can integrate all data that involves hospitals, patients, districts and integrated care organization and so on. And it can provide all services like medical service for users, prevention and monitoring, management of hospital, insurance service, and health care education for the middle-aged by the way of analysis and prediction, calculation and importing AI model and so on. Shown as the Fig. 4.

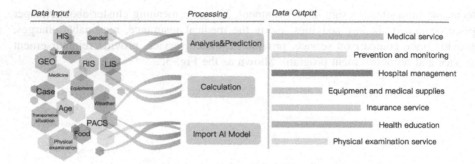

Fig. 4. The third platform data structure

The data of all the modules, which included treatment, prevention, management of hospital, providing equipment and medicine, insurance, education and physical examination service and so on, can be integrated on the platform, called the oral health care system designing for the middle-aged. It can meet users' needs effectively. The service system includes four modules: prevention, treatment, feedback and electronic archives. All of the roles can also be integrated on the platforms that involved in patients, doctors, hospitals, insurance companies, manufactories, police station, physical examination centers and so on. These modules can be promoted each other and recycle to form a close loop so that all the resources can be coordinated to form a complete oral health care service system for the middle-aged. The Fig. 5 shown the whole process about the service system.

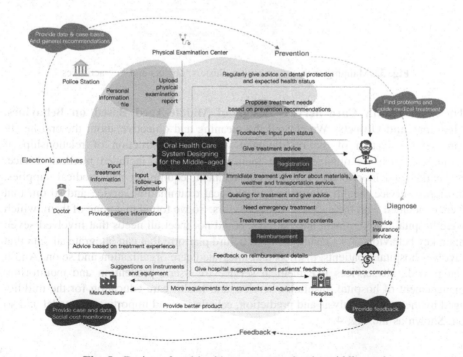

Fig. 5. Design of oral health care system for the middle-aged

In the prevention stage, the personal information file would be recorded by the police station in details from birth. The personal information would be send to the physical examination center. And the users' physical examination report data would also be shared on the platform. The user would receive the information about tooth protection and prevention suggestion regularly by the system which has synthesized the user's physical examination report and physical data. The user would take some actions of even raise some need about treatment according to the suggestions.

In the treatment stage, it includes two modules: the oral health care service and the oral treatment service. These two modules have similar process, so we take the process of oral treatment service as an example. When the user have some toothache, he would put his situation into the system. Then the system would give some treatment suggestions. The patient would enter one key registration based on it later. Then he would be recommended the most suitable hospital and doctor by the system that it decided according to the patient's need and the source status of the recommended hospital. And the patient would be suggested to carry the treatment documents, the most convenient and quickest path and provided the travel services to arrive at the hospital by the system that is decided according to the transportation and weather at the same time. At the end of the treatment, the patient can one key reimbursement to reduce his payment. The insurance company would recommend the most suitable insurance service to the patient according to the reimbursement situation.

In the feedback stage, the patient would have a comment on the treatment process. The system would help hospitals optimize their service according to the patient's feedback. It would have a further optimization for the algorithm so that it can develop a more suitable treatment plan to the patients next time. The staffs in hospital would also optimize their treatment service according to the feedback from the system. The doctors would also have some suggestions about the optimization of medical device and order some medicine according to their treatment experience. Manufactories would continue to optimize their device design and research on medicine according to doctors' suggestions. And they would supply the medicine to the hospital to meet their needs.

In the electronic archives, users' treatment information is synchronized to the system. It is combined with the personal information file uploaded by the police station and physical examination reports and they form the electronic archive together. The electronic archive provides some about prevention and health care service according to the data and cases. It also give the guidance for medical treatment. The data of treatment would also be synchronized on the system. Then the system would provide feedback and data to hospitals and manufactories, which would make them improve their service and products continuously.

All the data would be promoted and synchronized to the database that followed the process from prevention to feedback. This would make the system improve the algorithm continuously and provide more efficient service. As a result, the operating cost would be down continuously.

4 Conclusion

With the more and more serious problem about oral health care of the middle-aged, it would be urgent to improve their oral health situation by all kinds of effective methods. Moreover, it can be easy to ignored and the needs of taking care of their teeth is also increasing. But the existing system can't provide the suitable service to satisfy them. So we need to study the whole process of oral health care for them in a new perspective. Fortunately, we found the SAPAD theory framework, which can analyze the user behavior deeply, which establish a user-center product construction strategy. Then we combine the PCA method with the SAPAD theory framework, which can not only make use of the SAPAD to analyze the user behavior deeply, which establish a user-center product construction strategy, but also combine the quantitative research characteristics of the PCA. We provide a feasible scheme for improving SAPAD framework. In the practical aspect, we also provide a more scientific and feasible scheme for improving the oral health care of the middle-aged, and constantly improves the quality of life of the middle-aged.

References

1. Wang, X.: The Fourth National Oral Health Epidemiological Survey Report. People's Health Press, Beijing (2018)
2. Herrmann, G., Mueller, K., Behr, M., et al.: Xerostomia and its impact on oral health-related quality of life. Z. Gerontol. Geriatr. 50(2), 145–150 (2017)
3. Bidinotto, A.B., dos Santos, C.M., do Nascimento, L.H., et al.: Change in quality of life and its association with oral health and other factors in community-dwelling elderly adults-a prospective cohort study. J. Am. Geriatr. Soc. 64(12), 2533–2538 (2016)
4. Ehtesham, H., Safdari, R., Mansourian, A., et al.: Developing a new intelligent system for the diagnosis of oral medicine with case-based reasoning approach. Oral Dis. 25, 1555–1563 (2019)
5. Shimpi, N., Ye, Z., Koralkar, R., Glurich, I., et al.: Need for diagnostic-centric care in dentistry: a case study from the Marshfield Clinic Health System. J. Am. Dent. Assoc. 149 (2), 122–131 (2018)
6. Suebnukarn, S., Chanakarn, P., Phisutphatthana, S., et al.: Understanding information synthesis in oral surgery for the design of systems for clinical information technology. Br. J. Oral Maxillofac. Surg. 53(10), 968–975 (2015)
7. Tynan, A., Deeth, L., Mckenzize, D., et al.: An integrated oral health program for rural residential aged care facilities: a mixed methods comparative study. BMC Health Serv. Res. 18, 515 (2018)
8. Aro, T., Laitala, M., Syrjala, A.M., et al.: Perceptions of older people's oral health care among nurses working in geriatric home care. Acta Odontol. Scand. 76(6), 427–432 (2018)
9. Ju, X., Brennan, D., Parker, E., Mills, H., Kapellas, K., Jamieson, L.: Efficacy of an oral health literacy intervention among Indigenous Australian adults. Community Dent. Oral Epidemiol. 45, 413–426 (2017)
10. Kohli, R., Nelson, S., Ulrich, S., Finch, T., Hall, K., Schwarz, E.: Dental care practices and oral health training for professional caregivers in long-term care facilities: an interdisciplinary approach to address oral health disparities. Geriatr. Nurs. 38(4), 296–301 (2017)

11. Åstrøm, A.N., Ekback, G., Ordell, S., Nasir, E.: Long-term routine dental attendance: influence on tooth loss and oral health-related quality of life in Swedish older adults. Commun. Dent. Oral Epidemiol. **42**, 460–469 (2014)

12. Ordell, S., Ekbäck, G.: Smoking cessation and associated dental factors in a cohort of smokers born in 1942: 5 year follow up. Sci. Res. Rep. **69**, 107–112 (2018)

13. Kang, J., Wu, B., Bunce, D., Ide, M., Pavitt, S., Wu, J.: Cognitive function and oral health among ageing adults. Commun. Dent. Oral Epidemiol. **47**, 259–266 (2019)

14. Guo, J., Ban, J.H., Li, G., Wang, X.: Status of tooth loss and denture restoration in chinese adult population: findings from the 4th National Oral Health Survey. Off. J. Sci. Sect. Chin. Stomatol. Assoc. (CSA) **21**(4), 267–273 (2018)

15. Wang, C.X., Ma, L.L., Yang, Y., et al.: Oral health knowledge, attitudes, behaviour and oral health status of Chinese diabetic patients aged 55 to 74 years. Off. J. Sci. Sect. Chin. Stomatol. Assoc. (CSA) **21**(4), 249–257 (2018)

16. Hu, F., Sato, K., Zhou, K., et al.: From Knowledge to Meaning: User-centered Product Architecture Framework Comparison between OMUKE and SAPAD. Atlantis Press, pp. 877–885 (2016)

17. Hu, F., Zhou, K., Liu, Z.S.: Service design of community rehabilitation for the elderly based on SAPAD framework. Packag. Eng. **29**(2), 1–7 (2018)

18. Wang, Y.: Umbrella design research for driver based on SAPAD. Guangdong University of Technology, Guangzhou (2014)

19. Driver, H.E., Kroeber, A.L.: Quantitative Expression of Cultural Relationships. University of California Publications in American Archaeology and Ethnology, Inc. (1932)

20. Wang, Y.: System Engineering, 4th edn. China Machine Press, Inc., Beijing (2008)

21. Liu, J., Ma, A., Wang, N.: Product structure module clustering method based on design structure matrix. J. S. China Univ. Technol. (Nat. Sci. Ed.) **2**(11), 45–48 (2016)

22. Ariel, M.: Defining Pragmatics. Cambridge University Press, Inc., Cambridge (2010)

Consumers' Digital Capability and Demand for Intelligent Products and Services

Seonglim Lee, Jaehye Suk[✉], Hee Ra Ha, Yue Huang,
and YuanZhou Deng

Department of Consumer Science, Sungkyunkwan University, Seoul, Korea
jaehye.s@skku.edu

Abstract. This study investigated the effects of consumers' digital capabilities on demand for intelligent services and products in Korea using data from the 2018 Survey on Digital Divide collected by National Information Society Agency. Digital capabilities consisted of three dimensions, ability to use ICT, confidence, and ability to solve problems in using ICT. Dependent variables were whether consumers need voice assistant, biometric authentication, autonomous vehicles, and smart home. Seemingly unrelated probit analysis was conducted. The major results were as follows. First, ICT has been used mostly for digital shopping and consumption. Korean consumers were relatively confident on using new technology, but not quite confident on protection of information privacy. More than three-fourths of the respondents gained help from social network for problems solving using ICT. More than half of the sample solved problems by oneself. Second, there existed significant demand for intelligent products and services as at least more than half of the sample needed intelligent products and services considered in this study. Third, the effects of the sources of help for solving problems in using ICT were consistent across the different types of intelligent products and services: self-problem solving and having someone to provide help from intimate social network were positively associated with having a demand for intelligent products and services. The effects of use of ICT for various activities didn't show a consistent result. This study confirmed the important role of social network and social capital as a part of consumers' digital capability.

Keywords: Digital capability · Intelligent products · Intelligent services · Social network · Problem solving ability

1 Introduction

With the introduction of smartphones to consumers, various intelligent technologies have been rapidly spread into consumers' daily life. Recently intelligent services such as voice assistant and biometric authentication have been released in the consumer market, and intelligent products such as autonomous vehicle and smart home devices are on the verge of market launch. Intelligent products and services are expected to bring consumers convenience and efficiency that they have never experienced. However, intelligent products and services are not widely used among consumers.

© Springer Nature Switzerland AG 2020
C. Stephanidis and M. Antona (Eds.): HCII 2020, CCIS 1226, pp. 654–662, 2020.
https://doi.org/10.1007/978-3-030-50732-9_83

According to the 2018 Survey on Information Security in Korea, only 18.7% of internet users used AI services and only 3.8% used IoT products and services.

The benefits of intelligent products and services may be enjoyed by those segments of the population who have the requisite ability to use them. The ability to use ICT has been 'the indispensable grammar of modern life [1]. So called, digital capabilities increasingly have become part of the toolkit necessary to participate and prosper in a ICT based society [2]. They help consumers to use a variety of technologies, appropriately and effectively in different spaces and situations.

This study examined the effects of digital capabilities on the demand for intelligent products such as autonomous vehicle and smart home, and for intelligent services such as voice assistant and biometric authentication. Intelligent products and services are defined as those with the intelligence to take autonomous action and make decisions based on interactions with the environment. This study distinguishes between intelligent products and services in the form of existence: intelligent products exist in the form of physical objects and intelligent services are provided in the form of softwares.

In general, digital capability is defined as the skills, knowledge and understanding which help people to live, learn and work in a digital society [3]. This study seeks to broaden the concept of digital capability beyond the cognitive components such as knowledge and skills following the classical concept of consumer competencies. According to Moshes & Roy [4], consumer competencies that contribute to the individual's effectiveness as a consumer in the marketplace include specific behavioral acts and attitudes as well as cognitive components. Consumer scientists define consumer capability as a combination of knowledge, attitude, and behavior necessary to make sound market decisions [5].

Selwyn [2] argued that developing and sustaining an individual's use of ICT depend in large parts on an individual's network of relevant social contacts who can offer advice, encouragement and practical support. Individual's ability to draw upon social capital from the networks of friends, relatives, neighbors, other significant others, membership of groups and organizations, and technological expertise has been recognized as an important element of individuals' ability to effectively engage with ICT and become a critical factor in people's sustained use of ICT [2, 6, 7]. In the era of hyper connected society, being a consumer who is 'connected' or who remains 'disconnected' from technology makes difference in the ability of individuals to make meaningful use of ICTs [2].

Finally, incorporating the behavioral and attitudinal aspects, this study defines digital capability as a combination of attitude, behavior, and skills which help people to live, learn, and work in an ICT environment. The behavioral aspect of digital capability refers to actual uses of ICT for various digital activities including shopping, social networking, and productive activities. The attitudinal aspect refers to psychological confidence on ICT as many previous research has shown that the confidence is an important predictor of acceptance of new technologies. Skills reflect the social context of digital capability which refers to problem solving ability in relation with social network which works as a source of help to solve problems in using ICT.

2 Methods

2.1 Sample

Data from the 2018 Survey on Digital Divide conducted by National Information Society Agency was used for the analysis. The Survey on Digital Divide is designed to track the digital divide index in Korea and collects information about access to digital devices and services, use of ICT. This study used a nationally representative sample of general Korean population aged more than or equal to 7 years old. Among 7,000 subjects participated in the survey the sample for analysis was restricted to 6,245 internet users. The descriptive characteristics of the sample are shown in Table 1.

Table 1. Descriptive statistics of sample, N = 6,245 (Weighted)

Variables		Frequency	(%)
Gender	Female	3066	(49.10)
	Male	3179	(50.90)
Age	<= 10 s	949	(15.20)
	20 s	965	(15.45)
	30 s	1045	(16.73)
	40 s	1239	(19.83)
	50 s	1163	(18.62)
	>= 60 s	885	(14.17)
Education	<= High School	4122	(66.00)
	>= College	2123	(34.00)
Region	Seoul	1210	(19.38)
	Metropolitan	1637	(26.22)
	Capital area	1356	(21.71)
	Rural area	2041	(32.69)

2.2 Measures and Analysis

The dependent variables were consumers' demand for intelligent products and services. The dependent variables were measured with four dummy variables of which each was coded as 1 if respondents answered "necessary" to the question that how much the intelligent products and services such as voice assistant, biometric authentication, autonomous vehicle, and smart homes were necessary in their lives, and coded as 0 for the answers of "not necessary".

The independent variables included consumers' digital capabilities and sociodemographic variables. Digital capabilities were measured in terms of three aspects: behavior, attitude, and problem solving abilities in the social context. The behavioral aspects were measured with uses of ICT for digital shopping & consumption, social participation, economic activities, and public administration. Use of ICT for shopping and consumption was measured with 10 items in which responses were given on a 4-point Likert scale, with 1 = totally disagree and 4 = totally agree. We had 4 items to measure the use of ICT for social participation, 3 items for economic activities, and 2 items for public administration. Responses to the questions were given on a 4-point Likert scale, with 1 = totally disagree and 4 = totally agree. Attitudinal aspects of digital capability reflected consumers' confidence on dealing with ICT and consisted with two sub dimensions- confidence on using new technology and confidence on the protection of information privacy. Confidence on using new technology was measured with 5 items and confidence on the protection of information privacy was measured with 1 item in which item responses were given on a 4-point Likert scale, with 1 = totally disagree and 7 = totally agree. Problem solving abilities in the social context were measured with three dummy variables of which each was coded as 1 if respondents were able to obtain advice or help from oneself, intimate social network, and professional experts for problem solving in their using ICT, and coded as 0 if not.

We included whether consumers had perceived or known the four types of intelligent products and services as a control variable. Gender, age, education, household income, and region were included as covariates in the model. Seemingly unrelated probit analysis was applied because the dependent variables may be correlated. We used statistical package for STATA 14 to analyze that data.

3 Results

3.1 Digital Capabilities of Consumers

The level of the use of ICT for shopping and consumption was relatively high as the mean usage score of digital shopping and consumption was 2.88 out of 4. However, the mean scores of usages of ICT for social networking, economic activities, and public administration were less than 2 indicating that, on average, consumers had rarely used ICT for these activities. Except for digital shopping and consumption, ICT had not yet seemed to be penetrated in humans' daily life in Korea.

The mean score for consumers' psychological confidence on the use of new technology was relatively high approaching 3 out of 4. Regarding the protection of information privacy, consumers might not feel confident, as of which the means score was 2.44.

Regarding the consumers' problem solving capability in the use of ICT in the social context, about 77% of the sample solved the problem with a help from the intimate social relationship such as family, friends, and colleagues, 55% solved the problem by oneself. Only 17% of the sample responded that they depended on the professional experts. Digital Capability of the sample are shown in Table 2.

Table 2. Digital capability of the sample, N = 6,245 (Weighted)

Variables		Mean	(SD)
Use of ICT	Digital shopping & consumption	2.88	(0.61)
	Social participation	1.71	(0.80)
	Economic activity	1.92	(0.81)
	Public administration	1.72	(0.82)
Confidence	Use of new ICT	2.83	(0.64)
	Protection of information privacy	2.44	(1.00)
Variables		N	(%)
Problem solving of ICT use	By oneself	3442	(55.12)
	Intimate social relationship	4835	(77.42)
	Professional experts	1066	(17.07)

3.2 Demand for Intelligent Products and Services

As presented in Table 3, about two thirds of the sample responded that they needed biometric authentication and smart homes. The demand for voice assistant was relative low in that slightly more than half of the respondents indicated that it was necessary in their lives. About 61% of the sample responded that autonomous vehicles were necessary.

Table 3. Consumer demand for intelligent products and services, N = 6,245 (Weighted)

Intelligent Services	Voice assistant		Biometric authentication	
	N	(%)	N	(%)
Not necessary	2773	(44.40)	2112	(33.81)
Necessary	3472	(55.60)	4133	(66.19)
Intelligent products	Autonomous vehicles		Smart home	
Not necessary	2436	(39.00)	2180	(34.90)
Necessary	3809	(61.00)	4065	(65.10)

The results of the seemingly unrelated probit analysis of the demand for intelligent services, i.e., voice assistant and biometric authentication were presented in Table 4. Those who used ICT for digital shopping and consumption and economic activities and those who were confident on using new technology were more likely, but those who used ICT for public administration were less likely to have demand for voice assistant. Those who solved problems in using ICT by oneself and with the help from the intimate social network were more likely, but those who solved the problems with the employment of the experts were less likely to think voice assistant necessary. In addition, those who perceived voice assistant, whose age were in 10 s or 50 s + than whose age in 30 s, and who had higher education were more likely to have demand for voice assistant.

Table 4. The effects of digital capability on demand for intelligent services

		Voice assistant		Biometric authentication	
		Coefficient	Robust(SE)	Coefficient	Robust(SE)
Constant		−1.190	(0.274)	−0.697	(0.279)
Perception of services		0.533	(0.035)***	0.780	(0.036)***
Gender	Male	0.128	(0.034)	0.055	(0.036)
Age	10s	0.284	(0.071)***	0.166	(0.075)*
	20s	0.084	(0.063)	0.133	(0.067)*
	40s	0.116	(0.062)	−0.029	(0.065)
	50s	0.157	(0.063)*	0.036	(0.066)
	60s	0.171	(0.074)*	−0.060	(0.076)
Education	High school	−0.114	(0.044)**	−0.100	(0.045)*
Log (Income)		−0.024	(0.044)	−0.023	(0.044)
Region	Seoul	0.043	(0.056)	−0.115	(0.057)*
	Metropolitan	−0.138	(0.038)***	−0.093	(0.039)*
	Capital Area	−0.042	(0.578)	0.019	(0.058)
Use of ICT					
Digital consumption		0.081	(0.039)*	0.030	(0.040)
Social participation		−0.014	(0.030)	−0.070	(0.032)*
Economic activity		0.147	(0.031)***	0.068	(0.032)*
Public administration		−0.058	(0.027)*	0.013	(0.028)
Confidence					
Use of new technology		0.163	(0.034)***	0.135	(0.035)***
Protection of information privacy		−0.018	(0.022)	−0.022	(0.022)
Problem solving					
By oneself		0.280	(0.041)***	0.227	(0.042)***
Social network		0.231	(0.044)***	0.280	(0.046)***
Expert		−0.330	(0.044)***	−0.121	(0.046)**
ρ		0.633 (0.015)***			
Log-pseudolikelihood		−7047.315***			

The effects of digital capabilities on demand for biometric authentication were similar to those on demand for voice assistant except for a few points. Those who used ICT for social participation were less likely to have demand for biometric authentication. The effect of using ICT for public administration and digital shopping and consumption did not significant for the demand for biometric authentication. Youngsters were more likely to demand for biometric authentication than the elders.

The results of the seemingly unrelated probit analysis of the demand for intelligent products such as autonomous vehicles and smart homes were presented in Table 5. Those who used ICT for social networking and economic activities were more likely

Table 5. The effects of digital capability on demand for intelligent products

		Autonomous vehicles		Smart home	
		Coefficient	Robust(SE)	Coefficient	Robust(SE)
Constant		−1.148	(0.270)	−0.592	(0.277)
Perception of services		0.576	(0.040)***	0.587	(0.038)***
Gender	Male	0.066	(0.034)	−0.041	(0.035)
Age	10s	0.114	(0.071)	0.176	(0.073)*
	20s	0.057	(0.064)	0.097	(0.065)
	40s	−0.008	(0.062)	0.050	(0.063)
	50s	0.128	(0.063)*	0.154	(0.065)*
	60s	0.083	(0.073)	0.086	(0.075)
Education	High school	−0.184	(0.044)***	−0.167	(0.044)***
Log (Income)		0.060	(0.043)	−0.010	(0.044)
Region	Seoul	0.167	(0.056)**	−0.069	(0.057)
	Metropolitan	0.047	(0.038)	−0.040	(0.039)
	Capital Area	−0.058	(0.056)	−0.036	(0.058)
Use of ICT					
Digital consumption		0.041	(0.039)	0.112	(0.039)**
Social participation		0.064	(0.031)**	0.033	(0.032)
Economic activity		0.081	(0.031)**	0.061	(0.032)
Public administration		−0.062	(0.027)*	−0.016	(0.028)
Confidence					
Use of new technology		0.036	(0.035)	0.019	(0.034)
Protection of information privacy		−0.036	(0.022)	−0.010	(0.022)
Problem solving					
By oneself		0.292	(0.041)***	0.149	(0.042)***
Social network		0.242	(0.044)***	0.152	(0.045)**
Expert		−0.215	(0.045)***	−0.058	(0.045)
ρ		0.635 (0.015)***			
Log-pseudolikelihood		−7187.436***			

but who used for ICT for public administration were less likely to demand for autonomous vehicles. Those who solved problems in using ICT by oneself and with help from the intimate social network were more likely but who solved the problem by employing experts were less likely to demand for autonomous vehicles.

Regarding the demand for smart home, those who used ICT for digital shopping and consumption were more like to have demand for smart homes. The modes of problem solving by oneself and with helps from social network had a positive effect on demand for smart homes. Confidence did not show a significant effect on demand for intelligent products considered in this study. The effects of perceiving the intelligent products, age and education of the respondents were significant.

4 Conclusion

This study investigated the effects of consumers' digital capabilities on demand for intelligent services and products in Korea using data from the 2018 Survey on Digital Divide collected by National Information Society Agency. Digital capabilities consisted of three dimensions: ability to use ICT, confidence, and ability to solve problems in using ICT. Ability to use ICT was operationally defined as the use of ICT for digital shopping and consumption, social networking, economic activities, and public administration; Confidence was measured as psychological confidence on the use of new technology and protection of information privacy. Problem solving ability was defined in the social context and focused on three sources of help, by oneself, intimate social network, and professional expert.

The major results were as follows. First, ICT had been used most for digital shopping and consumption, and not been frequently used for social networking, economic activities, and public administration in Korea. Korean consumers were relatively confident on the use of new technology, but the confidence level on protection of information privacy was not high enough. More than three-fourths of the respondents gained help from the intimate social network when they had problems using ICT. More than half of the samples were able to solve problems in using ICT by oneself. Less than one fifth needed professional experts in solving problems of using ICT. Second, there existed significant demand for intelligent products and services as at least more than half of the sample needed intelligent products and services considered in this study. Third, those with higher education and aged in 10 s and 50 s tended to be more likely to demand for intelligent products and services. Fourth, the effects of the sources of help in using ICT were consistent across the different types of intelligent products and services: self-problem solving and having someone to provide help in the intimate social network were positively associated with having a demand for intelligent products and services. The effect of use of ICT for various activities did not show a consistent result. It may be partly because the levels of ICT usage were not high enough to generate a significant difference.

This study confirmed the important role of social network and social capital as a part of digital capability of individuals and as a stimulus to enhance the demand for intelligent products and services.

References

1. Wills, M.: Bridging the Digital Divide, Adults Learning 10–11 December (1999)
2. Selwyn, N.: Reconsidering political and popular understandings of the digital divide. New Media Soc. **6**(3), 341–362 (2004)
3. Mishra, C., Pandey, S.: An assessment of Digital Capability Training Programs among Higher Education Institutions in India. Library Philosophy and Practice, pp. 1–23 (2019)

4. Moschis, G.P., Moore, R.L.: An analysis of the acquisition of some consumer competencies among adolescents. J. Consum. Aff. **12**(2), 277–292 (1978)
5. Kim, M.R., Hwang, D.S.: Consumer competencies of urban wives and related variables. Korean J. Korean Home Econ. Educ. Assoc. **1**(2), 23–36 (1998)
6. DiMaggio, P., Hargittai, E., Neuman, W.R., Robinson, J.P.: Social Implications of the Internet. Ann. Rev. Sociol. **27**, 307–336 (2001)
7. Murdock, G., Hartmann, P., Gray, P.: Conceptualising home computing: resources and practices. In: Heap, N., Thomas, R., Einon, G., Mason, R., Mackay, H. (eds.) Information Technology and Society, pp. 269–283. Sage, London (1996)

Product Innovation Redesign Method Based on Kansei Engineering and Customer Personality Type

Yihui Li[✉], Meiyu Zhou, and Xiaohan Wu

East China University of Science and Technology, Shanghai, China
ingrid_yhl@163.com

Abstract. Most companies in modern society redesign to create new products. Redesign can improve product quality and shorten cycle time, but most redesign product innovations only modify a relevant reference element of the product, ignoring opportunities for redesign innovation brought about by factors affecting customer personality. This research introduces a product innovation redesign method based on kansei engineering and customer personality types. Based on customer personality types, three research goals were proposed. Based on the results of the analysis, a linear quantitative model was established for each personality type to explore the relationship between the customer's emotional experience and the elements of product redesign. From these models, design support information is generated to assist product designers in redesigning innovations.

Keywords: Kansei engineering · Customer personality type · Redesign

1 Introduction

1.1 Background and Motivation

Products can be redesigned to improve quality, reduce costs, extend product life, or reduce environmental impact. Therefore, redesign is an important part of the product development process. However, current redesign technologies may also limit product innovation. Redesign usually focuses on resolving conflicts between current product requirements and previous design capabilities [1]. Another aspect that plays an important role in product development is product design elements, which make product differences directly impress customers.

This study introduces a new approach to product redesign. The fuzzy quantification theory type 1 is used to synthesize the three dimensions of sensibility. According to the personality type of the customer, this method obtains suggestions for the combination and proportion of new redesign innovation points. In modern society, sunglasses are no longer just an indispensable product for people's sunshade, but also gradually appear as fashion items. This paper uses the research method of perceptual engineering to integrate the user's personality type into the redesign of sunglasses products, so as to improve the redesign level and customer satisfaction. Kansei engineering is the perceptual combined technology mainly designs products based on the sensitivity of

© Springer Nature Switzerland AG 2020
C. Stephanidis and M. Antona (Eds.): HCII 2020, CCIS 1226, pp. 663–670, 2020.
https://doi.org/10.1007/978-3-030-50732-9_84

people. It is a product development method based on consumer needs. It is a comprehensive interdisciplinary discipline between design, engineering and other disciplines [2].

1.2   Application of Kansei Engineering in Glasses Design

Eyewear design is a popular product that changes over time, focusing on personality and emotional experience, and belongs to the research area of perceptual engineering of product design technology. However, the research and analysis of perceptual engineering in eyewear design is not complete, mainly as follows, Emphasizes the relationship between human face shape and glasses, and ignores the in-depth understanding of the personality preferences of different consumer groups. Although the shape of glasses is important, it needs to be combined with the individual needs of customers, so that it is more relevant to its research and enhances the value of research and the practical significance of the redesign and development of eyewear products.

2   Method

(1) Use principal component analysis (PCA) to generate new concepts for eyewear product redesign, (2) use Relief method to identify relevant product design elements, and (3) use fuzzy quantification theory type 1 (FQTT1) to generate quantifications for product redesign model. By using the Relief method, identifying design elements generates related design elements. Based on the results of FQTT1 analysis, a linear quantitative model was established for each personality type to explore the relationship between the customer's emotional feelings and product design elements. From these models, design support information is generated to help product redesign.

In this research, sunglasses are in the field of product development. The research framework is designed in parallel to solve problems that begin with problem definition, research goals, methodology, results discussion, and conclusions. The method aims to achieve research goals. In this study, SPSS 21 was used as a data processing tool. The framework details and process of the research method are shown in Fig. 1.

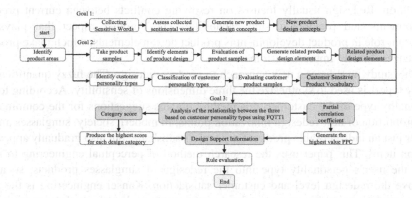

Fig. 1. Research method flow.

The research started by identifying the product area as the research object. After that, the perceptual vocabulary was collected through a questionnaire, and then new product redesign concepts were generated to achieve the first goal. Then, to achieve the second goal, for each collection the samples of the design elements were determined and evaluated based on the new design concepts to obtain relevant design elements. Finally, new design concepts and product design elements were synthesized for each customer's personality type to achieve the third research goal.

Four product design students and thirty customers with experience in buying sunglasses products participated in this research. The customers who participated in the survey were selected according to the purpose of sampling. The criteria are as follows: (1) Research sunglasses products, (2) Select or purchase sunglasses products, (3) Use sunglasses products, (4) Have the need to purchase sunglasses products. The evaluation steps are performed by using Likert scales.

3 Research Process

First, the adjectives describing sunglasses were extensively collected through the Internet and print media. After preliminary selection, 24 adjectives were obtained. After group research and discussion and analysis of the meaning of the perceptual imagery of the vocabulary, the words with similar meanings were deleted to obtain 10 perceptual products Image adjectives are "fashion", "simple", " delicacy ", "softness", "classic", "practical", "streamline", "lightweight", "stable", "cute". In addition, 10 antisense words were selected to match with them to obtain the subject's perceptual image space. The vocabulary group is shown in Table 1. After that, all the sentiment words obtained were evaluated on 30 customers using Likert scale (level 5). The results of the evaluation were then analyzed using the principal component analysis (PCA) method to reduce the collected sensible words.

Table 1. Screened 10 pairs of perceptual words.

Fashionable – rustic,	Simple – tedious,	Delicate – rough,	Mellow – sporty,	Classic– unique,
Practical – beautiful,	Light – heavy,	Streamlined – angular,	Calm – gorgeous,	Cute – sexy

3.1 Screening of Samples

In order to achieve the second research goal and conduct sample screening, firstly collected 48 sunglasses samples from the Internet, fashion magazines, periodicals and other channels, involving all the best-selling sunglasses brands in the market. Number these samples separately and use the online questionnaire, asked 30 subjects, let them choose 12 samples of their own preference, and finally choose the top 12 samples. By asking experts and designers, and according to different premise of the style, the final 12 samples were selected as Research object. Screening results are shown in Fig. 2.

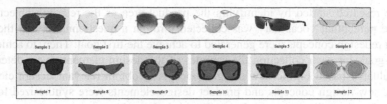

Fig. 2. Sample screening results.

3.2 Selection of the Test Target Group

The target group for this study is young people, which collects basic information of the testees based on several aspects, such as age, gender, knowledge background, and work status. Because young people are fashion and personality seekers, they have sunglasses design the higher requirements are the main consumer groups of sunglasses. Choosing this group as the research object has high research value. According to the semantic difference method, Likert summated rating scale was used to make the questionnaire. In this example, there are 30 test subjects initially, and their ages are mainly distributed between 19 and 35 years old. The basic conditions of the test subjects are shown in Table 2.

Table 2. Table captions should be placed above the tables.

Variable name	Category	Amount	Percentage (%)
Gender	Male	12	40%
	Female	18	60%
Profession	College student	15	50%
	Designer	3	10%
	Teacher	5	16%
	Seller	7	23%
Education	PhD student	2	6%
	Graduate student	21	70%
	Bachelor student	7	23%

3.3 Preliminary Data Analysis

Through preliminary analysis of 10 samples in Excel, the corresponding data between the samples and the sentiment words. Summary data available, among the 120 scores, there are 53 positive values, 3 values are 0, 64 negative values. Because the trend of negative values is the first 10 words after the previous screening, negative values account for 53.3%. It is verified that the samples selected in the previous stage are consistent with the research topic. Find the mean value of all negative values is −0.90, and the mean value of all positive values is 0.64. Select the data with an absolute value greater than 0.64 and less than −0.90. A value greater than 0.64 indicates that the sample tends to the right term, less than −0.90 The data indicates that the sample tends to the left vocabulary, which indicates that the testees has a stronger response to those words describing the sample.

Through the above analysis, we can obtain the subject's perceptual image data for sunglasses, and the design development direction that should be grasped in the redesign of sunglasses for young people. Using principal component analysis (PCA), the original data was used to perform dimension reduction analysis with SPSS software. The resulting eigenvalues of each component are shown in Fig. 3a, and the PCA variable factor map is shown in Fig. 3b.

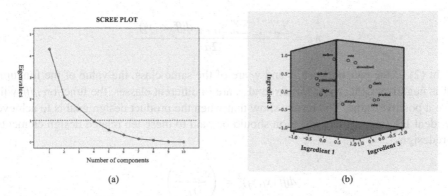

(a)   (b)

Fig. 3. (a) Results of eigenvalues; (b) Variable factor graph (PCA).

According to the results of PCA, three principal components with eigenvalues greater than 1 were generated. A vocabulary that appears more frequently in each sample is used as a general vocabulary. Combined with original data and SPSS output charts, it is derived from the factor analysis table. The key words are: *stylish, classic, simple, practical, light, streamlined,* and secondary vocabulary is: *calm, delicate, and feminine.* It shows that customers' perception of these words is higher for the emotional images of sunglasses.

3.4 Identification of Related Design Elements

The results of the design element recognition phase are shown in the table. The Relief algorithm is used to determine the relevant product design elements of the BT image. Basically, the Relief method is a method based on feature weights, inspired by instance-based learning, which detects those that are related to Statistically relevant characteristics of the target concept [3] (Table 3).

The equation is shown in (1). First, define the ith design element as f_i, where $F = (f_1, f_2, \ldots f_m)$, the weight of the ith design element is w_{f_i}, where $w = (w_{f_1}, w_{f_2}, \ldots w_{f_m})$, and the customer has m dimensional features ($i = 1, 2, \ldots, m$) and n sample sizes ($t = 1, 2, \ldots, n$), expressed as x_{ti} where $X = (x_{t1}, x_{t2}, \ldots, x_{tm})$ [4].

Table 3. Results of design element recognition

Design element	Type				
Glasses frames × 1	Half frame	Frameless			Full frame
	Square	Round	Oval	Sector	Bat-shaped
Spectacles × 2	Geometry		Irregular shape		
Nose pads × 3	Frame separation type		Fixed type		
Bridge of the nose × 4	Big arc shape		Micro-arc shape		
Pile head × 5	Geometry		Irregular shape		
Lens color × 6	Dark brown	Gray black	Green	Blue	Rose pink
Frame color × 7	Cool colors		Warm colors		
Decoration × 8	Color decoration	Jewelry decoration			Pattern decoration

$$w_{f_i} = \frac{\sum_{t=1}^{(n-1)} \sum_{j=(t+1)}^{n} diff(x_t, y_j)^2}{2a} \tag{1}$$

In (2), if the pair between x_t and y_j are of the same class, the value of the function diff is negative. Otherwise, when x_t and y_j are in different classes, the function *diff* will have a positive value. The results show that when the product design goal is to achieve the ideal BT image, more attention should be paid to these ten related design elements in redesign.

$$diff(x_t, y_j)^2 = \left(\frac{x_t - y_j}{r_{f_i}}\right)^2 \tag{2}$$

3.5 Redesign of Sunglasses Products Based on Customer Personality Type

At this stage, the personality type of customers is determined according to Hippocrates and Galen theory, and personality is divided into four basic personality types: (1) optimism (animation, cheerful personality, humor, outgoing, leading the trend); (2) Testy (strong, risky, powerful, dominant); (3) Melancholy (consideration, individualism, detail, planner, perfectionist); (4) Indifference (friendly, easygoing, peaceful, shy, adaptable Strong) [5]. Evaluations were performed using the personality questioner test. Evaluations from 30 respondents showed that the study had 9 optimistic, 10 Melancholy, 3 irritable, 8 indifferent.

Then, execute fqtt1 to find out the relationship between the descriptive variables that are defined in the value of [0, 1] and the numerical object variables in the fuzzy group given in one sample. As shown in (3) The illustrated FQTT1 model means a linear function that determines the category that best expresses the data structure by minimizing a given object change and its error variance.

$$y(w) = \sum_{i=1}^{k} a_i u_i(w) \tag{3}$$

In the above model, after further model calculations, FQTT1 method is used to find out the relationship between product design elements and customer personality types, and is used to describe a given image. In the model and Fig. 4, the category score indicates the degree of preference of optimistic emotional feelings for each category variable. If the grade is positive, the customer's emotions tend to BT images.

In Fig. 4, the partial correlation coefficient (PCC) indicates the degree to which the design element influences the design concept. According to the results in Fig. 3a, the maximum PCC of the optimistic "BT" image tends to the lens color (x6). The results indicate that the design element "lens" The relationship between "color" and "BT" images is the closest. Based on the obtained model, design support information is generated to determine the combination of product design elements based on the given new concept. The results of the design support information are shown in Table 4.

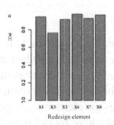

Fig. 4. PCC for optimistic design.

Table 4. Results of design support information for BT images.

Design element	Optimistic	Testy	Depressed	Indifferent
Glasses frames × 1	Half frame	Full frame	Frameless	Full frame
	Oval	Round	Square	Square
Spectacles × 2	Irregular shape	Geometry	Irregular shape	Geometry
Nose pads × 3	Frame separation type	Fixed type	Fixed type	Fixed type
Bridge of the nose × 4	Big arc	Slightly curved	Slightly curved	Big arc
Pile head × 5	Irregular shape	Geometry	Geometry	–
Lens color × 6	Dark brown	Blue rose pink	Gray black	Gray black
Frame color × 7	Warm colors	Warm colors	Cool colors	Cool colors
Decoration × 8	Jewelry decoration	–	Pattern decoration	–

Table 5. Design impact elements for four personalities.

Parameter	Optimistic	Testy	Depressed	Indifferent
Highest PCC	Frame color	Nose pads	Decoration	Glasses frames
Design standards	Dark brown	Fixed type	Jewelry decoration	Half frame/square

According to the results shown in Table 5, the most influential design elements tend to be optimistic "lens color", irritable "nasal pad", melancholic "decorative" and indifferent "frame". Generally speaking, all results show the relationship between each personality and its most influential design elements, these relationships often reflect their personality.

4 Conclusion

In this article, the redesign of sunglasses products is studied to show how perceptual engineering applies FQTT1 analysis to help product designers make decisions for new product designs for each personality type. The results of the PCA method show the collected perceptual vocabulary the extraction is reduced to a small range. By using the Relief algorithm, eight related design elements are generated. Based on the results of the FQTT1 analysis, a linear quantitative model is established for each personality type to explore the emotional feelings of customers and the product design elements. Relationships. From these models, design support information is generated to help product designers redesign their products. Overall, the results show that by developing a more scientific analysis of emotional vocabulary and product development of customer personality types, the Design level and customer satisfaction.

References

1. Li, Z.S., Kou, F.H., Cheng, X.C., Wang, T.: Model-based product redesign. Int. J. Comput. Sci. Netw. Secur. **6**(1), 99–102 (2006)
2. Cui, M.: Research on Female Eyewear Design Based on Perceptual Engineering. Yanshan University (2014). (in Chinese)
3. Kira, K., Rendell, L.: The feature selection problem: traditional method and a new algorithm. In: AAAI, pp. 129–134 (1992)
4. Djatna, T., et al.: Balinese aromatherapy product development based on Kansei Engineering and customer personality type. Procedia Manuf. **4**, 176–183 (2015)
5. Vorkapić, S.: Electrophysiological differences in sanguine, choleric, phlegmatic, and melancholic. Rom. J. Psychol. Psychother. Neurosci. **1**, 67–96 (2011)

An Evaluation Model of Commercial Ring Designs from Cognitive and Emotional Aspects Based on the Quantification Theory I

Ting Liu[✉] and Jian Shi

Shanghai Jiao Tong University, Shanghai, China
liuting9623@sjtu.edu.cn

Abstract. To better cater to aesthetic and emotional needs of contemporary customers, measurement of their subtle and sentimental evaluation and prediction of their perceptual values of commercial jewelries are of growing importance. Rings account for a great majority of jewelry sales. It is representative to research on the relationship between ring design and customers' perception. The ring form is decomposed into 4 items under morphological analysis. Three bipolar perceptive criteria are identified based on Kansei theory and through literature study and KJ method. 15 samples are selected via manual selecting and cluster analysis. Lastly, an evaluation model based on quantification theory I to predict consumers' sentimental evaluation of commercial rings is introduced. In this way, user's subtle cognition and attitude of a ring can be quantified and predicted. Designers can identify dominant design factors and improve their design more efficiently.

Keywords: Applied cognitive psychology · Quantification theory I · Kansei Engineering · Jewelry design evaluation

1 Introduction

Nowadays, significance of jewelry gradually shifts form material aspects to spiritual level. Consumers' cognitive and emotional evaluation of products matters much in making purchase decision. Many researches have investigated the relation between consumers' perception and design factors to predict consumers' affective evaluation. Related studies often consist of three main procedures which involve Kansei experiment, establishment of evaluation model and design verification. Kansei Engineering (KE) [1, 2] is firstly utilized to investigate people's psychological feelings and desires and then other methods is applied to analyze relationship between the psychological factors and design factors. Models are further built to measure and predict people's affective evaluation [3–7]. Hsin-His Lai, Yang-Cheng Lin *et al.* [6, 7] compared three different models' performance of predicting the simple–complex (S-C) product image value of different personal digital assistants (PDAs) forms. The three models are respectively founded on quantification theory I (QTI), grey prediction (GP) theory and neural networks (NN). Results suggested that the QTI model outperformed the other two models. The methods are also applicable to evaluate other kinds of products.

© Springer Nature Switzerland AG 2020
C. Stephanidis and M. Antona (Eds.): HCII 2020, CCIS 1226, pp. 671–679, 2020.
https://doi.org/10.1007/978-3-030-50732-9_85

Through literature study, it can be found that such research is few in commercial ring design. However, it is anticipated that the jewelry market will witness a remarkable growth and ring is reported the most crowd-pleasing jewelry and it shared 28.9% in the jewelry market in 2018 [8]. Customers with more disposable income and new perception of lifestyle regard rings more as a daily accessory. Ring's signification is gradually more concerning consumers' cognitive and emotional needs. Unfortunately, numerous rings' designs fail to satisfy the customer's needs and end up as a drug on the market.

Under research combined QTI with other theories and methods, this paper examines the relationship between consumers' psychological perception and form design of commercial rings. This study focuses on ornamental finger rings, excluding engaging ring or other rings which are of certain use.

2   Method

2.1   Morphological Analysis of Ring Forms

Ring form is decomposed into parts with sets of possibilities through morphological analysis [9]. Based on the analysis of the structure and form features of rings in market, the ring form is divided into 4 parts with 12 possibilities in total. Parts include inlay, hoop color, overall shape of ring hoop (small decorative patterns on the hoop are not considered) and image elements of the ring. Possibilities of inlay are classified into "No inlay", "Inlay with white diamond or other colorless gemstones" and "Others". Hoop colors involves silver white, pink gold, gold, and other colors. Single closed hoop without decorations and fancy hoop are two kinds of the overall shape of ring hoop. Image elements of rings include "Abstract figures", "Concrete image elements (such as animals and plants)", and "No decorative elements".

2.2   Perceptual Evaluation Criteria of Rings

Customers' cognitive and emotional perception of products can be described by Kansei words [2]. 46 Kansei words of rings are preliminarily collected by summarizing and integrating Kansei adjectives from related journal articles, papers, advertisements, etc. The words are then clustered through the first two steps of KJ method [10]. Combined with preceding related researches, three Kansei bipolar adjective pairs are identified: modern and traditional, simple and gorgeous, feminine and masculine.

2.3   Quantification Theory I

Quantification theory I (QTI) [11] is used to predict quantitative criteria based on the qualitative items. In the field of quantification theory, the Hayashi methods of quantification are widely used. Variables are classified into qualitative explanatory variables and quantitative criterion variables. In QTI, explanatory variables are named items and their possibilities are categories. The notation system of QTI is shown in Table 1. The three bipolar pairs are three criterion variables and samples' observations of the three criteria are indicated as vector y_1, y_2, and y_3, respectively. The four parts of ring's form are items and the possibilities are categories. The indices are listed in Table 2.

Table 1. The notation index of QTI

Notation	Definition
i	The ordinal number of a sample
j	The ordinal number of an item
k	The ordinal number of a category
y_i	The quantitative criterion value of sample i
x_j	The j-th item
C_{ij}	The i-th category of item j
r_j	The total number of categories in item j
$\delta_i(j, k)$	Dummy variable of category k in item j of sample i
b_{jk}	A constant coefficient that relies on category k in item j
ε_i	A random error in the i-th spot-check

Table 2. Indice system of ring design

Item		Category	
x_1	Inlay	C_{11}	No inlay
		C_{12}	Inlaid with white diamond or other colorless gemstones
		C_{13}	Inlaid with other kinds of gems
x_2	Hoop color	C_{21}	Silver white
		C_{22}	Pink gold
		C_{23}	Gold
		C_{24}	Other colors
x_3	Overall shape of ring hoop	C_{31}	Single closed hoop without decorations
		C_{32}	Fancy hoop
x_4	Image elements of the ring	C_{41}	Abstract figures
		C_{42}	Concrete image elements
		C_{43}	No decorative elements

On the basis of popularity and representativeness, 100 samples are initially selected from 10 jewelry manufactures, including Tiffany, Swarovski, Chow Tai Fook, Chow Sang Sang, Cartier, TASAKI, Bvlgari, Chaumet, Damiani, MIKIMOTO. Through Jaccard distance-based hierarchical clustering, the 100 samples are classified into 15 groups. A Kruskal-Wallis H test indicates that the 15 groups have a statistically significant difference on the 12 design features, with $p = 0.014$ of category C_{24} and the others $p = 0.000$. Then 15 representative samples were selected randomly from the 15 groups, respectively. Dummy variable $\delta_i(j, k)$ is introduced to quantify the response between category k and its related item j of sample i.

$$\delta_i(j,k) = \begin{cases} 1, \text{ if sample } i \text{ has the category } k \text{ of item } j \\ 0, \text{ otherwise} \end{cases}, \begin{cases} i = 1,2,\ldots,15, \\ j = 1,2,3,4 \end{cases} \quad (1)$$

Categories of the 15 samples comprise a 15×12-order matrix which is called the response matrix X.

$$X^T = \begin{pmatrix} 010000000010000 \\ 001110111101001 \\ 100001000000110 \\ 100010010000000 \\ 010000001101101 \\ 001001100010000 \\ 000100000000010 \\ 111001010010100 \\ 000110101101011 \\ 010100010010101 \\ 101010101100000 \\ 000001000001010 \end{pmatrix} \quad (2)$$

2.4   Questionnaire Survey of QTI

Questionnaires are made to acquire consumers' personal assessments of the three criteria, which involve modern and traditional, simple and gorgeous, feminine and masculine, of the samples. It is found that a semantic differential format scale out-performs a Likert one in many respects and respondents' reaction is more homogeneous in the semantic differential version [12]. A seven-point scale which admit a neutral choice is commonly applied in attitude tests [13]. A scale with 7 points is used to measure the three criteria of each sample in a semantic differential format.

The questionnaires were issued via a link to respondents one-by-one and 55 valid questionnaires have been collected. 85.5% of respondents are aged between 18 to 25 and the rest are over 25 years old. Women account for 83.64% of the total. 56.36% among respondents are exposed to jewelry at a fairly high frequency.

2.5   Data Preparation

To get a more accurate measurement of respondents' Kansei feeling, statistics defined as outliers are replaced with the mean of the category they subordinate to. Data on the high end of the distribution in boxplots are regarded as outliers in the explore procedure in SPSS. Mean scores of the three criteria of 15 samples are calculated without outliers to generate the three criterion vectors as followed.

$$y_1 = (4.25, 2.42, 2.20, 4.89, 2.11, 2.84, 2.71, 4.49, 3.11, 2.15, 4.29, 2.25, \\ 5.79, 3.67, 2.73)^T \quad (3)$$

$$y_2 = (2.96, 1.67, 5.00, 2.87, 2.32, 3.11, 3.65, 2.76, 2.11, 4.95, 3.71, 6.60, 4.67,$$
$$4.02, 3.33)^T \tag{4}$$

$$y_3 = (3.73, 6.04, 3.15, 5.74, 4.64, 6.37, 5.68, 6.27, 5.22, 4.41, 5.42, 4.33, 5.56,$$
$$4.93, 5.91)^T \tag{5}$$

Vectors y_1, y_2, and y_3 denote the average scores of respondents' evaluation of the 15 samples on the three criteria: modern and traditional, simple and gorgeous, feminine and masculine, respectively.

3 Results

3.1 Establishment of Evaluation Model of Ring Designs Based on QTI

According to QTI, the measured value of criterion y_i of sample i has the following relation with categories.

$$y_i = \sum_{j=1}^{4} \sum_{k=1}^{r_j} \delta_i(j, k) b_{jk} + \varepsilon_i, i = 1, 2, 3, \ldots, 15. \tag{6}$$

Take the first criterion, modern and traditional, as an example to establish the evaluation model. Predictive equation of criterion one can be written as Eq. (7).

$$\hat{y}_1 = x\hat{b}_1, x = (\delta(1, 1), \delta(1, 2), \ldots, \delta(4, 2), \delta(4, 3)) \tag{7}$$

Vector $\hat{b}_1$ consists of estimated value of coefficient $\hat{b}_{jk}$ of each category. Based on the method of QTI and the least-squares principle, vector $\hat{b}_1$ satisfies the following equation.

$$X^T X \hat{b}_1 = X^T y_1 \tag{8}$$

With the help of the mathematical statistical analysis software MATLAB, matric $\hat{b}_1$ can be work out.

$$\hat{b}_1 = (-9.962, -8.390, -7.117, 5.091, 6.670, 7.060, 6.332, 3.860, 3.152, 1.633,$$
$$1.700, 0.936)^T \tag{9}$$

Evaluation prediction model of the first criterion can be established.

$$\hat{y}_1 = x\hat{b}_1 = -9.962\delta(1.1) - 8.39\delta(1,2) - 7.117\delta(1,3) + 5.091\delta(2,1)$$
$$+ 6.67\delta(2,2) + 7.06\delta(2,3) + 6.332\delta(2,4) + 3.86\delta(3,1) + 3.152\delta(3,2)$$
$$+ 1.663\delta(4.1) + 1.7\delta(4,2) + 0.936\delta(4,3)$$

$$(10)$$

Similarly, evaluation models of the other two criteria are obtained as follows.

$$\hat{y}_2 = x\hat{b}_2 = 14.72\delta(1.1) + 14.642\delta(1,2) + 13.554\delta(1,3) - 7.385\delta(2,1)$$
$$- 6.979\delta(2,2) - 8.755\delta(2,3) - 8.052\delta(2,4) - 4.046\delta(3,1) \quad (11)$$
$$- 4.596\delta(3,2) + 1.305\delta(4.1) + 0.486(4,2) + 2.885\delta(4,3)$$

$$\hat{y}_3 = x\hat{b}_3 = 17.71\delta(1.1) + 19.919\delta(1,2) + 20.312\delta(1,3) - 11.595\delta(2,1)$$
$$- 10.969\delta(2,2) - 11.278\delta(2,3) - 11.975\delta(2,4) - 5.286\delta(3,1) \quad (12)$$
$$- 5.516\delta(3,2) + 1.6943\delta(4.1) + 2.579\delta(4,2) + 1.842\delta(4,3)$$

3.2   Contribution of Items

The contribution value of item j to a certain criterion is measured by the range of its coefficient $\hat{b}_{jk}$. Contribution values of items are listed in Table 3.

$$range(j) = \max_{1 \le k \le r_j} \hat{b}_{jk} - \min_{1 \le k \le r_j} \hat{b}_{jk}, j = 1, 2, 3, 4; \ k = 1, \ldots, r_j \quad (13)$$

Table 3. Contribution values of items

Item	x_1	x_2	x_3	x_4
Criterion				
y_1	2.845	1.969	0.708	0.764
y_2	1.167	1.776	0.549	2.399
y_3	2.602	1.006	0.230	0.885

4   Discussion

4.1   Importance of Design Elements

In the evaluation model, design elements are denoted as items. Range of item's coefficient $\hat{b}_{jk}$ represents the degree of importance of the design element to a certain criterion. From Table 3, it can be inferred that "Inlay" has the greatest influence on customers' perception of "modern and traditional". "Image elements of the ring" is most decisive on people's feeling of "simple and gorgeous". Consumers' feeling of "feminine and masculine" is most closely related to "Inlay". However, "Overall shape of ring hoop" has the least impact on all the three perception criteria mentioned above. Roughly, "Inlay" plays a significant role in people's perceptive evaluation of rings while "Overall shape of ring hoop" has the least influence. The sign of coefficient $\hat{b}_{jk}$ indicates the polarity of design feature's influence. It is obvious in Eq. (10)–(12) that feature "No inlay" has the greatest positive impact on the feeling of "modern" and "simple". Gold ring hoop makes people feel more traditional and gorgeous. Rings inlaid with other gems, such as colored stones, pearls, etc., look more feminine. Silvery ring hoop is more masculine than gold or pink gold ones. In this study, although results show that rings with other colored hoops arouse feeling of "masculine" most, it is hard to draw the conclusion as samples of hoops in other colors are mainly in black, which may confuse respondents' evaluation.

4.2 Discussion on Efficiency of the Evaluation Model

Correlation analysis and significance test between the observations and predictions of the three criterion values are conducted with SPSS to examine the efficiency of the model. Table 4 shows the Pearson correlation coefficient, the Spearman's rank correlation coefficient and p-values of one-tailed statistical significance test of the two kinds of correlation analysis between the observed value and the predicted value of each criterion. Take the scores of criteria as continuous variables, the closer the absolute value of Person correlation coefficient is to 1, the more efficient the model is. Take the scores as ordinal variables, the closer the Spearman's rank correlation coefficient is to 1, the more efficient the model is. Except for Spearman's rank correlation coefficient of criterion 3 is a little lower than 0.8 but well higher than 0.7, the other two criterion evaluation model's coefficients are both higher than 0.8. Results of significance test reach the significance level, where p-values are all near to 0. It implies that models of the three criteria have a good performance on predicting customers' feelings.

Table 4. Results of corelation analysis

Criterion	Criterion 1	Criterion 2	Criterion 3
Pearson correlation coefficient	0.870	0.852	0.847
P	0.000	0.000	0.000
Spearman's rank correlation coefficient	0.861	0.839	0.789
p	0.000	0.000	0.000

5 Conclusion

Distinct design elements function differently and their various features evoke varied feelings. The evaluation model established on QTI theory achieves a better mutual understanding with empathy between designers and consumers and clearly pictures the relationship between ring design elements and customer' perception of "modern and traditional", "simple and gorgeous", and "feminine and masculine". It is interesting to find that "Inlay" and "Hoop color" have relatively higher influence on people's feeling while "Image elements of the ring" and "Overall shape of ring hoop" plays a less important role. This finding may explain why there are more and more patterns of inlay and more colored ring hoops but the hoop shapes and image elements are relatively less varied in commercial ring market. Customers may be more responsive to gems and colors of rings. To some degree, the model may help ring designers improve and innovate their design more efficiently and designers can also verify their design.

However, more efforts are still needed in the future. QTI has been proved to be a good method of analyzing relationship among factors. The preparation of QTI analysis is vital to generate efficient outcomes. As for the sample selection, there is no standard method or procedure in the literature. This study tries manual selecting and clustering analysis to find representative samples, but uncertainty about whether the samples are representative or not still exists. Future study is needed to develop an efficient way of selecting representative samples from a large quantity of products.

Acknowledgements. Thanks for the help of all the participants in this study.

References

1. Nagamachi, M.: Perspectives and the new trend of Kansei/affective engineering. TQM J. **20**(4), 290–298 (2008). https://doi.org/10.1108/17542730810881285
2. Nagamachi, M.: Kansei engineering and its applications, **32**(6), 289 (1996). https://doi.org/10.5100/jje.32.286
3. Lin, K.C., Wu, C.F.: Practicing universal design to actual hand tool design process. Appl. Ergon. **50**, 8–18 (2015). https://doi.org/10.1016/j.apergo.2014.12.008
4. Shieh, M.D., Li, Y., Yang, C.C.: Product form design model based on multiobjective optimization and multicriteria decision-making. Math. Probl. Eng. **2017**, 1–15 (2017). https://doi.org/10.1155/2017/5187521
5. Chou, J.R.: A Kansei evaluation approach based on the technique of computing with words. Adv. Eng. Inform. **30**(1), 1–15 (2016). https://doi.org/10.1016/j.aei.2015.11.001
6. Lai, H.H., Lin, Y.C., Yeh, C.H.: Form design of product image using grey relational analysis and neural network models. Comput. Oper. Res. **32**(10), 2689–2711 (2005). https://doi.org/10.1016/j.cor.2004.03.021
7. Lin, Y.C., Yeh, C.H., Wang, C.C., Wei, C.C.: Is the linear modeling technique good enough for optimal form design? A comparison of quantitative analysis models. Sci. World J. **2012**, 1–13 (2012). https://doi.org/10.1100/2012/689842
8. Jewelry Market Size, Share & Trends Analysis Report By Product (Necklace, Earrings, Ring, Bracelet), By Material Type (Gold, Platinum, Diamond), By Region, And Segment Forecasts, 2019–2025. https://www.grandviewresearch.com/industry-analysis/jewelry-market
9. Ritchey, T.: General morphological analysis. In: 16th Euro Conference on Operational Analysis (1998)
10. Scupin, R.: The KJ method: a technique for analyzing data derived from Japanese ethnology. Hum. Organ. **56**(2), 233–237 (1997). https://doi.org/10.17730/humo.56.2.x335923511444655
11. Tanaka, Y.: Review of the methods of quantification. Environ. Health Perspect. **32**, 113–123 (1979). https://doi.org/10.1289/ehp.7932113

12. Friborg, O., Martinussen, M., Rosenvinge, J.H.: Likert-based vs. semantic differential-based scorings of positive psychological constructs: a psychometric comparison of two versions of a scale measuring resilience. Personality Individ. Differ. **40**(5), 873–884 (2006). https://doi.org/10.1016/j.paid.2005.08.015
13. Al-Hindawe, J.: Considerations when constructing a semantic differential scale. La Trobe Pap. Linguist. **9**(7), 1–9 (1996)

Designing a New Interactive Outdoor Light Installation for a Recreational Urban Trail

Marthe Victoria Paulsen, Anja Holter Gigernes,
and Susanne Koch Stigberg[(⊠)]

IT Department, Østfold University College, Halden, Norway
{marthe.v.paulsen, anja.h.gigernes,
susanne.k.stigberg}@hiof.no

Abstract. Interactive outdoor light installations change how we experience places and invite people passing by to engage with them. In this project, we investigate how we can design such an interactive light prototype to enhance a recreational urban trail. We applied a user-centered design process to develop a solution that fits our users' needs and demonstrate how the concept of northern lights can be used to create a more secure and inviting urban trail. Here, we present our design process and prototype to inspire future work in the field.

Keywords: Ambient lighting · Interactive lighting · Outdoor lighting

1 Introduction

New technology such as micro controllers, RGB leds or video projection and advanced laser technology have started to make their presence felt in the world of architectural light installations. They provide new ways of ambient experiences and can change the way we interact with our environment. The purpose of this thesis is to investigate how to make an urban trail in close proximity to our University College more attractive. We applied a user-centered design process to understand why the urban trail is not used that much and find a solution that makes the urban trail more attractive to students and staff. Section 2 present related work that inspired our design process. We outline our methods in Sect. 3, before presenting our design concept in more detail in Sect. 4. We conclude this poster paper with some initial findings from a field trial and suggestions for future work.

2 Related Work

Here we present two related projects [3, 4] that inspired us in our design process. Both projects use lights to create new experiences. They interact with people passing by constantly changing. They both have a lightweight feeling and integrate into their surroundings. In the following we describe each project in more detail.

© Springer Nature Switzerland AG 2020
C. Stephanidis and M. Antona (Eds.): HCII 2020, CCIS 1226, pp. 680–684, 2020.
https://doi.org/10.1007/978-3-030-50732-9_86

2.1 Dune

Daan Roosegaarde, a Dutch artist, presented a project called "Dune" [3], which aimed to create a natural landscape of technology. LED lights and sounds were interactive, controlled by people passing by. Motion sensors detect peoples' position, lighting up the installation at that location and creating soothing chimes. The installation was easy to move and tested in different environments in the Netherlands.

2.2 The Passing on Project

«The Passing on Project» from Milano is a collaborative project between the architect Makoto Tanijiri, lighting designer Izumi Okayasu and media producer Yahoko Sasao. They created an interactive installation called «Turn Light Into Delight» [4]. Visitors were asked to carry an acrylic LED cube when entering the installation that was shaped as an indoor pool. When people placed the cubes onto the water, they started to glow, creating a constantly changing experience as visitors come and go.

3 Method

We applied a four-step design process consisting of the stages "Research", "Ideate", "Build" and "Testing" [2]. The design process followed a user centered approach to ensure that our solution corresponds to actual user needs. We involved users during all four steps of the design cycle steps [2] using several iterations of user interviews and evaluations. Furthermore, we applied the prototyping framework by Houde and Hill [1] to create multiple prototypes, exploring our design concepts and evaluating our design choices. During the research phase we looked at related work presented in Sect. 2, interviewed people that lived nearby the trail and consulted a lighting expert regarding principles and guidelines for interactive lighting installations. From the interviews we established the concept of security for our lighting installation. During ideation we used sketches to explore different design dimensions. After several iterations of sketches and user feedback, we agreed on "Northern Lights" as metaphor for our design concept. During prototyping we created a 3D model using Autodesk Maya and investigated different materials for digital fabrication. Furthermore, we created and tested construction files for building the prototype. Finally, we tested our prototype in the field.

4 Final Design Concept

Our concept was inspired by the northern lights and its colors. The model is designed to reflect the natural appearance of the northern lights. The installation shall be pure and elegant, not disturb nature or the environment around the installation, instead integrate gracefully into its surroundings. To create this experience, we prototyped a physical model using plexiglass and a wooden base with lights illuminating the plexiglass. We engraved a geometrical pattern into the plexiglass using a laser cutter and implemented an animation simulating northern lights moving over the sky. The animation is controlled by sound from people's footsteps. In the following we present the look & feel as well as the implementation of the prototype in more detail.

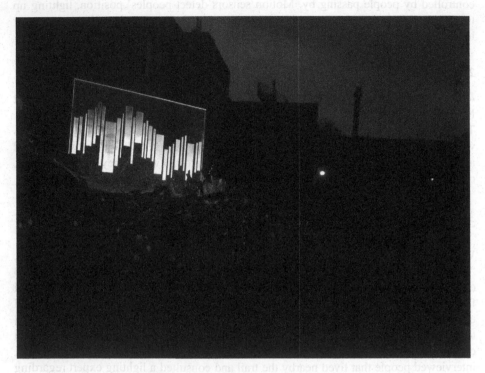

Fig. 1. Final prototype placed outdoors

4.1 Look and Feel Prototype

The prototype is made up from engraved plexiglas and a mdf base. The stand has an integrated neopixels[1] connected to a micro:bit[2]. Figure 1 shows the final prototype placed in the urban trail environment.

Material. We selected plexiglas as material, because it is light weight and transparent, making it almost invisible in nature. Only the engraved areas stand out as solid pattern. The base was made out of mdf, a natural material, provided support for the plexiglas and had space for the integrated technology.

Size and Shape. We explored different sizes as well as bending the plexiglas to create a wavy look without success. The final prototype was rather small to almost disappear in the environment if not lighted up, but still big enough to be noticed.

---

[1] https://www.adafruit.com/category/168.

[2] https://microbit.org.

Color. The choice of color was important to us, to create a feeling of security and reflects the northern lights. We choose colors ranging from blue/green to purple/pink.

4.2   Implementation Prototype

To create an interactive prototype we used two micro:bit, one as input device and one as output device. See Fig. 2 for a wiring diagram.

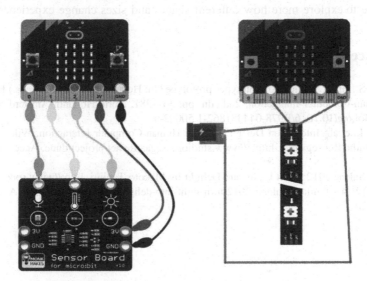

Fig. 2. Wiring diagram for input device (on the left) and output device (on the right)

Input Device. The animation was triggered by people's footsteps. We used the microphone sensor from the MonkMakes[3] sensor board. The input device was placed on the side of the trail in a watertight transparent plastic bag. We needed some testing to find the right threshold to trigger the animation. If the threshold is passed the input device sends a signal to the output device using the built-in radio functionality. We implemented a second micro:bit as backup input device for testing purposes, enabling a wizard of oz testing scenario, if the sensor would not trigger. If the A or B button was pressed, the micro:bit send a signal to the output device using the built-in radio functionality.

Output Device. We implemented a listener in a second micro:bit. If a new radio message was received an animation was started. The brightness of the animation was adapted to the environment using the built-in light sensor. The Neopixel stripe had external 5 V power supply. The electronic components were stored in a watertight transparent plastic bag.

---

[3] https://www.monkmakes.com.

5 Initial Findings and Future Work

From the initial field test, we received overall positive feedback. People passing by expressed that the prototype fits nicely in the environment and felt that the combination of colors we chose were harmonic, calming and comfortable. However, the prototype was rather small and did not provide a feeling of security for the whole trail. In future work, we would like to explore adding several prototypes as a series of animation following the users footsteps, similar to the project by Dune [3]. Furthermore, we would like to explore more how different shapes and sizes change experiences.

References

1. Houde, S., Hill, C.: What do prototypes prototype? In: Helander, M.G., et al. (eds.) Handbook of Human-Computer Interaction, 2nd edn, pp. 367–381, North-Holland, Amsterdam (1997). https://doi.org/10.1016/B978-044481862-1.50082-0
2. Sharp, H., et al.: Interaction Design: Beyond Human-Computer Interaction. Wiley (2019)
3. Dune|Studio Roosegaarde. https://www.studioroosegaarde.net/project/dune. Accessed 19 Mar 2020
4. Milano Salone 2012: Turn Light Into Delight by Makoto Tanijiri. http://www.spoon-tamago.com/2012/04/19/milano-salone-2012-turn-light-into-delight-by-makoto-tanijiri/. Accessed 19 Mar 2020

Study on the External Ear Size of Chinese Minors for Product Design

Linghua Ran$^{(\boxtimes)}$, He Zhao, and Zhongting Wang

SAMR Key Laboratory of Human Factors and Ergonomics (CNIS),
China National Institute of Standardization, Beijing, China
ranlh@cnis.ac.cn

Abstract. In this study, 532 minors from northern China were selected to measure their facial ear length and width. Data statistics showed that there was significant difference in the length of facial ears between different genders (P < 0.05), and there was no significant difference in the width of facial ears between different genders (P < 0.05). The length and width of facial ears of boys and girls increased with the increase of age, but there was no significant difference between different ages (P < 0.05). The research results can provide data support for the ergonomic design of earphones, earmuffs and other ear products.

Keywords: Chinese minor · External ear · Size

1 Introduction

In China, there are about 120 million people with hearing impairment at present, a considerable part of the causes of hearing impairment in young people are related to long-term use of earphones. Bad habits of using earphones and long-term wearing of uncomfortable earphones will cause ear injury [1]. So it is very important to minimize the physical damage of earphones and to improve the comfort of wearing earphones for a long time.

Studies have shown that 45% of headphone users consider the comfort of headphones as the primary consideration when purchasing headphones [2]. Unreasonable earphone shape is not only easy to fall off when wearing, but also easy to cause discomfort such as local pressure and swelling pain of the wearer. Recent research has found that extending the shape of earphone and earplug can make the wearer feel more comfortable, but also not easy to fall off [3].

The data of minors' ears is the basis of the design of earphones, earmuffs and ear protection articles. The length, width and proportion of minors' external ear contour should be fully considered in the design. At present, most of the researches on the characteristics of the ear are on adults, but few on minors. Qi Na [4] et al. studied the auricle morphological characteristics of 202 adult women and 202 adult men, and gave the representative average ear details according to the statistical results, but did not include the ear data of minors. Yin Xingzhong [5] and others measured the auricles of 120 young students aged 19-23. The measurement tool is Martin caliper, and the measurement items include 6 indexes of left and right auricles. Jiancai [6] et al. studied

© Springer Nature Switzerland AG 2020
C. Stephanidis and M. Antona (Eds.): HCII 2020, CCIS 1226, pp. 685–688, 2020.
https://doi.org/10.1007/978-3-030-50732-9_87

the auricle development of 110 children in Changsha area. The subjects were 2–12-year-old minors, mainly providing data reference for plastic surgeons to choose the time of ear reconstruction and the size of cartilage scaffold carving.

In this paper, 532 minors in northern China were studied in order to provide data support for the design of earphones, earmuffs and ear protectors.

2   Experiment Method

The measurement items include ear length and ear width. The definitions of these two measurement items come from GB/T 5703:2010 [7]. We have made a manual measurement with a Martin scale. Each measurement personnel have been trained in the early stage and have passed the measurement assessment. During the measurement, the subjects sat on the chair with their eyes flat in front of them and remained motionless. The tester held the Martin ruler on the right side of the subject and measured the length and width of the right ear.

3   Experimental Subject

The sample of this sampling is 532 minors aged 12–17 in northern China. The distribution of subjects is shown in Table 1.

Table 1. Information of subjects

Age group	Boys	Girls	Total
Age 12–13	75	73	148
Age 14–15	120	38	203
Age 16–17	102	79	181

4   Data Analysis

4.1   Ear Data Differences Between Different Genders

The statistical values of ear length and width for boys and girls are shown in Table 2.

Table 2. The statistical values of ear length and width

Gender	Ear length		Ear width	
	Mean value	Standard deviation	Mean value	Standard deviation
Boys	62.33	4.247	35.48	2.681
Girls	58.93	4.145	33.49	2.533

It can be seen from Table 2 that the average ear length of boys is 62.3 mm, and that of girls is 58.9 mm. The average ear length of boys is 3.4 mm larger than that of girls. The mean ear width of boys was 35.5 mm, that of girls was 33.5 mm, and that of boys was 2 mm larger than that of girls.

Independent sample test was conducted. It was found that there was a significant difference in the ear length between different genders (P < 0.05), and there was no significant difference in the ear width between different genders (P < 0.05).

4.2   Ear Data Differences of Different Age Groups

The data of ear length and ear width of different ages are shown in Fig. 1.

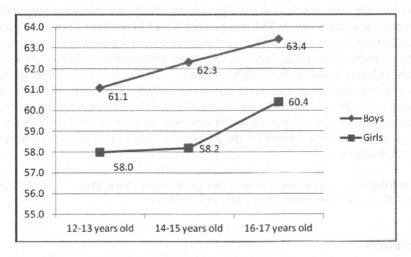

Fig. 1. Ear length of minors of different ages

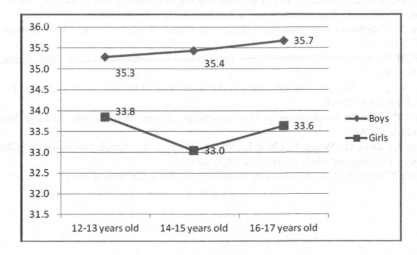

Fig. 2. Ear width of minors of different ages

It can be seen from Fig. 1 and Fig. 2 that the ear length and ear width of boys increase with age. The length of ear increased from 61.1 mm in 12–13 years old to 63.4 mm in 16–17 years old, and the width of ear increased from 35.3 mm in 12–13 years old to 35.7 mm in 16–17 years old, However, there was no significant difference between the two groups ($P < 0.05$), the difference between the two groups was not significant ($P < 0.05$).

5   Conclusion

The data of minors' ears is the basis for the design of earphones, earmuffs and ear protectors. The length, width and proportion of the external ear contour of minors should be fully considered in the design. In this study, we measured the facial ear length and facial ear width of 532 minors aged 12–17 in northern China, and grouped them according to age and gender, and analyzed them by statistical methods. The statistical results showed that there was significant difference in the length of facial ears between different genders ($P < 0.05$), and there was no significant difference in the width of facial ears between different genders ($P < 0.05$). The length and width of the ears increased with age, but there was no significant difference between the appearance ear length and the appearance ear width between the ages ($P < 0.05$). The research results can provide data support for the ergonomic design of earphones, earmuffs and other ear products.

Acknowledgment.   This research is supported by "Presidents Fund Project" (522018Y-5984), National Key R&D Program of China (2017YFF0206602).

References

1. Bo, D., Yan, Z., Yusheng, W., et al.: Epidemiological investigation of hearing impairment and ear disease in Jilin Province research. Chin. J. Otol. **5**, 20 (2007)
2. Lei, Y.: Interpersonal relationship and acoustic design of earphones. Speakers Microphones **35**, 2 (2011)
3. Liu, B.S.: Incorporating anthropometry into design of ear-related products. Appl. Ergon. **39**, 115 (2008)
4. Qi, N., Li, L., Zhao, W.: Morphometry and classification of Chinese adult's auricles. Acoust. Technol. **29**(5) (2010)
5. Jian, C., Auricle development of Han nationality children in Changsha. Xiangya Medical College (2008)
6. Yin, X., Zhao, D., Wang, J., Chen, L., Wang, P., Chen, K.: Auricle observation of Chinese youth. Heilongjiang Med. Pharm Acy **32**(1) (2009)
7. GB/T 5703:2010 Basic human body measurements for technological design

Impression Estimation Model for Clothing Patterns Using Neural Style Features

Natsuki Sunda[1], Kensuke Tobitani[1], Iori Tani[1], Yusuke Tani[1],
Noriko Nagata[1(✉)], and Nobufumi Morita[2]

[1] Kwansei Gakuin University, 2-1, Gakuen, Sanda, Hyogo, Japan
nagata@kwansei.ac.jp
[2] Couture Digital Ltd, Sankyo Sakaisujihonmachi Building F9 1-8-2, Bakurou-machi,
Chuo-ku, Osaka, Osaka, Japan

Abstract. In product design, the impressions evoked by surface properties of objects attract attention. These impressions are called affective texture and demand is growing for technologies that quantify, index, and model it. Even in the fashion industry, the diversification of user needs necessitates the customization and personalization of products. Consequently, there has been a focus on custom-made services. However, enormous amounts of time and human costs are needed to find clothing patterns to suit one's own preferences and ideas from among the countless patterns available. This research focused on affective texture related to visual impressions, and we proposed a method for automatically estimating the affective texture evoked by clothing patterns. To this end, we conducted the following steps: (1) quantified the visual impressions for patterns; (2) extracted style features as physical characteristics; and (3) modeled the relationships between visual impressions and physical characteristics. Afterward, based on the obtained models, we estimated the impressions for unlabeled patterns. Then, we verified their validity through relative evaluation and absolute evaluation, and we confirmed that our models estimated the impressions corresponded to the impressions that people actually felt. In addition, we implemented a system to enable users to intuitively search for patterns.

Keywords: Fashion · Texture · CNN · Lasso regression

1 Introduction

In product design, not only designs, such as colors and shapes, but also the impressions (e.g., "luxurious" or "antique") evoked by surface properties of objects attract attention. These impressions are called affective texture, which is an important factor in preference for or the quality judgment of an object. Therefore, demand is growing for technologies that quantify, index, and model affective texture.

Even in the fashion industry, the diversification of user needs necessitates the customization and personalization of products. Consequently, there has been a

C. Stephanidis and M. Antona (Eds.): HCII 2020, CCIS 1226, pp. 689–697, 2020.
https://doi.org/10.1007/978-3-030-50732-9_88

focus on services that allow customers to order custom-made clothing on the Internet. However, enormous amounts of time and human costs are needed to design unique clothing. For example, it is difficult to find clothing patterns to suit one's own preferences and ideas from among the countless patterns available.

This research focuses on affective texture related to visual impressions, and we propose a method for automatically estimating the affective texture evoked by clothing patterns. To this end, we model the relationships between visual impressions and physical characteristics. In addition, based on the obtained models, we implement a system to enable users to intuitively search for patterns.

2   Previous Research

Research on texture analysis has been conducted for a long time, and various texture features have been proposed [1,2]. In recent years, Gatys et al. [3] has been proposed an algorithm for transferring an image style using VGG-19 [4], which is a convolutional neural network used for object recognition. In their research, it is suggested that content features are necessary for object recognition and that style features represent the detailed appearance in images, such as multi-scale color information and the pattern information, and are not as important for object recognition.

Thereby, Takemoto et al. thought that style features were strongly related to affective texture based on unique texture properties (uniformity, density, coarseness, roughness, regularity, linearity, directionality, direction, frequency, and phase [5]). Thus, they proposed a texture synthesis method with the desired affective texture using style features and showed high-precision results [6].

In this research, we think that clothing patterns are also part of texture. Therefore, based on Takemoto et al., we use style features as physical characteristics representing patterns and clarify the relationships with the visual impressions they evoke.

3   Proposed Method

In this research, we propose a method for automatically estimating the affective texture evoked by clothing patterns. Figure 1 shows an overview of our approach. First, we conducted a subjective evaluation experiment and a factor analysis, and quantified the visual impressions of a small number of patterns. Next, we extracted style features as physical characteristics using a VGG-19 network. Afterward, we conducted a lasso regression and constructed impression estimation models. Finally, using our models, we estimated the impressions for a large number of unlabeled patterns.

4   Quantification of Visual Impressions

4.1   Subjective Evaluation Experiment

We conducted a subjective evaluation experiment in order to quantify the visual impressions evoked by patterns.

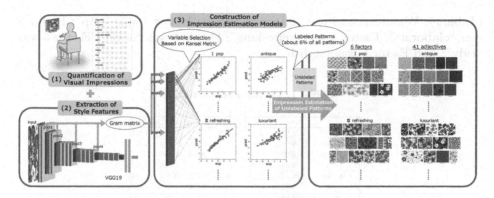

Fig. 1. Overview of our proposed method

First, it was necessary to gather and select comprehensive and representative words for evaluating visual impressions. Based on Tobitani et al. [7], we conducted a free writing experiment using 10 pattern images. Then, we verified whether the obtained words were suitable for visual impressions. As a result, we selected 28 adjectives with high fitness. We also added 12 adjectives that previous research used for clothing materials and the feel of materials [8–10] and "cute" from the viewpoint of actual use. Finally, we used 41 adjectives as the evaluation words in this experiment.

Next, we specifically focused on flower patterns and collected 1,158 such images. Then, in order to select comprehensive and representative stimuli, we conducted clustering based on style features extracted from the images. Based on the divided clusters, we selected 75 images as the stimuli. The extraction of style features is described in Sect. 5.1.

A total of 40 graduate and undergraduate students (18 men; 22 women; average age: 21.9 ± 2.8 years) participated in this experiment. The participants observed stimuli shown on an LCD monitor and evaluated their impressions on a seven-point Likert scale. In order to reduce the burden on them, we had them use 10 or 11 out of the 41 evaluation words. To take the order effect into consideration, the order of the evaluation words was randomized for each stimulus, and the order of the stimuli was randomized for each participant.

Through this experiment, we obtained data for 10 participants per stimulus and per evaluation word. Then, we scored each scale from -3 to 3 in one-point increments. For each evaluation word, we calculated the average score, and defined it as the evaluation score for the impression of each stimulus.

4.2 Factor Analysis

In order to extract and quantify latent factors that contributed to the impressions evoked by the patterns, we conducted a factor analysis of the evaluation scores using the maximum likelihood method and promax rotation. As a result, six factors were extracted, and the cumulative contribution ratio was 81.1%

(Table 1). We interpreted each factor as follows: Factor 1 was "pop"; Factor 2 was "elaborate"; Factor 3 was "refreshing"; Factor 4 was "novel"; Factor 5 was "tidy"; and Factor 6 was "stylish".

Table 1. Factor analysis results

	Factor1	Factor2	Factor3	Factor4	Factor5	Factor6
cheerful	0.971	-0.171	-0.083	0.120	0.194	0.034
bright	0.916	-0.202	0.075	0.090	0.291	-0.001
gloomy	-0.906	0.145	-0.134	0.084	-0.155	-0.149
dark	-0.881	0.240	0.109	-0.272	-0.414	-0.024
mature	-0.864	0.177	0.070	0.011	0.280	0.442
vivid	0.852	0.256	-0.006	-0.138	0.116	0.121
plain	-0.845	-0.182	-0.104	0.050	-0.005	-0.083
stand-out	0.844	0.158	-0.023	-0.142	-0.296	0.003
lively	0.830	0.276	-0.046	0.005	0.109	-0.065
flashy	0.775	0.326	-0.148	-0.065	-0.079	0.060
calm	-0.736	-0.131	0.151	-0.054	0.340	-0.009
glittering	0.727	0.273	0.004	-0.050	-0.114	-0.109
colorful	0.691	0.275	-0.282	0.041	0.274	-0.118
Japanese-style	-0.634	0.260	-0.003	0.005	0.292	-0.374
modest	-0.593	-0.459	-0.153	0.074	0.209	-0.038
antique	-0.564	0.046	-0.320	-0.165	0.125	-0.214
luxuriant	0.556	0.427	-0.133	-0.222	0.458	0.261
rustic	-0.489	0.142	-0.268	0.034	-0.392	-0.290
contemporary	0.433	-0.078	0.335	0.274	-0.019	0.222
eccentric	0.392	0.286	-0.138	0.332	-0.341	0.052
complex	-0.142	0.987	0.084	0.204	0.186	-0.135
simple	0.056	-0.955	-0.035	-0.232	-0.202	0.068
multilayered	0.100	0.869	0.232	-0.110	-0.009	-0.126
rattling	0.325	0.748	0.148	-0.166	-0.204	-0.269
gorgeous	0.218	0.613	-0.241	-0.171	0.023	0.464
commonplace	-0.122	-0.598	0.009	-0.365	0.107	-0.058
mysterious	-0.495	0.530	-0.130	0.466	-0.119	0.118
cool-looking	-0.008	0.042	0.973	-0.091	0.179	-0.218
cool	-0.323	0.217	0.965	-0.026	-0.189	0.070
breezy	0.184	-0.035	0.696	-0.025	0.466	0.001
typical	0.029	-0.099	0.083	-0.915	-0.014	0.188
free	0.501	0.054	0.013	0.696	0.281	-0.206
unique	0.054	0.590	-0.076	0.602	0.101	-0.247
futuristic	0.222	0.254	0.115	0.587	-0.105	0.071
cute	0.271	-0.152	-0.013	0.186	0.851	-0.171
elegant	-0.563	0.293	-0.080	-0.154	0.695	0.290
beautiful	0.159	0.261	0.405	-0.166	0.638	0.237
sophisticated	-0.176	-0.232	0.323	-0.067	0.102	0.610
Western-style	0.360	-0.209	-0.152	-0.417	0.081	0.537
attractive	-0.074	0.216	0.362	0.221	-0.131	0.413
modern	0.213	0.192	0.180	0.186	-0.036	0.347

Finally, we defined the evaluation scores obtained from the subjective evaluation experiment and the factor scores obtained from the factor analysis as the quantified impressions (impression values) for the patterns.

5   Modeling the Relationships Between Visual Impressions and Physical Characteristics

5.1   Extraction of Style Features

We used the style features proposed by Gatys et al. [3] as physical characteristics representing patterns. The style features were Gram matrices of feature maps output from hidden layers of a pretrained VGG-19 network. Since they represent the detailed appearance in images, such as multi-scale color information and pattern information, they can be considered to be strongly related to visual impressions for clothing patterns. We extracted style features from pooling layers 1, 2, 3, and 4 of VGG-19 using the images labeled in Sect. 4. Their dimensions were 64×64, 128×128, 256×256, and 512×512, respectively.

5.2   Lasso Regression

We considered a regression problem to model the relationships between visual impressions and physical characteristics. In this research, over-fitting was expected since the style features were high-dimensional features with respect to the number of labeled patterns. Therefore, we adopted a lasso regression based on Takemoto et al. [6]. In a lasso regression, significant parts are selected from independent variables, and regression models are constructed, while over-fitting is prevented.

We conducted a lasso regression by setting the impression values as the dependent variables and the style features extracted from each pooling layer as the independent variables. Then, we used the penalty parameters obtained when mean square errors were minimized during K-fold cross validation (K = 7). For each factor and adjective, we constructed a regression model for each pooling layer and adopted the model with the greatest coefficient of determination among the four models as the impression estimation model. The impression estimation models were as follows: "bright," "breezy," and "cool-looking" were pooling layer 1; all six factors were pooling layer 2; "rustic" and "cool" were pooling layer 3; and the other 36 adjectives were pooling layer 4. The average coefficient of determination for all of the impression estimation models was 0.84 for six factors and 0.70 for 41 adjectives, and we confirmed that our models had high precision.

6   Validity of the Proposed Method

6.1   Impression Estimation for Unlabeled Patterns

Based on the models constructed in Sect. 5.2, we estimated the impressions for the remaining 1,083 unlabeled images. First, we extracted style features from the pooling layer adopted as each impression estimation model used them. After that, we input style features into the models and had the models calculate impression values for each pattern. In addition to the right side of Fig. 1, Fig. 2 shows the top 20 patterns with high calculated impression values for several of the factors and adjectives.

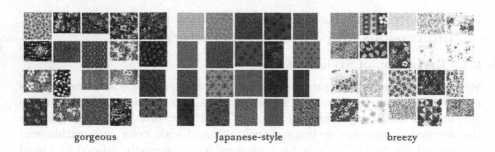

gorgeous   Japanese-style   breezy

Fig. 2. Examples of the estimated results

6.2 Verification Experiment by Relative Evaluation

In order to confirm whether the results estimated in Sect. 6.1 corresponded to impressions that people actually felt, we first conducted a pairwise comparison experiment using Thurstone's paired comparison. Then, we psychologically scaled the actual impressions and obtained their ordinal structure. Finally, we compared it with that of the estimated impressions.

Among the evaluation words, after considering the number of adjectives included in each factor and their factor loadings, we selected the following 10 adjectives: "cheerful," "bright," and "colorful" in the "pop" factor; "complex" and "multilayered" in the "elaborate" factor; "cool-looking" in the "refreshing" factor; "free" in the "novel" factor; "cute" and "elegant" in the "tidy" factor; and "sophisticated" in the "stylish" factor.

Then, we selected the top two, the two around zero, and the bottom two of the calculated impression values for each evaluation word, and we used a total of 60 images as the stimuli in this experiment.

A total of 10 graduate and undergraduate students (5 men; 5 women; average age: 22.3 ± 1.1 years) participated in this experiment. The participants observed two stimuli shown on an LCD monitor and evaluated which one was applicable for each evaluation word. They used six images per evaluation word, and each participant conducted 150 trials. To take the order effect into consideration, the order of the stimulus pairs and evaluation words was randomized for each participant.

Figure 3 shows the psychological scale value of each pattern for each evaluation word. For "elegant," "bright," and "cool-looking," we confirmed that our models accurately estimated the ordinal structure, including for pattern groups whose calculated impression values were around zero. In addition, statistically significant differences existed between groups with high and low calculated impression values in seven out of 10 words.

6.3 Verification Experiment by Absolute Evaluation

We conducted a subjective evaluation experiment with the unlabeled images used in Sect. 6.1, and had people actually give them impression values. After

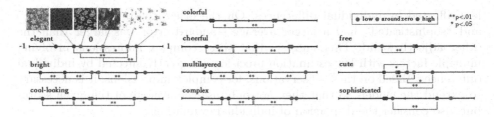

Fig. 3. Pairwise comparison results

that, we calculated the correlation coefficients between the impression values
given in this experiment and the impression values calculated in Sect. 6.1, and
then verified the validity of our models.

A total of 25 graduate and undergraduate students (15 men; 10 women;
average age: 22.7 ± 3.3 years) participated in this experiment. The participants
evaluated in the same procedure as in Sect. 4.1 with the evaluation words used
in Sect. 6.2. However, in order to reduce the burden on them, we had them use
one of the five stimuli sets into which the 1,083 images were divided.

Through this experiment, we obtained data for five participants to per stimulus and per evaluation word. Then, we obtained impression values in the same
procedure as in Sect. 4.

Table 2 shows the correlation coefficients between the given impression values and the calculated impression values. There were extremely strong positive
correlations for "cool-looking" and "bright," as well as positive correlations for
"colorful," "cheerful," "complex," "cute," and "multilayered." "Free," "elegant,"
and "sophisticated" had weak positive correlations.

Table 2. Correlation coefficients results

cheerful	bright	colorful	complex	multilayered	cool-looking	free	cute	elegant	sophisticated
0.574	0.791	0.597	0.563	0.476	0.818	0.341	0.528	0.336	0.298

6.4   Discussion

From the results in Sect. 6.2 and Sect. 6.3, we confirmed that our models had high
generalizability. In particular, models such as the "bright" and "cool-looking"
models had high precision. On the other hand, models such as the "free" and
"sophisticated" models had lower estimation precision than the other adjectives.

We considered individual differences in evaluations caused by ambiguities
of words. Therefore, for each evaluation obtained in Sect. 4.1 and Sect. 6.3, we
calculated the standard error between the participants for each stimulus and
calculated its average between stimuli (Table 3). "Bright," "colorful," and "cool-
looking" had a smaller average standard error than the other adjectives did.
This suggests that these simple impressions with high estimation precision are

less affected by individual differences. On the other hand, "free," "elegant," and "sophisticated" had a larger average standard error was larger than the other adjectives did. This suggests that these complex impressions involving multiple factors with low estimation precision are greatly affected by individual differences. Based on these observations, for complex impressions, it is necessary to extend the models so that they not only use the average of the given scores but also consider the dispersion of individual evaluations.

Table 3. Standard error results

	cheerful	bright	colorful	complex	multilayered	cool-looking	free	cute	elegant	sophisticated
Sect. 4.1	0.362	0.356	0.352	0.451	0.451	0.410	0.378	0.425	0.498	0.491
Sect. 6.3	0.346	0.312	0.337	0.365	0.346	0.312	0.399	0.380	0.399	0.435

6.5   Implementation a Pattern Search System

Since we confirmed the validity of our proposed method, we implemented a pattern search system using the estimated results. This system enables users to intuitively search for patterns with the words used in Sect. 4 as queries. It was applied to the fashion-on-demand app COUTURE made by digital fashion ltd. and is already being used in practical application (Fig. 4).

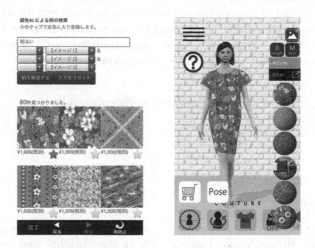

Fig. 4. The app COUTURE

7   Conclusion

We have proposed a method for automatically estimating the affective texture evoked by clothing patterns and conducted the following steps: (1) quantified the visual impressions of a small number of patterns with a subjective evaluation experiment and a factor analysis; (2) extracted style features as physical characteristics using a VGG-19 network; and (3) modeled the relationships between visual impressions and physical characteristics with a lasso regression. Afterward, based on the obtained models, we estimated the impressions for a large number of unlabeled patterns. Then, we verified their validity through relative evaluation and absolute evaluation, and we confirmed that our models had high generalizability. In addition, we implemented a system to enable users to intuitively search for patterns.

In the future, we will extend our models to consider individual differences and correspond with general patterns and shapes.

References

1. Julesz, B.: Textons, the elements of texture perception, and their interactions. Nature **290**(5802), 91 (1981)
2. Portilla, J., Simoncelli, E.P.: A parametric texture model based on joint statistics of complex wavelet coefficients. Int. J. Comput. Vis. **40**(1), 49–70 (2000). https://doi.org/10.1023/A:1026553619983
3. Gatys, L.A., Ecker, A.S., Bethge, M: Image Style Transfer Using Convolutional Neural Networks. In: IEEE Conference on Computer Vision and Pattern Recognition, pp. 2414–2423 (2016)
4. Simonyan, K., Zisserman, A.: Very deep convolutional networks for large-scale image recognition (2014). arXiv preprint arXiv:1409.1556
5. Tuceryan, M.A., Jain, A.K.: Handbook of Pattern Recognition and Computer Vision. Texture Analysis, pp. 235–276. World Scientific (1993)
6. Takemoto, A., Tobitani, K., Tani, Y., Fujiwara, T., Yamazaki, Y., Nagata, N.: Texture synthesis with desired Visual impressions using deep correlation feature. In: IEEE International Conference on Consumer Electronics, pp. 739–740 (2019)
7. Tobitani, K., Matsumoto, T., Tani, Y., Fujii, H., Nagata, N.: Modeling of the relation between impression and physical characteristics on representation of skin surface quality. J. Inst. Image Inf. Telev. Eng. **71**(11), 259–268 (2017)
8. Doizaki, R., Iiba, S., Okatani, T., Sakamoto, M.: Possibility to use product image and review text based on the association between onomatopoeia and texture. Trans. Jpn. Soc. Artif. Intell. **30**(1), 57–60 (2015)
9. Mori, T., Uchida, Y., Komiyama, J.: Relationship between visual impressions and image information parameters of color textures. J. Jpn. Res. Assoc. Text. end-uses **51**(5), 433–440 (2010)
10. Mouri, C., Ueda, E.S., Terauchi, F., Aoki, H.: Relationship between Mimetic words and kansei and sensory characteristics. Bull. Jpn. Soc. Sci. Des. **58**, 209 (2011)

Design Aid of 3D Wire Art Using 3D Models

Satoshi Tsuda[✉], Yuta Muraki, and Ken-ichi Kobori

Graduate School of Information Science and Technology,
Osaka Institute of Technology, 1-79-1 Kitayama, Hirakata City, Osaka, Japan
m1m19a23@st.oit.ac.jp

Abstract. In this paper, we propose a method of automatically determining the wire art curve shape along the shape of the 3D model. Moreover, the wire art curve shape is determined from several evaluation index. In our method, we define multiple infinite planes from an oriented bounding box of the input 3D model. After that, the intersection line between the polygon mesh of the 3D model and the infinite plane is calculated, and the curve of the wire art is automatically determined based on the evaluation index of length and complexity. By showing a set of 3D contour curves from the input 3D model, automatic design of wire art with maintaining the shape feature of the 3D model is realized. We apply the proposed method to various 3D models and verify the effectiveness of the proposed evaluation index.

Keywords: Computational design · 3D model · Wire art

1 Introduction

In recent years, it has become popular to create interior goods and decorations by hand. wire art is one of handicraft. Wire art is an art formed by bending according to the design drawings designed using aluminum wire. This art is attractive molding goods because it is low cost and easy to get by mail order. However, a high technique is necessary for producing 3D wire art, and it is often produced by the hand of an expert and the craftsman.

In this paper, we propose a method of automatically determining the wire art curve shape along the shape of the 3D model. Moreover, the wire art curve shape is determined from several evaluation index. In our method, we define multiple infinite planes from an oriented bounding box and Gaussian Curvature of the input 3D model. After that, the intersection line between the polygon mesh of the 3D model and the infinite plane is calculated, and the curve of the wire art is automatically determined based on the evaluation index of length and complexity. By showing a set of 3D contour curves from the input 3D model, automatic design of wire art with maintaining the shape feature of the 3D model is realized. We apply the proposed method to various 3D models and verify the effectiveness of the proposed evaluation index.

© Springer Nature Switzerland AG 2020
C. Stephanidis and M. Antona (Eds.): HCII 2020, CCIS 1226, pp. 698–703, 2020.
https://doi.org/10.1007/978-3-030-50732-9_89

2   Related Works

Digital Design Method. In recent years, there are many tools to support materials and production methods using computers in hand-made fabrics and handicrafts that can be produced by hand. In the support tool, it is possible to produce original handicrafts by using CAD system etc. Therefore, the demand for design support systems for simulating designs and deliverables is increasing.

Design Aid of Wire Art. As a study to aid the design of wire art, there is a study that present feasible wire art from 2D line drawing by Iarussi et al. [1]. In addition, there is a study that automatically fabricated 3D wire art using a wire bending machine from 3D model and its contours by Miguel et al. [2]. In this study, they calculate the curves that can be fabricated by wire bending machines. However, due to the limitations of the wire bending machine, it is not possible to express complex contours. In our method, it is possible to express a complex contour from the intersection of the plane and the 3D model, and automatic design of the wire art curve which maintains the shape characteristics of the 3D model is performed.

3   Proposed Method

3.1   Overview

In the proposed method, the polygon mesh of the 3D model and the accuracy of the output are input. First, we calculate the OBB of the input model and the Gaussian curvature of each vertex. Next, a plane for each xyz axis is generated at the vertex position where the Gaussian curvature is the largest. This plane has a slope along the direction of OBB. Moreover, we generate planes symmetrically from the generated plane according to the accuracy of the output. Then, the wire art curve of the output is determined by calculating the cross-sectional line between the generated plane and the polygon mesh of the input model and evaluating its group. (see Fig. 1).

3.2   Oriented Bounding Box

In this method, the wire art curve is determined using the curve along the input model. Therefore, it is necessary to calculate OBB of the input model. we calculate OBB, it is possible to enclose the model in as small a square as possible, regardless of which direction the model is facing. OBB can be calculated by using principal component analysis for the model. According to principal component analysis, the orientation and length of each xyz axis can be obtained by treating the scattering of each vertex of the model as a variance covariance matrix.

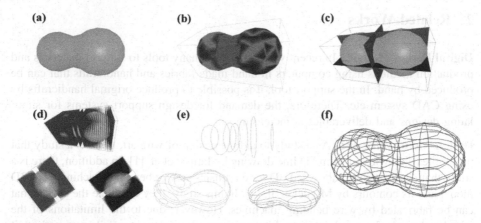

Fig. 1. Given a 3D model (a), our system calculates OBB and Gaussian curvature (b) and generates a reference plane (c). Moreover, generate a plane evenly based on a reference plane (d) and determine the wire art curve by the evaluation value (e). The result of combining the wire art curves for each xyz axis is the final output (f).

3.3   Gaussian Curvature

In this method, the reference position of the wire art is determined by the curvature of the model. Therefore, it is necessary to calculate the Gaussian curvature of the input model. We confirm the curvature of the mesh by calculating the Gaussian curvature. The Gaussian curvature is calculated from each vertex of the input model. In addition, when the absolute value of Gaussian curvature is large, the unevenness of the mesh becomes remarkable. Therefore, the reference position of the wire art is the vertex position where the absolute value of the Gaussian curvature is the largest. We calculate Gaussian curvature by Meyer et al. [3].

3.4   Reference Plane

We generate three planes at the reference position determined in Sect. 3.3. In addition, this plane has normal direction for each axis of the OBB. We generate planes worth the number of output precisions on the left and right of the three generated planes. This output precision is 30.

3.5   Cross-Sectional Line

We calculate the cross-sectional line. The cross-sectional line is a line segment where the mesh of the input model and the plane of each xyz axis generated in Sect. 3.4 intersect. The intersection is calculated as:

$$X = A + \overrightarrow{AB}\left(\frac{|PA \cdot N|}{(|PA \cdot N| + |PB \cdot N|)}\right) \tag{1}$$

Where, X is the intersection of the plane and the line of the mesh, AB is the line of the mesh, P is the point on the plane, and N is the normal of the plane. (see Fig. 2).

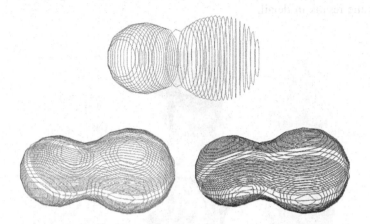

Fig. 2.   Cross-Sectional line group calculated for plane of each xyz axis.

3.6   Layout-Wire

We use the cross-sectional line group calculated in Sect. 3.5 as wire art curve candidates and determine the wire art curve to be output based on the evaluation value. However, the cross-sectional line with the reference plane is determined as a wire art curve, regardless of the evaluation value. The evaluation value is the sum of the circularity and the normalized perimeter of the cross-sectional line. This evaluation value is calculated for the calculated cross-sectional line group. The evaluation value is calculated as:

$$E(l) = E_{circularity}(l) + E_{contour}(l) \tag{2}$$

In addition, the circularity is calculated as:

$$E_{circularity}(l) = \frac{4\pi S}{l_{length}} \tag{3}$$

Moreover, the normalized perimeter of the cross-sectional line is calculated as:

$$E_{contour}(l) = \frac{l_{length}}{Max_{length}} \tag{4}$$

Then, the wire art curve determines the number of 30% of the cross-sectional line group in the order in which the evaluation value is high. However, the cross-sectional line with a high evaluation value may be concentrated. When concentrated, the wire art curve has biased. Therefore, the cross-sectional line adjacent to the determined cross-sectional line is not selected.

4   Experimental Result

We calculated several wire art curves using this method. (see Fig. 3). The following describes the results in detail.

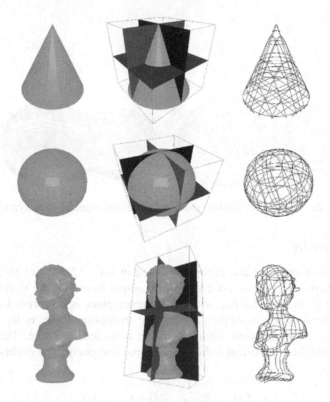

Fig. 3.   Determined the wire art curve. From left to right: input model, reference plane, the wire art curve.

We consider that the shape characteristics of the input model can be reflected by using circularity and normalized perimeter as evaluation values. In addition, we consider that the balance of the wire art curve is maintained by using the reference plane as the position where the unevenness of the input model is remarkable.

However, if the input model is a complex object, the curve is not determined in the part shown in Fig. 4. In this method, the cross-sectional line of the wide area of the model is determined by the evaluation index. Due to the local area of the model is not considered. Therefore, it is necessary to segment mesh the input model and disassemble wide-area parts and local parts [4].

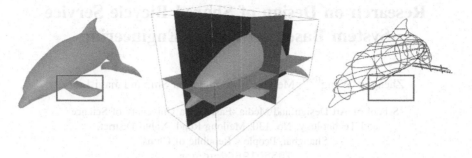

Fig. 4. Problematic the wire art curve. From left to right: input model, reference plane, the wire art curve. There is no wire art curve in the area surrounded by the red rectangle.

5 Conclusion and Future Work

We proposed a system to assist in the design of the wire art curve with 3D models and output accuracy input. The shape characteristics of the input model were captured from orientation and curvature. In addition, the wire art curve which maintained the shape feature by the evaluation values of the cross-sectional line group between the plane and the mesh was determined.

For future work, to disassemble 3D model in order to be able to calculate the shape characteristics of local areas of the 3D model. At the present, it does not consider the support when assembling from the decided wire art curve. Therefore, we consider that support the assembly procedure through animation and viewer.

References

1. Iarussi, E., Li, W., Bousseau, A.: WrapIt: computer-assisted crafting of wire wrapped jewelry. ACM Trans. Graph. **34**(6), 1–8 (2015)
2. Miguel, E., Lepoutre, M., Bickel, B.: Computational design of stable planar-rod structures. ACM Trans. Graph. **35**(4), 1–11 (2016)
3. Meyer, M., Desbrun, M., Schröder, P., Barr, A.H.: Discrete differential-geometry operators for triangulated 2-manifolds. Vis. Math. **3**(3), 34–57 (2002)
4. Kalogerakis, E., Averkiou, M., Maji, S., Chaudhuri, S.: 3D shape segmentation with projective convolutional networks. In: CVPR, vol. 1(2) (2017)

Research on Design of Shared Bicycle Service System Based on Kansei Engineering

Zhengyu Wang[⊠], Meiyu Zhou, Zhengyu Shi, and Jiayi Lian

School of Art Design and Media, East China University of Science
and Technology, No. 130, Meilong Road, Xuhui District,
Shanghai, People's Republic of China
753501966@qq.com

Abstract. With the development and progress of the society, user's consumption conception is also quietly changing. Nowadays, users are increasingly paying attention to the emotional satisfaction brought by products and services. The quality of products and services depends greatly on the user's satisfaction and enjoyment. As a user-oriented shared bike product service system, it has always been a difficult problem to promote enterprises to continuously maintain the differentiated and dynamic development of their services in an increasingly competitive market. The present article aims to offer a solution to this problem. Firstly, this paper starts from the emotional needs of users and takes the shared bicycle service system as the research object. The perceptual image space of the shared bicycle product service system was established by using the theory and method of Kansei engineering. Secondly, quantitative analysis method is used to calculate the collected perceptual image questionnaire data of product service system, and the key perceptual image is extracted using principal component analysis method. Finally, based on users' emotional demands for the product service system, we analyzed the stakeholders and their relationships in the product service system, combined with the design requirements of service contact. We explored the service blueprint planning method and the process carding principle of the overall service, based on the user's behavioral process. We also put forward the content and method of service optimization design for the shared bicycle product service system.

Keywords: Shared bikes · Product service system · Service design · Kansei engineering

1 Introduction

At the present stage, the social service industry has become an important economic pillar. Its importance is increasing. The development of service design provides good support for the service industry. However, service design is different from those tangible, physical products that can be felt by human senses. And the intangibility of service design makes it more difficult for researchers to design services to meet customers' emotional needs, therefore, to provide users with a better service experience in complex service design has become more critical.

© Springer Nature Switzerland AG 2020
C. Stephanidis and M. Antona (Eds.): HCII 2020, CCIS 1226, pp. 704–713, 2020.
https://doi.org/10.1007/978-3-030-50732-9_90

The involvement of the kansei engineering provides research tools, perceptual information collection and related data processing methods for service design [1]. Researchers can obtain customers' real feelings about products or services by using the research methods of kansei engineering [2], and establish the dynamic relationship between user's emotional feeling and design features through the experimental data of Kansei adjectives [3]. Therefore, based on the above research, we believe that the method of guiding product service system design with user's perceptual needs can provide new ideas for the design of shared bike product service system.

Through literature research, the author found that the number of articles using Kansei Engineering in the field of service design is very limited, and most of the research only focus on a single aspect of service system design [4], and neglected the value of combination of products and services, correctness of service assumptions, the dynamic virtuous circle of contacts in the service process, and the combing of user needs. For example, Rostlinger and Goldkuhl proposed in 1999 that the research of Kansei Engineering should include the application of service orientation. In the same year, Nishino applied Kansei Engineering to explore the design of Internet business services, and found that the combination of Kansei Engineering and service design has wide applicability [5]. In 2012, Hartono [6] proposed a comprehensive framework including Kano model and QFD for luxury hotel service research. In 2017, Hsiao used a combination of Kansei Engineering and online text-mining techniques analysis to study the design of transnational logistics service [7].

Based on this, this research adopts the Kansei Engineering research method to study the design practice of shared bike product service system. Firstly, researchers will observe and interview users according to the actual situation of product service system to explore the user demand of shared bike product service system. Secondly, we use the research method of perceptual engineering to clarify the perceptual image of the shared bike product service system. Through quantitative statistical analysis, we study the influence of user demand on each perceptual image, and extract the key perceptual image using principal component analysis. Finally, this paper proposes an effective system design and development direction which combines products and services for the shared bike product service system.

2   Research Overview

Product Service System (PPS) was a pre-designed business model that turns the original "split" mode of design, sales and service into a comprehensive system of integrated products and services [8]. Compared with the traditional business model, it has the advantage of lower environmental impact [9]. Product service systems are divided into three categories: product-oriented, use-oriented, and results-oriented. Among them, the use of orientation and results-oriented services as a service to replace products has great potential for development. The most typical examples of use-oriented services are lease and shared services, For example, the shared bike product service system provides users with product usage service through enterprise resource allocation [10]. The product service system integrates the service into the product, which not only extends the value of the product, but also helps the company to enhance its value chain.

With the improvement of people's living standards, people gradually begin to pay attention to the quality of life, the content of spiritual life and emotional needs. Therefore, Kansei engineering emerge as the times require. It is a translation method that can transform users' blurred visual experience into product details. The reason why kansei engineering is widely used in the field of product design research is that, on the one hand, it has put forward guiding research results for the development of product design, on the other, product design can expand the research horizon based on mature Kansei engineering research methods. Its application in service design was first proposed by Nagamachi in 1980 and the application framework was summarized by Hartono [11]. Subsequently, on the basis of Hartono, some Singaporean researchers added and integrated SERVQUAL model, Kano model, QFD and kansei engineering research methods to propose perceptual service attributes, such as "surprise", to establish the relationship between service attributes and users' emotional experience [12]. Hsiao provides a reference example for kansei engineering in the service field by establishing the corresponding relationship between consumer feelings and cross-border logistics service elements [7].

3   Research on Users' Emotional Demand of Shared Bike Product Service System

3.1   Establishment of Kansei Image Space

Collect Kansei adjectives from books, papers, reviews, etc., and 96 Kansei adjectives were initially selected. After screening them by card sorting method and focus group method, 20 Kansei adjectives with appropriate number were finally sorted out. Likert five-order scale was used to make 20 Kansei image words into a five-order Kansei image questionnaire, and a total of 60 copies were sent out, and 54 valid questionnaires were finally collected, the Kansei adjectives in the top 8 of the selection rate are selected to describe the shared bicycle product and service system, according to the order, it is convenient, affordable, safe, reliable, smooth, relaxed, friendly and intelligent.

3.2   Principal Component Analysis of Kansei Image Adjectives of Shared Bike

In order to understand users' perceptual cognition of shared bike product service system and accurately grasp users' perceptual demands, this paper uses principal component analysis to calculate the data and obtain the key Kansei image of the user.

Firstly, Kmo and Bartlett tests are carried out on the data to determine whether the data is suitable for principal component analysis. Secondly, use the maximal rotation of variance method and perform the orthogonal rotations, and finally the factor space of the perceptual vocabulary data is constructed, the operation results are shown in Table 1. The three principal component factors of principal component 1, principal component 2 and principal component 3 are extracted, and three customer expectation factors are determined. This three principal component factors respectively explain

39.701%, 19.789% and 18.152% of the total variance, and the principal component accumulation explained 77.641% of the variance, reflecting that the higher recognition of this three principal component factors.

Table 1. Total variance

Component	Initial eigenvalues			Extraction sums of squared loadings			Rotation sums of squared loadings		
	Total	% of variance	Cumulative %	Total	% of variance	Cumulative %	Total	% of variance	Cumulative %
1	3.176	39.701	39.701	3.176	39.701	39.701	2.230	27.874	27.874
2	1.583	19.789	59.490	1.583	19.789	59.490	2.098	26.222	54.096
3	1.452	18.152	77.641	1.452	18.152	77.641	1.884	23.546	77.641
4	0.589	7.359	85.001						
5	.430	5.377	90.378						
6	.329	4.107	94.484						
7	.267	3.342	97.826						
8	.174	2.174	100.000						

3.3 Result Analysis

It can be seen from Table 2 that principal component 1 is correlated with "reliable", "intelligent" and "safe", among which the "safe" can best represent principal component 1, so it is called "trust factor". Principal component 2 is associated with "convenience", "smoothness" and "ease", among which the "relaxed" can best represent principal component 2, so it is called "efficiency factor". Principal component 3 is associated with "affordable" and "friendly," and "friendly" can better explain principal component 3, so it is called "affinity factor".

Through the above principal component analysis to prove that the "trust factor", "efficiency factor" and "affinity factor" has great influence on the principal components, and we can safely draw the conclusion that three key Kansei image, "safe", "relaxed" and "friendly" can represent the eight Kansei image adjectives participated in this survey. It indicates that in the current shared bike product service system, the Kansei image which users pay most attention to is "safe", "relaxed" and "friendly", these conclusions provide the design direction for further design work.

Table 2. Rotated component matrix

	Component		
	1	2	3
Affordable	.126	.139	.894
Convenient	.110	.792	.304
Reliable	.697	.127	.318
Smooth	.619	.622	−.115
Relaxed	−.020	.879	.098
Intelligent	.739	.459	−.090
Friendly	.088	.105	.914
Safe	.883	−.230	.158

4 Design of Shared Bike Product Service System

4.1 Stakeholder Analysis and System Map

Focusing on the shared bike service provider, the stakeholders of the shared bicycle product service system can be divided into seven groups: "users", "shared bike service providers", "strategic partners", "capital holders", "competitors", "shared bike industry chain", "government", "relevant agencies" and "environment", the detailed information is shown in Fig. 1.

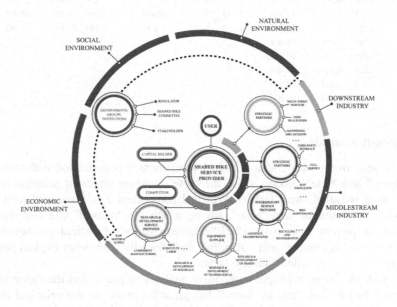

Fig. 1. Stakeholder analysis chart

By sorting out the connection relations among various stakeholders, this study constructs a shared bike product service system map. In this system, the main core stakeholders are service providers and users, and the remaining stakeholders mainly exist to promote the interaction between them. The details are shown in Fig. 2.

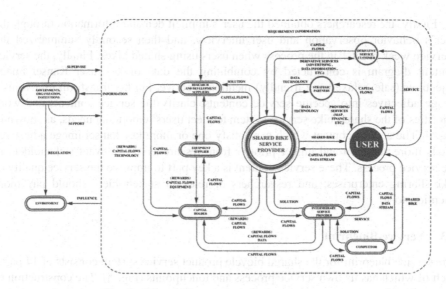

Fig. 2. Shared bike product service system map

4.2 Service Touchpoints and Service Content Diagrams

In order to understand the service touchpoints in the shared bike product service system and clarify the functions, responsibilities and relationships of stakeholders in this system, this study builds a key contact diagram for the shared bike product service system, as shown in Fig. 3, which provides basic information for the following service contents.

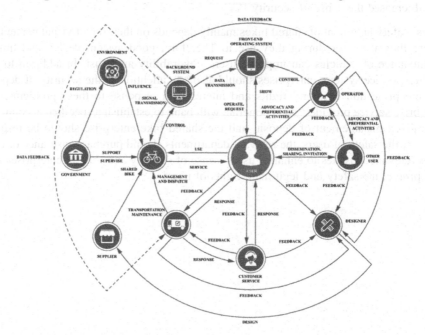

Fig. 3. Key service touchpoints diagram of shared bike product service system

Firstly, the researchers obtained the user's implicit demand information through the user's behavior observation and user interview, and then secondly summarized the "service weak points" in the process when users using shared bikes. Finally, the service content diagram is constructed by combining the data of key user Kansei image adjectives (safe, relaxed and friendly) mentioned above. Further transform user Kansei image adjectives into specific service contents, clarify the service contents and work priorities of the shared bike service system to meet users' emotional needs, as shown in Fig. 4. The service content which can satisfy one or more key kansei image adjectives needs more attention and higher priority from researchers or relevant stakeholders in the service process. These service content is a key part to improve the service quality of bike-sharing enterprises, and researchers or relevant stakeholders should pay more attention to it.

4.3 Service-Blueprint

The service blueprint for the shared bicycle product service system consists of 14 parts, each of which has its own service process and touchpoints (Fig. 5). The construction of the service blueprint is conducive to the timely response of the system to changes such as users and environment, which facilitates the follow-up modification of the system and also can improves the quality of service.

4.4 Design Suggestions for Shared Bike Product Service System

Based on the conclusion of the above research and the emotional needs of users, the following strategies are proposed for the design of shared bike product service system.

(1) Increased the sense of security

Users' safety judgment of shared bikes mainly depends on their direct visual perception before they use it or during they use it. Therefore, good system design and timely maintenance of vehicles can improve users' favorability and trust. In addition to the product service system, enterprises should also pay attention to the security of deposit and the protection of users' rights and interests. In response to these problems, the enterprise service providers can cooperate with bank to establish a specified account for centralized management of deposit, and the shared bike enterprise should be responsible for the safety of users, the relevant departments should purchase insurance or take other relevant activities to enhance users' sense of security and trust in enterprises and also protect the safety and legitimate rights of users.

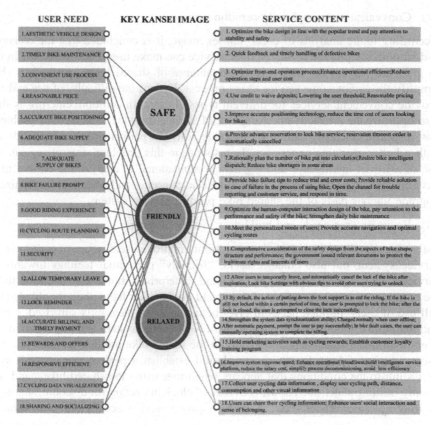

Note: The "user need" and "service content" of the same serial number correspond to each other.

Fig. 4. Service content diagrams

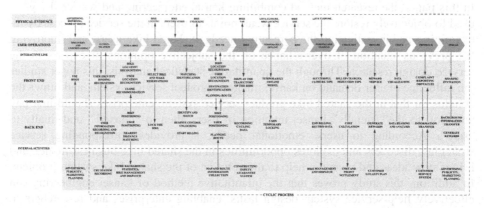

Fig. 5. Shared bike product service system service-blueprint

(2) Convenient and simplified operation process

According to the analysis of users' kansei image, it is concluded that the convenient and smooth use process of shared bike service can make users feel "relaxed", in order to give full play to the convenience advantages of shared bikes, enterprises should simplify the cumbersome service usage process, Reduce the difficulty of use and better provide convenient services for different types of users. In addition, enterprises should also optimize the interactive performance of service software to reduce the problem of low response efficiency caused by unstable software performance, and provide users with a better operating experience. In response to this problem, enterprises can make use of artificial intelligence and big-data computational to analyze the current market environment, logically predict and estimate user needs, and effectively optimize and upgrade various parts of the shared bike product service system.

(3) Focus on user needs and build user loyalty program

Satisfying users' perceptual needs can not only improve users' sense of trust in product service system, but also enhance users' "friendly" perceptual feelings towards their services. This requires that on the one hand, enterprises should pay attention to meet the explicit and necessary needs of users, and on the other hand, they should also make full use of users' implicit needs to give them a sense of pleasantly surprised, establish and maintain a good interaction mechanism between the system and users, and improve users' emotional attachment and loyalty to the shared bike product service system. For users with special needs, enterprises should establish a perfect management system according to the conditions that appears when user using the shared bikes, and set up loyalty training plans, such as the activities of clock in cycling for discount, sharing and inviting new user rewards, etc., so as to improve users' viscosity and utilization rate.

5 Conclusion

In this paper, the research method combining kansei engineering and service design is used to objectively restore the service weak points of users in the service process by re-examining and investigating the perceptual needs of shared bike users, and improving the previous situation of over-reliance on the subjective opinions of experts in the service design research. Through the quantitative statistical analysis, this paper studies the influence of user demand on kansei image in product service system, and draws the conclusion that in the shared bike product service system, enterprises should first pay attention to the "friendly" kansei intention of users, then to "relaxed", and finally to "safe". According to users' emotional needs, it provides corresponding service strategies, discovers and explores opportunities in the shared bike business model, and brings new ideas and potential help to the solution of the shared bike system problem. In addition, this study proves that the quantitative method of kansei engineering can effectively help service system design tasks, enabling enterprises and researchers to understand users' perceptual needs from a more complete perspective, and promote the consistency of product and service elements, so as to comprehensively improve service quality. In future research, the author hopes that the conclusions and methods obtained in this study can be extended from bike-sharing industry to other types of industries, so as to demonstrate the applicability of the proposed method.

References

1. Tsuchiya, T., et al.: A fuzzy rule induction method using genetic algorithm. Int. J. Ind. Ergon. **18**(2–3), 135–145 (1996)
2. Dahlgaard, J.J., Schütte, S., Ayas, E., Dahlgaard-Park, S.M.: Kansei/affective engineering design: a methodology for profound affection and attractive quality creation. TQM J. **20**(4), 299–311 (2008)
3. Demirtas, E.A., Anagun, A.S., Koksal, G.: Determination of optimal product styles by ordinal logistic regression versus conjoint analysis for kitchen faucets. Int. J. Ind. Ergon. **39**(5), 866–875 (2009)
4. Maussang, N., Zwolinski, P., Brissaud, D.: Product-service system design methodology: from the PSS architecture design to the products specifications. J. Eng. Des. **20**(4), 349–366 (2009)
5. Nishino, T., Nagamachi, M., Ishihara, K., Ishihara, S., Ichitsubo, M., Komatsu, K.: Internet Kansei engineering system with basic Kansei database and genetic algorithm. In: Proceedings of TQM and Human Factors (Linkoping, Sweden: Centre for Studies of Humans, Technology and Organization), pp. 367–372 (1999)
6. Hartono, M.: Incorporating service quality tools into Kansei engineering in services: a case study of indonesian tourists. Procedia Econ. Finan. **4**, 201–212 (2012)
7. Hsiao, Y.H., Chen, M.C., Liao, W.C.: Logistics service design for cross-border e-commerce using Kansei engineering with text-mining-based online content analysis. Telematics Inform. **34**, S0736585316303136 (2017)
8. Mont, O.: Clarifying the concept of product-service system. J. Clean. Prod. **10**(3), 237–245 (2002)
9. Roy, R.: Sustainable product-service systems. Futures **32**(3), 289–299 (2000)
10. Tukker, A.: Eight types of product-service system: eight ways to sustainability? Experiences from SusProNet. Bus. Strategy Environ. **13**(4), 246–260 (2004)
11. Hartono, M.: A proposed integrative framework of Kansei engineering and kano model applied to services. In: Proceedings of the 2nd International Research Symposium in Service Management - Service Imperatives in the New Economy (2011)
12. Hartono, M., Chuan, T.K.: How the Kano model contributes to Kansei engineering in services. Ergonomics **54**(11), 987–1004 (2011)

A Comparative Study on the Preference Model of Users and Designers for Scissors Modeling

Xiaohan Wu[✉], Meiyu Zhou, and Yihui Li

East China University of Science and Technology, Shanghai 200030, China
1712496875@qq.com

Abstract. With the rise of e-commerce, buying some daily necessities online has become an indispensable part of People's Daily life. The aim was to study how consumers and designers perceive scissors when they only see their appearance. Research method is to use the questionnaire to collect data, scissors, the shape of the elements is obtained by morphological analysis and using the SPSS software to independent sample t-test and Pearson correlation analysis, the results of three groups of data as a result, designers and users of two emotional vocabulary associated data and two sets of modeling elements and the emotional vocabulary associated data, conclusions are designers and consumers have different view of part of x scissors, and gives Suggestions for the design of the scissors.

Keywords: Scissors modeling · Cognitive differences · Designers · Users

1 Research Background and Purpose

Perceptual engineering is a technology that combines perceptual and engineering. It is a theory and method that uses engineering techniques to explore the relationship between the sensibility of 'people' and the design characteristics of 'things'. It can be used to quantify the user's sensible needs. The image is transformed into a morphological element of detailed design [1]. Perceptual engineering originated from a lecture by Kenichi Yamamoto of Mazda Corporation in Japan in 1986 at the International Symposium on the Operation of the Automotive Industry in the United States. In this lecture, Kenichi Yamamoto first proposed the concept of perceptual engineering, which caused the automotive industry. It is generally valued [2] regarding the study of perceptual engineering, SI Shiharas [3] applies fuzzy back-propelling theory in automotive design and derives its corresponding theory and method based on perceptual imagery; Akinori et al. [4] tested and validated the automobile driving system with the help of perceptual engineering Zhao Yanyun et al. [5] applied analytic hierarchy process and fuzzy evaluation method to research the design of material image in product design; Du Hemin [6] introduced perceptual engineering in product design evaluation and conducted application research; Jing Nan et al. [7] used morphological analysis to innovate product styles; Xu Yanqing et al. [8] applied perceptual engineering methods when analyzing consumer needs; Wonjoon Kim et al. [9] used correlation analysis and the SD method analyzes and compares the preference models of automotive leather

C. Stephanidis and M. Antona (Eds.): HCII 2020, CCIS 1226, pp. 714–721, 2020.
https://doi.org/10.1007/978-3-030-50732-9_91

designers and customers. Here we introduce the perceptual engineering theory and methods into the analysis of household scissors.

According to a survey [10], as of July 11, 2019, only on Taobao's e-commerce platform, the monthly sales volume of a capable stainless steel household scissors was 4,685, with a cumulative evaluation of 29321 people; Zhang Xiaoquan's household red handle scissors The cumulative evaluation of 77814 people shows that online shopping has become one of the sales channels of practical tools such as scissors. However, the e-commerce platform also has its shortcomings, that is, it is not possible to experience the use of scissors in real time. Consumers need to judge the pros and cons of scissors and use experience based on pictures or videos. In the case of consumers, designers and consumers 'perceptual perception of their appearance, study the differences between designers and consumers' perception of X-shaped scissors, and analyze the correlation between morphological elements of X-shaped scissors and perceptual cognition.

2 Research Methods

2.1 Recruitment of Experimental Subjects

A total of 55 participants were recruited, including 29 designers and 26 consumers. A total of 55 questionnaires were received, including 52 valid questionnaires, 28 valid designer questionnaires, and 24 valid consumer questionnaires. Participants representing designers are currently design students or practitioners, each of whom has more than 4 years of design experience. Gender is almost evenly distributed: 12 men and 16 women. Their average age is 25.5 years. Consumers are represented by people who have bought scissors, 12 men and 14 women. Their average age is 34.5 years.

2.2 Using the SD Method Questionnaire to Obtain Designer and User Sentimental Evaluation

Vocabulary Selection. Before designing the questionnaire, we must first select the adjective pairs, and first classify the shape needs of the scissors using the method of analytic hierarchy process. Divided into three levels of function, form and aesthetics. Then collected 65 perceptual adjectives about scissors from websites such as customer evaluation and magazine description. Three experts in related fields were then invited to screen adjective pairs.

In the end, a total of six adjective pairs were selected: 'delicate-rough', 'modern-traditional', 'sharp-dull', 'laborious-laborsaving', 'lightweight-heavy', and 'durable-fragile'. Subjects evaluated the tactile perception of each sample on a scale of 1–5 based on each adjective and preference.

Sample Selection. More than 300 scissors samples were collected through magazines, the Internet and supermarkets. According to the types of links, they were divided into three categories: x-shaped scissors, u-shaped scissors and special-shaped scissors. Due to the large number of samples, the panel finally decided to use x scissors for sample screening. Through analysis and screening, the typical samples were divided into 9 categories. Select a sample from each category. A sample product is shown in Fig. 1.

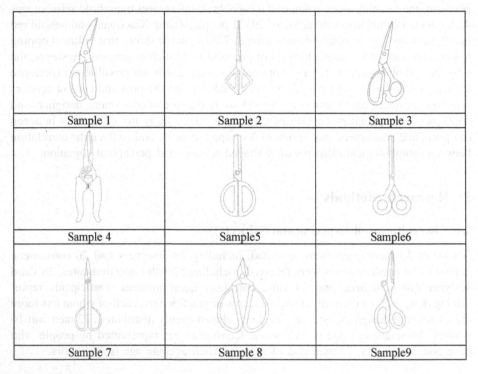

Sample 1	Sample 2	Sample 3
Sample 4	Sample5	Sample6
Sample 7	Sample 8	Sample9

Fig. 1. The samples of scissors

Data Statistics and Analysis. In order to identify the perceptual differences between the designer and the client on the shape of the scissors, independent sample t-test analysis and correlation analysis were performed. The average and standard values of each sensory evaluation of designers and users are shown in Table 1 and 2. For each sample, descriptive statistics of each tactile attribute are performed. For independent sample t-test analysis, the scores of the perceptual evaluations of all samples from the designer and the customer were compared. Get Table 1.

It can be seen that, on a delicate-rough set of perceptual words, the sig of the designer and the user is sigma 0.095 > 0.05, so check the rows with equal variances and the sig value is 0.638 > 0.05. It shows that there is no statistically significant difference between the designer group and the user group in the delicate-rough set of perceptual words. On the modern-traditional set of perceptual vocabulary, the sig for designers and users is 0.015 < 0.05. We consider the variances to be unequal, so if you look at the rows with unequal variances, the sig value is 0.150 > 0.05. It shows that there is no statistically significant difference between the designer group and the user group in the 'modern-traditional' set of perceptual words. In this way, we have significant differences between 'sharp-dull', 'laborious-laborsaving' and 'durable-fragile'.

Table 1. Mean and standard value of designer and user perceptual evaluation

	Occupation	N	Average	Standard deviation	Standard error mean
Delicate	Designer	29	25.5172	5.48778	1.01906
	User	23	24.6522	3.35219	.69898
Modern	Designer	29	24.0690	5.85498	1.08724
	User	23	22.5652	3.77583	.78732
Sharp	Designer	29	24.1034	5.90003	1.09561
	User	23	26.6957	4.91227	1.02428
Light	Designer	29	26.2759	5.57992	1.03616
	User	23	25.8261	5.78126	1.20548
Durable	Designer	29	24.8621	5.01942	.93208
	User	23	28.2174	4.58214	.95544
Laborious	Designer	29	25.1379	4.98372	.92545
	User	23	27.3043	5.49739	1.14629

Table 2. Significant differences between users and designers in the six vocabularies

	Delicate		Modern		Sharp		Laborious		Light		Durable	
	e	u	e	u	e	u	e	u	e	u	e	u
Sig	.095		.015		.137		.089		.081		.906	
Sig (2-tailed)	.638	.543	.299	.15	.015	.006	.022	.006	.196	.11	.004	.004

For correlation analysis, select Pearson's correlation and use the sample's perceptual cognition as a variable. Correlation analysis of perceptual vocabulary word pairs for the designer group and the user group, respectively, to obtain Table 3 and Table 4.

Table 3. Correlation test results of user group sensible word pairs.

	Delicate	Modern	Sharp	Laborious	Light	Durable
Delicate	1	.576**	.385**	.419**	.470**	.406**
Modern	.576**	1	.286**	.330**	.402**	.201**
Sharp	.385**	.286**	1	.600**	.480**	.516**
Laborious	.419**	.330**	.600**	1	.639**	.537**
Light	.470**	.402**	.480**	.639**	1	.282**
Durable	.406**	.201**	.516**	.537**	.282**	1

** Correlation is significant at 0.01 levels (two tailed).

In the results we can see that the significance of all data pairs is less than 0.05, so all the data are statistically significant. Therefore, it can be concluded that six pairs of adjectives have a positive correlation between each other. The relationship diagram is drawn as shown in the figure. The thickness of the line represents the strength of the

Table 4. The correlation between the six vocabularies of the designer

	Delicate	Modern	Sharp	Laborious	Light	Durable
Delicate	1	.631**	.327**	.402**	.382**	.234**
Modern	.631**	1	.212**	.418**	.369**	0.116
Sharp	.327**	.212**	1	.559**	.280**	.442**
Laborious	.402**	.418**	.559**	1	.358**	.411**
Light	.382**	.369**	.280**	.358**	1	.159*
Durable	.234**	0.116	.442**	.411**	.159*	1

* Correlation is significant at 0.05 levels (two tailed).
** Correlation is significant at 0.01 levels (two tailed).

correlation. That is, users believe that there is a strong correlation between 'sharp-dull' and 'laborious-laborsaving', and there is a strong correlation between 'laborious-laborsaving' and 'lightweight-heavy'. Therefore, users believe that the lighter and more labor-saving, the sharper the more labor-saving.

The correlation between the six vocabularies of the designer is shown in Table 2, 3 and 4. There are two groups of data with significance greater than 0.005, which is not statistically significant. The remaining data are statistically significant. Therefore, we conclude that the teacher's group has a strong positive correlation with the 'elaborate-rough' and 'modern-traditional' perceptual vocabulary groups. Therefore, the designers think that the more refined means the more modern.

2.3 Determination of Morphological Elements

The morphological analysis method was proposed by Swedish astronomer physicist Fw Fritz Zwicki in 1942. This method first decomposes a complex system into several independent elements; then finds out the form or means that may realize each element; finally, arranges and combines the elements and possible forms or means to form a morphological matrix [11]. The shape of the scissors is composed of a combination of multiple morphological elements. In order to more comprehensively analyze the various possibilities of morphological combinations, the morphological analysis method is used to decompose the shape of the scissors into three elements, such as the handle shape and the scissors blade morphology and the overall shape. Each of the sub-elements are elements listed below, there are elements of the sample is referred to as 1, is not referred to as a 0, as shown in Table 5 to obtain, for the emotional vocabulary and structural elements Laid the foundation for correlation analysis. *The following* Table *gives a summary of all heading levels.* The lowercase letter 'a' presents a semicircle, 'b' represents a ellipses (including circles), and so on. The other letters in sequence represent rod, triangle, straight rounded corners, straight square angles, long arcs, short arcs, and symmetry and asymmetry.

Correlation Analysis of User Perceptual Evaluation and Morphological Elements. Correlation analysis was performed on the evaluation data of each sample in the questionnaire and the morphological data in the sample to obtain Table 6.

Table 5. Distribution of morphological elements of each sample.

Sample	Handle shape				Blade shape				Overall shape	
	a	b	c	d	e	f	g	h	i	j
S1	0	1	1	0	0	0	0	1	0	1
S2	0	0	0	1	0	1	0	0	1	0
S3	0	1	0	0	0	0	0	1	0	1
S4	0	0	1	0	0	0	0	1	1	0
S5	1	0	0	0	1	0	0	0	1	0
S6	0	1	0	0	0	1	0	0	1	0
S7	0	1	0	0	0	0	1	0	1	0
S8	0	1	0	0	0	0	1	0	1	0
S9	0	1	0	0	0	0	0	1	0	1

Table 6. Correlation analysis between user perception and morphological elements

	Rough	Traditional	Dull	Laborious	Bulky	Fragile
a	−0.156	−0.255	.753*	0.534	0.182	0.341
b	0.12	.688*	−0.47	−0.227	−0.305	0.023
c	0.548	0.379	0.14	0.192	0.536	−0.242
d	−0.132	−0.372	−0.061	0.023	−0.209	0.292
e	−0.132	−0.426	0.489	0.599	0.101	0.618
f	−0.027	0.381	−0.336	−0.343	−0.403	−0.052
g	−0.133	−0.166	−0.173	−0.123	0.311	−0.432
h	0.548	0.379	0.14	0.192	0.536	−0.242
i	−0.205	−0.439	−0.169	−0.061	0.023	−0.03
j	0.497	0.634	0.311	0.377	0.431	0

* Correlation is significant at 0.05 levels (two tailed).
** Correlation is significant at 0.01 levels (two tailed).

The statistically significant data pairs that less than 0.05 are as follows: geometric semicircular handles are positively correlated with 'sharp-blunt' handles, 'ellipses (including circles)' handles are 'modern-traditional' Positive correlation. In other words, the user group believes that a geometric semicircular handle means dull, and a oval (including circles) handle means tradition.

Correlation Analysis of Designer's Perceptual Evaluation and Morphological Elements. Correlation analysis was performed on the evaluation data of each sample in the questionnaire and the morphological data in the sample to obtain Table 6 and 7.

Statistically significant data pairs show that the streamlined semi-circular handle has a strong positive correlation with 'modern-traditional', the straight rounded blade has a strong negative correlation with the 'delicate-rough', and the long arcs, so as the rod handle is strongly positively related to 'lightweight-heavy', that is to say, the designer

Table 7. Analysis of correlation between designer perception and morphological elements.

	Rough	Traditional	Dull	Laborious	Bulky	Fragile
a	−0.454	−0.348	0.611	0.507	−0.33	0.451
b	0.289	.819**	−0.424	0.37	−0.184	−0.302
c	0.42	0.173	0.115	0.099	.670*	−0.437
d	−0.201	−0.291	0.32	−0.037	−0.167	0.524
e	−.763*	−0.526	0.532	0.326	−0.351	0.492
f	0.437	0.591	−0.071	0.3	−0.204	0.144
g	−0.015	−0.134	−0.424	−0.522	0.4	−0.386
h	0.42	0.173	0.115	0.099	.670*	−0.437
i	−0.188	−0.346	0	−0.381	0.119	0.205
j	0.294	0.462	0.227	0.649	0.311	−0.321

* Correlation is significant at 0.05 levels (two tailed).
** Correlation is significant at 0.01 levels (two tailed).

group believes that a streamlined semi-circular handle means more traditional, a straight rounded blade means more delicate, and the long arcs and rod handles mean more bulky.

3 Conclusions

In summary, for the overall data, after independent sample T test, it can be known that the designer group and the user group are in the perceptual vocabulary group 'sharp-dull', 'laborious-laborsaving' and 'durable-fragile' There are significant differences. As for the correlation between perceptual words, the Pearson correlation analysis test shows that the designer group has 'modern-traditional' and 'durable-fragile' and 'lightweight-heavy' and 'durable' There is no statistical significance of the correlation data on the two perceptual vocabulary groups of 'durable-fragile'. Among the other pairs, the designer group and the user group show a positive correlation. In terms of correlation, designers Believes that the 'delicate-rough' and 'modern-traditional' pre-sentations have the strongest positive correlation, while the user group believes that there is a strong correlation between 'sharp-dull' and 'laborious-laborsaving' There is a strong correlation between 'laborious-laborsaving' and 'lightweight-heavy'. For the morphological elements of scissors, due to the limited number of questionnaire samples, only a small number of data sets have a significance of less than 0.05, which is statistically significant. Designers and users think that the oval handle means more traditional, and in other on the one hand, the designer believes that straight rounded blades mean more refined, the long curved blade and rod handles mean more bulky. The user group believes that a geometric semi-circular handle means dull.

This study shows that there is indeed a difference in perceptual cognition between designers and users, and there are indeed differences in perceptual cognition caused by morphological elements. Therefore, in future design activities, designers need to introduce the method of perceptual engineering to In the product shape design process, the correlation between the product's morphological elements and the user's emotional needs can be effectively analyzed, and the emotional changes that different morphological features can produce for the user can be studied, so as to find a better one based on a clear design positioning The combination of morphological elements achieves great satisfaction of user needs.

References

1. Liu, S.: Design Psychology. Shanghai People's Art Press, Shanghai (2009). (in Chinese)
2. Zheng, J., Li, X.: Design Methodology. Tsinghua University Press, Beijing (2012). (in Chinese)
3. Ishihara, S., Ishihara, K., Nagamachi, M.: An analysis of Kansei structure on shoes using self-organizing neural network. Int. J. Ind. Ergon. **19**(96), 93–104 (1997)
4. Akinori, H., Takamasa, S.: A Kansei engineering approach to a driver/vehicle system. Int. J. Ind. Ergon. **15**(1), 25–37 (1995)
5. Zhao, Y., Bian, F., Li, J.: Research on product material image based on perceptual engineering. Mech. Des. **32**(8) (2015). (in Chinese)
6. Du, H.: Perceptual engineering and fuzzy analytic hierarchy process product design modeling evaluation. J. Xi'an Univ. Technol. **30**(3), 244–249 (2014). (in Chinese)
7. Jing, N., Fang, H., Zhang, Q.: Research on innovative design of product style based on typology. Mech. Des. **32**(4), 121–125 (2015). (in Chinese)
8. Xu, Y., Chen, K., Peng, Z.: Analysis of consumer demand based on perceptual engineering. Des. Art Res. **2**(3), 1–5 (2012). (in Chinese)
9. Kim, W., Lee, Y., Lee, J.H., Shin, G.W., Yun, M.H.: A comparative study on designer and customer preference models of leather for vehicle. Int. J. Ind. Ergon. **65**, 110–121 (2018)
10. https://uland.taobao.com/sem/tbsearch?refpid=mm_26632258_3504122_32538762&clk1=5abaa6b7fecf619626892945a40198f5&keyword=%E5%89%AA%E5%88%80&page=0
11. Wei, Y.: Design of electric hand drill based on perceptual engineering. Packag. Eng. **37**(24), 108–113 (2016). (in Chinese)

Extracting Kansei Evaluation Index Using Time Series Text Data: Examining Universality and Temporality

Runa Yamada, Sho Hashimoto[✉], and Noriko Nagata[✉]

Kwansei Gakuin University, 2-1, Gakuen, Sanda, Hyogo, Japan
nagata@kwansei.ac.jp

Abstract. In recent years, affective needs, such as usability and comfort, have attracted attention, along with conventional manufacturing needs, such as function, price and reliability. Therefore, when designing products, it is necessary to accurately and efficiently reflect user's affective needs on product design. To that end, we clarify the user's emotions and impressions, in terms of the ways that people feel about products. However, they are assumed to be constant regardless of time-series, impressions that are influenced by time-series and impressions that are used universally within a certain period are mixed. As the user's emotions and impressions depend on time-series, it is necessary to deal with them separately, by time-series. In this study, based on time-series changes in the appearance frequency of evaluation words, we classified the Kansei evaluation index, according to whether it changes by time-series or not. In the proposed method, for each evaluation word, a state-space model is first used to extract the information of seasonal and trend variations. Second, by clustering this information, the evaluation terms are separated into several clusters. This method was applied to the fashion field, where time-series effects are believed to exist. The results confirmed that there were two patterns of seasonal variation and four patterns of trend variation in the impression of fashion in general, and eight universal impressions were extracted.

Keywords: Text mining · Time series · Kansei evaluation index

1 Introduction

In recent years, with the diversification of user needs and preferences, products have attracted attention, not only for their value in conventional manufacturing, as with functions and prices but also for their sensibility values, such as usability and comfort [1,2]. The Kansei engineering approach is recognized as the most reliable and effective method to handle affective needs and can be applied to various domains [3]. One specific approach to model Kansei evaluation that expresses the relationship between physical features and impressions of products [4–6]. It is expected that clarifying a user's affective evaluation (impression

© Springer Nature Switzerland AG 2020
C. Stephanidis and M. Antona (Eds.): HCII 2020, CCIS 1226, pp. 722–729, 2020.
https://doi.org/10.1007/978-3-030-50732-9_92

and emotion) of products and providing feedback to their design will improve product's quality and brand image. These studies are based on the assumption that people's impressions of products or services is constant. However, some of the impressions that compose the model include seasonal variation and trend variation; there may be a mixture of those affected by time-series effects and those used universally within a certain period.

As an example of analyzing time-series effects of value, there are some studies about grasping long-term trend information on items and coordinates in the fashion field. With the development of artificial intelligence, research is being conducted actively to predict the future of fashion trends using machine learning tasks [7,8]. As the main focus of these studies is on the future of fashion trends, modeling Kansei evaluation quantitatively is not considered.

Therefore, in this study, we work on the classification of the Kansei evaluation indexes according to whether it changes chronologically, based on the time-series change of the word appearance frequency. In this study, we assume seasonal variation and trend variation as time-series effects, and classify universality and temporality based on how they are affected.

2 Previous Study

In a study to quantitatively model the user's impression using text mining [5,6], a hierarchical structure, consisting of three layers, is assumed: (1) "Emotion" layer that expresses the preference of the product, (2) "Impression" layer that expresses the characteristics of the product, and (3) "Physical element" layer that expresses the physical features of the product. According to this hierarchical structure, the impression structure of the target product field is clarified from the product review text. Specifically, to model the impression structure, words representing the evaluation of the target product (evaluation words) are divided into emotions and impressions, using multiple dictionary information, and topics are extracted for the evaluation words corresponding to the impressions (impression words). However, the user's impressions are thought to be influenced by time series, such as seasonal variation and trend variation. As these factors are not considered in the modeling, we must model the impression structure separately by time-series.

In the case of predicting long-term trends in the fashion field, there are studies to discover trends in realway using the similarity of coordinated images by investigating the relationship between cutting-edge fashion "runway" and general fashion "realway" in fashion shows [7] and to predict the future popularity of styles discovered from fashion images taken in an unsupervised manner [8]. In these studies, time-series modeling of the visual feature of fashion style is possible, but the structure of the impression that causes the trend of the visual feature is not known.

3　Methods

We classify the Kansei evaluation indexes according to whether it changes chronologically, based on time-series changes in the appearance frequency of evaluation words.

The method consists of four steps. First, we collect and select evaluation words, using word classes and Japanese dictionaries of evaluation expressions. Second, we estimate the state-space model that decomposes the appearance of evaluation words into each factor component (seasonal variation and trend variation). Third, we classify the appearance of evaluation words by clustering each factor component. Finally, we cluster evaluation words with small time-series changes using embedding words. In this method, we classify the universal Kansei evaluation indexes according to whether it changes chronologically.

The state-space model in this study is indicated by the following formula:

$$y_t = \mu_t + \gamma_t + \epsilon_t \tag{1}$$

$$\mu_t = \mu_{t-1} + \beta + \eta_t \tag{2}$$

where y_t is the evaluation word appearance probabilities vector at time t, μ_t is the trend component, γ_t is the seasonal component with the so-called the four seasons of spring, summer, autumn and winter (In this study, according to the four seasons of the Japan Meteorological Agency, spring is from March to May, summer from June to August, autumn from September to November, and winter from December to February), ϵ_t is the irregular and $\epsilon_t \sim N\left(0, \sigma_\epsilon^2\right)$, μ_t is a generalization of the intercept term that can vary dynamically across time, β is a generalization of the time-trend that is constant, η_t is the irregular and $\eta_t \sim N\left(0, \sigma_\eta^2\right)$. The seasonal component is modeled as:

$$\gamma_t = -\sum_{j=1}^{s-1} \gamma_{t+1-j} + \omega_t \tag{3}$$

where ω_t is the irregular and $\omega_t \sim N\left(0, \sigma_\omega^2\right)$.

y_t is calculated for each year and the four seasons and standardized to $N\left(0, 1\right)$ for each evaluation word. This model shows what factor y_t is decomposed into and that it changes in x year. In addition, the state-space model consists of two equations: an observation Eq. (1) that determines how an internal state is observed from a certain internal state, and a state Eq. (2) that determines how the internal state changes with time [9].

The clustering of seasonal variation γ_t and potential internal state transition μ_t by k-means method is used to classify the time-series variation of evaluation words. By modeling the time-series relationship of the appearance frequency and bundling the evaluation words with similar models, it can be estimated as an evaluation index with the same time-series tendency.

In the classification results obtained by the above processing, the time-series variation can be interpreted, but evaluation words with different meanings are mixed into the cluster, making them difficult to interpret. For this reason, we interpret each cluster using the distributed representation of words and hierarchical clustering. Word2Vec [10] is used as a learning method for the distributed representation of words. Word2Vec is a technique to obtain a distributed representation of words, using a two-layer neural network, called a Skip-gram model. Next, we calculate the cosine similarity between the evaluation words in each cluster, using the distributed expression of the evaluation words obtained by Word2Vec, calculate the distance based on the cosine similarity, and perform hierarchical clustering by the longest distance method. The number of clusters in this study is determined, such that the evaluation words with a cosine distance in the top 30% of the whole belong to the same cluster.

4   Experiment

4.1   Data

The data included in this study are fashion news articles written at Fashion Press[1] between March 2012 and November 2019, 20,357 pages. There is a structure in which fashion trends are transmitted from top designers and collections in a top-down fashion. Therefore, we analyze fashion news articles that are located in a position that connects users and top designers. Fashion Press has seven categories of news articles: fashion, beauty, gourmet, art, film, music, and lifestyle. In this study, we perform analysis focusing on time-series features in fashion categories.

4.2   The Collection and Selection of Evaluation Words

To extract the evaluation words necessary to extract the evaluation index in the fashion field, we collected and selected evaluation words suitable for expressions to evaluate fashion. First, to extract evaluation words related to the impression, the words with a POS that is a main adjective or noun (adjective base) are collected from all words after morphological analysis. Next, evaluation words of other POS are collected using the following three Japanese dictionaries: (1) EVALDIC ver. 1.0.1 [11,12], (2) Japanese Sentiment Dictionary (Volume of Verbs and Adjectives) ver. 1.0 [11], and (3) Japanese Sentiment Dictionary (Volume of Nouns) ver. 1.0 [13]. The conditions of the collection are as follows: (1) included in EVALDIC; (2) included in the words given the "evaluation" tag in the Japanese Sentiment Dictionary (Volume of Verbs and Adjectives); (3) included in the words given the "evaluation" tag in the Japanese Sentiment Dictionary (Volume of Nouns); and (4) appear in the fashion category more than 0.5% higher than those in the non-fashion categories.

In a related study [5], evaluation terms are classified based on the Japanese Appraisal Dictionary-attitudinal evaluation ver. 1.0. [14] which category information of evaluation expressions is attached. In this dictionary, there are two

---

[1] https://www.fashion-press.net/.

categories of evaluation expressions: "externalized evaluation" and "internalized evaluation". Internalized evaluation expresses the evaluator's feelings and feelings for the evaluation target, such as "happy" or "fun" and externalized evaluation indicates the characteristics of the evaluation target, such as "soft" or "beautiful." In this study, as in the previous study, evaluation words corresponding to externalized evaluation were selected to clarify the impression factors that lead to the user's emotions.

As a result, 117 evaluation words were selected as evaluation words suitable for expressions that evaluate fashion.

4.3   Time Series Clustering Using State Space Model

As some evaluation words are strongly influenced by trends and seasonal fluctuations, we classify the evaluation indices using a state-space model and the k-means method.

The parameter estimation of the models described in Sect. 3 is performed by the BFGS method, and the potential internal state transition μ_t and seasonal variation γ_t obtained from those models are clustered. The optimal number of clusters was determined using AIC (Akaike Information Criterion). As a result, the number of clusters of potential internal state transition was 4, the number of clusters of seasonal variation was 2, and evaluation indexes with time-series tendency of all 8 patterns were extracted. Figures 1 and 2 show the cluster centroids of potential internal state transitions and seasonal variations, respectively.

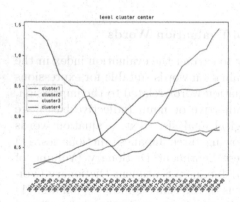

Fig. 1. Potential internal state transition

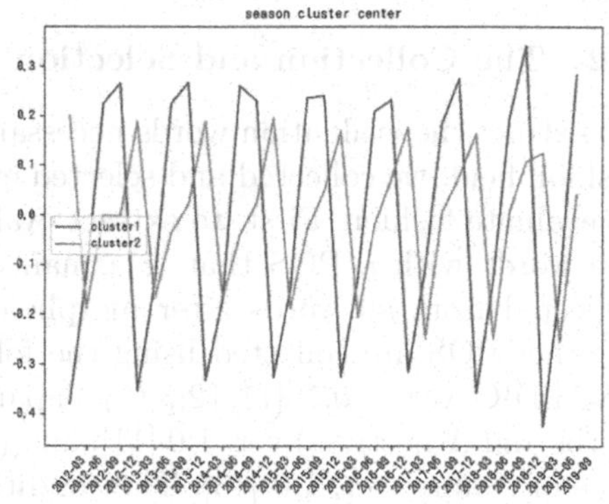

Fig. 2. Seasonal variation

Looking at Fig. 1, it is possible to estimate that there are clusters 1 and 2, which have relatively small fluctuations and are relatively stationary, as well as cluster 3, which has an upward trend, and cluster 4, which has a downward trend. Looking at Fig. 2, it is possible to interpret cluster 1, which has a strong seasonal variation, and others.

4.4 Interpretation of Evaluation Index by Word2Vec

Clustering was performed on the evaluation words belonging to cluster 2, which is a group of evaluation words with small seasonal variation in Fig. 2, among the relatively stationary clusters 1 in Fig. 1. Table 1 shows the results of these interpretations. It was possible to extract eight universal evaluation indices, except for clusters containing fashion-specific words like cluster 3 and clusters with only one word in the cluster, such as cluster 10, which are difficult to interpret.

The clusters obtained from this result are: (1) impression on services and assortment (Clusters 1, 2); (2) impression on physical characteristics (Cluster 4); (3) impression on comfort (Clusters 5, 7); (4) tactile impressions (Cluster 6); and (5) visual impressions (Clusters 8, 9). It was possible to interpret all clusters as a set of evaluation words related to fashion, so reasonable results were considered to have been obtained.

Table 1. Interpretation result

Cluster	Interpretation	in Japanese	Impression Words	in Japanese
Cluster 1	Sense of security	安心感	prepare, comfortable, stable, enhanced	備える, 快適だ, 安定, 向上
Cluster 2	Richness	豊富さ	rich, prepared	豊富だ, 備える
Cluster 3	noise	ノイズ	best, down	ベストだ, ダウン
Cluster 4	Feeling of size	サイズ感	big, long, short	大きい, 長い, 短い
Cluster 5	Feeling of wearing	着こなし感	rough, can handle	ラフだ, こなせる
Cluster 6	Soft feeling	ソフト感	soft, supple, soft	柔らかだ, しなやかだ, ソフト
Cluster 7	Active feeling	アクティブ感	casual, light, active, effective, sporty, hard, neat, elegant	カジュアルだ, 軽やかだ, アクティブだ, 効く, スポーティーだ, ハード, 端正だ, 上品だ
Cluster 8	Presence	存在感	presence, attract, glow	存在感, 惹く, 光る
Cluster 9	Pop feeling	ポップ感	vivid, pop, pale, shines	鮮やかだ, ポップだ, 淡い, 映える
Cluster 10	noise	ノイズ	reminiscent	彷彿たる

From these results, we extracted eight types of evaluation indices (sense of security, richness, feeling of size, feeling of wearing, soft feeling, active feeling, presence, and pop feeling) that are commonly used in fashion during the target period.

5 Conclusion

In this study, we propose a method to classify the Kansei evaluation index, which is influenced by time series, from the fashion news articles existing on the web and the Kansei evaluation index, which is universal within a certain period. In the proposed method, evaluation words were first collected and selected, based on the category information and the evaluation expression dictionary. Next, we modeled the time-series changes in the appearance frequency of evaluation words using the state space method, and clustered seasonal changes γ_t and potential internal state transitions μ_t using the k-means method. Finally, the validity of this method was verified by interpreting the evaluation index using Word2Vec.

In this experiment, we analyzed fashion news articles for 9 years and applied this method. As a result, it was confirmed that there were two patterns of seasonal variation and four patterns of trend variation in the overall impression of fashion. We extracted clusters with small fluctuations in internal state and small seasonal fluctuations, and performed clustering to interpret their semantic information. As a result, we were able to confirm the evaluation indices that are universally used in the evaluation of eight fashions.

Future tasks include improving the accuracy of the state space model, modeling the relationship with emotions and improving the diversity and usefulness of the information obtained by investigating clusters that were not used in the interpretation in Figs. 1 and 2.

References

1. Qu, Q.X.: Kansei knowledge extraction based on evolutionary genetic algorithm: an application to e-commerce web appearance design. Theor. Issues Ergon. Sci. **16**(3), 299–313 (2015)
2. Toyota, N., et al.: Objective evaluation about texture for cosmetic ingredients by direct shear testing of powder bed. J. Soc. Powder Technol. Jpn. **52**(12), 694–700 (2015)
3. Chen, C.H., Khoo, L.P., Chen, K., Pang, J.H., Huang, Y.: Consumer-oriented product form creation via Kansei engineering. In: Proceedings of the International Symposium for Emotion and Sensibility-Emotion Research in Practice, pp. 184–191 (2008)
4. Yanagisawa, H.: Quantification method of product emotional quality considering its diversity (application to quantification of emotional quality in product sound design). Trans. Jpn. Soc. Mech. Eng. Series C **74**(746), 273–282 (2008)
5. Hashimoto, S., Yamada, A., Nagata, N.: A quantication method of composite impression of products by externalized evaluation words of the appraisal dictionary with review text data. Int. J. Affect. Eng. **18**(2), 59–65 (2019)

6. Yamada, A., Hashimoto, S., Nagata, N.: A text mining approach for automatic modeling of Kansei evaluation from review texts. KEER 2018. AISC, vol. 739, pp. 319–328. Springer, Singapore (2018). https://doi.org/10.1007/978-981-10-8612-0_34
7. Vittayakorn, S., et al.: Runway to realway: visual analysis of fashion. In: 2015 IEEE Winter Conference on Applications of Computer Vision. IEEE (2015)
8. Al-Halah, Z., Stiefelhagen, R., Grauman, K.: Fashion forward: forecasting visual style in fashion. In: Proceedings of the IEEE International Conference on Computer Vision (2017)
9. Durbin, J., Kpoopman, S.J.: Time Series Analysis by State Space Methods. Oxford University Press, Oxford (2012)
10. Mikolov, T., Chen, K., Corrado, G., Dean, J.: Efficient estimation of word representations in vector space. In: ICLR Workshop 2013 (2013)
11. Kurohashi, S.: Improvements of Japanese morphological analyzer JUMAN. In: Proceedings of the Workshop on Sharable Natural Language Resources, Nara, pp. 22–28 (1994)
12. Kobayashi, N., Inui, K., Matsumoto, Y., Tateishi, K., Fukushima, T.: Collecting evaluative expressions for opinion extraction. J. Nat. Lang. Process. **12**(3), 203–222 (2005)
13. Kobayashi, N., Inui, K., Matsumoto, Y.: Designing the task of opinion extraction and structurization. IPSJ SIG Technical report, NL171-18, pp. 111–118 (2006)
14. Sano, M.: The construction of "Japanese dictionary of appraisal -attitude-" Development of language resource to capture diversity of evaluation. In: Proceedings of the 17th Annual Meeting of the Association for Natural Language Processing, pp. 115–118 (2010). (in Japanese)

Behavioral Research and Service Innovation of Cinema Viewers in China

Xiaofang Yuan and Qiujie Jiang[✉]

Wuhan University of Technology, 122 Luoshi Road, Wuhan, Hubei, People's
Republic of China
qiujie1202@gmail.com

Abstract. The current popularity of online movie and the homogeneity of
movie theater services have led to the client loss of movie theaters in China.
This essay takes advantage of service design methods to analyze film viewers'
physical behavior, psychological behavior, and contact points in different movie
watching stages. A cinema service system map and service blueprint are proposed in this paper based on the behavioral characteristics of viewers and further
proposed SPTE cinema service framework and strategy. The research on the
behavior of viewers and the discussion of service strategies not only provide the
basis for the theater to create products and services that meet viewers' needs, but
also provide valuable reference for theaters to build service innovation system.

Keywords: Viewing · Behavioral research · Service design

1 Introduction

The three major changes in movie consumption behavior summarized as improved
convenience, enhanced social consumption atmosphere, and increased impulse consumption in people's real life have led to an overall increase in the online rate of the
Chinese movie industry [1]. More and more viewers are choosing to watch movies
online or view through personal devices, and the attendance of traditional theaters has
been greatly challenged. To date, most of the practice and research on viewing services
are based on marketing, which provides new marketing methods for enterprises. This
method often uses marketing data to determine the content and focus of marketing,
which lacks a comprehensive study on the viewer experience and the service provision.
And the practice of this method may cause mismatch in product and service provision
and a further loss of viewers at market is predictable.

This study analyzes the behavior of viewer and the interactive relationships of
stakeholders in the service link by using service design methods. In order to innovate
the existing theater service model, new service strategy is suggested in the research
finally.

2 Relevant Work

2.1 The Service Mode of Chinese Cinema

Since the reform of the cinema in China in the 21st century, the industry has changed the previous division method, distribution level and industrial structure, and the number of viewers has increased significantly. At the same time, the rise of the Internet has enabled the online ticketing platform to fully penetrate from upstream production to downstream viewers. From the content point of view, the theater's services include projection services, viewing services and supporting services [2]. The projection service is closest to the main body of the film, and the effects of its projection equipment directly affect the audience's audiovisual experience. Viewing services mainly exist in the ticket sales area, ticket inspection area, and projection area. In this link, the contact between employees and customers is positive, and customer satisfaction is directly proportional to service quality. Supporting services are a series of equipment and personnel services provided by the theater to expand its service and marketing scope, such as leisure seats, merchandising, parking services, etc. At present, the supporting services of most theaters are the reverse development of viewer needs, and this top-down development method deviates from the actual needs of viewers, and it is also easy to cause decline in resource utilization, homogeneity of products and services, and ultimately lead to the loss of audience to theaters.

2.2 Innovation on Cinema Service

Scholars have proposed innovative ideas and practices for cinema viewing services from viewers' experience effecting factors and technical support. In the study of effecting factors of cinema customer experience, Wen Tao proposed that in the research model of cinema customer experience effecting factors and its mechanism, promotion, display effect, convenience and reasonable price have a direct positive impact on viewing experience [3]. Lin Jiaju believes that the reconstruction of the supporting products around the theater can create a comprehensive service experience for viewing and entertainment and promote the well-round development of theaters and shopping malls [4]. FVAE (Factorized Variational Autoencoders), as a neural visual network system technology, is used to analyze the expressions of live audiences to connect with the movie scene, which allows temporary changes to the plot or even determining the final direction of the movie [5].

Some scholars also innovated in the marketing strategy for theater. Zhang Denan proposed a seven-dimensional marketing strategy of implementing differentiated marketing, experiential marketing, VIP membership services, combined flights, theme marketing, public welfare activities, and expanding theater functions by summarizing the new theater marketing model [6]. Zhou Ying subdivided from the behavioral level of viewing viewers and proposed corresponding marketing strategies for different timing and occasions, different viewing directions, and five factors that affect brand loyalty [7]. The North American film industry is the leader in the world film industry. And AMC, Regal, Cinemark and other theaters are using technology to transform theaters, upgrade seats and catering services, increase audience loyalty, and establish diversified profit channels to cope with the loss of viewer and market decline [8].

In general, the innovation of viewing services requires the joint promotion of technology, service and marketing. Facing the current opportunities and challenges, this research will take the viewing experience as a beginning to explore cinema service design countermeasures in different scenarios and move the innovation process of cinema service forward.

3 Methodology

3.1 Behavioral Research on Viewers

Service design was first proposed in the field of management, and with the continuous intersection of design thinking and service marketing concepts [9], service design methods and tools have further advanced and optimized. In the research phase of viewer behavior, the shadow tracking method and the route of viewer are used to analyze the behavior of the viewer's entire viewing process.

In this research, after taking shadowing to some selected typical viewers for a period of time, some problems in viewer behavior can be observed as much as possible [10]. With the viewer's permission, their behavior is recorded. Kat Kaplan defines the user journey map as a research method that combines storytelling and visualization [11]. This study uses the user journey map to summarize the behaviors and feelings of viewers at different stages and lists the corresponding pain points and design ideas.

3.2 The Development of Service

In order to build the overall framework of products and services in the viewing system, the service system map and service blueprint are used to illustrate the relationships between stakeholders in the system, as well as the delivery and circulation of products and services.

The system map can visualize the participants (including the flow of materials, information, etc.) involved in the service delivery. Combining the product service system design framework previously proposed by this team with the five experience design areas [12, 13] in the service proposed by Leonieke G. Zomerdijk, a cinema service system diagram is expected to build.

At the same time, service blueprints is applied to subdivide services. The service blueprint was first used to record and analyze the service process of the enterprise [14], by studying the service delivery, building the overall framework of all parties and service delivery. In the cinema service blueprint, the physical behavior is divided into tangible display and viewer behavior, while the service personnel are subdivided in behavior and function, and service delivery includes front and back-end contact.

4 Implementation

4.1 Behavioral Research on Viewers

According to the *"Analysis of the Development Status and Development Trend of China's Cinema Industry in 2018"* released by China Industry Information Network, viewing consumption is mainly concentrated in post-85-95 populations [15]. We randomly selected three from 25 home theaters in Hongshan District of Wuhan City for investigation, mainly using user interview and shadowing. Participants of the study included 20–35-year-old moviegoers and cinema staff. Aiming at viewers, a typical persona was set as a study model. Finally, the user journey map is used to summarize and analyze the data (see Fig. 1), which helps us better understand the feelings, thoughts and behaviors of the target viewers, summarizes the pain points of the viewers, and obtains the design opportunities corresponding to the problem.

The user journey map records the whole process of the viewing from the intention of a viewing plan to leaving the theater and analyzes the spent time and behavior of the viewer at each stage. The user journey map is divided into five stages as follows: before buying tickets, after buying tickets, while waiting, while watching movies, and after leaving. The viewers have shown more of the following: there are more consumption choices and entertainment needs before and after the ticket purchase. And sometimes viewers feel confused to pick up tickets and find the exact seat in the theater. At this stage, there are more potential creative marketing space. The viewing is the stage where viewers spend the longest time in the theater. Viewers have shown a direct need on their viewing experience, such as the quality of the projection, the seat, the environment, and light.

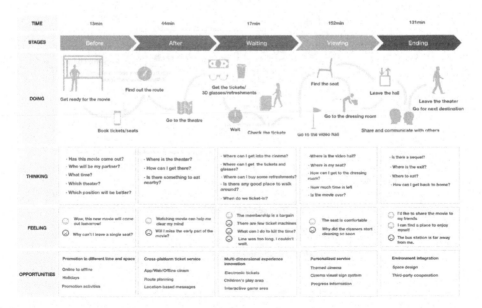

Fig. 1. Viewer journey map

Through the in-depth excavation and analysis of the contact points of the viewers' behavior, the pain points of the viewers in the entire service process is summarized and refined in this paper. The pain points mainly are listed bellows: the ticket purchase platform is not easy to use; the lack of clear route guidance; the equipment is hard to use; the viewing is not personalized; and the service is interrupted before and after the movie. According to the behavior analysis and pain points of viewers, design opportunities on different scenarios in the entire viewing process have been developed: on-demand promotion in different time and space, cross-platform ticket service system, multi-dimensional experience innovation, personalized services and environment integration. Aiming at the design opportunities in different scenarios, we combed the cinema service elements to build a cinema service system and cinema service blueprint.

4.2   The System of Theatrical Service

The whole service system map shows the service provision and information exchange between stakeholders (see Fig. 2). The main path is that viewers receive the information forwarded by the theater, then viewers purchase tickets through multiple platforms, and go to the theater according to the system's recommendations. After the viewing, the entire service was continued through the conversion of the theater and external passenger flow. In the process, a movie theater-centric model is formed. These stakeholders include potential users, ticketing platforms, service data centers, regulators, producers, food suppliers, and various supporting categories in the external environment.

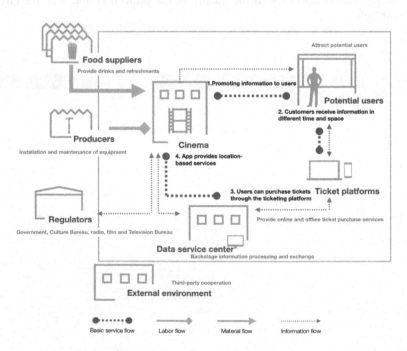

Fig. 2. Cinema service system map

After conducting a research on service delivery, we have drawn a service blueprint for the cinema (see Fig. 3) to provide a platform for service quality management. The visible and invisible support activities and services from online booking, ticket purchase to viewing until departure are listed in the figure. Visible employee behavior includes ticket sales, food sales, ticket checking, facility maintenance, cleaning, and location guidance. Correspondingly, the invisible service provision area includes material distribution, content generation and management, data analysis, server and third-party platform support, etc. The cinema service blueprint provides an overall service delivery and support framework. Through this platform, cinema staff and other stakeholders can clearly understand their respective services and complete the corresponding tasks. Furthermore, it continuously improves and optimizes in the service implementation, and continuously provides better service experience for viewers.

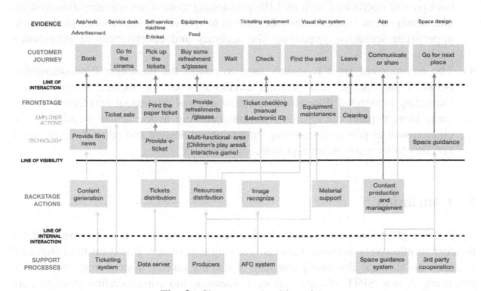

Fig. 3. Cinema service blueprint

4.3 Service Innovation Strategy for Theaters

This study proposes a Service-Promotion-Technology-Environment (SPTE) service framework by re-integrating different levels and different supporting elements under the viewing process. Exploration towards the cinema service strategy is made from four dimensions: service, promotion, technology and environment.

1) The service layer is designed to serve from multi-sensory channels and the satisfaction of viewer differences. Multi-sensory channels include the design of all the visual content of the theater, the ergonomic considerations of the theater hardware facilities, the division of the olfactory experience in different areas, the provision of food and the creation of the auditory experience in the projection area. The viewer

difference is to provide products and services that meet the needs of various types of viewer as much as possible.

2) The promotion layer mainly includes three scenarios. The promotion before the viewing can be divided as follows: point, line and surface. Points refer to the information provided by the platform to individual viewers. Line refers to the dissemination of video news at special occasions such as festivals, movie events, or related spaces. The surface is the distribution of movie information in the traffic distribution center. The viewers may have a long fragmentation interval in the waiting area, which allows advertisements, merchandise, and entertainment activities to promote multiple consumption. Thus, the theaters can provide a lasting service experience through the mobile platform on viewers after finishing their watching in cinema theaters.

3) The technology layer collects and analyzes viewer usage data and relies on background operations such as LBS positioning system, recommendation system, and management system to provide content to viewers through mobile platforms in appropriate scenarios, improving the accuracy and effectiveness of information push.

4) The environment layer is mainly used to realize the passenger flow conversion between the internal and external environment of the theater. Cross-scenario marketing is targeted through internal and external contextual correlation. At the same time, expand the cinema function according to the actual situation of the cinema such as providing catering, entertainment, leisure and other comprehensive services to increase revenue growth.

5   Conclusion

As the rise of various new media viewing methods, there is an increasing need for theaters to effectively improve viewers' viewing experience. Based on the behavioral research on viewers, this study conducts a cinema service system map and service blueprint. A new SPTE cinema service framework and corresponding strategies are also introduced in the study. Through a more comprehensive understanding of viewer needs and the provision of corresponding services, the attendance and viscosity of theaters can be improved. At the current stage, the research mainly focuses on the behavioral analysis of a fixed group viewers. A hierarchy model of viewing needs towards different groups of viewers can be built afterwards.

References

1. Yueming, Y., Li, L.: On new ecosystem of popular film consumption in the context of "internet+". Contemp. Cine. **11**, 92–96 (2017). (in Chinese)
2. Siyu, H., Chuanguo, F.: 4 + P model: the transformation and development of domestic cinema in the post-cinema era. Movie Lit. **19**, 4–10 (2016). (in Chinese)

3. Tao, W.: An empirical study on customers' experiential influencing factors and the mechanism in respect to cinemas. J. Northeast. Univ. (Soc. Sci.) **11**(3), 230–235 (2009). (in Chinese)
4. Jiaju, L.: Research on the status reconstruction of shopping center's supporting categories under the background of experiential marketing—taking cinema as an example. Commer. Times **6**, 38–40 (2017). (in Chinese)
5. Deng, Z., Navarathna, R., Carr, P., et al.: Factorized variational autoencoders for modeling audience reactions to movies. In: IEEE Conference on Computer Vision and Pattern Recognition (CVPR). IEEE Computer Society, pp. 2577–2586 (2017)
6. Denan, Z.: Research on cinema innovative marketing model. J. Liaoning Econ. Manag. Cadre Inst. **6**, 35–37 (2015). (in Chinese)
7. Ying, Z.: The Research of Wanda Cinema's Marketing Strategies. Xi'an University of Architecture and Technology (2015). (in Chinese)
8. Kan, P.: On the american cinema industrial development strategy in the era of experience economy. Contemp. Cine. **9**, 70–75 (2017). (in Chinese)
9. Xin, X., Cao, J.: Positioning service design. Packag. Eng **39**(18), 55–61 (2018). (in Chinese)
10. Bella, M., Hanington, B.: Universal Methods of Design. Rockport Publishers, Beverly (2012)
11. Customer Journey Maps – What They Are and How to Build One. https://www.toptal.com/designers/product-design/customer-journey-maps. Accessed 02 Mar 2020
12. Yuan, X., Wu, Y.: The framework for sustainable product-service system design. Packag. Eng. **37**(16), 91–94 (2016). (in Chinese)
13. Zomerdijk, L.G., Voss, C.A.: Service design for experience-centric services. J. Serv. Res. **13**(1), 67–82 (2013)
14. Shostack, G.L.: Design service that deliver. Harv Bus. Rev. **62**(1), 133–139 (1984)
15. Analysis on the Development Status and Trend of China's Cinema Industry in 2018. http://www.chyxx.com/industry/201802/613362.html. Accessed 02 Mar 2020

Interactively Solving the Takeout Delivery Problem Based on Customer Satisfaction and Operation Cost

Liuyang Zhang[1] and Wenzhu Liao[2(✉)]

[1] Department of Industrial Engineering, Chongqing University,
Chongqing 400044, China
1144399455@qq.com
[2] Department of Engineering Management, Chongqing University,
Chongqing 400044, China
liaowz@cqu.edu.cn

Abstract. Based on the development needs and realistic environment of o2o meal delivery industry in China. In this paper, the takeout distribution problem (TDP) has been proposed, and the most important customer satisfaction and operation cost in the process of o2o distribution are taken as the optimization objectives. The constraints of this problem are analyzed. Then, A mixed integer programming model with bi-objectives can be established. On this basis, a two-stage solution strategy based on human-computer interaction (HCI) is proposed, and the key technical methods are shown in detail, including coding method, order merging strategy and solving algorithm. Finally, in order to verify the effectiveness of the proposed model and algorithm, the key points of the instance design are proposed. In addition, the display method of the algorithm results is given. Through the Gantt chart display, it is easy to find the problems in the distribution and put forward the improvement methods. In general, this study provides strong support for the sustainable development of o2o distribution platform scheduling system.

Keywords: Takeout delivery problem · Bi-objectives · HCI solution strategy · Heuristic algorithm

1 Introduction

With the rapid development of the Chinese takeout industry, the number of orders in the peak period has multiplied every year since 2015 [1, 2]. Now, "Mei Tuan", "Eleme" and " Star Eleme" basically occupied 90% market share of Chinese takeout industry [1]. The major takeout platforms transferred the core competition from the cultivation of customer consumption habit to the promotion of customer experience gradually. Therefore, Intelligent scheduling system has been vigorously developed by each takeout platform. The statistical data shows that compared with the early manual scheduling, the average delivery time has shortened to 26 min, the average single running distance of riders has reduced by 7%, and the maximum income of rider has increased by 40% since the intelligent scheduling system was deployed [1]. However,

© Springer Nature Switzerland AG 2020
C. Stephanidis and M. Antona (Eds.): HCII 2020, CCIS 1226, pp. 738–745, 2020.
https://doi.org/10.1007/978-3-030-50732-9_94

some social contradictions are covered up by the beautiful data. As is known to all that it is impossible that the intelligent scheduling system consider the real-world situation well at any time. Some unreasonable scheduling will cause the order delivery delay, however, the riders, who are completely used as tools, have to be punished even if it is not their mistakes. In the long run, it has resulted in the high turnover rate and low happiness index in the takeout industry.

The problem of takeout delivery can be regarded as a kind of expansion problem of Vehicle Routing Problem with Time Windows and Simultaneous Pickup and Delivery problem (VRPPDTW). VRPPD has an important attribute: the vehicle must pick up the goods before delivery; this is obvious in the delivery process. In addition, the location of the rider in the delivery problem is not fixed, namely, the rider will not return to a distribution center after the delivery completed, which is the difference between TDP and general VRPPD problems. Through literature search, it is found that the research on delivery is still limited. Su et al. [3] and Jian et al. [4] have addressed the multi-objective model about the supply chain, coordination mechanism was proved as important to the logistics system. Chen et al. has studied the problem of delivery based on customer satisfaction [5], but it is not enough to only focus on customer satisfaction of time window, and more goals should be considered in the math model. Reyes et al. introduced the meal delivery routing problem firstly, a rolling horizon algorithm has been developed to solve the dynamic meal delivery problem, the computational results showed a nice work of it [6]. LI et al. addressed the delivery problem with an objective function of minimum cost, including the fixed cost, delivery cost and time penalty cost of the new order [7]. However, all of the researches don't attach the importance of rider's delivery experiences to the dispatching process. Thus, the bi-objective math model and dispatching method based on Human-Computer Interaction (HCI) have been proposed in this study. In practice, the solution of the TDP would benefit platforms, riders, customers in different aspects: 1) the fuel consumption and total operating cost can be decreased by minimizing the travelled distance and the number of riders employed; 2) the delivery efficiency can be improved enormously 3) the customers satisfaction can be maximized so that the reputation and competitiveness of the platform will be effectively guaranteed; 4) riders will be dispatched with effect and balanced, and their income will increase, most importantly, the riders would find their achievement in the works.

2 Model and Methodology

2.1 Model Construction

This study focuses on two main optimization objectives in the delivery process, namely, cost and satisfaction. Bi-objective function is transformed into single objective optimization by linear weighting method [4]. The objective function is showed in Eq. (1).

$$\min f = a(Z_{11} + Z_{12} + Z_{13}) - b(w_1 Z_{21} + w_2 Z_{22}) \tag{1}$$

In Eq. (1), a and b are sub-objective function weights. Z_{11} represents the vehicle operating cost which includes the cost of vehicle depreciation and the salary of the personal. Z_{12} represents the cost of fuel consumption. Z_{13} represents the cost of penalty, due to the strict time requirements, a soft time window is used in this study, the order should be delivered within $[e_{P_i}, l_{P_i}]$, otherwise, additional costs will be incurred and customer satisfaction will be reduced. Z_{21} represents the customer satisfaction of time. Z_{22} represents the customer satisfaction of food quality. w_1 and w_2 are sub-objective function weights. Besides, compared with the traditional VRPPD, most of the constraints of the TDP are similar. While the order merging strategy is considered in the delivery problem, some orders will be merged into one task and then delivered by a rider. Therefore, some constraints are added, that is, an order can only exist in one task, and a task can only be delivered by one rider.

In order to quantify customer satisfaction, and use the algorithm to solve conveniently, the fuzzy evaluation method is used to solve the problem. The relationship between customer satisfaction and membership is shown in Table 1.

Table 1. Relationship between membership value and customer satisfaction

Function value	0–0.4	0.4–0.6	0.6–0.8	0.8–1
Customer satisfaction	Not satisfied	Good	Satisfied	Very satisfied

2.2 Solution Strategy

In this section, due to the rider's experiences are considered, the two-stage strategy is introduced to solve the TDP model. As it shown in Fig. 1. In the first stage, insertion detection method and heuristic algorithm are used to solve the initial delivery scheme of the problem. When the rider received the dispatch scheme, the rider can choose to accept the system instruction or some of instructions according to his own distribution experience and current situation. Then, the feedback will be sent back to the system. In the second stage, the problem is solved again by the combination of fixed local solution method and local search algorithm. This scheduling strategy not only makes use of the powerful computing power of the intelligent algorithm, but also combines the personal delivery experience of the rider and real-time environment feedback. Riders with certain autonomy can improve the efficiency and stability of delivery process, more importantly, it will enhance the sense of participation and self-identification of riders and make them enjoy their work finally.

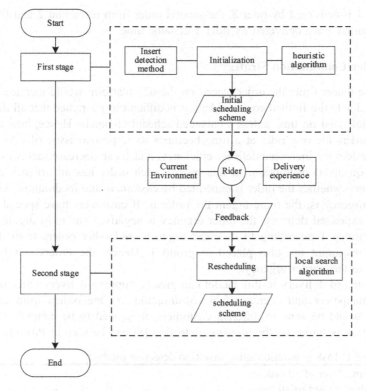

Fig. 1. The HCI solution strategy for takeout delivery problem

3   Relevant Algorithms and Technical Means

In order to achieve the above solution strategy, the key technical methods have been fully studied. In this section, all key technical methods will be shown in detail.

3.1   Encoding

The two layers coding method is developed in this study, including the order layer and rider layer. there are 6 orders from 3 o2o restaurants and 3 riders are available. There are 3 orders sent to the first restaurant, 2 orders sent to the second restaurant and 1 order sent to the third takeaway restaurant. Hence, an initial delivery plan is given in Fig. 2. It means the first order and second order from the restaurant 1 are delivered by rider 1 at same time, the first order from restaurant 2 is delivered by rider 2, the third order from

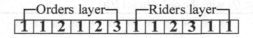

Fig. 2. Two-layer coding method

restaurant 1 is delivered by rider 3, the second order from restaurant 2 and first order from restaurant 3 are delivered by rider 1 at same time.

3.2   Order Combination Strategy

Around the dinner time, the order placed on the o2o platform would increase sharply. However, due to the limited cost of riders, it is difficult to guarantee that all the orders could be delivered on time unless a balanced schedule is made. Hence, how to merge multiple orders for one rider at a time becomes an important issue of o2o delivery system. Besides the increased delivery efficiency, it also can decrease fuel consumption and food quality consumption. In this model, each order has an urgency attribute, which reflects whether the order is expedited by customers and its duration. The lower the order urgency is, the more urgent the order is. If customers have special require-ments for expedited delivery, the order urgency is negative. The most urgent order is placed in group 1 according to its order urgency, and other orders from the same takeaway restaurant are also placed in group 1. Hence, the orders can be sorted according to their order urgency.

Consolidated delivery in this model can greatly improve delivery efficiency, save delivery manpower and decrease fuel consumption. As the orders from same o2o restaurant would be send to different customers, they need to be merged. The com-bination strategy based on the insertion detection [8] can be seen in Procedure 1.

Procedure 1: Task generation using insertion detection method

1: Input: P, set of all orders.
2: Output: Q, set of all tasks.
3: Calculate the urgency of each order
4: Generate the set Ub
5: Sort the orders in Ub by non-decreasing urgency value.
6: Calculate the order number n of Ub
7: $j = 1$
8: **while** $n \geq 2$ **do**
9:    Select two orders with the highest urgency P_r P_s
10:    Generate initial task Q_j
11:    **for** $t = 3 \rightarrow n$ **do**
12:       If the order P_t can be merged
13:          Move order P_t from set Ub into task Q_j
14:             t=t+1
15:       **else**
16:          Break
17:       **end**
18:    j=j+1
18:    Calculate the order number n of Ub
19: **end**
20: Generate task Q_j with the order in set Ub

3.3   Heuristic Method

A hybrid heuristic algorithm Adaptive Multi-population Genetic Algorithm (AMGA) with two layers coding and adaptive adjustment method to dynamically control crossover rate and mutation rate is developed for order combination and routing planning. Immigrant operator is one of the important operators in AMGA, which can realize the migration operation of excellent chromosomes between different populations and make the optimization speed faster. The immigration operation process is shown in procedure 2.

Procedure 2: Immigrant operator

   1: Input: MP1, set of all population (before immigration).
   2: Output: MP2, set of all population (after immigration).
   3: for $i = 1 \rightarrow MP1$ do
   4:   B=find the best chromosome in population i.
   5:   W=find the worst chromosome in population $i + 1$.
   6:   W=B
   7: end

---

4   Simulation Instance Design

Due to the fact that the data of takeout involves the trade secrets of platform competition, there is a lack of standard cases of takeout distribution in the existing instance base. Therefore, combined with the design principles of international standard instance and the service characteristics of Chinese takeout industry, the design of test instances of takeout distribution problem is helpful to test the effectiveness of the proposed model and algorithm. Based on the real environment of Chinese o2o takeout delivery market, we assume that there are 30 customers, 5 restaurants and some riders randomly distributed in a 5-km rectangular range, and the customers send orders to different restaurants at 0. Riders are required to deliver all orders within 40 min. The quantity and type of food ordered by customers should be taken into consideration. Different types of takeout food have different preparation times for the restaurant. The distribution speed of riders can be simplified to uniform driving, but it should be different in peak traffic and flat hump traffic. Customers have a soft time window for food delivery, i.e., overtime is allowed but will be punished. Riders' service time at each customer should also be considered.

Finally, the solution algorithm can give the following distribution Gantt chart (seen in Fig. 3.). Through this chart, we can clearly know the order consolidation, task allocation, delivery time, rider loading and other data, which will help to identify the problems in the delivery process and formulate improvement plans in the future.

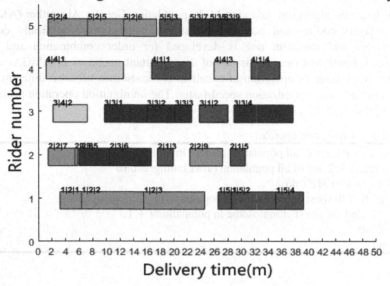

Fig. 3. Gantt chart of the meal delivery

5   Conclusions

Based on the brief description of TDP and the comparison with VRPPDTW, this paper puts forward the main characteristics of TDP and constructs the bi-objective mathematical programming model of TDP with the objective of minimum cost and maximum customer satisfaction. In addition, a heuristic genetic algorithm with two-layer coding and adaptive rate of crossover and mutation is proposed. Insertion detection method is used to generate good initial solution. The two-layer coding method is an improvement on traditional VRP coding method, which could solve the problem of order combination and delivery order at the same time. Meanwhile, a Gantt chart is given to indicate the specific delivery sequence of different riders to verify the effectiveness of this proposed method. In further research, a more in-depth and realistic delivery problem might consider a continuous time period to construct a more practical delivery model.

Acknowledgment.   This work is supported by project of science and technology research program of Chongqing Education Commission of China (No. KJQN201900107) and project of Chongqing Federation of Social Science Circles (No. 2019PY43).

References

1. Erie Consultation: Development report of China takeaway O2O industry, vol. 2016, pp. 2–49 (2016)

2. Jiang, F., Xu, M., Cui, D.: Scheduling system based on takeaway logistics big data. Big Data Res. **01**, 109–115 (2017)

3. Su, J., Li, C., Zeng, Q., Yang, J., Zhang, J.: A green closed-loop supply chain coordination mechanism based on third-party recycling. Sustainability **11**(19), 5335 (2019)

4. Jian, J., Guo, Y., Jiang, L., An, Y., Su, J.: A multi-objective optimization model for green supply chain considering environmental benefits. Sustainability **11**(21), 5911 (2019)

5. Chen, P., Li, H.: Optimization model and algorithm based on time satisfaction for O2O food delivery. Chin. J. Manag. Sci. **24**, 170–176 (2016)

6. Reyes, D., Erera, A., Savelsbergh, M., Sahasrabudhe, S., O'Neil, R.: The meal delivery routing problem. Optim. Online (2018)

7. Li, T., Lyu, X., Li, F., Chen, Y.: Routing optimization model and algorithm for takeout distribution with multiple fuzzy variables under dynamics demand. Control Decis. **34**(2), 406–413 (2019)

8. Pan, L., Fu, Z.: Insertion detection method for vehicle routing problem with time window. Syst. Eng. Theory Pract. **32**(2), 319–322 (2012)

Author Index

Printed in the United States
By Bookmasters